Greta Garbo and the Rise of the Modern Woman

Scott Reisfield

VENDELA

Nonfiction

Originally published in United States of American in 2026 by Wildeve Press.

Hardcover Edition ISBN: 978-1-972059-99-9
Paperback Edition ISBN: 978-1-972059-98-2
Large Print Edition ISBN: 978-1-972059-97-5
eBook Edition ISBN: 978-1-972059-96-8

Cover design and interior page production by Mike Hamers, www.Lightspeedca.net
Cover photographs by: (left) Garbo family photo, (right) Clarence Sinclair Bull.

Advance Praise for *Greta Garbo and the Rise of the Modern Woman*

Bookshelves groan under the weight of books about Greta Garbo. She has been characterized as, variously, a loner, a sphinx, a depressive, a victim, a lesbian, and essentially unknowable. Those bookshelves can be considerably thinned out, as Scott Reisfield's biography of his great aunt, based as it is on impeccable research and her own letters, gives us Garbo as a recognizable human being – ambitious, dedicated, sure of her worth, a good friend devoted to her family and her privacy. Bravo!
— Scott Eyman, Author of *Joan Crawford: A Woman's Face.*

There have been many books about Greta Garbo, but Scott Reisfield's *"Greta Garbo: The Modern Woman"* is one of the essential ones, and for several reasons. Reisfield places her in the context of her time and correctly assesses her cultural impact and influence. He makes a strong case for her as, not only a one-off original, but as a great artist whose operatic vision in combination with her naturalistic truthfulness pointed the way to a new kind of screen acting. And he knew her, a fact whose importance must be emphasized. There are things Reisfield knows about Garbo, just from having been in her presence, that we will never be able to know. But, fortunately, he tells us.
— Mick LaSalle, author of *Complicated Women: Sex and Power in Pre-Code Hollywood.*

In 2005 Scott Reisfield together with Robert Dance published *Garbo: Portraits from Her Private Collection*, a fantastic coffee table book with lovely pictures seldom seen. Now Scott Reisfield has written a history of his great-aunt. Informed by research in archives around the world, he has put the pieces together for the final book on "the Divine Woman" – telling the story of both the star and the woman.
— Bo Florin, Professor in Cinema Studies, Stockholm University

Scott Reisfield, Garbo's grand nephew, reveals how and why Garbo transformed society through her art. Garbo drove forward the evolution from the Victorian Era because her acting was believable. Two generations of women around the world looked to Garbo to understand how to be a Modern Woman.

Her personal story is compelling. Garbo rose from a working-class Stockholm to conquer first theater, then European film and finally Hollywood. She had unmatched talent, honed by the finest training. Garbo fought over contracts with MGM and won. An independent woman, she was the bane of censors and social conservatives until they derailed her career. Hers was one of the most remarkable lives of the twentieth century.

Table of Contents

Note on Sources
Introduction .... *i*
1 Growing Up 1
2 Formulating a Life 19
3 Dramaten 39
4 Swedish Theater and Film 51
5 Gösta Berling 63
6 The Odalisque Project 86
7 Triumph in Berlin 112
8 MGM or Film Europe? 128
9 Two Months in New York 137
10 MGM Sells the Unknown Garbo to America 152
11 Naturalistic Acting 166
12 The Temptress 175
13 The Modern Age 183
14 The Garbo Audience 193
15 Flesh and the Devil: Garbo Meets John Gilbert 208
16 Loew's and the First-Run Theater 223
17 Tumult 235
18 Anna Karenina Becomes Love 250
19 Working With Garbo 260
20 The Death of Stiller 276
21 A Visit to Sweden 285
22 The Quest for a Private Life 293
23 The Production Code 307
24 Garbo Talks 313
25 Garbo's Popularity Explodes 324
26 Independence 335
27 Queen Christina 349
28 Censorship 367
29 The Costume Drama Strategy 381
30 Garbo Turns Thirty 397

31 Ninotchka 417
32 End of an Era 426
33 The War Years 434
34 A Parasocial Life 444
35 The Duchess de Langeais 459
36 The Miracle 466
37 Fade to Black 473
Appendix 1 486
Appendix 2 493
Appendix 3 497
Appendix 4 500
Acknowledgements 501
About the Author 504
Endnotes 506
Index 543

Dedication

For Cathy, as always.

Greta Garbo and the Rise of the Modern Woman

A Note on Sources

For readers unfamiliar with Greta Garbo, this book stands on its own. People familiar with Garbo from earlier biographies are sure to notice that I have eliminated a number of stories about Garbo that were made up years ago and became part of the canon. I was able to disprove them. The Garbo revealed here is far more interesting.

While prior biographers made plenty of errors in their Garbo books, we must give them some grace as Garbo's actual history is difficult to establish. Much of the problem has to do with Garbo's life in Europe. Vast stretches of her early life were reported in magazines and newspapers from 1928 on, and most of the information was made up out of whole cloth or altered in some way. For a researcher reading not-quite-contemporaneous articles about Garbo's youth, their assumption is that they would be accurate. But they are not.

The source of most errors is the Swedish magazine *Lektyr*. While actual elements of Garbo's life were included in *Lektyr* articles, they were mostly fanciful fictions. But there are also real interviews with people who knew her, so one must try to find validation for each article. *Lektyr* published numerous articles about Garbo each year for a decade. Though Garbo had been friends with Lars Saxon, the publisher of *Lektyr*, she had turned down his romantic advances. The quantity of articles may reflect his unhappiness at being jilted. Though for his magazines the Garbo articles were also good business.

Then there were people like Erik Petschler and Arnold Genthe who did work with Garbo but wrote stories that put them in the center of Garbo's professional progress, despite facts to the contrary.

Cecil Beaton and Mercedes de Acosta are often quoted regarding Garbo. Their relationships with Garbo were rather different, but both wrote, and told friends, stories about Garbo that they made up. Both were known by their contemporaries to be notoriously unreliable chroniclers of their own lives, and their diaries and autobiographies are not factual documents. There are a few other minor writers (e.g., Christopher Isherwood, who would go back and rewrite his diaries) whom I don't rely upon without some kind of corroboration.

I spent a decade probing the truth of each story, eliminating those that were made-up. I let stand stories that I could not disprove. While there are a hundred or so books about Garbo, there are only eleven serious biographies that added valuable new research. There are also two critical appreciations that added useful interviews. In appendix one, I explain what these books got wrong and sometimes why this transpired. Appendix one is not an exhaustive list of prior errors. I wanted to give the experienced Garbo reader a sense of the magnitude of the problem. I also acknowledge some of the fine research writers did. For example, Norman Zierold's interviews with Garbo's co-stars and others at MGM are a wonderful resource.

I will cite one example here. Every biography quotes a story by Erik Petschler about how Garbo entered the Royal Dramatic Theatre in Stockholm (Dramaten) as a student due to his intercession. The real story was completely different and shows how intentional Garbo was in her approach.

Garbo had been working for a different producer/director named Ragnar Ring, making industrial films as a side gig to her job as a salesclerk at the Paul U. Bergström Department store (PUB). She had started working at PUB in July 1920, and Ring had cast her in a film for PUB that he made in December that year. Ring kept hiring her for other industrial films. From at least January 1922, and possibly earlier, Garbo had been taking her money from these films and investing in acting lessons with an eye toward becoming a stage actor. She had hired the retired head of the Dramaten school, Frans Enwall, as her coach. Enwall became ill, so by July Garbo had switched to taking lessons from his daughter.

In June 1922 Ring asked Paul Bergström if he would give Garbo three weeks' leave to make a feature-length advertising film. Bergström declined and wrote to Ring that Garbo (only sixteen) was one of his best salesclerks and therefore he could not give her the time off. Further, he told Ring he was giving Garbo ideas about an acting career that were going to lead her away from her promising, and predictable, sales career.

Therefore, Ring would withdraw his offer. Garbo was already planning to leave PUB to become an actor. She wanted to make a film to have money for school. Instead of working for Ring, she signed on to make Petschler's film *Luffar-Petter* (1922). She quit PUB on July 22, 1922. She would make Petschler's film, and also apply to Dramaten on August 18. Auditions for those invited based on the applications took place on September 11. Somewhere between July 23 and September 10 she spent three weeks filming *Luffar-Petter*. Corroborating this, years later Bergström would write a note to Ring basically saying they had both been wrong about Garbo's future.

Erik Petschler created a different version of this story that can't possibly fit into the timeline. According to Petschler he offered Garbo the role in *Luffar-Petter* and Bergström wrote the letter to him. Garbo decided to make the film anyway and quit PUB. Sometime weeks after production, Petschler ran into Garbo on the street and she poured her heart out about how she didn't have a job and she still hoped to be an actor. Petschler claims that he then arranged for her to take lessons from Frans Enwall and encouraged her to apply to Dramaten.

Where is the time for this? If filming had started the Monday after Garbo quit PUB, there would have been just one week from the end of filming until Dramaten applications were due. That's assuming filming began on July 24. All we know is that it was concluded before Garbo undertook her audition seven weeks later. In July 1922 Frans Enwall was ill, so the lessons were with his daughter Signe. Finally, Garbo herself told interviewers that she took acting lessons for months before applying to Dramaten.

Does it matter? In the actual story Garbo executed a plan to become an actor that took at least a year to come to fruition. She had talent, but she worked hard and made her break. In the Petschler version he is the hero who created her career for her.

It's not that hard to count up the weeks and realize Petschler is lying. Biographer John Bainbridge clearly did, and his solution was to ignore the date Garbo quit PUB, writing it as "in early summer" when he had access to, and quoted from, Garbo's PUB personnel record. Why obfuscate? He knew that she resigned on July 22.

All the subsequent biographies used the Petschler story as if true. No one cross-checked the story against Ragnar Ring's story. To disprove it you have to go to all the source information and search for errors. The number of fabricated or incorrect stories about Garbo is nearly endless.

All images are courtesy Scott Reisfield unless otherwise noted.

Greta Garbo signature courtesy Harriet Brown and Company, Inc.

"The cinema has given precisely one great artist to the world, Greta Garbo. Unless you also count that damn mouse." [1]

— Louis B. Mayer, President, MGM Studios

Greta Garbo driving a car.

Introduction

Comes the hour, comes the woman.

In the early 1970s Garbo and my mother traveled to the Coco Point Lodge on the island of Barbuda for the first time. It was an upscale island resort.[2] Coco Point had a dinner dress code of formal wear for women. As they readied to dine their first night my mother realized that Garbo was dressed in pants and asked if that was what she planned to wear. Garbo responded, "Yes, these should do."

The resort was already buzzing with the news of Garbo's arrival. When they entered the dining room, all eyes turned to her. Every woman there wondered: Would she be turned away for violating the dress code? She wasn't. The next evening, half the women wore pants. My mom related that Garbo was quietly pleased. Another social restriction for women removed.

Greta Garbo was my great-aunt. To write this book I have taken what I knew of her, letters and information from my family and new research, to create a fuller portrait of this remarkable person. After her death I read what other people wrote about her. The picture didn't match the person. Nothing captured her essence. I didn't initially plan to do so, yet I spent years assembling Garbo's story. I have stripped away incorrect information that muddied the picture.

Greta Garbo was a highly trained stage actor who transitioned to films early in her career. She worked hard to get into the best theater school and made two remarkable films in Europe before coming to Hollywood. She had immense natural talent and her training was in a naturalistic style of acting. In Hollywood she would transform, well, almost everything.

She was brought to Hollywood to be a star—though I don't think Louis B. Mayer and Irving Thalberg, who ran the MGM studio, quite expected GARBO. By the age of twenty-one, three films into her American career, she was arguably the best actor in the world. The naturalistic style she used would take over Hollywood.

Garbo was able to use her acting skill to paint relatable women on the screen in film after film. Her audience tried to be like her or fell in love with her. She was only considered beautiful because beauty bent toward her. Before her stardom the public preferred smaller-boned, delicate women like Lillian Gish.

From the moment they first saw her on-screen, her Hollywood peers stood in awe of what she was doing. Lionel Barrymore, a co-star in four films, wrote, "She had the true nimbus of greatness."[3] His brother John Barrymore told a reporter, "The physical power she expends in her work is amazing."[4] Bette Davis would tell writer Whitney Stone, "Her instinct, her mastery over the machine, was pure witchcraft. I cannot analyze this woman's acting. I only know that no one else so effectively worked in front of a camera."[5]

Where other stars took years to build their careers, Garbo achieved stardom from her first film. Women—Garbo's fan base was mainly urban women—thought they could read her thoughts on the screen due to her acting ability. The intensity of fan attachment to Garbo and how she represented to them the various modern ways a woman might live her life are hard to appreciate today.

Once it was clear in late 1926 that Garbo was a star, she entered into a months-long contract standoff with MGM. She was just turning twenty-one. MGM blinked first.

Fans believed in the characters Garbo portrayed. For example, in 1930, one year into her near-decade-long total dominance of fan attention, Garbo received 3,000 fan letters per day, dwarfing the 800 letters President Hoover received, many of which only needed to be forwarded to the correct government department. If it took someone five minutes to handle and respond to each Garbo letter, it would require a staff of thirty-two to manage the multitude of letters arriving daily. Eleanor Roosevelt would report that she received 300,000 pieces of mail in 1933, which was 821 per day.[6]

Her message was also timely, arriving as women were trying to sort out exactly what their new social freedoms were. With her characters Garbo destroyed the Victorian conception of women whose worth was based on their chastity. The audience believed in the imperfect women she portrayed and the underlying humanity Garbo displayed. The requirement for virginity and sexual innocence is stripped from the Modern Woman.

By the age of twenty-five she had transformed society. Women dressed like her characters, and they wanted to live like her characters lived. Women bought millions of dollars of clothing and furnishings derived from her film's costumes and sets. Her presence on-screen and in magazines, and what people perceived as her private persona, were forces for social change. They resonated with women in a wide variety of phases in their lives, on issues beyond just their hair, clothes, and eyebrows. Women used Garbo to redefine what a woman was in an early proto-feminist way.

Restored to her rightful place, Garbo is revealed as a towering figure in the first half of the twentieth century. Garbo has been hidden by forty intervening years of social conservatism that rejected the Modern Woman.

Almost unrecognized was how Garbo transformed the way people created portraits. She acted for the camera; she didn't merely pose. While elements of this evolution existed before Garbo worked with Arnold Genthe in New York, their 1925 sessions are the marker of this transformation.

The closest modern parallel to Garbo's remarkable cultural impact on women would be Taylor Swift, though comparison is difficult because the mechanisms of fan engagement have transformed.

Was it just by acting that Garbo changed the world? The simple answer is yes. The more complex answer is that she changed all acting in Hollywood and made it have more impact regardless of the actor. The public perception of her, both in and out of character, goes beyond her work in film, though it springs from it. Finally, she consciously made feminist choices when she earned control.

In 1932 Garbo became independent, free to sign with any studio. Garbo only made one film with this independence before censorship began to transform Hollywood, constraining how women could be portrayed on the screen. That film was *Queen Christina* (1933). Garbo delivered an independent woman, a queen. The film transgressed on many levels. Garbo agreed to include a lesbian kiss, and her lover initially, and acceptingly, thinks he is aroused by a man, as the queen is in male disguise. The queen makes many nontraditional choices. This led directly to the creation of the Production Code Administration, the office that would provide a steel backbone to the social conservatives' drive for censorship. Her late career is a rear-guard action against social conservatives.

Working by project, Garbo would only make seven independent films over nine years. Within this period Garbo made choices with intent. One will see how she was more the architect of her career than she is often credited with being. Garbo intentionally chose film roles that caused censorship challenges. She and Irving Thalberg cleverly used three costume dramas to turn censorship against itself. Then Garbo pivoted to comedy. *Ninotchka* (1939) wasn't just funny. It was sophisticated, lampooning Stalinism with a deft touch.

In 1941 Garbo's final film was inexplicably condemned and then censored. The script had been pre-approved and the film was not particularly bawdy. At the time it didn't seem to mark the end of her career.

Over the next fifteen years there are seven projects she clearly agreed to make; one can find the written agreements for four of them. Of her unrealized projects, several clearly were intended to push the boundaries of censorship, though we don't have the scripts to understand how the difficult issues were to be addressed. Garbo never backed down from her desire to portray interesting women.

Garbo registered with the audience as a complete, complex woman who held many thoughts and emotions in her mind. A Modern Woman. She resonated with the audience both in the roles she portrayed and in the person the audience believed was behind those roles. While she did not plan to have this effect on society, she pushed it forward throughout her career.

I travel for work and over the past twenty-five years I would add an extra day to a trip and visit an archive. I slowly assembled these resources, both learning important facts about Garbo's life and raising new questions. Using translations, I was able to add resources from Sweden and Germany. I had the family letters my grandmother had given to me translated. I was stunned by what I eventually figured out. Garbo's story had been lost. While several biographers have found important information about her life, they also were led astray by a sea of misinformation. Many of these fake stories take away Garbo's agency. Others present her as a changeling, talented but detached from the world. They are clear in presenting Garbo as someone with savant syndrome whose success had nothing to do with her intelligence, skill, or effort. One recent biographer actually wrote of Garbo as "a Swedish peasant girl, uneducated, naïve and always on her guard."[7]

This book reveals Garbo and all her power. She was a key touchstone for two generations of women, an impact she achieved because of her talent, belief in the emancipation of women, and hard work.

Then there is the question of what it means to have what seems like half the world decide that you represent them. Garbo, she didn't need a first name. The woman she represented to her audience was Modern. A woman who was both feminine and assertive. This was not without personal consequences for Garbo. Men pursued her with romance in mind, even men she had never met. One bequeathed her his small house.

Reading this, those of you who have read other Garbo stories might be thinking, "That's not what I recall about Greta Garbo at all." And you would be right. The understanding of her impact on the lives of women has been forgotten. Today Garbo has often been reduced to a meme about reclusiveness. As you will see, the characterization is not particularly accurate.

The conventional evolution of the Garbo history has been something akin to a ball that rolls down a hill gathering things that stick to it. A modern parallel is Ingrid Schorr's story of what it has been like to be the "Rockville Girl" from the R.E.M. song "(Don't Go Back To) Rockville." Schorr recalls how every new biography of R.E.M. or interview with someone who lived in the Athens-Clarke County area in the last quarter of the twentieth century accreted new "facts" to the story of Rockville Girl. For example, Schorr was surprised to learn that instead of being a lyrical invention about her return home to trendy, tech-savvy, and factory-free Rockville, Maryland, she actually had returned to a mythic Rockville with factories. Life there was miserably blue collar. Once added to a biography, it becomes part of the canon the next biography is built upon. People will tell her directly, and she can read about, an entire alternative life she never lived.[8]

While there are other women who may have had as much impact on how women fit into society in the first half of the twentieth century, they can be counted on one hand, perhaps two. Hopefully I deliver a more complete synthesis of Garbo's life and importance that puts her impact on art, culture, and society in context.

Many histories of Greta Garbo have already been written. Her real life was more interesting. The hour came. Garbo was there. This is the story.

Chapter 1 – Growing Up

"There were several of us children who used to visit the Salvation Army on the South Island of Stockholm—that's where I did my first performing and singing. This led to my being invited to sell Stridsropet. It worked to some extent in the building we lived in, but I was never any great shakes as a newspaper-seller."[9]

— Greta Garbo

Greta Garbo age nine.

The reporter could see that the woman was overcome with emotion. That seemed reason enough to talk to her. So he did. The woman, Gullan Johansson, had come to watch the internment of her childhood friend's ashes. She entered into an easy conversation with the reporter, who had come to cover the event for his magazine. Greta Garbo was being laid to rest. Though the event was being televised live nationally, Gullan wanted to be there.

He asked the question reporters had been asking about Greta Garbo for eighty years: What was she like?

Gullan went on to describe her childhood friend and their shared backgrounds.

> "We used to play store with rocks just to entertain ourselves," she began. "We didn't have any fancy toys. The only thing that separated our inner courtyards was a row of outhouses. We used to climb up on top of them and stand there talking.
>
> "But Garbo was the leader! She was bossing the other kids around. At times we dressed up, or rather, made spectacles out of ourselves, and we played theater. She was more forward than the rest of us. She was adventurous. Once she went to Uppsala. No one knew where she was."[10]

She related that the two friends started working at barbershops. Greta at Götgatan and Gullan at Åsögatan. "The task we had was to lather up men before they got shaved."[11]

* * *

They had met around age five. As teenagers they drifted apart. Different lives, different friends. Gullan was now ninety-four, the last of the girls from the old Söder neighborhood. The bonds of their old friendship stretched over the intervening years, and she had come to Skogskyrkogården (Forest Cemetery) on this beautiful day in June 1999.

The reporter went up to Garbo's niece after the ceremony and informed her that Gullan was outside. Introductions were quickly made. To his disappointment, they stepped away to talk privately. The two chatted in Swedish for twenty minutes or so. Then Gullan went home. There was no one else left from her childhood or working life to add to their reminiscences.

What has emerged from the stories told over the years by her childhood friends was a portrait of a tall girl who was serious, bossy, kind, playful, and so intelligent she hardly had to study to get by in school. She liked playing at theatre from a young age, and grew to dream of being an actor. Before she was twenty, and with the encouragement of Mauritz Stiller, her dream changed. Now it was to be the greatest actor.

Garbo's childhood was framed out by the Sweden of her youth. It both constrained her options and gave her opportunities that had not existed for young Swedish women a generation earlier. During her childhood women gained suffrage, and economic opportunities began to expand both for women and working-class Swedes as the country rapidly industrialized. The other natural variable was her family, warm and supportive. They would be a fixture in her entire life. To properly see the young Garbo, one must focus in on what she herself would say about it, while stripping out the fanciful stories that were created about her.

The period from about 1850 through the start of World War I was a time of great demographic and social upheaval in Sweden. Birth rates increased and infant mortality rates decreased in the second half of the nineteenth century. The once mainly agrarian population was transformed, either moving to the city looking for work in the new industries being created or emigrating. In conjunction with the greater economic opportunity in the city, social unrest related to class structure developed.

Due to the country's wealth in hydro power, iron, and forests, Sweden's GDP doubled between 1880 and 1905.[12] Whereas 30 percent of Swedes lived in towns or cities in 1900, that percentage grew to 45 percent by 1920.[13] The population of Stockholm more than doubled from 168,000 in 1880 to 342,000 in 1910. In moving to Stockholm in the 1890s, Karl and Anna Gustafson had been on the leading edge of Swedish urbanization.

The combination of dislocation and economic change led to a twinned political and national transformation that was notionally tied to the turn of the century in the minds of Swedes.

Swedes termed this combination of social, economic, and political changes that their society went through *sekelskifte* (the turn of the century). No longer was top-down social control acceptable to large segments of the population.

All kinds of movements shaped Swedish society. New organizations represented many groups, including professions, industries, and neighborhoods. The Free Church movement rejected the official state church. The army demanded a say in who its officers were. Women organized social groups within and across class lines without deferring to men.[14]

The very notion of what it meant to be "Swedish" was crystalized in the Swedish National Romantic movement. National Romanticism in Sweden tied the rural past (or a somewhat mythical version of it) to the modern through a shared sense of a Swedish character and community. The Romantic movement in Sweden was liberal in character. In addition to the economic forces that in part drove this creation of a new national identity, several events occurred to reinforce the process. In 1905, Norway peacefully seceded from Sweden to become an independent country. While the separation ended up being non-violent, it was contentious and led to a resurgence of Swedish nationalism. The adoption of Sweden's national anthem that year was not a coincidence.[15]

The Romantic movement would directly inform the theatre and film of Sweden. The story-telling Swedish films with which Mauritz Stiller and Victor Sjöström redefined the art of film in the late 1910s were National Romantic films.

Sweden was dependent on trade prior to World War I. Its two largest trading partners, Germany and Britain, were on opposite sides of the conflict. At the outset of the war, Sweden declared itself neutral.

Both Germany and Britain blockaded trade with Sweden by the other, as well as Swedish trade with other countries. The practical impact for Sweden was that it was reduced to selling Germany iron and timber. Germany could sell little to Sweden in return. Items like grain that it had formerly exported to Sweden were now needed for domestic demand. Swedish ships traveling between the two countries were occasionally sunk in the Baltic by the British or Russians.

Sweden continued to sell iron ore to Britain by way of the Norwegian port of Narvik. Yet the British blockaded Swedish imports, as they feared that imported food would be sent on to Germany, with Sweden as just a transfer point.

Greta Garbo age ten.

At the time, Sweden imported a third of its grain and all of its tropical foodstuffs, including coffee, spices, sugar, and tropical fruits. Sugar, bread, meat, eggs, milk, and butter were all rationed. Whereas in 1907, the average Swede consumed 6 kilos of butter and 126 kilos of meat per year, by 1917 butter consumption had dropped to 3 kilos and meat consumption to 26 kilos. The bread ration for a Swede in a neutral country was only 75 percent of that for a German.[16]

The war, therefore, caused significant economic hardship for Sweden, most importantly in terms of food. Garbo's youth, ages nine to fourteen, would be defined by this time.

The effects of the war led to a political crisis. In the aftermath of the 1917 election in which the Liberal and Social Democratic Parties won a decisive majority, King Gustaf V attempted to appoint the leader of the Conservative Party prime minister. This gambit failed disastrously and the king was left with no choice but to appoint Liberal Party leader Nils Edén as prime minister. The Liberal-Social Democratic coalition forced through numerous reforms, including universal suffrage, and claimed for the Riksdag (the Swedish Parliament) what had formerly been the king's political powers. From this point forward, Sweden was a constitutional monarchy. Women gained legal equality within marriage in 1921.

The immediate post-war economic situation was not much better for Sweden than the hardships during the war, as financial crises, joblessness, and industrial problems affected all of Europe.[17] While Sweden became ever more progressive during the interwar period, it remained "stratified by class, hobbled by deference, rigid with formality and xenophobia."[18]

The other big change during Garbo's childhood was the flow of women into the Swedish workforce. Between 1920 and 1930, the female labor participation rate increased from 26.9 percent to 30.7 percent. Women dropped out of the formal labor force upon marriage. In 1920, only 3.8 percent of married women were employed; by 1930, this figure rose to 8 percent. Previously married women, primarily widows, now also re-entered the formal workforce.[19]

Garbo's idea of women's role in society came from the Swedish Social-Democratic ideals. While they were not universally accepted in Sweden itself as Garbo grew up, she clearly believed she had the right to work and live an independent life from an early age, and her family supported her in that belief.

It is in this context that Garbo, a working-class woman, could make her way to a good working-class job and then get admitted to a prestigious national theatre training program committed to developing the country's culture.

Greta Garbo grew up in a tight-knit family with three children. She was the youngest, born in 1905. Sven was born in 1898 and Alva in 1903. The family was working-class, with all that meant in the Stockholm of the early twentieth century, when society was socially stratified and only the middle class had educational opportunities beyond primary school.

Her parents, Karl Alfred Gustafson and Anna Lovisa Karlsdotter, both came to Stockholm from rural farming communities, though they were separated by a hundred miles (161 kilometers). Karl arrived in 1890 and Anna in 1895.

Karl and Anna met and fell in love sometime after Anna arrived in June 1895. They were married on May 8, 1898, just under three months before the birth of their son, Sven Alfred Gustafson. Though a few of their siblings would eventually follow them to Stockholm, Karl and Anna met, married, and had three children completely on their own.

Karl was born in Frinnaryd, Jönköping County, 200 miles (322 kilometers) south of Stockholm. Karl's full siblings either remained in southern Sweden or emigrated to America. By the time the first of Karl's younger half siblings permanently moved to Stockholm in 1904, Karl had already been there for fifteen years. Karl's family, Johan Gustafson and his second wife Joanna, had moved to Hyltinge in 1902, but that was still 70 miles (113 kilometers) away. It seems to have been a three-hour train ride at the time, so visits were more of a possibility.[20] Garbo occasionally visited as a child.

Anna's entire family was 250 miles (402 kilometers) farther south in Kalmar. Her younger sister, Sigrid, did not move to Stockholm until 1907. The rest of Anna's family either emigrated to America or remained in southern Sweden.

In 1900, they were living at Gotlandsgatan 44 and Karl was working as a butcher.[21] Their second child, Alva Maria, was born September 20, 1903, and at the end of the month they moved to Renstjernasgaten 22[22] (now Renstiernas gata) for a year. The records list Karl's employment status as "worker." Then, in December 1904, the family moved to Blekingegatan 32,[23] the Stockholm address most famously associated with Greta Garbo. The building had been constructed that year expressly to house city workers, so Karl must have been a city employee at the time. Garbo was born September 18, 1905.

All of these addresses are in Södermalm (*söder* is Swedish for south), an island neighborhood on the south side of Stockholm that was solidly working-class at the time. Karl and Anna were a working-class couple. Several jobs have been associated with Karl; it is not clear how frequently he changed jobs, or if record keeping was just not specific. He is clearly identified at one point as a butcher. After 1903, Karl is mostly identified as a laborer or worker. Anna worked in some capacity before getting married, but after she married Karl she is always identified as a wife in government documents. Anna worked informally once the children were in school, which was common Swedish practice at the time.

The Gustafson apartment at Blekingegatan 32 was on the third floor (the second floor when counted the European way where the first floor is above the ground floor). The apartment was accessed from the central area through a door that opened to a small hallway. On the left was a kitchen and on the right was a bedroom. Between the two double-room apartments at either end of the building were a set of one-room apartments and a stairwell.[24]

In addition to their apartment on Blekingegatan, the Gustafsons rented a cottage in the Dalen Allotments in Enskede, about 4 miles or 6.5 kilometers south of their apartment. Dalen was a philanthropic urban garden project cre-

The Gustafson family cottage at Enskede.
Courtesy of the Greta Garbo family archive.

ated to give working-class families in the city a place to garden and spend time in the outdoors. Allotments were rented at subsidized rates starting in 1912.[25]

The allotment movement spanned northern Europe and Dalen was one of several in Stockholm. While designed to help working-class families, they were out of reach for the truly poor, who didn't have kitchens, couldn't afford even the subsidized rent and didn't have the time to attend to the garden.[26] For a working-class family like the Gustafsons the subsidized rent gave them access to a green space for growing some food and recreation. Dalen was also a social space.[27]

While the apartment was small for a family of five, Dalen gave them space during the summer. They could take a tram from Söder to Enskede and walk to Dalen. Garbo and Alva would spend much of the summer there gardening, playing, and socializing. Years later Garbo would relate the following:

> We used to have an allotment in where Alva and I liked to spend time in the summer. We used to grow carrots and beetroot and potatoes there. We had red currant bushes and two raspberry canes. Occasionally we had such a bumper harvest that we were able to sell some of our potatoes.[28]

Of the few relatives who would follow Karl and Anna to Stockholm, the family was closest to Anna's sister Selma Sigrid Johansson (Sigrid), who was eight years younger than Anna. In 1907 she moved to Stockholm and joined the Salvation Army, where she worked until 1915. Garbo sang with and sold papers for the Salvation Army while Sigrid was employed there. After leaving the Salvation Army, Sigrid eventually moved to Nykroppa in Värmland in 1917. Garbo visited Sigrid for the summer of 1921, and perhaps at other times.

After Anna's death in 1944, Garbo returned to Sweden in 1946 and visited Sigrid. An uncle, Axel, passed away in 1956, leaving small bequests to Garbo and her brother, Sven.[29] Garbo was surprised at this bequest. She asked her sister-in-law Peg to make arrangements to remove her from the bequest, or direct it toward Sigrid or other heirs.[30]

Karl's half sister Maria moved to Stockholm in 1904. She was the sibling that Karl was the most fond of. A half brother, David, would move to Stockholm in 1911 and several other half siblings would follow, though some only stayed for a few years before returning to Hyltinge.

Garbo's path was not easy, but it was possible because of how Swedish society had evolved. Greta Garbo was a product of her time. The Sweden where she grew up was evolving rapidly from an agricultural society run by a monarch into an industrialized social democracy.

Growing up Greta Garbo quickly earned the family nickname "Kata," from the Swedish firebrand suffragette and socialist Kata Dalström.[31] It would be her family nickname all of Garbo's life. It was how she signed family letters.

Garbo spoke only infrequently about her family. She told author Sven Broman (whom she met in Klosters later in life), "Alva, my sister, and I always called our mother Anna. All three of us were so very close to one another. By the way, I always called my sister Alva 'Lillan' [little one]. She was two years older than me almost to the day."[32] While Alva and her father, Karl, passed away while Garbo was young, she would always remain close to her mother, her brother, and his family.

As was then typical of Swedish children, Garbo started school at the age of seven in 1912. World War I started just before Garbo turned nine. As Sweden experienced food shortages and worker unrest, there were protest marches over the lack of food.[33]

Garbo spoke about this with Sven Broman later in life:

> While we were growing up during the First World War, most things were in short supply. Of course, we did live in modest circumstances, but we always had enough food for the day.[34]

Garbo has mistakenly been portrayed as having an impoverished childhood. Her childhood was nothing like the destitution experienced by Charlie Chaplin, Joan Crawford, or Clara Bow. Rather, the Gustafson family was a stable working-class family. Her parents remained married until Karl's premature death. By the time Karl died, Sven and Alva were out working.

Interviews given by her uncle, David Gustafson, were one factor leading to this perception of family poverty. Instead of speaking about a working-class family that, beginning in 1914, had two incomes (father and son), lived in a relatively modern building, and could afford to rent an allotment, David spoke of them as poor. He also positions himself as a bit of a savior. The first of Garbo's many "rescuers," in their telling.

He presents the general deprivation that many working-class people in Stockholm faced during the war as somehow specific to the Gustafson family. He is correct that the family worried about access to food, neglecting to mention that this was the general wartime condition.

Biographers have used the lack of indoor plumbing at Blekingegatan 32 as a marker of the family's poverty. The fact that the Blekingegatan building didn't have toilets in the apartments is true, but misunderstood. While Stockholm had piped water beginning in 1861, the apartment building at Blekingegatan 32 was built during a citywide moratorium on installing plumbed toilets in Stockholm.[35] As a city surrounded by lakes, sewage had become a critical public health issue for the growing metropolis. It took decades to implement a sewage system that didn't foul the drinking water intakes. Stockholm's working-class neighborhoods universally had communal sewage disposal systems based on outhouses. Poverty was not having a kitchen. The Gustafson apartment kitchen had running water and sinks with drains.

In addition to tending to their modest farming plot in Enskede, Garbo had the kind of jobs working-class children of the era often had.

She became a runner for Agnes Lind, who ran a stationery and tobacco shop down the block from the Gustafson apartment on Blekingegatan.[36] Lind was friendly with Anna Gustafson, so she kept an eye on the young child from work as Greta traveled home from school. Greta didn't earn much cash this way, but she did get postcards of actors.

Sigrid's job with the Salvation Army led to Garbo performing with other children at the temple, her first experience with public performance. This led to a brief career selling newspapers.

Discipline in the Gustafson household was not harsh. The family was kept together by love and supportive interaction. Garbo told Sven Broman: "I cannot remember my mother ever saying a cross word to me. She was widowed early and her health was poor. I was always worried about her when I was in Hollywood."[37]

Childhood friend Ebba Antonsson, in an interview in 1990, recalled the following:

> We lived near one another and I spent a lot of time with the Gustafson family. Greta's father worked nights and slept during the day. Greta and her sister, Alva, slept in the kitchen, while their parents slept in the living room. Since their father had to sleep during the day we had to be quiet and we mostly kept to the kitchen.[38]

She had a youthful sense of justice. It is apparent in this childhood story she related later, which is corroborated by an interview with a childhood friend:

> One night when I was going home, I saw two men fighting. They were drunk. I can't stand people who are drunk! One was big and the other little. The big man was hurting the little one. I went up and pulled on the big man's sleeve, asked him why he was doing it. He looked down on me. I was eight years old—
>
> "That's all right. You can go home now. Here's your little daughter." Then I ran away. I wasn't his little daughter.[39]

Garbo herself described her childhood on one occasion to reporter Ruth Biery:

> I have always been moody. When I was just a little child, as early as I can remember, I had wanted to be alone. I detest crowds, don't like many people. I used to crawl into a corner and sit and think, think things over. When just a baby, I was always figuring, wondering what it was all about—just why we were living.

> Children should be allowed to think when they please; should not be molested. "Go and play now," their mothers and fathers tell them. They shouldn't do that. Thinking means so much to even small children. [40]

Garbo was a tomboy. Two childhood playmates from her building, Oscar Lönn and Erik Schytt, would relate;

> For us boys, she was the girl of all times, We got on really well with her and she with us. She would rather play with boys than girls. In the winter, she was wild about sledding.[41]

Regarding the allure of acting, Garbo was clear that she was captivated from a young age. She gave Biery a long and detailed description of how she fell in love with acting.

> When I wasn't thinking, wasn't wondering what it was all about, this living; I was dreaming. Dreaming how I could become a player.
>
> No, none of my people were on the stage. It was just born in me, I guess. Why, when I was just a little thing, I had some water colors. Just as other children have water colors. Only I drew pictures on myself, rather than on paper. I used to paint my lips, my cheeks, paint pictures on me. I thought that was the way actresses painted.
>
> Long before I had been in a theater, I did this. I don't know where I got it; from pictures, from others talking—or just from me, the inside of me. I didn't play much. Except skating and skiing and throwing snowballs. I did most of my playing by thinking. I played a little with my brother and sister, pretending we were in shows. Like other children. But usually I did my own pretending. I was up and down. Very happy one moment, the next moment—there was nothing left for me.
>
> Then I found a theater. I must have been six or seven. Two theaters, really. One was a cabaret; one a regular theater—across from one another. And there was a back porch to both of them. A long plank on which the actors and actresses walked to get in the back door. I used to go there at seven o'clock in the evening, when they would be coming in, and wait until eight-thirty.

> Watch them come in; listen to them getting ready. The big back door was always open even in the coldest weather.
>
> Listen to their voices doing their parts in the productions. Smell the grease paint! There is no smell in the world like the smell of the backyard of a theater. No smell that will mean as much to me—ever.
>
> Why, last night, for the first time since I came to this city, I went to a theater. Went down to the Biltmore in Los Angeles. Went behind and talked with the girls; watched them make up; smelled the backyard of the theater just as I used to when I was little.
>
> Night after night, I sat there dreaming. Dreaming when I would be inside—getting ready. [42]

The two theatres that Garbo used to hang around sat back to back near Mosebacke Square, a short three quarters of a mile (1.1 kilometers) from her apartment. The Mosebacke Theatre was a cabaret theatre that catered to a more general audience. The Södra Theatre, Stockholm's oldest private theatre, ran plays for a middle-income audience. Since they backed each other, one could see a bit of the backstage workings of both theatres from this vantage. This was an era when a seven- or eight-year-old might have the run of their neighborhood without any parental concern.

Garbo did what children always do: She played with other children. She also went to the movies, which were new. She recalled the following:

> And I went to the movies, just like other children. I didn't see a regular theater—inside—until I was twelve. But I went to the movies often. I usually paid for my tickets. but sometimes, just sometimes, the man at the door could be persuaded to be kind, and money wasn't necessary. [43]

Elements of the draw of theatre for the young Greta Garbo have already come to light. Childhood acting, collecting theatre actor cards, evenings sitting outside the stage door, and finally attending shows. "Ever since I can remember I must be an actress," she told Biery. [44]

As Greta Garbo grew into her teenage years, she towered over her classmates. She was self-conscious because of this. As she told Biery, "I was just the same size I am now when I was twelve years old. I haven't grown a bit since then.

Isn't that lucky? Everywhere I went as a child, I was pointed at because I was so big—so very big."[45]

She told Broman a slightly different story. "I really did grow too fast as a child. I was taller than all the other children of my age. I think I reached my full growth as soon as I was fourteen."[46]

Since the 1955 Bainbridge biography it has been written, and copied, that Garbo dropped out of school when she was fourteen. In fact, seven years was the length of public primary education in Sweden at that time. This early end to formal education in Sweden was not much different from other countries at that time. For example, in 1920 only 17 percent of Americans completed high school.[47]

Garbo had finished her seven years in the spring of 1919, at age thirteen. She went to a church-run primary school, called a *folkskolan*, as did 95 percent of children in Sweden. Fewer than 1 percent of female Swedes of the time had

Garbo in an undated (but likely 1919) photo of her class at Katrina South School.

any further schooling beyond primary school. Sweden's secondary school program was for wealthy families. A working-class child such as Greta Garbo had no realistic path to further education past the seventh grade in Sweden until after 1927.

Her Katrina South School is open to this day. The walk from the Gustafson apartment is fewer than ten minutes. Garbo was an above average student. She was well behaved, for the most part. Her trip up north to Uppsala was the only unexcused absence on her school record. [48]

Garbo's childhood friend, Ebba Antonsson, told Barry Paris, "I didn't find school as easy as Greta: she seemed never to do any homework but knew all the answers anyway." [49] However, school did not captivate her. In 1928, she summed up her education in a way that makes one feel that she just coasted through.

> I hated school. I hated the bonds they put on me. There were so many things outside. I liked history best. But I was afraid of the map—geography you call it. But I had to go to school like other children. The public school, just as you have in this country. [50]

One final consideration from this part of Garbo's life: Her health was not robust. She told Broman, "I was a sickly child, as well. My mother used to give me cod-liver oil." [51] Garbo dealt with various health issues for her entire life. Most critically she would be diagnosed with pernicious anemia in 1927. A condition that can be treated but not cured. Prior to the development of the first treatments in 1926, it was nearly always fatal within a few years.

As Garbo neared the end of her time as a school student in 1919, a new concern troubled the Gustafson household. Karl was in failing health. He developed kidney disease, a condition that the medical community of the time was ill-prepared to treat. There was no understanding of his condition and no money to treat working-class people with what were considered at the time terminal conditions.

Fortunately, Sven was working as a baker and Alva was an office clerk. Garbo's mother, Anna, worked part-time as well.

"She did several hours cleaning at a local jam factory every day. She also had a paper route early every morning in the area around Blekingegatan," [52] Garbo's friend Antonsson recalled.

While Karl's illness eventually precluded him from working, the household continued to function because of the incomes brought in by Sven, Alva, and Anna. "Despite these issues, Anna, Greta's mother, always had freshly baked bread to offer us and we all thought she was lovely,"[53] related Antonsson.

After Garbo graduated from school at thirteen in spring 1919, she sought work. Swedes were not supposed to start full-time work until they were fifteen, so Garbo found part-time work at local barbershops.

"They've written a lot about my working as a child at a barber's shop, lathering the faces of the men to be shaved," Garbo recounted to Broman in later years. "I didn't just work at one barber's shop, but at three—mostly on Götegan, where they had the most customers. No one forced me to work. I gave my earnings to mother but spent the tips mostly on chocolate."[54]

One of these barbershops was that of Arthur F. Ekengren on Götegan. Ekengren's wife, Sally, ran the cash register and recalled that Garbo made about 4 crowns in salary (about $16.60 in 2025 US dollars[55]) and about the same in tips each week.[56]

Mrs. Ekengren had fond memories of her former employee: "None of her customers ever complained, but they probably wouldn't have, even if she had scalded them. She was really one of the most beautiful creatures I have ever seen. She was more filled out in those days, almost buxom, and she simply radiated happiness. I remember she was wild about Carl Brisson. She used to sing his songs—she knew them all—and she had her locker, where she kept her smock and wraps, covered with pictures of him. We were all very fond of her. She was a sunbeam."[57]

Carl Brisson, a Danish boxer who had transitioned to cabaret singer, broke through with Swedish audiences in 1918 and had become a regular headliner at the Mosebacke Theatre. He sang well and his stage routine resonated with working-class Swedes. Later in life, Brisson and Garbo became friends.

Mrs. Ekengren received two complimentary tickets to a Brisson show at Mosebacke in 1919 and gave them to her daughter and Garbo. Garbo was reportedly such a raucous fan that the audience cheered her as well as Brisson.

Working as a barbershop assistant was a typical entry-level job for working-class women in Stockholm. Most young Swedes only gravitated to more serious jobs in specific trades in their twenties. For the Gustafsons, Garbo's flexible hours in a barbershop close to home meant she could help with her father when he needed care.

Karl Gustafson's kidney disease progressed. During the course of his disease over several months, possibly over a year, Garbo took him to the local clinic several times. Max Behrman recounts that she told him she took her father to the Maria Sjukhus, where they waited in line despite the fact that her father was too weak to stand. Garbo thought he would die as they waited. When they reached reception, the questions were mostly about the family's ability to pay.[58]

Job flexibility was important because her brother, Sven, was fulfilling the first part of his military service in 1919. He trained for four and a half months as a machine gunner with the Vaxholm Grenadier Regiment, based just outside of Stockholm.[59]

Garbo was protective of her family and generally did not discuss them with either the press or most friends. As she told one reporter:

> Why should I tell the world about them? They are mine! No, I am the youngest, but they have always treated me as the oldest. I can't remember being young, really young, like other children. I always had my opinions, but I never told my mind. No one ever seemed to think I was young.[60]

Her brother Sven had a child out of wedlock with a woman named Elsa Hagerman in 1919, so Elsa and their child moved into the Gustafson apartment. The relationship did not last so Elsa and the child moved out. Garbo herself was the first of the siblings to move away from home when she went to Hollywood.

Garbo wrote her family constantly, as her household staff related to Rilla Page Palmborg.[61] Later she sent hundreds of letters to her sister-in-law. Her family was who she most wanted to visit when returning to Sweden, and she bought a farm with her brother so she could live with her family when in Sweden.

Other stories about Greta Garbo as a child have been published. One can't say all of them are wrong, but neither can one establish that they are accurate.

Many were initially published in the Swedish magazine *Lektyr*, which ironically was published by Lars Saxon, a man she had once been close to. From 1930 on, *Lektyr*, a cross between *National Enquirer* and *People*, published mostly fanciful Garbo stories on a near-monthly basis.

That is not to say *Lektyr* should be completely discounted. Saxon knew Garbo, and she probably told him stories of her youth in Söder. People did give interviews about her, which were published in *Lektyr*, the Swedish film fan magazine *Filmjournalen*, and other publications. Memories, however, are fallible. For example, one story printed in the 1930s had a friend remembering when Garbo came home for Christmas 1924 before she left for America. That was the Christmas Garbo spent in Istanbul. Is the story just mixed up with Garbo's next visit to Stockholm in 1928, or is it a complete fabrication?

Garbo's life would now abruptly exit childhood.

Chapter 2 – Formulating a Life

"It was obvious from the start that she had very convincing dramatic talent. The fact that her knowledge of the drama was not wide didn't matter. What really counts in an actress is contact with real, everyday life and an ability to feel and understand it. In that sense Greta Garbo, or Greta Gustafson as she was then, was extremely well equipped. She was very mature for her age." [62]

— Signe Enwall, Garbo's acting coach

Teenaged Garbo at Skansen Park.

The time between the death of Garbo's father and her admission to the Royal Dramatic Theatre School was just over two years. On one hand she had precociously found a good department store job months before she was technically old enough to be employed full time, and years earlier than most Swedes settled into career jobs. On the other hand she spent most of these two years working to leave that job behind and transition into acting. She would develop the people skills necessary to excel at sales. Garbo would stumble into a chance to make industrial films, and take full advantage of it. Garbo would take professional acting lessons, doing everything she could to prepare for her transition. Finally, she would apply to the Royal Dramatic Theatre (Dramaten) School.

Greta Garbo's father died on June 1, 1920, at Maria Hospital, only forty-nine. The cause of death was listed as an inflammation of the kidneys. The underlying cause could have been anything: environmental toxins, bacterial infections, or diabetes.

The event transformed her life in many ways. The youngest child, she had been the one to stay near home to help out with his care needs. Her mother, brother, and sister were all out at work.

> My father died when I was fourteen. God, what a feeling. Someone you love is there, then he is not there. Gone where you can't see him, can't talk with him. You go to the studio, work all day, come home to the hotel, lie down, turn out the lights, and think about him.
>
> The same flesh, the same blood—yet he is gone, never to return. Gone my God, what a feeling.[63]

This loss of a member of her small family must have been difficult for Garbo, but it also opened up opportunities for her to work in a more exciting and lucrative position than that of barber's assistant. In fewer than two months she found a good job at Paul U. Bergström department store (PUB), one of the finest department stores in Stockholm. She was young to land such a well-regarded position.

> It was only a few days from my fifteenth birthday when I started the job at PUB and mother said it was the best birthday present I could get. My future would be assured. I would be able to work at PUB for the rest of my life, which might have been just as well.[64]

Earning a job at PUB as a fifteen-year-old was quite an accomplishment. Working as a clerk was preferable to factory and domestic jobs in the eyes of most Swedes. Service jobs had less drudgery, dirt, and health risk, though the pay was not necessarily better.[65]

Technically Garbo violated employment regulations by starting at PUB two months before she was of age for a full-time job. The more interesting observation is that Garbo was taking a career job when most Swedes didn't begin their careers until their mid-twenties, as they worked in less demanding entry-level jobs for a few years. Beginning a career at fourteen, even fifteen, was the move of a serious and industrious Swede.

The key to success as a salesclerk was to develop a skill in social interactions. Unlike manufacturing jobs where output could be measured every hour, salesclerks had to build relationships with customers over time. As historian Susan Porter Benson writes,

> Saleswomen constantly heard their supervisors emphasize the critical importance of skilled selling, and understood from their daily experience their ability to make or break a sale, but as women workers they remained low-paid and low-valued in the labor-market hierarchy.[66]

Department stores believed that skilled selling led to higher sales. In the United States, the executive secretary of the National Retail Dry Goods Association estimated that the salesperson's powers of persuasion clinched nearly two-thirds of all sales.[67] Therefore, most salesclerks received some kind of performance bonus or product discounts as part of their compensation.

Salesclerks received training in the historical development of products, manufacturing, care, and fabric properties, knowledge Garbo carried with her the rest of her life. Salesclerks also had to manage the class divide between themselves and their middle-to-upper-class customers, simultaneously bonding with them in female comradeship while discussing products. Garbo would excel at this, becoming a salesclerk that the store president and owner was aware of and wanted to retain.

For most women, a job as a salesclerk, like all formal female employment, ended with marriage. Between women leaving for marriage, those fired for poor performance or rules violations, and women who just left for their own reasons, turnover rates in department stores were high.[68]

We don't know much about Garbo's state of mind at the time. She did write a letter before she applied to work at PUB to a childhood friend, Eva Blomqvist, who was spending the summer in the northern town of Sävast. In it, she scolds Eva for what seems like a series of bitchy transgressions. Eva had ignored her when she was out with other friends and their paths crossed. Garbo also perceives Eva as trying to create a division between her and her older sister, Alva. Garbo directly lays down the gauntlet, calling for Eva to behave more as a friend in the future.[69]

A month later, she wrote to Eva again. Clearly Eva has made her amends by post, but they had not met in person. Garbo tells Eva she is now working at PUB, and suggests that Eva apply there as well. In a third letter to Eva, Garbo describes herself as feeling "like I have lived forever and not like a joyful 14-year-old."[70] She has an eye on Paul Bergström's son, and she is aware that her coworkers are evaluating her. "Bergström has a son who is a manager there and he is very stylish. You see, Greta's heart is lost for humanity. Everyone at Bergström's are following me with such an interest, but imagine, I am just fifteen [technically still fourteen] years old."[71]

Regarding a future in acting, Garbo writes, "But, don't worry, I have not given up my dreams of the theater. No, these dreams are still as alive as before."[72] Then just a week later in another letter to Eva, Garbo wrote, "Every moment when I am left on my own, I am longing for the theatre, because there, Eva, is everything I ever wanted."[73] Within two years, through work and study, her theatre dreams came to fruition.

Despite Garbo's desire that Eva join her at PUB, Eva ended up working elsewhere when she returned to Stockholm.

Garbo started on July 26, 1920, her brother's twenty-second birthday. She was initially assigned to the hat department as a paid intern making SEK126 ($400) per month. As store manager Fredric Hellberg would relate;

> But in a large department store, people can easily be short of people, especially during rush hour, and so it happened that Greta had to step in and serve customers.
>
> And then we noticed a strange sales talent in the girl. When she stepped up to the customer, she underwent a sudden transformation. It was as if she had played a "role" — that of a clerk.

> And with inspiration. She felt in the air how each particular customer would be received, the usually quiet girl found the right words and demonstrated the hats in the right way.[74]

Finally able to work legally, she was assigned to the women's ready-to-wear department as a salesclerk. Her manager was Magdalena Hellberg. Fifty years later, when she was in her nineties, she remembered the young Garbo clearly.

> She was one of ten girls working in my department. She was conscientious about her duties, but she was always dreaming of movies and the theatre. She once told me, "It is all I ever think about."
>
> She was very ambitious, quiet, and always took great care about her appearance. Even at her young age one could sense her self-restraint.[75]

While the two years Garbo spent working at PUB were not directly related to theatre, the job would lead to advertising work and provided her a level of comfort interacting with a wide range of people, many of whom came from better economic circumstances than did Garbo. She was able to closely observe and interact with middle-class and upper-class Swedes.

After Garbo had been at PUB only a few months, management came looking for a hat model. Hellberg later related the following:

> One day Mr. Bergström, the big boss of PUB, came asking me if I could suggest a suitable girl to model hats for our spring mail-order catalogue for 1921. Without hesitation I answered, "Miss Gustafson should be perfect for that. She always looks clean and well-groomed and has such a good face."
>
> Greta was thrilled when I told her about her new assignment. Knowing that it was I who had recommended her, she told me, "Aunt Hellberg can arrange anything for me. Oh, how happy I am!" It was probably the longest sentence I ever heard her say at any one time.
>
> So it happened that five pictures of Greta Gustafson appeared in fifty thousand copies of our spring catalogue, distributed all over Sweden. She was still only fifteen, but looked more like twenty.[76]

Another comment about Garbo's work as a salesclerk at PUB came from the man who reported that he had been the one to hire her. In an interview Ernst Lundgren recalled: "I can remember walking past one of the changing rooms where Garbo, then fifteen, was attempting to persuade a customer to buy a dress. She was very persuasive and considerate. 'A good salesgirl,' I said to myself. 'She'll go far.'" [77]

Garbo modelling a hat in 1922.
Courtesy of the Swedish Film Institute.

One final letter from Garbo to Eva Blomqvist exists. Garbo wrote it in August 1921 while in Nykroppa, a small village on the eastern edge of Värmland County. She was staying with her maternal aunt, Sigrid Johansson, who had moved there. Garbo was recovering from an unknown malady while taking an extended break from her job at PUB. Garbo has described herself as being a sickly child and apparently this continued into her teen years. "I am not completely healthy. I am quite pleased to be here, and I am not longing for Stockholm. I wished to come to a place where there would not be so many people, to be able to rest up and recover a bit." [78]

Sigrid Johansson was a wonderful presence. Author Stig Berg, who grew up across the street from her, wrote in his memoir about growing up in Nykroppa: "She was divinely kind to us little boys who ran around there and did one naughty thing after another. Not only that, we almost always got good juice and buns when we came on our visits." [79]

Greta Garbo's film break came in her first months at PUB when Ragnar Ring (John Magnus Ragnar Ring), also known as Lasse Ring, cast her in a minor role in an advertising film he was making for PUB.

Ring had gotten into film over a period of years. Initially he was an officer in the Royal Västernorrland Regiment, based in Sollefteå, a town significantly north of Stockholm. In this capacity he trained military dogs. In 1912 the director, Mauritz Stiller, who will feature significantly in this story shortly, started development of a film that focused on military dogs in the Swedish Army, *När larmklockan ljuder* (When the alarm bell sounds, 1913). While in Sollefteå, Stiller met then-Lt. Ragnar Ring, who explained how the dogs were trained and used. These discussions led to Ring writing the script, as he alone understood what the dogs could be commanded to do.[80]

Ring had done some theatre acting and directing on the side, another reason Stiller thought he could handle the script. Ring, Stiller, and cinematographer Julius Jaenzon seemingly spent many happy evenings at the Hotell Appelberg near the Sollefteå military base, discussing dogs, theatre, and film. The friendship they established producing *När larmklockan ljuder* endured for the rest of Stiller's life.

The film featured three actors, only one of whom, Lilly Jacobson, went on to act in additional films. The cast was fleshed out by officers and soldiers from the Royal Västernorrland Regiment and their trained dogs. The basic plot of the film was that a patrol is sent to fend off an attack, and the military dogs valiantly assist in the defense. *När larmklockan ljuder* ran twenty-two minutes (two reels) and premiered April 17, 1913. It was well received in Sweden and did a significant amount of export business.

Stiller continued making films for Svenska Bio. Ring, intrigued by the work he had done for Stiller, directed a single film for Pathé in 1913, and then was fully mobilized for the duration of World War I.

Ring retired with the rank of captain when he was demobilized after the war ended. He went to work for the publisher AB Hasse W. Tullbergs. Initially, Ring was hired to supervise foreign sales of the series of books Tullbergs published on various Swedish industries.[81] For example, Ring edited a book on Swedish industry that was published in Finnish, and coordinated sales to Finnish officials, purchasing associations, major companies, hotels and restaurants, libraries, and business clubs.[82]

In 1920, Ring was tasked with creating the Tullbergs Film business unit. Initially, this was an extension of their Swedish Industry publishing line, taking what had been a print series and extending it into another medium using film. Ring also pursued additional advertising clients. PUB was one of the first new clients he landed. In December 1920, he was at PUB establishing how he would shoot the advertising film he had in development. As he explained years later,

> Yours truly saved 20 Swedish crowns for a large department store by substituting a paid extra with a sweet and chubby 15-year-old teenager that I pulled out from a sales table, obviously wearing make-up she had put on herself, putting her in the spotlight of the duplex light in front of the film camera.[83]

He also recounted to his granddaughter what that encounter was like. Lillemor Ring related,

> Lasse observed the young girl who was fully engaged in wrapping the perfume for his wife Ruth. He thought she had an interesting appearance. She was a little light-haired, wore a light blue blouse and a dark blue bow loomed from her back-combed hairstyle. At the hairline of her forehead and next to the ears on both sides of her face, her face was framed by beautiful curls that only a curling iron can achieve. She had perfect eyebrows and Lasse was fascinated by her blue eyes and dense long black eyelashes. Her lips were well-shaped and full. She really had unusually beautiful facial features no matter what angle he looked at her from. Maybe she would fit?[84]

Garbo in costume for her first film role.

The idea of the film was to advertise the breadth of products that could be bought at PUB. The storyline was that a family had lost everything in a fire and were now shopping at PUB to outfit their entire lives. Filming took place December 1, 1920,[85] and it became a public event as many people descended on the store to see the process take place.

Garbo figures into a segment where she models a variety of

clothes. This segment was apparently not in the original script. Ring later related that at five feet, seven inches she was too tall to play the part he had cast her in: the family daughter. So, they improvised.[86]

Ragnar Widestedt, one of the actors in Ring's contingent related what had happened later: "When she put on her black and white checkered costume, I thought the effect was exaggerated and absurd. She looked grotesque . . . I leaned toward Ring and suggested that we shouldn't use her. 'She's impossible,' I said."[87]

Widestedt claimed that Lasse Ring shared his opinion, "but [he] was a decent fellow, he didn't want to disappoint Greta or break his promise. 'We can always leave some film on the cutting room floor,' he answered. But then something remarkable happened. When she started acting we noticed that she had studied the situation so carefully and played her role with such intuitive feeling that the result was far too good to throw away."[88]

The years of childhood playacting, the years of watching actors from backstage at Mosebacke, finally found an expression in the way Garbo delivered her performance for Ring. At this point she still had no formal training. She had never worked in film. But she had an intuitive sense as to how to deliver a performance, and Ring did indeed have to keep it.

In Garbo's scene, she models outrageously mismatched and unattractive outfits. She is understated, but clearly delivering on the humorous aspects of the bit.

There are several versions of the PUB film. One film, titled *Herrskapet Stockholm ute på inköp* (Mr. and Mrs. Stockholm go shopping, 1920), ran forty minutes, and was shown against a white background in a PUB storefront window.[89] It premiered December 12, 1920. Another version ran as a short before films in theatres.

Even while untrained, Garbo had something special on film. When Ring's boss, Hasse Tullberg, saw the film, mismatched outfits and all, he said, "She is so beautiful that it hurts my heart to just see her."[90]

Ragnar Ring was always clear that the Greta Garbo who worked for him didn't have the training she shortly received. He wrote, "First and foremost—I have not discovered Greta Garbo. I only discovered Greta Gustafson when she was fifteen years old. I let her act in lighter roles in commercials for a couple of years before all the romantic 'discoveries' of the big star took place."[91]

Garbo connected with Max Gumpel while she was making *Herrskapet Stockholm ute på inköp*. Gumpel was at PUB because his nephew was cast as the family's young son. Born in 1890, Gumpel was fifteen years older than Garbo and accomplished. He had competed as a swimmer in the 1908 Olympics and then won a silver medal in water polo on the 1912 Swedish Olympic team when the Olympics were held in Stockholm. He had just won another water polo medal (bronze) in the 1920 Olympics.

Gumpel came from a wealthy family. He trained as an engineer and then co-founded the successful construction company Gumpel & Bengtsson. From the outside, they had nothing in common, but they went on to become lifelong friends until Gumpel passed away in 1965. If their relationship began as a romantic one, and reports regarding this vary, it quickly faded into a genuine friendship. At the time they met, Gumpel was single. He married Ingeborg Oskara Olsson in 1922.

There is a trend that one can see from this point: Garbo struck people. They noticed her. They found her interesting and engaging. While she was physically attractive, her charisma was what made people interested in Garbo. Whether she was selling clothing at PUB, talking a director into casting her in her first film, or chatting with Gumpel on the set, Garbo was able to relate to people.

Only a few of Ragnar Ring's industrial films remain.[92] In 1928, Ring stated that he had made three hundred to four hundred films for Tullbergs.[93] Whether they were separate film productions or separate edited versions is not known. Tullbergs' industrial films fit into several, often overlapping, categories.

Ring categorized his films by type. In different interviews, he used slightly different definitions; it is not clear if the market changed over time or if he was just giving examples. These categories included advertising, archival, industrial, business, educational, home, family, propaganda, and technical films.[94] In addition to the projectors used in theatres, there was a booming business in smaller projectors and films were shown everywhere. Companies screened films for visitors, associations screened films at meetings, and retailers showed films in store windows.

Tullbergs frequently used the same recorded film in multiple projects. These could be films with slightly different audiences, including films for export that needed proper intertitles in the right language. For example, he made tourist films for the state railways and films for the Swedish Transportation

Association.[95] Many export films were just variants of a Swedish film with some altered scenes. So, version control of the historic record is difficult.

For example, the 1921 film *Sverige och Svenska Industrier* (Sweden and Swedish industries) was recut and retitled as *Tokiofilmen* (The Tokyo film, 1922). This version included Greta Garbo presenting each section.

If Ring produced three hundred to four hundred films between 1920 and 1928, he probably produced seventy-five to one hundred during the nearly two years between the first film he made with Garbo in December 1920 and the start of her Dramaten student years in September 1922.

Only thirteen Tullbergs films in this date range exist in the Swedish Film Database.[96] Many of Tullbergs' films were for overseas customers. Additional Tullbergs films have been found in both the Finnish and Norwegian archives. None of the available films feature Garbo, but many of the films in the Finnish and Norwegian archives are not available to watch. Denmark and Germany were also markets that Ring mentioned in interviews, but no Tullbergs films have been found in either country so far.

Greta Garbo was involved in four productions for Tullbergs that have survived. The first, the December 1920 job for PUB, was released in several versions. There are two censorship numbers for consecutive dates for *Paul U. Bergström AB Stockholm* (December 11) and *Herrskapet Stockholm ute på inköp* (Mr. and Mrs. Stockholm go shopping) (December 12).[97] The Paul U. Bergström version was about half the length of the theatrical version.

Konsums nya bageri (Konsum's new bakery) was released in 1921, though the exact date is not known. The film was for a subsidiary of Konsumtionsföreningen. Konsumtionsföreningen was a co-op that was in several businesses and used Tullbergs Film frequently.

Another surviving film is *Konsumtionsföreningen Stockholm med omnejd* (Consumer's association, Stockholm and surroundings). This film premiered on September 25, 1921.[98]

Tokiofilmen was delivered to the Swedish government by Ring in January 1922.[99] It was based on footage from prior industrial films. Whether new footage was shot, in addition to the sequences with Garbo, is not known. This twenty-minute film was designed to be shown in five parts, each focused on an aspect of Swedish industry. Garbo's task was simply to introduce each segment by pointing to the relevant location on a map of Sweden. Garbo was given leave from PUB for her work on this film as it was considered to be in the interests of Swedish industry and the government.

Did she appear in any of the lost films? The odds seem high based on Ring's comments and contemporary press.

The fourteen extant Tullbergs films from 1920 through 1922 represent about 15 to 20 percent of their total production during the window in which Greta Garbo worked for them. Since Garbo appears in four of these fourteen films, there could easily be a dozen lost Garbo industrial films. The known Garbo films were saved because they received special handling in the 1930s due to her presence in them. The PUB and co-op films were re-edited and released in theatres as shorts. Tokiofilmen was a government project and therefore was archived.

In 1942, Ring was invited to give a speech at an event honoring him upon his sixtieth birthday. He recalled working with Garbo: "At first, she was an extra in some film advertisements, but soon we found that she should get more time on film and for the next two years we hired her for several film advertisements."[100]

Garbo was also spoken of as one of the "Tullbergs film girls" in a 1922 article on Tokiofilmen,[101] implying an ongoing relationship between Garbo and Tullbergs.

In yet another article, Ring recounted that, "The little shop assistant was able to cash in on several film roles at rather reasonable cost to me during the following two years, and I have never seen anyone so profoundly joyful and proud of two extra ten crown bills as she."[102]

Finally, Ring explained, he and Garbo worked "nights and weekends." While this is a Swedish colloquialism for hard work, it might also be literally true, as Garbo was moonlighting from PUB for the two Konsumtionsföreningen productions.

Therefore, it is likely that Garbo had much more experience acting in film than previously thought. Ring did not provide her with the kind of training she later received, but she would have been comfortable on camera.

Lasse Ring also provided Garbo with her first experience on a theatrical film. He had many contacts in the film industry beyond Mauritz Stiller, one of whom was director John W. Brunius. His project in December 1920 was the film *En lyckoriddare* (A knight of fortune, 1921) with Gösta Ekman and

Mary Johnson in the lead roles (therefore filmed immediately after Garbo's work for PUB). Lasse told Brunius how well Garbo had performed for him and that she and her older sister, Alva, wanted to be extras.

The filming location was the studio Skandiaateljén, in Stocksund. This was then an ultra-modern film stage that was built as a huge greenhouse in order to receive as much light as possible. The sisters were given minor roles, Greta as the maid and Alva as a girl at the pub. The film premiered on March 14, 1921.[103]

Ragnar Ring and Greta Garbo clearly developed a friendship beyond their professional relationship. Magdalena Hellberg observed, "I could see that he was growing very fond of the young Greta, and I noticed that she, although still only sixteen or seventeen, responded to his attentions. I cautioned her, saying, 'Miss Gustafson, you shouldn't be seeing a man so much older than yourself.' Her short reply to my warning was, 'Well, I'll always learn something.'"[104]

When Garbo learned that her immediate supervisor at PUB, Magdalena Hellberg, was related to a well-known stage actor, she pumped her for information about acting. Hellberg ended up as an intermediary between the two of them:

> To my surprise she discovered very soon that I had a close relative who was an actor at the Royal Dramatic Theatre. His name was Ivar Kåge [a well-known Swedish stage, and later film, actor]. Greta was always putting questions to me about the theater which I could not answer, but I would promise to ask Ivar when I saw him. Soon I became an intermediary, transmitting questions from one and bringing back answers and advice from the other.[105]

PUB had an amateur theatre club for its employees, but Garbo never joined it. Instead, she took her Tullbergs earnings and invested in private acting lessons. This demonstrates that Garbo's intent even while working at PUB was to find a way to transition to an acting career. In going to Frans Enwall, she was working with the best freelance acting coach available in Stockholm. Garbo later related:

> And that's all I knew of the stage until I was sixteen. Then I met an actor. And I told him, just like millions tell actors, that I wanted to go on the stage. Asked him, just like all the others, how I could do it.

> He called upon another actor, better known, and sent me to him.
>
> It was Frans Enwall.
>
> He is dead now, but he has a daughter on the stage in Sweden. He said he would ask if they would let me try to get into the Dramatic School of the Royal Theater [colloquially known as Dramaten] in Stockholm.[106]

Frans Enwall had been a Dramaten student, followed by a long career on the Dramaten stage. He started teaching at the school in 1897, rising to head in 1907.

Garbo herself stated that she had taken acting lessons for six months. Given that she applied to Dramaten in August 1922, she probably started the lessons in late 1921 or early 1922, soon after he retired.

All of these commitments added up. Garbo would typically have worked about 48 hours per week in a job like the one she had at PUB.[107] To this, she was adding both private acting lessons and freelance film work for Tullbergs.

In the summer of 1922, Ragnar Ring asked Paul Bergström to give Garbo three weeks off to make *En vikingafilm* (A viking film), a feature-length film that was an advertisement for Viking Shoe Polish. Ring was offering her 1000 crowns ($5,000). Bergström responded to Ring that he would not give Garbo time off to make the film, writing, "Miss Gustafson, in spite her youth, is one of the best saleswomen in my entire company."[108]

While no record of Garbo's commission earnings at PUB has ever been found, it is likely that she earned commissions in addition to her salary, as that was typical for department store salesclerks then in Sweden.[109] If she was, as Bergström wrote, one of the best salesclerks, those commissions would have been a nice supplement to her wages and one reason that Bergström could argue with Ring that Garbo would be giving up a promising and steady job for a riskier career as a film actress.

Despite the fact that he was offering to pay her more than she was making at PUB, after his exchange with Bergström Ring was concerned that Garbo would be left without income after the short three-week production. He counseled her to keep her job at PUB. Ring recounted,

> But that was when her boss came and told me what was on his

> mind. I was severely reprimanded for "giving the girl crazy ideas about the movies," she who had the best future in film. So, we all know what happened. As an honest man, I felt like it was my duty to tell her to drop her dreams to be a movie star and focus on her job. This made Greta angry.[110]

That Bergström was moved to keep Garbo is by itself interesting. In America, the turnover of department store sales staff between 1925 and 1930 varied between 67 percent and 250 percent annually.[111] Sweden would not have been much different. Clearly, Garbo had made an impression at PUB.

Ring also later said, "The girl did as she had always done; she took control of the situation herself. She left the department store and went to the movie industry by free will, because that was her destiny."[112]

A career in acting would have an additional benefit for Garbo if it were to work out. Acting was one of the few vehicles for Swedish women to achieve recognition and financial independence in the early twentieth century. A 1914 book on Swedish career women featured ten actresses.[113]

At the time she was evaluating her options before quitting her job at PUB, she clearly already hoped to be admitted to Dramaten. She had been taking lessons for at least six months, first with Frans Enwall and then, after his health deteriorated, with his daughter, Signe. A Dramaten graduate herself, she was a member of the Dramaten ensemble. If Garbo were to be admitted, she would pay no tuition, but she would receive no salary either. At best, she would earn small amounts for appearing in minor roles supporting the company.

Garbo had wanted to be an actor for many years, literally since childhood. But it had always seemed unrealistic for a child without the advantages of secondary schooling that many Dramaten actors had. She had a solid job at PUB, where she was successful. She had gotten into industrial films—not the usual path to an acting career, but at least it had given her exposure and contacts. The constancy of her desire to be an actor came out in several interviews she gave to Ruth Biery.

Garbo never addressed the issue, but being cast in a film in the summer of 1922 would provide her more money than she could make working for PUB for a few extra weeks. If she got admitted to Dramaten, this money would help her until she could start working as an actor.

Since she was not part of the cast for *En vikingafilm*, another low budget film going into production in the summer of 1922 caught her eye. Erik Petschler had written the script for a comedy film that followed the Mack Sennett formula of filling the screen with slapstick comedy and beautiful women.

The Dramaten entrance applications were due in August. She may have already met Erik Petschler and had an offer to act in *Luffar-Petter* (Peter the Tramp) before the application deadline arrived. Garbo decided that now was the time to commit to a career as an actor. She resigned from her job at PUB on July 22, 1922, four days shy of exactly two years.

Applying to the Dramaten school was the culmination of Garbo's efforts to find a way to transition to a career as an actor. Her career options fell into a couple of possible solutions. She could get into Dramaten, where she would gain additional stage training and assurance that she would at least have a chance to make it as a professional actor. Acceptance at Dramaten was the most positive outcome possible because of its stature and the nature of its program.

If she did not get in, she could apply to work for the Ranft organization, which ran many of the remaining high-end theaters in Sweden. Based on her prior work with Ring, she could continue to work with him on industrial films. As some of them became more "feature film like," the pay became more reasonable, as *En vikingafilm* had shown her. Finally, working with Erik Petschler would give her a role in a theatrically released film, which could hopefully lead to others. While at this point Garbo clearly saw herself as a future stage actress, she had to find a way into the business. A chance at one of these options, or some combination, was enough for Garbo to take the risk and quit her nice, secure job at PUB.

Signe Enwall took over Garbo's lessons from her father, who had taken ill. Enwall found her to be a talented, though raw, pupil: "It was obvious from the start that she had very convincing dramatic talent. The fact that her knowledge of the drama was not wide didn't matter. What really counts in an actress is contact with real, everyday life and an ability to feel and understand it. In that sense Greta Garbo, or Greta Gustafson as she was then, was extremely well equipped. She was very mature for her age."[114]

She recalled preparing for the audition with Garbo: "Don't forget that she was only sixteen years old, and that she was not from a theatrical family. But she was so anxious to succeed that she was completely receptive to assistance. We picked out the parts for the audition together after discussion. They were things I felt she was able to do."[115]

Of the applications submitted by the August 18 deadline, twenty-five candidates were approved for auditions,[116] down from forty-five auditions in 1921 due to the tough new admissions procedures instituted for this class[117] Gustaf Molander reported that twenty-two of the aspirants granted auditions were women.[118] The odds of surviving the cut to the final four women were daunting, less than one in five. By contrast, both men who auditioned were admitted.

Reflecting back on Dramaten several years later, Garbo talked about the school and the audition:

> The School is a part of the Royal Theater of the King and Queen of Sweden. No, it doesn't cost anything to go there, but you are not paid for your work either. You take a test to get in. There is a jury of about 20 people. Newspapermen, critics, theatrical people, actors, the heads of the school, and others. I studied for six months. They gave me a Swedish play by Selma Lagerlof. The auditions took place on September 11 and 12.[119]

School started six days later on September 18, a compressed timeframe that seems amazing today. Garbo recalled the following:

> My test came on a beautiful day in August [actually September]. It wasn't cold, but it wasn't hot either, as it is in this country. I remember it was right after noon. I was just seventeen [actually sixteen]. And I was frightened. My knees shook. I trembled all over. Oh. I almost fainted afterwards!
>
> I couldn't see a person. They were down in front. All I could see was that black pit—that black open space. All I could hear was whispering. I was so shy! I had never tried to act. The one-year pupils were on the stage. They read the lines of the parts which were not mine. I said my speech, all right. Then I just ran off. I forgot to say good-bye. And I was so frightened. I thought they would think I had not been polite because I had forgotten. In a couple of days, they telephoned that I had been admitted.[120]

After resigning her job at PUB, Garbo would make her first major theatrical film before starting school. She would be unhappy with the process and the final product. However, it would provide money for her to live on while in school.

* * *

Erik Petschler was born in 1881 and was acting in theatre in the late 1890s. Primarily he was a stage actor. He had minor roles in a number of Swedish films before he starred in his own film productions in the early 1920s.

Luffar-Petter (Peter the Tramp) was the first theatrical film to feature Garbo in a visible role. She played one of three bathing beauties. Petschler produced, directed, and starred in the film. It was filmed primarily in August 1922 and released that December.

The production records for *Luffar-Petter* have not been found. But a few records for the Petschler film *Värmlänningarna (Värmlanders*, 1921) exist.[121] *Värmlänningarna* is a six-reel film compared to the five reels for *Luffar-Petter.* It took three weeks[122] and was filmed in Ransäter, a small town not quite midway between Stockholm and Oslo in the heart of Värmland. So, one could assume that *Luffar-Petter*, which had two filming locations, would have taken about as long because of the second location.

Värmlänningarna is based on a classic Swedish play and the story has been remade multiple times, Petschler's being the second of five Swedish-language versions. The story is about two young lovers separated by family antagonisms and class.

Petschler's records also give one an idea as to what various roles in a second-tier Swedish film might pay. The leads received 2,000 to 3,500 crowns ($10,000 to $17,500). Featured players received 1,500 crowns ($7,500).[123]

As Ring wrote that he had offered Garbo 1,000 crowns ($5,000) for the role in *En vikingafilm*, it seems likely that Garbo received 1,000 to 1,500 crowns ($5,000 to $7,500) for her work in *Luffar-Petter*. Enough to ease her life at Dramaten when added to her family's support.

Värmlänningarna was a successful film, receiving both good reviews and strong ticket sales. It also did well when exported to other countries. This success either allowed Petschler to self-fund *Luffar-Petter* or simplified his ability to raise the necessary funds.

Petschler later spun a tale of how he came to cast Garbo in *Luffar-Petter*, and how he subsequently counseled her to apply to Dramaten, that could not possibly be accurate.

Garbo in costume for *Luffar-Petter*.

Instead of ending up at Dramaten because of the patronage and good efforts of Erik Petschler, Garbo executed a long-term plan to prepare herself for a career as an actress. Being accepted to Dramaten was a break she made for herself.

Garbo clearly felt working with Petschler was unsatisfactory. In a September 1926 letter to Mimi Pollak, she asks Mimi to tell Mona Mårtenson that she recommends turning down a job offer from Petschler.[124] Mårtenson did take a lead role in the Petschler film *Bröllopet i Bränna* later that year.

While we don't have a record of how Garbo networked, she had made connections that could not have hurt her application. She had studied with Frans Enwall and his daughter Signe, both well connected to Dramaten. She had become friendly with the actor Ivar Kåge. She had worked for Ragnar Ring, who knew Gustaf Molander's friend Mauritz Stiller. She had been an extra for the director John Brunius. Not a bad set of connections for a sixteen-year-old salesclerk. If one cared to ask more broadly among the well-to-do, both Paul Bergström and Max Gumpel thought well of her.

That fall after school started, Dramaten classmates watched Vera Schmiterlöw (class of 1921)[125] in *Thomas Graals myndling*, which premiered October 9, 1922. Then at the end of October came a premiere with classmate Mimi Pollak as one of the leads in *Amatörfilmen*. Tore Lindwall and Georg Funkquist (class of 1921) both had supporting roles. These two films, both directed by Dramaten school head Gustaf Molander, were not acclaimed by critics as masterpieces, but had done reasonably well.

By contrast, *Luffar-Petter* was decidedly lowbrow. The concept was stolen blatantly from Mack Sennett. Critics panned it as art, but they recognized that it might have commercial appeal. Petschler lacked Sennett's deft touch. The film's release seems to have been delayed by censorship issues. The initial trade publicity came well before the film's release. *Luffar-Petter* was financially successful and played for several months around Sweden, perhaps because it was clearly homegrown. Garbo and the two other bathing beauties were presented in the two-page trade ad for distributors in the trade magazine *Filmbladet*. Consumer ads focused on Petschler, who starred as the comic fulcrum of the film. Garbo received but brief mentions in reviews. The reviews focused on the director and how the film was both funny and derivative.

Garbo went to the premiere of *Luffar-Petter* on December 22 with schoolmates Alf Sjöberg and Mimi Pollak. It was a difficult experience for her. Sjöberg recalled being befuddled when Garbo confided that her part was that of a bathing beauty. He already considered her the premiere student in her class after just four months.[126]

They left before the credits rolled. Sjöberg recalled how they consoled Garbo as they wandered the city: "We pulled the poor girl out of the theatre before the lights went up. Wandering the streets we made her make a holy promise that she would never again do anything with film. Her right place was, and remained, the theatre."[127]

Garbo was unhappy with the process of working for Petschler and the product created. Being cast as mere eye candy isn't quite universal for women trying to break into film acting, but it is close. In this sense Garbo's experience isn't exceptional. What came next was. The Dramaten school would allow Garbo, just seventeen, to develop her immense talent in a supportive environment, and from this point forward producers and directors would treat her as a professional.

Chapter 3 – Dramaten

"She was gifted, of course;
though it seemed as though she did not dare show it,
as though she did not have the courage to be truly herself.
But at times it would flash out,
especially if something fired her imagination." [128]

— Gustaf Molander, Director of the Royal Dramatic Theatre School

Greta Garbo and her classmates during her second year at Dramaten.

Garbo could not have been more fortunate than to be trained at Dramaten. There were other theatre schools in the world in the 1920s, but most actors learned by working their way up in the profession by starting in small roles while learning on the fly. Dramaten, and its school, were funded by the state and the school didn't charge tuition.

Dramaten was part of a unique Swedish approach to theatre. Theatre was attended more broadly there than elsewhere. Actors had better social status. Finally, Sweden had been developing a more naturalistic style that was modern and rooted in psychology. The naturalistic style was then uncommon, ascendant in the Nordic theatre and at Stanislavski's Moscow Art Theatre. Naturalistic acting appeared elsewhere in Europe, but it was not dominant yet. The transition to naturalistic acting will be addressed below.

The Royal Dramatic Theatre in 1930.

* * *

Dramaten put Garbo on the road to Hollywood. There she was trained at the highest level as a naturalistic actor. This would open all the professional doors she walked through. Garbo's first day at Dramaten was September 18, 1922, her seventeenth birthday. Apparently as they were going through the initial introductions of the relatively small student group, she blurted out this fact, breaking the ice. She made lifelong friends among this small group.

Her talent was obvious to Gustaf Molander and the staff. This would come across both in how her teachers would later speak of her and how quickly they put her on stage. Garbo was given roles rapidly, which was uncommon.

The six students in the class of 1922 were an unusually talented mix, among whom Garbo still stood out. A seventh student, Alf Sjöberg, was actually admitted in 1922 as a second-year student, the only time this happened in the history of the Dramaten school.[129] The base Dramaten program was two years. During Garbo's first year the members of the eight-person class of 1921 mingled with the class of 1922 in everything they did. Dramaten occasionally invited students for a third year after their two-year commitment. In 1922, Märta Ekström was a third-year student.

Of these sixteen students, eight would leave indelible marks on Swedish film and theatre. Alf Sjöberg, from the class of 1922, went on to a great career, primarily as a director and writer, though he acted as well. In turn, Sjöberg's protégé, Ingmar Bergman, would write and direct a string of classic Swedish films in the fifties and sixties. Mona Mårtenson, Arnold Sjöstrand, Georg Funkquist, and Tore Lindwall all went on to long and significant careers in Swedish theatre, film, and television. Vera Schmiterlöw first had a successful film career in Germany. She returned to Sweden when the Nazis took power, but she did not resume her film career until later in life, when she appeared in several miniseries in the sixties and seventies.

Garbo's classmate Mimi Pollak would play many film and theatre roles, but would become best known as a director and instructor, teaching at Dramaten for over twenty years. Karl-Magnus Thulstrup had a long acting career in film, theatre, and TV.

The new class of 1923, when it arrived the following year, was only four students. Two of them, Sten Lindgren and Holger Löwenadler, had brilliant careers in Sweden.

Of this group Garbo was closest to Pollak, Sjöberg, and Schmiterlöw. She remained in touch with them for years.

Garbo loved Dramaten, both the program and her fellow students. Reminiscing to Sven Broman years later, she described Dramaten: "It was rather different. It was a good school. Perhaps the happiest time of my life."[130]

In her extensive interview with Ruth Biery in 1928, she spent a lot of time talking about Dramaten and her failings as a student. Garbo recounted the following to her:

> "Oh. God. I was happy! I almost died. Oh, now, even now, I can hardly breathe when I remember. For now, pretty soon, I knew I was to be a real actress!" But, her voice became wistful, perhaps, a little regretful. Then she laughed and her eyes twinkled. People do not often see Greta Garbo's eyes twinkle.
>
> "But I was a very bad child. I upset the whole school. I liked to go out at night. We lived right in Stockholm and distances are not as far there, you know. You can take a taxi and be almost anywhere in five minutes. Any theater in the city. I liked to go to the theater in the evening. So I was late almost every morning! Exercises came first—and I almost always missed them. The other pupils were charming, lovely girls who were always on time. Then, in would come Garbo, late as usual. I'd come in the door and say, 'There's a rumor about that this school is still here. But I'm so tired; Garbo's so tired—'
>
> "And nobody would say a word to me!
>
> "Then it became serious. I started being late. If one had the privilege, you know. No, they didn't scold me. If I had been scolded. I'd have been there. I cannot stand to be scolded. Usually, we'd go out and drink coffee, all together, when I finally got there. Yes, they taught us dancing. But I can't dance. I was ashamed to dance. . . . The school was wonderful. We had the very best teachers. We were given plays to study. Two pupils and a teacher would study together. No, we were never on the stage. Oh, we were on the background of the Royal Theater. We never said anything. Just went on to learn what you call stage presence."[131]

Dramaten tolerated her tardiness. Molander once jokingly told an interviewer that he didn't remember her from class as she always slept through it.

A school like Dramaten was not how the vast majority of actors of the time were trained; it was a unique program. Most actors learned the craft in small theatres and touring troupes, working their way up over years of practice.

Instead, Garbo had joined one of the finest acting schools in the world. Garbo had excellent teachers and they taught a naturalistic acting style. In the curriculum at Dramaten, students studied diction, portrayal, deportment, movement, dance, fencing, and history.

Molander kept notebooks on the school each year. His first mention of Garbo in the 1922–23 notebook refers to her as "Greta Garbo [Gustafson]." So, contrary to many later claims of who suggested the name, she was already transitioning to using the name Garbo from the day she started Dramaten. In the remaining places where Molander assigns Garbo to roles, he transposes the order to "Greta Gustafson [Garbo]."[132]

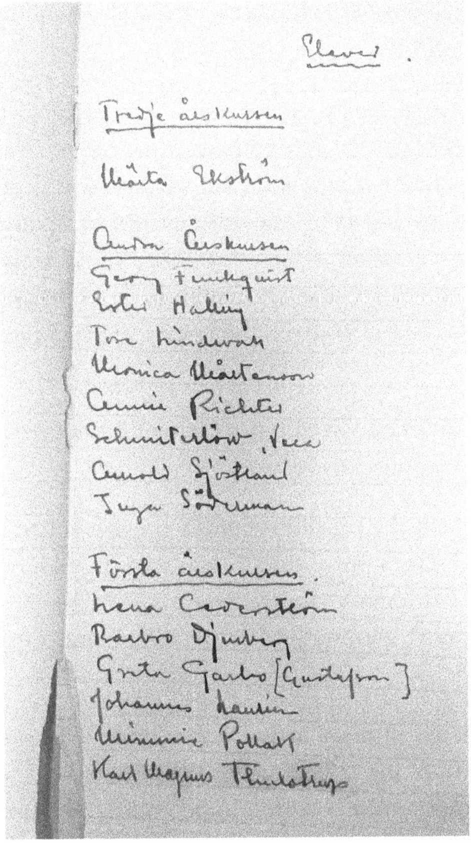

The first page regarding students from Gustaf Molander's notebook on the Dramaten class of 1922. Photo by Scott Reisfield. Courtesy of Stockholm University of the Arts.

In his notebook for 1923–24, Garbo appears under only the name "Greta Garbo" from its start in September." The transition is complete, though legally she did not change her name until December 1923.[133]

Garbo was keenly aware that her social circumstances were different from those of her Dramaten classmates. While Dramaten did not charge tuition, students had to pay their own living expenses. Garbo had the money she had saved from working at PUB and from *Luffar-Petter*. She was living with her family and they were investing in her future.

Dramaten was a way into acting for the middle class. In some ways it was a privileged shortcut, quicker than working one's way up in normal theatres. The other students in her class had all gone to private schools at some point. They spoke middle- or upper-class Swedish. They were older. At seventeen, Garbo was a year and a half younger than any other student. Several had been acquainted with each other before becoming Dramaten students.

Garbo was sensitive about this. In an undated letter to Mimi Pollak, she wrote, "Misse [Mimi Pollak's nickname] I am afraid that I shall never understand what I read. I've read something the last days but really don't understand what I read. But I want to try again—won't you darling when you have a chance advise me from your experience what I should buy in books. Not just prose. If you will I will be very grateful."[134]

Garbo was not the first working-class student to attend. Tora Teje had grown up in the same Söder neighborhood as Garbo. Teje gained admission to Dramaten at the age of fifteen by lying about her age, and then went on to a fabulous career on various Stockholm stages. In 1913, she shifted from Dramaten to working for the Albert Ranft organization, which controlled most of the theatres in Sweden at this time. She returned to Dramaten in 1923, briefly overlapping the end of Garbo's time there. However, they never appeared together on stage.

Garbo saw Teje act in the October 25, 1923, Swedish premiere of *Anna Christie,* in the role Garbo immortalized on film in 1930.

The school itself was in a small area on the third floor of the theatre. It had a classroom, a rehearsal space, the director's office, and a coatroom. It did have easy access to the third balcony of the main theatre, from which students could watch rehearsals. Students didn't comingle with the actors, and were not allowed in the actors' lounge.[135]

First-year students primarily appeared in plays as uncredited extras. Garbo was an exception.[136] Given the talent of her schoolmates, this is notable. She had a minor role in *Äfventyret (The Beautiful Adventure)* beginning November 4, 1922. She hadn't been at Dramaten for even two months. She got two additional minor roles in the first half of 1923.

By contrast, the two actors from the class of 1921 who went on to the most significant careers on stage, Georg Funkquist and Arnold Sjöstrand, didn't get a single named role at any point in their first year. Neither did the women in the class of 1921, Vera Schmiterlöw and Mona Mårtenson.

From her own class of 1922, Mimi Pollak and Lena Cederström each appeared in the fall 1922 production of *The Beautiful Adventure* with Garbo. No one else was cast in any role during the first year.

"Greta was the youngest in age in our litter—but still the oldest," Mimi Pollak recalled. "Quiet, thoughtful, scared, fearless, curious about life and very ready to laugh, an absolutely wonderfully composed person."[137] This brings to mind comments made by Garbo herself, and others, about how her siblings treated Greta, the youngest, as the most mature even during her childhood.

Garbo's classmates wrote surprisingly little about their friend, protecting her. Many would only ever talk about their Dramaten years with fellow actor Fritiof Billquist, not knowing he was writing a book about Garbo. In their more public comments, they remember her impact, particularly her voice. The great Swedish director, Alf Sjöberg, remembered the first time she acted on stage as a student. "On stage [Gustaf] Molander had begun with *Den osynlige*[138] *[The Invisible]*, Greta had a small part but it came as a shock for many. The voice, the low-pitched voice."[139]

Lena Cederström recalled, "When we first were extras at the theater, and Greta had a couple of lines to say, how everything turned completely silent around her, and all actors were listening to the young student, and all of us were probably thinking about what would become of this beautiful blond girl."[140]

Garbo wrote to Mimi Pollak about her fond memories of the years at Dramaten, being backstage and chatting with her classmates, drinking coffee or beer, and smoking cigarettes while gossiping at restaurants. Mimi recalled the following:

> One of my fondest memories of Greta from our time as students was from a big party that the Royal Dramatic Theatre arranged for Halfdan Christensen in the large ballroom at [the] Strand Hotel. Students were also invited, and we felt so joyful to be at a party with all the stars of the theater. The students were of course placed together at the end of the table. We had a very good time, and when dinner was over, a small, improvised cabaret took place. Imagine my horror when I saw Greta step up in the ball room to sing the latest cabaret song *"Fru från Hagalund" ("I am the Lady from Hagalund")!* Greta was wonderful! She always did what you least suspected."[141]

Pollak also recounted how they watched established actors on the Dramaten stage:

> As soon as Greta and I had a few break hours between lessons, we slipped out on the third balcony and watched what was happening on the dimly lit stage.[142]

Karl Nygren, Dramaten's speech instructor, recalled the following:

> In the classroom she was very quiet. Sometimes I wished she would show more initiative. I remember that now and again she seemed very depressed and troubled. She often blushed, especially when we were discussing things that she wasn't acquainted with. I think this was probably due to the fact that her schooling had been meager, and she was acutely conscious of that. I was often sorry for her in the classroom. But when I would meet her by chance in the halls or in the theatre she was not at all bashful.[143]

He remembered the time one day during class when he was trying to explain the way to make certain tones.

"I wanted to show how to speak with a kind of nasal twang. In trying to get this across I imitated the popular cabaret stars, Hansi and Jean Moreau. Always after that, whenever I met Greta outside the classroom she would greet me in those nasal tones, saying, 'Good morning, Director Nygren. Is this the right way to say it?' She had a very pleasing personality, very attractive."[144]

Garbo also used to entertain her fellow students with the adventures of two imaginary rabbits. Fingal and Agaton. Fingal was a clever small brown rabbit, while Agaton was a large white silly one. She could hold the entire group in a thrall with their newest tale.[145]

Dramaten was an important crucible for her development. The quality of her education there, and its focus on the naturalistic style, was not an accident. Rather it was the result of the development of Swedish society and national feeling. Sweden had a long history of theater, going back to King Gustav III, who moonlighted as a playwright. The king founded Kungliga Dramatiska Teatern (the Royal Dramatic Theatre), colloquially Dramaten, in 1788, in part to put on his own plays. Theater took on a more important role in Swedish culture from that point. Dramaten was created expressly for the people; prior to its creation, almost all theater had been staged at court. Gustav III specifically called for a Swedish theater about Swedish life with Swedish playwrights and Swedish actors.[146]

While the institution of Dramaten was over 130 years old by the time Garbo became a student, the building itself had only opened in 1908. After the original building burned, Dramaten had been housed in other theaters, and had lost its royal patronage. All this changed in the 1890s due to the rise of the National Romantic movement and its focus on Swedishness. This culminated in the renewed royal patronage and a new theater building.[147]

Swedish society was very theater oriented. Between 1890 and 1910, Stockholm had more theatre seats per capita than any major city in Europe, serving a literate, eager, and cosmopolitan public. [148]For example, in 1910 Stockholm, with a population of three hundred thousand, had nine spoken-word theaters. Copenhagen had but seven theaters to serve its population of half a million.[149]

As explained by theater historian John Lewis Austin, the growth of development of new theaters and theatergoing was part of the progression of the Swedish Romantic movement in creating the modern Swedish nation.

> The best evidence that the modern project did not lack ambition in other areas was to be found in the material formation of the city itself. The most serious, and arguably most successful, project at the sekelskifte was the creation of a modern capital, and the invention of modern Stockholm had a great significance to formations in the theatre.[150]

The way theater in Sweden developed—in fact, the way the very city of Stockholm was developed—flowed from the National Romantic movement that defined the nation at that time. Austin summed it up succinctly:

> The city's pressing need for new residential as well as institutional structures coincided with the nation's need to advertise its claim to modernity, both domestically and internationally. This process did not begin at any specific moment, of course, but a periodization is useful. For purposes of this study, the pivotal phase of the sekelskifte can be said to have begun with the Stockholm Exposition of Art and Industry in 1897.[151]

Where in the nineteenth century theaters had been situated in local neighborhoods, such as the Södra and Mosebacke Theatres in Söder that Garbo visited in her youth, the new theatres were built in the city center, which was accessible due to the new network of streetcars.

Stockholm offered many types of theater. Dramaten offered state-sponsored highbrow productions. The theater network of Albert Ranft offered spoken-word plays at a variety of price points, both downtown and in the neighborhoods. Not classed as theaters in the same sense were neighborhood cabarets. Stockholm also had a fine opera. By 1920, Stockholm supported fourteen spoken-word theatres, an opera, fifteen summer theatres, and numerous cabarets.[152]

Swedish theater originally followed the conventions of French theater, deferring to France culturally as many countries in Europe did. But in the late nineteenth century Scandinavia, and specifically Stockholm, brought forth a new style of theater that came to dominate stages around the world. Known as modern theater, it was typified by "psychologically motivated, naturalistically detailed acting."[153] It is this naturalistic acting style that Garbo would use to revolutionize Hollywood.

Two playwrights emerged who turned Swedish theatre toward modern theatre. Both Henrik Ibsen (Norwegian) and August Strindberg (Swedish) wrote plays that were more realistic and required actors to communicate with more subtlety from the stage. Their work was in some ways not wholly original. Theater scholars have found plays that shaped this movement in earlier French productions, and Strindberg was well acquainted with the Theatre Libre in Paris. Finnish-Swedish playwright Julius Wecksell had written the early naturalistic play *Daniel Hjort* in 1862.

What Ibsen, Strindberg, and to a lesser extent Bjørnson did was to produce a body of significant plays so as to make modern theater an everyday experience instead of an oddity.[154]

Modern theater encompassed writing, acting, and production. Writers sought to create plays that addressed modern social problems. The plays were innovative, handling character with more subtlety and through clearly psychological prisms. The writers employed stark realism and then symbolic and expressionistic devices to make points. Frequently bold technical experimentation would be included, in portrayals, in staging, or in the flow of the performance.[155]

The greatest expression of this practice was Strindberg's Intimate Theater, whose impact extended far beyond its two brief incarnations. Founded in 1907 and refounded in 1915, the Intimate Theater was small and brought spectators closer to the stage. While both Dramaten and the Ranft theaters put on modern plays by Ibsen, Strindberg, and others, the Intimate Theater was a space specifically designed for them.

Garbo herself was never on the stage of the Intimate Theater. The style of acting she learned, her whole conception of what made good theater, was formed by people who had worked there and been influenced by its impact on Stockholm. Mauritz Stiller spent a year managing the Intimate Theater and, while still a director for Svensk Filmindustri, directed a number of modern plays at both the Intimate Theater in Stockholm and the similar Lorensberg Theatre in Gothenburg.[156]

Sweden also learned from developments in theater pioneered in other countries. Max Reinhardt's touring productions of *The Pelican* and *A Dream Play* in the years before Garbo started at Dramaten had a huge impact on Swedish theater and set design in 1920 and 1921.[157] Stanislavski brought the Moscow Art Theatre to Stockholm in 1921 and 1922 just before Garbo started at Dramaten, putting on several of his classic plays: *Uncle Vanya, The Cherry Orchard*, and *Three Sisters*, as well as some other plays.[158] Stanislavski in turn had modeled the acting at the Moscow Art Theatre on Swedish acting.

Dramaten put on naturalistic plays by Eugene O'Neill starting with *Anna Christie* in 1923. Dramaten's connection to O'Neill remained exceptionally strong for the rest of his life.

A cross-fertilization of ideas and people dominated the culture of Dramaten, the Intimate Theater, and all Ranft theaters. Further, where Broadway was a four-day train trip away from Hollywood, Dramaten was a twenty-minute tram ride from the Svensk Filmindustri sets at Råsunda. People moved between them on annual contracts and for specific performances. The film world in Sweden was just part of the theater world. Actors participated in films during their traditional summer break. Directors moved back and forth as well.

Swedish film directors Victor Sjöström and Mauritz Stiller, both veteran stage directors, used a naturalistic style in their films after 1917. Finally, theater directors such as Stanislavski codified the process of naturalistic acting for wider dissemination. All of those threads, now commonly referred to as naturalistic acting, run through Greta Garbo, but not Garbo alone. Fellow Swede Lars Hanson was a skilled naturalistic actor, and they acted together in a play and three films. Naturalistic acting was prevalent throughout Swedish theater and film. The entire troupe at the Moscow Art Theatre was beginning to work this way. Elements of naturalistic acting had begun to spread through the European theater world. Because of her talents, and because Garbo was a female actor, her skill would resonate with a female audience in a powerful way in the coming years.

All of these elements worked together to provide training and support at the beginning of Garbo's career. Successful people stand on the shoulders of those who came before, and Garbo, with all of her natural talent, also stood on some big shoulders. Theater was a profession where a Swedish woman of the time could have a career. Actors were respected. Swedish society supported theater with attendance and the financing of Dramaten. A body of professionals in acting and the other crafts could teach you the ropes at a high level. Finally, the practice of theater in Sweden was modern and the naturalistic style of acting was exactly what film did not yet know it needed.

Garbo had grown up watching golden-age Swedish films. Three seminal figures of the golden age were Mauritz Stiller, Victor Sjöström, and Gustaf Molander (of Dramaten). They worked together before Garbo was on the scene, and shared a somewhat common history. Garbo would work with all of them, become Stiller's romantic partner, and become a good friend of Sjöström and his family. The rise of the golden age would give Garbo the advantages that came from the cross-fertilization between Swedish theatre and film. The end of the golden age would send her to America.

Greta Garbo, Mimi Pollak and Ingalill Söderman
in a Dramaten publicity photograph.
Photo by Jensen. Courtesy of the Swedish Film Institute.

Chapter 4 – Swedish Theatre and Film

"You know, I have been thinking many times over here, that I can't say I exactly miss Sweden— and that's simply because the conditions in the movie business have changed so much during the past few years."[159]

— Victor Sjöström, director, in a letter to Hjalmar Bergman after arriving in Hollywood

Left to right: Victor Sjöström, Mauritz Stiller and Gustaf Molander (standing) and three unidentified people at the Råsunda studio in 1914.

A large impact on Garbo's life and career from when she started at Dramaten until she left for Hollywood just three years later came from three people who dominated Swedish film and theatre. Their paths crossed often in Stockholm. However, their theatre careers were each incubated in Helsinki at a time when Swedish was the predominant language of the city.

Gustaf Molander trained her at Dramaten, Mauritz Stiller cast her in *Gösta Berling* (1924)[160] and guided her early career, and Victor Sjöström would direct her in *Divine Woman* (1928). Both Stiller and Sjöström were important in her personal life. Garbo could get artistic and business counsel from some of the most experienced people in the business.

Finland had been politically attached to Sweden from the Middle Ages but was lost to Russia during the Swedish-Russian War of 1808–1809. Swedish had been the language of administration and trade, spoken in the cities; by contrast, large swaths of the interior spoke Finnish. When Finland gained independence in 1917, both were made official languages.

Swedish-language theatre was an important cultural institution in Helsinki and Turku. Swedish actors and directors often took jobs for a season in Finland.[161] One of the key institutions, Helsinki's Svenska Teatern (Swedish Theatre), stands to this day, putting on Swedish-language plays.

In 1886, Gustaf Molander's father, Harald Molander, arrived from Stockholm to take over management of the Svenska Teatern. He took what had been a sleepy organization and transformed it into a great institution. Under Molander's leadership, it was regarded on equal terms with the elite theatres in Copenhagen, Stockholm, and Oslo.[162]

Victor Sjöström

In 1896, Victor Sjöström arrived in Finland to try his hand at acting. He was born in 1879, and Sjöström's family had emigrated to New York when he was an infant. After his mother's death in 1893, he returned to Sweden at the age of thirteen and moved into the house of an aunt in Uppsala. When his father returned to Sweden two years later, Sjöström moved to his father's house in Stockholm. That did not work out, so Sjöström moved out on his own. Upon his father's death in 1895, Sjöström decided to join a theatre troupe departing for a tour of Finland, where he seems to have worked until he joined a Gothenburg-based touring theatre in 1899.

Mauritz Stiller was four years younger than Sjöström. Born into a Jewish family in Helsinki, his early life was difficult. As a child of the city, he was fluent in Swedish. He was orphaned at a young age and brought up by friends of his parents. The year Sjöström left for Gothenburg, Stiller joined a Swedish-language touring theatre.

Mauritz Stiller

World events interrupted Stiller's early theatre career. In 1904, Russia and Japan went to war with each other. Finland was still part of Russia. When Stiller was drafted into the military, he resisted conscription and was arrested. In 1905, Stiller escaped from prison and fled to Sweden, where he was given shelter in Stockholm by a female actor who knew him from Helsinki. He then began working as an actor in Sweden.

Gustaf Molander

Gustaf Molander was born in Helsinki while his father ran the Svenska Teatern there. In 1896 his father was hired to manage a theatre in Stockholm for Albert Ranft, and the family moved back to Sweden.

Stiller returned to Helsinki in 1907 to join the company at Svenska Teatern. Both Stiller and Molander were on stage at Svenska Teatern in 1909. The son of Harald Molander was now grown up. He had trained at Dramaten and, upon completion of his studies, joined the Svenska Teatern company.

In 1909, Sjöström became the director for one of Albert Ranft's touring companies. The following year, he struck out as an independent director. In 1910, Stiller left Helsinki to become the director of the Intimate Theater in Stockholm.

In December 1911, Charles Magnusson, who ran Sweden's largest film company and became one of the seminal figures in the worldwide film industry, hired Stiller as a director at Aktiebolaget Svenska Biografteatern (commonly referred to as Svenska Bio).[163] Then, as the new year began, Magnusson hired Sjöström as well. The following year, Gustaf Molander joined the ensemble at Dramaten, and the three were finally all in Stockholm at the same time.

Of the three, the career of Stiller from this point is the easiest to describe. He was a director because his acting skills were limited. He directed films and occasionally plays. He wrote or cowrote scripts for his own productions.

Sjöström was accomplished at everything. He was a fantastic actor, working in both his own films and those of Stiller. He continued acting on both stage and screen into his later years. He may have delivered his finest performance at the age of seventy-seven in the classic Ingmar Bergman film *Wild Strawberries* (1957). He wrote many of his scripts and he directed for both theatre and film.

Molander is remembered as an actor, director, and writer, though he never reached the stature of Sjöström or Stiller. In 1917, Molander and Sjöström cowrote the script for the seminal film *Terje Vigen (A Man There Was),* which Sjöström directed and starred in. This was Sjöström's first film of the Swedish golden age. Molander then wrote the two *Thomas Graal* films (*bästa* film, 1917 and *myndling,* 1922), which were directed by Stiller and starred Sjöström. In 1919 and 1920, Molander cowrote with Stiller the scripts to *Sir Arne's Treasure* and *Sången om den eldröda blomman* (Song of the scarlet flower).

From this point, forces pulled their professional associations apart. Molander was focused on running the Dramaten school and developing his own career as a film director. Sjöström was working with ever bigger budgets on his own films and stopped acting for other directors. Stiller would find new writing partners and was also writing and directing bigger-budget films.

While Gustaf Molander's later career is seldom followed, he wrote scripts and directed many Swedish films, most notably *Intermezzo* (1936) with a young Ingrid Bergman.

Stiller and Sjöström had a worldwide impact on film. In addition to directing a string of remarkable Swedish silent films from 1917 on, they shaped how films were made elsewhere. Their technical command of the art was unsurpassed during this time. They developed storytelling conventions that were copied widely. After their original successes in Sweden, both went to Hollywood and directed important films. Irving Thalberg, head of production at MGM, pointed out Sjöström to other MGM directors and told them to just do as Sjöström did.

The three knew each other and had shared common experiences in both Helsinki and Stockholm. Their lives were intertwined. For example, in August 1926, Molander cabled Stiller that Sjöström had decided not to rent Stiller's place in Lidingö while Sjöström visited Sweden, but that he himself would like to rent it.[164]

Though Garbo, Stiller, and Sjöström never worked together on a project, both directors were an important part of her life. Stiller sought Sjöström's counsel while deciding if he should leave Sweden for MGM. Once there, he and Garbo were frequently together with the Sjöströms. Garbo and Victor's wife, Edith Sjöström, became good friends.

Sjöström was probably Stiller's closest friend other than Garbo. He wrote of Stiller in 1951 that "in spite of all these twenty-three years my memory of him is so vivid, so sharp and strong. Because he was such an extraordinary outstanding personality. So many different kinds of man were gathered within him."[165]

As Garbo and Stiller became collaborators, friends, and then romantic partners, it also gave her an entrée into the collective world of three of the main personalities and decision makers in Swedish film.

Stiller and the Swedish film industry contributed greatly to Garbo's development as an actress. This happened in a context that reflected the naturalistic Swedish style of acting, the use of Swedish nationalism to tell film stories, and the feminist nature of many of those stories.

Svensk Filmindustri made films that tried to capitalize on the nationalistic feeling in Sweden and developed what has been called the "Swedish style." This distinct style came from several inputs. Svensk Filmindustri used stories from the Swedish Romantic movement, particularly the novels of Selma Lagerlöf, as source material. The resulting films had complicated stories that required more sophisticated direction to work. Not inconsequentially for Garbo, both as a film viewer and in her role in *Gösta Berling*, Lagerlöf wrote female characters with both agency and complex lives. Svensk Filmindustri happened to have two directors who, by 1917, were among the best in the world. Therefore, the stories resonated with their home audience, but they were also exportable because they were good films and their storytelling, lyricism, and production quality were new to the audience of the time. From 1917 to 1924 the Swedish film industry, led by Svensk Filmindustri (first as Svenska Bio, and then from the 1919 merger with competitor Filmindustri AB Skandia as Svensk Filmindustri) created marvelous and entertaining films. The period is often called the golden age of Swedish film.

Film historian Bo Florin summed this up:

> The "Swedish Style" was characterized in particular by its ways of handling cinematic subjectivity, but, above all, it seems to express a national—or at times rather nationalistic—striving to create a genuinely Swedish cinema, possible to distinguish from other, international productions.[166]

Svenska Bio hired Charles Magnusson as the production manager in 1909. Magnusson became one of the first early film pioneers to grasp the entire scope of what a film studio needed. Unfortunately, his business was in Sweden, not America. This strategic problem crippled his growth opportunities as the film industry evolved. Magnusson was a leader in building a theatre empire to control exhibition. He spent years trying to build an export business. He understood the need for longer dramatic stories earlier than most peers. He just couldn't achieve sufficient enterprise scale with Sweden as his home market.

Sweden was always a market that was primarily served by imported films. First France, then Germany, and finally the United States provided the bulk of films shown in Sweden. By controlling the key theatres, Magnusson was just doing what every other film magnate of the era did to maximize profits, because most of the profits were in exhibition.

He decided that Svenska Bio's future was in longer films with better stories and better production values. Magnusson wanted to make films that were more like *Birth of a Nation* (1915), which he had distributed in Sweden. He selected Stiller and Sjöström as his two best directors and let most of the others go. Magnusson had decided to make fewer films, but ones that could make better exhibition profits. The rest of the time he filled his theatres with imports. This marked the beginning of the Swedish silent film golden age (roughly 1917–1924), driven by the studio built by Magnusson producing films directed by two of the silent film era's great directors, Stiller and Sjöström. It ended with the departure of both directors for America.

The Stiller film *Balettprimadonnan* (released as *Wolo Czawienko* in the United States, and under a wide array of titles in other markets; November 1916) was only three reels, but it was the first one audiences would see that used this new production strategy. Audiences were struck by the carefully constructed plot and excellent acting by Lars Hanson and Jenny Hasselquist. Universally praised by reviewers, *Balettprimadonnan* did well in Sweden and had strong export revenues.

Magnusson had acquired the film rights to the Henrik Ibsen poem, *Terje Vigen* (A Man There Was). He gave Sjöström a large budget and the time to turn it into a film with a complex story. It arrived in theatres just two months after *Balettprimadonnan. Terje Vigen* (1917) ran four reels and featured shots that delivered the natural world as a character in the film.

Confirming this new direction, Svenska Bio announced in 1917 that "the directorate has decided to rearrange the approach to filming, in such a fashion that a smaller number of films than earlier will be produced this season. Instead, much more qualified artistic efforts will be spent on these films."[167] Those films—*Thomas Graals bästa film* (Thomas Graal's best film), *Tösen från Stormyrtorpet (The Girl from the Marsh Croft)*, and *Alexander den store (Alexander the Great)*—were produced in the summer of 1917 and reached theatres that fall. Each was a hit.

By allowing Sjöström and Stiller to create high-quality narrative films, Magnusson had films he could market as specials to the Swedish audience at higher ticket prices. In addition, Magnusson believed that these higher-quality films would be more successful in export markets.

To a great extent, Magnusson was placing his bet on the skills of Stiller and Sjöström. Sjöström recalled the following:

> Both Stiller and I had the great good fortune to stumble upon directing careers at a time that was so suitable for us. Suitable to break away from the muck, to question the assumptions behind what I was so often to hear in Hollywood later on—"give the public what it wants." We also had the good fortune to work for a studio whose president, Charles Magnusson, was an intelligent man. So intelligent, in fact, that he eventually discovered that the best way

> to deal with us was to leave us alone, trust us and let us do what we wanted, what we thought was right. In other words, every film we made was a one-man job. That was undoubtedly a boon both for us personally and for our work. And I have to say that public taste was different back then.[168]

Stiller and Sjöström became close friends, yet worked independently. "We used to talk about completely different things when we met," said Sjöström. "What we talked about least was film. Maybe we read each other's scripts and, of course, we went to each other's premiers and were pleased about each other's successes—we were, and remain, friends—but that was all. There was never any kind of artistic partnership."[169] The Finnish group of Stiller, Sjöström, and, from 1917 when he started scriptwriting, Gustaf Molander, drove forward the creative efforts to transform the way film told stories. In addition, Svenska Bio had assembled talented technicians like the cinematographer Julius Jaenzon, and had access to a group of strong actors.

Mauritz Stiller watching Victor Sjöström (with megaphone) direct a film.

The Swedish golden age films did well in European markets. Svenska Bio's problem was that it had inconsistent access to the American market. As an example of how valuable the American market could be for Svensk Filmindustri, forty-four prints of the film *The Girl from the Marsh Croft* (Sjöström 1917) were sold to the American distributor, which by itself covered about 25 percent of the film's production costs.[170]

The access issue was primarily political. The American film companies didn't want imported films in their market. Sweden was small enough that the United States could deny its distributors market access and Sweden had little leverage to counter this action. A larger market, like Germany, could negotiate reciprocal access or American investment. Sweden was just too small. Consequently, Svenska Bio films received only infrequent access to the American market.

The arguments about the accessibility of Swedish films to the American audience miss the fact that, across the large international audience in many countries, there was a market for visually beautiful, well-filmed stories that were based on complex plots and were well acted. The fact that this type of film might skew to the higher end of the market just meant that it took away the most profitable slice of the revenue pie.[171] Swedish films didn't have to compete in the mass market to be successful. If Svenska Bio had been able to even come close to replicating the American revenues from *The Girl from the Marsh Croft* across all of its golden age films, it would have remained a major industry force a lot longer.

Swedish industrialist Ivar Kreuger invested millions of Swedish crowns in Svenska Bio in June 1918. Then, in December of 1919, Svenska Bio bought out its main competitor, Skandia. The merged company was named Svensk Filmindustri. Its capitalization had grown from 2 million crowns ($146 million) to 35 million Swedish crowns ($655 million) in eighteen months.[172] In 1920, Svensk Filmindustri built an entirely new studio in the Stockholm suburb of Råsunda.

With the creation of Svensk Filmindustri, Charles Magnusson pushed for grander epic films with larger budgets. The planning took longer, the sets took longer, the shooting took longer, and now it involved more locations. The result was fewer finished films by the two directors. For example, whereas Victor Sjöström had delivered two films per year from 1917 to 1920, in 1921 he produced just a single film. He delivered two in 1922, then left for

America in 1923 after producing his final film for Svensk Filmindustri. Stiller delivered two films per year from 1917 to 1923, except for 1918, when he delivered a single film, and 1922, when he produced none.[173] Between 1913 and 1921, with the exception of 1918, these two directors had always delivered at least four films per year to Svensk Filmindustri, often many more. With their reduced output from 1921 through 1923, Magnusson now had trouble covering his overhead costs.

In January 1922, Svensk Filmindustri restructured and formed a production subsidiary, AB Svensk Filminspelning, co-owned by Charles Magnusson, Olof Andersson (Svensk Filmindustri's financial manager), Victor Sjöström, and Mauritz Stiller.[174] The company produced three of the films distributed by Svensk Filmindustri in 1922–1923. Svensk Filminspelning produced the final two Victor Sjöström films before he left for America and the Stiller film *Gunnar Hedes Saga (The Blizzard,* 1923), his second to last Swedish film. While we don't know what their earlier compensation arrangements looked like, inside Svensk Filminspelning they more or less functioned as independent producers. They were responsible for costs and they received some of their compensation from a percentage of revenues. However, the entire terms of these complex relationships between the companies and the directors are obscured by incomplete historical records. What is clear is that few Hollywood directors had as complete an understanding of every aspect of production as did Stiller and Sjöström.

Because the records are incomplete, it is hard to determine exactly how this changed the business relationship of the directors to Svensk Filmindustri. What is clear is that Sjöström was entirely dissatisfied. In Sjöström's correspondence with his wife while he was traveling to Italy in March 1921, he acknowledged that working conditions at Svensk Filmindustri had changed considerably.[175] They each then left Svensk Filmindustri, Sjöström in 1922 and Stiller in 1924.

In a letter to writer Hjalmar Bergman, he mentions that "because of the newly established company [Svensk Filminspelning] I am more tied down than ever. It is impossible to escape from it."[176] In his November 9, 1922, letter to Bergman, Sjöström comments on his sticky financial arrangements with Svensk Filmindustri. Unfortunately, we don't have Bergman's understanding of the state of play, so the letter is less than clear on details:

> I would of course prefer to follow the old road, but I have to provide the financial support, which is not possible. I sometimes think of breaking free of the company and trying to do something on my own, but I am too much of a coward. And taking Edith and the children into consideration, I can't risk the money we have been able to save. Moreover, I am now so financially involved with the company that it will take years to settle. And whatever the result will be is completely unpredictable.[177]

Through November 1922, negotiations between Joe Godsol, who had replaced Sam Goldwyn as the chair of Goldwyn Pictures, and Victor Sjöström took place regarding a director's job at Goldwyn. Negotiations were complicated by the intercession of Charles Magnusson, who had his own agenda.

Godsol arranged for his representative in Stockholm, Oscar Rosenberg, to negotiate a deal for Sjöström's services. Rosenberg ended up negotiating with Anders Jordahl, who actually represented Svensk Filmindustri. His draft of the contract added rights for Svensk Filmindustri to distribute Sjöström-directed films in what should have been a simple deal between Sjöström and Goldwyn Pictures. On November 15, Goldwyn Pictures cabled directly to Rosenberg that any distribution deal was unacceptable. The deal, without distribution rights, was finally hammered out on December 4.[178]

Sjöström did not learn of this until he arrived in New York in late January. In a letter to his wife, he lays out Magnusson's duplicity and asks her to not tell Stiller about these events.[179]

On the day Sjöström departed Stockholm, he also signed agreements with Svensk Filmindustri that addressed the distribution rights to his American films in Sweden. The agreement also seems to have addressed outstanding debts Sjöström owed to Svensk Filmindustri;[180] and an implied parallel agreement resolved his equity position in AB Svensk Filminspelning.

We don't have access to Stiller's thoughts regarding Charles Magnusson and Svensk Filmindustri at the time, but his long letter to Magnusson in August 1925 details one way he believes Magnusson took advantage of him. In a damning statement, Stiller writes, "In particular when I see what percentages you have been debiting Svensk Filmindustri abroad—against all agreements. In several cases, I know what you have paid and what you have debited Svensk Filmindustri."[181]

Some Stiller financial documents survive in the archives of Victor Sjöström. These few pages are incomplete and reflect a re-creation in 1926 or 1927 of Svensk Filmindustri's financial claims against Stiller from 1922 to that point. Two big issues are revealed. First, Svensk Filmindustri charged Stiller directly for some costs that seem to be more appropriately billable to the production. The effect was that Stiller took more financial risk. The other was that German film companies were willing to offer him much more lucrative deals.

In retrospect, the creation of Svensk Filminspelning seems to have been a clever move by Magnusson to give his directors the perception of being more involved in the revenue stream from the films they created while really not giving them such a great deal. In the end, it bought him a short amount of time. Sjöström left for Hollywood as soon as he felt he could extract himself. Stiller stayed to make *Gösta Berling*, and then looked to Germany. But his relationship with Magnusson would trouble him for years. The problems at Svensk Filmindustri would be a major factor in Garbo's decision to move to Hollywood.

As the 1920s progressed, the advantages of the "Swedish style" became less unique. American and German writers and directors began delivering high-quality stories, and newly integrated film companies funded their own longer films, spending budgets on production values that had previously been the province of the Swedes. While Swedish films had always been distributed in Europe, market access and profitable arrangements had always been difficult to obtain. They were rarely given access equal to that of domestic firms in these export markets. Swedish films often received less theatre exposure, shorter bookings, less advertising, and limited distribution. American firms worked to cut Sweden out of their market by not giving Swedish firms import rights. What was left after 1924 was a company, in Svensk Filmindustri, that could still find and tell stories that resonated with its home audience, but without the creative advantages it held a decade earlier.

Garbo benefited from the skills and resources of the golden age at the start of her career. The money flowed through both Swedish film and theatre. Then quickly, it was gone, for Svensk Filmindustri wasn't able to overcome the advantages Hollywood held at the quality end of production. For Garbo, her career was just starting as the golden age was ending. But before the end, she was cast in a magnificent classic film.

Chapter 5 – *Gösta Berling*

"You get a face like that in front of a camera only once in a century."[182]

— Mauritz Stiller, director, in a letter to a Svensk Filmindustri executive

Greta Garbo as Elizabeth Dohna in *Gösta Berling*.

During Garbo's first year at Dramaten, everyone seemed to believe in Garbo's potential. The summer between that first year and her second is when that potential began to be realized. Mauritz Stiller, the most important film director remaining in Sweden, cast her in *Gösta Berling*. Her professional and romantic relationship with Stiller would become one of the most important in her life.

She formally changes her name to Greta Garbo. She would return to Dramaten and take on bigger roles. Critics of both film and theatre thought well of her performances. Other actors' and film writers' comments about Garbo and her own recollections show that her confidence and belief in her talent were growing.

Garbo would also have an important impact on portrait photography. The first inklings of her novel approach are seen in work she does with noted photographer Henry Goodwin.

The Dramaten season ended in mid-June, leaving Garbo free for the summer.[183] On June 30, 1923, Mona Mårtenson and Greta Garbo jointly wrote a letter to Mimi Pollak. They were waiting for Mauritz Stiller to arrive for auditions.

Stiller had already seen Garbo on film, on stage, and in person. From 1920, when Tullbergs Film was started, through at least 1923, Stiller used to come and watch his friend, Ragnar Ring, edit his films in his home in Fältmarskalksvägen.[184] In all likelihood, he saw one or more of her Tullbergs films being created.

Both Garbo and Stiller said in interviews that he saw her on stage. Garbo spoke with Palmborg in 1926 and said that Stiller saw her in a school play before casting her in *Gösta Berling's Saga (The Saga of Gösta Berling)*.[185] At the time, her goal was to be a stage actor. Her decision to take the part in Stiller's film reflects her perception that Svensk Filmindustri films were of a different caliber than Erik Petschler films

Gladys Hall (writing under the pseudonym Faith Service) interviewed Stiller in July 1925, and she summed up the conversation about how he found Garbo: "He was, it seems, about to cast *Gösta Berling* from the story of Selma Lagerlöf. He was looking, specifically, for the main character, that of Elisabeth Dohna. Elisabeth Dohna had, too, to look a very special way. His search led him to the School of the Royal Dramatic Theatre where, instantaneously, and just like that, he spied the fugitive personality of Greta Garbo. 'Ah,' he must have thought, 'Ah, 'tis she!'"[186]

Even before her formal audition, Garbo had gone to Stiller's house before the Dramaten term ended at Molander's direction. "That day, after school. I went up to his house to see him. I had never seen Mr. Stiller. To me he was just a very big man."[187]

What was this first meeting between Garbo and Stiller like? She related it as follows:

> He was not at home. So I sat down and waited. Pretty soon he came in with his big dog. I started trembling all over. He seemed such a funny person. He looked at me, looked me up and down. Looked me all over. He has told me since, exactly what I had on, even to my shoes and stockings. I had on black, low heeled low shoes, with black stockings. He just said a few words about the weather and things in general. At times it seemed as though he looked away, but I know he was really looking at me every moment. After quite a few moments, he said, "Well, can't you take off your coat and hat?"—just as though he had asked me a dozen times before, when he had said nothing about it. Then he just looked at me some more and said, "What's your telephone number?" Then I knew it was all over. "He isn't interested," I thought. "When they're not interested they always ask your telephone number." So I put on my hat and coat and went out. No, I wasn't worried. I just didn't think any more about it.[188]

But Stiller seems to have concluded that Garbo might be a fit. In responding to Faith Service's questions in July 1925, Stiller said, "In the first place, it was because Miss Garbo so perfectly looked the part, the character." Service goes on to say that Stiller "got the impression that she had something in the head. He added that her quality of grace was also very marked."[189]

When Hyltén-Cavallius first wrote his memories of Garbo's audition for *Gösta Berling* in *Stockholms Dagblad* in 1933, he wrote a longer piece that reflected the process Stiller went through to cast Garbo:

> In reality, things did not happen in such a spectacular way. Stiller was, as all of his old friends and colleagues can confirm, not a particularly theatrical man, he did not have any epiphanies, and

> he rarely worked himself up to excitement. In his own way, he was a genius. But he was also a sharp critic, and his natural starting point was usually that of doubt. When he saw Garbo for the first time, he did not fall into a prophetic epiphany. He was just sitting at his desk wrapping up the final scenes of the film script of *Gösta Berling* when he told me: "You know, I just got hold of a girl, a student at the Royal Dramatic Theater, she is young and does not know much. But I wonder, I am thinking: Should I dare to cast her as Elisabeth Dohna? She is very cute. You will get a chance to see her soon, because she is coming over to show what she can do." She came over, and she was quiet, shy and definitely very attractive. But she was still not a large movie personality. On the other hand, we were still debating if little Greta Garbo would be able to handle the role of Elisabeth Dohna.
>
> Stiller set aside his concerns and decided to give her the role and she started to shoot. But every time we were in doubt, we consoled ourselves with the fact that she was so beautiful: "Everything is beautiful on her! Her feet, for example, have you noticed those? She has incredibly beautiful heels, in one straight beautiful line!" I am citing this from Stiller to show how Stiller first and all was fascinated by her appearance. And both of us realized she was not common eye candy, but her beauty was at once lovely and special, and she was intriguing and fascinating as a type of woman. And Stiller had a strong eye for the common. He was always afraid of banal theatricality in his films, he was searching for originality. And Garbo had her peculiar beauty naturally.[190]

In his 1960 memoir, which is more commonly used as a source, Hyltén-Cavallius compressed the story. He recalled that she was already going by Garbo at the time of the audition. While Stiller seemed set on Garbo for the Elisabeth Dohna role, Hyltén-Cavallius was not as sure based on the audition. "She came, she was seen, but she did not conquer immediately. She was certainly very pretty, but extremely shy. Stiller discovered that this personality trait was an advantage. 'You see, she is so timid that the audience will feel sorry for her, it becomes touching,' he exclaimed. He examined her like a foal at a horse market: 'Look at her feet! She has such beautiful heels in one single, straight line! And such long eye lashes! Right?'"[191]

GÖSTA BERLINGS SAGA PÅ FILM

Majorskan (Gerda Lundequist) bland kavaljererna på julmiddagen på Ekeby.

Vi meddela i detta nummer de första fullt färdiga bilderna ur Gösta Berlings saga, sådan den gestaltar sig på filmen, som sannolikt kommer upp på nyåret. Det är ju både färgrika och intagande scener, bilderna återge. Här ovan t. v. Gösta Berling (Lars Hanson) och Marianne Sinclair (Jenny Hasselquist). T. h. hjälten och Ebba Dohna (Mona Mårtensson). Den tredje av systrarna Dohna spelas av friherrinnan Cederström. Filmen utgår från Svensk Filmindustri, och regissören Stillers namn borgar för att det blir ett vackert verk.

1097

Garbo is so unknown that she is misidentified in an early magazine article.

Garbo at the time was unsure how the audition had gone, as she had not initially risen to the assignment in the audition. "And I was ashamed. I was ashamed to try and put myself over, as you say it. I had never done anything to put myself over before, and it made me very ashamed to do it. Mr. Stiller waited a few moments, and then said, 'My God, can't you be sick? Don't you know what it is to be sick?' Then I knew it wasn't play and it wasn't funny. I knew it was necessary in the movies and I became a very sick lady."[192]

According to cinematographer Julius Jaenzon, Garbo approached him at the Råsunda studio the next day. She was anxious to know how the screen test he had filmed had gone. Would she get the part? Jaenzon said he doubted Stiller was going to pick her.[193]

Then Stiller called. Garbo related, "Then, in a few days he called me and told me he had a place for me. I had it in my hands; now I could get a little excited."[194]

Gösta Berling is a classic of Swedish literature. Published in 1891, it was the debut novel written by Selma Lagerlöf. Though Lagerlöf didn't win the 1909 Nobel Prize in Literature for a specific work, *Gösta Berling* is considered her finest novel.

Lagerlöf's work was solidly in the Swedish National Romantic movement. The stories resonated with a wide cross section of Swedish society. For Svenska Bio, and then Svensk Filmindustri, producing films based on these stories captured the attention of the Swedish market.

Further, the way Lagerlöf constructed stories made them translatable into film. Lagerlöf's stories are melodramatic. They feature well-developed characters with an underlying psychological resonance. For the audience of her day, Lagerlöf's female characters face difficult circumstances. Frequently they are cast out, and the story follows what happens to their characters as a result. The evolving rights of women and how women fit into society are central to Lagerlöf stories.[195] While *Gösta Berling* is set in the past, its message about women as individuals with agency is contemporary for its time.

Both Victor Sjöström and Mauritz Stiller adapted Lagerlöf novels as films, though Lagerlöf decidedly preferred work done by Sjöström, who hewed to her novels more precisely. The first Lagerlöf film project by Stiller, *Herr Arnes Pengar (Sir Arne's Treasure,* 1919), follows the novel faithfully. However, after

Stiller's next Lagerlöf story, she was so upset with his changes that she insisted he release it under a different name, so *En Herrgårdssägen* became *Gunnar Hedes Saga* (1923).[196] Stiller's changes didn't really hurt the appeal of the story and reflected the difference between novels and films as Stiller perceived them. The film was successful with critics and audiences.

Lagerlöf asked Charles Magnusson to assign someone other than Stiller to the film production of *Gösta Berling.* However, Victor Sjöström had already departed for America.

Magnusson, or even Lagerlöf, seemed to have looked for alternatives. German playwright Bertolt Brecht was working on a script for a film version of *Gösta Berling* in 1923 for German film director Ellyn Karin, who had told Brecht she had secured the rights from Selma Lagerlöf. Brecht's July 1923 letter to Arnolt Bronnen asks for his intervention in finalizing his financial arrangement with her.[197] Clearly Karin had misled him, as she had not finalized a deal on the rights. At the time Brecht wrote this letter, Stiller was finalizing the cast and preparing for production.

Stiller and Hyltén-Cavallius's script for *Gösta Berling* had to cut down and simplify the sprawling plot of the book. Even then, the finished film ran three hours and was shown in two parts at the premiere.[198] The main story arc is the platonic relationship between *Gösta Berling*, a defrocked priest, and Margareta Celsing, the wife of Major Samzelius (and, therefore, usually referred to in the story as Majorskan). Majorskan's trysts with her true love before her arranged marriage are revealed at a Christmas dinner and she is cast out. The point of the rest of the story is that both *Gösta Berling* and the Majorskan are redeemed through their actions.

The dramatic tension in *Gösta Berling* is provided by the relationship between *Gösta Berling* and the Majorskan. The story revolves around them. Garbo's role as Elisabeth Dohna is a critical supporting role as it allows for *Gösta Berling's* redemption. In order to make the story work, Elisabeth has to love Gösta but not act on her feelings. Elisabeth, who finds *Gösta Berling* attractive, does not stray. But they do develop a mutual admiration.

Garbo understood that Elisabeth was a great role. She would tell Ruth Biery, "And he gave me the part of Countess Dohna in *Gösta Berling*. The very best part for my very first picture!"[199]

Elizabeth Dohna removing her wedding ring.

The story shows that Henrik Dohna is not worthy of Elisabeth's love. Through an improbable legalistic device, her marriage to Henrik is deemed defective; they are technically no longer married. In order to be properly married, Elisabeth and Henrik must say their vows again.

But, when offered the opportunity to make their married life legal, Elisabeth declines. She is then forced to live life on her own, but in a way that works for the socially conservative audience, which was a tricky balance in 1924 Sweden. Stiller did not have fifty typed pages to explain emotional nuance and interior thought as Lagerlöf did in the novel. Garbo was able to deliver the purity of soul, drawn to Berling but remaining faithful to her husband until she is freed from her marriage, that Stiller needed from her.

This opens the chance for *Gösta Berling* and Elisabeth to finally become a couple. Along the way are a slew of additional subplots involving a web of characters. In one classic scene, wolves chase the sled carrying *Gösta Berling* and Elisabeth Dohna across a frozen lake. The manor at Ekeby, where both *Gösta Berling* resides and the Majorskan once lived, is intentionally burned in a spectacular fire. In the end, Majorskan is restored to the Ekeby manor, which she gives to *Gösta Berling* and Elisabeth.

While the subplots are difficult to describe briefly, they add to the story and interact among themselves. The simplification of the story from incredibly

Elizabeth Dohna confesses her love of Gösta Berling to Margareta Celsing.

intricate to merely intricate upset Lagerlöf and some reviewers. The film did well in Sweden and was successful in export markets, particularly in Germany. Its success, however, was not spectacular.

The cast for *Gösta Berling* was announced in all the Swedish papers on July 17, 1924. Garbo was announced as Greta Gustafsson. She and Mona Mårtenson were described briefly as students at Dramaten. The focus was rightly on the balance of the all-star cast that Stiller had assembled. *Svenska Dagbladet* included photographs of Mårtenson and Garbo.

Why did the newspapers use Gustafsson rather than Garbo? This was due to the somewhat legalistic nature of Swedish society at the time. Before she legally changed her name to Garbo, she couldn't just use it as a stage name. By convention, no Swedish publication would use anything but her legal family name.

Legally her name was still Gustafson. Perhaps even Gustafsson. Many Swedes, particularly those who thought themselves modern and liberal, had dropped the second letter s that was present in so many family names. Before they were family names, they were merely patronymic descriptors. Greta Gustafson would have been Greta Karlsdotter (Karl's daughter). Her brother would have been Sven Karlsson (Karl's son).

With both evolving practice and the transition in 1901 to the use of family names that continued through generations, the possessive letter s was redundant. When you look at modern Swedish family names, they come in both one s and two s variants. Worldwide, roughly two-thirds of people using a variant of the Gustafson surname use the two s version. The Swedish bureaucracy refused by and large to accept this new one s variant at the time. Therefore, on Garbo's November 13, 1924, application to officially change her name from Gustafson to Garbo, you have the bureaucrat writing her name as Gustafsson right above where she has signed it as Gustafson.

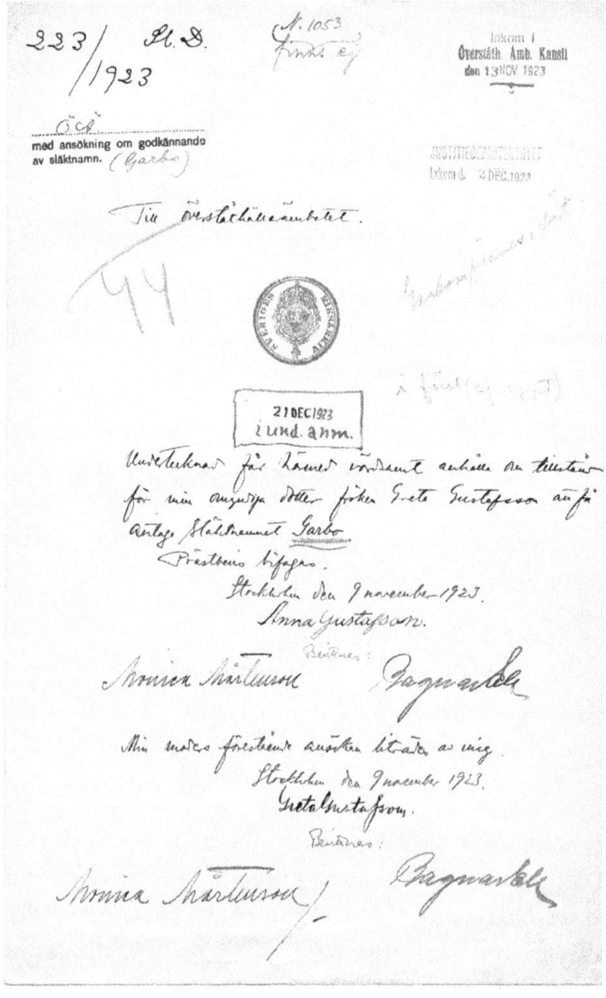

223/1923

Inkom t
Överståth. Amb. Kansli
den 13 NOV 1923

med ansökning om godkännande av släktnamn. (Garbo)

Till överståthållareämbetet.

21 DEC 1923
i und. anm.

Undertecknad får härmed vördsamt anhålla om tillstånd för min omyndiga dotter fröken Greta Gustafsson att få antaga släktnamnet Garbo.
Prästbevis bifogas.
Stockholm den 9 november 1923.
Anna Gustafsson.

Bevittnas:
Amina Mårtensson

Min moders förestående ansökan biträdes av mig.
Stockholm den 9 november 1923.
Greta Gustafson.

Bevittnas:
Amina Mårtensson

Greta Gustafson changes her name to Greta Garbo.

The two main actors were spectacular. Gösta Berling was played by Lars Hanson, the leading Swedish male actor of the time. Majorskan was played by Gerda Lundequist, a legendary and, at this point, middle-aged stage actress who had just been widowed. While she dominated Swedish stages for six decades, this was the first of only eight film roles she undertook. The rest of the cast were established actors who fit their parts well. Initial filming happened in August and September 1923.

The start of filming was difficult for Garbo. She was unsure of herself and certainly felt underqualified given the rest of the cast. Later in life she described her experience as follows:

> The first days of work I was so scared that I couldn't work. I was sick in earnest. Finally, everyone went out and left me. The electricians, the prop boys—even Mr. Stiller. He told me to practice alone. But I knew he was in some corner watching. I looked all around and could not see him, but I knew he was there. So I would not practice. I would not rehearse all by myself.—I would not look so stupid.[200]

The rest of the cast was sympathetic to her plight, though some did not see her talent in the way Stiller saw it.

Karin Swanström, who had an important role in one of the film's subplots, certainly didn't see anything special in Garbo at that time. Years later she recalled the following:

> Frankly, we were inclined in those days to think Greta's good luck [was] her greatest asset. None of us could understand why Stiller was so interested in this little nobody, because he had never paid any particular attention to anyone before. To us she appeared to be just an awkward, mediocre novice. Our desire to make her one of our little family here was never fully realized, because of Stiller's jealous care of Greta. He scarcely permitted anyone else to even speak to her, and would hardly leave her out of his sight for a moment.[201]

Ragnar Hyltén-Cavallius wrote a brief datebook entry about filming on August 6, 1923. On this day they filmed the Christmas dinner at Ekeby. He wrote, "Greta Gustafson unimaginably pretty."[202]

Six weeks later, on Sept. 18, her birthday, when he recorded her name in his datebook, it is as Greta Garbo. As noted earlier she is recorded as Greta Gustafson Garbo as early as September 1922 in Gustaf Molander's Dramaten notebook.

Stiller lavished attention on Garbo when she was on set. He was keen to get exactly the portrayal from her that he needed. At some point during the production, Stiller had realized her immense talent. Now he was working not just on the role of Elisabeth Dohna, but on training an emerging star to realize the full range of her talents. Ragnar Hyltén-Cavallius may have reflected his somewhat dated views of the relation between a teacher and pupil, but his basic point that Stiller was drawing everything he could from Garbo is clear when he wrote,

> This was the potter in front of his clay—it could be shaped into a beautiful vessel. Technically, she did not know anything, but Stiller trusted his powers as an instructor, and it did not fail him. He was screaming and bugging her, and with time, she was like wax in his hands, his large, clumsy hands.[203]

Stiller invested infinite amounts of time. As Karin Swanström recalled, "I can see them—forever walking up and down, up and down in the shade of that little grove [outside Filmstaden] . . . Stiller was always teaching and preaching, Greta solemnly listening and learning. I never saw anyone more earnest and eager to learn."[204]

A behind-the-scenes look appeared in *Filmnyheter* describing the effort that went into producing one short scene. They wrote the following:

> One scene, full of poetry and graceful pleasure, is the one when Elisabeth gets her lesson in the Swedish language from *Gösta Berling*—and it is the verb "love" that he chose as the example. The lesson takes place in the park and the sun shines between the trees of the teacher and his pupil. A wonderfully beautiful scene, just too short!
>
> To get these few film meters in the camera, to get the right lighting on the two young figures, was not done simply. The daylight alone was not enough, artificial lighting must also be added. For that reason, a lighting car drove out and was set up behind two strong lamps, and a couple of smaller lights. The power was switched on and now the sun received the help that it needed to get the right effect. A whole day's work—the result a few meters![205]

Stiller filming the scene where Gösta Berling teaches
Elizabeth Dohna to conjugate the verb love.

Garbo was a quick student. Cinematographer Julius Jaenzon would tell film writer Bengt Idestam-Almquist that while Garbo was initially shy, she didn't fear the camera. Within a few days from the start of filming she was generally good on the first take.[206]

Somewhat unusually the production of *Gösta Berling* was broken into two shooting windows. The first window was in August and September. All of the winter scenes were then shot in November and December. During the production break, Garbo returned to Dramaten and resumed her studies. Now she was cast in regular Dramaten productions in more significant roles.

A photo of Garbo appears in the November 18, 1923, issue of *Idun* magazine as part of a photo series from the filming of *Gösta Berling*. She is identified mistakenly as Mona Mårtenson. In all likelihood, no one outside the theatre and film worlds noticed the error.

When production was underway during the second window, Garbo sat for her first interview. Inga Gaate, working for *Filmjournalen*, spoke with several cast members. In an amusing forerunner of Garbo's relationship with the press for most of her career, her apparent first words were "interview! No, I have nothing to say."[207]

But then Garbo went on to speak in some depth about working for Stiller, making it clear she valued the time and attention he was investing in her. "Terrible. I've had a Gethsemane, but Stiller is the coolest man I know. You do not get angry or sad no matter how much bark you get."[208]

Garbo wasn't always a compliant novice. She could also snap back. Gaate distilled their conversation as follows: "It had been very heated between the director and the aspiring actress out at Råsunda. But no one opposed Stiller not even the temperamental Gurra [one of Garbo's nicknames among Dramatic students]. She remained quiet and suffered. But from her tight lips could be heard, 'Damn Stiller, I hate you!' That was in the heat of the moment. Otherwise he is her idol, 'The most elegant person there is.' I believe her, the slender Gurra, when she says, 'Everything is so different! One day you feel one way, and the next day just the opposite. It is as though you had a dozen different beings in you, each one fighting for superiority.'"[209]

As the film came together in the editing room, Hyltén-Cavallius remembered that Stiller was happy with the way his gamble in casting Garbo had turned out:

> When editing the film, Stiller was pleased by the fact that his new protégé was not a fully formed artist, she was never ever fake. What she expressed was always genuine. "And you feel touched by her, you feel sorry for her!" he exclaimed triumphantly. As time passed, Stiller learned to believe in this quiet, shy and lovable girl.[210]

Just as Garbo, after her initial timidity, had grown into her position at Dramaten, now she grew as a film actress under Stiller's guidance. She later told Ruth Biery about making *Gösta Berling*: "The picture took a long time. There were snow scenes and we had to wait until it was winter. When it was over, I was no longer frightened."[211]

In her second student year Garbo was cast in better roles in more plays with the main Dramaten company. She had minor roles in *Den beundrandsvärde Crichton (The Admirable Crichton,* 1902) in October and *Äfventyret (The Beautiful Adventure)* in November (Garbo performed in *Äfventyret* during her first and second years at Dramaten. She had different roles in the different productions of the play).

In December, after the second production window for *Gösta Berling*, Garbo and Lars Hanson appeared together on the Dramaten stage in *Ett Resande Teatersällskap* (A traveling theatre company, 1848).

In addition to the regular productions, Dramaten also had student recitals performed on the same Dramaten stage in front of friends, family, teachers, other actors, directors, and anyone else with an interest.[212]

Garbo gave a remarkable performance during her recital on February 17, 1924, as evidenced by reviews in all the major newspapers. Garbo and Arnold Sjöstrand acted out a key scene from the famous Swedish-Finnish play *Daniel Hjort*, written by Josef Julius Wecksell in 1862, which was one of the most significant Swedish-language plays before those of August Strindberg. While now considered dated and creaky, it had a modernist feel, with important psychological aspects that were a new approach to the stage when it was written. Every theatre fan in Stockholm at that time would have been familiar with this play. Reviews would be comparing Garbo's performance with that of a legion of established actors.

The scene Garbo and Sjöstrand played for the audience is a pivotal one from the first act. Sjöstrand played Daniel Hjort and Garbo his mother.

The basic plot outline is that when Hjort was an infant, his father had gone to his lord, Klaes Fleming, whom he fervently supported, to complain that Fleming's troops had pillaged his farm during the ongoing war. For his troubles the father was executed, and Hjort's uncles were either executed or jailed. Hjort was taken and raised by Fleming as his own.

In the scene Garbo and Sjöstrand acted, Hjort's mother comes to him and reveals these truths to the now-adult Hjort. She bids him to seek revenge against the Flemings, which, for the balance of the play, he does, but not without four more acts of love, betrayal, battle, and other melodrama.[213]

"Miss Greta Garbo," stated *Stockholms Dagblad*, "was such a capable Katri (Daniel Hjort's mother), as one can ask of a twenty-year-old girl, who by the character of her feminine charm seems to be destined for a completely different repertoire."[214] Although the reviewer found it strange that a young actress played an old woman, this was common for students at the school as all of the students were young.[215] As was typical of people who evaluated the young Garbo at the time, this reviewer was apparently not aware she was just eighteen.

The other Stockholm papers took notice of Garbo's performance as well. *Dagens Nyheter* said, "Garbo in Daniel Hjort deserves to be talked about. She has a deep beautiful voice and a good stage presence."[216] *Stockholms-Tidningen* said, "Greta Garbo gave a natural and passionate performance."[217]

Svensk Filmindustri used photographs to publicize *Gösta Berling.* This had become common practice worldwide, so in that sense the photos of Garbo that were released were not unique or remarkable. Scene stills with Garbo had been used to publicize *Luffar-Petter*. Garbo emerged as an actor as both the creation of these images and their usage were changing. While the most dramatic impact of these changes for Garbo would take place in America, one can see the beginnings in Sweden.

Garbo had appeared in a layout of four scene stills in the August 20, 1923, issue of *Filmnyheter.* The September 17, 1923, issue included a scene still of Garbo and Mårtenson, among several, under the caption *"Are Swedish Actresses Beautiful?"*

The January 14, 1924, issue of *Filmnyheter* had a one-page article on Garbo titled "Who Is Greta Garbo?" Though she had been using the Garbo name since starting *Dramaten* in September 1922, this was the first time she was recognized by that name in a publication after her formal name change in December 1923. The majority of the page was a photo from the set of *Gösta Berling* with a short write-up about her.[218]

The coverage of *Gösta Berling* proceeded with minimal photographs in newspapers. Where photos were used, in magazines and occasionally newspapers, they were scene stills. The advertising with graphics featured Lars Hanson, who after all was the lead.

Greta Garbo was in photographs from a young age. Class pictures and portraits further demonstrate that, while the Gustafson family was working class, they could afford some of the amenities of the time. Garbo does not seem to have had portraits made to further her acting career while she worked for Tullbergs. Her earliest portraits after she began school were taken by photographers known to have worked with Dramaten. She sat for Ferdinand Flodin, Sture Ekstrand, and a photographer with the surname Jensen. The portrait images are not precisely dated.

Jensen also took behind-the-scenes, posed "candids" of the Dramaten students. Some of these appeared in theatre and art magazines. They can be roughly dated by the group of students in the image.

The cover of the March 17, 1924, issue of *Filmnyheter*, published as *Gösta Berling* was released, was a scene still of Lars Hanson and Greta Garbo. It was the first of many Garbo magazine covers.[219]

None of the photographers who made portraits of Garbo up until this point created any remarkable images. They were nice workmanlike images. As we will see shortly, Garbo soon changed her approach to photography. Initially the difference is a minor glimmer. The true evolution would happen in New York.

The transformation of Garbo as a photography subject begins with Henry Goodwin. His work appears in the March 30, 1924, issue of *Filmjournalen*.[220]

The Goodwin portraits are the first in which the photographer and Garbo work to create something more than a person sitting while photographed. Henry Goodwin was one of the great European pictorialist photographers. The pictorialist technique emerged toward the end of the nineteenth century and was a reaction to the increasing volume of literalist photographs that emerged as the technology of photography was simplified and disseminated. By 1888, anyone could take a photograph and send film to Kodak for development.

Goodwin wanted to make photography an independent art form that could be compared to any other type of visual art, and not simply regarded as a mechanical reproductive technique—a view he shared with other pictorialists. As the name implied, the "pictorial" presentation was their chief concern.

The early pictorialist photographers, like Julia Margaret Cameron, sought to create portraits that sum up the essence of the subject. Pictorialists delivered an image that combined the carefully composed visage of the person with props that communicated the personality, profession, and accomplishments of the subject. The final product was rendered by extensive manipulation of the negative. This approach reflected the technology of the time, and mimicked the art of painted portraiture.

Pictorialism was partially a way to overcome deficiencies in cameras, lenses, and paper that by Garbo's time were being cleared away steadily by technical advances. By viewing the captured image as the raw material to be worked into final form, pictorialists worked around these technical issues. Intentionally using soft-focus lenses and fabrics, and by staging the image with props and through composition before the darkroom and printing manipulations, they thought of themselves as more like painters or graphic artists.[221] The realism that replaced pictorialism was only possible after technical advances in cameras and lenses.

Garbo's career began in the midst of this transformation. The changes were multifaceted, encompassing what tools photographers used, how they worked, and how the photographs were used. Technical advances in cameras, lenses, and lighting meant that photographs could have greater depth of focus and subjects didn't have to hold poses for long stretches. The creation of readily available developing chemicals and standard papers, both of which could be purchased at a store, simplified the workflow and lowered costs. The cost of reproducing images, both individually and in mass media, constantly dropped.

This changed the use of photographs. In 1920 photos were a rare accent in newspapers. By 1930 they were common, with sections devoted to photographic collages on Sundays. Magazines had adopted photographs earlier, and the drop in photo costs allowed them to sell issues to readers at lower prices.

A pictorialist photographer took a few expensive exposures and manipulated them extensively to achieve an expression of the person in a portrait. As technology made the approach possible, a realist photographer would take hundreds of inexpensive exposures and, after selecting the best, present them with minimal alteration as a version of the person.

Garbo's role in the evolution of photography was to be on the leading edge of how subjects posed for portraits. Garbo would act for portraits. The beginnings of this can be seen in her work with Henry Goodwin. A year and a half later her sessions with Arnold Genthe would transform portrait photography.

Goodwin was born Heinrich Karl Hugo Bürgel in Germany. In Stockholm, he became the leading Swedish portrait photographer of his era.[222]

Goodwin used the negative as simply a starting point for artistic creation. His composition was usually concentrated by a predominantly dark tonality, and the detail was reduced in favor of soft outlines and a lack of sharp focus.[223]

He wrote about his creative process:

> A photographic portrait is, if not a contradiction, then nonetheless a combination of two things whose natures are unalike and unreconcilable. Photography is an automatic process, applied science, optics, chemistry. Portraiture is a spiritual activity of the most pronounced humankind, above all the depiction of a personality, with everything that this involves in terms of knowledge of people and contemporary cultural history.[224]

Goodwin's portfolio consisted of several themes. He photographed the cityscape. He photographed nature and the countryside. Later in life, he concentrated almost exclusively on botany. He has an extensive oeuvre of artful nudes. The vast majority of his revenue, however, came from portraits. In his society portraits, the subject sits passively while Goodwin tries to extract some essence of them in his photography and darkroom manipulations. The other portrait subjects were from the arts: actors, dancers, directors, and writers. With actors and dancers particularly, Goodwin often added elements from their art. Some are posed in costume. Others caught as if in mid-performance.

Goodwin spoke of the difficulties involved in making portraits tell a story: "They require a knowledge of the role, of the author, and an understanding of theatre as a distinctive art form. A conventional studio image can, at most, achieve an objective record, but never a portrait, which requires pictorial effect, composition, a proper distribution of tone, rhythm, confident framing, all of them things that require the intervention of a supervising hand."[225]

He also talked about the effort involved in a photographic session that might yield one or two images after he finished with his manipulations. "Rarely has such a huge apparatus been set in motion in my home, so much space been needed, so many different lighting and optical devices been in use. The result, however, was meagre: from an inconceivable number of negatives and after more or less meticulous re-working, three, possibly four fully satisfactory pictures. [. . .] It was nothing beyond what could be expected given the skills of the model and oneself."[226]

The Garbo portraits are unique in two respects. These unique elements will later be amplified in the portraits Garbo creates with Arnold Genthe in New York. First, in the two more standard portraits, where Garbo is looking at the camera. Goodwin crops the image of Garbo close to the face. There is little else. This is unusual for Goodwin portraits. Most of his portraits are half- or full-body shots. That he focused in on Garbo's face so closely is clearly a

A typical half-body shot compared to the tightly cropped final version of a portrait of Garbo by Henry Goodwin.

choice. The result is two beautiful headshots, in slightly different poses. It would be hard to argue with his results.

The negative to one of these headshot images is in the Stadsmuseet Stockholm. It is a standard half-body pose. Goodwin is making the conscious choice to focus in on Garbo's face by cropping. He will not be the last photographer to do so. He doesn't need anything else; Garbo doesn't need a costume to express her personality.

The final two portraits from the session are the most interesting. One is a headshot with Garbo's arm raised. The position of her body implies motion, almost like she is dancing. It is most definitely not the standard "Sit here in this chair and I will point my camera at you" portrait. While Goodwin has taken portraits of dancers on stage, the tightness of his focus on Garbo's face is unique.

Finally, Goodwin creates a very different portrait of Garbo posed in an awkward way. Her body extends out of frame to the right (as viewing the image). Her hands are in unnatural positions and she is leaning on an elbow. The printed image was a significantly cropped version of the original negative. By cutting away the top of Garbo's torso and bringing the focus in on the face and the motion of her arms, Goodwin seems to have reached into his experience with dance photographs to capture something. Garbo's face and body have an expressiveness that allow him to use close cropping and motion in a way he hasn't with other subjects. He realized that the malleability of Garbo's face was what made her a unique photographic subject. This subtle difference in how Goodwin cropped and printed the photographs is only apparent when you look at his whole body of work.

Garbo and Goodwin have done something unusual that Goodwin emphasizes through tight cropping. It evokes Goodwin's images of modern dancers in motion, though those are primarily shot to include the entire body.

Most subjects ended up with one or perhaps two images from any portrait session. For example, Goodwin took hundreds of photos of the actor Jenny Hasselquist over many years to deliver what ends up being a fair collection of images, built one or two images at a time. Goodwin found five images of Garbo worth printing from a single session.

Goodwin was the most talented photographer Garbo had worked with up to that point. They created a set of interesting portraits. A few of them, when looked at in retrospect, are a precursor to the leap that Garbo would take with Arnold Genthe in a year and a half.

Upon the release of *Gösta Berling* in Sweden, local reviews fell into two basic camps, sometimes in the same review. The main complaint was that Stiller's film did not follow the book. Stiller streamlined the story, dropping many secondary storylines. Those who expected fidelity to the original story were disappointed, including Selma Lagerlöf herself. How it would be possible to faithfully follow the novel in a normal-length film isn't discussed. Stiller's two-part abbreviation of the story clocked in at three hours.

Reviews that focused on the story as told found the film delightful. When the film was released overseas, where the audience had minimal knowledge of the source material, *Gösta Berling* was well received both critically and by audiences. The trade publication *Filmbladet* caught the balance between the two camps.

The *Gösta Berling* movie may have its faults and shortcomings—unfortunately nothing is infallible in this the most flawed of worlds—but it is a magnificent work, created by one of the most knowledgeable and brilliant directors and with many of the most distinguished performing artists as the main. It should be received with gratitude and sympathy rather than with petty criticism and sour lines.[227]

Gösta Berling was successful, in both Sweden and Europe—though, to be clear, the film was not a blockbuster success along the lines of a film like *Ben-Hur* (1925) and earned less than Svensk Filmindustri had hoped in its home market.

Most reviews did not address Garbo's performance because the focus was on the performances of Lars Hanson and Gerda Lundequist, but she held her own in a difficult role to get right. One reviewer wrote, "Greta Garbo will probably be a name which will be looked for in film, after her portrayal of the young Elisabeth Dohna, and we will have the right to expect something from her. She has intelligence and is beautiful, natural, piquant, charming."[228]

Later Garbo would tell Ruth Biery the following:

> When we had finished *Gösta Berling*, there were no more pictures, so I went back to school. We have to make our pictures in the summer except for the snow scenes—No, school was not any different. I was still the naughty Garbo and still late in the morning.[229]

She finished the school year with two performances. *La Malquerida* (The Unloved Woman by Jacinto Benavente, 1913, listed in the Dramaten role book as *Mors Rival* [Mother's Rival]) ran fifteen performances during which, for the only time, Garbo shared a stage with legendary Norwegian actor Harriet Bosse (muse to and third wife of August Strindberg). It is a psychological thriller about murder and incest. Bosse later wrote to Arvid Paulson, "Garbo on the other hand (comparing her with Ingrid Bergman), was a genius—she was wonderful."[230]

The theatre year wrapped up with a revival of the 1913 Lucien Besnard play *Mon ami Teddy* (Min vän Teddy/My friend Teddy). Garbo played Mathilde. Ivar Kåge, the Dramaten actor who her boss at PUB, Magdalena Hellberg, had introduced her to three years earlier, was in the cast, as was her former drama coach Signe Enwall.

After her success in *Gösta Berling,* the Swedish film industry wondered why Garbo didn't follow up her success with a role filmed during the summer of 1924. The answer came in an August magazine article:

> After Greta Garbo's great success as the young and beautiful Elisabeth Dohna in the *Gösta Berling* film, she had been expected to see her name on the casts for several of this year's films. But the name Greta Garbo has been bright with her absence. Now comes

> the explanation. She had promised her director for her first film, Mr. Stiller, to be at the disposal of the film he will be making this year, and she has kept that promise.
>
> Miss Garbo will thus make a role in the Stiller film, there is always something of interest that can be communicated regarding this recording, which is still kept quite quiet. However, it can also be mentioned that the document will largely be played out in the Eastern environment and that Constantinople[231] can't wait to receive a Swedish film squad as guests. [232]

While Garbo was still in Sweden, she did some work for advertisements. All of these modeling jobs took place while she was at Dramaten. Her modeling work was limited to three advertisements: a fashion photo in *Idun's* September 23, 1923, issue; an ad for Lancia Lambda cars with fellow Dramaten student Vera Schmiterlöw in 1923; and twin ads for YVY Soap with her sister Alva that ran in *Filmnyheter* in 1924.

Once Garbo arrived in America, she ceased doing advertising work, other than photography in support of her film career. Garbo gave up the potential to earn significant extra income by making this choice. Most well-known actors did some advertising work, and it was lucrative. Garbo also decided to not work on radio, where most stars made money from advertising or dramatic enactments of stories. From 1927 on, her contracts even excused her from radio interviews.

As Garbo wrapped up her second year at Dramaten she would commit to working with Stiller in his next film production. Events would send her to Istanbul and Berlin. She would make a classic German film, but not for Stiller. Their personal relationship would flounder, though they remained in professional contact. As financing for films became challenging in both Sweden and Germany, she and Stiller would turn toward America.

Chapter 6 – The *Odalisque* Project

"I liked to be alone in Constantinople. I went to the bazaars. I had a guide with me. They are so big you could never find your way out of them without someone to guide you.

I was so restless. It was a very big disappointment not to have the money for our picture. But I was not lonely. I walked around the old city by myself mostly." [233]

— Greta Garbo

Garbo photographed in costume for *Odalisque.*

Given the financial problems that now beset Svensk Filmindustri, Stiller looked to Germany to finance his next film. Trianon, a German film company, would offer him a better deal than he ever had in Sweden. He would bring Trianon grand new script for a film to star Garbo. However, the financing for this project would evaporate and leave Garbo stranded in Istanbul.

Garbo rarely spoke about the *Odalisque* project. Reconstructing it through letters and court documents gives us insight into the events that would transform her career, from stage actor to film star.

Stiller and Garbo found themselves on their way to Hollywood sixteen months after the premiere of *Gösta Berling.* At the point where they left together, they were no longer a romantic couple. Garbo and Stiller each separately realized that to have the most impact, they had to be in Hollywood.

In many ways, the process that led Garbo and Stiller to leave Sweden for Hollywood was simple. That's where the money was. For example, the production cost of Garbo's first American film was 67 percent higher than the cost of *Gösta Berling.* Despite a brief resurgence of filmmaking in Europe after World War I, the film industries in every European country were marginalized by the import of American films, which came to dominate the global market. Concurrently, American production companies found much of the talent they needed to make films in Europe and brought them to America. Film production was becoming an international business centered in Hollywood; film financing and distribution were becoming international businesses centered in New York.

In 1924, Garbo was tied to Stiller professionally and romantically, so she was going where Stiller went. She was young and learning. In addition to her own experiences, she was close to Dramaten schoolmate Vera Schmiterlöw, who was now starring in Swedish films.

After *Gösta Berling*, Stiller asked Garbo to not accept other offers for film work over the summer. He had an idea for a new film that she would star in.

Around this time Garbo and Stiller became a romantic couple. They stepped out together among Stiller's social circle. Ragnar Hyltén-Cavallius wrote, "Stiller was working on making the girl into an artist with all his energy. He exposed her to what the art of movies really is, and he shared all his experience with her."[234]

Years later, Hyltén-Cavallius discussed the social aspects of Garbo's integration into Stiller's social world:

> Stiller sought to broaden her horizons in art and culture, and also in the social sphere of Stockholm, where her lower-class background was apparent in her accent and manners. But he also shaped her in other ways. He wanted to foster her as an artist, refine her taste, teach her to admire everything he liked, hate what he found banal, look at things and people with his original and independent view. And she learned this slowly but surely.[235]

They attended the Swedish film industry dinner honoring the visit of Mary Pickford and Douglas Fairbanks on June 21, 1924. She wrote the following to Mimi Pollak:

> Then I was at a dinner, a movie-dinner with the whole Råsunda clique with Mary and Doug. [This was] also an unusually nice night. [I had] Moje [Mauritz Stiller's Swedish nickname] at the table. He and I and Karl-Gerhard ended up at K-G at 6 AM. The day after little Mrs. K-G had a son. Wasn't that great. So, there you hear, something is always happening.[236]

Garbo's romantic involvement with Stiller is apparent in Stiller's letter to her on August [incorrectly written as September] 13, 1924, informing her that she needed to prepare to leave the next Saturday for the *Gösta Berling* premiere in Berlin on the 20th. He closes the letter with the following:

> I hope you feel rested after all the parties you have experienced in Stockholm lately. And your friend is longing for you.
>
> — Moje[237]

While it is fair to ask if Stiller took advantage of Garbo, a young actor who worked for him, it doesn't seem that Stiller was a casting couch lothario. Instead, they fell in love despite their consciousness of the twenty-four-year age difference. When Garbo periodically withdrew from their romantic relationship, Stiller continually gave her all the space she desired. Their professional relationship proceeded without regard to their romantic status. Finally, when Stiller had returned to Sweden and left Garbo in Hollywood, it is Garbo who wrote Stiller to rekindle the romance.

Garbo and Stiller

In September 1924, at the beginning of her third year at Dramaten, Garbo wrote a letter to Mimi Pollak as she sat backstage at Dramaten about to go onstage in *The Violins of Autumn*. Mimi was working in the southern Swedish city of Helsingborg for the season. Garbo writes about Stiller in a familiar way, at one point proposing they have dinner together: "I love you, and if you love Nisse [Pollak's future husband], then I love him too. And Moje. I would love to have dinner with you and him. He likes those small, strange, easy to handle people, judging by his conversations, so that would probably be a success."[238]

Garbo then goes on to report that she discussed the small size of Mimi's hands over dinner.[239]

Regarding plans for *Odalisque* [the film Stiller was planning] she wrote Pollak in September, "Moje had traveled to Berlin, perhaps it will happen now."[240]

In March 1924, right after the premiere of *Gösta Berling* in Stockholm, Stiller had received a letter from David Schratter, the president of the Berlin-based German film company Trianon-Film AG. Schratter had just hired the Swedish actress Mary Johnson, who had earlier appeared in two of Stiller's great films. After outlining the positive attributes of Trianon, Schratter invited Stiller to Berlin to discuss the possibility of Stiller directing Johnson in a Trianon production.[241]

Stiller and Sjöström were considered the great directors of early silent film in Europe. After World War I, a set of German directors who had found inspiration in the Swedes had emerged. Schratter's problem was they were unavailable to work for Trianon. Leading German director Ernst Lubitsch, like Sjöström, had already left for America. The other two great German directors working in 1924, Fritz Lang and F. W. Murnau, worked for or were about to work for the German film company UFA. Landing Stiller would give Trianon added credibility.

Also in March, Stiller looked for a property in which he could feature Garbo. He purchased the rights to make a film from the short novel *I livets virvlar* (Swirls of life, 1925), written by Vladimir Semitjov, a Russian expatriate living in Stockholm. Semitjov had sought out Stiller as someone he could speak to in Russian upon his arrival, and Stiller had found him work at the Råsunda studio.[242] The story was a fictionalization of actual events.[243]

This Stiller project never had an official title, as it was never filmed. It was frequently referred to as "The Constantinople Project" and as *A Tale from Constantinople* in the script donated to the Swedish Film Institute by Hyltén-Cavallius years later. The most frequently used title to describe the project has been *Odalisken från Smolna* (The odalisque from Smolny, which also translates to The concubine from Smolny). This was the title of a slightly different version of the story that was serialized in *Stockholms-Tidningen* under the byline of Bengt Idestam-Almquist.[244] It will be referred to here as *Odalisque.*

The Smolny, in this tentative title of the film, is an upscale neighborhood within the city of St. Petersburg. A more descriptive title would be something like The Concubine from the Smolny Neighborhood, implying by coming from Smolny that the protagonist was well to do before the revolution.

In early April, Stiller found himself the guest of Trianon and Schratter at a dinner at the Hotel Esplanade in Berlin. He needed a producer and Schratter needed a director.

David Schratter and his company had become a medium-sized player in the German film industry. Schratter was born in 1893 in what is now Chernivtsi, Ukraine. Schratter left before the start of World War I to see the world. He eventually founded a successful export-import business in Shanghai. Most of his business was exporting to the United States. During the war he applied for and was granted American citizenship.

Shanghai in the 1910s was a rapidly industrializing city dominated by Western commercial interests. A wide array of labor-intensive products were manufactured for export. On May 27, 1918, Schratter married Alma Lowenthal in Chicago. By 1921, he relocated to the United States and turned his attention to Germany, first as an import agent, then as a business owner.

Schratter may not have been the most straightforward businessman and he may have skirted the law. In October 1921, Schratter was charged with fraud in New York for misrepresenting the value of imported textiles from Germany.[245] The resolution of this case is unknown.

In spring of 1923, Schratter had a chance meeting with the owners of the original version of Trianon while they were on location filming. They were halfway through production of a film and experiencing financial difficulties. Schratter took over financing of the film and, in August 1923, he reincorporated the new Trianon.[246]

Initially, Trianon met with success. Trianon entered 1924 with a plan to make eight films. By this standard it ranked as a medium-sized German film company. To finance this growth, Trianon took out a new set of loans. The general economic conditions for the German film industry had soured by 1924. Until November 1923, German film companies had relied on inflation to cut the burden of their up-front costs against later revenues. The actor who cost 300 marks in January would have cost 600 marks in March when the film was released. Revenues adjusted upward with inflation, but costs had already been incurred. Therefore, the production costs of films were low compared to their eventual revenues. The introduction of the Reichsmark in November 1924 brought hyperinflation to an end, and the production economics of the German film business, particularly regarding export, now had to be more realistic.

With the end of hyperinflation, it became difficult for film companies to access capital. The industry was considered a risky bet. Schratter had capital for investment from his other ventures. He also took out personal loans to finance production. Trianon's first two films of 1924 were major successes and generated significant revenue.

This profitability allowed Trianon to roll out a plan to become an integrated studio, working in production, distribution, and exhibition. Schratter founded a production company, Trianon-Film-Ateliers GmbH, and a distribution subsidiary, Trianon-Film Verleih GmbH. Trianon published its own consumer magazine, *Filmsignale.*

All of this required money. Trianon found an interesting source for its funds. Erich Bretschneider, one of the people who had loaned Trianon money, was the CEO of Wohnstätten GmbH, a building society, which had just received 2.5 million marks ($11.3 million) from the Labor Ministry to be used for construction loans for apartments. For various reasons, Wohnstätten had been unable to deploy these funds in construction as intended. Concerned that bank interest was not generating a sufficient return, Bretschneider decided to loan funds to Trianon. Investing in seventy-seven incremental steps, Bretschneider's investment grew to 3,615,254 RM ($16.3 million) over the course of 1924.[247]

Two important developments flowed from the April 1924 meeting between Stiller and Schratter. Svensk Filmindustri, through the efforts of Stiller, was able to strike a deal with Schratter to grant Trianon a five-year license to exhibit *Gösta Berling* in Germany, Austria, Hungary, Czechoslovakia, Yugoslavia, Poland, Turkey, Egypt, and some additional small countries. This deal was crucial to Svensk Filmindustri as *Gösta Berling* needed the sales from these markets to finally turn a profit.

Gösta Berling had cost 555,000 crowns ($2.8 million) to make. Svensk Filmindustri also spent 157,000 crowns ($800,000) on advertising and distribution in Sweden and Norway. Svensk Filmindustri only made 548,000 crowns ($2.8 million) in Sweden and Norway, so in its home markets it was underwater by 157,000 crowns ($800,000).

The film's profits rested on the international distribution deals that netted an additional 244,000 crowns ($1.2 million), the lion's share of which was the deal with Trianon.

In total, the net profit from *Gösta Berling* was 80,000 crowns ($400,000), out of which Stiller received 39,000 crowns ($200,000), calculated obscurely from the net after all costs. The remaining 41,000 crowns ($200,000) was Svensk Filmindustri's profit.[248]

These financials demonstrated the basic problem Svensk Filmindustri and all European film companies faced. *Gösta Berling* was successful, though not spectacularly so, and yet Svensk Filmindustri only made 6 percent on its costs. Without robust export sales, the film would have been a financial disaster. Though the summary financial sheets for the film production that have survived possibly understate the actual revenue.

Stiller's deal with Svensk Filmindustri for *Gösta Berling* was for 33 percent of domestic profits in Sweden, but only 10 percent of export profits.[249] Schratter made a written offer to Stiller on April 10 for a two-film deal. Compared to what Stiller got from Svensk Filmindustri, the deal was wonderful. He received both 100,000 Swedish crowns ($500,000) and 30 percent of net receipts. He also received the rights to distribute the films in Scandinavia. This arrangement probably helped Stiller to manage his relationship with Svensk Filmindustri. It also gave him more revenue than his *Gösta Berling* deal gave him. Germany had ten times the population of Sweden, so the 30 percent for the domestic market was across a larger first-exhibition market.

Stiller did not sign this April deal. Schratter wanted to start production of the first film on May 1, three weeks into the future. Stiller needed more preparation time. Schratter immediately departed Berlin to sell *Gösta Berling* and his other films to distributors throughout Europe. Toward the end of his trip, Schratter met with Stiller again in Stockholm. On May 22, Stiller wrote out a draft agreement to make four films for Trianon.[250]

By August Trianon was apparently riding a wave of success based on three factors. First, Trianon's films had been successful domestically, including enough prestige films to garner good press. Second, Schratter had purchased distribution rights for films by other companies so he could deliver more complete programs to theatres. Third, he had assembled nearly all of the elements to be a fully integrated film company: a studio, stars, production staff, marketing, and distribution. All of these elements delivered revenue. The only element that Trianon never had was a chain of theatres.

A deal with Stiller was a major accomplishment. Even before his "golden age" films, he had been highly regarded in German film circles. His films were well received by German audiences. Stiller's 1920 film *Erotikon* was the template for numerous light comedies filmed in Germany. Stiller had visited Germany frequently and was a figure in the German press. He was on friendly terms with several German directors, particularly F. W. Murnau.

Unfortunately, this apparently growing and successful company imploded by the end of the year.

In April 1924, striking a deal with Svensk Filmindustri for the distribution rights to *Gösta Berling* was actually a needed lifeline. The rights to *Gösta Berling* eventually generated about 600,000 RM ($2.7 million) in revenue against a licensing cost of 130,000 marks ($585,000). But not quickly enough.[251]

The first problem was that the production of *Orient* (1924), Trianon's first on-location project, ran woefully over budget.[252] It was filmed in Egypt and production dragged on for months, so the film wasn't ready for release until October. This created a cash-flow problem for Trianon just two months after it had seemed flush with cash. Without additional loans from Wohnstätten, authorized by Bretschneider, Trianon would have failed.

Not only could Trianon not pay its existing loan obligations, but it had also mortgaged every available asset. Wohnstätten already had as loan collateral its land, its cars, the film negatives, and the equity.[253] Wohnstätten was so stretched financially that it needed a new loan from the Labor Ministry, ostensibly for the construction business in which it wasn't actually investing at this point.

Garbo had been waiting for Stiller and Stiller had been waiting for Schratter. After signing the deal in May with Schratter to begin production of *Odalisque* in July or August, Schratter pushed Stiller off to a later start, as he needed the *Gösta Berling* revenue to produce *Odalisque*.[254] As part of his strategy to delay, Schratter created an advertising campaign for *Gösta Berling* that included a September premiere in Berlin. This in essence pushed production of *Odalisque* into the fall.

In mid-August, *Aftonbladet* reported that Stiller had completed work on the *Odalisque* script. Garbo had already been cast and veteran Swedish actor Einar Hanson was to be the male lead. Stiller hoped to film on location in Istanbul if budgets permitted.[255]

Somewhat untruthfully Garbo later related the following to Ruth Biery:

> When it came toward summer again, I had a telegram from Mr. Stiller. "Do not make any plans for the summer," he told me. Of course, there were other companies who might want me.
>
> So I made no plans. I went away into the country. Oh, yes, I was alone. I always went away alone. That is what I like—to go away, far into the country, alone. An old couple to cook for you, look after your things for you.[256]

Garbo was withholding the fact that by this time she and Stiller were a couple. This window from the Swedish premiere of *Gösta Berling* in March 1924 through September 1924 is basically the only window in time where they would have had the opportunity to be a social couple in Stockholm. When

Stiller wasn't working to close the Trianon deal or finalizing the *Odalisque* script with Ragnar Hyltén-Cavallius, Garbo and Stiller spent most of a pleasant summer at Stiller's house on Lidingö. While there are no photos of Garbo and Stiller together, Garbo kept a set of snapshots from that summer. They mostly show Stiller at leisure: snuggling with his cat, another with his dog and cat, and a photo of a relaxed Stiller sitting on a rock.

The Stiller house still stands on Lidingö, the windows still the same as in Garbo's snapshots.

Garbo returned to Dramaten for the remainder of her second year, which ended in June. Garbo and Stiller stepped out for the dinner thrown by the Swedish film industry for Douglas Fairbanks and Mary Pickford on June 21, 1924, at the Saltsjöbaden's restaurant. The who's who of the Swedish film industry were there. Garbo wrote Mimi Pollak about that evening shortly after in the letter quoted earlier.

Mauritz Stiller and his cat. Photo by Greta Garbo.

On September 13, 1924, Stiller wrote Garbo a letter:

> My dear little Greta,
> Pack all your things as soon as you get this letter. You will travel to Berlin with me on Saturday, and before then you have to get your passport. I have worked myself half crazy to get the play ready, but

> I am still working on the last act. *Gösta Berling* will be shown on the 20th in Berlin. Then, we can attend the opening and the reception and party after.[257]

Garbo recalled her first trip out of Sweden to attend the Berlin premiere in an interview in 1928:

> I received a letter from Mr. Stiller. They wanted me to come to Berlin for the opening of *Gösta Berling*. I went back to Stockholm and Mr. Stiller came for me—I have everything in the world to be grateful to Mr. Stiller. I have never seen a more beautiful inside of a person!
>
> No, I had never been out of Stockholm except to my own country before. I was not so excited.[258]

While not initially excited about the trip, Berlin would impress her.

> Berlin was wonderful to us. Oh, yes, it was a very big opening. Everything that Mr. Stiller does in Europe is big. There, he is the master. Everybody goes to see his pictures.
>
> We went on the stage. They sent us many flowers. They had sent away to Stockholm for us and they made it a very big time for us. The German people are wonderful. They do not touch you, yet they have their arms around you—always.
>
> And Berlin! I will never forget when I came to it. The smell of the city. An amazing smell that has everything in it. You can feel it in your breast, when it is coming. I had not been in a big city before—where there were so many, many people. But I could feel the smell long before we were really inside the city—it was as though I had smelled it before.[259]

Stiller's traveling party included just Garbo and Gerda Lundequist from the cast of *Gösta Berling*. Garbo was fond of "the very big Swedish actress," whom she described as "the most marvelous person. She has the most amazing eyes of any person. So much soul and so tired, always."[260]

They did all of the standard things one does for the promotion of a film. They were photographed and they gave interviews. Artur Rosenthal, then the editor of Kinematograph, later recalled, "The Swedish woman [Garbo] was dragged to the editorial offices of all periodicals and she spent two hours with us in the Scherl building, chatting about the past and future of international film."[261] Apparently, no one cared enough about what Garbo thought about international film to print a word of this interview.

With a premiere date in September, Schratter was hoping to use initial publicity for *Gösta Berling* to set the stage for theatre owners to buy his whole fall program.

The fact that a German company was leading its program with a Swedish film, and that it had directly contracted with a Swedish director to make four films, fed thoughts of the creation of a "Film Europe." After years of discussions about how European film companies might band together to challenge the American firms, this might have been a first step in that direction. Noting the introductory remarks by Hanns Brodnitz, the Mozartsaal theatre's director, the magazine *Der Film* wrote the following:

> The start of the season. A festive audience to welcome Mauritz Stiller, one of the most active and zealous pioneers of cinematography. One of those who showed the way to the higher development of film. Hanns Brodnitz pointed out the importance that Stiller in particular has for the development of film and with what love and care he devotes to his artistic work. The slogan that Brodnitz put in the foreground for the evening, "European films for Europe," may be interesting but now is not the right moment to be so eagerly engaged in this topic.[262]

Some reviewers did not stint in their praise:

> We let the images pass us by in breathless suspense, we feel captivated by numerous visual moments, we experience the all too human through the art of acting of the main characters. It is a film that is not easily forgotten. It can offer infinite things in quiet, thoughtful hours. Not only by the way Stiller wielded the director's baton, not by the way he offered us delicious subtleties, but by the overall line, by the attitude to the main moments of the plot. What we are offered pictorially at many points in the film is excellent and of impressive force. It is like a delicious jewel that has been given to the film industry.[263]

Other reviewers had quibbles. It diverged from the original novel. It had too many intertitles. It was more of a straight historical film than a lyric Swedish film. The plot wandered. With these reviews, Schratter had not obtained all of his objectives, because the distribution trade read the reviews.

Reviewers, however, were not the same as the audience. Reviewers represented an artistically focused minority, whereas the general audience just wanted to be entertained for two hours. Fortunately for Schratter, the public was happier with the film.

European reviewers tended to focus on the director as auteur, so few wrote about the acting. Those who did write about the acting in *Gösta Berling* all agreed: Garbo was fantastic.

Perhaps the reviewer to go the furthest in praise was Fred Hildenbrandt, whose quirky review in *Berliner Tageblatt*, written as if the Ekeby cavaliers were transported to contemporary Berlin, was primarily about Garbo.

> The cavaliers sit silently around the table in the corner, the table staring at bottles, and they first drink one glass after another, each looking sheepishly past the other. Beerencreutz is lying with both arms over the program of the film, cursing softly to himself; *Gösta Berling* looks over his shoulder and says, "Greta Garbo is her name, Greta Garbo, Greta Garbo." And he doesn't look unkind about it. But then he empties his glass, shakes the hair out of his forehead and jumps up.[264]

In *Vorwärts* the reviewer picked out Garbo, after the leads Lars Hanson and Gerda Lundequist, above all others: "But the gallery of beautiful women is all the more interesting. Above all Greta Garbo, the young Countess Elisabeth Dohna full of delightful charms."[265]

The reviewer for *8 Uhr-Abendblatt* wrote that Garbo possessed "the loveliest countenance to appear on screen in a European film in years."[266]

Louis B. Mayer was not yet in Europe, but in August 1924 while in Berlin for the *Gösta Berling* premiere, Stiller apparently met with MGM agents. Garbo recalled the following:

> While we went there, that one week for the opening, people spoke to Mr. Stiller about our coming to America. He talked, but he did nothing. We went back to Stockholm, to get ready to make a German picture.[267]

Garbo had signed a contract for a third year at Dramaten back on February 3, 1924, before *Gösta Berling* had even been shown. Her salary for the theatre year was to be 1,200 Swedish crowns ($6,000).[268] At that point, Garbo's career thoughts were that she would remain on stage. Perhaps she could make films in the summer during the theatre break as other actors did. From her perspective, when she signed up for a third year almost nothing in her career plan had changed.

Garbo had waited all summer for a Stiller project, and none had developed. So in September, she returned to Dramaten. She clearly missed her friends from the first two years. She wrote to Mimi Pollak:

> I am sitting in the dressing room at the theatre. In an hour, Barbro [Djurberg], [Britta] Vieweg and I are going onto stage where we're extras. God, it is so terrible, no Misse wherever I am, and when I am sitting here at night, I just want your seat to be occupied by you. It's dead here, literally. No playful people laughing and smoking, screaming and swearing.[269]

Stiller next wrote to Garbo on October 19, 1924, from Berlin. He had been sick. This illness delayed him by about a month. He needed to scout locations in Istanbul, but he could not until he recovered.

> Dear, dear Greta,
>
> I am longing for you, and still I don't get in touch with a single line—Can you forgive me? I can't understand it myself. But nowadays I blame everything on my illness.
>
> Of course, I have to rest as soon as I arrive in Berlin. And I am still by far not cured. I walk around unable to make any decisions. My mood is changing as my stomach pleases to feel. However, I will try to travel to Constantinople in a few days. Someday I have to recover, especially since the doctors here say it is nothing dangerous. I am suffering terribly from having lost the energy I had before though. Imagine if I will never get it back!
>
> I have been so tempted to ask you to come for a long time, that had at least cheered me up a bit in my misery, but then I decided that I should at least be healthy first. But it is terribly boring to be completely alone. Nobody patting my belly. As times comes, you have to notify Svaneberg that you will leave Stockholm . . . ? To be

> more precise, . . . November. Oh, dear Greta, it will be so much fun to have you on international water! If I could just recover and be healthy! So the play could run with life and speed. It is terribly difficult to get a hold of the real characters here, but everything will work out in the end. If I may say so myself! Write some lines to me. And above all, do not forget me. Kiss me.
>
> — Moje[270]

Garbo appeared in *Knock or the Triumph of Medicine* at Dramaten for the premiere on October 31, 1924.

In letters to Mimi Pollak, she describes how student life at Dramaten had changed. Her former classmates were scattered to their new jobs. The school is still there, but the chairs are filled with new faces.

> I wanted to write something beautiful darling, but they are chatting so much here in the dressing room, it drives me crazy. No such nice things as we were talking about at times—wait a bit—they are talking about being nervous—ha![271]
>
> In Berlin, it was not fun because of the language, and it is such a large city, I felt a bit deserted. I was homesick then, but when I am at Dramaten all day and see everything stomping at the same speed year after year, I don't know what I feel.[272]

The unspoken difference from February 1924, when Garbo was willing to commit to a third year at Dramaten in anticipation of a stage career, to November 1924, when she was released from her Dramaten contract, was her relationship with Stiller, and her belief that her future was with him.

Odalisque was to be a big-budget film. The production plan involved location shots in and around Istanbul, as well as studio production in Berlin. Schratter and Stiller argued about how to produce sets. Some were made at Råsunda and shipped to Berlin.

Garbo was to play a Russian aristocrat, Marja Ivanova, fleeing the revolutions in Russia. She stows away on a ship, but the crew sells her into slavery. She is bought as an odalisque (concubine) by a Turkish prince, whom her lover murders to free her from slavery. One of the questions the film asks is whether as a now-impure woman Marja is worthy of being loved. In the end she and her lover go their separate ways.

He asks her, “Where will you go now?”

Marja responds, “I am a wanderer. The world is my home.”[273]

While Garbo was important to the project, the more established actors, Conrad Veidt and Einar Hanson, were signed to higher salaries.

Stiller traveled to Berlin in September. In her September 15 letter to Mimi Pollak, Garbo mentions that Stiller has departed.[274] He probably looked in on arrangements there, but he was intent on going to Istanbul to look for shooting locations. Stiller took ill, however, and was bedridden for a month. In October, Garbo writes to Mimi, “And life is difficult in other ways as well. Moje is ill, and if he does not recover, I don’t think anything will happen. (If and but in life) But if everything turns out OK, Misse, then I will come for a visit before I leave.”[275]

Garbo was nevertheless optimistic. She wrote to Mimi: “I am studying German and trying on lots of clothes at NK.”[276]

Finally, Garbo writes Mimi in November 1924 that she has received a letter from Stiller and she expects to be leaving soon. Stiller returned to Stockholm about November 11. In the meantime, MGM had sent Stiller a telegram on November 8 asking if he would be free to meet with Mayer. Mayer was in Rome reviewing the production of *Ben-Hur*, which had gone drastically over budget. He was available to meet Stiller any time before he departed for America at the end of the month.[277] A meeting was set for when Stiller and Garbo were in Berlin on their way from Stockholm to Istanbul.

With the final agreement to proceed with *Odalisque*, Stiller now needed to get Garbo released from her Dramaten contract. Alma Söderhjelm, the Finnish historian and friend of Stiller, recalled that he was at her house for a series of phone calls and negotiations with Molander over the course of an evening that included “moans and sighs” as Stiller tried to persuade his friend to release Garbo for his project.[278]

Gustaf Molander’s notebook shows that Garbo withdrew from Dramaten in November 1924.[279] Trianon paid for her release as part of its contract with her.

Stiller came back to Stockholm, assembled his twelve-person traveling party, and returned to Berlin in time to meet Mayer on either November 25 or 26.

The meeting of Louis B. Mayer, Mauritz Stiller, and Greta Garbo was important, though it did not seem so at the time. Mayer had seen any number of Stiller films. His job was to keep up with what his competitors were doing in the United States and Europe. MGM had a copy of *Gösta Berling* because, as we shall see shortly, people at MGM were watching it.

Irene, Louis B. Mayer's daughter, recalled her father's reaction to seeing *Gösta Berling*:

> We went on a Sunday afternoon to a projection room to see *The Atonement of Gösta Berling*, Stiller's most recent film. The only advance reservation my father had about him was the stipulation that he wouldn't come to Hollywood without his new leading lady, an obstacle my father thought that he could overcome. Instead, Miss Garbo overcame him in the first reel. It was her eyes. He said, "She reminds me of Norma Talmadge." There was no resemblance, but what they had in common and what he must have meant was the capacity to convey feeling through their eyes. Dad said, "I'll take Stiller all right. As for the girl, I want her even more than Stiller. I can make a star out of her. I'll take them both."[280]

Garbo later said that the discussion was primarily between Mayer and Stiller. She didn't talk much at all. "When I met Mr. Mayer, he hardly looked at me. I guess he looked at me out of the corner of his eye, but I did not see him. All of the business was done with Mr. Stiller."[281]

The meeting ended with a verbal outline of what a deal might look like, but no agreement. Stiller and Garbo left for Istanbul; Mayer and his family returned to Los Angeles.

It seems clear that Stiller would have preferred to remain a European director. While he had met with Louis B. Mayer, he probably did not give Mayer's offer much thought. As we will see, even knowing Trianon's difficult financial position, Stiller preferred to work with them on *Odalisque*.

Stiller's group left Berlin for Istanbul on November 27 and arrived on November 30. The financing of *Odalisque* had always been precarious. In retrospect what is clear is how committed all of the parties were to the production, until the moment it collapsed. In November, prior to returning to Stockholm to ready for the trip to Istanbul, Stiller met with Otto Busch, the production manager for Trianon. Busch informed Stiller that Trianon was in financial straits and unable to meet its obligations. At the time, Trianon was only paying fixed costs because Wohnstätten had reduced its loan exposure to Trianon.

The situation was potentially a recipe for recriminations and the termination of the deal. However, the parties all believed in the project and wanted it to move forward. Stiller and representatives of both Wohnstätten and the government met on November 20 at Schratter's apartment to negotiate a deal that would allow the production of *Odalisque*. Against the projected costs of 400,000 marks ($1.8 million) that they agreed to as a production budget, Stiller said revenues should top a million marks ($4.5 million). Schratter was even more optimistic, expecting 1.5 million ($6.8 million).[282]

Stiller, Trianon, Wohnstätten, and the German state agreed to proceed with the production of *Odalisque* with a budget of at least 400,000 RM ($1.8 million), and possibly 450,000 RM ($2 million). Wohnstätten committed to pay 100,000 RM ($450,000) in production costs. Trianon would pay the balance of 300,000 RM ($1.4 million) out of revenues it assured everyone were coming shortly. Even with this uncertainty Stiller preferred continuing with Trianon over signing with MGM. One week later, Wohnstätten advanced Stiller 120,000 RM ($540,000) and he departed for Istanbul.

Bretschneider transferred most of the remaining funds to Trianon in December, but Stiller never saw any of it. Trianon used it to pay current expenses and to establish a British distribution organization. Then Wohnstätten withheld the final sums it had promised.

The traveling party took the train from Berlin, and Hyltén-Cavallius remembered that he and Stiller had continued to refine the script during the journey south. "As soon as we stepped off the train in Stambul, Garbo would show her magic powers. In spite of her ugly travel dress with the ugly flight cap, model 1924, she got carriers and the customs to stare at her in delight and serve her with a not-eastern rapidity."[283]

While preparations were made to begin filming, Garbo toured the city with Hyltén-Cavallius and Hanson.

Ragnar Hyltén-Cavallius observed as well "that people on the street in Constantinople, who would have no earthly reason to know who Garbo was, or care, took notice. When we went to the bazaar in old Stambul for the first time, Turks and Armenians, from old men to our 15-year-old guide, the little serious Mahomed, were all taken by the beautiful stranger, we were convinced that Garbo's beauty really would be admired by the whole world."[284]

The party were guests at the Swedish legation for a dinner. Stiller had to deal with permit issues, and he was trying to get his lighting equipment out of customs. The filming locations had to be finalized.

Stiller soon realized he had a problem, though. The November revised production agreement was less than a month old. The initial 120,000 marks ($542,000) had been spent on transportation, initial arrangements, and preliminary filming. A portion may also have been used for production costs in Berlin, and possibly an up-front payment to Conrad Veidt. At this point, Trianon had not contributed a thing. Stiller had already commissioned and built sets at Råsunda for shipment to Berlin. These were eventually billed against Stiller's Svensk Filmindustri account.[285]

No one answered Stiller's cables to Berlin. Needing additional money to keep production going, he and Hyltén-Cavallius boarded a train back to Berlin. Hyltén-Cavallius recalled the scene at the train station: "I remember how Garbo was leaning herself crying into Stiller's chest."[286]

Garbo in Istanbul in 1924.

It has often been written that the failure of *Odalisque* was Stiller's fault for overspending. This does not hold up to scrutiny. The finances are tough to track without accounting detail, which is missing. The summary finances that were tracked in the subsequent legal case brought by the German state against Trianon, and that are cited by Florin and Vonderau, are from the accounting records, but probably presented in court in a way to cast blame for the problem on Stiller, who was not a party to the lawsuit and did not get an opportunity to answer in court.

The generalization comes from spreading the 400,000 DM ($1.8 million) budget over seventy production days, and ignores all other costs. Stiller's total commitment to production in Istanbul was about forty days, from his arrival in Istanbul on November 27. Well-known actor Conrad Veidt had been contracted to start shooting in Berlin on January 15, 1925, so Stiller had to return by then. Veidt's contract was for one month. This provided for thirty days shooting in Berlin. In the broadest sense, production in Istanbul would have to be about 60 percent of the budget, or about 240,000 marks ($1.1 million), though the actual budget detail is unknown.

Several costs, an up-front payment to Conrad Veidt and perhaps some costs in Berlin, may have come out of Stiller's initial draw. Stiller had departed Berlin with at most half of the money he needed for Istanbul had everything gone according to plan. Stiller expected to receive these additional funds from Trianon at some point in early to mid-December. Trianon did not have the cash flow to deliver on its commitment. Any of it. It didn't send a single mark.

That is not to say Stiller made no mistakes. He may have been over budget and behind schedule. Turkish customs had held up his lighting equipment. He may not have had the permits he needed. He had never shot outside Sweden; the environment may have been more challenging than he had anticipated. The production might not have been as crisply organized as would have been ideal, but Stiller didn't waste money, as has been speculated. He didn't have the time. After twenty days in Istanbul, Stiller returned to Berlin.

Years later, Ragnar Hyltén-Cavallius donated the script for *Odalisque* to the Swedish Film Institute, where it is in the archives. He wrote a brief explanatory note about how the script came to be, and the general events. He writes clearly that "in October [actually November] 1924, Stiller, Garbo, I, Einar Hanson and photographer Julius Jaenzon traveled to Istanbul to prepare the recordings, and soon everything was ready for launch. Then suddenly the whole company was stopped."[287] Stiller had proceeded with all of the preparatory steps, only to not receive the balance of funding required for production.

Stiller traveled back to Berlin, probably leaving on December 21, accompanied by Ragnar Hyltén-Cavallius.[288] Garbo and the other ten people remained behind in Istanbul.

Schratter was not in Berlin when Stiller arrived. He did meet with a Trianon lawyer on December 26. Stiller met once again with the Germans, this time including Schratter, on New Year's Eve. Despite the problems due to Trianon's inability to recover its investment in distribution, it was clear that all parties were still committed to the creation of *Odalisque.*

At this meeting disagreements arose over how funding would flow into the production. Schratter wanted any funds paid to Trianon first, so Trianon could continue funding new distribution, and that *Odalisque* would be funded out of subsequent revenue. Since Schratter had not funded production as he had agreed just the prior month, Stiller wanted to be funded directly by Wohnstätten.

At this point, events took a dramatic and unexpected turn. The publisher of a German film magazine wrote a letter to Schratter asking him to clarify loan arrangements, which the publisher ascribed to being between Trianon and a totally different company, not Wohnstätten. The named third-party company was embroiled in a very public financial scandal. While in a technical sense Wohnstätten was a private company and it was merely not following its charter to invest in building apartments, in the political environment of Germany at the time, this was a bad look. No more loans would be made by Wohnstätten, and the *Odalisque* project was dead.

On New Year's Day 1925, Garbo wrote a letter to Vera Schmiterlöw:

> Here are a few lines from a sad Turkish lady. Things really suck here, it rains and is shitty in all ways. It is actually so nasty here that you wouldn't believe it is true. I shouldn't even mention all animals that are walking right into you when you are out in public. No shooting of films yet, everything is so stupid.
>
> I am longing so for you, imagine if you and Mimmie were here. Then, we would just laugh at all the misery. There is no Christmas rush here, I miss that so much. But if you would write and tell me about Christmas, it might cheer me up a bit. Write when you've got the time, I would love to tell you about everything here.[289]

Garbo spent a month in Istanbul on her own. She found the city fascinating. "Yes I would like to go back to Constantinople. But I would not like to live there. The colors of that country. You cannot describe them. I would like to see them again, but not stay longer than the one month I was there then." [290]

Garbo clearly expected Stiller to successfully solve the financial issue with Trianon. She asked Vera to have a mutual friend send some books for her to read:

> Imagine I am already looking forward to seeing you—I will tell you everything about these damned people. Ask Göstis to send me a couple of books. I don't have a single line to read. Only stare at the ceiling. Would you dare to do that? *En kvinna på 40 år* (A Woman at Forty), Paul Lange and F? P, i.e many plays, no trashy novels? And fancy books by fancy authors. I would be so happy then. I wait longingly to hear from you. [291]

Reporting in the German press regarding Trianon, the loan, and *Odalisque* was often horribly inaccurate. *Das Tagebuch's* article on January 27, for ex-

Garbo, Einar Hanson and Ragnar Hyltén-Cavallius in front of the Süleymaniye Mosque.

ample, couldn't even get basic details correct. They didn't understand that Svensk Filmindustri did not get German government support, they misconstrued the reason Stiller returned to Berlin from Istanbul, and they believed that Conrad Veidt had traveled there.

The article bemoans the financial straits in which Trianon and Westi (another troubled German film company) found themselves and blames the profligate ways of both firms. The article concludes by praising the financial strength of the largest German film company, UFA, which must have amused anyone then looking at the holes in the UFA balance sheet. UFA would be desperately looking for an emergency cash infusion inside six months.[292]

Garbo later recalled the following: "It was a shock, about not making that picture. But it was none of my fault. Although I was so restless, why should I have worried? There were other companies and I was young and was alone in a big, wonderful city.[293] . . . I have had troubles the same as other persons. The company went broke in Constantinople, but I found another."[294]

While Stiller was in Berlin standing amid the wreckage that was Trianon, he looked to find a way forward. He had three options. One option was to try yet again to rescue *Odalisque*. He considered, and rejected, asking Magnusson for funding.

There were two remaining options, and Stiller took both. He met with Georg Pabst and they came to an agreement that Garbo and Einar Hanson, his two stars currently stuck in Istanbul, would star in Pabst's new film project, *Die freudlose Gasse (The Joyless Street*, or, sometimes, *The Street of Sorrow*, 1925).

The third option was to follow up on his November meeting with Louis B. Mayer and go to America. Stiller ended up choosing this option as well. He sent a cable to Victor Sjöström to ask how he found working for Metro-Goldwyn-Mayer. Sjöström's original contract with Goldwyn had been assumed by Metro-Goldwyn-Mayer in their 1924 merger.[295]

Events did not move quickly and Garbo and the whole traveling party remained stuck in Istanbul. Finally on January 20, 1925, Stiller sent Garbo a telegram. "Pack my things, trunk, money is arriving today to the Swedish legation Istanbul five hundred 500-dollars to each."[296] Of the traveling party, nineteen-year-old Garbo is the one Stiller notified.

Upon arriving in Berlin, Garbo signed a contract with Pabst for the role of Grete in *Die freudlose Gasse*. The short contract, dated January 26, 1925, formalized the verbal agreement Pabst reached with Stiller. The production window was February 12 to March 26 and included a photography day on March 30 for portraits.

Garbo's fee for the six weeks' work for this role was 15,000 Swedish crowns ($74,000). The common practice in Germany was to pay actors by the role, though, as we will see, Garbo would be shortly offered an annual contract in Germany. If one translated the *Die freudlose Gasse* contract into a weekly rate, as was the common practice in the United States, she was making $650 ($12,000) per week for the role—though treating this as an apples-to-apples comparison is a bit misleading, as her *Die freudlose Gasse* contract was for only six weeks. American contracts were for a forty-week year, not all of which were spent on active projects. The main observation is that Garbo was being paid good money for her work in *Die freudlose Gasse*. Einar Hanson, back from Istanbul as well, also signed with Pabst.

The one-off film deal with Pabst did not solve Stiller's basic problem. At that moment, he apparently did not see a solution in either Sweden or Germany. *Gösta Berling*, though not a failure, had not been as critically successful as some of his earlier films. He was probably aware, as was everyone in the German film industry, that every German film producer, not just Trianon, was in some kind of economic difficulty due to both the end of inflation and the competition with the larger and better organized American companies.

On January 30, 1925, Garbo and Stiller signed letters of intent to work for Metro-Goldwyn-Mayer.[297] In retrospect, Stiller did not understand the difference in the pay rates between the European and American film industries. While not lavish for Hollywood, the MGM offers were good money from a European point of view. Stiller would be offered more upon his arrival in New York by First National. It seems clear that he did not yet understand how much more valuable his talents were in Hollywood compared to in Europe.

Writing about the value of Garbo's skills at this point is difficult. Her compensation in the MGM letter of intent was $400 ($7,500) per week for a standard forty-week year. She was receiving feature-player compensation based on her performance in a single film. As initially conceived by MGM (as we shall see, this letter of intent does not reflect the final deal signed in New York), her contract gave them a lot of upside earnings potential if Garbo was even mildly successful. If all Garbo had become in Hollywood was a featured player on a five-year contract, MGM would have accomplished the minimum it set out to do by hiring her. While it had annual options for a further four years after the initial one-year term, it could also just let its option expire if Garbo didn't succeed in Hollywood. The options of hundreds of newly signed Hollywood actors expired before the second year.

While major stars like Lillian Gish could command salaries as high as $6,700 ($125,000) per week at MGM in 1924, many lesser stars earned much less. Norma Shearer, just emerging as a star with top billing at MGM, earned $1,000 ($18,700) per week.

While Stiller was still at the Hotel Esplanade in Berlin, Sjöström sent him a telegram on February 7, apparently answering a question Stiller had wanted to have answered before he signed with MGM. Sjöström writes that his treatment at what was by then MGM was "splendid." Further, he did not receive a percentage [of revenues] yet, but he did get a bonus.[298]

The fate of Trianon is an interesting tale. It is an example of the financing problems facing all the European film producers. The campaign to investigate the loans that propped up Trianon was begun by Karl Wolffsohn, publisher of the film magazine *Lichtbild-Bühne*, to weaken it so that a different publishing company, Ullstein, could take over the film company. Ullstein was a 33 percent owner of *Lichtbild-Bühne*.[299]

Shortly after the *Odalisque* debacle, however, revenue from Schratter's efforts to gain additional distribution for *Gösta Berling* finally started to bear fruit. For several months, Trianon was again a functional company, but bankruptcy followed in 1926. Trianon was eventually absorbed by Wohnstätten as a subsidiary. Trianon-Wohnstätten was involved in film until 1967.

The entire affair ended up in court in June 1925. After a seventeen-day trial, Trianon and Schratter were found not guilty of any crimes. They had borrowed money and spent it legally.

David Schratter and his family left Germany for Paris in 1926. His son, Herman, was born in New York in 1928 and, at some point, Schratter relocated to Romania. His daughter, Mary, was born in Bucharest in 1930; Schratter is listed as a merchant on the birth certificate. In 1934 the Schratters returned to

America, where David was still a naturalized citizen, moving to Los Angeles. In 1935, Schratter sued Garbo to recover money he claimed was due to him. The suit was settled out of court.

Here Is "Miss Sweden"

MLLE. GRETA GARBO, above, of Stockholm, Sweden, was declared in the recent national beauty competition to be prettiest woman in the country.—*P. & A. photo.*

Trianon placed an article announcing that Greta Garbo won an imaginary beauty contest in August 1924. This version is from the *Oakland Tribune* August 27, 1924.

There is one final fascinating loose end regarding Trianon. After Stiller and Schratter reached agreement on their contract, Trianon issued a press release that was picked up by only a few newspapers in America and Britain. In it Greta Garbo was hailed as the newly crowned "Miss Sweden." A photo with a caption declaring her the winner of this fictitious contest ran in the *Oakland Tribune* (and other papers) in August 1924, almost a year before Garbo even arrived in America.[300] Clearly Trianon had big plans for overseas distribution that were never realized once the company ran into financial difficulties.

The delays and eventual implosion of the *Odalisque* project kept Garbo unexpectedly off the screen for months, though she had worked at Dramaten. Delay would be a feature of her career for the next two years. But the next step for Garbo would be a triumph, a starring role in one of the greatest German silent films.

Chapter 7 – Triumph in Berlin

"Greta Garbo as I first saw her, gave me a clue, a new angle,
and a new sense of elation. This is beauty,
and this is a beautiful and young woman
not exaggerated in any particular,
stepping, frail yet secure across a wasted city." [301]

— Hilda Doolittle, poet

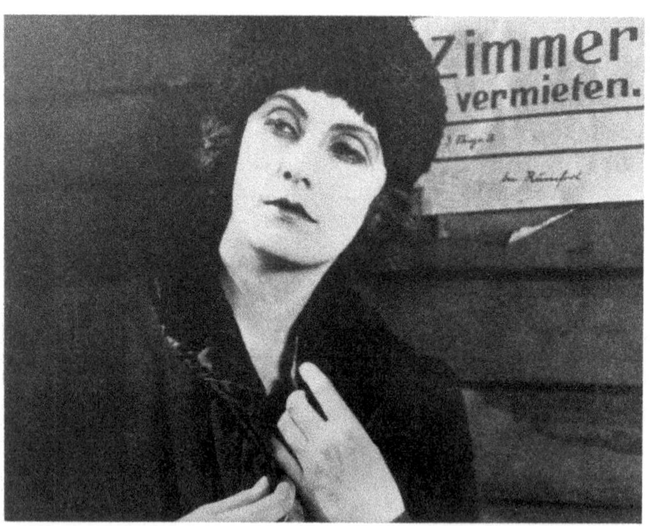

Greta Garbo as Grete Rumfort in the 1925 film *Joyless Street.*

Even though Garbo had not been in a film since *Gösta Berling*, she clearly had been working on her craft. Her acting in her next film, *Die freudlose Gasse*, is mature and confident. *Die freudlose Gasse* would be revolutionary, introducing the New Objectivity style that would transform German film and art. It was controversial and brought attention to the lived lives of women. There is hardly any record of what Garbo thought of the film, though she would spend most of the rest of her career creating more roles that portrayed real women with sexual agency, complex lives, and difficult life decisions.

The film *Die freudlose Gasse* was based on a book by the same name. The story is a harrowing tale of life in the then-recent past, during the postwar hyperinflation in Vienna.

The book was written by Hugo Bettauer, an Austrian Jew who had converted to Protestantism and moved to America, where he started writing. He moved to Berlin after a few years and worked as a newspaper reporter specializing in corruption and bribery. He then returned home to Vienna, where he founded a magazine and focused on writing novels. He was one of the best-selling authors of his day. Nine of his twenty novels were turned into films.[302]

Bettauer was controversial for a few reasons. He was considered Jewish, even though he had converted. He wrote openly about sex and sexual issues in his magazine, *Wochenschrift Probleme des Lebens* (Weekly problems of everyday life). He covered homosexuality, abortion, and other hot-button issues. He had a liberal attitude toward sex and women's roles. He wrote about the ills of society, crime, sex work, the decadence of the elites, and moral decline.[303]

He wrote to provoke. Most people in authority on all sides of the political spectrum disliked him because of something he wrote. He could be wickedly satirical. He wrote a book, *Die Stadt ohne Juden (The City Without Jews*, 1922), in which he described how boring life in Vienna would be if all of the Jews were to be removed by train. He was also a keen social observer, as fifteen years later the Jews of Vienna were removed by train.

Die freudlose Gasse was serialized in the Viennese daily newspaper *Der Tag* between October and December 1923.[304]

Both the book and the film are intensely political, though with clearly different stories.

In an interview given during the later reconstruction of the film, the film's editor Mark Sorkin explained how he discovered the book. According to Sorkin, a Russian friend talked to him about the novel and lent it to him to read. Sorkin read the novel without stopping, and at the end of the day he called Pabst and recommended the book as excellent movie material. He described how Pabst, also fascinated by the book, decided to do an "inflation-time movie." From his first discussion of the book, Pabst wanted to focus on inflation and the despair that led to crime.[305]

Georg Wilhelm Pabst had completed only two films when he undertook *Die freudlose Gasse*, but he had extensive theater experience dating back to 1906. He happened to be in France at the start of World War I and spent the entire war as a prisoner of war, staging prison camp plays. After the war, he was deeply involved in the experimental theater movement. He directed his first film in 1923 at age thirty-eight, and a second in 1924.

He had been planning to make a different story, *Der Dybuk*, and had already invested five months of pre-production work. Pabst's financial backers for the project, film distributors Michael Salkin and Romain Pines, were financing their first film. In a meeting with Pabst in December 1924, Pines expressed hesitancy regarding the marketability of *Der Dybuk*. Pabst suggested shifting to *Die freudlose Gasse* and contracts were modified to this end.[306]

After Pabst persuaded them that *Die freudlose Gasse* was a better investment, he needed a cast.[307] It is assumed that Pabst and Stiller conversed shortly after the decision to film *Die freudlose Gasse.*

The remainder of the cast includes some of Germany's finest actors of that time. Asta Nielsen was the leading female actor in Germany, Ágnes Esterházy was a well-known starring and supporting actor, and Valeska Gert was famous for her stage work. Among the male actors Werner Krauss was one of the most famous and successful German stars, appearing in over a hundred films. Jaro Fürth and Henry Stuart typically worked as supporting actors, and they were well-known, solid artists. Einar Hanson had worked in leading roles in Sweden and Germany.

The plot of *Die freudlose Gasse* follows several threads. Some key characters never meet. The structure has six different subplots, though the stories of Grete and Marie predominate. Garbo plays office clerk Grete Rumfort. Her father, Hofrat (Jaro Fürth), a formerly bourgeois government employee, trades his pension for a lump sum so he can invest in a stock being kited by profiteers. Thinking he has inside information and that the price of the stock will rise, he encourages Grete to buy an expensive new fur coat. Her boss at the office takes the appearance of the new coat to indicate that Grete has been engaging in sex work. When she rejects his advances, she is fired.

Grete Rumfort's boss makes aggressive sexual advances in the film *Joyless Street.*

The recommended stock then crashes and Hofrat's investment is wiped out. Lieutenant Davy (Einar Hanson) appears and rents a room in the Rumfort apartment. Sparks fly between Grete and the lieutenant, but Hofrat drives him off because of a misunderstanding. To save the family from destitution, Grete decides to become a sex worker; she is saved when Hofrat realizes she has been paying the family debts with the rent money from Lieutenant Davy.

In the major parallel story arc, Marie Lechner (Asta Nielsen) lives with her abusive, crippled father. She is in love with Egon Stirner (Henry Stuart), who is responsible for spreading rumors in order to cause the stock price decline that victimizes Hofrat. Marie turns to sex work to earn money for Egon to invest in the scheme. Then she catches him with another woman, whom she murders. Egon is accused, but eventually Marie confesses.

Other subplots revolve around the character of Regina Rosenow (Ágnes Esterházy), the daughter of the banker organizing the stock fraud, who loves Egon. Another follows an abusive butcher, played by Werner Krauss, who trades meat for sex. And the brothel owner, Madam Greifer (Valeska Gert), has her own story as well.

The more minor characters are well drawn and provide a point. For example, Gregori Chmara's role as Kellner, an impoverished Russian emigrant, probably of noble origin, working as a waiter in the brothel, uses typical Europeans' stereotypes of Russians to underlay the dual nature of his relationship with Grete.[308]

Madam Griefer tries to get Grete Rumfort to join her brothel.

Historically, Pabst is a difficult director to appraise. Pabst made a string of socially relevant and successful silent films, starting with *Die freudlose Gasse*. Disenchanted with the Nazis, in 1933 he left Germany for France. He made one unsuccessful film in America, and then had the misfortune to be in Austria when Anschluss happened. He ended up agreeing to work in the German film industry under the Nazis. While his films under Hitler were not political, this stained his reputation. Further, the films he made after he left Germany in 1933 were not of the high caliber of his early films. His later failings shouldn't detract from his earlier accomplishments.

Because of censorship cuts, *Die freudlose Gasse* had been a difficult film to analyze prior to its reconstruction in 1998. It was one of the most popular and most controversial Weimar-era films. Only now, with the reconstructed version, can people appreciate its brilliance. In his silent films after *Die freudlose Gasse* Pabst would be better at avoiding censorship while still delivering pointed social commentary. In Pabst's best films, he framed the story in a more leftist context than any of his contemporaries. His attack on social ills of the time and his early feminism seem modern today.[309]

The script for *Die freudlose Gasse* was written by Willy Haas, who recalled how he got involved:

> One day, in 1924, the movie director G.W. Pabst called me and asked me to read a novel by the Viennese author Hugo Bettauer,

> *Die freudlose Gasse*. He thought it would make a good film. I read the book. It was a terrible crime story, a sensationalist piece from the Viennese period of inflation. But I immediately knew why Pabst with his brilliant sense for contemporary taste was drawn to that book: it was the crass social image of the inflation, the bankruptcy of the old families of the higher officials and academics, the corruption, and the moral decline we had also lived through in Berlin. We agreed to focus on the social issues and consign the criminal aspects of the novel to the background.[310]

Therefore, Haas's script changed the original plot, which was more of a mystery story in which a reporter solves a murder case while at the same time rescuing the Grete Rumfort character from life as a sex worker. Haas dispenses with the reporter altogether. Instead, the plot focuses on three female characters and their paths throughout the economic and social destruction of their worlds. Haas and Pabst added and subtracted other characters as well. The butcher, Geiringer, the villain of the film, is their invention. Instead of a male-centered detective story, *Die freudlose Gasse* morphed into a female-centered social drama.[311]

The novel directly attacked antisemitism. This element is entirely absent from the film.

This film was one of the first to present events from a female point of view. Pabst chose to not make a stylized Expressionist film, the popular style for upscale German films in the first half of the 1920s. *Die freudlose Gasse* was an early film in a style that would be known as New Objectivity (Neue Sachlichkeit), an artistic movement that spanned media as diverse as painting, literature, architecture, and film. New Objectivity is grounded in realism and the practical. A wordier translation of Neue Sachlichkeit would be something like "the new matter of factness." This style came to dominate German film in the late 1920s and requires naturalistic acting.

The film's interwoven storylines are driven by hyperinflation in all of its forms. It's not just money that has been devalued. Women's virtue, social position, personal integrity—everything intangible is now nearly worthless. Only tangible goods like the butcher's meat have value.

Historian Bernd Widdig expresses the parallel between inflation and sex work that was established in the Weimar cultural context:

> More fundamentally, we can think of prostitution itself as a "sexual inflation." If we consider for a moment sexuality within the terms of economic analogies and understand the sexual act as a currency, then prostitution resembles the inflationary dynamics because it is based on the potentially unlimited duplication of the sexual act. The sexual act during prostitution defies the concepts of both uniqueness and individuality; rather, it stresses quantitative sameness and multiplicity: it is defined by the very fact that other men came before and will come afterward. Thus, prostitution is regarded as devaluing the sexual act by violating the very rules that make the act valuable within a patriarchal society; namely, it is a non-circulating, unique, qualitative, not quantitative event between two people. The third characteristic, circulation, is also a constitutive moment of prostitution and becomes symbolically coded in the site of the street.[312]

The powerlessness of the women in *Die freudlose Gasse* in the face of their losses of all the values they had once known is what drives the story forward. How the three female protagonists face this changed society captivated the audience. Film historian Sara F. Hall wrote this:

> The challenges they face constitute the emotional, dramatic, and symbolic focus from the very beginning of the film, where, in the opening sequence the camera follows Grete as she meets up with her father and Marie as she tries to avoid hers. The first shots orient the viewer to the fact that these women's efforts at social and economic catch-up and self-protection will play out as the physical navigation of their "joyless street," whose labyrinthine spaces become a social and moral minefield for those women who seek a better life.[313]

Many contemporary reviewers found *Die freudlose Gasse* to be designed for female spectatorship, and it seems likely that the original audience did as well.[314] What were women seeing on the screen? Film historian Alexandra Seibel phrases it most succinctly: "Then this very experience of witnessing one's own objectification is made transparent in *Die freudlose Gasse.*"[315] However, Pabst's tale has a somewhat happy ending, as Grete Rumfort ends up with the American lieutenant.

By directly portraying the challenges to the female half of the population during hyperinflation, Pabst explicitly makes them, probably for the first time in their experience, the spectators being addressed.[316]

The cast announcement from the Film Kurrier special issue on *Joyless Street.* The three leading women are featured across the top.

Pabst was clearly conscious of the concept of the "New Woman." To have a "New Woman" also implied the evolution of a "New Man," and Pabst drew the Lieutenant Davy character as a feminist hero.

The role of women in society was a particularly fraught issue in the Germany of the time because of inflation. In some ways, young women were dealing with the same changes in society as other countries. German women had been given the right to vote for the first time in the Weimar constitution. Young women were filling the same office jobs and factory jobs as young women in other countries.

Film historian Jenelle Troxell sums this up: "*Joyless Street* becomes an exploration of the lengths to which the women will go to deliver themselves from their dire economic situations—an exploration which puts both of them into conflict with prewar codes of morality."[317]

While much of the dramatic arc of the story is driven by class differences and the exploitation of the lower-class poor and the formerly bourgeois newly poor by the upper class, the sexual exploitation dimension is keenly attuned to the "New Woman" and her ill-defined fit into society.

Die freudlose Gasse was shown in its original run time of about 151 minutes (3,738 meters in length) only infrequently. The film was extensively censored because of its provocative nature. The German censorship report for the film runs thirteen pages, one of the longest censorship reports from the Weimar era. Censorship changes for *Die freudlose Gasse* were similar in extent to those for the notorious pro-communism film *Kuhle Wampe* (1932). Making these changes required re-editing the film to make a story with the remaining footage. Intertitles were changed or new ones were created.

After the initial drastic revisions due to censors before its release, *Die freudlose Gasse* was censored again because the film still caused a public sensation. Seven additional scenes were cut. These cuts removed much of the feminist impact of the film. Film historian Sara Hall noted the following about these censorship cuts:

> All seven sequences display one or more of the following qualities: they show a man taking violent sexual advantage of a woman with no financial resources; they show women's bodies in varying states of undress; they display female sexual appeal in an overt manner; or they represent a desperate act of violence on the part of a dis-

> traught and impoverished woman. The selection of such scenes reveals a deep anxiety toward and about women as sexual and financial agents in the tumultuous inflation years, displaying a conflicted sense of protectionism surrounding female virtue, which coexists uncomfortably with fear toward the potential excessive tendencies of a femme fatale.[318]

Pabst implies that "for every Grete, there are numerous other women who will never find a place in the patriarchal bourgeois moral order."[319] This is the essence of the message that Garbo spent the rest of her career refining, though usually from the position of a "fallen woman." Her character stays true to her own heart in difficult circumstances. After all, Grete barely avoids sliding into sex work herself. Her salvation is not because of her morals, though she has those. Grete is willing to sacrifice and become a sex worker to protect her family. Events conspire, through the intercession of Lieutenant Davy, to make her life less desperate than that of Marie.

Every export market also censored the film extensively, though the required changes could be wildly different. For example, France cut 20 percent of the film, including every scene of the "street" itself. Austria demanded the removal of the Werner Krauss character entirely.[320]

A truncated version was released in America in 1928 to take advantage of Garbo's fame. It was edited down to one-third of its original length to focus just on Garbo's Grete Rumfort story.

By the time World War II began, no available version of the film was anything like the original. The result was that many critical reviews, even from the year of initial release, critique less than the original film. Critics knew the film had been important, but they could not view the film that had been.

Many later critics wrote about *Die freudlose Gasse* while not really understanding its full power. Only truncated versions were available until a nearly complete version was reassembled in 1998 after nearly a decade of curatorial work. Seventy years of film criticism (1928–1998) regarding *Die freudlose Gasse* can more or less be safely set aside.

The Munich Filmmuseum was able to create a single restored version from five different negatives. The museum was guided by the original script (which was not always followed in production), censorship documents, and knowledge that the film was actually initially filmed as two simultaneous originals, referred to by Pabst and Sorkin as negatives A and B.[321]

In order to show what his characters are thinking in *Die freudlose Gasse*, Pabst uses the device of a close-up. He tries to draw on the character the mental anguish of their situation as shown by their expressions.[322] Pabst wanted Garbo so he could use this technique.

Pabst had seen Garbo in *Gösta Berling* and thought she was the right actor for the role of Grete Rumfort. When he learned she was available, he quickly came to an agreement with Stiller, who had returned to Berlin from Istanbul, to get her under contract.

A film writer was given access to the set of *Die freudlose Gasse* and the article appeared in the March 1, 1925, issue of *Der Film*. While the writer is fluffing the film, the choice of the article's focus is the female actors:

> The Sofar film company is an exception in this respect, as it has managed to build up a "Joyless Street" in Staaken, where a few days ago a generating triad between the three stars of Sofar could be noted. Namely, one saw the Countess Ágnes Esterházy, Asta Nielsen and Greta Garbo in a unanimous interplay. On this occasion it must be emphasized that the order of the stars mentioned here is not connected with any value judgment. All three women are among the best actresses we have today and the contrast between the black Asta, the brown Ágnes and the blonde Greta gives a picture that the experts and the general public can expect with interest. After what has been seen so far in Staaken from the joyless street this film should be one of the best quality performances to be expected in the new season.[323]

Bettauer was assassinated during the production of *Die freudlose Gasse*. Austrian National Socialists (Nazis) had explicitly called for his death due to his liberal, feminist, and pro-Jewish views. They got their wish when he was shot on March 10 by a young Nazi party member, Otto Rothstock, who had quit the party before the shooting to obscure his membership.

At the trial, Rothstock was defended by Walter Riehl, chair of the Austrian Nazi Party. He had not left the scene of the crime and in court claimed no real defense as he was proud of having killed Bettauer. He was sentenced to only eighteen months in a psychiatric facility.

Garbo was not in Germany for the May 18, 1925, premiere of *Die freudlose Gasse*. She had lived through a difficult four months since her departure from Stockholm in November to make *Odalisque*. While still in production with Pabst, she wrote to Mimi Pollak indicating her unhappiness with her work on the film:

> Here I am in a movie that I will probably be so ghastly in that you won't recognize me if you'll see it. No director myself, I have no technique, no courage. I never forget these four months I have lived abroad. I have experienced so many bad things—or should I blame it all on my own temperament. I don't know.[324]

She continued: "I am done here in the end of this month, will travel directly to Stockholm."[325]

Pabst and Sorkin edited *Die freudlose Gasse* during April, and the premiere in May was a great success. Garbo's work was well received by reviewers.

Pabst's *Die freudlose Gasse* is remarkably sophisticated in its contrast of the stylized brothels, mysterious stairways, and dark backstreets with the moving, realistic portrait not only of the Asta Nielsen and Greta Garbo characters, but of the well-developed minor roles as well. The relatively restrained acting styles of Nielsen and Garbo convincingly portray their characters' despair and misery.[326]

Most film magazines in Germany were trade oriented. The goal was to place films with distributors and theaters, and magazines were how they discerned which films to carry or show. A sample of German reviews show the impact of both the film and Garbo.

Trade magazine *Der Film's* review focused on Garbo's achievements in her portrayal of Grete:

> The main character is characterized by Greta Garbo. She has never been better than this. She seems to have learned a great deal already in the German speaking milieu. In any case, she has in her performance art a number of registers which are very finely graded by the director.[327]

Other reviews, like that of the trade magazine *Reichsfilmblatt*, focused on the impact of the harrowing story. For Germans, this was recent history:

> There are scenes of gripping force that make the viewer's throat choke. Yes, that's how it really was. I heard whispering behind me. For even if the action of the film takes place in Vienna, the location is secondary. All the big cities that were hit by the tide of inflation experienced the same thing. The unrestrained pleasure-seeking of the inflation winners, those fools who thought they were rich and became poorer every day. In contrast, the misery of the declining middle class, the starving proletariat. Queuing for a piece of meat, a bit of butter, bleak hopelessness, dwindling morals and faith, desperate sinking in the current of time. Pabst lets it arise again in milieu-safe artistically seen pictures from our eyes.[328]

Reichsfilmblatt also called out the overall excellence of the cast:

> The acting cast of the film is excellent. A long list of great names: Asta Nielsen in her unique art draws the shattering tragedy of a harlot, Werner Krauss as a butcher shows the naked brutality of that time, Valeska Gert is a bawdy woman and Greta Garbo in simple chaste beauty is the girl who is tossed in the whirlpool of meanness to and fro. Jaro Fürth provides the type of the official who uncomprehendingly feels the time pass over him.[329]

Another magazine with a film industry audience, *Deutsche Filmwoche*, actually found the cast too good, distracting focus from the stars:

> *Die freudlose Gasse*: a film of juxtapositions: here poverty, murder and hunger, there wealth, love and splendor from the inflationary period of Vienna. Willy Haas adapted the novel from Hugo Bettauer for the film that G. W. Pabst carefully and nuanced directed. This film has one flaw: its cast is too good. This is not meant to be a paradox, because a cast that stars every little waiter role takes away interest in what is happening and draws attention to the actors. . . . Greta Garbo shows the mental and external suffering of a small civil servant's daughter. She is unearthly without being pathetic; beautiful without being "sweet," an actress without difficulty.[330]

Film-Kurier, a major magazine that appealed to fans, wrote about Garbo's performance:

> Greta Garbo as the court councilor's daughter is captivating through the poetry of her appearance. The chastity of the figure becomes palpable in her portrayal—something of the folk song mood blows around this figure.[331]

The key to Garbo's role as Grete is that the audience is privy to the knowledge that she is virtuous, while she is continually placed in situations where those around her question her virtue. The resolution of these various mistaken assumptions drives her part of the story and makes the Grete character accessible to the female audience, all too familiar with assumptions about their virtue.[332]

Even extensively edited, *Die freudlose Gasse* was a sensation in Germany.[333] By June of 1925, just weeks after the premiere, *Die freudlose Gasse* was playing in twenty-three theaters just in Berlin, including in working-class neighborhoods.[334] Working-class and female viewers found the story resonated even with the edits.

The audience in Germany was differentiated. As in other markets, an urban, modern city audience went to expensive showings of films at newly constructed, large theaters. Residents of working-class neighborhoods saw films at small local theatres with few amenities. At the other extreme, a rural audience might still watch a scratchy spliced-together print of that same film months later on a sheet in a barn. *Die freudlose Gasse* did well everywhere. It was running in theaters a year after release and might have run in rural distribution for years. As long as the print fed through the projector, someone somewhere would show it.

These audiences had different social orientations, and preferred different films. *Die freudlose Gasse* resonated perhaps most strongly with an upscale, artistic, feminist, and internationalist group that included the poet Hilda Doolittle, *Die freudlose Gasse* opened their eyes to the artistic possibilities of film, an art form they had previously dismissed as too plebeian.

Doolittle (who wrote under the name H. D.), Bryher (born Annie Winifred Ellerman), and Kenneth Macpherson founded the magazine *Close Up* in 1927. It was an international avant-garde journal that carried erudite writings on film. Written in English and distributed throughout Europe, *Close Up* was antiwar and anti-fascist. Contributors included Gertrude Stein and Dorothy Richardson.

Bryher wrote in the December 1927 *Close Up*,

> I came late to the cinema and I came because of *Joyless Street*. . . . One wet dismal afternoon in Switzerland I went to *Joyless Street*. And I saw what I had looked for in vain in post-war literature, the unrelenting portrayal of what war does to life, to the destruction of beauty, of (as has been said) the conflict war intensifies between those primal emotions, "hunger and eroticism."[335]

And again in March 1929: "[Nothing] could affect us more than our first film, our introduction, we might say, to the whole possibility of screen art—*Joyless Street*, seen here in Montreux some five years ago. *Joyless Street* was my never-to-be-forgotten premiere to the whole art of the screen, and G. W. Pabst was and is my first recognized master of the art."[336]

Doolittle rhapsodized about Garbo in *Die freudlose Gasse*, comparing her to Helen of Troy. She used Garbo as the model for her own acting. Doolittle was disappointed when Garbo left Europe for Hollywood and panned Garbo's performance in *Torrent* (1926) as having destroyed her pure beauty by acting and dressing in the Hollywood fashion.[337]

All of the various reviewers found Garbo's acting to be a more nuanced, realistic style than they were accustomed to. It delivered more impact than one might have expected based on her work in *Gösta Berling*. The year between the two films had been spent honing her craft, at Dramaten, with Stiller, and now with Pabst.

Garbo's acting is now fully mature. She has become a master of psychological portrayal in silent film. Yet she is only twenty. Plenty of twenty-year-old actors appear in film, but not with her command. It is the result of talent, luck, and hard work.

In the four years since Ring first filmed Garbo she has been trained at the best school for naturalistic acting, risen to perform significant roles on the Dramaten stage, and worked for two of the best film directors of the era. Both of whom excelled at bringing psychological nuance to films.

Die freudlose Gasse also featured technical innovations that captured the audience. The Debrie Sept camera was a 35mm French camera introduced onto the market in 1922 for both still and moving images. Guido Seeber adopted the little hand-held camera for *Die freudlose Gasse*. He recalled that *Die freudlose Gasse* was "a film in which many transition shots of the characters moving from place to place were recorded with the [Debrie] Sept."[338]

In 1928 when Louise Brooks was with Pabst in Germany to film *Pandora's Box* (1929), Pabst asked her if she knew Garbo. She said they had met several times, though they were not friends. Pabst went on to rave about Garbo. She recalled a later tea at Pabst's apartment, where he showed her his Garbo photographs that he had been collecting for the three and a half years since they had worked together. Pabst again talked about her talent at some length.[339]

In Paris, *Die freudlose Gasse* premiered as the first feature film at the Studio des Ursulines on January 21, 1926. This famous theater, founded to show experimental and art films, exists to this day. It was an immediate sensation there, in part due to an intertitle inserted into the film decrying the censorship the film had undergone. The censor himself was in the audience and had to depart abruptly.[340] *Die freudlose Gasse* ran at the theater for several months.

The edited export versions of *Die freudlose Gasse* were successful in many European markets. In Russia, due to its treatment of social issues and class exploitation, it was one of the few German films to be authorized for viewing. It circulated there until 1932 and suffered only light censorship[341] This version contained scenes depicting nudity and violence, so it received an adults-only rating.

After two films Garbo was now an established European star. She was at a career crossroads. Europe or America? She had signed her letter of intent with MGM while underage, so it was not enforceable. She would receive offers to work in Europe. Eventually Garbo decided to go to Hollywood. The deciding factor was Stiller.

Chapter 8 – MGM or Film Europe?

"When you read this, I will be ready (I think) to travel to America." [342]

— Greta Garbo in a letter to Mimi Pollak

Garbo's U.S. Silver Certificate with the notation "Berlin April 9, 1925."
Photo by Scott Reisfield. Courtesy of the Greta Garbo family archive.

For many people the assumption is that as a nineteen-year-old woman, Garbo must have come to America in Stiller's baggage. This has been presumed in prior biographies. It is fair to ask how much control a young Garbo exercised over her own career.

She did admire Stiller, and she did entrust aspects of her career to him. Stiller cast her in *Gösta Berling*, Stiller cast her in *Odalisque*, and Stiller arranged for her to film on *Die freudlose Gasse*. On the other hand, Garbo earned the third year at Dramaten on her own. She negotiated with UFA over a contract and, as we will shortly see, she came to America with different objectives than did Stiller. Garbo might not have ventured to America if Stiller had not gone as well. He provided her counsel and support. Stiller was more experienced. She and Stiller came together to take care of their separate situations, which arose from their letters of intent with MGM.

From the time Garbo signed to work on *Die freudlose Gasse* in January until she left for America in June, she and Stiller clearly vacillated as to whether to go to America or not. Both Garbo and Stiller took active steps to try and continue in Europe rather than sailing for America. While Garbo and Stiller each signed a letter of intent with MGM on January 30, 1925, they had different situations. Only nineteen, Garbo was underage, her letter of intent was not valid, and she was aware of that fact. Stiller had a valid letter of intent, but he thought he could avoid turning it into a contract if handled adroitly. Tracking how Garbo and Stiller pursued their decisions between Sweden, Germany, and America can be done in a general sense based on documents and letters.

Stiller and Garbo had clearly become romantically involved at some time around the Swedish premiere of *Gösta Berling* in March 1924. After the failure of the *Odalisque* project, their relationship foundered. In Garbo's March 9, 1925, letter to Mimi Pollak she wrote:

> "You asked about M. I can't tell you anything about this because it is too difficult, too complicated to touch on. But I probably have mainly myself to blame."[343]

In that same letter Garbo wrote to Pollak, "I travel to another world and then you don't know anything about the future. I don't believe that I can keep up in the battle over there but I have to try."[344] So while Garbo is still working on *Die freudlose Gasse*, she seems committed to America.

The break with Stiller seems to have been Garbo's decision. On March 20, Stiller wrote from Stockholm to Garbo in Berlin, "Are you better? Do you

Stiller sitting in front of his home at Lidingö, 1924.
Courtesy of the Greta Garbo family archive.

take care of yourself? I long so after you." After covering some other points, he closes, "Dear Greta, under the current conditions I dare not long for you but I do anyway."

Regarding America, in the same letter, Stiller wrote, "No, we should seek to go over the Atlantic. It will be best."[345]

Perhaps the most interesting artifact is an American one-dollar silver certificate that Garbo kept her entire life. On it she had written "Berlin April 9, 1925." Garbo was in Berlin on March 31 for photography. We don't know the exact date of her return to Sweden. It seems it was a token of the plan to go to Hollywood as she departed Berlin.

In 1925 MGM aggressively raided the Swedish film and theater worlds for talent because the newly integrated company was short of directors and actors. Victor Sjöström had signed with the then-independent Goldwyn Pictures in 1923. Mayer and Thalberg thought highly of him as a director and they asked Sjöström about whom else to bring to Hollywood. Mauritz Stiller, Lars Hanson, Einar Hanson, and Greta Garbo all signed MGM deals in 1925. That same year, MGM offered contracts to actors Mona Mårtenson, Gösta Ekman, and Ivan Hedqvist,[346] but they chose to remain in Sweden (though

Mårtenson briefly came to Hollywood in 1927, she left without making a film). MGM also tried to lure cinematographer Julius Jaenzon to America.[347]

Both Garbo and Stiller then changed their attitude toward America. From April until the final decision to leave for America in June, an incomplete record of discussions exists, but the partial record is fascinating. Charles Magnusson and German interests, including at least the UFA company, sought to have Stiller remain in Europe, forsaking MGM despite his letter of intent.

At some point in 1925, Victor Sjöström received a telegram from Charles Magnusson and UFA proposing that he join a European film consortium that Svensk Filmindustri, UFA, and others were developing. In the mid-fifties Swedish film writer Bengt Idestam-Almquist would, without attribution, name Vladimir Wengeroff and Hugo Stinnes company Westi Film, and Swedish industrialist Ivar Kreuger as the potential investors.[348]

Sjöström was offered $100,000 per year ($1.9 million), but he viewed the prospects for this consortium as uncertain and turned them down.[349]

Stiller's later August 2, 1925, letter to Magnusson is one of the few surviving documents that reveal anything about the early 1925 discussions regarding the creation of a "Film Europe" enterprise, a pan-European consortium centered on Svensk Filmindustri and two German companies, UFA and probably Westi, to compete with American studios.

Stiller wrote,

> Pommer, whom I have negotiated with earlier, comes to mind. To the Germans, that I have no sympathy for, I did not want to travel. You convince me to do that as well, . . . We are making a deal, and there in Berlin, I see for a moment suddenly clearly and do not want to sign before my lawyer has looked into everything. You state that the contract will no longer be valid if I cancel it on April 23, the same day as we arrive to Stockholm. I hurry to Nilsson on my arrival, but in my confusion, I have forgotten Metro's contract in the countryside. I tell him that we need to write a letter to you and cancel the contract anyway, and he can go over the paperwork later. Nilsson responded to me that it can be cancelled orally, and we are both heading over to you in order to cancel it. Puh, Nilsson and I agree on having dinner at Royal, when he will go over the paper and tell you the result. He finds the paper being dangerous for me, and the break of the contract some hours earlier, alright. "I

> have tried to help Magnusson as much as possible," I tell him, "now I probably have to go to America?" "Is that what Mr. Stiller wants?" "No, I do not feel like it," I say, "but it can't be helped." To this Nilsson responds: "Magnusson seems pretty strange to Pommer." I admit this, at the same time pointing out that I have ended up in a terrible position, just because I have wanted to help others out.[350]

Despite all issues raised by the uneven reception of *Gösta Berling* and the failure of the *Odalisque* project, Stiller remained one of the most important directors in Europe. His association with a Film Europe project would give it gravitas. His more cosmopolitan films like *Erotikon* (1920), though a Swedish production, had had a pan-European appeal.

A portrait of Garbo taken in Berlin by Albert Binder in March 1925.

At about the same time Garbo was also talking to UFA, but we can't establish that Stiller was involved. An unsigned version of a contract between Garbo and UFA, dated April 20, 1925, promises Garbo a starting salary paid in dollars of $450 per week (with no unpaid weeks) ($8,400) for the first year.[351] Denominating the contract in dollars protected Garbo against the risk of inflation returning.

This would amount to $23,400 ($438,200) for the first year of the contract. By comparison, most German film actors couldn't expect to earn more than $4,800 per year[352] ($90,000). Unlike the UFA offer to Garbo, most actors worked per project, not per week, indicating that UFA valued Garbo highly. For comparison, leading German star Henny Porten earned between $30,000 and $36,000 ($561,800 and $674,200) per year at the time on per-project contracts.[353] We will return to Garbo's contract with UFA shortly.

On April 25, 1925, Garbo officially terminated her contract with Trianon, which had technically been in force this entire time. The company was far behind on salary payments. The settlement letter states that the original contract ran from November 1, 1924, to October 31, 1925. By mid-March, Trianon was either three or four months in arrears. To terminate the contract Trianon committed to paying Garbo 1,000 RM ($4,500) a month for six months.[354]

While we don't know exactly when Stiller started working on the Film Europe project, we do know that Stiller began to work on the screenplay for the story of the Swedish King Gustav III. Stiller brought in a young Swedish writer and actor to collaborate on the development of the script. Carlo Keil-Möller had made a name for himself in southern Sweden. Keil-Möller started as an actor on the stage in Helsingborg, and he had just been lauded for the script of a successful comedy. Keil-Möller went on to be a successful writer and director of plays. He was a major director at Dramaten during World War II.

Garbo was aware of Stiller and Keil-Möller's project and wrote to Mimi Pollak on April 11 asking for her perception of Carlo Keil-Möller.[355] Nils Lundell, Mimi Pollak's future husband, had acted with Keil-Möller in the comedy *En piga bland pigor* (A maid of maids, 1924), a film for which Keil-Möller also wrote the screenplay. Even if Mimi Pollak herself had not crossed paths with Keil-Möller during her year on stage at the Stadsteatern in Helsingborg, she now knew many of his friends from the city where he began his stage career.

While Stiller is working on the Gustav III project, Garbo's plans are less clear. Garbo wrote to Mimi Pollak's father, Julius, in Karlstad at the beginning of June. She declines an invite to visit him, writing, "But I am a bit nervous just now and it would be boring to see me. I still don't know where I shall land so it is not easy to be calm."[356] Garbo asks Julius to have Mimi Pollak write as soon as he sees her. "Little Uncle Julius when Misse comes home [from Italy], ask her to write me at once—she is, you see, the only person who can help me with something of great importance to me."[357] She closes by hoping she and Mimi can be on the stage in Stockholm together that fall.[358]

It seems that the Film Europe project between Svensk Filmindustri and German interests didn't collapse until about the beginning of June 1925. Hugo Stinnes untimely death in April 1925 was the likely reason. Without his dynamic leadership, Westi ceased operations in July 1925.[359]

Sjöström's concerns about financial viability were not without merit. UFA aalso had financial challenges. UFA would need to be bailed out by American competitors at the end of 1925. The financial straits UFA was in must have been apparent in June.

UFA's financial problems in 1925 had three main causes. First, the German home market did not deliver the profits that American film companies could ring out of theirs. A successful film in Germany might be seen by four or five million people across the country's 5,000 theaters. In America, with 22,500 theaters, a similar film would have an audience of eighteen to twenty million people.[360]

Second, all German firms had trouble in the export market. Some countries Germany had fought against in World War I were still resentful. The American market was tough to crack due to import restrictions on foreign films and returned only limited revenue.

Third, UFA had trouble managing costs. For example, in Germany, where the standard top end of film production cost was considered 400,000 marks ($1.8 million), Fritz Lang spent 6 million marks ($26.4 million) making *Metropolis* (1927, but already well into production in 1925). It would be impossible for UFA to break even on the film. By mid-1925, UFA was headed toward a financial cliff.[361]

Finnish historian and writer Alma Söderhjelm stayed at Stiller's house with him and Carlo Keil-Möller.[362] She had cowritten the script for the Stiller film *Gunnar Hedes Saga* (1923).

Söderhjelm wrote that Garbo came by Stiller's house in Lidingö and Garbo asked her if Stiller had talked to her about America. She wanted Söderhjelm to "put in a good word" for her. Söderhjelm told Garbo her understanding was that Stiller intended to go to the US alone.[363] Stiller's letter to Magnusson in August 1925 made clear that he had hoped to travel to New York only to extract himself from his MGM letter of intent and then return to Sweden.

Söderhjelm seems unaware of the up-and-down nature, or even existence, of the personal relationship between Stiller and Garbo. In Söderhjelm's telling, she is perhaps the person to have had a hand in creating Garbo's Hollywood career by getting Stiller to take her along. Söderhjelm writes that she did give Stiller Garbo's message that she would like to travel with him to America.

This leads to the natural question of what was Garbo's plan? She knew what MGM wanted from her letter of intent. It seems that Stiller's decision to go to America to get out of his letter of intent motivated Garbo to travel with him. Yet Stiller's plan was to exit his contract and return to Europe. They were not romantically involved at the time yet remained professional associates. The logical conclusion is that Garbo traveled to New York to negotiate a better deal. She might not have gone to New York on her own, but was comfortable if she was going with Stiller.

Consider the audacity of Garbo's plan. She intends to travel to New York and negotiate a different contract than one based on her letter of intent. It seems clear that Garbo's main objective is, and it would remain so when in New York, to reduce the number of years she commits to below the five in the letter of intent. Garbo probably already knew that her sister Alva had lymphoma.

She clearly was banking on the idea that MGM realizes she is more valuable than what it offered her earlier in the year. Despite the technical defect in the letter, MGM would certainly consider it a negotiated arrangement. While she had an offer from UFA, she was aware of its tenuous finances through Stiller. Garbo's gambit to travel to New York to negotiate a different contract was a bit like Frodo walking into Mordor, both naïve and audacious.

Magnusson had for years tried to get distribution rights to American films for his theaters. In 1922 he had asked Sjöström to finalize a deal Magnusson thought he had in principle with Goldwyn Pictures. This had failed. Now in 1925, it appears Magnusson sought to leverage Stiller's departure to gain the distribution rights to his MGM films in Sweden.

We don't know how Magnusson asked MGM or Loew's for these Swedish distribution rights, but we know that MGM sent a telegram to Stiller expressly telling him to not negotiate distribution rights for films he made in America with Svensk Filmindustri.[364]

In August 1925, Stiller wrote a long letter to Charles Magnusson from New York.[365] In it, Stiller ascribes his change of heart regarding working for MGM:

> It was the only right way for me to go after all that I had been through. But that is not what destiny wanted. I come to Stockholm. You talk about the falling out between you and Metro. You tell me about it, please note, after I have signed the unlucky contract with Metro. You know me, know what I am like—I do not have any particular urge to go to America—and light-handed as I have always been regarding anything concerning myself, I am immediately willing to stand by your side without thinking about what dangerous adventure I am getting into.[366]

Magnusson wanted to dictate more than just the terms of any deal Stiller finalized with MGM. As a condition for fronting the money Stiller used to travel to New York, Magnusson made Stiller agree to follow his negotiating strategy, which we will cover shortly.[367]

Unfortunately, Garbo and Pollak did not connect in the short time between Garbo's letter to Julius and her departure from Stockholm on June 25. Therefore, Garbo wrote another letter to Mimi on June 21:

> I thought for a while that we would be able to be together for the next season but . . . a couple of days ago Moje called me for the first time in two months and told me about the trip to America. I will leave as quite a sad young lady, as you know! I would have loved to talk to you before I go.[368]

The other person that Garbo spoke with before she left for America was the publisher, Lars Saxon. They had been friends at this point for at least a year. Saxon had had a romantic interest in Garbo, but it does not seem to have ever been reciprocated. Saxon published general interest magazines that became racier and more gossipy in later years. He understood the entertainment business and seems to have answered her questions and speculations about the possible futures before her.

They did spend midsummer of 1925 together. Just before her departure she wrote to Saxon:

> Yes, Lasse boy you have been sweeter to me than you realize. I think fate sent you to be my little guardian angel for what would I have done if I had not had Lasse? Of course you will have fun on this trip [he is leaving Stockholm for business]. Perhaps you will have forgotten who I am when you get these lines. But I absolutely believe you should make a study trip to America. Egotistic like all women. Don't forget that you are terribly welcome. Little Lasse I haven't left yet but when I arrive I shall try to get together my address—if you receive mail that looks like it has been written by me.[369]

Keil-Möller does not seem to ever have been part of the American option. When Stiller finally commits to America, he will breach his contract with Keil-Möller for script writing services. Keil-Möller will then pursue him for the unpaid balance on the contract. However, this must have been resolved, as when Stiller returned to Sweden they reconnected, and Keil-Möller would speak well of Stiller over the years.

Garbo and Stiller sailed for America on June 26. She could not have known how fantastical her next two years would be.

Chapter 9 – Two Months in New York

"They had this picture from Sweden, fourteen reels with Swedish subtitles, a very complicated story called The Saga of Gösta Berling. *There were about seven or eight of us in the room. Nobody could follow the story. It was complicated, the titles were in Swedish, and nobody would have sat through the picture if it hadn't been for this girl. They just waited for her to come on. Every time she came on, all the cutters went "Ahhh."* [370]

— Albert Lewin, director

Greta Garbo and Mauritz Stiller arrive in New York, July 1925.

Garbo and Stiller were only supposed to spend two weeks in New York before continuing on to Hollywood. Instead they would spend two months. The holdup was primarily Garbo's contract. This period of Garbo's life has been misunderstood by prior Garbo biographers, ins ways that serve to reduce her agency and the perception of MGM's interest in her. The main point they miss is that Garbo arrived with negotiating leverage, and used it.

Garbo arrived in New York July 6, 1925, on the MS *Drottingholm.* Famously the only people to greet her as she disembarked were an MGM publicity man, the photographer he hired, and Kaj Gynt, a Swedish actor hired as a translator. The arrival of Garbo, director Mauritz Stiller, and Axel Nilsson, a Swedish lawyer who traveled with them, had generated a total of zero press attendees.

Garbo was unknown to the American public. But within two years she would become one of the leading actors in Hollywood, generate enormous profits for Loew's, the company that owned both the studio she worked for and the best chain of first-run theaters, redefine film acting, embark on a celebrity love affair with John Gilbert, and walk out on MGM for six months in a contract dispute before finally signing a new lucrative star contract.

Garbo had already been announced in the trade press months before she arrived in New York. Variety misspelled her name. On April 8, 1925, the article stated that "MGM would spring a new screen star on their American public very shortly in the form of Greta Gerber, a Swedish picture star. Out at the Culver City studios plans are being formulated for an extensive exploitation and publicity campaign to be used in her behalf."[371]

Perhaps MGM learned from this that it would be better off holding its publicity fire until it had a film to work with. Garbo received limited press mentions until the release of her first film.

New York was just a waypoint on the trip to Hollywood. The initial plan as reported in the July 6 *New York Daily News* was for Garbo and Stiller to depart for Hollywood in two weeks' time. Due to contract issues Garbo would be there for nearly two months. Both she and director Mauritz Stiller wanted contracts that were different from the letters of intent they had signed in January.

Hollywood was already talking about her. In August, while Garbo and Stiller were delayed in New York, *Aftonbladet's* Hollywood reporter wrote back to

Sweden, "Of Miss Garbo it has been said that she is undoubtedly the most beautiful and talented actress that film has."[372] One must conclude that this was the in-house MGM view regarding the potential of its new acquisition based on her European films.

Garbo would later tell magazine writer Ruth Biery, "I thought that America will be all flowers. I thought there would be almost carpets of flowers on the streets of New York City. I wasn't terribly excited. I do not get excited. But I was ready to see the flowers on the streets of the American cities."[373] MGM publicist Hubert Voight would report about her time in New York that "she was effervescent, fun-loving and enjoyed all the fanfare and publicity."[374]

In these first two weeks Voight arranged her first American interview, with Gladys Hall (using the pseudonym Faith Service), for the September issue of *Movie Magazine*. Though Stiller did most of the talking. Her husband, freelance photographer Russell Ball, took a set of portraits and then a set of fashion shots. Both sets of images, along with the images from their arrival at the dock, were the first ones added to the MGM Publicity Department files.

In a later interview with Ruth Biery, Garbo related that she was taken aback by the summer heat of the city. She said, "I spent all of my time in the bathtub thinking about how it would be when we got to California and I would start working in American pictures."[375] Garbo told her that she had already gone to "The Follies" and to the Winter Garden. "I liked that. It was fun to watch the American people."[376]

A portrait of Greta Garbo by Russell Ball.

The Gladys Hall interview, the parallel Russell Ball photo shoot, and a second minor interview with W. Adolphe Roberts seem to have happened in the first few days that Garbo was in New York. Then activity paused as Garbo and Stiller each became involved in contract negotiations with MGM. The Garbo contract would not be resolved until the end of August. The key to resolving Garbo's contract was J. Robert Rubin, the general counsel for both Loew's and MGM, and he was then in London negotiating to buy London theaters and film rights to novels.

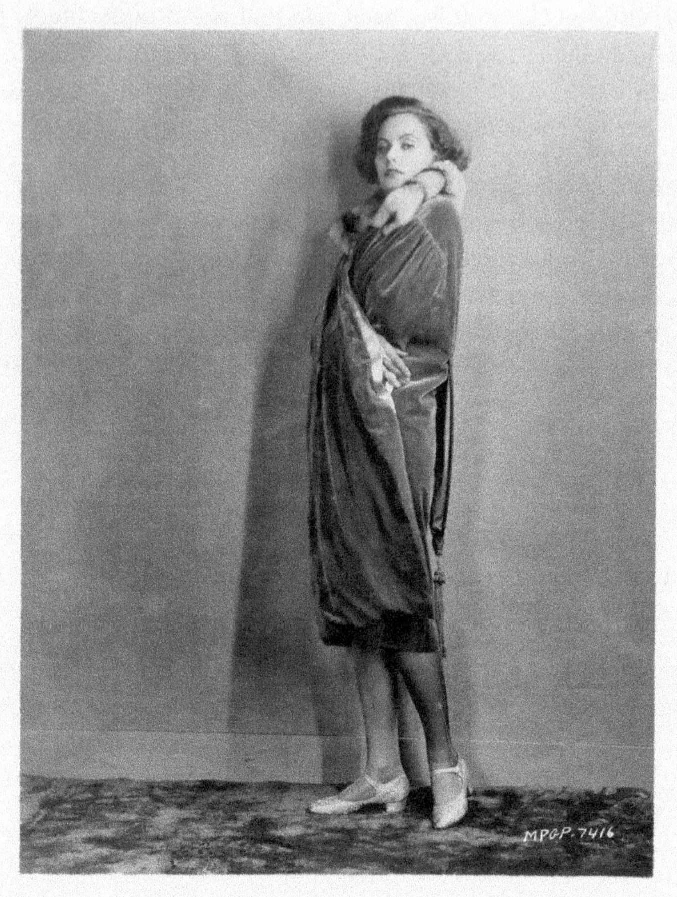

A fashion image of Greta Garbo by Russell Ball.

The long delay that ensued while everyone awaited the return of Rubin allowed for Garbo and Arnold Genthe to transform portrait photography. Film would be the second art Garbo transformed. Even before reaching Hollywood Garbo was beginning to command the power of her talents in new ways.

Modern portrait photography as we now see it in magazines flows in large part from the work Garbo did, first with Arnold Genthe, and then with a succession of talented portrait photographers. In part because she became one of the finest portrait subjects of the era in an artistic sense, and in part because the world wanted billions of her images, Garbo was one of the most important portrait subjects of the twentieth century.

Photographers at the time worked to get a single image of a portrait subject. For example, when one looks through the entire collection of Arnold Genthe portraits from his New York studio, in most instances the entire portrait session yielded a single or perhaps two images. The rest were discarded. Genthe worked in a pictorialist manner, hand working the original negative, lightening and darkening areas, to finalize the image produced for the client.

There is a certain simplicity to the concept of a visual representation of a person. Yet, portraits have been produced in a vast array of variations on this basic theme. Because of the technical limitations, the practice of posing subjects for their portraits led to the output of static images from the pictorialist era of photography until the 1920s. Portrait subjects in this era were carefully posed people who had to hold still for several seconds to produce the image. Garbo arrived as the technology to capture more expressive images and the means to print them cheaply both evolved.

While most portraits were still formal and posed, an entire army of amateur photographers were using Kodak Brownie cameras to take candid photographs. Some of these images were presented as art, an entire body of new photography. However, photographic portraits from this era mostly remained static and separate from candids. Subjects were being still for the camera, not acting for the camera. While Arnold Genthe himself, for example, was able to take portraits with very short exposures as early as 1900, the actual practice of most portrait photographers lagged far behind.

Garbo would sit for a limited number of photographers. But the list covers many of the best portrait photographers of the era. Their Garbo portraits are often among the best examples of their work. In addition to the portraits taken for MGM by Ruth Harriet Louise, Russell Ball, Clarence Sinclair Bull, and George Hurrell, Garbo sat for Arnold Genthe, Edward Steichen, Nickolas Muray, Cecil Beaton, George Hoyningen-Huene, Horst Horst, and Antony Beauchamp. Only Beauchamp is a relative unknown. She would even get Beaton and Hoyningen-Huene to take her passport photos. Garbo sat for portraits through the early-1960s, long after her last film.

Garbo worked hard at photography. She understood how photography communicated her image to her fans. Many other stars looked down on portraits as a marginally useful obligation.

Garbo had made some interesting portraits working with famous Swedish photographer Henry Goodwin in 1924. They presage what she and Genthe would achieve, though her sessions with Genthe clearly go further. Genthe was born in Berlin, Germany, in 1869. He was educated as a classics scholar, receiving a doctorate from the University of Jena in 1894. The following year, he was offered a position as a tutor to the children of a well-to-do German family moving to San Francisco. Shortly after arriving in San Francisco, he taught himself photography. His reputation grew and some of his photographs were published. When his job as a tutor ended in 1897, he opened a photographic studio rather than returning to Germany.

Genthe wrote about the state of portrait photography in his essay "Rebellion in Photography."[377] He described the standard studio of the day as one in which the patron arrives and ponders which stock background they would like to be seated in front of for their portrait. The patron was posed in one of a dozen poses, their body held in place by clamps and stays while the exposure was made.

By contrast, Genthe believed that "the sitter shall be allowed to assume any position that pleases him."[378] Genthe also discusses how he uses conversation and distractions to keep his subject occupied while he takes several exposures before they are even aware that the camera is at work. Genthe observed that most people unconsciously reverted to a rigid expression in anticipation of being photographed.[379]

When one scrolls through his entire body of portraits taken in New York, one sees that, for most of his subjects, he has printed a single image from the sitting.[380] Occasionally he has two or three images. Sometimes for a particularly prestigious subject he has more. His 1918 session with John D. Rockefeller netted five images. He sits in the same chair for all five. His subjects are captured as they are at the moment. But they remain static.

One photographic subject seems to have fascinated him. Genthe took many pictures of dancers while dancing. He created 2,755 dance-related images, most from 1910 to 1930. Some are standard portraits, but many capture dancers at work.

All the leading modern dance photographers, Arnold Genthe, Edward Steichen, and Nickolas Muray in New York and Henry Goodwin in Stockholm, were trying to capture two things in their dance photographs that were absent in their portraits: movement and emotion.

Breaking free from the conventions of ballet, modern dance sought to express emotion on the stage. Dancers such as Isadora Duncan, Maud Allan, and Loie Fuller started this revolution in the 1880s and it quickly spread to Europe.

The modern dance photographs of all four of these photographers have a different feel from their portrait work. All are trying to find ways to capture the communication of movement, emotion, and feeling embodied in modern dance in the photographs they make of the art. Initially, they seem to have separated modern dance out from portraits as much as they did landscapes.

Isadora Duncan, for one, felt that Genthe did capture what she was trying to express in dance. As Duncan wrote in her autobiography *My Life* (1927), his "pictures were never photographs of his sitters but his hypnotic imagination of them. He has taken many pictures of me which are not representations of my physical being but representations of conditions of my soul."[381]

Anna Duncan dancing.
Photo by Arnold Genthe

Another way to capture emotion was to fake it. Around this time in New York, photographer Lejaren à Hiller was working in commercial photography just blocks from Genthe, trying to create "the psychological moment"[382] in advertising photographs that he spent hours, or even days, carefully staging.

Genthe was one of the best known and most expensive portrait photographers in the city. He supplied portraits of actors to *Vanity Fair* and other publications as a part of the standard publicity system. While Garbo's first sitting with Genthe probably was arranged by MGM, this is not known for certain.

Genthe didn't have one portrait session with Greta Garbo in July 1925. He had three. This by itself is unusual. The process by which they decided to expand the standard single portrait session into a series of sessions that delivered stunning photographs is unknown.

It is possible to identify the three separate sessions because the Library of Congress has copies of the original negative sleeves. Therefore, we know that the first session produced a single portrait.

Unfortunately, when the deteriorating negative sleeves were copied, no mechanism had been established to match sleeves with the negatives that had been contained within. Many of the negatives did not survive, just the resultant prints. But the sleeves reveal that Garbo and Genthe had three sessions, July 21 (one negative), July 27 (nine negatives), and July 31 (four negatives). From this, we can match the clothing Garbo is wearing to the number of negatives with each costume. Descriptive notes on a few negative sleeves help as well.

The July 21 portrait session produced a portrait rather in the vein of most Genthe portraits of actors. It is nice, solid work. Garbo wore a sleeveless, patterned top. How and why Genthe and Garbo scheduled a second sitting would be fascinating to know.

The work they created on July 27 was totally different in nature from that single portrait. Garbo acts for the camera on the 27th. Genthe was attuned to capturing gestures and emotive movement from his dance photographs. Portrait photography is an interaction between the photographer and the subject, and here Genthe and Garbo seem fully engaged with each other, pushing the boundaries of what each could do.

The single image from Garbo's photo shoot with Arnold Genthe on July 21 1925.

Garbo wore a simple black chiffon gown that she folded and draped a variety of ways, so it takes a bit of study to realize it is all the same garment. The achievement is not just capturing a single emotive moment, but rather the range that Garbo exhibits in the different images. Each image tells a different story, and they all deliver visual power. Whereas typical Genthe portrait sessions yielded one or two usable images, July 27 yielded nine.

Years later, Clarence Sinclair Bull described how his portrait sessions with Garbo worked, and it seems similar to how Garbo worked with Genthe on July 27:

> I never tell her how to do this or that. Instead, I just let my imagination run riot, and, with her cooperation, usually manage to get something different. For instance, in my last sitting of her, I made ninety exposures. Not once during that time did I ask her to pose a certain way. Before we began I explained to her what I was trying to record, and she did the rest.[383]

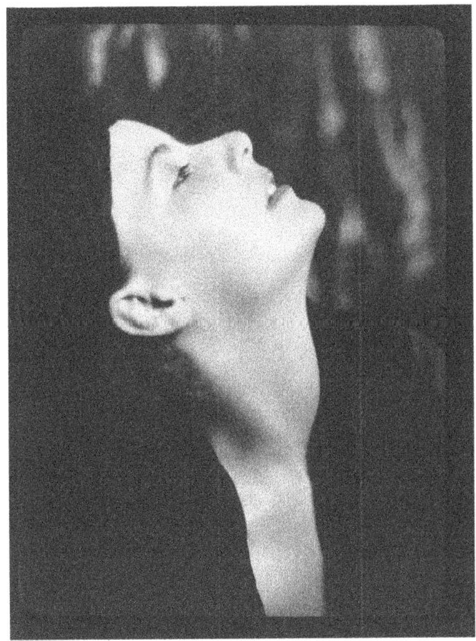

One of the expressive images from the July 27 session.

This is what Genthe and Garbo worked to achieve on July 27. The results are breathtaking. Nothing like this had been presented in standard portrait photography before. While the Henry Goodwin image from 1924 had gone part of the way there, these images moved portrait photography into a new era. There is nothing stilted or static about them.

Garbo and Genthe capture something else. They create a connection between Garbo and the viewer that more or less bypasses the photographer. Karen Vedel quotes Barthes to explain how early modern dance photographers (she writes about Goodwin, but it is also true of Genthe, Steichen, and Muray) were disconnecting the photographic creation from the details of a particular dance to deliver to the viewer something greater.[384]

Matthew Reason captured what Genthe is doing in his essay on dance photography. The photograph "might have mechanically frozen its subject in time, but the photograph communicates movement beyond the moment it depicts—beyond, in a sense, what it reveals photographically to what it evokes in the mind of the viewer."[385]

Genthe wrote about photographing Garbo: "Her face had an unusual mobility of expression and in the course of an hour my camera had captured a number of distinctive poses and expressions, all so different that it was hard to believe they were of the same girl."[386]

Garbo and Genthe connect the viewer to the model more directly in the July 31 session.

It went so well that, apparently, they decided to do it all again four days later. The third and final portrait session on July 31 has Garbo wearing a simple V-neck top. The material is flat, but there is a visible hem where the material overlaps at the collar and lapel. The four images that Genthe and Garbo produced from this session are more subdued than the images from July 27. This restraint renders them even more powerful. It is as if Genthe and Garbo are fine-tuning the balance between acting for the camera and taking portraits with the camera.

These four images are not as clearly "acted" as the nine images from earlier that same week. But there is also no question that Garbo is not merely posing.

While Genthe, Goodwin, Steichen, Muray, and other photographers had captured modern dancers in motion, and while those same photographers had taken portraits of actors in costume, even posed, no one fused acting and portrait photography in quite the way Garbo and Genthe did on July 27.

The balance that was achieved in July 1925 would drive high-end portrait photography forward from that point to today.

This approach had other uses as well. The entire discipline of fashion photography, all of the images of an Avedon-like photographer capturing mercury as a model moves around, throwing poses, is derived entirely from this set of portrait sessions. Richard Avedon's entire oeuvre of dynamic images of women in motion couldn't have happened without the Genthe photo shoots with Garbo.

As *Dance* and Robertson pointed out,

> what Genthe does with Garbo is technically little different from the romantic drape shots he has made of other young players, like Norma Shearer: there's the same soft focus, the same attention to the flowing hair, even similar poses. But the effect of the photographs is very different, and the difference resides in Garbo. Garbo, in Genthe's photographs, is intense and dramatic. Her hair is thick, even fierce; there is nothing softly languorous about her appearance whatsoever. Garbo's partial nudity here projects not vulnerability, but abstract idealism. She radiates tragedy, not sexuality; she moves through a tremendous range of moods and emotions, from penetrating intelligence to glowing beauty.[387]

As the images Garbo and Genthe created in July 1925 made their way into various publications, photographers started to mimic what they had done. Edward Steichen, who as photo editor for *Vanity Fair* had probably seen all the Genthe images, copies one pose in the December 1925 issue. Since his subject was Gloria Swanson and not Garbo, it didn't have the same power. *Vanity Fair* was probably the most important showcase for celebrity portraits in that era.

In appendix two assembled portraits of female actors from 1925 issues of *Vanity Fair* and the portraits from Genthe's sessions with Garbo. The differences are striking. In time other photographers would deduce how Genthe and Garbo had done it, few more successfully than the very photographers with whom Garbo was going to work with in Hollywood.

The difference is clearly Garbo. Arnold Genthe seems to revert to his former techniques in subsequent portrait sessions, though from time to time you can see a glimpse of more animation in a subject. Even most of his later photographs of actors do not reflect what he and Garbo accomplished in 1925.

With the return of J. Robert Rubin in late August, the focus now turned to her contract. Stiller had promised Magnusson that he would allow the Swedish lawyer, Axel Nilsson, to develop the negotiating approach toward MGM. In his lengthy letter to Magnusson from August 2, he recounted how Nilsson's negotiating strategy had been a mistake, and how it had left him unable to either get out of the letter of intent or secure the distribution deal for MGM films in Sweden that Magnusson had requested. It seems that Stiller was financially indebted to Magnusson after the Trianon debacle and had to acquiesce to this approach as Svensk Filmindustri fronted Stiller the money for the journey.

Analysis of the data from the 1920s that remains has shown that in Europe the creative inputs, directors and actors, were typically 20–30 percent of a film's budget. In America, which was already spending bigger budgets on the average film, the creative inputs ran 30–40 percent of a film's budget. Moving to Hollywood was therefore lucrative for European directors; MGM's letter of intent with Stiller purchased his skills at a discount by American standards.[388]

Stiller had figured this out on the trip over from Sweden, as the ship had several film executives traveling on it. So, he was now both reluctant to move to America and feeling underpaid. However, once Nilsson had botched the negotiation, Stiller had no alternative but to sign his contract with MGM. Stiller would get $1,000 ($18,500) a week.[389]

Garbo's situation was completely different. It caught MGM off guard to realize that Garbo was only nineteen. Given the mature performances Garbo was delivering, apparently no one considered the possibility that Garbo was a minor. So, her letter of intent was not enforceable in the United States, Sweden, or Germany.

There is no proof Garbo came to New York to negotiate a better deal, but there is no other reason for her to have left Sweden. If Stiller's plan was to not sign a deal with MGM, but to just negotiate to an impasse and return to Sweden, why did Garbo go on the trip? She knew her letter of intent was unenforceable; she didn't need to travel to New York. The most plausible explanation is that Garbo wanted to work in Hollywood for a year, even if Stiller returned to Sweden. She would have the Sjöströms to look out for her in Los Angeles.

Under this plan, there was every chance that her next film would not be directed by Stiller, but by a different MGM director. Garbo had taken control of her career.

The main objective Garbo brought to the negotiating table was that she only wanted a one-year deal, as her sister, Alva, was suffering from recently diagnosed lymphoma. While the MGM calculation was based on the number of years it wanted the contract to run to pay back its investment in establishing Garbo in the American market, her position was based on personal concerns.

Seven months later in March 1926, as MGM was asking her for a contract extension, she told an interviewer, "For the first time my parents [written as such in Motion Picture, though in reality her father was deceased] are sorry I am actress. They do not want me so far from my home. But I plead with them—'just for one little year'—so I am here."

"And will you stay but one year?" the interviewer asked.

"If America like me, maybe longer, but I must go home to visit first," she replied.[390]

In negotiating with Rubin, Garbo could reference the competing offer from the German studio, UFA. The MGM letter of intent was for a one-year contract with four studio options. UFA had offered a two-year contract with a single option year and for slightly more money each year. Both contracts were in US dollars, a hedge against the possible return of inflation in Germany, so they are easy to compare. The only advantage of the MGM contract was that MGM paid for all costumes and UFA only paid for costumes for period dramas. The weekly salary terms offered Garbo were as follows:

In 1925 Dollars

	MGM letter ($)	UFA draft contract ($)	MGM final contract ($)
Year one	400	450	400
Year two	600*	650	600*
Year three	750*	1,000*	750*
Year four	1,000*	n/a	n/a
Year five	1,250*	n/a	n/a

Note: n/a is short for "not applicable."   ** = Studio option*

In 2025 Dollars

	MGM letter ($)	UFA draft contract ($)	MGM final contract ($)
Year one	7,500	8,400	7,500
Year two	11,200*	12,100	11,200*
Year three	14,000*	18,700*	14,000*
Year four	18,500*	n/a	n/a
Year five	23,100*	n/a	n/a

Note: n/a is short for "not applicable."   ** = Studio option*

THE SAN FRANCISCO EXAMINER:

"American Peepul So Na-ice"

Greta Garbo, cinema star of Sweden, who, with Mauritz Stiller, Swedish director, at left, arrived in San Francisco yesterday to "conquer America." At right is Sam Stiller, brother of Director Stiller, whom he had never met before.

Garbo and Stiller visit his brother in San Francisco on their way to Hollywood.

Garbo signed her deal on August 26 and she and Stiller left for Los Angeles four days later. The contract was signed by Edwin Bowes, but the title page is on Robert Rubin's stationery. Her original salary and option schedule from the letter of intent remained in place, but only for three years. This gave her the shortest contract for a new potential star that MGM signed during the studio era.

While Louis B. Mayer must have agreed to this shorter timeframe, it troubled Garbo's relations with Mayer and MGM for the next year and a half. All that remained after the agreement was reached was to get her mother Anna's signature on the contract. Garbo was still only nineteen and would not turn twenty-one until September 18, 1926. In 1925, this meant sending a paper copy to Stockholm by ship, getting the signature, and returning the contract to New York, again by ship.

Waiting for her mother's signature left plenty of time for Stiller and Garbo to make a leisurely, circuitous journey to Hollywood. They left New York by train on August 30, using a route that took them to Chicago, Minneapolis, and Vancouver, rather than the direct four-day route through Chicago and then southwest to Los Angeles. They spent six days in Canada, visiting Banff and Victoria. From Vancouver, they traveled to San Francisco, where Stiller had two brothers.

At some point, Nick Schenck met Garbo and Stiller while they were in New York haggling over the contracts. Schenck was functionally in charge of Loew's, as Marcus Loew was ill. In essence, while they were signing contracts with MGM, everyone worked for Schenck. He later recalled:

> I met Miss Garbo when she came through New York on her way to Culver City, and I met Mauritz Stiller then also. My reactions toward Miss Garbo were instantaneous. She was unusually beautiful and her personality had an intriguing effect.[391]

Garbo summed up her time in New York as follows:

> We lived in New York for two months and were just at the point of returning home. Everything went sort of haywire. Stiller has been unlucky lately. It has been a pity for him.[392]

Garbo and Stiller finally arrived in Southern California on the morning of September 10. A contingent of MGM's Scandinavian employees welcomed them, complete with public relations photographers. Both Garbo and Stiller settled by the ocean in Santa Monica. This was close to the MGM studio, and among most of the others in the Hollywood Scandinavian community. Garbo found a bungalow at the Miramar Hotel. Stiller started there as well, but shortly found a house in Santa Monica.

Maybe a hundred, at most a few hundred, people in Hollywood had seen Garbo on film when she disembarked the train on September 10. Among this small group, there was a more or less universal belief that Garbo might change everything. Louis B. Mayer and head of production Irving Thalberg now had Garbo on the lot. The film cutters must have been happy too.

The production of *Torrent*, Garbo's first MGM film, was rather straightforward. The marketing of the film and its reception were both completely unusual.

Chapter 10 – *Torrent*: MGM Sells the Unknown Garbo to America

"From the moment Torrent *went into production, no actress was ever again quite happy with herself. The whole MGM studio, including Monta Bell, the director, watched the daily rushes with amazement as Garbo created out of the stalest, thinnest material the complex, enchanting shadow of a soul upon the screen. And it was such a gigantic shadow that people didn't speak of it."* [393]

— Louise Brooks, actor

Greta Garbo and Ricardo Cortez in *Torrent.*

The newly created MGM had few female film stars in 1925. Garbo's first film was a calculated risk to address that deficiency. From the casting to the budget to marketing, MGM bet on Garbo. Based on previews, and his own eyes, Thalberg knew he had a star even before its release.

Stardom was usually built over years. Actors worked their way up from supporting roles or came to Hollywood with lengthy European or stage resumes, and the press that came with those careers. Garbo blew past all of that in one film. The thing that had struck Mayer when he first saw her in *Gösta Berling*, her capacity to convey feeling on film, would strike everyone.

People have speculated about what MGM expected from Garbo once she was cast in a film. Several writers have theorized that Garbo's success surprised MGM. Much of that comes from the erroneous and often repeated theory that MGM was at a loss about what to do with her. That she was a throw-in to the Stiller deal. The evidence shows that Mayer hired her because he thought she could possibly be a star. Once the fact that she was in New York without a valid letter of intent was revealed, Mayer agreed to sign Garbo to an unusual three-year contract. Finally, once she got to Hollywood, Thalberg cast her in a relatively significant film.

That film was *Torrent*. MGM handled her carefully and Garbo's acting would carry the film. The result was a resounding success and the creation of a new star.

In the early film industry budget was a rough proxy for expected quality of the final product. Marcus Loew defined a first-grade film as one having a budget above $150,000 ($2.8 million), so by Loew's own definition, *Torrent* was a major film.[394] With a production cost of $250,000 ($4.7 million), probably close to the budget, *Torrent* ranked tenth in terms of actual cost for the forty films MGM produced that year. Mayer and Thalberg had the confidence in Garbo's potential to cast her in significant films from the start.

Two other Garbo films in the 25–26 MGM film year that followed *Torrent* ended up ranking first and fourth in production costs for the season. The cost of one, *Flesh and the Devil* (fourth, 1926), was planned, and the cost of the other, *The Temptress* (first, 1926), was an accident, as will be shown shortly.

MGM could have opted to cast Garbo in lower-cost vehicles to see how she would fare with American audiences. The decision to cast her in *Torrent* was a riskier choice, as MGM had no audience feedback on her appeal in America.

MGM surrounded Garbo with an acceptable cast in *Torrent*. While male lead Ricardo Cortez is mostly forgotten today, he had just signed a star contract with MGM in 1925. The supporting cast included well-known actors Gertrude Olmstead, Lucien Littlefield, and Mack Swain, among others.

Even before the film was released, the daily rushes were a silent earthquake in Hollywood. Everyone at MGM wanted to see them. Everyone else in Hollywood was talking about them. Garbo's acting was unlike anything they had ever seen.

Torrent is a slightly unorthodox story: The boy and girl do not live happily ever after. Garbo plays Leonora Moreno, a poor Spanish girl growing up in a small town. Ricardo Cortez is her love interest, Don Rafael Brull. His wealthy family happens to rent out the house Leonora lives in with her parents. Implicit in the story is that the two have grown up together.

Don Rafael's mother breaks up the couple and evicts the family from their home. Leonora goes off to Paris and becomes a famous singer, La Brunna. In addition to her fame and talent, it is implied that she's had numerous lovers.

Leonora, now rich and successful, returns home to try her luck with Don Rafael once again. He rejects her and immediately proposes to the woman he has been courting. Then the torrential storm referenced by the title occurs. Concerned for her, Don Rafael looks for Leonora to ensure that she is safe. She is home and the floods have not reached her. Don Rafael, however, is wet and cold. In a wonderful scene, she challenges him. Leonora displays the trophies of her fame, she points out that he has come to her out of concern, then she professes her own love and her willingness to sacrifice it all for him. But Don Rafael departs, shaken by her transformation from Leonora to La Brunna, and perhaps a bit scared of his mother.

Torrent is a story of unrequited true love, and Don Rafael is just not up to the task. One would think that would have been enough for Leonora, but she goes to Don Rafael's engagement party and finds him alone to declare her love one more time. Rejected, she says, "Why can't I just hate him?"

The film closes with an encounter years later in Paris. Don Rafael has five children and lives in comfortable middle age with his wife, but he confesses that he still longs for Leonora. After she performs, she departs for home alone as an intertitle reports the conversation of two observers that she "has everything she wants," when clearly, she doesn't.

Two years later, Garbo recalled making *Torrent*:

> It was very hard work, but I did not mind that. I was at the studio every morning at seven o'clock and worked until six every evening. I was so tired. I did not go anywhere. I moved down to Santa Monica to be near the ocean.
>
> I would go home and lie down and think, think about my sister and my brother and my mother, back home, in the snow in Sweden.[395]

Ricardo Cortez had been disappointed that his wife, Alma Rubens, had not been cast as the female lead. He found himself playing opposite Garbo, an unknown actor he had never heard of. As filming progressed, he began to realize that he was not the star of *Torrent*. The director and producer were focused on Garbo's character. It became obvious that MGM employees, including senior managers such as Eddie Mannix, were wandering onto the set to watch Garbo at work, not Cortez. He became irritable and resentful, demanding that he too be accorded star treatment.[396]

Garbo had been practicing her English. She would talk with cinematographer William Daniels, usually about film-related topics. She was making it a point to try to overcome the language barrier. Daniels noted the language progress was uneven. One day Garbo said to him, "I'm important." Smiling to himself, Daniels replied, "Why, you're the most important person around." Garbo's follow-up was, "Important Garbo—important sardines—just the same."[397]

Upon completing *Torrent*, Loew's was confronted with an interesting problem. It had a great film with a great star, yet no one knew who she was. Garbo had been given only minor publicity upon her arrival. At the beginning of 1926, a photo of Garbo, Stiller, and Sjöström from the day she arrived in Hollywood was printed in Exhibitors Herald. All they could say about her in the caption was "abroad she had become popular."[398]

Factors like the track record of the film's other stars and the director could also boost interest in a new film. Another angle was if the source material was a known work. Here, *Torrent* worked at a particular disadvantage, not just because there was no history of prior Garbo films. Ricardo Cortez was an acceptable, but not extraordinary, leading man, and excelled as a bad guy in his later career. He was a known quantity, but his name was not going to draw significant business. Monta Bell had been trained by Charlie Chaplin and had only made the jump to directing his own films in 1925. Few people went to see a film by a new director.

Of all the principal names associated with *Torrent*—actors Garbo and Cortez, book author Vicente Blasco Ibáñez, and director Monta Bell—only Ibáñez meant anything to the public at large in 1926. Therefore, publicity focused on the fact that the source material was from a popular author and the film was marketed as *Ibáñez' Torrent*. This also addressed the issue of a 1924 film with the same title.

Despite the quirkiness of the script and the unknown cast, *Torrent* was a resounding success. MGM recorded billings of $668,000 ($12.1 million), making *Torrent* the ninth-highest-earning MGM film of the 25–26 production year.

As a studio, MGM didn't sell a single theater ticket. Its revenue came from renting its films to distributors, who then rented them to theaters. Film distribution was competitive. Not every film could be shown for a week on a first-run screen. There were too many films. Since no integrated major film company owned theaters in every market, the integrated majors conspired to show each other's films as part of their monopoly, but they still fought to get their films into the best theaters. Therefore, MGM had a challenge releasing *Torrent* given its cast.

Irving Thalberg had a practice of using early previews to gauge audience reaction. The second known preview of *Torrent* was on February 5 at the nine-hundred–seat Marquis Theatre in what is now West Hollywood. A reviewer for the *Hollywood Daily Citizen*, who went by the initials C. E. N., may have been invited, or may have just stumbled upon it. The reviewer, who had no preconceived notion regarding Garbo, wrote, "Individual honors rest with Greta Garbo, enacting the character of Leonora Moreno. She carries a difficult part well. From the beginning to end the work of Greta Garbo nearly overshadows all else."[399] So Thalberg knew he had something.

An article in the January 27 issue of *Variety* magazine[400] summarized an interview with Irving Thalberg the day before. Thalberg talked about the MGM actors who he thought should be treated as stars in the coming year. Film industry readers would have heard of Conrad Nagel and Sally O'Neil. Nagel had been on the screen since 1918, and O'Neil had broken through in a number of screen roles the prior year. They had not yet even seen Greta Garbo when Thalberg told *Variety* that, going forward, Garbo would receive star billing.[401]

Garbo had not yet received the seal of approval from audiences; perhaps a thousand people in America had seen her on-screen. Thalberg knew what people liked; he had been to the previews. She was like nothing that had ever appeared on the screen. Thalberg, Mayer, and Schenck only had one question: How big would Garbo be?

Torrent received almost no pre-publicity. However, the support it received during its rollout reveals what promise Loew's thought the film, and Garbo, had.

Any film not properly marketed during its launch was a missed opportunity. There were no second chances. The plan had three parts. *Torrent* premiered at the Capitol Theatre in New York on February 21. *Torrent* was actually shown as early as January 21 in previews and early release. But its success at the Capitol was the basis of a trade ad campaign that focused on the fact that *Torrent* had set the one-week box office record at the theater. *Torrent* was held over for a second week, which was not uncommon, but it was a second indicator that the film was a hit.

The ad in the New York Daily News for the New York premiere of *Torrent* lists Garbo's name first.

The success of *Torrent* at the Capitol Theatre and in first-run theaters in key markets was used to sell the film into other first-run theaters in smaller cities and then into subsequent-run theaters.

Six weeks before its general release, *Torrent* was described as a "special" in *Exhibitors Herald.*[402] MGM dropped three trade ads supporting either *Torrent* or Garbo in February and March, two of which were two pages. MGM chose to advertise the film to the exhibitor trade at the level of its special pictures. Once released, MGM supported *Torrent* with a two-page ad and a cover in Exhibitors Herald. This was a common support level in the trade press for a film that a studio was confident about, so advertising *Torrent* this way signaled to the exhibitors that they could take the risk of booking it in their theater.

The total effect of this effort is explained by film historian Andrea Comiskey:

> For studios' biggest releases, successful early runs in the keys—and particularly in New York and Los Angeles—were crucial to generating desirable bookings and solid box-office returns further down the distribution hierarchy. Studios gave higher-budget films more tightly coordinated releases across key cities in order to capitalize on national publicity campaigns. The higher a film's budget, the more likely it was to receive substantial coverage outside the film industry trade press.[403]

Once the premieres and advertising had brought the theater bookings, MGM had to get people into the theaters. Whereas people might have a favorite star or a perception of how an actor might fit a role, with Garbo there was no reference point. MGM had to find a way to translate the theater bookings into an audience in a timeframe measured in days or weeks. It had to convert advertising, reviews, the other acts on the theater program, and word of mouth into ticket sales.

Once *Torrent* had been placed in a theater, MGM and Loew's spent heavily to draw patrons to see the film. For *Torrent*, MGM booked the best bands and acts. For example, when *Torrent* was shown at the first-run Capitol Theatre in Detroit the week of April 18, 1926, the film was paired with an elaborate Kunsky-Publix stage presentation that featured Eduard Werner and his thirty-five-piece Grand Orchestra, as well as the organist Robert Clark.[404]

There were musical and vaudeville acts before the film and music during the film. Musical support for a film could vary considerably. Better music would draw more patrons. Silent film was not silent. Some combination of musicians played the music for the film. In a first-run theater, it might be a full band or a smaller group, depending on the budget. At smaller theaters, the music might be a small band or just a piano player. In a small theater, sometimes they played the film's score and sometimes they played whatever music they felt like playing.[405]

Public relations dropped a few made-up interviews with Garbo about silly topics. According to these, she was a newly converted fan of pumpkin pie, she had arrived in Hollywood looking for a furnished room to rent, and her hobby was exploring the state of California in her free time. A story about her speeding ticket in Santa Monica was real.

The last part of the Loew's strategy was to give audiences a view of Garbo the week before *Torrent* arrived in their theater. The one-minute trailer for *Torrent* is heavy on Garbo, with her in four different costumes.[406] It is probable that Loew's ran an extensive and effective street-level campaign of one-sheet posters and other exploitation gimmicks, though no record of the extent of this ephemeral effort survives. Finally, strong word of mouth boosted attendance.

It became clear quickly that the film, in the sense of a story on the screen, was not the draw. It was Garbo. *Photoplay* wrote about *Torrent*, "The only extraordinary thing about the picture is that it is not above the average, which is most extraordinary for MGM."[407] All while suggesting readers go see the film for Garbo.

It seems, based on the limited ticket revenue reports in *Variety*, that attendance for *Torrent* was stronger in first-run theaters.[408] Loew's, the owner of the best and most first-run theaters, could only have benefited from this.

A good marketing plan can get people interested, but the product has to deliver, or sales will quickly fall off. *Torrent* received mixed reviews from early critics. In fact, Variety carefully distinguished between its praise for Garbo and its belief that the film itself was weak:

> The Ibáñez name may pull some money, and while *Torrent* is well played and capably directed there is nothing about the picture that is going to make the public crazy about it. . . . There are other "names" in the cast, and although veterans they could not overshadow Greta Garbo. Hail this girl, for she'll get over.[409]

Exhibitors Herald wrote, "Garbo a hit in her first American screen portrayal. The Cosmopolitan production from MGM studios accomplished the feat of piling up a gross business at the Capitol theater of $30,685 [$575,000] the first two days of its engagement there. Will be held over for second week."[410]

As *Torrent* opened in key city after key city, positive reviews of Garbo rolled in, one after another. They emphasized her plasticity, with Garbo described as resembling several stars in turn. A sample review stated:

> Probably the most important feature of the film is the latest Greta from Sweden. This is the Greta Garbo, a pretty, wistful, and intensely feminine young person, who suggests a composite picture of a dozen of our best-known stars. Making her debut in the film, she registers a complete success. She is not so much an actress as she is endowed with individuality and magnetism.[411]

The two trade papers, *Variety* and *Film Daily*, agreed that the film was unlikely to do well at the box office, and the *Film Daily* reviewer explicitly tied its lack of appeal to the fact that the love story "fizzled out in disillusionment."[412]

Overall, *"Ibáñez' Torrent* was rather coolly received by reviewers. They saw the ridiculing of heroic postures and use of anticlimax as failed realizations of genre conventions."[413]

The response to Garbo was much more positive: "Greta Garbo, making her American debut as a screen star, might just as well be hailed right here as the find of the year. This girl has everything with looks, acting ability and personality."[414]

Below I will go into more depth about what Garbo delivered to the audience that changed Hollywood. One can see the impact in the reviews of, and audience response to, *Torrent*. Film historian Alexander Walker captured the uniqueness of what Garbo achieved with the audience in just one film:

> It is the sure sign that a new type of film star has arrived when reviewers are forced to compare her with an old type. That the comparison is made at all is evidence of her impact; a little later will come evidence of her individuality; and then of her uniqueness. Greta Garbo telescoped all three stages into one with her first American film, *Torrent*.[415]

Even reviews that panned *Torrent*, and the reviewer for the *St. Louis Post-Dispatch* positively hated it, found Garbo, though in this case not her name, fascinating:

> As leading woman, Greta Garbo, as pretty a screen star as has been seen in many years. Miss Garbo—that must be her right name, for no one could imagine an actress picking it for stage purposes—

> has a pair of eyes which look right through you and button up the back, but even they fail to pull *Torrent* in out of the wet.[416]

Patron reactions to Garbo can be observed. First, they bought a lot of tickets. Garbo sold more tickets to exhibitions at the highest priced first-run theaters. Her audience was upscale. Her new fans also wrote letters to both fan magazines and the studio. For example, the June issue (which would have been sent to the printer in mid-April) of *Photoplay* magazine featured the following letter of the month from Mrs. L. E. Sanborn:

> One day I went to see *Torrent*, in which there was a wonderful person called "Greta Garbo." I wish I had a thousand dollars to invest in futures: I'd put it all on her. She has everything the others have, and more—piquancy, sprightliness.[417]

A Portrait of Greta Garbo for *Torrent*. Photo by Ruth Harriet Louise. Courtesy of the Greta Garbo family archive.

In 1926, there was no systematic reporting of theater ticket revenues. *Variety* did report ticket revenues for some theaters in some markets, mostly the first-run theaters. Even then in New York, the reporting was just for a few large theaters in Manhattan. Brooklyn, with nearly the same population, didn't exist in these reports. This spotty data does show that *Torrent* did well in most first-run theaters. It did especially well in cities with large numbers of clerks, half of whom were women.

In New York, in just two weeks at the Capitol Theatre, *Torrent* drew a strong $117,000 ($2.2 million).[418] No data exist for all of the other Loew's theaters in the broader metro area. Chicago was America's second-largest city. At the Roosevelt, *Torrent* "started briskly at $20,000 [$375,000] with new star, Greta Garbo, creating world of comment among fans."[419]

In Los Angeles, America's fifth-largest city at the time, *Torrent* premiered at the Loew's State Theatre paired with a stage act. Variety reported, "House with stiff competition could have had no better combination than this picture and Rube Wolf. They stood the test. Gross of unusual proportions at $29,000 [$524,900]."[420]

But a film could have widely different receptions in different cities. *Torrent* did only pedestrian business in Kansas City.

Confusing any evaluation of a film's draw was the fact that in first-run theaters films were paired with live acts most of the time. MGM had done a good job of pairing *Torrent* with strong live acts, which cost it money but drew in more patrons. To the extent that these people became Garbo fans and turned out for her subsequent films, it was money well spent. But there is never an apples-to-apples comparison between the drawing power of films because the show was never just the film.

Speaking about Garbo's abilities and how they had a unique impact on her audience, Betsy Erkkila wrote,

> In *Torrent*, in which Garbo transforms herself from amorous adolescent to diva, to vamp, to woman alone, she reveals not only her plastic and mercurial power but her capacity to shape the film in her own self-generated image. Garbo eroticized the stylized unreality of the film vamp and radicalized the mere surface freedom of the 1920s' flapper, creating the powerful image of a passionate and worldly woman who seemed ultimately disillusioned by the romantic adventures to which she was irrevocably doomed.[421]

This ability to portray the character while simultaneously representing something more to her audience would be her hallmark.

Torrent was released one week after the Norma Shearer vehicle *The Devil's Circus* (1926), and they make for an interesting comparison. Shearer had just made the leap from B player to star at MGM. She had been in leading roles in lesser films since 1922, so audiences were familiar with her. She had joined MGM in 1924. Her first two films of the 25–26 production year cost just under $150,000 ($2.8 million), Marcus Loew's budget floor for an A film. Her final three films in the 25–26 production year cost $150,000 or above. The Devil's Circus cost $204,000 ($3.7 million).

While *The Devil's Circus* was Shearer's most expensive vehicle to date, it still cost less than *Torrent's* $250,000 ($4.5 million), reinforcing Garbo's status at MGM from her first production.

Costs and Profits (1926 dollars)

	The Devil's Circus	*Torrent*
Release	Feb. 15, 1926	Feb. 21, 1926
Earnings (domestic)	$375,000	$460,000
Earnings (foreign)	$244,000	$208,000
Total earnings	$619,000	$668,000
Total production cost	$204,000	$250,000
Under-the-line costs	$224,000	$292,000
Profit	$191,000	$126,000

Source: Eddie Mannix Ledger, Margaret Herrick Library, Academy of Motion Picture Arts and Sciences, Beverly Hills, CA.

Costs and Profits (2025 dollars)

	The Devil's Circus	*Torrent*
Release	Feb. 15, 1926	Feb. 21, 1926
Earnings (domestic)	$6.8	$8.3
Earnings (foreign)	$4.4	$3.8
Total earnings	$11.2	$12.1
Total production cost	$3.7	$4.5
Under-the-line costs	$4.1	$5.3
Profit	$3.5	$2.3

Note: All dollar amounts are in the millions.

Most interesting is the difference in under-the-line costs, which would be primarily marketing. As Garbo was unknown, MGM spent heavily, nearly $70,000 more, to bring in patrons. This amount is basically the difference in the profit between the two films. It also clarifies that MGM had a notion of what Garbo was going to do for it in *Torrent* and subsequent films. It invested in her future success.

Torrent did better domestically, and *The Devil's Circus* did better in foreign markets. The domestic strength of *Torrent* was certainly helped by the heavy marketing, though Garbo's resonance with the audience was immediate and word of mouth mattered more. Marketing can't make people see a bad movie.

In foreign markets, where MGM had less distribution power than in the United States, Norma Shearer was the known quantity. Foreign distributors already had a sense of what a Shearer film could deliver in their market, so they paid accordingly. In 1926 Loew's had no easy way to overcome foreign distributors' unfamiliarity with Garbo.

Between the end of production for *Torrent* and the start of filming for *The Temptress*, Garbo spent time watching other actors at work, as she always wanted to see what the most talented people were doing. She spent time on the set of *The Scarlet Letter* (1926), where Lillian Gish and Lars Hanson were filming under the direction of Victor Sjöström. This film went into production in late January 1926. No longer the neophyte, she was good friends with Sjöström and Hanson by this time. The Danish actor Karl Dane was also in the cast.

Garbo's other big accomplishment was to get another ticket for speeding in Santa Monica on February 23, 1926. She was traveling thirty-five in a twenty-miles-per-hour zone. The ticket and court appearance were her first venture into Hollywood reporting, as a speeding ticket for anyone else would hardly have been news. The process of getting caught speeding was not educational: In January 1927, she collected her third speeding ticket.[422]

Not much else is known specifically about the time between Garbo's first two movies. A letter to Lars Saxon dated February 14 does reveal an interesting detail. Garbo reports that she "had a talk with the chief yesterday and he was mad at me because he thought I am needlessly worried over everything."[423] There is no other context, and we don't know if the conversation was with Mayer or Thalberg.

Lars Saxon, a Swedish magazine publisher with whom she was friendly at the time, arrived in Los Angeles on a visit in January 1926 while Garbo was between films. He carried with him baked goods and gloves from Garbo's family. Garbo had valued his friendship in Stockholm, and he had given her advice at times. His main publication, the magazine *Lektyr*, had not yet veered off into the fanciful Garbo stories that it featured almost monthly in the 1930s.

Garbo wrote a long letter to Mimi Pollak on March 4, 1926.[424] She mentions that she likes Saxon, but that he keeps wanting to marry her, and Garbo is not romantically inclined toward him.

She is still depressed about being in America and her situation there. She writes, "I am very lonely. I do not want to and cannot get to know the Americans."[425] Her gray mood seems to flow as well from her belief that she has messed up her romantic life. Since Stiller is the only romantic partner in the picture at this point, this must be in reference to him. She writes, "I have been, and am still sad about my heart. I do not think it is often a woman has ever felt more inferior and worse than I have felt. I have humiliated myself, been bitter, mean, crazy, but I will never be free from what destiny has thrown to me."[426]

As she is about to start *The Temptress*, she writes of her concern regarding working for him (their romance was an on-again, off-again affair). "I will soon start working for Stiller. I am grateful and scared. I don't know what it will be like to work for him."[427] Grateful, one supposes, because she thinks he is a better director than Monta Bell.

The letter reveals that Garbo is surprised at *Torrent's* success, as she feels her work was mediocre. "My movie has been shown here, the critique was strangely kind, but I did not think I was anything, so I can't find pleasure in what I don't think I deserve. All the Swedes know that I was not pleased with myself. I was not photographed so well as I could have been, and my acting was nothing."[428] She is astonished that *Torrent* has been such a commercial success, and that MGM clearly believes this success is because of her.

Garbo's relationship with Stiller was complex. Their twenty-two-year age difference complicated the on-again, off-again romantic element of their relationship. After the romance began following *Gösta Berling*, it sputtered out before they decided to travel to America. Somewhere in transit it was rekindled. Their mutually supportive professional relationship would remain in place regardless of the state of romantic affairs.

Finally, Garbo mentions that she has considered asking Alva to come to Los Angeles, but she knows that would make her mother sad. So, she won't.[429] Garbo is unaware just how ill Alva has become, so her family must have been withholding the seriousness of her condition.

As Mayer had hoped, Garbo's naturalistic acting style did resonate with the audience. It did more than that. It would transform Hollywood acting itself.

Chapter 11 – Greta Garbo and Naturalistic Acting

"I've been down watching that new girl work.
I don't know what it is she has but I do know
that everyone on the lot who can get away for a few moments
from whatever he is supposed to be doing goes to watch her.
There is a stillness about her. A power, or—oh, I don't know." [430]

— Unnamed MGM executive

Greta Garbo, as Leonora, leaving her parents, played by Edward Connelly and Lucy Beaumont, in a scene from *Torrent.*

As Irene Selznick had recounted, when Louis B. Mayer first saw Garbo onscreen he likened her to Norma Talmadge.[431] Talmadge was the best-known naturalistic actor in Hollywood at the time. While Talmadge was effective and had her own fan base, Garbo was more talented, better trained, and benefited from technical changes in camera lenses and film stock.

The naturalistic style is more accessible to a viewer who wants to identify with the character. Garbo's skill allowed her to portray realistic, strong women whose emotions were visible and understandable. In contrast to her peers in 1926, Garbo was believable and relatable to the audience. The effect on the audience was immediate. Garbo gained fans with a single film.

Garbo was so good that one reviewer of *Torrent* wrote,

> Her technique is so perfect as to be imperceptible, and her mobile features express the most subtle shades of emotion. Few native actresses are so gifted.[432]

Reviewers of *Torrent* split into two camps. Some thought Garbo didn't act at all, that she was somehow just a personality that worked well on the screen. Laurence Reid's review of *Torrent* in *Motion Picture* magazine stated, "She is not so much an actress as she is endowed with individuality and magnetism."[433]

In his review for *Life* Robert Sherwood wrote, "She may not be the best actress on the screen—I am powerless to formulate an opinion on her dramatic technique—but there is no room for argument as to the efficacy of her allure."[434]

Other reviewers were clear that Garbo was delivering a performance. Mordaunt Hall wrote, "Miss Garbo may lift her head the fraction of an inch and it means more than John Gilbert's artificial smile or his wide-eyed expression. Miss Garbo may not be wholly unaware of her personal charm but she never for an instant gives one the idea that she is thinking of how she looks before the camera."[435]

In *Motion Picture Classic* Frederick Smith observed, "This Garbo has a fine abandon, a splendid fire, a surprising sense of characterization. She isn't afraid to act. That she was able to stand out of an inferior story, poorly directed, is all the more to her credit."[436]

One of the few female film critics in the 1920s, Elise Dufour, caught the essence of Garbo's acting in her review of *The Temptress*:

> "Many actors seem to think that a great deal of moving about or of facial working is effective; but such a genuine artist as Greta Garbo can stand almost motionless, and with scarcely a flicker of the eyes or lips, and yet invisibly pulsate such feeling that the audience inwardly trembles. Without moving from her position she easily relates herself to the other actors and to every inch of the set. Such living and inward unity is not mentally recognized, it still takes the breath of the beholder."[437]

Garbo herself was surprised that her first directors didn't give her direction as to how to portray her characters. In her first films, before the industry caught up with the Swedish approach to naturalistic acting, Garbo had to create the emotional underpinnings of characters herself.

She commented on the difference between working for Stiller and working for Monta Bell and Fred Niblo in a September 1, 1926, letter to Mimi Pollak:

> If you knew how strange directors are here. Many of them certainly know nothing about emotional life and so forth. You only get direction on how you should go, stand, sit, speak and so forth. Then you do as you please even if you do it poorly. It is not like when Stiller was with and motivated me to feel something.[438]

In her first interview with Mordaunt Hall of *The New York Times* Garbo told him,

> Over here the director permits the players to show much more individuality in acting than where I come from. The American director tells his players to act the scene as they feel it—and then he makes suggestions. In Sweden we are instructed exactly how the scene must be played before the camera is turned. Of course we have the liberty of arguing with the director, supposing it occurs to us that the action is not suitable to the scene.[439]

In naturalistic acting the actor tries to "be" the character. The dominant form of stage acting at the time was stylized. In theater the actors declaimed from the stage. The actor in no way tried to inhabit the life of the person they were portraying. Instead, they performed in a theatrical fashion, playing to the audience and standing front and center to deliver speeches directed at the audience rather than fellow actors. The audience expected this; the height of acclaim was for the audience to demand, through applause, an encore of the speech just completed.[440] Stylistic acting was not intended to represent everyday reality. The artificiality of the performance was not only accepted, but it was also expected and delivered within codified norms that included over-dramatic physical movements and broad gestures.

Film acting in the early days was stylistic and melodramatic. In addition to deriving acting style from theater, film acting also had to account for the lack of sound. However, by the 1910s, film acting was becoming more naturalistic. These changes were related to the development of the short narrative feature, the emergence of recognizable film stars, and the building of large theaters.[441] These changes happened despite the fact that silent films had no dialogue.

Greta Garbo and Ricardo Cortez in a scene from *Torrent.*

Naturalistic acting requires the actor to inhabit another personality for the portrayal. Film and theater had always had some blend of naturalistic and stylized performances. Neither style has ever completely vanished. Naturalistic performances on stage are now ascendant for several reasons. Changes in lighting techniques gave audiences a clearer view of the stage. Broad societal changes that flowed from the end of the Victorian era and allowed for a more nuanced view of a person's personality and motivations made understanding the interior life of a character more important to audiences. The interest in human motivations flowed from the development of the fields of psychiatry and psychology.

For the film industry specifically, technical developments in cameras, lighting, lenses, and projection screens gave the audience an incremental, ever-crisper visual experience. These developments helped Garbo deliver naturalistic performances. For example, panchromatic film, introduced in 1925, renders tones in a more true-to-life way. Her subtle gestures were therefore more recognizable than they would have been just the year before. Close-ups were more effective because of the technical advances. Faces were not washed out by bright lighting or hard to keep in focus.

Cinematographer William Daniels would say, "Yes, I think everybody recognized that Garbo had something different from the very beginning."[442]

It is not just that she showed up and, using a more naturalistic style of acting, won over audiences. There were other naturalistic actors and directors looking for those actors in Hollywood. She was just so confoundingly much better at it that reviewers, audiences—literally everyone—either thought she was the most talented actress on-screen or not acting at all. Ironically, in the case of the second group, the point was to look like she was not acting at all.

Modern writers who don't acknowledge Garbo's acting skill are willfully ignorant of what her peers thought. It's hard not to view this dismissiveness as anything other than misogynistic. Name a male actor whose skills have been similarly ignored. Or they denigrate her skill because they don't like what she achieved through talent and hard work. Biographers have written that Garbo's acting was a random gift to her from the gods. Barry Paris quoted Lawrence Quirk that she was "almost an idiot savant."[443] Robert Gottlieb asked in his first paragraph, "Was she even an actress, or merely a glorious presence?"[444]

Garbo's training had been to be a naturalistic actor. First the Dramaten theater school, and then directors Mauritz Stiller and Georg Pabst had her work in a naturalistic style. Her early industrial films for Tullbergs Film are not naturalistic at all, but she learned the craft of acting for film. What she had in abundance and what her teachers channeled into the actor who arrived at MGM was immense natural talent.

Garbo related how Stiller told her to work:

> He did have some simple rules he used to preach. He was concerned that I should grow more self-confident. [His rules]
>
> > Don't take notice of other people.
> > Be yourself.
> > Don't try to be like anyone else.
> > Every person is unique.
> > Don't try to be like Norma Shearer.
>
> Yet what I most remember is Moje warning me and other people not to overact. We were taught just to suggest various emotional states; it was the viewer who was to be given the chance to fill it out.[445]

Ragnar Hyltén-Cavallius, who knew her over many years from the *Gösta Berling* days, observed,

> Not until later would I understand that the secret about Garbo's incredible success was that she represented the "romantic woman" as imagined by both the young and the old in the 20s and 30s, perhaps now as well [1960], but you cannot demand too much of a prophet. Also, she turned into that kind of actress after a couple of years, and they are the best—who by intuition, in a sleepwalker's confident way, walks, or rather floats into her roles.[446]

As for a thread that runs through all of Garbo's performances, film historian Alexander Walker wrote,

> She presented an imperfect human being—hence a far more credible one than the vamp whose eyes flashed out her brand of fully-fashioned evil as if they were two sky-signs.[447]

Garbo didn't need a lover for a love scene. In many instances, her character demonstrates her love to an object rather than an individual. Betsy Erkkila observed that "Garbo transforms physical passion into a form of spiritual communion that is most intense when the male figure is not its immediate object."[448]

Greta Garbo on the MGM lot in 1925.

In one famous scene from *Flesh and the Devil*, Garbo, at the communion rail next to her lover, turns communion into a public sex act in church. In *A Woman of Affairs* (1928), Garbo holds a bouquet of flowers as if they were human, and to the viewer it seems as if those flowers are mortal. In *Queen Christina*, Garbo touches every object in the room she shares with John Gilbert in order to memorize the night they have spent together. She seems to absorb something from each object.

She was a keen student of her craft. Garbo not only watched

how others worked, in film and on stage, she watched herself. Her housekeeper, Gustaf Norin, recalled that he would take Garbo to her own films two or three times each. While she wouldn't go to the premiere, she would have Norin drop her off at a theater in Long Beach or Pasadena where she watched the film alone.[449]

She told Mordaunt Hall that she liked to think about acting even when she wasn't on the set.[450]

Following the release of *The Divine Woman*, a nameless reporter for the *Santa Monica Outlook* interviewed Victor Sjöström. He reflected on Garbo's acting:

> She has not appeared in innocent roles by any means, but she has succeeded in playing sophisticated roles in such manner that she has drawn sympathy for her character no matter how many of the social or moral standards that screen character violates. Miss Garbo's characters always have such positive redeeming traits that they almost counterbalance the ultra-sophistication of her roles. When you stop to think she has never failed to deliver, and that not one of her pictures has been a failure, one can't help but believe that the success of Greta Garbo is due to herself, rather than to direction, vehicles, insignificance of wardrobe or elegant settings. She is the only screen star I have ever known who has succeeded in every characterization she has attempted.[451]

Famous Russian director Sergei Eisenstein thought Garbo was a master of improvisation, not a person who followed an "academic technique." He thought Garbo's acting was similar to Chaplin's.[452]

Garbo seems to have felt compelled to act, noting a point where she finally felt she could live without acting. In 1945 she wrote to her sister-in-law Peg Gustafson that "sadly I do not feel like making movies anymore."[453] Though we know that she tried to make films for another decade.

Perhaps more astounded than reviewers in their evaluation of Garbo as an actor were the industry professionals who had to work with her and compete for roles against her. The first element was just the impact of seeing someone do what you do for a living at a totally different level. Lois Wilson, who had a half-century career in film, said of Garbo after her second film:

> I'm willing to work. I have been willing to serve my apprenticeship. But when I see a girl like Greta Garbo, for instance, step into pictures and in two roles accomplish more than I have in twenty, I have to think it's time for me to pause.[454]

The actors who worked with her found her unique. For instance Robert Taylor, who co-starred with Garbo in *Camille* (1936), would say to an interviewer in the 1960s:

> Working with her was perhaps my greatest acting lesson, though I probably didn't learn enough from it. . . . If she ever makes another picture, I want to buy the first ticket.[455]

Just months after starring with Garbo in *Anna Christie*, George Marion would tell an interviewer:

> She has a distinctive genius for characterization that brings the breath of life into the puppets of the dramatist's imagination. Hers is a personality that literally walks into the roles she imparts. She seems to possess an insight into the soul of the character and she renders herself to its portrayal with little thought of self, content to register by the sympathy she feels for the character presented.[456]

While Alec Francis would say:

> Garbo has the most expressive personality of anybody at present on the screen. She is truly a great artist, who can convey more with one look, one word, or one touch of the hand than most actresses can get across in a whole reel of film.[457]

Bette Davis would never work with Garbo, but is an actor from the Studio Era who matched up with her in terms of talent. She viewed Garbo as one of a kind:

> I don't think anyone has truly transcended a role. Maybe one or two scenes, but not the whole picture. Garbo, of course, transcended—but not the whole role, because she was playing only to herself. She was everywhere. In a peculiar way, she was behind the camera, in front of the camera, the cameraman—she was the whole thing. She never fed a line to anyone. She said the line. It was up to the other actors to play off her; she never played off them. But that's a fluke. It never happened to anyone else—except maybe Duse on the stage. She was to theater what Garbo was to pictures.[458]

There are dozens of these quotes from her co-stars, her peers, and her directors. They could be a book in themselves. I'll close with one from a director. Richard Boleslawski directed Garbo in *The Painted Veil* (1934). He was also a leading naturalistic acting theorist and teacher.

He would say,

> She was so completely thorough in her art, that one found her almost as marvelous as the camera itself.[459]

Watching the response to *Torrent*, Thalberg and Mayer now knew what MGM had in Garbo. Thalberg would take inordinate care in Garbo's second film to get how she was used in film exactly right. It turned out to be more difficult than he thought.

Leonora embraces her mother in a scene from *Torrent*.

Chapter 12 - *The Temptress*

"It is a mistake to call Garbo mannish. Or masculine. But it is difficult to find exactly the right word to describe a certain something about her which calls those words to mind. Perhaps bigness will do. She is a big person, mentally and physically, and she likes bigness." [460]

— Adela Rogers St. Johns, writer

Garbo dressed for tennis circa 1927.

The *Temptress* is important for what happened around the production, rather than for the film itself. Mauritz Stiller would start as the director, only to be fired after completing nearly an entire film. Irving Thalberg would spend months on reshoots and re-edits. What should have been a two-month project stretched out to six.

Garbo's role in her second American film was a completely different character than Leonora had been. The audience still loved her because of her authenticity. Anyone who thought that her success in *Torrent* had been somehow fortuitous now could see that Garbo was using an underlying acting skill.

Stiller had been assigned to *The Temptress* as his first American film. It had been bumped back behind *Torrent* because MGM was waiting for the arrival of Einar Hanson to play the male lead. However, Einar Hanson had contract issues with MGM, and he never made a film for the studio.

The Temptress was another Ibáñez potboiler. Garbo plays Elena Fontenoy, who draws men to her like moths to a flame. Three men die directly for her love. Others have their lives destroyed. Garbo's character doesn't mean to have the effect she has on men. It just happens. The story revolves around her love for Antonio Moreno's character, Manuel Robledo. It is set in Paris and Argentina.

Stiller never finished *The Temptress*. He was fired after completing about three-quarters of the film. Fred Niblo was then hired as his replacement. The scene stills created during production provide a daily record that can be used to show the order in which the scenes in the final film were shot.[461] Niblo reshot all of Stiller's work in the first half of the film, but important Stiller-filmed scenes for the second half were retained.

Hanging over Garbo's head while *The Temptress* got underway was her sister's sickness. Lymphoma was poorly understood in 1926. The five-year survival rate was between 10 percent and 30 percent, but the prognosis for a newly diagnosed person to live more than one year was relatively high.

With her new income, Garbo sent money home for medical care for her sister. Unfortunately, Alva's illness progressed rapidly, and she would be dead less than a month after Garbo started filming *The Temptress*.

Ingrid Stocklassa recalled,

> I can remember Garbo talking about her sister Alva, to whom she was deeply attached. Garbo was tortured by letters from Sweden

> telling her she was getting more and more sick until she finally died.[462]

Still, Alva's death came as a surprise to her. In an undated letter to Lars Saxon, she told him, "Do not forget Lasse, if you call my sister, to tell her that I will come home quite soon and that it seems like I have only been here for two–three weeks, and that it is best for me to stay a while, just for a little longer."[463]

Thalberg fired Stiller shortly after Alva's death after a long and contentious meeting. At this point he had been filming for twenty-four days. This is half as many days as Niblo would spend on primary photography. However, we can identify that Stiller filmed the whip fight scenes, which are two-thirds through the film as released. By that measure he was working efficiently.

Albert Lewin, then head of the story department and later a director and producer, happened upon the fateful meeting between Thalberg and Stiller:

> I came walking down the alley and it was dark—we all worked late in those days—and I looked up into Irving's office. He and Stiller were talking. Irving was walking back and forth—he always walked around when he talked—and he was tossing that $20 gold piece of his up in the air, catching it and tossing it up again. I couldn't hear what was being said, of course, but it was plain that a very lively discussion was in progress. It was a curious sight, a kind of dumb show. As I stood there I saw Greta Garbo walking up and down the asphalt street alongside the old wardrobe building. She would look up into the office where Irving and Stiller were talking, watch the characters inside for a moment and then walk away again. I watched her for quite a time as she continued that pacing up and down, up and down.[464]

In getting himself fired by Thalberg, Stiller actually achieved his original objective of separating from MGM and making more money. Stiller left MGM to make *Hotel Imperial* (1927), starring Pola Negri, for Paramount. Erich Pommer, newly arrived from UFA as a Paramount producer, trusted Stiller with his first American project.[465] Stiller had his pay bumped up to $2,500 ($45,800) per week from the $1,000 ($18,300) per week he had been unhappy with at MGM.[466] For this film Stiller created groundbreaking cinematography techniques to move the camera from room to room on overhead rails. The film did well and had good reviews.

The relationship between Garbo and Stiller was complicated. It changed over time and when they arrived in the United States, what had been a chilled romance heated up again. While their romantic relationship would wax and wane, their friendship and professional relationship remained strong through Stiller's twenty-seven months in Hollywood. Garbo would tell Biery,

> Mr. Stiller had to go back to Europe. How I miss him. He talked in my own language. I owe everything to Mr. Stiller. I have not understood everything over here, but now everything is settled and we are all working together. I cannot stand trouble.[467]

Yet, despite their romance, Garbo is sure that she and Stiller will not marry. This seems to have been due to Stiller's view that their age gap was too big and that over time Garbo would stumble over that difference. He did not want to detract from what he saw as her brilliant future. She wrote of this to Pollak:

> I wrote that I would get married. I can still not describe anything in more detail in this letter, but I will probably never get married. Believe me, my head is turning around and around with thoughts of misfortune. I do not want to see a single person.
>
> Isn't it horrible, Misse, but I never look at any men (but of course not any women either). I would not be interested in any of them. For me, the only one who is there for me is my old Moje, isn't that a tragedy. I will probably become a little spinster. What do you think about that descriptive word?[468]

Outside observers could see their love for what it was. Victor Sjöström once said that "there is no doubt that Moje for a while was in love with Garbo and she with him."[469]

Stiller had worked on *The Temptress* for twenty-four days. It took Fred Niblo another fifty-nine days to reshoot most of the scenes and finish the film. Given that June 2 was the likely start date for Niblo and that he wrapped up primary filming July 30, there were only forty-nine shooting days, at most, during primary production. Therefore, *The Temptress* had at least ten days of reshoots during postproduction, perhaps more. That represents over 15 percent of the time Niblo spent on *The Temptress*.

It took quite a while for Thalberg to be satisfied that he had the best possible version of *The Temptress*. Just based on the time involved his editing must have been extensive. At the end of July, right as production wrapped, MGM announced its plan to release *The Temptress* on September 5.[470] That allowed a month for editing, a reasonable timeframe in the silent era. However, a notice in *The Film Mercury* announced that, due to the significant editing that remained, this opening was being postponed.[471] After several more announced delays the New York premiere took place on October 3.[472]

Elena attends to Manuel after the whip fight. A Stiller-filmed sequence retained in the final film.

Prior to *The Temptress,* it had been problematic to end a film with the female star either dying or dissolute. For example, the Pola Negri film *Bella Donna* (1923) ended with Negri, who had accepted the affections of her Arab host and then tried to murder her husband, wandering out into the desert to meet her death. Reviewers and audiences were appalled.[473]

MGM eventually decided to film a second ending after the New York premiere. In the original sad ending, Garbo is observed by Moreno back in Paris. She is dissolute and barely aware of the world around her. She thinks the man sitting at the next table is Jesus. In the happy ending, Garbo and Moreno find a way to stay together. Other than where directed by censors, the exhibitor generally could select the ending that fit with their audience. They didn't always have an option: Ohio censors chose the sad ending for all screenings in the state.[474]

Garbo rode a horse for a lost scene from the Stiller version of *The Temptress.* There are scene stills of Garbo riding, and she mentions in a letter that she had never ridden sidesaddle before and had to learn. She wrote to Saxon, "The horse fell on me yesterday, but I was not injured, I was on my feet five minutes after it happened, and I was thinking about mom and then, got up on the horse again. Oy, oy, the instructor thought I was good, he did not know that I was thinking about my mom."[475] Actor Joel McCrea, who performed stunts on *The Temptress*, remembered her protesting that one stunt was too dangerous for McCrea to do because he was "a youngster," and did it herself.[476] Ironically, they were the same age.

There is a theory that Stiller and male lead actor Anthony Moreno clashed over Stiller's insistence that Moreno shave his mustache, a story told as partial justification for the eventual removal of Stiller from the film. This theory seems improbable, while Moreno had a mustache in *Beverly of Graustark*, the film immediately before *The Temptress*, in *Mare Nostrum*, filmed right before that film, Moreno appears mustache free. In the Stiller version of *The Temptress* Moreno is mustache free in Paris and has a costume mustache in Argentina. He has a natural mustache in all the Niblo filmed scenes.

Despite the many positive reviews and the enormous audience response, Garbo herself was critical of her work in *The Temptress*. She wrote to Mimi Pollak, "My last film that is now showing was poor and I was rotten. You will pity me when you see it."[477]

Reviewers and audiences would disagree. *Photoplay* wrote that *The Temptress* "is all Greta Garbo. Nothing else matters."[478] Newspaper reviewers generally liked the film, particularly city papers. *The Los Angeles Times* review stated, "*The Temptress* is a fascinating picture—because its star is a fascinating personality."[479]

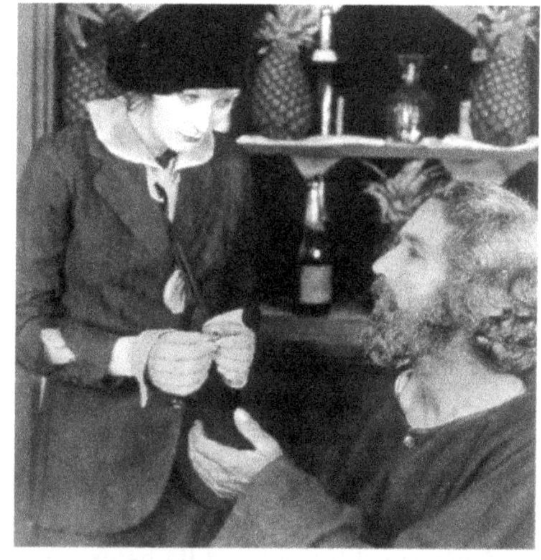

The closing scene of *The Temptress*. Elena hallucinates that the man at the cafe is Jesus, and gives her ring to him.

Garbo's understated acting drove this success. In his review of *The Temptress* in *The New York Times*, Mordaunt Hall wrote, "There are moments when Miss Garbo reflects a characteristic mood by the slightest movement of one of her eyelids." He elaborates later in the review: "Miss Garbo is not only remarkably well suited to the role, but with a minimum of gestures and an

In this Stiller filmed scene set in Argentina Moreno has a costume mustache. It is set flush to his lip.

In this Niblo filmed scene set in Paris Moreno has natural mustache. It curls away from his lip at the tip.

unusual restraint in her expressions, she makes every scene in which she appears a telling one."[480]

Garbo commanded the film. Just twenty-one when *The Temptress* was released, she already defined her characters, and the other actors reacted to her lead.

Garbo was no longer the unknown actor asked to carry *Torrent.* She had established herself in a single film, and rentals for *The Temptress* reflect this. In total, net revenue increased 50 percent in Garbo's second MGM film. While domestic rentals increased 27 percent, export rentals almost doubled.

Garbo was naturally unhappy with the situation in her private life as production of *The Temptress* proceeded. During this time, Garbo was still mostly keeping to herself. She remained depressed about how things had worked out in America, with Stiller, with her career, with being without her old friends. To Dramaten classmate Vera Schmiterlöw she wrote, "I never go out and sit home like an old lady see no one here, no friends, don't wish any either of those that are here. I only meet Stiller who is still unboundly kind and the Hansons, Lasse [Lars] and Karin. But not often. I am really alone. I also wish I could take over Mama and my brother for the time that's left."[481]

Her loneliness would end when she started her third film. She would meet John Gilbert. But before we proceed to that fateful encounter, I want to explain why Garbo appealed to the women of the modern age.

Chapter 13 – The Modern Age

"Sex is no longer news. And the fact that it is no longer news is news." [482]

— Frederick Lewis Allen, author

Greta Garbo in *Flesh and the Devil.*

Garbo resonated with her audience because she fit with the changing times. They saw in her roles, and in their perception of her as an individual, answers to fundamental questions they faced. The end of the Victorian age set in motion a change in the role of women in society in terms of their work, their very presence in the public sphere, the conception of femininity, and their lifestyles, spending habits, and sexual behavior. Garbo, in her film roles and public persona, enabled many of these changes.

Garbo helped to create permissions to redefine female life. She was a key communicator of a proto-feminism that gave women a new agency. The heart of this was a new view of female sexual desire.

The first wave of feminism had brought the right to vote. Female emancipation would not begin to be an ascendant point of view for half a century.[483] Society would bend to a reaction by social conservatives, fueled by the Depression, war, and then the threat of nuclear annihilation. But within this regression, the Modern Woman was continually redefined, and women's sexuality and sexual expression became acknowledged.

Life in the Victorian age revolved around separate social spheres for men and women. A concern of middle-class Victorians was that women who must work for themselves may be subject to moral compromises in pursuit of economic stability. The concept of female purity was a central tenet for middle-class Victorians. To avoid temptation, women shouldn't work.

The Modern Woman drove cars. Here Garbo drives in a MGM publicity photo.

Before industrialization, the poor, people of color, and those otherwise disenfranchised lived lives often just above a subsistence level. The mass of poor people were not expected to live to Victorian standards because they were poor. Realistically, poor women needed jobs.

The rise of the modern age was directly tied to industrialization. The scale of the transformation was breathtaking. The work of Victorian women was often informal, on farms, for example, or in domestic service. In the modern age, a higher percentage of women worked in formal jobs.[484] Women shifted to jobs in offices, factories, and shops. Increasing wages allowed more families to enter the middle class. Freedom from mundane tasks that had defined the female sphere of familial life meant opportunity. This led to the acceptance of women in the public sphere and a transformation of relations between men and women, both before and in marriage.

The streets of any town literally had more women. Photographs of urban landscapes feature quantitatively more women from the 1890s to the 1930s. The most dramatic increase took place in the 1920s.[485] The shift to the modern age merged the male and female spheres. The new patterns of school, work, and socialization led to a greater familiarity between men and women. It was almost inevitable that some form of greater equality had to emerge.[486]

These social changes were not confined to Western industrialized nations. For example, similar change was taking place in Brazil and Japan;[487] though in some regions and countries, such as Africa, South America, and China, industrialization was not widespread but, rather, was concentrated to the limited geography of major cities.

Industrialization did not completely leave the farming communities behind; they had automobiles and some of the modern conveniences, such as mincers, which didn't require electricity. But the urban life that resulted from industrialization had two distinctive features not present in rural life: higher incomes for the new jobs, and the social and sensory dynamics of the city.[488]

One element of the Victorian age that was overthrown was the concept of immutable virtues. It was replaced by the concept of values that might be flexible in the face of circumstance, as articulated by Friedrich Nietzsche, Max Weber, and others. In the Victorian age, there was no excuse for cowardice. A Victorian would die to preserve honor. In the modern age, it depended on circumstance. For women the immutable virtues were chastity before marriage and monogamy within marriage.

The modern feminist idea is that, while there are sex differences, there are not innate male advantages. Women are entitled to social, economic, and political equality. While women of the twenties in Western countries were able to vote and had more agency than their grandmothers, they were confronted with a sex-based hierarchy in which men held a privileged position.

Women earned less, they were restricted from certain jobs, and it was assumed that, when they married or had children, they would stop working and focus on domestic life.

Historian of culture and gender Peter Filene explained how the separate social spheres merged while still not yet embracing female emancipation. "By regarding motherhood as only a phase of their careers, they extended the female role far beyond Victorian definitions. As one feminist mother and career woman said, instead of being thrust into the singular job wifehood they were choosing 'wife-ing it' as one profession among others."[489]

What also changed was how women got to the point of marriage. In the Victorian construct of upper- and middle class society, the sexual purity of a woman before marriage was paramount. Flowing from this belief were restrictions on dress, work, appearance in social spaces, and courting. Ideally, a woman would only ever be sexual with the man she married. *Love* was nice, but secondary to the business of marriage as a means to have and provide for children.

Where did a respectable Victorian woman meet her future husband? Usually through social circles, including at church and community events. At supervised venues such as these, the scope for romantic interaction was limited. Some Victorian women married men they barely knew, often through arranged marriages.

In the post-Victorian world, instead of meeting a future spouse at church or in a parlor, couples created themselves by meeting for dates. Their interactions as a married couple were more companionate. But the activities of their day-to-day lives once married were little different from their mothers.

The journey to marriage was restructured. A space was created to explore sexual interests while on that journey. This started with feminine display. Women wore sleeker, and fewer, clothes. They used nail polish, toothpaste, makeup, and perfume. They cut their hair. Dating, which had been uncommon in the nineteenth century, became the way couples were created by 1925.[490]

Women stepped out on dates without chaperones. Dating permitted couples to explore compatibility. Petting became socially acceptable, within certain boundaries regarding partner familiarity and situation. Petting described a range of erotic physical contact from kissing to extended physical fondling. Intercourse was still considered immoral except when a couple was well on their way to marriage after a serious courtship.[491] The youth of the 1920s considered none of this promiscuous:

> The new order was about sex, sexuality, self-display and relationships. Yet these issues between men and women also extended to the concept of the family, with the development of the idea of companionate marriage and more equality between men and women. Women of the twenties were interested more in the concept of "freedom," the right to self-expression, self-determination and personal satisfaction than in political rights or economic opportunities. The standards borne by their feminist [women's voting rights supporting] mothers.[492]

A seductive portrait of Garbo by Russell Ball from 1927.

Dating was public in a way that meeting in a family parlor (which might not even exist in the new urban neighborhoods) or making a social call was not. The couple was anonymously in the public sphere at restaurants, amusement parks, theaters, and dance halls. The downside of this new approach to courtship was that it required money. Since men had more money than women, it put women at a disadvantage.[493]

Therefore, in a way that it had not been in the Victorian era, dating was a commercial relationship. Men could more readily afford the admission price to the new attractions. Women could barely exist economically on their more minuscule wages. As a Chicago waitress explained, "If I didn't have a man, I couldn't get along on my wages."[494]

Finally, they had sex. Whereas only 14 percent of the women who turned twenty before World War I admitted that they had had premarital sex, 36 percent of women who turned twenty after the war reported that they had.[495]

The Victorian notion of female purity didn't even allow for imagining sex before marriage. The new Modern Woman may not have had sex before marriage, or at least not broadcast the news, but she was aware of sex, aware of her appeal to men, and might try her appeal out on some number of potential mates before choosing a husband.

Whereas in the 1910s and 1920s, discussion of changing sexual mores and interpersonal relationships was an ongoing topic in newspapers and magazines, by 1930, it was no longer topical.

An important element of this transformation was birth control. Birth rates declined in industrializing countries even in the Victorian age. In Europe and the United States, birth rates had been broadly declining since the mid-1800s.[496] Over the nineteenth century, the number of children born to the average American woman dropped from 5.3 to 3.5 children. Birth control pioneer Margaret Sanger's book, *Happiness in Marriage* (1926), brought home the point that marriage was not just about children. It was also about companionship, romance, and pleasure.

The changing landscape for women focused on what would be acceptable in a moral sense in this new modern world. Almost every discussion of feminine attitude and behavior came back to a question of either what action was moral or what personal morality was signified.

The Victorian age was morally black and white. In the modern age, the same behavior, as virtues were replaced by values, could be moral or immoral depending on context. Sex was no longer innately immoral:

> The unwavering understanding of the bad girl as "other" even permitted Rosa Jensen, who at the age of seventeen had a child outside of marriage, to consider herself "basically a nice girl." Moreover, because respectability was such a fluid concept under which a broad range of behaviors could be categorized, young women's participation in activities that were by their own admission not entirely proper, or even slightly risqué, did not necessarily challenge their identity and perception of themselves as fundamentally nice girls.[497]

Garbo, and the film industry overall, spent the years between the wars addressing this topic, from scenario to scenario. The process of creating the Modern Woman played out in stories told on movie screens.

Because many films were speaking to women, and film was a new medium with an appeal to a broader audience than books or theater, there were calls for censorship from the earliest days of the industry.

Film censors blocked scenes that were derived from plays and books that weren't themselves subject to any censorship because they viewed the audiences as different. While moral crusaders railed against scantily clad women on-screen in New York, topless shows were available elsewhere in the city.

In the censors' minds, the universal popularity of film called for greater oversight than that afforded to literature or theater. Because films were watched by all elements of society, filmmakers could not be permitted broad freedom of expression. Their task was to model behavior for the masses and reinforce that one should live within an ordered society with the church, the family, and authority as the foundation.[498]

Martin Quigley, one of the prime movers in the Catholic Church's campaign for censorship stated this directly: "All other dramatic forms have comparatively negligible patronage. The printed word and the spoken word are largely dependent for their effectiveness upon capacity for understanding on the part of the reader and the audience. Both are unequal to the potency of the cinema in its access to and impress upon a public numbered in the many millions."[499]

One problem with censorship was the absence of agreement as to what should be censored, if anything. There was no general support for government regulation of films. Only a vocal minority of people wanted to restrict what was shown in films. In the only time censorship was put to a statewide vote, Massachusetts voted overwhelmingly against censorship in 1922. After that, reactive pressure groups that wanted more censorship understood they had to achieve their goals in other ways.

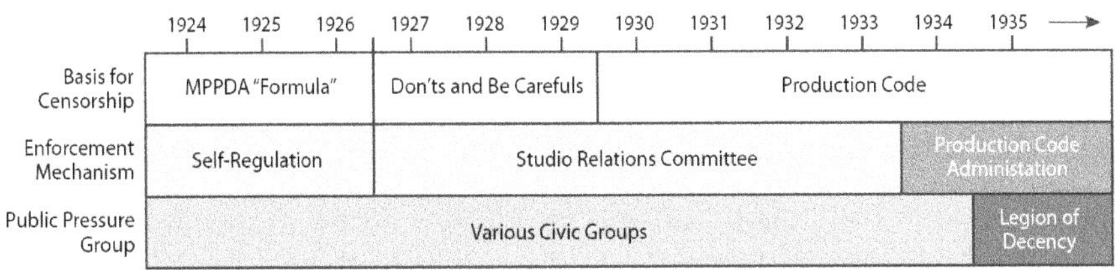

A chart showing the evolution over time, from 1924 through 1936, top row: the document that was the basis for censorship, middle row:the enforcement mechanism, and bottom row: the emergence of the Legion of Decency as a public pressure group.

The film companies created an industry organization, Motion Picture Producers and Distributors of America (MPPDA), which hired Will (William Harrison) Hays as the chair. Hays was a politically astute former postmaster general. Beginning in March 1922, Hays tried to work with both sides, the studios and the censors, to give the studios an idea of the kinds of scenes that would be censored and to get pre-approval of the treatment of scenes before they were filmed. National guidelines were not developed until 1924 and there was no central authority overseeing censorship at the studios until 1927. What all early censorship attempts had in common was that they only looked at the product in its finished form and censored that. There was no administrative connection between production and censorship until the institution in 1930 of the first version of the Production Code.

The evolution of American censorship proceeded in three related areas between 1924 and 1934; the basis for censorship evolved, as would the enforcement mechanism and the application of public pressure. This progression can be somewhat confusing because the word "code" appears in both the basis for censorship (the Production Code) from 1930 and the enforcement mechanism (the Production Code Administration) from 1934. The people involved appear again and again over time in slightly different roles. The progression from 1924 through 1934 is always toward more censorship and a move to intervening earlier in the production process. It is always driven forward by the Catholic Church.

The MPPDA's self-censorship programs were designed to manage both domestic and international pressures. The self-censorship guidelines went through three iterations. In 1924, the first version (referred to specifically as "the Formula") codified an agreement to not develop screenplays from salacious books and to refrain from controversial advertising.

This agreement was replaced in 1927 by what is now referred to as the "Don'ts and Be Carefuls," a form of pre-production guidance for scripts being submitted for approval before filming. Finally, the Production Code (the Code) as the standard for evaluation was introduced in 1930. The Studio Relations Committee technically could enforce censorship, but in practice they were toothless.

Development of the Code was heavily influenced by American Catholics, both the formal hierarchy of the church and Catholic laypeople involved in the film exhibition business. This was the result of several factors. Many Protestant denominations were pushing for full censorship. Catholic bishops had realized that any formal role in censorship would only make them a target, and they were willing to exercise more indirect control of film content.

Actual censorship was rather light until the advent of the Production Code Administration in 1934. First, public taste led studios to show restraint on content. Before a national approach that started with scripts, the effects of censorship were easy to avoid or defer, as discussed in a later chapter: "Censorship." Since such a high percentage of profits were generated in the first days of exhibition, anything that delayed censorship of a film lessened the effect of that censorship.

For Garbo's first three MGM films, any censorship came from local censorship boards. *Torrent* was not risqué; Garbo's affairs were alluded to, but no second lover appears on camera. *The Temptress* and *Flesh and the Devil* pushed every boundary. In *The Temptress*, Garbo is a destroyer of men. Her husband pimps her out. The one man she does fall in love with sees her power and does not, in the end, reciprocate her love. Every other man in the film is willing to kill others for her. Garbo is definitely not the sweet girl next door.

In *Flesh and the Devil*, Garbo cheated on not one but two husbands. She is not remorseful about her actions in the slightest. Her character is more classically vampish than in *The Temptress*.

Before Garbo, feminine desire on film was often cartoonish. After *Flesh and the Devil*, Irving Thalberg developed roles for Garbo that took better advantage of her abilities. The stories Thalberg found for her used her acting skills to the fullest. She explored desire in nuanced performances. With just a few exceptions, in film after film, Garbo constructed a sexuality within each role that served as a challenge to the status quo. She was not submissive and trapped in domestic roles. Thus, Garbo was a guidepost for women constructing their modern identities. Exactly what social conservatives were worried about.

Early on, Garbo created a dilemma for the censors. How does one censor thought? The viewer thought they knew what the actor thought, but what could a censor they see that was actionable? While playing a part, Garbo goes further into sin and redemption than other actors with the same basic role. "She becomes the symbol of sexual appeal rather than any particular bad woman," wrote a National Board of Review critic about the time of *Flesh and the Devil*.[500]

Where Garbo's behavior on-screen was transparent, censors seemed to have had trouble grappling with the meaning of the action.

Take, for example, the classic scene from *Flesh and the Devil* where the four main characters are at a church service. By this point, Garbo is married to Hanson, and Gilbert is just her former lover. Gilbert is comparing in his mind the innocent Barbara Kent to Garbo. As they kneel at the communion rail, Gilbert drinks from the chalice and passes it on. Before Garbo drinks, she intentionally turns the chalice so she drinks from the exact edge that Gilbert drank from. As Garbo acts it, the scene is sensual. At the same time, how do you censor communion performed as per ritual?

The three romantic rendezvous between Garbo and Gilbert in *Flesh and the Devil* are highly charged and erotic. But, in a technical sense, they are not that different from other love scenes in other silent films. How can a censor say Garbo's kisses go too far? They clearly are closer to sex than other silent-era love scenes because that thought is planted in the viewer's mind by Garbo.

The rest of Garbo's silent films, and *Anna Christie*, her first sound film, were made under the "Don'ts and Be Carefuls" regime. While MGM cast her in several roles that pushed boundaries, *A Woman of Affairs* is the only one of the seven silent films in this group where the existence of the Hays Office made any difference at all.

While MGM made business decisions regarding scripts and editing, the decisions were based on its plan to manage the local censorship boards. Through this period, the Hays Office was less a censor and more an industry guide to local censorship. This changed with *Queen Christina* in 1933. Garbo, and her roles, became a focus of the forces that demanded the movies become less prurient. Censorship became more powerful and constraining, and Garbo would be more directly associated with selecting her roles.

From that point censorship would become central to her career. Until then it was an issue dealt with between MGM on one side and censors on the other. Her roles would push the boundaries, but for the entire industry censorship was an issue to be managed. Meanwhile, the central figures on the pro-censorship side would spend years planning to gain control over how the industry told stories. Their eventual success would transform both film and America.

In this changing social landscape Garbo found a large and appreciative audience. The core of this audience was the female clerk.

Chapter 14 – The Garbo Audience

"The prism to view Garbo, with several of her female acting contemporaries, was an actress whose "star text" was, in part, tied to her link to broad social changes. She embodied a new type of film persona—one that invested aspects of the classic temptress (an evil alluring female) with elements of the new woman (a sophisticate who operated with sexual and social autonomy)" [501]

— Lucy Fisher, film historian

A portrait of Garbo taken for the MGM film *The Mysterious Lady.* Photo by Ruth Harriet Louise. Courtesy of the Greta Garbo family archive.

Garbo arrived in Hollywood at an interesting time for women. The first wave of feminism had crested with the passage of suffrage. Second-wave feminism was a half century in the future. The separate female sphere of life that was a feature of the Victorian age was gone, but how women would live in the single social space of the modern age was still being figured out. Greta Garbo provided an important part of the answer to the question about how to live as a Modern Woman.

When she arrived in Hollywood, she was far from the standard conception of female beauty, either in real life or on-screen. Her face was not pixieish enough, and she was too tall and too flat chested. Beauty at the time was exemplified by Mary Pickford, Clara Bow, and Gloria Swanson. At five feet seven, Garbo was one of the tallest female actors in Hollywood. Most of her contemporaries were no taller than five feet four.

Given how beauty came to be defined by Garbo in just a few years, it is interesting to note how the initial impression was that she was successful despite not being beautiful. In the *Minneapolis Star Tribune* review of *Torrent,* the reviewer commented,

> This lady is by no means handsome, judging by the accepted standards of American screen beauty. She can act, however, and act well.[502]

Writer Jim Tully described her thus:

> She is broad shouldered, flat-breasted, awkward in her movements. Her form is the despair of the wardrobe mistress.[503]

Her technical ability, combined with the fortuitous timing of her arrival on the scene, led to Garbo being more than just an actor to her audience. Garbo's ability to become a star in record time flowed directly from her acting style. She also brought a message. She was the representation of the Modern Woman. Without speaking dialogue Garbo still communicated to the audience with complexity, depth, and subtlety. One reviewer wrote, "Mona Lisa's smile is childishly frank compared to Garbo's."[504]

Decades after her last film, Garbo's Dramaten classmate, film director and film theorist Alf Sjöberg, tried to get at the transcendent impact Garbo had on the audience:

> I believe it is difficult with the current historical situation to get an accurate grasp of her importance for the world public during the

> thirties. One must leave film analysis. Here as always a sole work of art can't be taken out of the time frame when it was created.
>
> Rather, open a world history and see her portrait beside Einstein and Churchill. Her face, this one primitive landscape that at the same time identifies its alienation. The anguish and forgiveness that Sartre analyzes in Existentialism [1946]. Her voice, the golden voice, that we thought was meant for our little corner of the world, had an echo in it, which beyond the words spoken would fascinate the whole world.[505]

Sjöberg is capturing the idea that Garbo had an impact beyond playing a character in a film. During Garbo's career, people didn't perceive culture as coming from popular entertainment. The conservative argument was that film stood only in opposition to traditional culture. There was no concept of cultural transformation. Raymond Williams would not publish "Culture Is Ordinary" until 1958. While Garbo was changing culture, it wasn't yet an academic discipline.

Garbo did not arrive and then by herself change a static culture. Before film spoke to the Modern Woman, books and magazines already did. Narrative film only emerged in the middle of the 1910s. Before this development, Modern-Woman stories were told in print. Often, stories first published in print then made their way to film.

This was the era of magazine fiction. Maureen Honey, who has written widely on early twentieth-century gender and class issues, surveyed more than six hundred stories from *Delineator*, *Good Housekeeping*, *Ladies' Home Journal*, *McCall's*, and *Pictorial Review* for the years 1920 through 1929. These stories almost uniformly delivered a narrative based on non-Victorian gender roles. Standard plot elements were as follows:

- The introduction: women yearning for change in their home environment and rebelling against parents, family, tradition, and simple country life
- The gambit: leaving home for the city, often New York, and new jobs, freedoms, friends, and romance
- The challenge: dangerous men, conservative disapproval, the loss of simplicity, and sexism[506]

The emergence of narrative stories in film in the 1910s led to the creation of the vamp: a dangerous, independent, and sexual woman. The original vamp was Theda Bara, who assumed this persona around 1914. Vamps were sexual vampires, which is how they got their name. They made wonderful film bad girls. In the early twentieth century, men were counseled that their strength and vitality came from their semen, and to discharge semen wantonly would lead to weakness. Men needed to guard these vital juices from women out to steal power from men through sex.[507] Though, of course, the draw of the character in a story was that there was sex.

The story of a gallant lady—a lady who was perhaps foolish and reckless beyond need—but withal a very gallant lady.

An intertitle from the film *A Woman of Affairs* that captures the essence of a Modern Woman character.

It didn't stop there. Gibson Girls, flappers, any variety of poses tried to capture what it was to be a Modern Woman. They were a distinct break from the Victorian era, each presenting a facet of a modern conception of gender relationships.[508] *Ladies' Home Journal* defined this Modern Woman as "someone who knew the rewards of both the workplace and the home and who made the 'right' choice of her own free will."[509] They lived adventures outside the domestic sphere. These stories portrayed a more emancipated woman out in the masculine world.[510] The Modern Woman was never returning to a separate domestic sphere, and believed that she should be able to develop that part of her that led to happiness regardless of her gender.[511]

The role that these stories played in the evolution and eventual triumph of the Modern Woman offered a sandbox in which to work out women's place in modern life. Innumerable films by Garbo, Shearer, and others took the statement "This could never be acceptable behavior for a woman" and crafted a story using that behavior that gained sympathy for the female character in the hearts of the audience.

Film historian Jackie Stacey wrote, "Spectator/star relationships all concern the interplay between the self and the ideal."[512] Since other Modern Woman stories were being written and other actors would portray Modern Women, what made Garbo unique? The foremost thing was that when Garbo arrived in America, no one had the combination of talent and training to allow them to deliver a naturalistic performance that the audience could relate to by mentally projecting themselves into the character. She created a connection from the screen to the audience that had not previously existed. This connection can be observed by their level of interaction with her through letters, ticket purchases, media consumption, and self-presentation.

For well over a decade Garbo was the actor on-screen fans wanted to be in real life. For the six years that MGM controlled her career it placed Garbo in films that catered to Modern Women. Once she gained a degree of control in 1933 and began selecting scripts, she made a string of films that addressed female authority and sexuality in clever ways.

Garbo's naturalistic acting was more effective in establishing a connection between the artist and the viewer. The audiences were able to discern her thoughts, or what they perceived as the character's thoughts. This intensified the impact of her work. What Garbo seemed to think on-screen was what they thought they might think in a similar situation. There was a congruence.

Her roles seemed real. Initially, this is all due to Garbo. In *Torrent* and *The Temptress*, we have seen how the directors did not give Garbo guidance on how she was to emote. They were unconcerned with her internal portrayal because, in their experience, actors didn't have the ability to communicate their internal thoughts through the film medium. But Thalberg could see what was happening; from *Flesh and the Devil* on, he makes full use of her abilities. This was likely the reason for the extended edits and reshoots on *The Temptress*.

In a rather quick development, with Garbo, MGM found itself presenting Modern Woman stories to urban, female audiences who were going to Loew's first-run theaters, and it was extremely profitable.

That Garbo resonated right from the start can be seen by a report in *Film Spectator*[513] that ranked actors based on their box office for eighteen months through July 1927. The exact methodology is lost, but the idea was to capture the revenue generated from the percentage of seats available to sell that were filled rather than to rank stars based on reviews. This was likely accomplished through data collected from a nonscientific subset of theaters.

At this point, only three American Garbo films have been released and Garbo ranks ninth. She is the second-ranked female actor, after Norma Talmadge.[514]

Film historian Patrice Petro commented about Weimar-era German audiences: "The existence of a patriarchal power structure rendered the very choice of rebellion or submission highly problematic for women, and necessarily different than it must have been for men. Whether the dilemma of female emancipation was addressed in fantasies of ethical conflict as in *Die freudlose Gasse* . . . the appeal of the film melodrama derived from its attempt to speak to the promises and failures of sexual and economic liberation in Weimar, and thus to the fundamental contradictions in women's lives."[515] While Petro is writing about the Weimar audience, the condition was universal.

Lois Weber, an early silent-era director and later story editor, returned to Hollywood in 1925 from a European sojourn and proposed, in an article entitled "Exit Flapper, Enter Woman" that the opportunity existed for Hollywood to develop roles that presented a more well-rounded woman on the screen. She had found European actors to express more of a depth of personality in their portrayals. She wanted to create a type of "womanly woman" who was neither flapper nor vamp.[516]

Famously, Garbo's complaint after *Flesh and the Devil* was that she didn't want to always play a "bad woman." Rather, she wanted to play an interesting woman. Garbo did not play a vamp in *Torrent*; her character's only sin is that she didn't stay in the village and await Don Rafael's eventual realization that she was his true love.

Instead, Leonora goes to Paris, becomes a famous singer, and has lots of sex (off-screen and only inferred) with her admirers. She has lost her true love by pursuing a career. The real sadness in *Torrent* is the Don Rafael character. He gives up his true love because his mother browbeats him, which was certainly no less "emasculating" than Leonora's affairs. While Leonora has had lovers, her heart has stayed true to Don Rafael. It is Don Rafael who has been inconstant and has fallen short.

It is the complex persona that Garbo created in Leonora that captivated audiences. She wasn't good or bad, just a woman. Leonora was a more complete, multifaceted person as a character. And you could see her thinking on the screen.

This delicacy of portrayal is not in the script. It was created by Garbo and Stiller. Garbo chose to do the unusual and creative on the set. She was explicit about this in a letter to Mimi Pollak written just after starting her third American film, *Flesh and the Devil*:

> If you knew how strange directors are here. Many of them certainly know nothing about emotional life and so forth. You only get direction on how you should go, stand, sit, speak and so forth. Then you do as you please even if you do it poorly. It is not like when Stiller was with me and motivated me to feel something.[517]

Garbo's character, Elena, in *The Temptress* is not really a vamp. She destroys men left and right. Yet, while she is a direct threat to the self-control of the male characters she encounters, through her actions Garbo goes about it in a new and fresh way. She comes across less as evil and malicious, which is the Theda Bara version of a vamp, and more as a woman lost in herself and reacting to her internal forces.

To the extent that movies were social commentary on the key questions of the day, Garbo helped to address them, including the question of what it meant to be a woman in the 1920s and 1930s. The *Exhibitors Herald* reviewer, writing on *The Temptress*, spoke directly to the issue of appropriate female behavior:

> Ibáñez sets out to prove, apparently, that the worst woman in the world is as good as the next one and quite fit to share the final fadeout with the upright engineer [clearly in Chicago he saw the alternate happy ending to *The Temptress*]. I have no objection to his proving that, or whatever he may feel like proving next, within the privacy of his book covers. But I've seen so many hundreds of motion pictures proving the opposite conclusion that I'm sold on the virtue thing.[518]

Other reviewers wrote,

> What Garbo offers her worshippers is a vision of life without compromise, love without disenchantment, sexuality without scabrousness.[519]

> Garbo arouses her audience to the expectations of a real sexual relationship. Like no other star of her time, Garbo is definitely beyond innocence.[520]

Garbo had played a virtuous, but complicated, heroine in both *Gösta Berling* and *Die freudlose Gasse*. Irving Thalberg related to Louella Parsons that Garbo did not like the vampish Felicitas character in *Flesh and the Devil* and was reluctant to play the part.[521] She wanted to play characters with more complexity.

Some critics have viewed Garbo as a cipher, merely allowing the audience to project their own ideas of the new *Modern Woman* into being. Digging deeper, Garbo was more of a clarifying presence for the audience. Garbo showed them the truths about feminine life and sexual power dynamics that they already knew to be true. Garbo was not innocent or sexually unaware, but she was pure of heart. What Garbo brought to the audience was her behavior in the situation. They could see her thought and, since they weren't conversing with her, that "sight" was a projection by the audience. But rather than a cipher process, it was great acting.

The Temptress could have been played as a vamp role, either as an evil woman or in a camp fashion. Instead, Garbo plays it straight up. She is merely living. Yes, she has been with many men, but she has been living life as best she can.

In the climax to the story, Robledo confronts Elena after Canterac has killed Pirovani while fighting over Elena. For a silent film, this is a lot of title cards to throw on the screen in just ninety seconds. Garbo's acting between cards sells the story.

> **(Robledo)** "Tonight a man killed his friend—another life upon your soul!"
>
> **(Elena)** "Why upon my soul? What have I done?"
>
> **(Robledo)** "Your husband met his death because of you!"
>
> **(Elena)** "Because of me, perhaps—but not through any fault of mine!"
>
> **(Robledo)** "You let Fontenoy ruin himself for you! You sent him to his damnation!"
>
> **(Elena)** "My husband—sold me—to Fontenoy."
>
> **(Robledo)** "Men have died for you—forsaken work and honor—for you!"
>
> **(Elena)** "Not for me—but for my body! Not for my happiness, but for theirs!"
>
> **(Elena)** "But there is one thing about me that is a part of God—my love—for you."[522]

For her fans, Garbo's role is that of a woman making the best of her situation. She is "bad" in the sense that she has allowed her husband to sell her body, had sex out of wedlock, been the unintending agent of death. But she is just a woman trying to find her way, who thinks she has finally found love. The audience could imagine either being that woman or loving that woman. Garbo's acting made this believable. Garbo between these title cards is the key to the resonance of her character.

Because Garbo could deliver the underlying essence of the character, she could play unfaithful women, sex workers, and kept women while still presenting herself on-screen as a woman looking for true love.

From the very beginning, in *Torrent*, Garbo demonstrates obvious intent in creating her characters. Despite this, the fan magazines would focus on her power with her fans, without ever considering how such a relationship came about. Even later (male) critics have frequently attributed Garbo's success to her ability to allow the (male) viewer to do the actual construction of art. Garbo was merely a naïve vessel instinctively bearing secret epiphanies to the viewer.[523]

The people who worked with Garbo reported that she was anything but naïve. Instead, they report a woman employing fantastic concentration to deliver subtle, nuanced performances that some actors who had been on the set had to go back and see on film to understand what they had just experienced in person. With the faintest muscle movement or repositioning of her body, Garbo could communicate chapters to the audience. One sees in Garbo's roles not a passive actor but rather an actor presenting the element of a character necessary to drive forward the story, often using the most infinitesimal quantum of motion possible.[524]

While the character had appealed to men, it came as a surprise to some that Garbo in *The Temptress* was a hit with women.[525] Part of this success was Garbo's ability to transcend the details of the role and to speak directly to women about how women might live. Garbo's women had agency. Speaking about Garbo, Fred Niblo observed that what had transpired was "the banishment of the demure little heroine the screen has done so well by for a generation. The new heroine is the sophisticated woman. It is now the hero's turn to succumb to new fascinations. She is the one who conquests. The screen heroine of today has outgrown her ginghams and is all dressed up in evening gowns now. Her innocence is put away with her curls and dimples."[526]

One of the few female reviewers of the time, Tamar Lane, writing for *The Film Mercury*, thought that in *The Temptress* MGM had completely missed the value of Garbo as an actor. "Garbo has a rare combination of beauty, charm and sincerity. Why not let her express these qualities in her screen portrayals? Why present her in roles foreign to her inherent screen personality? Greta has a warm, sympathetic appeal. She is not a vampire type."[527]

Laura Mulvey later astutely wrote that Hollywood films were constructed for the male gaze. Garbo provided an ongoing aside to the female viewers about being a Modern Woman. She is an unparalleled figure of identification for the female audience. Richard Lippe observed the following:

> In many of her films, including the Cukor projects, Garbo is exceedingly sympathetic and vulnerable projecting a direct expression of her feelings and physical desires but without denying her intelligence, integrity and fortitude. The close-up shot is used often to capture Garbo's ability to register simultaneously the mental and emotional responses she has to a given situation.[528]

An ad from the *Los Angeles Times* (Feb. 8, 1934) for dresses sold at the Cinema Shop inspired by the film *Queen Christina.*

The review of the New York premiere of *Love* (1927) in *Variety* started with a recap of who was in the audience. The film was "a clarion call to shoppers. Shoppers mean women, and women mean matinees. Big ones. Try and keep the femmes away from this one. They've all apparently got a Gilbert-Garbo complex tucked away somewhere. The men too. They like Garbo, but the girls are going to pay off this production cost, and some more besides."[529]

These women were coming to see a real woman address a life problem to which they could relate. Not the sex, though that didn't hurt. Not her dying for her sins. To see Garbo act the part of an imperfect woman living through her desires and choices.

Variety pointed out that *Love* drew a middle-class audience, by focusing on the fact that present in the theater were women who could spend the afternoon at a movie.

For its review of the 1929 film *The Single Standard*, *Variety* began, "What some girls do today, and a lot more would like to do, Greta Garbo does in *The Single Standard*."[530]

But unlike some of her contemporaries, Garbo didn't just portray licentiousness. "The appeal of Garbo, however provocatively she might array herself, was romantic rather than sexual, and that is the reason women liked her. Her spirit leaped first and her body, in total exquisite accord, leaped after. She yearned not for pleasure in bed but for love in eternity."[531]

No one dreams of throwing themselves in front of a train because their life has run out of viable options. Yet, Garbo did so successfully in *Love*. Women saw in Garbo a pure femininity that triumphed over the petty moral strictures that focused on the inevitable shortfall of the individual against the ideal. Garbo was great in her imperfection. Since each fan was similarly imperfect, Garbo showed how to rise above one's imperfections with grace. They recognized a version of themselves.

One usually thinks of fans finding transcendence or aspiration in their favorite stars. While Garbo fans would copy her, identify with her, and wear clothes inspired by her, what they found in the role itself was an identification with human imperfection. MGM dressed her in stunningly beautiful clothes, and she appeared on gorgeous sets. The Art Deco style represented modernity in the 1920s and 1930s. Garbo was tied to the Art Deco style in the clothing she wore and the chairs upon which she sat.[532] Millions were made selling Garbo-adjacent merchandise.

Many film reviewers of the time wrote of Garbo's impact on men, not women, often because the reviewers were men themselves. In 1974, film historian Molly Haskell was able to look at Garbo as a Modern Woman, while writing from a modern perspective herself. Her question was, why does Garbo resonate today? "And yet, to those of us who like to think of ourselves as 'liberated,' what can Garbo mean today? In one sense, her very perfection as the embodiment of the 'feminine ideal' is a notion we resist. We have traded in our pedestals, our stars as divine beings, for concrete identities within history with the same ambitions and options as men."[533]

A photo essay from *Vanity Fair* magazine (November 1932) showing how Garbo has influenced the self-presentation of other female actors.

Haskell's answer was "Garbo was an existential heroine, a woman ready to flout social convention and embark, radical and fearless, on the adventure of love. There is something almost frightening in her passion, particularly in the silent films, where it is more explicitly sexual. In *Flesh and the Devil*, kneeling beside John Gilbert at the communion rail, sheathes the chalice and nuzzles it with a gesture that is provocatively, and unmistakably, erotic."[534]

Haskell's conclusion was:

> It remains for others to show us the day-to-day realities of love, the power struggles, the neuroses, the varieties of sex, the hangups and hanging on between men and women, men and men, women and women. Garbo embraces us all. Adds their ideal made flesh, she is a once-in-a-lifetime fusion of sexual passion and courtly love. The notion of total love. So utterly absent in contemporary films, is one that women respond to. But doesn't Garbo also appeal in the same way, to the best in men? Isn't it her eyes and face—her soul—to which, first and last, they respond? At a time of sexual doubt and uncertainty and fragmented relationships, when we are trying against improbable odds to "put it together," we could do worse than doing deep of her spirit.[535]

Garbo's fans may not have even bought tickets for the actual movie. They bought tickets for Garbo, to see what life might be.

But if narrative closure in Garbo's films, most of which were written by women, is brought about by rewarding the devotion of the good woman and punishing the passion of the bad woman, Garbo projects an infinity of desire and yearning that transcends the exigencies of the vamp plot. While the plot seems to contain or kill off Garbo's power, Garbo continually reinscribes her potency by evoking the possibility of something beyond the frame and the ultimate inadequacy of the system that seeks to contain her. Even when Garbo dies in these early films, as she does at the end of both *Flesh and the Devil* and *Love*, her death seems not so much a punishment as a judgment of the world's inadequacy.[536]

The first impact of Garbo, and there would be others, was to transform the kind of story Hollywood told and the way actors acted in film. Norma Shearer shifted from pedestrian female roles to portraying a more Modern Woman after the arrival of Garbo. Her original skill was light romances. For example, in *The Student Prince in Old Heidelberg* (1927) Shearer falls in love with the crown prince, only to lose out to tradition when he marries the bride his father selected. By *The Divorcee* (1930), Shearer has been transformed into a Modern Woman negotiating a plot that revolves around adultery and the difficulty of love gone wrong.

This transition worked for Shearer because she never tried to be a clone of Garbo. She took the modern attitude, fashioned it around her own persona, and worked on her acting.

When Marlene Dietrich was hired by Paramount in 1930, the company definitely had Garbo in its sights. But she and Josef Sternberg, the director who

Garbo in a scene still from *The Single Standard*. She came to exemplify the Modern Woman for most people in the 1920s and 1930s.

guided her career, were smart enough to establish a separate personality for her. Dietrich succeeded because she didn't try to copy Garbo. She portrayed her own version of a Modern Woman. Fan magazines wrote endless head-to-head comparisons of the two because they were both Germanic and blonde. If she had had a less distinct personality, these articles might have torpedoed her career.

Those actors who were hired to copy Garbo, and then did so slavishly, were unsuccessful. Anna Sten didn't resonate with audiences. One didn't have to copy Garbo to be a Modern Woman, just her modern attitude. Joan Crawford, Carole Lombard, and Katharine Hepburn couldn't have been more different from Garbo, or each other, yet they were modern and learned to act in a naturalistic fashion.

By 1932, *Photoplay* wrote about the emergence of this new heroine: "You will realize that this new type is an outgrowth of modernity. . . . The new cinema heroine can take care of herself, thank you, since she combines, with her mysterious allure, many of the hard-headed attributes and even some of the physical characteristics—the tall, narrow-hipped, broad-shouldered figures—of men. . . . Nowadays it's the heroine who falls. These new vamps are not vamps in the strictest sense of the word, since they are the heroines of the picture. The bad woman—the shady dame is today's heroine."[537]

It took a woman to more completely capture the zeitgeist. Helen Appleton Read wrote the following:

> It isn't merely because Garbo is beautiful and glamorous that she had set a fashion—created a type. She has crystalized an idea that was already forming. She is its symbol. It is a combination of out-of-doors and the eternal feminine-age-old allure without a trace of fussy feminine vanity—independence without the blight of feminism.
>
> And let me add that the Marlene Dietrichs, the Tallulah Bankheads, Joan Crawfords and Hope Williamses haven't reached stardom because their producers presented them as out Garbo-ing Garbo in her own special line of beauty and manner, but they have stirred the imagination of the public because they too, symbolize the taste of the period.[538]

To get a sense of how important Garbo had become to MGM in just one season, the following chart shows the rough contribution to total rental revenue of the leading female actors at MGM for the 25–26 production year. What is clear is that MGM needed Garbo.

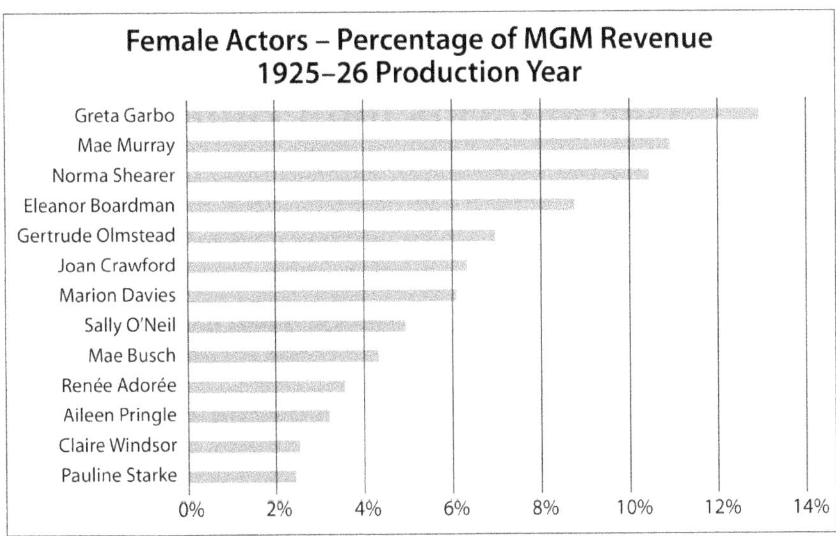

There are some quirks to the data because I chose to double count female actors who co-starred in films. For example, both Joan Crawford and Sally O'Neil starred in *Sally, Irene and Mary* (1925). Therefore, the numbers don't total to 100 percent. The point is the relative revenue.

Another element that a simple chart doesn't capture is that Mae Murray was forty-two and near the end of her drawing power as a female lead. Finally, not everyone was in the same number of films. We are comparing Garbo's three films with four from Norma Shearer, Gertrude Olmstead, and Eleanor Boardman. Several of these actors only made two MGM films in this time-frame. With the exception of Sally O'Neil, who was also at the beginning of her career, all the other MGM leading female actors had been on-screen for at least five years, building their marketability.

In two films Garbo forcefully seized the attention of Modern Women. Her next film would turn that attention into a blinding spotlight.

Chapter 15 – *Flesh and the Devil:* Garbo meets John Gilbert

"I told her yes, I am in love with Garbo, I want to marry Garbo. She wants to leave the screen and buy a wheat ranch and have seventeen children and don't think she can't. I love people and cities and conversation—so I say I will not marry her unless she goes on being Garbo. She says she will not marry me unless she can leave the screen forever. So there we are." [539]

— John Gilbert, actor

The photo of Gilbert and Garbo from *Flesh and the Devil* that launched a million dreams.

When Garbo began filming *Flesh and the Devil* in August 1926, she had not yet been in Hollywood for a year. Making the film would be transformative. She would fall in love with John Gilbert and through him expand her social circle to include many of the most interesting people in Hollywood. It is her first film with first-rank co-stars and would mark a new confidence in how she dealt with MGM.

Between the end of main filming for *The Temptress* and the start of filming for *Flesh and the Devil*, Garbo dashed off a letter to Lars Saxon. She starts by asking if he can spare a Swedish-language copy of the Dostoevsky novel *The Idiot* (1869). She confirms that production of *The Temptress* took about six months, and she is about to start again.[540]

Garbo writes that she must get a manager. She expresses that she has trouble explaining to MGM management what she needs from them. Part of her problem, as she sees it, is that she doesn't understand how MGM works.[541] She is discontented with the situation. Garbo would always discuss professional issues with Stiller. She trusted him. Here we see Garbo looking to cast a wider net so she can negotiate effectively.

For her third American film, Garbo was cast in yet another melodrama, *Flesh and the Devil*. This time she was cast opposite John Gilbert. As pleased as Garbo might have been with the improvement in co-stars, she felt betrayed by Mayer. She went to the studio chief and objected to the role. She wanted better parts in better movies just as Mayer had promised. But MGM did not want to alter the formula that was spinning box office gold. Mayer held Garbo to the letter of her contract.

Felicitas was a classic vamp role, but the cast was stronger, including both Gilbert and Garbo's friend, the Swedish actor Lars Hanson, who had played the eponymous *Gösta Berling*. The director was the well-regarded Clarence Brown. After briefly refusing to report to the set, a disappointed Garbo dutifully began work on the picture.

Garbo related to Ruth Biery in some detail her interactions with Louis B. Mayer regarding her contract before the start of production for *Flesh and the Devil*:

> Mr. Mayer called me in and said I was to start right away. My sister had died while I was making *The Temptress*. My poor body wasn't able to carry on any longer. I was so tired, so sick, so heart broken.

> I went to Mr. Mayer and said, "Mister Mayer, I am dead tired. I am sick. I cannot do another picture right away. And I am unhappy about this picture—"
>
> And they said, "That's just too bad. Go on and try on your clothes and get ready."
>
> If people are not happy, I should think you would try and make them happy. "I am sick," was all that I answered.
>
> I am not the kind of a girl who can powder my nose and say, "Ah. Go on with you." What couldn't I have given to have been born an American girl. To have understood the American language and the American business.
>
> What could I do? I went to the hotel in Santa Monica and lay down to think. I did not think I could go on. I had heard of a manager. So I got one! Somebody who could talk the English language.
>
> He saw how sick I was, how tired. "Poor lady, why don't you go home and rest?"—he told me.
>
> So I went home for two days. Then I heard about the papers. They say, "Greta Garbo goes home—She is temperamental—she cannot be handled." I did not understand that, so I went to my manager and said, "Maybe I better go back to the studio. I have rested two days. It does not make any difference here whether I am tired and sick and have lost my sister. I do not understand and I will go back."[542]
>
> So I went back and said nothing.
>
> And there I met for the first time, except to nod to him, John Gilbert. And he was so terribly good to work with! He has such vitality, spirit, eagerness. Every morning at nine o'clock he would slip to work opposite me. He was so nice, that I felt better; felt a little closer to this strange America.[543]

While Garbo backed down over *Flesh and the Devil*, she had made her position clear to MGM. She wanted the better roles in quality films that she had been promised. In an interview with writer Doris Markham, she elaborated on this point:

> I do not want to be bad woman—on the screen, you know. That is my only trouble in America. People say I am what you call a "vamp type." I know what they mean, but I do not think I am. I do not like to play "Bad Woman!" Oh, much rather, I played good women—good, but interesting—you know?[544]

The MGM payroll records document that Garbo started on *Flesh and the Devil* on August 15.[545] *Flesh and the Devil* was based on an 1894 novel, *The Undying Past*, by Hermann Sudermann. The novel is a clunky melodrama that was trimmed to fit into the standard length of a feature film. Initially, Gilbert was not interested in playing the part of Leo von Harden, but the addition of Clarence Brown as the director and Greta Garbo as Felicitas apparently swayed him to agree to the role.[546]

Garbo and Gilbert in a scene still from *Flesh and the Devil.*

The plot of *Flesh and the Devil* is based on a love triangle. Leo (John Gilbert) and Ulrich (Lars Hanson) are childhood friends now in the military. There is an introductory scene to establish their friendship and give them some character. Leo meets Felicitas, played by Garbo, and is smitten. He pursues her and falls in love. Rather quickly he ends up killing her husband in a duel. Leo must then serve a three-year banishment to Africa. Leo lies about the cause of the duel to protect Felicitas, so Ulrich is unaware of their tryst. Upon Leo's return, he finds Felicitas and Ulrich have married. Felicitas tries to contrive a way to stay married and keep Leo as a lover. Leo rejects this but, in the ensuing argument, Ulrich appears, and the net result is a planned duel between the friends. In the end, the two can't go through with the duel, and Felicitas drowns while trying to interrupt the duel as well, thus permitting a somewhat happy ending, at least for the men.

John Gilbert, known as Jack except on official documents, was a gregarious person who had friends everywhere he went. Born to traveling actors in Logan, Utah, in 1897, Gilbert ended up in Hollywood working as an extra in 1915, while still in his teens. He worked for a variety of film companies and important early industry figures, including Thomas Ince and Maurice Tourneur. In 1921, he signed a multi-film contract with Fox. There, Gilbert became a star.

This success was followed by a long-term deal with Louis B. Mayer Productions in 1924. By the time his first film under this deal was released, Louis B. Mayer Productions had been merged into the newly created MGM.

Gilbert then worked on a string of significant films with excellent directors and his acting matured with these experiences. He backed Lon Chaney in Victor Sjöström's *He Who Gets Slapped* (1924). After two now-lost films, he starred in successive blockbusters, *The Merry Widow* (1925) and *The Big Parade* (1925).

By the time Gilbert finished *The Big Parade*, he had been married and divorced twice. His Hollywood social circle was composed of interesting people from all facets of the industry. He had a hard-living lifestyle, with lots of adventures, romances, and drinking. He thoroughly enjoyed being a film star. When Rudolph Valentino passed away on August 23, 1926, a week after Garbo reluctantly arrived on the set of *Flesh and the Devil*, Gilbert became the leading male star of the time.

Garbo and Gilbert got along from the start, and soon their friendship developed into a romance as torrid as the one their characters were sharing on the screen. Fueled by the MGM publicity department, which took full advantage of the romance to promote its film, the Hollywood press reveled in the love affair. The resulting publicity elevated Garbo to the highest level of celebrity.

Flesh and the Devil is one of those films that came together perfectly. That was no accident. Clarence Brown was a good director. The cast was strong, and not only was Garbo a naturalistic actor, but Lars Hanson was as well. Jack Gilbert was reasonably good at the naturalistic style and didn't seem out of place.

Garbo and Gilbert had seen each other around the MGM lot but had not been introduced. Clarence Brown later recalled the exact moment he realized they had become lovers:

> When they got into that first love scene, well, nobody else was even there. Those two were alone in a world of their own.[547]

The first scene is remarkable. When Gilbert first meets Garbo, he breaks off a flower from her bouquet; she looks at him with surprise, then amusement, then modesty; then he smells the flowers; then the carriage pulls away—in one take.

Garbo was now working on a third consecutive film with cinematographer William Daniels. He filmed all or most of twenty-two of Garbo's twenty-six MGM films. Well respected by his peers, Daniels was nominated for four Oscars, winning once. He was good at solving problems and balancing the artistic and technical needs of a scene.

Brown and Daniels had developed a visual schema for *Flesh and the Devil* that included mattes, montage editing, chiaroscuro lighting, and silhouettes. All propelled the story along.[548]

This led to creative solutions such as lighting a love scene. Brown recalled the following:

> In *Flesh and the Devil* for the arbor love scene I just wanted a faint glow to illuminate Garbo and Gilbert's faces. So I gave Jack Gilbert two tiny pencil carbons to hold. When they kissed the carbons lit up. His hands shielded the mechanism from the lens.[549]

This solution makes the scene incredibly intimate.

Barbara Kent, in only her second role (as Ulrich's younger sister, Hertha), later spoke about how Brown worked with Garbo: "He was especially careful with Garbo and would almost whisper his instructions to her."[550] Brown quickly learned that the best way to direct Garbo was to do so minimally.

Garbo and Gilbert illuminated by just pencil carbon lights.

Garbo arrived already understanding the scene and her role in it, but also not over-rehearsed. Most scenes only needed a take or two. In situations where Brown thought Garbo had not quite captured what he sought in the scene, they would just discuss it and then shoot again.

Garbo was already limiting her press availability, so fan magazine writer Doris Markham was given a unique invitation to the set of *Flesh and the Devil.* She described the filming of the communion scene this way:

> A few minutes later she was kneeling at a communion rail, John Gilbert beside her.
>
> Again they were caught up in the magic cloud of their own making—they played a scene that tightened your throat with its intense beauty—even there in that most prosaic and disillusioning of all places—a motion picture set.
>
> "They have done that in every love scene they have played," said Clarence Brown, "it's marvelous."
>
> The scene was over and Greta had slipped down from her knees into a pathetic little heap on the altar steps. Her face was dead white. Her eyes, big and solemn and tragic—for the scene she had just played was part of the story of a woman who is interesting

> but not—good—"and when people see me on the screen, they will think I am like that," says Greta. "Oh, yes, they will! They will write me letters about it—that is why some days I am sad, but most days I am very, very happy—I am very happy—" she was looking up—John Gilbert was standing there.[551]

Markham asked Garbo about her lunch with the Swedish crown prince, who visited MGM on his tour of America:

> Yes, and I had never seen him before in my life. Not on the street, not in a procession, not anywhere. And in Sweden, I would never have met the Crown Prince. It would have been too difficult—but here in America, I sit beside him, I talk to him—oh, he is charming, and he had such a good time here.[552]

Clarence Brown was the earliest of her directors to talk about what working with Garbo was like. "It was all there," he recalled. "She had this remarkable ability to register thoughts and emotion without doing much of anything."[553] Monta Bell and Fred Niblo seem to have been taken unawares regarding her ability to deliver a nuanced performance in her first two films, even after they had captured it. By contrast, Brown clearly saw what Garbo could do on film and immediately used it.

A Lobby Card advertising *Flesh and the Devil.*

Garbo attended the February 3 Los Angeles premiere at the Forum. She wore a chiffon and ermine wrap and arrived with Gilbert.[554] It was the last premiere she arrived at publicly, though she surreptitiously attended others.

Variety wrote of *Flesh and the Devil*, "Here is a picture that is the 'pay-off' when it comes to filming love scenes. There are three in this picture that will make anyone fidget in their seats and their hair rise on end."[555]

The reviewer went on to forecast that the film was "certain to be a box office smash, no matter where they play it. It looks as though it should be big enough to smash the record at the Capitol this week and possibly hold over next week for another record. After they get a load of this love making the audiences are going out and talk about it, and send others in."[556]

According to *Photoplay*, "Here is the picture filmed when the romance of Jack Gilbert and Greta Garbo was at its height. Naturally, the love scenes (and there are several thousand feet of them) are smolderingly fervent."[557]

Mordaunt Hall in *The New York Times* pointed out director Clarence Brown's ability to have "analyzed the feelings of the characters and flashed an idea of their thoughts upon the screen."[558] A trick easier to turn if you have Greta Garbo and Lars Hanson in the cast. Gilbert holds his own in this respect as well.

At least one reviewer compared Garbo's performance to Theda Bara, the vamp of old. According to the reviewer, Garbo's portrayal is subtle. She goes about her seduction in a more roundabout way without the full-on voluptuousness of Bara. It is believable that men fell in love with Garbo, whereas Theda Bara was always a caricature of a woman. Garbo's ability to suggest through her acting makes the portrayal believable.[559]

Much later, the British critic who wrote pseudonymously under the name E. E. Laing would say of *Flesh and the Devil*, "It was not Art in the Stiller-Sjöström sense. It had, however, punch and one of those overheated plots which Hollywood managed with awful adroitness."[560]

Flesh and the Devil was a tremendous success for both MGM and Loew's. For MGM, the film rental revenue of $1.3 million ($23.3 million) was second only to that of the Erich von Stroheim spectacular *The Merry Widow* for the 25–26 production year. It was also second in profits, netting $466,000 ($8.4 million) after costs.

It is not possible to derive a number for either ticket sales or profits that accrued to Loew's from an individual film. The data are lost. But at just the Capitol Theatre in New York, *Flesh and the Devil* set the all-time ticket revenue record of $248,296 ($4.5 million) over four weeks. Reports in the trade press indicate that *Flesh and the Devil* did exceedingly well in first-run theaters. The very theaters that Loew's owned and that delivered outsized ticket revenue.

Garbo had quickly developed a unique characteristic of performing better in first-run theaters in urban markets with large concentrations of middle-class and upwardly mobile women. The value of this characteristic to Loew's has been underappreciated. Garbo films were almost perfectly matched to the Loew's theater customer profile.

In Washington, DC, a city where Loew's controlled the first-run theaters and where the workforce included a very high percentage of clerical workers, *Flesh and the Devil* delivered a box office of $26,000 ($470,000) for the Palace Theater and sold tickets to one-third of the city's White population (which at the time was tracked separately from Black film attendance, which may not have been tracked at all).[561]

The Gilbert-Garbo love affair, begun on the set of *Flesh and the Devil*, was the gossip news of the year. It was discussed in fan magazines and newspapers and on radio. Even before *Flesh and the Devil* was released, how the couple would appear on the screen was of national interest. Articles such as this one from Motion Picture primed the publicity machine:

> It was as amazing, as electrifying, as poignant as that—the look between John Gilbert and Greta Garbo.
>
> No wonder Clarence Brown says he is getting the greatest love scenes that have ever been screened, in *Flesh and the Devil*. He is working with the raw material. They are in that blissful halcyon stage of love that is so like a rosy cloud that they imagine themselves hidden behind it, as well as lost in it—they are not even self-conscious—yet.
>
> And when two personalities such as John Gilbert and Greta Garbo love, there will either be a great idyl or a great tragedy—possibly both. It is hard to imagine their love story running along conventional lines—and as for denying it—they might just as well try to deny the existence of fire![562]

Garbo was in love with Jack Gilbert, at least for a period of time. A then-teenage Ingrid Stocklassa recalled,

> One Sunday while we were making lunch, Garbo whispered to me in confidence that she had met John Gilbert for the first time. She asked Garbo, "Well, what did you think of him?" Garbo's response was only "Ah!"[563]

Actor Eleanor Boardman married director King Vidor on September 8, 1926, in a small ceremony. Boardman recounted years later that Jack Gilbert and Greta Garbo were to marry at the same time, making it a double wedding. There is no other evidence for this improbable story.

There is a picture of the wedding party in King Vidor's biography, *A Tree Is a Tree* (1953). Gilbert is visible, but not Garbo. Garbo and Gilbert had only met on the set of *Flesh and the Devil* on August 15. To think Garbo would agree to marry him twenty-four days later seems unlikely. Though to think that Gilbert would have asked in that timeframe is entirely likely. Gilbert rushed into marriage all four times he was married.

The final reason to doubt there was ever a plan for a double wedding is that Garbo biographer Karen Swenson researched marriage licenses issued in Southern California and could not find one for them.

Adela Rogers St. Johns was a friend of Jack Gilbert's and, therefore, a frequent guest at his Tower Road home. Though she never considered herself close to Garbo, she wrote of how Garbo would spend an afternoon being part of the social group while still maintaining a distance:

> She rouses herself to come on the court, where she plays the best tennis of any girl in pictures. Hitting terrific drives like a man. Then swiping the sweat off her face with her forearm, she retires once more into herself.[564]

Tennis seems to have been her passion, as several people have stories about Garbo on the tennis court. King Vidor recounted that he taught Garbo to play tennis on the court at Jack Gilbert's house: "She was a bulwark of strength at the net."[565] The only woman who could beat her at tennis was Aileen Pringle.

Basil Rathbone wrote about one tennis match where he was her doubles partner:

> In due course, after lunch [at Jack Gilbert's house in June 1928] we

> played tennis and went for a swim in the pool. I was Garbo's doubles partner and rarely played a worse game! Garbo was not a large woman. She was beautifully proportioned and I think could best be described as being the aesthetic-athletic type. She swam like a fish and by the time we met in the water she was very friendly and most of my inhibitions had been overcome.[566]

Garbo and John Gilbert at his Tower Road home.

Screenwriter Carey Wilson played tennis with Garbo frequently and found her technique unorthodox but effective:

> I rather fancied myself as a promising tennis player. In fact, I thought I was pretty good. But with the "Fleek" [the diminutive of Gilbert's original nickname for Garbo, Svenska Flicka (Swedish Girl)] it was something else again. The Fleek played the most unorthodox tennis you can possibly imagine. Grasping the racket well up toward the throat, she would smack the ball so heartily that there wasn't much to be done about it in the event it happened to land in the court.[567]

A 1930 article would list Garbo's athletic interests. In addition to tennis she reportedly engaged in long walks, was an expert swimmer, and rowed well.[568]

Garbo became a semipermanent resident in Gilbert's guest room. She spent time there regardless of the state of their romantic relationship, which would fade over time. What they had was a deep understanding of each other that led to a friendship that endured until Gilbert's drinking undermined most of his friendships and his career.

Jack Gilbert was, at the time, one of the centers of Hollywood social life, hosting a regular Sunday brunch that was well attended. Garbo made her first American friends in this group. She was close with some, like Carey Wilson, Cedric Gibbons, Dolores del Rio, Frances Goldwyn, and Lilyan Tashman, and just chatted socially with others. Various people have listed this circle slightly differently.

Colleen Moore,[569] Carey Wilson,[570] and biographers Roland Flamini[571] and Eve Golden[572] reported a core group that gathered at Gilbert's, including many couples: Irving Thalberg and Norma Shearer, King Vidor and Eleanor Boardman, Carey and Carmelita Wilson, Colleen Moore and John McCormick, Basil and Ouida Rathbone, Sam and Frances Goldwyn, Cedric Gibbons and Dolores del Rio, Lilyan Tashman and Edmund Lowe, Herman and Sarah Mankiewicz, and Barney and Alice Glazer.

Others frequently at Gilbert's included Arthur Hornblow Jr., Juliette Crosby, David Selznick, Richard Barthelmess, Ronald Colman, Victor Fleming, Edmund Goulding, Paul Bern, and Anita Loos. These were just the regulars.

When Garbo's time on Tower Road is mentioned, she is described both as reserved and part of the social scene, depending on who was there and apparently how she felt that day. For example, Herman Mankiewicz would tell jokes and when Garbo would laugh he would claim she didn't understand them. He would coax her to explain the joke to show she wasn't just laughing along with everyone else, and her answers in her newly learned English would delight the group.[573]

By the end of 1926, Garbo and Gilbert had realized that they were ill-suited as marriage partners. Gilbert would reconsider from time to time, but Garbo seems to have decided definitively that she was not going to marry Gilbert:

> The only American man I have gone out with at all is Mr. Gilbert. Many things have been written and said about our friendship. It is a friendship. I will never marry. But should anyone say that? No one knows what tomorrow will bring. But now I think I will never marry. My work absorbs me. I have time for nothing else.
>
> But you may say that I think Jack Gilbert is one of the finest men I have ever known, American or otherwise. He is a real gentleman. He has temperament. That is, he gets excited—has much to say sometimes—but that is good.[574]

In a letter back to Mimi Pollak she summed up her relationship with Gilbert this way:

> You ask about Gilbert. Yes, there has been a lot in the newspapers but I can't do what the newspapers expect. I'm not suited to be married. I am too temperamental and too nervous. And soon enough the man who married me would discover that I am brainless. He is very sweet and angry because I don't want to get married. I've been very bad towards him. Without knowing what I wanted, I've promised many things which now make him unhappy because I can't go through with them. He has a very attractive home with everything you could want—tennis, swimming pool, servants, cars and everything else to make life easier. But I still return to my old, ugly hotel room. Why?[575]

In a late 1926 interview, Gilbert said, "No, we are not going to be married. Nevertheless, she is the most marvelous person in the world."[576]

Though one must consider it a bit of hyperbole, Gilbert went on to describe the effect Garbo would have upon entering a room: "When she comes into a room, every man stops to look at her. And every woman too, which is more remarkable. She is capable of doing a lot of damage—unconsciously of course. Upsetting thrones, breaking up friendships, wrecking homes—that sort of thing."[577]

Garbo and John Gilbert in a scene still from *A Woman of Affairs.*

Rogers St. Johns came to think their romance had almost a "piquant quality." "I have called their romance high comedy—but as I look at it I'm not so sure. The incongruity of this pair made for laughter both between them and for the rest of us."[578]

Gilbert and his friends respected Garbo's frequent desire for solitude, while also trying to get her out and involved in a broader social life. Colleen Moore recalled that Carey Wilson had invited her to his party at the Beverly Wilshire Hotel in early 1927. When he heard that she was not planning to attend, he drove to Gilbert's house to retrieve her:

> When Carey went to Jack's house to pick the two of them up, she said she didn't have an evening gown and couldn't go. She was wearing a long, dark green dress with a high neck and long sleeves. Carey took a scissors, cut a low back, cut across the front, and whacked off the sleeves. The result may not read like much, but with Garbo wearing it, who noticed? For she was, when she arrived at the party, all we had heard about and more—a radiantly beautiful woman, a girl-woman, young, shy. Unsophisticated, with the same childlike quality about her which has marked so many of the world's great artists.[579]

Gilbert and Garbo also went up to San Simeon at least one time for a weekend with William Randolph Hearst and Marion Davies. But often she was happy to remain at Gilbert's and read. Gilbert found this frustrating. Studio publicist Howard Dietz related a conversation he had with Gilbert about a time he tried to tease Garbo into going out with him:

> When I said, "I'm going out," the only thing she said was, "I'll leave the door open, Jack!" I said, "I'm going out to sleep with Anna May Wong!" "I'll leave the door open, Jack," was all she said. What in the hell do I do?[580]

When Garbo was with the group socially, her humor could be dry. Gilbert once chartered a plane for a scenic flight over Southern California for a dozen of his Hollywood friends. Carey Wilson recalled that, as the plane took off, Garbo wondered aloud, "If we crash, who gets top billing?"[581]

Garbo was a hit with the public. At twenty-one, she was a Hollywood star. She mingled with the other Hollywood stars. One further element of her appeal set her apart: She sold tickets at first-run theaters. The most profitable part of the business.

Chapter 16 – Loew's and the First-Run Theater

"We sell tickets to theaters, not movies." [582]

— Marcus Loew, president, Loew's

The marquee of the Astor Theatre in New York for the film *Grand Hotel.* The most important part of the film business was the theater experience.

The most important part of the entire film industry was the first-run theater. Loew's, which owned MGM, owned or controlled the most first-run theaters. These Loew's theaters were in cities full of female clerks. Garbo profitably filled those seats with female clerks.

The financial numbers used historically to discuss Garbo's success have been those from the MGM studio for film costs and rental revenues. These summary numbers are available for most major studio films from the 1920s and '30s. Today ticket revenues for films are reported on a weekly basis, but only incomplete exhibition revenue figures are available for these past years.[583]

Neither Loew's nor any other studio reported exhibition revenue by film. Focusing just on film rental revenues misses a major part of Garbo's financial impact. Garbo delivered higher average film rental revenue than did other actors, and then even more outsized exhibition revenues. Garbo's audience was uniquely profitable in theaters.

Zooming out to the total film industry in 1928 shows that the lion's share of film industry revenue, nearly half, came from first-run theater exhibitions. Subsequent-run theaters delivered only 16 percent of industry revenue. Together these two exhibition segments represented 64 percent of the total industry revenue. Film rental, where the studios made money, represented a still significant 31 percent of revenue. The balance of 5 percent was from physical distribution.[584]

First-run theaters got films first and they were protected from second-run and later-run theaters getting films before they had extracted the time premium that a new film received in the market. This distribution structure was called run-zone-clearance. It allowed for the maximization of theater revenues by controlling the timing of a film's exhibition as it traveled from the most profitable to the least profitable theaters.

Since first-run theaters made the most money, films made most of their money in the first weeks after release. Sidney Kent, a Paramount executive, elaborated in a talk at Harvard Business School in 1927:

> We can sell our first twelve hundred and fifty accounts within two- or three-weeks' time, but it takes us the remainder of the year to get the other eight thousand seven hundred to make up our average circulation.[585]

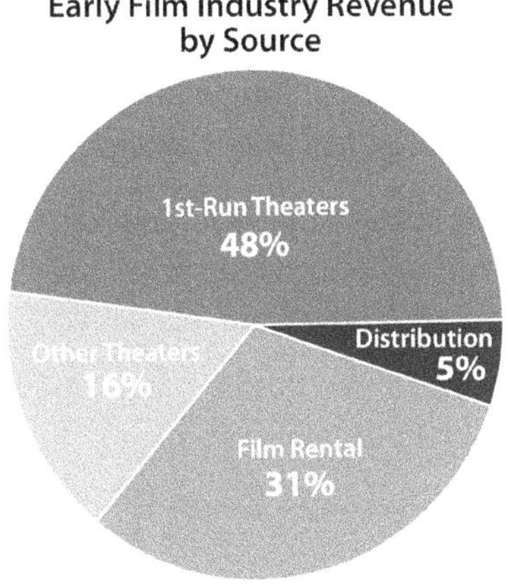

Figure: A summary chart created from The *Motion Picture Almanac* for 1929 that recapped the prior year. A distribution gross of $200 million ($3.7 billion) was reported. Of this, 15% went to the distributors and 85% to the studios, so the total gross for all studios was about $170 million ($3.1 billion).

On the exhibition side, admissions for the year were $550 million ($10.2 billion). After deducting the cost of renting the films (to avoid double counting), the total gross for theaters was $350 million ($6.5 billion).

For the combined Loew's/MGM organization, a Loew's spreadsheet for the year ending in August 1927 shows that the yearly gross income was $80 million ($1.5 billion), with $7 million ($128.6 million) in net income. The MGM subsidiary generated $29 million ($532.7 million) in film rental income for that year.[586] MGM's profit was about $3 million ($55 million),[587] $600,000 ($11 million) of which went to profit sharing for Mayer, Rubin, and Thalberg.[588] Therefore, only about $2.4 million ($44 million), 34 percent, of Loew's net income came from MGM.

The first-run audience was urban and female. The film industry only noticed that its audience was primarily women with the rise of Rudolph Valentino as a female-focused film star (*The Sheik*, 1921, was his breakthrough role).[589] The reason for this market phenomenon was the appeal of cinema itself. It was a new kind of social space created by industrialization. Movies were an inexpensive amusement that a woman could go to on her own.[590] It was also a modern era dating option. Industry insiders observed that between 60 percent and 75 percent of the film audience was female. The film companies therefore catered to women.[591]

Martin Quigley, the publisher of several major trade magazines (and one of the driving forces for censorship) would write that "the woman normally initiates theater attendance and, also, where a choice is available usually she determines what feature picture shall be seen."[592] In this context his call for censorship was clearly intended to limit what behavior women could see portrayed.

The urban market was not monolithic. Many recent immigrants and Black migrants from the South had not integrated into mainstream American society. Recent Catholic immigrants turned to the Catholic Church for guidance and support in their new land. Many rightly did not feel fully welcome.

Another major divide was between rural and urban. The rural market was poorer. It was further divided between the merely poor farmers of most of America and the really poor farmers of the rural South.

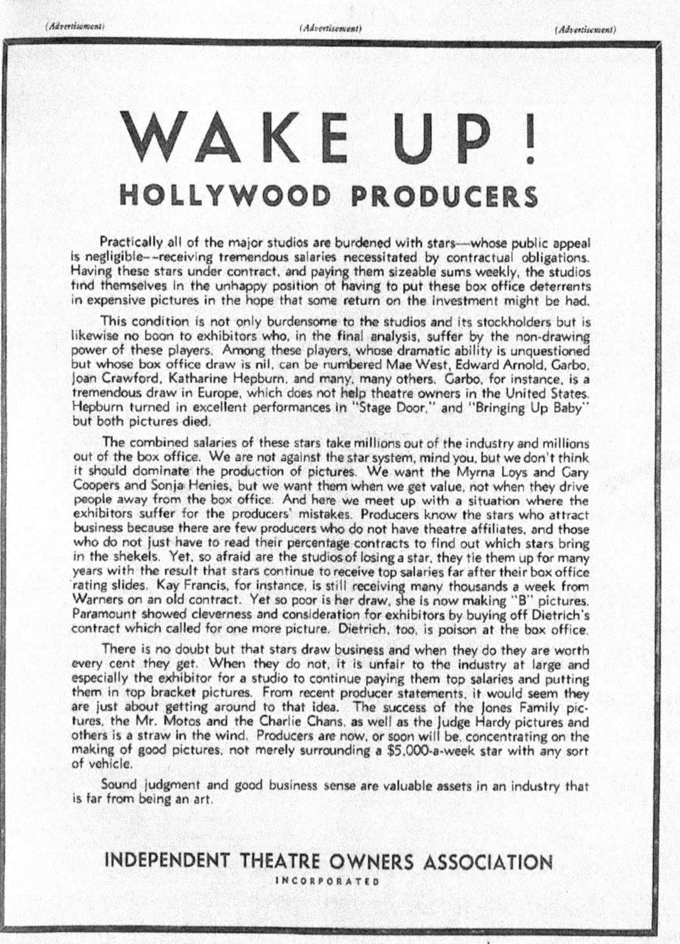

The May 1938 Independent Theatre Owners Association ad that claimed Garbo, and others, were box office poison.

Beyond the issue of its relative poverty, the rural market was also widely dispersed. Therefore, a key characteristic of rural America was that theaters were small. While the integrated film companies owned the big urban first-run theaters, the thousands of small independent theaters scattered across prairies or tucked into immigrant neighborhoods scratched out more meager revenues.

The importance of individual films could be totally different in each of the diverse distribution markets. Two films with similar rental income but different audiences would not deliver the same exhibition income. The margins were much better in first-run theaters. For example, a hypothetical Western that had the same rental income as a Garbo film would generate a lot less exhibition revenue because Westerns were more reliant on rural markets.[593]

The managers of these vastly different theaters followed different media. Whereas the managers of chain theaters learned about industry developments from *Variety*, *Film Daily*, and corporate sales meetings, the independent theater owner read about current events and new films in trade publications targeted specifically at them.[594]

When the Independent Theatre Owners Association took out an ad in May 1938 declaring that Garbo, Mae West, Joan Crawford, Katharine Hepburn, and others had no box office appeal, it spoke only for its subset of independent theaters. Managers of the theaters for the integrated film companies did not want to live without these very stars, as they filled their theaters' seats.[595]

In the ad, the Independent Theatre Owners Association claimed, "Practically all of the major studios are burdened with stars—whose public appeal is negligible—receiving tremendous salaries necessitated by contractual obligations. Having these stars under contract, and paying them sizable sums weekly, the studios find themselves in the unhappy position to having put these box office deterrents in expensive pictures in the hope that some return on the investment might be had."[596] Yet, both Garbo and Crawford signed lucrative new contracts by the end of that same year. Given the opportunity to not pay these stars at the end of contracts, the studios wrote new, bigger checks to them.

It was a great ad and generated commentary that resonates to this day. But it meant nothing to the integrated film companies, and it did not address their market reality. By this time, the smallest fifteen thousand theaters in America represented about 75 percent of the theaters, yet they were only generating at most 10 percent of exhibition revenue.

Attending a first-run theater like the Paramount Theatre in Seattle was a completely different experience when compared to a small theater like the Normal Theater in Chicago. First-run theaters were opulent, grand in scale and featured amenities for attendees.

Integrated film majors (initially Paramount and Loew's, but eventually including Warner, RKO, and Fox) owned or controlled most first-run theaters. These were large urban theaters that were able to charge premium prices. Therefore, these integrated major studios derived the most benefit from the run-zone-clearance distribution structure.

The logical question was why even more first-run theaters weren't built to compete for the most profitable slice of the market. One element was collusion. The integrated film companies, other chains of theaters, and bankers had a cozy oligopoly. When Paramount began building five new theaters in metro New York, Marcus Loew sat down with its president Adolph Zukor and delivered the message that this would be unacceptable, and he would have to add theaters in markets where Paramount didn't have competition.

The resolution was that Paramount rented or sold the five theaters to Loew's while they were under construction. Perhaps not unrelated, Loew's then sold several of its Canadian theaters to a Paramount subsidiary.

Another problem was financing construction. First-run theaters commanded expensive locations near transit hubs. While theoretically a competitor could open a theater across the street, in practice this was difficult. An independent developer was less likely to get financing in the face of established competition.

Integrated studios actively threatened proposed theater developments that would interfere with theaters in prime locations. In 1922, the builders of a new one-thousand-seat theater in Peekskill, New York, sued Loew's, several Loew's employees, and other film distributors for threatening their new theater. Theater owner Joseph Singer claimed that David Bernstein, Loew's CFO, said, "You made a big mistake by coming to Peekskill, because the town is not large enough for two [first-run] theaters. I am going to give you a fight." Bernstein's leverage was reportedly the threat that "you will not be able to get any pictures from anybody."[597]

After Loew's lost this case, it seems the integrated majors learned to not leave any evidence. Paramount's threats to small chains and theaters it wanted to buy were an open secret in the industry.

First-run theaters also had economies of scale in operation. They offered amenities besides just film. They had to have an audience that could afford to pay the higher prices. Before sound film, the theater's program usually included music and live acts to add value to the price of admission. Different theaters would use various blends of films, musicians, and live acts.[598] First-run theaters offered things, such as babysitting, that drew patrons. Finally, first-run theaters added air conditioning.

Data from an antitrust case fought over market conditions in Chicago in 1939 provide an insight into the profitability of first-run theaters. Because Chicago was a large city there were large second- and third-run theaters, so the comparison is of theaters with somewhat similar seating capacity. The first-run Chicago Theatre delivered three times the revenue per seat than the second-run Avalon, and more than six times that of the third-run Tower.[599] It is also possible to calculate that, when compared to the second-run theater, half of the higher revenue was due to higher ticket prices and half due to filling a higher percentage of seats.

A large percentage of audience members would pay a premium to see a picture when it was newly released. In the Chicago example, the second-run Avalon Theater is one commuter rail stop from the third-run Tower Theatre yet could charge 25 percent more per ticket because it had fresher films.[600] Appendix three goes into more detail.

Box Office per Seat Chicago Theaters

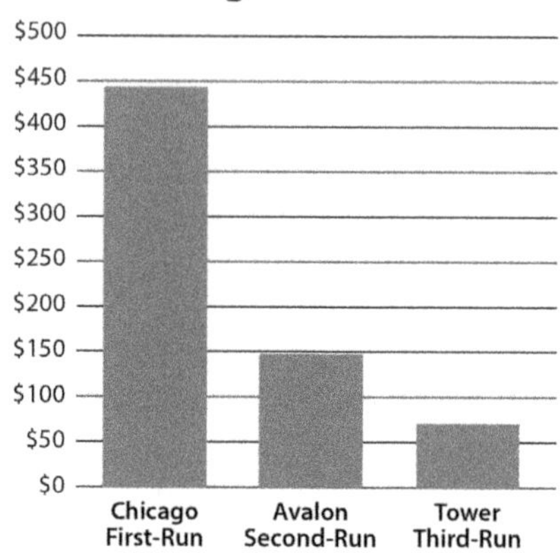

From 1920 on, the number of large first-run theaters grew rapidly.[601] While the building leveled off with the Depression, it never entirely stopped. Even in 1945, only around 1000 theaters of the total of 18,413 in the United States had over 1,500 seats.[602] This number was overwhelmed by the number of small theaters, but these small theaters mattered little to the total industry.

Number of Theaters by Seating Capacity: 1928

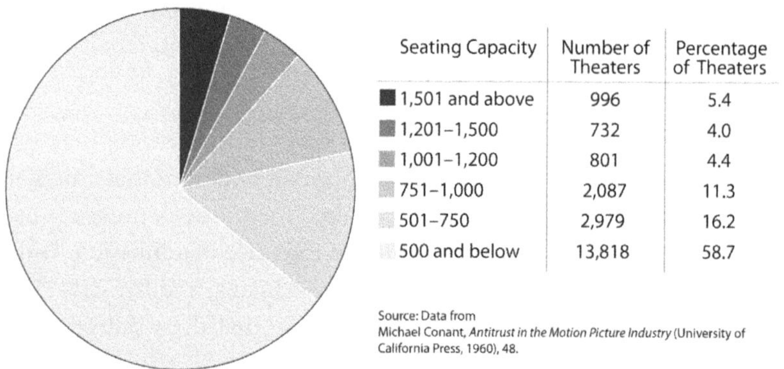

Seating Capacity	Number of Theaters	Percentage of Theaters
1,501 and above	996	5.4
1,201–1,500	732	4.0
1,001–1,200	801	4.4
751–1,000	2,087	11.3
501–750	2,979	16.2
500 and below	13,818	58.7

Source: Data from Michael Conant, *Antitrust in the Motion Picture Industry* (University of California Press, 1960), 48.

The profusion of small theaters was in part due to the dispersed nature of the American population at the time. A few years earlier in 1928, a survey showed that over 5,000 of the 20,303 total theaters counted that year were in towns with a population of 2,500 or fewer.[603] The 70 percent of Americans who lived in rural places or in smaller cities could not generate enough traffic for a large theater.

The great mass of small-town theaters, thousands of them, operated only on weekends.[604] This limited their potential income further. The average theater in a small town of less than 1,500 people generated $5,096 ($117,000) in annual income on average weekly attendance of 350.[605] The average admission ticket was a paltry $0.28 ($6.43). It would take 335 of these theaters to match the box office of the first-run Paramount Theatre in Aurora, Illinois.

Air Dome Theatre in Ellsworth, KS

First-run theaters had a presence unmatched by smaller rural theaters.

218-seat Dakota Theater in Seneca, SD

Marcus Loew developed a brilliant strategy of acquiring and building first-run theaters, primarily in New York. While he did acquire and build theaters in other cities, almost all his theaters were in cities with lots of a specific kind of patron, clerical workers. His theater patrons were Modern Women: the urban clerks and other middle-class women that Garbo's acting spoke to most directly. Being an office clerk was one of the few well-paying jobs open to women at the time.

Balaban & Katz Paradise Theater in Chicago

Loew's dominated the New York market and had a concentration of first-run theaters in other office worker–heavy cities such as Washington, DC, Los Angeles, Cleveland, and Baltimore. Garbo films filled these theaters for lucrative multi-week runs. As much as the profitability of MGM rested on Garbo films, Loew's was even more dependent on Garbo. This will be explored in depth for the film *Love* below.

The industrial economy ran on the work of armies of clerks.

There is no easy set of statistics that can show that clerical workers went to first-run theaters. It is a logical, compelling deduction. Clerical workers were concentrated in New York and a few other major cities. Clerks and middle-class wives were the two segments of the female population with the disposable income to routinely go to first-run theaters.

The largest cities had large populations, but the country was nowhere near as concentrated in urban markets as America is today. The top twenty-five cities held 20.7 percent of the population in 1930. The top five cities, New York, Chicago, Philadelphia, Detroit, and Los Angeles, held 12.3 percent of the population.

Large cities had more workers who were well paid, thanks to the emerging industrial economy. Clerical workers had the highest average pay of any occupational category in 1930. Clerical workers had their own census category, making them easy to track. They were the best-compensated job category at an average salary of $2,239 ($42,420) per year. All non–farm workers, with clerks included, made an average of $1,473 ($27,907) per year.[606] Farm workers had an average annual wage of $587 ($1,121) in 1925. At 24 percent of the labor force, farm workers were an important part of the economy, just poorly paid. Half of clerks were women. Even with the significantly lower pay of women in clerical occupations compared to men, a female clerk took home much more than a male farmhand.

The number of female clerks increased almost 300 percent between 1910 and 1920.[607] In 1930, 4.1 percent of all jobs were clerical. Half of all clerical workers were women, which amounted to two million female clerks. What tasks did clerical workers fill? Data from the 1931 Canadian census revealed that 54 percent of female clerks in Toronto were stenographers or typists and 18 percent were bookkeepers or cashiers.[608] Clerical work was so attractive to women that, in 1925, fully 34 percent of high school girls in Muncie, Indiana, aspired to be clerical workers.[609]

Over 17 percent of America's clerks were employed in just the five boroughs of New York City. The five largest cities employed one-third. The twenty-five largest cities held 20.7 percent of the population and employed 55.8 percent of all clerical workers.

Clerical workers were not the only people who went to first-run theaters. Anyone with disposable income contributed to the first-run theater audience. This concentrated mass of relatively well-paid workers of the new manufac turing and trade-based economy (professionals, manufacturing workers, and transportation workers) was primarily urban and provided the audience for first-run theaters.

New York was important to the first-run market because, in addition to having the most clerks, New York dominated the fields of finance, business services, and corporate management.[610] Trade and transportation employed a further half a million New Yorkers. New York's port remained the biggest in the nation.[611] The 156 shipping companies located along the city's waterfront were handling almost half of America's international trade.[612] Almost a million New Yorkers worked in apparel and other manufacturing sectors.

This is the genius of Loew's theater strategy. Loew's dominated first-run exhibition in New York with 312 theaters (31 first run) and had theaters in cities that had 36 percent of all clerical workers in the country in 1929. The Loew's patron was not the average American. They were the workers in the new economy.

There is only spotty information on annual box office revenue from this era. In 1928 *Film Daily* reported total box office for the industry at $800 million ($14.9 billion).[613] Film historians John Sedgwick and Michael Pokorny estimated 1934 total box office at $518 million ($15.2 billion), showing the

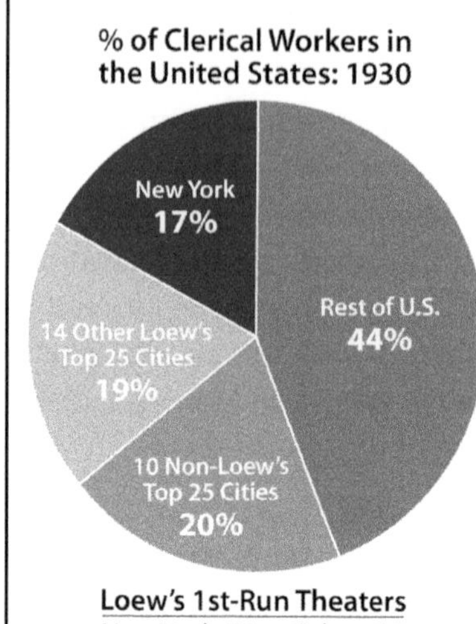

Sources: *"1930 Census: Volume 4. Occupations, by States. Reports by States, Giving Statistics for Cities of 25,000 or More,"* U.S. Census Bureau, accessed October 27, 2025, https://www.census.gov/library/publications/1933/dec/1930a-vol-04-occupations.

- *Film Daily Yearbook* (1930), 705–68;
- *Film Daily Yearbook* (1931), 707–821;
- *Cinema Treasures*, accessed October 27, 2025, www.cinematreasures.org.

devastating effect of the Depression on ticket sales.[614] We can estimate the importance of female clerks using reported information on frequency of attendance and ticket prices.

If America's two million female clerks (2 percent of the working population) attended first-run theaters forty times per year, paying $0.75 ($14.21) per ticket, they accounted for $60 million in ticket revenue. This would be about 9 percent of the industry ticket sales (assuming 1930 ticket revenue of $750 million [$14.2 billion today]) just by themselves, without dates, or middle-class wives, or women in other jobs. Therefore, while we don't have a modern audience analysis, female clerks, other women in professions like medicine and teaching, married middle-class women, and their dates and husbands were the core audience attending first-run theaters.

Garbo seems to have also resonated with the upwardly mobile Black audience in America. When six hundred guests of the Alpha Kappa Alpha sorority hosted a 1934 screening of *Queen Christina* in Houston, the audience was thrilled.[615]

In Garbo, Loew's and MGM now had the perfect actor to bring patrons to their first-run theaters. The only problem was that her contract only ran two more years.

Chapter 17 – Tumult

"I would like to do something unusual, something that has not been done. I would like to get away from the usual." [616]

— Greta Garbo to Mordaunt Hall,
film critic for *The New York Times*

A photo of herself that Garbo kept.

The six months after Garbo finished making *Flesh and the Devil* were personally and professionally tumultuous. She would fight with MGM over her contract, deal with Gilbert's erratic behavior, experience production problems on yet another film, and find herself deathly ill. Through this period the now twenty-one-year-old would display strength, grace, and composure.

By all accounts, the decision in October 1926 by MGM to cast Garbo in *Women Love Diamonds* (1927) was designed to pressure her into signing a long-term contract on its terms. The threat, either direct or implicit, was that MGM would feed her a series of second-rate roles, destroying her marketability by the end of her first contract.

Garbo told Ruth Biery about her reaction to being asked to film *Women Love Diamonds*:

> When I finished *Flesh and the Devil,* they wanted me to do *Women Love Diamonds* [originally titled *Diamond Handcuffs*]. I could not do that story. Four or five bad pictures and there would be no more of me for the American people.[617]

Garbo refused to report to the set.[618] After a short, informal standoff, MGM suspended her on November 6. She later said to an interviewer, "And I had a letter saying by not coming down to see the sketches I had refused to work and they could not pay me. What could I do?"[619]

Women Love Diamonds was put into production without Garbo and was a phenomenal flop when released in February 1927. One reviewer described the plot as "a silly opus that runs around in circles chasing its tail."[620]

Garbo knew how determined Mayer was to have his way. His manhandling of Mae Murray and others who crossed him over contract issues was well known. However, Mayer was not yet aware of how much Garbo wanted to have hers.

Garbo had come a long way in a very short time and had learned much about the way Hollywood did business. Back in Europe, Stiller had taken the lead in her negotiations with Mayer. Now, she was ready to speak for herself. It was a determined and decidedly less naïve person who arrived at the studio chief's office in late November 1926 for what Mayer had characterized as a little "chat."[621]

Mayer said he would get her better roles only if she scrapped her existing contract and signed a new five-year agreement. Garbo said she would consider it, but only if MGM both improved her roles and upped her salary to $5,000 ($92,000) a week, a figure still only half of that being paid to John Gilbert. Mayer offered $2,500 ($46,000), but Garbo held firm. Mayer fumed. He told her the idea of giving a "newcomer" that kind of money was out of the question. Furthermore, he threatened, her refusal of his offer meant that she would never get the kind of role she desired.

Finally, Garbo had heard enough and said something along the lines of, "I think I'll go home now."[622] And with that she did what few people had ever dared—she walked out on Louis B. Mayer.

Later, in a magazine interview, she said, "What I wanted was not to make a fuss. I hate fuss. I wanted only the opportunity to make good pictures."[623] Immediately, MGM placed her on suspension. Having rendered her, in effect, unemployed, the studio began hinting that she would be unable to renew her visa unless she capitulated.

Aside from Stiller, Gilbert, and a handful of others, the general view of the industry was that she was being unreasonable. If pressed, most would have agreed with—or been too fearful to dispute—Mayer's assessment that Garbo "had acted like a fool and ought to be spanked." This was representative of the paternalistic attitude studio chiefs took with their stars. Mayer probably thought he was unlikely to be bested by a twenty-one-year-old woman. "Unless she behaves herself," he concluded, "she will regret it."[624]

As Garbo's career was on the line, she sought advice and assistance from others: John Gilbert, screenwriter Carey Wilson, and Mauritz Stiller all advised her. The biggest addition to her team was Harry Edington, who became her agent in December 1926. Agents were a new force in Hollywood, and Edington, a pioneer in the profession, represented Garbo for free to build his reputation.

Outwardly, Garbo took all of this—the threats of deportation and the obstinate refusals to negotiate—with seeming indifference. To Mayer and MGM, she showed only stoic defiance. But her personal correspondence during this period shows a different Garbo, a young woman torn and exhausted by the loneliness of her situation. In a November 22, 1926, letter to her friend, Mimi Pollak, she wrote the following:

> I am so tired, so tired. I am so fed up with everything and so afraid because I am not old enough for all of this. I have also been very stupid. I have stayed at home from the studio for a while because

> I don't want to go there. They tried to get a hold of me and threatened me but I haven't gone there. . . . I hate being tied to the studio. Since I left, they have not paid me which I think is really cheap! . . . I don't know what the outcome will be . . . I do not know what will happen to me and to the studio situation.[625]

Seeking to help Garbo reach a reasonable resolution to her dispute with MGM, Mauritz Stiller penned a letter to Louis B. Mayer dated December 18, 1926. It reveals some interesting details of the developing situation. Stiller attempted to position himself as a neutral party, looking out for both parties' interests, though he would have spoken to Garbo about anything he sent.

His main point was that Garbo did not want to play only vamp roles. Stiller pointed out that Mayer hired her based on her performance in *Gösta Berling*, which was the antithesis of a vamp role. Stiller revealed that he had spoken to Thalberg on Garbo's behalf about her roles when he had been at MGM, and that Thalberg had assured him she would have more varied roles in the future.[626]

He reminded Mayer that Garbo had never been interested in a long-term contract, insisting on a three-year deal for the August 1925 contract.[627] A point not mentioned by Stiller in this letter was a key Garbo demand that she only make three films per year, rather than four.

Finally, Stiller delivered her proposed financial terms.[628] Taking his counsel, Garbo would sign a five-year contract that paid her $500 ($9,000) less per week for the first two years and $1,000 ($18,000) less per week for the final three years than what Harry Edington had proposed to MGM. However, we don't know the terms of Edington's financial offer. MGM declined Stiller's proposal.

In late January, Garbo agreed to return to MGM after it cast her in a silent version of *Anna Karenina* (1878), with Dimitri Buchowetzki as the director.[629] Since one of Garbo's issues had been the quality of the roles she was assigned, this gambit by MGM seemed to signify a change on its part. The Tolstoy novel was high literature, and the part of Anna Karenina was a good role. Edington counseled her to accept the assignment.

Variety used the headline "Greta Garbo Educated on Contract, Resumes."[630] As Garbo prepared to return to work, both *Variety* and *Exhibitors Herald* reported that MGM presented Garbo with a five-year contract and asked her to sign if she wanted to proceed with *Anna Karenina*. Otherwise, she would only get supporting roles.[631] Garbo departed again.

The original plan for this MGM silent version of *Anna Karenina* was to pair Garbo with Victor Varconi, a successful silent-era leading man, whom MGM had borrowed from Cecil B. DeMille to play Vronsky. However, Garbo's renewed walkout led MGM to abandon this pairing.[632]

Mayer launched a publicity campaign intended to cast Garbo's position in the worst possible light. It focused on her "unreasonable" position. MGM spun the story to make her look bad, with no corrective statement being offered by Garbo. While these articles were appearing in the press, the studio was sending Garbo a steady stream of reminders that her American work permit expired in July, which was just months away.

The tone media took in discussing Garbo during her contract disagreement with MGM is, not surprisingly for the times, dismissive of her. There was no discussion of Garbo's unique impact on MGM's and Loew's profits, or Garbo's willingness to finish her original deal.

Normally in the silent era, a star was made over time. For example, Mary Pickford first appeared on stage as a child, then appeared in her first film at the age of seventeen. At that point, in 1909, she made $100 ($3,000) per week. It was only five years later that she became a star, signing with Famous Players for $1,000 ($32,000) per week.[633] This slow climb to stardom was the path for most, including her most talented MGM contemporaries. It took Joan Crawford two years to reach stardom and Norma Shearer four.

In early March, MGM decided to test Garbo's stated proposition that she was willing to work as a supporting actress in a good film. She was cast in a small role in the Aileen Pringle film *His Brother from Brazil* (released as the lost film *Adam and Evil*, 1927). Pringle, who was friendly with Garbo from days spent together at Jack Gilbert's, objected. She realized that the publicity would naturally focus on Garbo, and not on Pringle.[634] Therefore, this plan was dropped, though Garbo had consented to working on the film. Through the entire confrontation Garbo proved willing to finish out her contract if MGM didn't undermine her career with bad roles.

Exasperated by MGM's tactics, Garbo cabled Robert Rubin at the Loew's office in New York on March 6, 1927. As Loew's managed the distribution of movies for MGM and was the studio's ultimate owner, in effect she went over

Flesh and the Devil packed theaters, making Garbo indispensable to MGM.

Mayer's head. Rubin was part of MGM management but was also Loew's corporate counsel.

She wrote,

> You no doubt already know that I have refused to sign the new five-year contract which Metro-Goldwyn offered me. Perhaps the New York office is not aware of the motive of my refusal to sign this contract and in order to stop false rumors I should like you to know what conditions really are. [MGM has] gone so far as to threaten me to the effect that I would not be given any good parts. . . . A five-year contract was ready several months ago, the terms of which were impossible and I immediately told them I could not sign it. The result was that every newspaper published long articles about my temperament and my refusal to playing roles. They also said that I refused to take the part of Anna Karenina which is indeed a false assertion as I asked them to let me take that part. . . . I was fighting to play three roles a year because my constitution is not strong and if I were to play as many roles as they see fit I know that I would break down under the strain and fail to do my work as it should be done. . . . To my deep regret I see that Metro Goldwyn has no understanding nor consideration for my situation though I have always tried to do my best in my pictures.[635]

Garbo was aware of the fact that the Loew's board was meeting two days after she sent her Sunday telegram. While MGM was a subsidiary of Loew's, the respective leaders, Nick Schenck and Mayer, didn't always have the same priorities. Garbo chose this moment to point out her value to Loew's. The one negotiating point she brings up is that, for health reasons, she only wants to make three films per year. The standard at the time was four. In the statement regarding "no understanding nor consideration," she is basically drawing a line. She further questions MGM's viability as a negotiating partner by bringing up its treatment of her in the press, implying it is unprofessional. She stops just short of calling Mayer unreliable.

Garbo Contracts Compared

	1925 contract			1927 contract		
Year	Weekly ($)	Annual ($)	2025 ($)	Weekly ($)	Annual ($)	2025 ($)
One	400	16,000	294,000	n/a	n/a	n/a
Two	600	24,000	440,000	2,000	100,000	1.8 million
Three	750	30,000	550,000	2,500	125,000	2.3 million
Four	n/a	n/a	n/a	4,000	200,000	3.7 million
Five	n/a	n/a	n/a	5,000	250,000	4.6 million
Six	n/a	n/a	n/a	6,000	300,000	5.5 million

Note: n/a is short for "not applicable."

Since all major decisions required the approval of Schenck, it must have been discussed, either at the March 8 board meeting or separately among Schenck, Rubin, and Mayer. They had to weigh the cost of a five-year contract more in keeping with Garbo's desires against the likely returns. The ticket sales from *Flesh and the Devil* must have made this an easy decision.

In late March, Robert Rubin came out to Hollywood from New York.[636] By March 29, MGM and Garbo had a new deal, hammered out by Rubin and Edington.[637]

In exchange for the five-year commitment it sought, MGM gave Garbo the money she had asked for, even backdating the contract to January of that year. In a face-saving gesture, however, the studio made weekly payments over fifty weeks, rather than the industry standard forty, thereby lowering the public perception of her salary. The straight math of being paid for fifty weeks instead of forty was equivalent to a 25 percent boost in annual pay.

There were several important differences between Garbo's new five-year contract and the original contract from August 26, 1925. The most obvious difference was money. Whereas the original contract had an escalating wage each year of $400/$600/$750, the new contract had both higher headline numbers—$2,000/$2,500/$4,000/$5,000/$6,000—and different parameters regarding when Garbo was paid. The 1925 deal required MGM to pay her salary for forty weeks per year and gave Garbo no guaranteed pause between films. The 1927 deal guaranteed Garbo fifty weeks' salary and a minimum of three weeks' rest between roles.

The net effect of the production and rest time provisions of the contract is that Garbo would make three films per year rather than the standard four. This is another way the value of her new salary was disguised. The 1927 contract addressed the possibility that Garbo would have to leave the country to renew her work visa status. If that requirement came to pass, MGM was obliged to pay her for eight weeks during her absence. In the event Garbo was not required to leave the country (which is what transpired), then she was entitled to a fifteen-week vacation after January 1, 1929. She was paid for eight weeks during her vacation.

Garbo standing by her home in Los Angeles.

In fact, Garbo made three films per year for 1928, 1929, and 1930. Due to vacation and contract timing, Garbo only worked on two films in 1931 and 1932.

Garbo's 1925 contract commenced basically at the start of

the 25–26 production year. Her work on *Flesh and the Devil* ran over into the next production year. The 1927 contract did not start so cleanly at the beginning of a production year. She did have a year of work at MGM under her belt, so one can't compare first years against each other as equal. One can observe that Garbo's pay for her second year at MGM increased fourfold with her new contract, from $24,000 ($440,000) annually to $100,000 ($1.8 million) annually. The following year exhibits a similar fourfold increase. The added years give Garbo a significant salary boost that increases in big steps with each additional year. All in the framework of a three-film output opposed to the prior four-film output.

There are four other ways the new contract differed from the first. Garbo was guaranteed star billing. MGM could buy insurance covering Garbo's death or incapacitation. Garbo no longer had to appear at premieres or other PR events. MGM could not loan her out to other studios. Although Garbo did not get contractual control over her roles, she was given some say in the selection of scripts, in the form of a verbal commitment.

Garbo had been considered star material from the start, and she hadn't disappointed in her first three films. When Garbo signed her five-year deal in 1927, MGM reframed its entire approach to her. This was a good business idea because it now had a significant financial commitment to her, and it wanted to get the best return possible.

Going forward, it would purchase or commission the best vehicles it could find. It assigned its top screenwriters to turn these properties into scripts. MGM assigned the best directors to Garbo projects. Garbo's leading men, though not always up to the task, were the best available. Huge sums were spent on sets, clothes, and jewelry. Cedric Gibbons and Adrian made Garbo shine through their skills in art direction and costume. Even the supporting casts were first rate.

Garbo projects were the focus of the studio in other ways. Many technicians worked on multiple Garbo projects. MGM had to arrange their schedules to make sure they were available.

During the silent film era, Garbo's movies returned more than twice the profit of the average MGM film, not accounting for Loew's exhibition profits. After the changeover to "talkies," they were at least three times more profitable than the studio's average production. The MGM ledgers reveal that her first three films delivered 13 percent of the company's revenue for the 1926 fiscal year (September to August). As discussed above, Garbo's importance to Loew's was probably even greater because her fans were more likely to see her films in Loew's-owned, first-run theaters; altogether, Garbo probably accounted for about 20 percent of Loew's consolidated revenue in the 25–26 year.

At this critical juncture after the formation of the integrated Loew's-MGM company, it could not afford to miss out on the potential Garbo offered. Loew's had just modified the executive bonus plans for the MGM management trio of Mayer, Thalberg, and Rubin to be based on a blend of Loew's and MGM's profits, not just those of MGM alone. Schenck wanted MGM to produce films with an eye toward filling his first-run theaters. Garbo continued to deliver the lucrative first-run audience to Loew's theaters throughout her time at MGM.

Garbo did eloquently sum up the experience in her interview with Ruth Biery:

> Then a very kind friend told me about a man who would understand both me and the people of this country. I had a lawyer to manage me up to this time. But this new man, they said, knew all about the studio and all about the making of pictures. He had been in Europe a long time and would sympathize and understand that all I wanted was no trouble and just a chance to make good stories. So I went to see Mr. Harry Edington, and after talking to me every day, almost, for more than a week, and coming to believe that I was not all the papers had said about me, he said he would handle all of my things for me. My contracts, my money, my work,—everything. You do not know what that means to a girl who knows nothing about this big country and this big American studio business.
>
> Since then, I have not had trouble. Because he understands both their business and me and my business.
>
> But before I employed him I was home seven months without pay. I did not say anything or do anything. And the papers always said I want money.
>
> I was terribly restless. I figured that maybe the next moment I would be packing my trunks. I was so low, as you say, that I thought would break. But it's like when you are in love. Suppose the man

> you love does something to hurt you. You think you will break it off; but you don't do it.
>
> Finally, they call me and say they have a story. I read it and went out and asked what part I was to play and they said the little part. Aileen Pringle and Lew Cody were to play the big parts. Mr. Edington tell me to do it, so I did not say a word, but tried on the dresses and was all ready to play the little part in the picture, when Miss Pringle said she would not do it.
>
> Then they called me and said I was impossible and could not be handled. For the first time I answered Mr. Mayer back. I said I had all my clothes fitted and was ready to play the little part. What more did they want? I am very sorry I answered back. I guess I did not understand them. It was all because I speak one language and they speak another. And the newspaper men who print all the bad stories, they could not understand either.
>
> They said it was a new contract they wanted. So Mr. Edington fixed up a new contract, for five years. Because it was not money I had wanted in the first place, money was not so important. But Mr. Edington's contract did give me more money than when I came to this country. They had a cartoon of me in my country, holding out my hand with many American dollars. They thought I get five thousand dollars a week. That is funny. Now Mr. Edington makes us understand one another and we are all very happy.[638]

In the midst of Garbo's contract negotiations, late in the evening of January 30, 1927, while returning from a weekend in Tijuana, Mexico, with three friends, Jack Gilbert rolled his car into a ditch north of La Jolla, California, by the Scripps Research Institute. The party included Donald Ogden Stewart, screenwriter and longtime friend of Gilbert's; Stewart's wife, Beatrice; and Beatrice's younger sister, Marjorie.

The two women received glass cuts and Beatrice suffered a broken kneecap. They were hospitalized at Scripps Memorial Hospital in La Jolla.[639] The two men were not reported to be injured.[640] Marjorie Ames's relationship with Jack Gilbert is unknown. In the accident report, she was described as a "member of the film colony"[641] and as "well known in motion picture circles."[642] But Marjorie Ames doesn't appear to have had any sort of Hollywood career. While she was about nineteen and Gilbert was twenty-nine, the age difference is not overly remarkable. Marjorie was only two or three years younger than Garbo.

The crash received brief coverage in a few papers in Southern California beyond the San Diego papers. No mention of the crash appeared in *Film Daily, Motion Picture News*, or *Moving Picture World*. In *Exhibitors Herald* and *Variety*, Marjorie was mistakenly identified by her sister's name, Beatrice, erasing Marjorie from the story. Beatrice herself appeared just as "Mrs. Stewart." Considering that at this point John Gilbert was one of the leading male actors in Hollywood, this lack of coverage must have been due to MGM's intercession.

While the crash and injuries were unfortunate, unspoken was that Gilbert had spent the weekend in Tijuana with a young and attractive woman. Whatever chance there might have been of a permanent relationship between Gilbert and Garbo slipped further from possibility.

Garbo and Gilbert remained friends and on February 3 attended the Los Angeles premiere of *Flesh and the Devil* together.

While everything regarding Garbo's relationship with Gilbert was falling apart, her romance with Stiller seems to have rekindled, according to an undated letter likely sent between April 18 and September 17, 1927. In this letter Garbo informs Pollak that she thinks she will be married to Stiller, but it is not a simple situation: "I believe I will already be married to Moje by the time you receive this letter. I am not exactly happy. My God, if I could just talk to you. I am going crazy, living without everything I like and care about."[643] However, she later writes to Pollak again, saying, "I am never going to marry!!"[644]

Whatever the duration of this rekindled version of the Garbo-Stiller romance, it didn't last. We know nothing else other than what Garbo recorded about this development in her letters.

At some point in mid-February, Gilbert was hospitalized. The ostensible reason was for appendicitis, but Gilbert maintained that he would not need surgery, and he could recover through nonmedical efforts. Gilbert reportedly got out of the hospital in mid-March and departed for a three-week vacation in Canada.[645]

Then Jack Gilbert got himself arrested the night of April 10, 1927. The details vary depending on whose account you read, but all agreed Gilbert was irrational, inebriated, and obsessed with Garbo. These accounts were related years after the events.

Colleen Moore recalled that an inebriated Jack had stopped by her house, just down the road from his own, to announce that he and Garbo were getting married, apparently that day. He doesn't seem to have bothered with formalities like marriage licenses or officiants. There was no wedding. Gilbert got even more drunk and then headed over to Garbo's apartment at the Miramar Hotel in Santa Monica. After he arrived, he decided to climb up the façade of the hotel to her balcony. As Gilbert climbed, Stiller, who was present, threw him back down to the ground. He then drove to Carey Wilson's house, where Wilson and his wife, Carmelita, patched him up. Gilbert wasn't done; he then got hold of a gun at Wilson's house and prepared to drive back to the Miramar to kill Stiller. Wilson got the gun from Gilbert but couldn't keep him from getting back in his car. At this point, the Beverly Hills police pulled him over and arrested him.[646]

Donald Ogden Stewart's version of events was that Gilbert left Colleen Moore's house and proceeded to his. There he drank brandy and was discussing a Pieter Bruegel reproduction that Donald and Beatrice Stewart had purchased in Vienna. He then suddenly departed for Garbo's apartment. Stewart said he had "that wild look in his eyes which betokened that the internal emotional pressure was approaching the safety-valve point."[647]

Stewart next heard from Gilbert indirectly: The police had Gilbert in a cell where he was lecturing on art. He had asked the police to call and ask Stewart to bring the Bruegel to make a point.[648] So at two a.m. they called Stewart, who went down to the station to see after Gilbert's status.

The story in the press washed out any mention of Garbo or Stiller and just had a drunk Gilbert appearing at the police station asking for an unnamed house guest of his to be arrested.

Gilbert himself said to the *Los Angeles Times* as he was released from jail, "I must have been laboring under a hallucination and looking for trouble."[649] Gilbert was quoted slightly differently in the *Los Angeles Daily News*: "I was just lonesome and went to the station and made an ass of myself."[650]

With Garbo signed, plans for *Anna Karenina* resumed. At the end of March, Ricardo Cortez was announced as the male lead, replacing Varconi.[651] Just before the start of filming the events leading up to the arrest of Gilbert took place. Filming began April 14, and Gilbert was sentenced to jail for a week on Tuesday, April 19.

MGM was forced to suspend filming on *Anna Karenina* after Garbo became ill and could not report to the set on April 25. Garbo's doctor told MGM that she had an intestinal infection due to pernicious anemia.[652] Pernicious anemia is an autoimmune condition where the body does not produce a protein called the intrinsic factor. It is incurable. Without intrinsic factor the body can't absorb enough vitamin B12 to create red blood cells. Untreated patients rarely lived for three years past the initial diagnosis.

Garbo was fortunate because treatments, based on eating raw liver or liver juice, had been developed the prior year. Liver concentrate injections were developed in 1935 and finally vitamin B12 shots would replace liver in the 1950s. Given how far Garbo's illness had progressed, several weeks of rest were the only solution.

Though she never talked about them, ongoing health issues related to pernicious anemia were a factor throughout her life. Pernicious anemia can lead to several gastrointestinal problems and also menstruation-related problems. Garbo suffered from both.

Ricardo Cortez briefly spoke about working with Garbo at this point. Writer Dorothy Calhoun wrote, "Ricardo Cortez, in white and gold uniform, strolled by. 'I like her,' he says; 'she never talks scandal, she never talks personalities, she never talks at all to speak of.'"[653]

Years later, Cortez told historian Kevin Brownlow, "We were on *Karenina* for six weeks and she became ill and Mr. Thalberg asked me to wait around. He called me in and said, 'I don't know how long this girl is going to be out, and I'd like to put you in a film with Lon Chaney. It's a good part, entirely up to you.' She was down with [pernicious] anemia of sorts. So I went into [*Mockery* (1927)], and they threw out what I had taken with her and began [Karenina] all over again."[654]

While Cortez had been assigned to *Anna Karenina* around March 22, only ten days of filming had taken place with this cast, as confirmed by the existence of scene stills with April 1927 negative dates. In a quick succession of changes, Buchowetzki was out as director, Edmund Goulding was brought in, and a whole new cast was assembled.

Garbo was not happy with Buchowetzki and wrote to Mimi Pollak during the filming of the scrapped version that he "is not a good director."[655]

Irving Thalberg and Dimitri Buchowetzki also had a difference of opinion as to the direction of *Anna Karenina* that seems to have come to a head while Garbo was ill. After a meeting between them, Buchowetzki either quit or was fired.[656] Buchowetzki had developed a reputation for being temperamental by this point in his career. There was a nearly four-year gap in Buchowetzki's life after he left *Anna Karenina* during which he directed no films. At some point he returned to Europe and, in 1930, resumed directing films for Paramount there. He left Europe in October 1931 and died in Los Angeles on January 1, 1932.[657] His return was unremarked upon and there were no press reports regarding his death.

Thalberg had spent the three-week break wrestling with ways to salvage the production with the already completed footage. When no practical solution was found, he started over.[658]

Chapter 18 – *Anna Karenina* Becomes *Love*

"I'd adore to eat right now, but I can't.
I happen to have a very peculiar stomach department,
I haven't got enough things to digest food with. . . .
If you don't have hydrochloric acid or whatever it is,
then the stomach goes on strike." [659]

— Greta Garbo

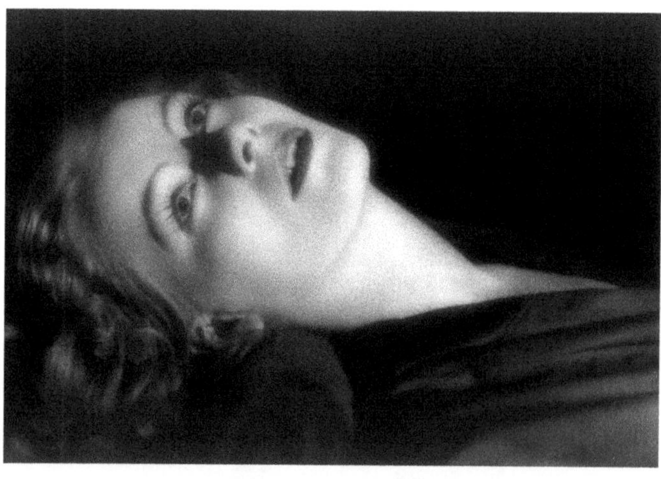

A portrait of Garbo by Ruth Harriet Louise for the MGM film *Love*. Courtesy of the Greta Garbo family archive.

The kind of close-up that troubled some reviewers.
The audience loved it. Photo by William Grimes.

Between the contract standoff, her illness, and production issues, a new Garbo film would not be released for nearly a year. Her return to the screen would be a silent classic.

Garbo missed three and a half weeks before she could return to work. Filming of the *Anna Karenina* project resumed about May 18 with a new script rewritten by Frances Marion. A new name for the film was adopted: *Love.*

Norman Kerry was cast as the male lead. Kerry was a serviceable actor who starred in many silent films. However, this version was also scrapped after June 7. There is no discussion in the trade press regarding what the issue was, but one would assume that Kerry was not the right actor for the part. In his place Thalberg brought in John Gilbert.

Thalberg's decision to replace Kerry with John Gilbert was a curious choice given the events of April. The Gilbert version didn't start filming until June 22.[660]

As adapted for film, *Love* has little relationship to the Tolstoy novel from which it was ostensibly derived. *Anna Karenina* tells a different story. Gone in *Love* are subplots involving other couples, which were Tolstoy's device for exploring what made a happy marriage. The focus in the film is on the course of Anna's life: finding Vronsky; falling in love; leaving Karenin; the conflicting forces of her maternal love for her son, her love for Vronsky, and the problems of social mores; her sacrifice for Vronsky's career; and the inevitable consequences of her illicit affair. Tolstoy's son, upon viewing a preview of the film in October 1927, objected to the changes and declared them an insult.[661]

Love uses close-ups extensively to reveal the shifts in Anna's state of mind. This is really the story of her thought process, exchanging security for love. Not everyone liked the emphasis on close-ups. *Film Spectator* complained, "If it had contained about half a dozen close-ups, instead of over three hundred, it would have been a good picture."[662]

While Edmund Goulding was the official director, he related that "every day at lunch and every evening at dinner while *Love* was being filmed, she, Jack Gilbert, and myself were together. We talked of nothing but the picture. I knew how I wanted it done, but I didn't give Garbo orders. She was given to understand that it was a mutual responsibility, this thing of directing. She rose to the suggestion like the great woman she is. The actual directing was done over the dinner table, not on the sets. When we assembled for work in the morning, it was all settled what we were going to do. We simply went and did it."[663]

Photoplay reported that Goulding let Gilbert direct portions of *Love*, particularly the love scenes with Garbo.[664] Gilbert had been a film actor since the mid-teens. He wrote and directed *Love's Penalty* (1921), an unsuccessful film, and had another half dozen writing credits.[665]

A lot of ground was covered between Stiller throwing Gilbert off Garbo's balcony in April and not only working together on *Love*, but perhaps even Gilbert directing Garbo in scenes instead of the appointed director. Garbo and Gilbert clearly were able to separate their personal and professional lives.

Love was a relatively quick production by all accounts, with filming wrapping up on July 25. The last dated scene-still negative is from July 21.[666]

While production details for August are not known, it seems that extensive retakes were required. In September, George Fawcett was called in to reshoot scenes that added a comic element to the story.[667] There may have been additional edits and retakes after that. The preview that Count Ilya Tolstoy viewed before complaining about the changes to the story took place in the first few days of October. The New York premiere was not until November 29.

Russell Ball was brought in to take additional portraits of Garbo in August 1927.

Love was filmed with two endings. The original ending flowed from the book, with Anna committing suicide. But at this time, rural audiences did not like films that ended in tragedy. Thalberg later related the following to students at USC:

> There was such a demand for the happy ending and there was a great deal invested in the picture.... It seems pointless to argue with the public, we acceded to the demand...which proved to be more successful in smaller towns.[668]

In this alternate ending, Anna and Vronsky are reunited after the untimely death of her husband. The ending shown was the choice of each exhibitor. Though in a few markets censors specified the ending.

Welford Beaton wrote in his Hollywood insiders' magazine, *Film Spectator*, that when Edmund Goulding took over production of *Love*, the production already had $220,000 ($4.0 million) charged against it for the Buchowetzki version, and that Goulding spent $180,000 ($3.3 million) on his version.[669]

However, this total combined cost of $400,000 ($7.3 million) doesn't add up to the $488,000 ($9.0 million) cost for *Love* recorded in the Mannix ledger. It's not even close. Where are costs for the two weeks of production with Norman Kerry? Plenty of additional potential costs may have been assigned to *Love* from the period before Garbo signed her five-year contract with MGM.

While Beaton may not have captured the full assigned cost, but rather some intermediate production cost, he seems to believe he has an apples-to-apples comparison of the costs for the Buchowetzki and Goulding versions. Based on the assigned cost, the film was made not just twice, but two and a half times.

The usual process was to use the scene stills to promote the film release and to use the portraits taken at the end of filming, often using the costumes, to build the fan base for the star. MGM's problem as it approached the release of *Love* was that it really didn't have enough images of Garbo. It had portraits and scene stills from three films and a few images from New York. By the time filming of the final version of *Love* got underway in June 1927, MGM had not created a fresh image of Garbo since the *Flesh and the Devil* portrait session in September 1926.

MGM rectified this situation by shooting on-set portraits during the filming in July. Clarence Sinclair Bull, at the time head of the scene-still department, took these posed portraits. Unlike with normal scene stills, Bull's images are not in the flow of the script. MGM also supplemented the standard post-production portraits by Ruth Harriet Louise with a set made by Russell Ball, who had moved to Los Angeles.

Loew's chose to open *Love* at the Embassy Theatre in New York on November 29. It was a smaller, intimate house with 556 seats. By comparison, the flagship Capitol seated 5,230. At the Embassy, *Love* was run without stage shows, prologue, or intermission, making it cost-effective for Loew's. *Love* ran at the Embassy even as the film made its way through the zone progression in general release outside New York. Demand was so high that ticket agencies handled sales, which was rare for films.[670] *Love* ran fifteen and a half weeks at the Embassy, selling out the theater for almost the entire run. For most weeks, the theater exceeded capacity with standing patrons.[671]

A few weeks after *Love's* run at the Embassy ended, it ran at Loew's large New York flagship theater, the Capitol. This two-week run included a stage show, as was standard for every film shown at the Capitol.

After a break in the schedule, *Love* went into general release in New York on May 10. The film worked its way through the various theaters over the following months.

Garbo films generated outsized exhibition profits. Her audience was primarily urban women who could afford a first-run ticket. As was shown earlier, first-run theaters delivered most of the profits in exhibition.

It is difficult to take the stated idea that Garbo drew an urban audience in first-run theaters and back it up with data. Ideally, there would be box office numbers by theater. Sadly, this data does not exist. However, Garbo's power to draw an audience to Loew's first-run theaters in New York may be demonstrated using the number of days a film was shown at a theater, available through *Variety* (for Manhattan premiere theaters and Brooklyn newspapers (for Brooklyn and Queens theaters).[672] This technique has been validated by film historians. Using a combination of ticket sale reports from the premiere theaters and theater schedules for the Loew's first-run theaters in Brooklyn and Queens the power of Garbo in New York's first-run theaters is clear.

A somewhat comparable film was the Ramon Novarro/Norma Shearer vehicle *The Student Prince.*[673] Norma Shearer was just emerging as a star for MGM. Her audience was like Garbo's, skewed toward female and urban. Comparing the exhibition results of the two films demonstrates Garbo's unique box office profitability.

The Student Prince was released right before *Love.* They are well matched in terms of their total domestic film rentals. *Love* delivered $946,000 ($17.4 million) while *The Student Prince* brought in $894,000 ($16.4 million). So, *Love's* domestic rentals were only 6 percent higher. Foreign earnings are left out of this analysis, though *Love's* foreign rentals were 10 percent higher.

Both films received similar distribution treatment in New York. They were first shown as a special feature, *The Student Prince* at the Astor Theatre and *Love* at the Embassy Theatre.[674] Then, each went on to a two-week run at the Capitol Theatre. Finally, they were released to the other first-run theaters in New York.

As a special feature, *The Student Prince* had ticket revenue of $170,700 ($3.1 million) at the Astor Theatre while *Love* had ticket revenue of $162,100 ($3.0 million) at the Embassy, one block away. Though these special runs were similar, there were important differences. The Astor was a larger theater, seating 1,141; and *The Student Prince* ran for thirteen and a half weeks. *Love* ran for fifteen and a half weeks at higher prices, at the cozy 556-seat Embassy. *The Student Prince* ran over both Thanksgiving and Christmas while *Love* ran over Christmas and New Year. *Love* screened just the film with an orchestra. The more elaborate show for *The Student Prince* had the orchestra plus a large male chorus, which also put on a prologue, so its so its performance costs were higher than those for the film-only Love. The assumption is that

Love* Exhibition Dates Compared with *The Student Prince

Theater	Seats	*Love* days	*Student Prince* days	*Love* seat total	*Student Prince* seat total
Metropolitan	3,500	7	13	24,500	45,500
Alpine	2,200	4	2	8,800	4,400
Bay Ridge	2,500	7	4	17,500	10,000
Bedford	2,100	7	4	14,700	8,400
Bijou	1,480	7	2	10,360	2,960
Broadway	1,559	7	2	10,913	3,118
Gates	3,000	7	4	21,000	12,000
Hillside	2,563	7	4	17,941	10,252
Oriental	3,000	7	4	21,000	12,000
Palace	2,500	7	4	17,500	10,000
Premier	3,000	7	4	21,000	12,000
Willard	2,168	7	4	15,176	8,672
Boro Park	2,750	4	2	11,000	5,500
Brevoort	2,000	4	2	8,000	4,000
Coney Island	2,500	4	2	10,000	5,000
Warwick	2,000	4	2	8,000	4,000
Total	**n/a**	**n/a**	**n/a**	**237,390**	**157,802**

Note: n/a is short for "not applicable."

the smaller theater also cost less to operate. Also working in favor of *The Student Prince* were publicity events. The wedding of Norma Shearer to MGM producer Irving Thalberg took place as *The Student Prince's* run at the Astor started. A theatrical version of *The Student Prince* was being exhibited in several Shubert theaters in metro New York as the film was released. Both worked to increase the audience.

Both films ran two weeks at the Capitol Theatre (seating of 5,230) at "popular prices" after their special presentations. Again, the results for the two films are almost indistinguishable. While *The Student Prince* brought in $137,700 ($2.5 million), *Love* brought in $137,000.

The advantage of *Love* in generating revenue for Loew's can be seen in its first-run theaters in Brooklyn and Queens. Both films appeared in the same set of Loew's first-run theaters, but *Love* ran for more days in most theaters.

Loew's was versed in maximizing theater revenues by booking films for exactly the optimal number of days in each theater. When a film's audience fell off, it was pulled and replaced. By looking at the number of seats and days the film was put before audiences, one can get a general idea of how well each film did in the outer boroughs of New York in terms of ticket sales. The number of days each film played in Brooklyn and Queens can be found in the Brooklyn newspapers. Across all but one of the sixteen Loew's first-run theaters in these two outer boroughs, Love played more days.[675] By multiplying the seats for each theater by the number of days each film ran, in total Love was shown to 50 percent more seats. While one doesn't know if those seats were filled, research has shown that this is a good proxy. The difference delivered profit to Loew's.

If they were all filled across all these theaters at $0.50 each, those eighty thousand additional seats delivered $40,000 ($735,000) in ticket revenue. Recall from earlier that a first-run theater seat delivered three times the exhibition revenue as a seat at a second-run theater, with not much difference in film rental cost. At equal rental revenue, a film that delivered a larger first-run audience was much more valuable to the exhibitor. Garbo was that difference maker.

The theaters would not have been dark, and there is no way to really capture the exact value of *Love* compared to the average replacement film. Loew's was running *Love* for full weeks because it filled more seats than a replacement. Sitting in those seats outside of midtown were the female clerks of New York.

This represents just the Loew's theaters in Brooklyn and Queens. Similar Loew's theaters existed in Manhattan and the Bronx, but their exhibition schedules are not as readily available.

Love was not an average film. It was one of the most profitable silent films MGM produced. MGM's rental profit from *Love*, which also included foreign revenue, was $571,000 ($10.7 million).[676] On the exhibition side, the net box office revenue for Loew's just at the Embassy and Capitol Theatres was $300,000 ($5.6 million), so the estimated profit from just these two theaters was probably about $100,000 ($1.9 million), alone equal to 17 percent of MGM's profit on the film worldwide. *Love* went on to generate ticket sales across the entire Loew's network of first-run theaters serving New York and other female clerk–dominated cities.

The upscale female audience that clustered around Loew's-owned theaters in New York and across the country delivered better ticket revenue to Loew's for every Garbo film.

Comparing these two films makes the strength of Garbo's appeal to the feminine urban audience crystal clear. The audience for *The Student Prince* wasn't that different from that for *Love*. Norma Shearer's appeal was not radically different from Garbo's. She delivered the same urban female fan base. Yet, *Love* dominated first-run ticket sales in the outer boroughs of New York.

Variety in its review spoke of the audience that *Love* drew:

> *Love*, plus Gilbert, plus Garbo, is a clarion call to shoppers. Shoppers mean women, and women mean matinees. Big ones. Try and keep the femmes away from this one. They've all apparently got a Gilbert-Garbo complex tucked away somewhere. The men too. They like Garbo, but the girls are going to pay off this production cost, and some more besides. And how often do the exhibits get a "matinee" picture?[677]

In most cities, *Love* was strong in first-run theaters (where it played to full houses), was held over for additional weeks, and drew many patrons to multiple shows.

In an experiment, MGM broadcast the entire film over the radio on December 20. Announcer Ted Husing described the action of the film as it took place, with a live orchestra performing the score. This was broadcast on New York station WPAP and over a network of stations in other cities.[678]

In the *New York Daily News*, the reviewer wrote that Garbo, in *Love*, "surpasses all other efforts in this altogether lovely screen interpretation of Tolstoy's *Anna Karenina*."[679] *The Film Daily* had no doubt of its box office potential: "Garbo and Gilbert make a striking team. The vehicle gives them both opportunities to display their talents and indulge in some hectic love scenes."[680]

Not everyone liked *Love*. To *Motion Picture* magazine, "This is a pretty bad movie." It found fault with the abridgment of the original Tolstoy story. Its only redeeming value was Garbo: "Because Greta is surprising, and her grace and beauty and fine acting make a cheap, melodramatic picture into something at least interesting, if not good."[681]

The New York Times focused on Garbo in its review of *Love*, pointing out that her characterization of Anna dominates the story:

> Miss Garbo's singularly fine acting held the audience in unusual silence. It can be said that Miss Garbo is ably supported by John Gilbert, but throughout this photo drama it is the portrait of Anna that is the absorbing feature. Other characterizations and even the story itself take second place when compared to the work of this Nordic player. Miss Garbo is elusive. Her heavy-lidded eyes, the cold whiteness of her face and her svelte figure compel interest in her actions.[682]

What Gilbert always had, regardless of the state of their romance, was a deep respect for Garbo as a person and as an actor. An unknown interviewer captured Jack Gilbert's analysis of Garbo's acting skill for the *Los Angeles Evening Express* in early 1928, after their second project together. Gilbert said,

Garbo and Gilbert in the film *Love*. Photo by William Grimes.

> Frankly I see nothing mysterious about Miss Garbo and her unusual ability. As an actress she merely combines intelligent thinking with her striking personality and without any more movement than is absolutely necessary portrays the characters assigned to her. If there is any secret to her phenomenal success on the screen it is in the fact that she is capable of making her thoughts register where a great many stars depend on definite action. Although she never makes a move in a closeup, for example, it is easy to read her thoughts and see the effect of some particular situation on her mind.[683]

Garbo had agreed to not return to Sweden until the end of 1928. She would make four additional films before she left. Garbo also began to settle into her American life.

Chapter 19 – Working with Garbo

"She sat out there [in an old whaling boat on location] and talked to us about our lives, our wives, our children. I thought to myself "Boy, if this had been Crawford or Bette Davis, they'd have been screaming; what the hell are you doing keeping me out here?" Because she was there from about 8:30 until noon before we ever got a shot. She just sat there and talked; it didn't bother her" [684]

— Gil Perkins, treasurer, Screen Actors Guild

Garbo and Clark Gable filming *Susan Lenox,* with the crew just off camera. Photo by Milton Brown.

The impact Garbo had on film professionals was extraordinary. From early in her time at MGM, everyone wanted to watch her work. They understood that she was special. Before her third film was even released Doris Markham wrote,

> Yet today, Greta Garbo is one of the most significant figures among the women of the screen—if not the most significant. It is nothing that has been said or written about her. It is nothing that she has done—yet. It is just the inexplicable charm and power of a rare personality. Everyone feels, without being able to explain the fact, that this slim girl is one of the children of Destiny—as definitely precious as a piece of pale green jade.[685]

She liked working with professionals in the technical crews. The set was the focus of most of her interactions when a film was in production:

> "I know so few American men," she answered frankly, sitting up attentively and clasping her knees with her slim, tapering fingers. "The carpenters, the electricians, all who work on the sets, I love. The many others who take part in the pictures—just a scene—I do not know them off the set. You do not believe what I say? But I am telling you the truth. When I am working, I see no one.—I cannot. I am too tired. I am at the studio at eight in the morning. I get home late in the evening. I go to bed exhausted."[686]
>
> "Between pictures I like to be quiet. I do not like many people. I cannot endure crowds and people peering at me while I dine and dance. No, when I go out it is to little places where I am not known. Also, I like to swim, to ride, to read. Always plenty to do, but not with the crowds."[687]

With her new contract, MGM gave Garbo its best resources. Garbo didn't just get MGM's best directors and actors. William Daniels, one of MGM's best cinematographers, worked on twenty-one of twenty-six Garbo films. She had costume designer Adrian's full attention. Cedric Gibbons personally worked on her sets.

The crews on Garbo films were often carried over to the next film. The same electricians, grips, carpenters, gaffers, sound engineers, and other specialists worked on Garbo film after Garbo film.

William Daniels would tell a writer, "Most of Miss Garbo's technical workers are veterans of many of her pictures, like myself. We have worked together so long that we have perfected systems of teamwork, and understand each other without having to pass around many orders."[688]

The ambiance was lighthearted, with several running gags. One example is an electrician who screamed whenever approached by Daniels, as if Daniels had hurt him.[689]

Clarence Brown recalled another running joke: "[There was] an electrician, and his face looked like the map of Ireland. Garbo used to kid him all the time. She'd say to him, 'Are you Scandinavian?'"[690]

When filming *Grand Hotel* (1932), director Edmund Goulding was acting through the scene where John Barrymore first kisses Garbo, playing her role. Barrymore said his line, "I love you." And he and Goulding brought their lips together but stopped short of a kiss. Garbo cracked up the crew by interjecting, "Well, Eddie, what are you waiting for?"[691]

Floyd Porter, who was Bill Daniels's gaffer on several Garbo films, recalled that after each scene, she would pat him on the back.[692]

While Garbo at times would be taciturn on the set for the entire shoot, she could also be playful. When her co-star in *The Kiss* (1929), Lew Ayres, arrived on set for their first scene, he was literally thrust before the camera to kiss Garbo. After the take, she turned to the assistant director and said, "I wonder if you would introduce me to this boy, we have not met." (Ayres was only three years younger.) For the rest of the production Garbo periodically turned to him and teasingly asked, "Have we met?"[693]

The crew didn't just stay on the set. They went out. Adela Rogers St. Johns reported,

> She likes to go with the gang on her picture—the men—to Italian restaurants where they serve good spaghetti, or to a Culver City lunch counter where the corned beef and cabbage is exceptional.[694]

When Garbo was filming *Flesh and the Devil*, the wife of one of the electricians went into labor and he had to leave the set. According to Clarence Bull,

> Five years later this same electrician, working on another Garbo film [either *Inspiration* (1931) or *Romance* (1930)], was amazed

> when the star came over and asked him how his little girl was doing and what her name was. This side of the so-called Swedish sphinx was rarely revealed to the movie public. But once the lovely woman touched you with this intimacy, you could never forget it. It involved the look in her eyes, the smile on her lips, even the color of her skin, as she expressed interest in you.[695]

Garbo clearly cared about her crews and was attuned to their morale on the set. During the filming of *Queen Christina* she was willing to sacrifice a full day of shooting for group morale. According to Gil Perkins, she had this conversation with the assistant director:

> "Charlie," she said, "the boys are very unhappy—they want to go to the football game today," and Charlie Darian said, "So what!" And she said, "Well, if I get sick and go home, can the boys go to the football game?" And he said, "No goddamnit, Greta, they can't! If you get sick and go home, we'll shoot something else. They're not going to go to the football game just 'cause you go home!"

A crowd gathers to watch Garbo film *The Single Standard.*
Photo by James Manatt. Courtesy of the Greta Garbo family archive.

> "Oh," she said, "well, all right, Charlie, but if it will get them to the football game, I will go home." But it didn't get 'em to the football game, so we worked all day.[696]

When filming ended, Garbo gave everyone in the crew a gift.[697] One crew member recalled getting a watch for one film, a tapestry for a second, and then an overnight case for a third.[698] Garbo gave Bill Daniels a beautiful gold cigarette case with an engraving inside that reads, "To 'Bill' Daniels, With Sincere Appreciation, Greta Garbo."[699]

One final story underlines Garbo's connection to her crews. In 1959, eighteen years after her last film, she had stopped by the home of director Jean Negulesco, a home Garbo had sold to him and his wife, Dusty. Negulesco had just wrapped a film for MGM and that night was hosting a party for the cast and crew. (Probably *Count Your Blessings* [1959], which starred two Garbo friends, Deborah Kerr and Maurice Chevalier.)

Negulesco related that he said,

> "G.G., this is still your house. The boys tonight are your friends. They worked with you and for you. Why don't you receive your friends in your house? Be the hostess. They will love to see you again."
>
> For a moment she was serious, remembering. I insisted: "Cole Porter is coming, too. He adores you."
>
> She smiled again. "Maybe."
>
> My sizzling Rumanian dishes in the kitchen called me. G.G. picked up her oranges and left.
>
> That evening she was the first one to arrive. We went straight to the bar and helped ourselves to another double iced Polish vodka.
>
> Dusty drifted away to meet the other guests at the door: "Garbo is here. Don't look surprised. Don't make much of it." And they didn't. They acted as if they had just left her at the studio that afternoon. Garbo was among friends. There was no tension from her. But there was held-in great excitement among her boys. What a story to tell friends: "We dined last night with Garbo."[700]

When Garbo first arrived in Hollywood, the technology of filming was such that the bright lights blotted out any observers watching the production.

Plenty of MGM employees wandered down to see Garbo at work for her first few films. As technology improved, actors were able to work under less intense lighting. Suddenly, the spectators behind the lights were no longer invisible. It was at this point that Garbo began insisting that sets be closed. She was hardly alone among actors in this sensitivity. Conrad Nagel, her co-star in two silent films, recounted, "She wasn't the only one. Nobody wants people to see them stumbling about in a scene, finding the way through."[701]

Garbo did, however, allow the fewest exceptions. She turned away studio executives and even close friends. For instance, Salka Viertel was not allowed on her sets. When Rex O'Malley asked her during the filming of *Camille* why she was so insistent on closed sets, she replied, "It destroys the illusion."[702] Yet she also felt comfortable having *New York Times* film critic Mordaunt Hall on set.

Somewhat surprisingly, Garbo was now an MGM Studio insider. She was comfortable with Mayer, Thalberg, Mannix, and other executives, and they with her. The crucible of contract negotiations led to a mutual respect and an appreciation of the talents each brought to the enterprise of filmmaking.

Much of Garbo's interaction with the executives took place either in formal meetings or less formal get-togethers on the studio grounds. For example, in January 1932 people assembled in Marion Davies's bungalow on the MGM lot. The group included Davies, William Randolph Hearst, Perc Westmore, Greta Garbo, John Gilbert, Louis B. Mayer, and Irving Thalberg. They were about to leave for a preview of the film Davies had just completed, *Polly of the Circus* (1932).[703]

The assembled group is interesting for two reasons. First, years after their romance had ended, Garbo and Gilbert still socialized together. Second, though it was clearly not a Garbo film work event, Garbo was present at these kinds of events with MGM executives. While these combined work and social functions have not been written about in detail, Garbo and MGM executives would have given everyone a familiarity one establishes with co-workers with whom one spends significant time. She wasn't management, but she was comfortable around management, and they were comfortable around her.

Garbo's sister-in-law, Peg Gustafson, related a story about one of Garbo's visits to her home. She spent over an hour wandering the garden of the house talking to herself. When she asked Garbo what she had been doing, Garbo responded, "Arguing with Thalberg."[704]

The MGM crowd at San Simeon Courtesy Marc Wanamaker/Bison Archives

Back row, left to right, partially obscured:
- King Vidor, MGM director and husband of Eleanor Boardman
- Beatrice Lillie, British stage actor
- Richard Barthelmess, actor for First National
- Eleanor Boardman, MGM actor and wife of King Vidor

Middle row:
- Frank Orsatti, talent agent
- E. B. Hatrick, general manager of Hearst Newsreels and Cosmopolitan Pictures
- Edmund Goulding, MGM director
- Margaret Talmadge, mother of actors Constance, Norma and Natalie Talmadge Garbo
- Nicholas Schenck, president of Loew's and MGM
- Norma Talmadge, actor, wife of Joseph Schenck (president of United Artists /not in photo)
- Harry Rapf, MGM producer
- Aileen Pringle, actor
- J. Robert Rubin, vice president of MGM and general counsel of Loew's
- Norma Shearer, MGM actor and wife of Irving Thalberg

Front row:
- Hal Roach, founder of Hal Roach Studios, which distributed through MGM
- Natalie Talmadge, actor and wife of Buster Keaton
- Eddie Mannix, general manager of MGM
- Constance Talmadge, actor
- Buster Keaton, actor, husband of Natalie Talmadge and recent MGM hire
- Paul Bern, MGM producer
- Irving Thalberg, vice president of production for MGM and husband of Norma Shearer

Foreground reclining:
- John Gilbert, actor

■ *Caption for image on left-hand page:*

The MGM crowd at San Simeon

Why is this photo so interesting? The executive power present.

- Garbo is arm in arm with the most powerful person present – Nick Schenck the president of Loew's.
- Four of the five most powerful people at MGM are present (Nick Schenck, Irving Thalberg, J Robert Rubin, Eddie Mannix). Only Louis B Mayer is missing.
- Two people with important distribution arrangements through MGM are present: E. B. Hatrick and Hal Roach.
- Two key MGM producers, Harry Rapf and Paul Bern, are present.
- There are also nine actors, including Garbo, who had significant careers as film stars.

Garbo was a fixture at the studio for years when she was in town. Walter Reich recalled that the day Mussolini announced Italy was entering the war (June 10, 1940) Garbo was sitting with him in producer Gottfried Reinhardt's office with Salka Viertel, composer Bronislaw Kaper, and writer John McLain.[705] She had no work commitment to be there as she didn't make a film that year.

Here one can perceive the emergence of two Garbos. Professionally she is a convivial part of the project, interacting with the rest of the crew and usually having a good time. She knows the key players on the business side of film and is comfortable with them. She is of the film industry. Not only does she know the brass at MGM, but she is also friends with producers like Charlie Chaplin, Sam Goldwyn, Orson Welles, and later Sam Spiegel. Garbo doesn't go to parties to network, because she already has all the connections she needs.

Garbo worked closely with costume designer Adrian, set designer Cedric Gibbons, the portrait photographers, and MGM's research department. She was focused on delivering the film, the publicity, and the tie-ins. Women adopted the clothing and household goods used in Garbo films as their own. Fashion trends were driven by her film costumes and MGM provided fans millions of Garbo photographs.

Cedric Gibbons and his wife, the actor Dolores del Rio, were one of the couples she was closest to in Hollywood. Beyond their friendship, we know she had significant input into the set designs for *Queen Christina* and *Two-Faced Woman.*

Adrian started working with Garbo for *A Woman of Affairs* and costumed her for the rest of her films. When Adrian brought his sportswear-based wardrobe for *A Woman of Affairs* to MGM, executives were aghast. Adrian later related, "They feared she would lose all her allure if she came down to earth." Adrian understood that Garbo's appeal transcended the costume, saying, "She is just as intriguing in a sweater."[706]

Garbo supported Adrian's wardrobe concepts, and MGM ventured to dress its leading star in sportswear instead of gowns, thinking it was a risk. The effect in the market was electric. From this point forward for more than a decade, what Garbo wore on-screen was the primary driver of fashion.

Adrian commented about working with Garbo, whose casual everyday clothes somewhat distressed him. He wrote in his journal about Garbo's approach to developing costumes for *Camille*:

> It takes all the imagination I possess to visualize the glamorous finished costume on this bedraggled woman. At times, watching her standing in the robes of a queen or wearing a devastating evening gown, with hop sneakers on and her hair unwashed, I have wondered how we would make it.
>
> We try on one hat after another on her. She shrieks with laughter. She puts a hat on backward. We like it. It becomes fantastic. I beg her to wear it that way. She pulls it in a more ridiculous fashion. We fit it like that. We laugh 'til we cry. We decide it must be worn like that. Slowly it begins to be taken more seriously. The ridiculous becomes the sublime. Her disheveled hair is forgotten. She for one fleeting moment crystallizes into something very beautiful and remote. I have learned from experience that on the day of shooting, when she finally washes her hair, puts on her film makeup, and steps into high-heeled shoes, she will once more look like MGM's Garbo.[707]

Women would see Garbo wearing a costume Adrian had created and want to dress in the same way. The studio, in cooperation with the American fashion industry, worked to make this as easy as possible for women to do:

A Cinema Shop ad for Garbo's coat from *The Painted Veil* (*The San Francisco News*, March 11, 1935, p. 22).

> Now and again the masses have their fling without either copying or being copied by the classes. There has been an epidemic of polo coats on Fifth Avenue of late. There is a girl named Greta Garbo who looks nice in a polo coat. She wears it for sport. But when a girl like Garbo looks nice in a polo coat, ladies who wish they looked like Garbo, but doubtless never will, are apt to take up polo coats for everything. The classes have been wearing polo coats for years. They're handy in the country over riding-clothes. But for town Vogue says no. Garbo goes serenely on her way to the studio . . . and young girls are thriving on them in all cities.[708]

Adrian sought to do the unexpected with Garbo's costumes. "It is out of the unexpected that style is born, and the influence comes."[709] Adrian believed that Garbo's influence of fashion was more far-reaching than that of any other actress.[710] His reasoning was that her individuality fired the imagination of women.

Adrian thought that it was Garbo's way of carrying herself that precipitated new fashion trends. "The most interesting thing about her was her ability to wear a thing and create a style—with complete unconsciousness. She wore them with a lack of self-consciousness."[711]

Garbo's impact on women's clothing was such that by 1930 British fashion writer James Laver would write,

> No one who studies the fashion magazines or even takes a walk in the streets could fail to recognize her influence. She has imposed her look with extraordinary completeness.[712]

Some of Garbo's most important professional relationships at MGM were with portrait photographers Ruth Harriet Louise and Clarence Sinclair Bull. Fans were invested in collecting her picture, and photographs were the basis for marketing campaigns.

Ruth Harriet Louise (her family name was Goldstein, but she dropped it professionally) was one of the few female age contemporaries Garbo would meet in her first years at MGM. Two years older than Garbo, she also arrived in 1925 and created the job of taking in-house studio portraits. Her brother, Mark Sandrich, also was in Hollywood and would eventually be the famous director of musicals. Like Ruth, he dropped his family name.

In a 1922 essay she wrote that the first job of a portrait was to "express personality."[713] Other than a single sitting Garbo did with Russell Ball in 1927, Louise would take all of Garbo's portrait photographs from her arrival later in 1925 through 1928, when Louise left MGM to get married.

In an early interview with Alice Tildesley, Louise would say, "Greta Garbo, the new Swedish discovery, had so much to give that when I first saw her I couldn't coordinate it into one picture. Later I learned to turn one side of her many-faceted personality to the camera at a time. She is a gorgeous subject, because she has so many moods. I have never seen a girl so young who seems so sad. Perhaps it is the heritage of the Old World, where no one is very happy, but even in her most joyous scenes I feel that sorrowful undercurrent."[714]

Garbo seems to have had a relationship with Louise outside the portrait studio. Once when angry she wrote a note on one of Louise's portraits of her: "I am not always yours. Greta Garbo. To Louise—isn't right most terrible [unintelligible] in the world. I am mad!"[715]

Of her portrait photographers, George Hurrell is the only one who didn't seem to click with Garbo. Hurrell's style did not involve the subjects acting for the camera. He preferred to just capture people unaware as they thought he was preparing.

Hurrell only made the portraits for the film *Romance*. They don't have the vitality apparent in the work of other photographers. Hurrell was a fine photographer and made excellent portraits of many other stars. The same year Hurrell took his Garbo portraits he took stunning images of Joan Crawford, Norma Shearer, and Ramon Novarro. Their lack of chemistry demonstrates that good portrait photography requires intent on the part of both the photographer and the subject.

Clarence Sinclair Bull recalled the first time he took over the responsibility for making Garbo's portraits after Ruth Harriet Louise had left MGM:

> The day Garbo walked into my portrait gallery [for *The Kiss* in 1929] she looked like a frightened schoolgirl. What she didn't know was that I was just as scared as she. For over three hours I shot her in every pose and emotion that beautiful face could mirror. Actually I had no control over myself and I wondered when she might say she'd had too much. She said nothing so I went on shooting. Finally I ran out of film.
>
> There had been no break. She hadn't asked for even a glass of water. As she rose and moved to the door, obviously tired yet somehow showing she had enjoyed our efforts, she said, "I was quite nervous, Mr. Bull. I'll do better next time." At the door I reached for her hand. It was as moist as mine. "So will I, Miss Garbo."[716]

Thus began a twelve-year partnership that created some of the most iconic photographs ever taken. Bull would later write about how Garbo worked as a subject:

> I would give her the general pose. She would look out of the corner of her eye to see if her interpretation was registering with me, and if so, she would hold it. I might make a gesture, and then she would repeat it, showing me how it was really done. We hardly spoke. Her eyes would roam and as she assumed a pose she could tell by looking at me whether it was what I wanted or not. She always knew.[717]

Garbo took a very businesslike approach to portraits. She arrived on time and ready to work. She knew how to pose. Other stars were late or diffident about the work, and some wanted a stiff drink or two.

Garbo took risks. She understood photography as an art, and how as the subject she could push boundaries. Bull thought Garbo was the most cooperative star at MGM. She could hold a pose for ninety seconds and would try unusual facial expressions:[718]

Garbo, John Gilbert, Edmund Goulding and others picnicking on the set of *Love*. Photo by William Grimes.

> I have never worked with any star as cooperative as Garbo. She was always willing to experiment with unusual lighting. Not many stars would submit to this brutal treatment, many being afraid their bad side might show. "Their bad side" I never showed them. . . . We enjoyed our work. She was the face and I was the camera. We each tried to get the best out of our equipment.[719]

Each session produced two to three hundred negatives. Garbo would come in to look at the proofs. When they started, Bull would hold back the images that displeased him. Garbo wanted to see them all, so from then on Bull showed her every proof.[720] She only rejected about ten percent.[721]

He would say this about her effort:

> Garbo actually works harder when posing for portraits than she does before the motion picture camera. . . . She considers the posing as part of her screen work and feels absolute concentration is necessary to get emotion over to the still camera.[722]

From 1927 to 1941 the world was awash in Garbo images. Fan magazines, general interest magazines, and newspapers all published her image frequently. Fans cut these out and saved them. Fans asked MGM for photos, and it sent them out by the hundreds of thousands. Fans bought cigarette cards. All of these were placed in albums or hung on walls. Because Garbo worked so hard at photography, there was no shortage of beautiful images. They were shot by the best photographers and the scene stills had amazing costumes and sets. The ubiquity of Garbo then led to the use of her image in art and it is suffused throughout popular culture.

Garbo signed the extension with MGM for two reasons. The obvious one was money. After five years, she would be financially set for life. In total, the contract paid her $975,000 ($18.5 million). Contractual time extensions added about a month, so the contract ended in late April 1932. She would still only be twenty-six years old.

Garbo now understood that Hollywood was the only place to be as a film actor if you wanted your work to have the maximum impact. No studio in the world, outside its Hollywood competitors, could match MGM for resources that could be placed at the disposal of a film production. Garbo used and enjoyed those resources. If Garbo just wanted to make art films, she would have returned to Europe. Garbo chose to stay in Hollywood because Hollywood films had the greatest global impact. We will see shortly how Garbo considered making *Queen Christina* in Europe, but realized that the resources didn't match what was available in Hollywood.

The most important thing Garbo had given MGM in signing a new contract was the five-year commitment. She exhibited mixed feelings about this in letters home. Garbo wrote to Mimi Pollak, "If I could only make movies in Europe."[723] But, of course, she could have if she wanted to. She could have let her original contract run out and signed with UFA in Germany, or any other European producer. When she signed her five-year deal, she was eighteen months away from the end of her original MGM contract.

Garbo complained in the same letter that "the sad thing is I am not even interested in my work. It's just a factory job here."[724] But Garbo clearly understood the trade-off, that these "factory movies" sold all over the world.

After *Love* Garbo made four films before she finally was able to return to Sweden for a vacation. First, she made *The Divine Woman* with Victor Sjöström. It was a project that sought to portray Garbo differently. The response was uneven, and it is the only lost Garbo film. The other three films, *The Mysterious Lady* (1928), *A Woman of Affairs,* and *Wild Orchids* (1929), stuck to the

Thalberg formula of providing a great Garbo scene as the pivot point of the story. These four films delivered Garbo to her fans in B+/B- vehicles. They weren't terrible; they just weren't remarkable.

These were successful films, just not great art. These films do deliver memorable Garbo scenes. This was in keeping with Thalberg's belief that a fantastic scene was the key to a successful film.

For example, the key scene in *A Woman of Affairs* that displays Garbo's full powers. Diana, played by Garbo, is in the hospital under the care of Dr. Hugh Trevelyan, played by Lewis Stone. Neville and Constance have come to visit. While Hugh, Neville, and Constance are standing in the hallway, Diana emerges from her room in a distraught state looking for a bouquet of flowers. She sees them and, oblivious of everyone there, walks toward them and lifts them out of the vase with a hug that one would give a child or a lover. She speaks to them about how she wants "only you."

Hugh interrupts her reverie with the flowers, and as she turns she sees Neville is there. Casting aside the flowers, Diana walks over to Neville and throws her arms around his neck. She tells him that her dreams have been answered and tells him she will get better if he stays with her. Neville tells Diana he won't leave.

Diana turns from Neville to tell Hugh that she is happy. Then she perceives for the first time that Constance is also there. Diana's happiness drains from her face as she recognizes Constance. Turning back to Neville, she readjusts the ring that, earlier in the film, she had slid off her finger on her wedding night, signaling her decision has been made.

She goes to Constance and insists that she is not in love with Neville, that she has been talking nonsense. This moves Hugh to shed a tear, as he sees the sacrifice that is being made by Diana. The attention of Diana and Constance turns back to Neville, who is clearly torn.

Diana thanks them for coming, as they have helped her. The flowers have been picked up and reassembled by a nurse, and Diana asks for them. Turning to return to her room she pauses, and takes Neville's hand in hers, before walking to her room. Constance and Neville are left together while Hugh and the nurse escort Diana back to her bed, where she falls asleep clutching her flowers.

No written description can adequately capture the power of this scene. Other than the period dress and lack of dialogue, it is modern and natural.

All of Garbo's remaining silent films would deliver about $1 million ($18.4 million) each in studio revenue.[725] The six silent films Garbo made after *Love* delivered almost 10 percent of MGM's total revenue for the 27–28 and 28–29 production years.[726] This even as Garbo had reduced her film output to three per year rather than the four other stars averaged. On to that Loew's would add its theater revenue.

Before Garbo returned to Sweden in December 1928, her tumultuous relationship with Stiller, which seemed on the cusp of clarity, would end with his death.

Chapter 20 – The Death of Stiller

"Your message made Moje happy he sends love his condition however absolutely hopeless Dear Greta seemingly only question of few days now becoming mostly unconscious no pain lung trouble everything possible being done for him much love."[727]

— Edith and Victor Sjöström in a telegram to Garbo, November 7, 1928

L to R: Edith Molander, Lars Hanson, Greta Garbo, and Mauritz Stiller. Courtesy of the Swedish Film Institute.

After Stiller was fired by MGM in April 1926, he and Garbo still saw each other with some frequency. They remained central to both the Scandinavian and German Hollywood communities. Moving to Paramount was wonderful for Stiller. He and producer Erich Pommer trusted each other and Stiller was allowed to work in his normal fashion. He was paid better than he had been at MGM and he even earned a $2,500 ($46,000) bonus for his first film.[728]

That film was *Hotel Imperial* (1927).

It was a Pola Negri vehicle. Lars Hanson later recalled,

> I saw Stiller when he was getting ready to start shooting *Hotel Imperial*. He was bursting with energy. He showed me the script of some scenes he was preparing—mass scenes of people in a square. According to the script, it would take three weeks of shooting. Stiller did it in three days. He was so very anxious to succeed that he worked until he was green in his face.[729]

It was released just after *The Temptress*. Stiller developed some novel filming techniques for the production. *Hotel Imperial* was a good film but not a world-class one. He followed that with another Pola Negri film, *The Woman on Trial* (1927). Einar Hanson co-starred in his last film before his untimely death.

Stiller decided to return to Sweden. He told Lars Hanson that he was going to "make one more picture. It will be genuine garbage, but I'll do that one and go home with the money."[730] While it seems that he planned a permanent return to Sweden at the point of this conversation, Stiller's answer to the question regarding his return to Hollywood changed based on the further evolution of the Garbo-Stiller relationship, which it turned out had longer to run. His death made the issue moot.

Stiller's final Paramount film was *The Street of Sin* (1928—lost), starring Emil Jannings and Fay Wray. Paramount clearly had confidence in Stiller. Not only did it have him produce the film, as Pommer had departed for Germany, they were trusting him with Jannings, who was at the peak of his career. Some scenes for the final edit were reshot by Ludwig Berger after Stiller's departure.

Shortly before he left Hollywood, Stiller said in an article in *Variety* that "I have not yet reached a position in American film affairs that will permit me to boast. . . . Had I remained in Europe, I think I would have continued to make pictures that the public looked upon as representative of life."[731]

Garbo was still close to Stiller and wrote a letter to Mimi Pollak: "I hope to keep Moje as he is for if he should leave me I don't know what I would do."[732] Yet Stiller's departure seems to be in part to expressly give Garbo independence.

Before Stiller departed Los Angeles, he wrote Garbo a letter. All his wisdom is apparent in it. While he wishes they were still together, he wants her to thrive on her own. He perceptively closes by predicting she will stay in America:

> My Dear Former Greta,
>
> I am now leaving Hollywood, the horror is I am leaving you here. Leaving you your freedom. You may, when I am gone, bloom again. The calm may return to your face. The strength will return to your lips and your mouth. Your eyes will not wrinkle so often—I am gone, struck from your life—you are free!
>
> But my thoughts are with you and I shall pray for you. That you may be protected from all evil, will sleep calmly and without guilt. Life is so horrible, but it will not be for you.
>
> I am leaving—you are free! As you have always been. And you should not think about me. You don't have to repeat "poor Moje" every time we meet. You are free! And to say it in your new mother tongue—everything is alright.
>
> — Moje[733]

Stiller departed New York on December 9, 1927, on the MS *Gripsholm*. Lars Hanson and Karin Molander sailed on the same ship. Einar Hanson had tragically died in a car accident on June 3 after completing his work on *The Woman on Trial*. The Swedish community in Hollywood was suddenly somewhat depleted.

He arrived, white haired and ill, in Stockholm shortly before Christmas 1927. He did not make any more films, although he was planning one. Instead, he successfully presented the George Abbott and Philip Dunning musical *Broadway* at the Oscar Theater in Stockholm in April 1928.

In January 1928, Garbo wrote a letter to Pollak in which she told her friend that the Sjöströms were still deciding whether to return to Sweden. She said about Stiller, "Perhaps you can meet Moje. Poor, dear Moje. In that case you will see what America has done to him. I care for him so dearly—and I have him to thank for being on the white screen."[734]

This romantic dynamic between Stiller, a man twenty-two years her senior, and Garbo has led some to speculate that their relationship was a real-life Svengali and Trilby situation. In the original novel, *Trilby* (1894), the Svengali character is Jewish (like Stiller) and the tone of the novel antisemitic. Though the reading of what a Svengali is has shifted over time to de-emphasize the antisemitic context of the original, what has remained is the idea of a controlling older man of evil intent manipulating a younger female artist. In the book, Svengali controls Trilby through hypnotism. She only has singing talent when under his spell.

There are several problems with that comparison. The main one is that Garbo had talent in abundance, and there was never any doubt about it. Second is that it removes any agency from Garbo, presenting her as yet another woman needing a man to get by. The final point is that Stiller's relationship as a director and guide never seems to have crossed the line into overbearing control.

Carlo Keil-Möller, after directly rejecting the Svengali-Trilby comparison, clearly stated that Stiller's aims were different. He saw that Garbo could be a transcendent actor:

> There is no doubt that Stiller was intensely interested in Garbo. But he lived essentially in the world of imagination and art. As the sculptor looks upon his block of marble or the painter on his colors, so did Stiller look upon Garbo. He realized what she could become; he knew how much his own cooperation could help her arrive at this goal. I do not think that I am guilty of any exaggeration if I say that she was his most beautiful artist's dream.[735]

At least since Stiller and Garbo had recommenced a romantic relationship after they sailed from Sweden for America, Stiller seems to have been a patient partner, waiting for Garbo to decide that their relationship had value. Though he told the Sjöströms that he thought he was too old for Garbo. Through their relationship's ups and downs, and the John Gilbert situation, their professional and personal friendship seems to have remained strong.

His letter to Garbo upon his departure for Sweden in 1927 speaks for itself. He hopes his departure will allow her to move forward. He points to her new life in America, and he reaffirms that he will always be there for her. It is possibly the best break-up letter ever penned. It confirms what Stiller's peers always said about him, that he was a prince of a man. Garbo kept this letter her whole life.

In early 1928, Garbo had a change of heart in regard to Stiller. We don't have the original letter she wrote to Stiller, but sometime in March he received a letter that clearly opened the possibility of Garbo and Stiller returning to being a couple.

Stiller wrote back:

> Stockholm March 6, 1928
>
> Dear missed Greta,
>
> How awful this distance and this longing for you are, these terrible years in America. Thank goodness these are now over and will never be repeated again—not for you and not for me. But why this letter to me? Shouldn't everything be forgotten? Would you like to continue? Why would you then write in that way to me? Why not write as it is? You might not be able to express your most secret thoughts and feelings in a letter to me—and I am certainly not asking for a confession from you—but write honestly—give me some facts.

A portrait from the film *Love*. Photo by Ruth Harriet Louise.

I am walking like a blind man, I don't know anything. This is by no means some kind of relationship from my part, you know that very well, you are free and can act as you please, but if you mean anything by what you are writing to me, I need to know this. Should something new sprout from the old? Will our emotions change skins? Will there be a spring in our senses? What do you want? I want to hear!

I have boundless feelings for you, something so mercilessly holy, and when I saw you in the Sjöström movie yesterday, I was so moved because it was you, and I was crying all night. Why? It is as if you were mine, my child, my beloved. . . . Every step you take, every emotion you express invoke an irresistible reflex emotion within me, I feel and I suffer with you. Is this not the highest point us poor human children can elevate ourselves to?!

Or perhaps my emotions are playing me a trick? Because I wanted to leave you—and this most of all for your sake—but I will not do this, dear Greta, not until I know how you feel, what you are thinking.

And now, far away from me, it should be easier for you, let me know! If we should stay together, we have to, which I first was against, get married. If not, there is no need for you to explain why. I will understand, and I will keep you in my heart forever—but then I don't want us to see each other again.

You should only take yourself in consideration, in the long run that is the only thing that matters. I do not want to write about my illness, because I feel much better, and in 3–4 weeks the doctors have probably gotten tired of me, and by then, dear Greta, I might have found out your thoughts about your Moje.

Farewell!
5Moje [736]

We don't have Garbo's response. But according to Colleen Moore, "Garbo asked Lilyan Tashman to help her buy some clothes. She was going to Sweden for a visit, and, as she confided to Lil, she wanted some beautiful outfits to 'startle Stiller.'"[737] So one must assume she hoped to marry Stiller in Stockholm.

They went to Howard Greer's shop. Greer recalls how Tashman announced their plan: "Garbo's getting ready for a trip back home. And she wants a flock of clothes to kick the natives dead!"[738] Greer and Tashman assembled a wardrobe of eighteen dresses for her.

At this point, Stiller believed that his health issues could be overcome. By all accounts, his doctors thought that he would recover. Then in the fall of 1928 Stiller's health took a turn for the worse.

There is also an envelope for another letter that Stiller sent to Garbo with a postmark of October 18, 1928, but the letter itself is lost.

Stiller's musical, *Broadway*, had opened on April 28, 1928, to very strong reviews. At some point during the five months following *Broadway's* premiere Stiller's health did decline. Stiller had been suffering from a lung condition that had required multiple surgeries.[739] But he thought that he would recover and continue working. He was hospitalized on October 2, 1928, at the new Red Cross Hospital in Stockholm. The choice of the Red Cross Hospital, which was more focused on rehabilitation reinforces the idea that his death was unexpected.[740]

Mauritz Stiller died November 18, 1928, while the filming of *Wild Orchids* was still underway.

Stiller had been planning to return to America to continue directing films.[741] Anticipating that he would be married to Garbo, his plan was to travel to Davos, Switzerland, and then on to Hollywood to resume work.[742]

Victor Sjöström had sailed from New York on October 12 and arrived in Stockholm about three weeks before Stiller's death.

Sjöström talked in depth about the last days of Stiller:

> The moment I entered the room I saw a man marked by death. What a homecoming. What a reunion. He had left Hollywood a year ago, so happy to go home. He knew now that I was coming and he had been expecting me impatiently. He cried like a child when he saw me and I had to exert myself to the utmost degree to control myself. We had a long talk—he did most of the talking—we even drank champagne in small sherry glasses—it was prescribed by the doctor—and when I left him that day he was cheerful and in good spirits. "If I live it will be thanks to you," he said.

> Of course, I went to see him every day—an old lady friend from Finland, professor Alma Söderhjelm and me were the only ones he would see—but he became more and more weak. One day when I came home after having been with him for several hours, the nurse at the hospital called me on the phone and told me that Stiller wanted to see me again. He wanted me to come back to him as soon as possible because he had something very important to tell me. I thought he wanted perhaps to talk to me about making his will. He had not made a will—so typical of him. I hurried back to the hospital again and was with him for more than an hour waiting eagerly for what he wanted to tell me. But he only talked about indifferent things. Then the nurse finally came in and said she could not allow me to stay longer, she must ask me to leave. But then Stiller suddenly got desperate. He grabbed my arm in despair and would not let me go. "No, no," he cried, "I want to tell you a story for a film, it will be a great film, it is about human beings and you are the only one who can do it." I was so moved I did not know what to say. "Yes, yes Moje," was all I could stammer, "I will be back with you first thing in the morning and then you will tell me." I left him crying in the arms of the nurse. There was no morning. Next day he was almost unconscious, he tried to talk but although I put my ear close to his mouth I could not make out what he said. And I don't know if he understood what I said. He only kept on staring at me. A day or two later he passed away.[743]

When news of Stiller's death reached Garbo, she was devastated. She wanted to stop production and leave for Sweden immediately. As the film was almost complete, MGM insisted she stay. Per her contract, MGM knew she was leaving for at least fifteen weeks when she departed for Sweden.

While production continued, Garbo was unhappy and not focused on work. Director Sidney Franklin recounted that Stiller's death "affected her profoundly—and it affected the picture. Our relationship, which wasn't too good to begin with, deteriorated. . . . It became so difficult that I went to see Irving to ask him to take me off the picture. He refused to relieve me and I struggled on as best I could to the end. It was not a happy picture. The results showed it."[744]

Stiller's death would have a lasting effect on Garbo. Two years later both John Loder and Wilhelm Sörensen would tell Rilla Page Palmborg that Stiller was Garbo's one and only great love.[745]

For her part, Garbo kept a table, a painting of Stiller by Arvid Fougstedt, and several personal photographs for the rest of her life.

Chapter 21 – A Visit to Sweden

"I never knew there were so many people in Gothenburg." [746]

— Garbo, upon seeing the dockside crowd for
her first return to Sweden

A wind-blown Garbo onboard the SS *Drottningholm* returning to New York in March 1929.

At the end of September 1928 as Garbo was making her plans to return to Sweden, she wrote Mimi and asked her to meet the ship in Gothenburg, if she was able.[747]

In her letter Garbo wondered, "Do you think people will be curious and come to the station?"[748] She was naïvely unaware that she had been transformed into a star in the eyes of Swedes as well.

Garbo left for New York as soon as the main filming for *Wild Orchids* wrapped. To the dismay of MGM executives, when they wanted Garbo to come in for retakes, she had already departed on December 2.

Mayer personally cabled her on the train on December 3, insisting that she could return for retakes and still make a ship in time for Christmas in Sweden.[749] The MS *Kungsholm* was scheduled to depart on December 8. It would have been impossible to make that departure if she had returned to MGM. Garbo did not turn around.

Garbo determined that the best way for her to travel to New York to catch the ship back to Sweden was to assume an alias. She traveled as "Alice Smith," and the ruse worked until an MGM employee noticed her in Chicago. He told the press and the hunt began.

Garbo poses for photographers on the MS *Kungsholm* as she leaves New York for Sweden in December 1928.

Garbo's solution to being unmasked was to leave the train at a station an hour north of New York. Joseph Buhler, her lawyer since the original 1925 contract, picked her up and she spent the night at his house in Greenwich, Connecticut. After a night in New York, she was able to evade the press and board the MS *Kungsholm*.

The trip began with rough weather, which added two days to the voyage. Everyone took to their cabins at first due to the rough seas. To Garbo's surprise, when the weather cleared and meals could be served, she found herself at the captain's table amid Swedish royalty.

She told the press this on arrival:

> We have had a wonderful time, however, some rough seas. Last night, I sang some songs at a little ship soiree. I love the ocean, this large infinite sea, not when the sun is shining on it, but the gray, overcast ocean. It is wonderful.[750]

A wedding party made up of many members of the Swedish royal family who had been on Long Island for the marriage of Folke Bernadotte to Estelle Manville, the daughter of industrialist Hiram Manville, was on the MS *Kungsholm*. Garbo, now a star rather than just a working-class Swede, socialized with the royal entourage that included Princes Gustavus (later king) and Sigvard.

Garbo and her mother on the train from Södertälje to Stockholm.

Another passenger was Lasse Ring, the man who had first put Garbo in front of a camera. Ring was onboard to film this maiden voyage of the MS *Kungsholm*. Three days after the return journey had begun, when Ring was taking a walk on the deck, he heard a voice jokingly say, "Good day Captain Ring. We have certainly seen each other before."[751] Garbo was at his elbow, dressed in her casual clothes and low-heeled shoes.[752]

The MS *Kungsholm* arrived in Gothenburg on December 19. The press boarded the ship as it approached Gothenburg harbor, and Garbo gave a brief press conference in the ship's library. While Garbo soon stopped giving interviews, for the rest of her career she often held press conferences when arriving in port.

In response to the question "How does it feel to be home?" Garbo responded,

"It's home!"[753]

Asked of her impressions of America, Garbo responded, "But you know how things have gone for me. It has been the same as anywhere else. One has had happy times and unhappy times."[754]

A few final questions were asked:

> *"What have you thought of your films?"*
>
> "One is always disappointed when one sees them cut and ready."
>
> *"Were you disappointed in Love too?"*
>
> "Yes, I should prefer to play quite different roles."
>
> *"Which?"*
>
> "Joan of Arc and Salome."
>
> *"And what American actor have you preferred acting with?"*
>
> "John Gilbert."
>
> *"What about Lars Hanson?"*
>
> Her artful response was "He's Swedish."
>
> When asked if she planned to marry, Garbo said, "I'm not going to marry."[755]

Garbo was mobbed at the dock and followed around town. The crowd broke two of the car's windows as the crowd crushed around it. The driver managed to push through the crowd and Garbo spent the evening in Gothenburg before catching the morning train to Stockholm. The entire Swedish press corps joined Mimi Pollak, who had met her in Gothenburg, and Garbo on the train.

South of Stockholm there is an important rail station at Södertälje, which is where Garbo's family and Mimi's husband Nils Lundell met them. Though they had originally planned to finish the journey to Stockholm by car, the traveling party elected instead to remain on the train to Stockholm Central Station. Photographers captured images of the family reunion on the train to run in the day's papers. There it seems most of Stockholm had turned out to welcome her home.

Garbo later recalled how this moment, arriving in the Nordic winter when the sun set around 2:45 p.m., moved her: "When I saw for the first time in the early dusk of the winter afternoon, with all of its lights shining from a thousand windows, I could have cried—it was so beautiful."[756]

Garbo settled into an apartment in a quiet neighborhood in the north of Stockholm that she had leased through Swedish film friends. Once reporters realized she was not staying at home they gave her, and her family, some peace.

Garbo's first trip home was her shortest while she was making films for MGM. She was only in Sweden for three months. She was constantly busy. She attended to the closure of her relationship with Stiller, met old friends, and made some new ones. She spent time with her family and went to plays. Stiller's *Broadway* was still running, and she took in that show and others.

Garbo had never been to Sweden. Yes, Greta Gustafson had. But the famous movie star from America was a totally different thing for Swedes, and this was not what Garbo expected. She had naïvely thought she could just slide into her old life with her old friends.

Garbo attended a Christmas dinner for the theater and film community at the Strand Hotel given by hotelier Julius Grönlund. Here she was reunited with Vera Schmiterlöw, who was working in Germany. The two were the guests of honor, with Prince Sigvard and industrialist Jacob Wallenberg as their tablemates.[757]

Garbo had met Nöel Coward at the Christmas party, and they got on rather well. They socialized for the weeks Coward was in Stockholm. While Garbo often wanted to stay in, or to affect a disguise, Coward would have none of it. He would drag her out to a restaurant or a party, sometimes literally pushing her through the door. He related that the minute she was inside she became her normal self, sometimes refusing to leave until three in the morning.[758]

She became reacquainted with Wilhelm Sörensen, whom she had first met during her time at Dramaten. Sörensen had been Prince Sigvard's classmate in school. Through the prince and Sörensen Garbo met Nils and Hörke (Martha) Wachtmeister. They remained close friends until the war. Garbo wrote Hörke letters and visited their home at Tilstad frequently when she was in Sweden.

She spent time with her old friends at holiday parties and at restaurants, bars, and coffee shops. Olof Molander, younger brother of Gustaf Molander and a director, invited her to a dinner party comprised mostly of her friends from her days before Hollywood. Here she was relaxed and playful. Molander recounted, "That evening she was as gay as anyone there. After dinner all the guests were supposed to put on a little individual performance. I remember Garbo sang an American cowboy song. She did it very cleverly."[759]

Crowds occasionally followed Garbo in the city, and she found the experience unnerving. It could be even worse than in America. On one occasion, after she had gone to a preview of Stiller's belongings, prior to their auction, Garbo and the executor of Stiller's estate, Hugo Lindberg, were followed by a crowd on the street, which grew to over a hundred people. Garbo and Lindberg picked up their pace. So did the crowd. Eventually they reached his office and escaped. Lindberg said, "When we got back in my office at last, Greta was very upset and nervous and seemed almost on the verge of tears. She sat down in a chair, took off her hat, and threw it on the futon, stating, 'People are mad.'"[760]

Lars Hanson had resumed his work on the stage after returning to Sweden at the end of 1927. While Garbo was in Stockholm, he gave a special performance of the Eugene O'Neill play *Strange Interlude* (1928) that she attended.

Garbo went to Northern Cemetery, where Stiller was buried in the Jewish section. She wanted to honor him, so she brought flowers. When she returned to the grave the following day, her flower arrangement had been torn apart and scattered. Garbo asked another visitor why this had been done. As she later explained, "When I asked someone standing nearby what this meant, he explained—what I in my ignorance had not understood—that the cross is a Christian symbol that has no place in Jewish life. That is why some Orthodox Jew had torn the arrangement apart that I had bought without knowing better."[761]

Abraham Stiller, Mauritz's only brother not in America, was still in Stockholm. He met Garbo then and they remained in touch for years. When Abraham told her that he hoped that Garbo would trust him to look out for her as he would a niece, she responded that she would rather be thought of as a sister-in-law.[762]

Garbo even contemplated the plot next to Stiller's as her final resting place for a time. Though when she told Abraham, he realized that Garbo's being Lutheran would complicate that plan.[763]

By this time Ragnar Hyltén-Cavallius was no longer just a screenwriter. He was beginning an illustrious career as a director for the Swedish Opera. Hyltén-Cavallius was a jack-of-all-trades. He wrote ten screenplays from 1923 through 1942. He directed four films. He was director at the Swedish Opera 1928–1952, and he was an instructor at the Opera school 1931–1956.

Garbo seated between Flight Captain Einar Lundborg and his wife Margareta. The man on the right is unidentified.

Hyltén-Cavallius reconnected with Garbo shortly before she left:

> In the spring of 1929, I met with Garbo again, by coincidence. She was now a chipper, liberated girl dressed in a trench coat and beret, and more beautiful than ever. She looked around, took me under the arm: "Come, Cavall, let us talk about old times, here where we will be left alone." And she gave me her irresistible, wholesome smile that could end in a little astute grimace—a glimpse of the lost South side girl—a real "gamin." One night we were going out with Calle [Carl] Brisson, he himself also at the height of his career. Garbo was joking about how much she had been in love with Calle—at a distance of course—when he was singing at a cabaret at Mosebacke. The night ended with Calle and Greta taking a cab and driving all around Djurgården to revive memories from their youth.[764]

Garbo spent time with her mother and brother. She convinced her mother to take a new apartment that had more amenities but was still in the old Söder neighborhood. The attempt to get her to move to a nicer neighborhood fell on deaf ears.

While she had come to expect publicity and attention in the United States, she was surprised that they also manifested in Sweden. She had recalled how actors could live their private lives in the Stockholm of her youth. Garbo related to actor John Loder that for her, Sweden was not like it used to be. She could not find peace because of the fans, and even Swedes gossiped about her, which she thought strange. Particularly since so much being written about her was fabricated.[765]

For Garbo, returning home changed some other relationships she had with the people she had known before America. While Mimi Pollak remained a friend for many years, their correspondence tailed off. There are only four letters from Garbo to Pollak from the entire 1930s. Though they clearly saw each other on Garbo's trips back to Sweden.

Garbo arrived back in New York on the SS *Drottningholm* on March 19, 1929. On this trip Nicholas Schenck himself, now the president of Loew's, met her at the dock.

While in New York Garbo granted her third interview to Mordaunt Hall, the film critic for *The New York Times*. He noted that "it was quite obvious after she answered a few questions that Miss Garbo's magnetism was just as impressive off the screen as on."[766] Garbo told him:

> I would like to do something unusual, something that has not been done. I would like to get away from the usual. I don't see anything in silly love-making. I would like to do something other people are not doing. If I could get von Stroheim! Isn't he fine?[767]

Garbo told Hall that she liked how *A Woman of Affairs* turned out as a picture.

One of the things she enjoyed about her return to Stockholm was wandering the streets looking into smaller shop windows and then going off to dinner without having to change her clothes. Garbo said that she knew only a few people in Hollywood. That she owned one car and played a little tennis.

On sound films, Garbo said, "I would love to act in a talking picture when they are better, but the ones I have seen are awful. It's no fun to look at a shadow and somewhere out of the theater a voice is coming."[768]

Chapter 22 – The Quest for a Private Life

"I don't understand why so much has to be written about me . . .
to be honest, I don't see how it can interest the public
to know what an actress does outside the studio,
or what her views on food are,
or what she thinks about people marrying."[769]

— Greta Garbo, to reporters at a shipboard press conference

Garbo standing between Karin Molander and Edith Sjöström in 1927.

The white-hot glare of celebrity was already focused on Garbo by 1928. It would only get more intense as years went by. Fan magazines printed articles and one-sentence observations. Newspapers covered her in innovative, new ways. She had a full biography published when she was twenty-six. Garbo's photos were everywhere. Initially these were just the MGM studio photos, but soon came photos of Garbo when she was walking around.

The Hollywood fan magazines weren't by any stretch interested in sourcing the truth of information. They were capable of printing diametrically opposing gossip snippets in the same issue, most anonymously sourced. They were sometimes accurate, but accuracy was not their objective. Historically, fan magazine interviews are the most interesting element. Garbo herself gave a few wonderful interviews and several of her co-stars spoke of her in their interviews.

The audience wanted to know the real person better. Who was Garbo really? What did she eat for breakfast and who did she like? Writers went out to answer these questions, and if they couldn't find the answer, often they made one up.

The media, particularly film fan magazines and national columnists, were clear on what they wanted from Garbo. They wanted her to talk to them. They wanted exclusives. They wanted access. When she wasn't working, she wasn't interested in spending all her time talking about what she did and how she did it. Therefore, almost everything else they wrote was either basic, such as when she started a film, or fabricated. Consider one example. In the November 1928 issue of *Photoplay*, there appeared a small piece on Garbo not being able to understand the dashboard of a car and, therefore, deciding to not learn to drive.[770] But anyone paying the slightest attention to Garbo would have known that she made the national news for collecting several speeding tickets in March 1926.

Many of the early Garbo interviews reveal nothing about the person. For example, Myrtle West interviewed Garbo in 1926, and the resultant article in *Photoplay* spends most of its time discussing her accent. Another 1926 interview in the *Los Angeles Times* by Katherine Lipke has so little content that it is stunning to realize that they actually spoke. Though it is clear she told Lipke that she didn't plan on marrying Jack Gilbert, all women like clothes, and she wanted better roles.

There are good interviews as well. Interviews with Rilla Page Palmborg and Adela St. Johns are interesting and contain good information. By far the best Garbo interview is with Ruth Biery. Garbo sat with Biery several times over two or so weeks and it was published as a single interview over three issues of *Photoplay* in 1928.

Lars Hanson, Garbo, Mauritz Stiller and Karin Molander in Santa Monica.

Garbo's most interesting relationship with an interviewer was with *The New York Times* film critic Mordaunt Hall. Starting with a first interview right after *Torrent* had wrapped production, he seems to be an interviewer Garbo felt comfortable talking to. Not only did Garbo give him multiple interviews, but she also had him on set while she was filming *The Kiss*. Rather than reporting it as an interview, Hall wrote it up as a discussion of her role and what she thought of some directors. He didn't ask about John Gilbert, which may have violated some interviewer code.

Otherwise, she didn't really give interviews after 1930. She did answer questions at press conferences. She gave several on ship while at the dock. These were in 1928, 1932, 1935, 1936, 1938, and 1946. In 1932 she answered press questions for an hour while changing trains.[771] She also held a press conference in 1938 in Italy in the hopes that by answering questions the press would leave Leopold Stokowski (a well-known conductor and her romantic partner at that time) and her alone. This didn't dissuade the Italian press at all.

The film fan media voiced their displeasure. Katherine Albert wrote that "she must now realize that her personality has become public property."[772] Another writer had this opinion: "It is probable that in the whole history of the world no artist ever grew to such great glory on utter heedlessness of what anybody thinks, says or writes."[773]

Given that Garbo had more publicity than she ever wanted without giving anyone interviews, she hardly saw much reason to change her mind. The last thing Garbo thought she needed was more public attention. Though she did understand what the publicity department was tasked with doing for the stars and the films. Her nickname for Vice President of Publicity Howard Dietz was vice president of poetry.[774] Later Garbo said, "I really did my best to make myself available. I wasn't so stupid that I couldn't see that publicity was sometimes necessary for a film and its actors. But what usually happened in America was that they simply invented things—whether I had spoken or not."[775]

In three short years she had become the queen of Hollywood. No other actor was held in such high regard either for her skill or her command of fans. Because of her contract dispute, illness, and production delays, *Wild Orchids* was only her eighth film for MGM. At a standard production pace she would have made twelve by that point.

Garbo with Berthold Viertel at the beach in Santa Monica.

Garbo didn't think being an actor gave her fans the right to enter her private life. Most of her interactions with fans were bothersome but not dangerous. Garbo rarely hired professional security, the one known instance being the time Garbo hired a bodyguard to protect her from the press while taking the train from New York to Los Angeles.[776] Garbo did worry about her personal safety. Once she became famous in Hollywood, several fans would cross the line into obsessive and dangerous behavior.

While there have always been men whose pursuit of a particular woman was unsound, and women who were killed by the man who was obsessed with them, film changed the way this played out. Suddenly there were millions of men who had sexual dreams about Garbo.

Celebrity stalkers can torment their victims, from unsolicited love letters to threatening tweets, break-ins, and kidnapping plots. Since the emergence of modern celebrity, famous people have been killed by fans who were obsessed with them: Selena Quintanilla-Perez, Rebecca Schaeffer, Gianni Versace, Christina Grimmie, Jill Dando, John Lennon. The list goes on. Then there are unfortunately also celebrities, like Monica Seles, Theresa Saldana, and George Harrison, who have been stalked and injured by obsessed fans without being killed.

What has changed since the emergence of modern celebrity is that many celebrities now live in a parallel world where they are protected from their fans. Garbo always rejected any sort of total separation from everyday life. While she did vacation in exclusive resorts and towns, she also frequently just walked about. She visited Gayelord Hauser in Wisconsin without taking any special precautions, and over repeated trips few recognized her.

However, over the years Garbo dealt with a number of deranged fans.

A girl from Texas began writing letters to Garbo in the fall of 1929. This escalated to phone calls and then one night, there she was at Garbo's house, asking for her to come down and talk, at 2 a.m.[777]

It wasn't just the fans. One Swedish journalist sent to Los Angeles to get a Garbo interview tried to run Garbo's car off the road, to get a chance to talk to her after the crash. Fortunately, the attempt was unsuccessful.[778]

In May 1931 a man stalked Garbo for several days, convinced that he was her brother. This led to his arrest, and a one-way ticket back home to Idaho.[779]

When asked in 1933, "How does it feel, Miss Garbo, to be so notable that one causes crowds to collect everywhere?" she replied, "I feel lonely and defenseless."[780] The prior year, Marlene Dietrich received extortion letters, threatening her safety.

Oscar Brosi was arrested climbing the wall surrounding her house in October 1933. He told the police that they had a spiritual affinity, and he wanted to give her a book of love poems he had transcribed from various books.[781]

Max Wengel came to Beverly Hills from Berlin expressly to marry Greta Garbo in 1941. He told the director of the Los Angeles County Lunacy Commission, after his detention, that while he had not yet met her, he had arranged the marriage through correspondence.[782]

In 1944 Garbo was awakened by the sound of burglars in her home. She climbed down a drainpipe and called out to neighbors for help. Spooked, the burglars, who seemingly thought she was away, ran, leaving two fur coats in the bushes. They did make off with some of her war ration coupons.[783]

When Edgar Donne passed away at seventy in 1947 his will read simply,

> I hereby give my entire estate to Greta Lovisa Gustafson, screen actress, whose stage name is Greta Garbo, to her and no other. If Greta Garbo becomes my wife, then it goes to Greta Lovisa Donne.[784]

This led to national news coverage. But digging deeper one can see how Donne could have easily crossed the line to being a dangerous stalker. He told neighbors that the postmasters were conspiring to keep his letters from reaching Garbo. His cousin Sissy Donne related,

> It was frightening every time he greeted us. Despite our ridicule he always said, "She'll be my wife soon."[785]

Donne had taken one trip out to Hollywood from Michigan in 1938. He never did get to meet Garbo on that trip.[786]

In 1952, a decade after the last Garbo film, she arrived at the dock in Portofino, Italy, on a small launch with George Schlee (a later in life romantic partner), actor Rex Harrison, and his wife Lilli Palmer. They had hoped to land unrecognized, but instead photographers and a wall of fans awaited them. Palmer recounted,

> For the first time in my life, I was physically afraid. I thought that any minute I would be crushed, smothered, or at best thrown into the water. The furious jostling of the people at the back thrust those in front hard up against us, and we couldn't give way, for there was nothing behind us, just boats and water a few feet below. Fortunately, the photographers at the front of the crowd were as badly off as we were; they were being pushed into us and thus couldn't take any pictures. They had a hard enough time protecting their cameras. "La Divina!" yelled the frenzied

crowd, surging forward. A minute more and we'd have all been in the water, with the photographers and the fans on top of us. Schlee had his arm around Greta, Rex was punching anyone within reach—but the rescue came from the photographers, who hit out at the crowd with their tripods, yelling wildly in Italian. Finally we made an opening and fought our way through to the jeep, kicking anyone who got in the way.[787]

Garbo tossing dice in the air. Courtesy of the Greta Garbo family archive.

Garbo could never totally let down her guard. Even when there was no ill intent on the part of her fans, the attention could be wearing. In 1964, over twenty years after *Two-Faced Woman*, producer Bill Frye took Garbo to a matinee of the play *Funny Girl*. He recounted the experience, marveling at the intensity of interest Garbo drew just trying to enjoy a play:

> We both enjoyed the first act immensely, and when the curtain came down for intermission I said, "Are we going to just sit here?"
>
> "Please, we mustn't move," she whispered urgently.
>
> I had been with Garbo often, but always in the privacy of my house or at the homes of friends. At the Winter Garden, I learned what her celebrity cost her in the world outside. Just minutes into the intermission, people realized that Garbo was in their midst. An audible buzz began to surround us. People walked down the aisle and crossed through the row in front of us, staring and talking and pointing.
>
> Trapped in a crowd soon numbering about 50, Garbo panicked. The moment the lights went down, she wanted to leave.

> "We're not leaving," I said. "The car won't be here and I don't know if we can get a taxi. It's hot outside, so we're not about to walk. Enjoy the show, and before the curtain comes down we'll run up the aisle and get out."
>
> But Garbo liked the second act more than the first, and when the curtain came down, I couldn't get her out of her seat. She applauded and applauded, and didn't seem to mind that the aisles were again jammed with people gawking at her.
>
> When we got to the street, the car was waiting. I put Garbo in the backseat, behind the driver, but before I could get around to the other side a woman opened Garbo's door and tried to climb in. I had to shove her forcefully out of the car. As we drove away, I realized I was exhausted. I'd been in public with any number of stars, including Tallulah Bankhead, Bette Davis, Rosalind Russell, and Joan Crawford, but I'd never witnessed anything approaching the frenzy we had just gone through.[788]

After Garbo returned from Sweden in 1929, Gustaf Norin and his wife Sigrid were hired as her household staff. Norin later worked as a makeup artist. During his career he was noted for his outstanding artistry and inventiveness with prosthetics. He worked on a long list of films and television shows.[789]

Rilla Page Palmborg would write a biography of Garbo in 1931 that leaned heavily on her interviews with the Norins. She provides an inciteful view into Garbo's private life. Gustaf told Palmborg that Garbo was very careful with her money. She gave him cash but asked him to keep receipts. He said, "She checked over all the bills at the end of the month, don't ever let anyone tell you that Garbo doesn't know how to handle money."[790]

The only time Garbo kept to a schedule was on the days she was filming. On those days she had to be at the studio at 9 a.m. She woke at seven and went out to the pool for a swim at a quarter past, placing her breakfast request with Sigrid on her way. After a brisk twenty-minute swim, Garbo ate breakfast and read the papers. When it was time, Gustaf drove her to MGM. She brought a lunch that Sigrid had made, usually a sandwich and fruit, with a tapioca dessert.

Garbo had a pet dog, Fimsy, that Ruth Jannings (the daughter of Emil Jannings) had gifted to her when the family returned to Europe. Garbo also had two cats and a parrot.

According to Norin, by this time Garbo was already in the habit of taking long walks. She particularly liked to go out in the rain.

When Garbo wasn't working, she swam more frequently and rode at the Bel Air stables three or four times a week. The stable was only 3 miles (4.8 kilometers) from her house, so sometimes she walked there.

Garbo with Ruth Jannings and Fimsy, the dog that Ruth left with Garbo when her family moved back to Germany.

Garbo did not entertain often. At this time her most frequent visitors were Harry Edington (her agent), Wilhelm Sörensen (visiting from Sweden), and film colony friends Jacques Feyder and his wife Françoise, Nils Asther, Edith Sjöström (who had returned to Hollywood with Victor in the fall of 1929), John Loder, and his wife Sophie.

Sörensen, who went by the nickname Sören, had traveled widely in Europe. When Garbo brought him to a dinner at Ernst Lubitsch's, he found that actor John Loder, whom he knew from Berlin, was also dining with them that evening. He and Sophie fit into the small Garbo social circle rather easily.

She spent time with the circle of people that congregated at the house of Belgian/French director Jacques Feyder. This included French writers Jacques Deval and Yves Mirande as well as director William Wyler and actor Charles Boyer (her co-star a decade later in *Conquest* [1937]). She remained friends with Edmund Goulding from when they met at Gilbert's house and through two films he directed. She had an open invitation to drop by his house for tennis or a swim.

Garbo first met Berthold and Salka Viertel at a party given by Ernst Lubitsch after she returned from Sweden in 1929.[791] The Viertels were central to her social life into the 1930s. Salka Viertel would be a pivotal writer in scripts Garbo chose to film once she concluded her five-year contract.

By this time Garbo was already being called a recluse, which in gossip speak of the day just meant one was not on the party circuit. Yet she clearly went out with her friends. Dinners at restaurants like the Russian Eagle were common. She spent many evenings at the Apex Club, a jazz venue in downtown Los Angeles. What these places had in common was that they were out of the way, non-Hollywood places where she could spend time without being noticed and bothered.[792] When Garbo was noticed, dense crowds gathered almost immediately.

Garbo and her friend Salka Viertel. Viertel would also write several Garbo screenplays and co-star in the German version of *Anna Christie.*

Garbo could turn up in unexpected places, with unexpected people. When Garbo first visited Frances Howard Goldwyn her husband, Sam Goldwyn, thought she didn't have real star potential because she first went back to the kitchen to talk to their Swedish cook.[793] Prior to the publication of this interview in 1969, no one was even aware that there was a social connection between Garbo and Samuel Goldwyn.

Sören recalled that she liked to go to movie theaters, because she could usually slip in unnoticed. She particularly liked Gary Cooper. She and Sören discussed the differences between the source material and the film they watched.[794] They could frequently be found at the Little Bit O Sweden Restaurant.[795]

After the premiere of *Anna Christie* Garbo took Sören out to La Quinta, a small hotel in the desert southeast of Palm Springs. There she rode a horse for hours through the dunes and canyons.[796] For Christmas in 1929 Garbo invited the Feyders, Nils Asther, Sören, and the Loders to her house and treated them to a traditional Swedish Christmas dinner.[797]

The Norins reported that "Garbo used to write to her mother and brother nearly every week."[798] Garbo's habit of writing to those close to her continued for much of her life, until phone calls took its place. The vast majority of these letters did not survive. However, we do have the extensive correspondence she sent to Peg Gustafson, her sister-in-law, in the years after 1940.

In the early 1930s Tallulah Bankhead hosted a dinner with Salka Viertel, Ethel Barrymore, and Greta Garbo. They played charades afterward. Bankhead recalled,

> She is excessively shy. When at ease with people who do not look at her as something begat by the Sphinx and Fridge, Norse goddess of the sky, she can be as much fun as the next gal.[799]

Garbo frequently went on a trip somewhere, either to study an upcoming part or after completing a picture. One vacation was to Yosemite, where she stayed at the recently opened Ahwahnee Hotel for a week hiking and horseback riding, before another guest realized who she was. The sudden attention ruined the vacation for her, and she sent a telegram to Norin to come pick her up.[800]

Garbo read articles about herself and Hollywood in general. She bought the American magazines from a local drug store. Her brother sent over Swedish magazines about once a month.[801] Garbo sent the American magazines home to her family.

The Norins told Palmborg that Garbo had two photographs in the house, one of Stiller and one of her brother Sven.[802] She was intensely connected to her family and closest friends.

Garbo had not been happy with her rental home on Chevy Chase Drive because her neighbors could, and did, peer into her yard. Her stay there became widely known and she found it difficult to maintain her privacy.

In April 1930 Sören found her a house at 1717 San Vicente Boulevard. Bounded on one side by a vacant lot and on the other by a tall cypress hedge, it was private. It backed the Riviera Country Club, which lay on the other side of Santa Monica Canyon Creek. She had walked the path along the creek, accessible from the house, many times.

The location suited her. The house was just under 2 miles (3.2 kilometers) from the Viertel house at 165 Mabery Road. It wasn't much farther to the beach. The MGM studio was just 10 miles (16.1 kilometers) away.

This move led to a fascinating vignette regarding Garbo told by a person who spent half a day with her without realizing who she was. From the San Vicente house Garbo had easy access to Santa Monica and Pacific Palisades. She walked to the sea frequently, and once writer Walter Taylor wrote about meeting her while out for a walk. Taylor was visiting Los Angeles. As an amateur botanist, he decided to walk north along the Santa Monica bluff with a gas station booklet of the wildflowers of California as his guide. Along the way he bumped into another amateur botanist carrying the same gas station booklet. Unknown to him at the time it was Garbo, and he described her as "a pale girl in muddy brogues, leather jacket and a tight little button of a hat." He described her as having a "well-scrubbed look and she wore no make-up."[803]

The 1932 Richfield Oil guide to wild flowers in Southern California that Walter Taylor and Garbo both carried on their walk

They had their interest in California wildflowers in common. They began to walk north along the bluff looking at flowers. Taylor recalled, "I found her a talkative companion. She monopolized the conversation, speaking with a slight accent and very precisely. She was a veritable encyclopedia about California wildflowers. She knew them all by sight and was able to give the Latin names of many."[804]

Learning that he was new to California, she told him of some other places that would have bountiful flower blooms at that time of year. Walking farther north, they came to a tearoom along the road. Probably the Olas Grande Inn, just east of the

Malibu Pier. The distance from Santa Monica to Malibu Canyon was 12 miles (19.3 kilometers), so they had walked some distance. They sat on the balcony overlooking the Pacific. On the way upstairs, they passed a parrot who amused her. While they had their tea, she recounted a parrot she had known and the funny things it said.

As they left the tearoom Garbo told Taylor that she was being picked up just a bit farther up the road. As they reached the intersecting canyon road where Gustaf Norin was waiting, a car driving by stopped because the occupants had recognized her. Garbo turned to Taylor and said, "Goodbye, my friend, and thank you for the lemonade."[805] Then she was in the car, and off her Norin drove. It was only when the autograph seekers had reached him that Taylor learned his companion had been Greta Garbo.[806]

Garbo was a physically active person. She was always known for her long walks. She swam both in the pool and in the ocean. She rode horses. She worked out with a medicine ball. She played tennis rather well. In addition to early games at Jack Gilbert's house she played at other locations. She routinely borrowed Edmund Goulding's court. Irene Selznick recalled Garbo beat Cedric Gibbons and David Selznick on the court in her backyard after the premiere of *Anna Karenina* in 1935, barefoot.[807]

A portion of the coast north of Pacific Palisades where Walter Taylor walked with Garbo.

Garbo is often described as having not gone to public events in Hollywood during this time, but there is plenty of evidence she did. Garbo took in lots of films, and she had perfected the art of sliding into the theater just as the lights went down. Since she preferred anonymity, the events that are known about tend to be the ones where her presence was noticed. The puppet theater on Olvera Street in Los Angeles was one such place, and of course it was reported. She was noticed at a performance by a Spanish dancer at the Philharmonic Auditorium. She had snuck in unnoticed, but some patron spied her and at intermission the entire crowd turned to look at her seated in a box with Harry Edington and Wilhelm Sörensen.

Garbo and Karin Molander in 1927.

Chapter 23 – The Production Code

"Our ideas of morality in entertainment differ radically from those held by the vast majority of the public." [808]

— Martin Quigley, censorship advocate and trade magazine publisher

Jeb Mondstruom (Alan Hale) intends to rape Susan (Garbo) in *Susan Lenox*. She escapes this time, but the film is full of forced sex.

In 1929 the ineffectiveness of the "Don'ts and Be Carefuls" censorship regime had become apparent and there was pressure for federal censorship regulation. There were two main issues. Some communities felt that their desire for less risqué films was overwhelmed by the overall popular taste. The second issue was the perception that Jewish executives in Hollywood were less moral than Christians. Some thought that federal legislation was needed to rein them in. This antisemitism was explicit. Iowa Senator Smith Brookhart viewed business competition in Hollywood as "a fight between two bunches of Jews."[809]

The arrival of sound had an impact on censorship issues. Silent films were easier to edit to accommodate some peculiar censorship issue in one region. Often cutting a single scene or changing a title card was enough of a fix. But with sound the dialogue had to have continuity, so censorship became a national instead of a local issue.

Initially Catholic censorship and input on films was diffuse. There was both the National Catholic Welfare Conference (NCWC) and the International Federation of Catholic Alumnae (IFCA) on a national level. Individual archdioceses commented on films as well. The NCWC lost funding at the beginning of the Depression. The IFCA had a policy of recommending films it approved of. This suited the studios, as those films not being approved were just not discussed by the IFCA.

Catholics are not the only people who recommended films. Both the Daughters of the American Revolution and the General Federation of Women's Clubs published lists of approved films.[810] Censorship concerns were found in many Protestant denominations. All of these groups communicated to the industry and to politicians, but for a variety of reasons (explained in several books on censorship during the mid-twentieth century), the mechanics of controlling the content of films ended up residing in institutions created by the Catholic Church and individual lay Catholics.

Beginning in 1929 a group of Catholics, comprised of both priests and laypeople, got together and created the Production Code. This group was organized by Martin Quigley, who owned *Motion Picture Herald*, the leading trade publication for independent theaters. His personal view was that movies should be entertainment and not social commentary. This was a view favored by many of his rural-theater-owner readers. His readership did not include the managers of integrated film company theaters in the cities.

Quigley thought that censorship had to take place during script development.[811] He found a sympathetic ear in George Dinneen, a Catholic priest in Chicago. Dinneen introduced Quigley to Cardinal George Mundelein. Quigley sketched out the mechanism by which a censorship code developed and supported by the Catholic Church would function. It was to be the collective action of twenty million Catholics directed by their priests and Catholic media.[812]

These three brought in Father Daniel Lord to write the draft code document. Additional input came from Joseph Breen, a lay Catholic who wrote articles against the decadence he saw around him, and Father Wilfrid Parsons, the editor of the Catholic magazine *America*. These people spent months developing the Production Code.

The Production Code (the Code) was a set of guidelines regarding moral issues and the portrayal of sex, violence, and relationships that film producers were supposed to use in the creation of films. It replaced the "Don'ts and Be Carefuls," though it was similar. The main difference was that whereas compliance with the "Don'ts and Be Carefuls" was only evaluated once the film was complete, the Code was supposed to be used at all steps along the way, from selection of material to final edit.

The plan that the group, which I will refer to as the Breen Group, had to get the industry to accept their Code as the guideline for all movie project development was to convince Hays and the studio heads that accepting the Production Code would reduce calls for censorship and improve their revenues. But behind this was the threat of concerted Catholic action.

At the same time the Catholic Church did not want to be directly associated with the Production Code. It explicitly wanted the benefits of censorship to its standards without being seen as the censors.[813]

The Production Code was adopted in March 1930. But the Catholic creators of the Code and the Hollywood studios had vastly different ideas as to how it was supposed to work. The Breen Group wanted to transform the film industry into a vehicle to promote a moral life, that stood by the sanctity of marriage, that rejected communism, and reinforced a top-down structure of an ordered society.[814] Lord, for one, wrote to Cardinal Mundelein that the producers had agreed to rigidly enforce the Code.[815]

This group of Catholics was virulently antisemitic, which made it hard for them to interact with the film industry. Wilfrid Parsons thought that Hays's problem was that he believed "these lousy Jews out here would abide by the Code's provisions."[816] Joseph Breen wrote to Parsons that Jews were "the scum of the earth."[817]

The initial mechanism for enforcement of the Code on its creation in 1930 was the Studio Relations Committee (SRC). The SRC ran the studio's self-censorship efforts until it was replaced by the Production Code Administration (PCA) in 1934.

The producers viewed the Code as just a slightly more intrusive set of suggestions. The one definitive change was that, before the institution of the Production Code in 1930, there wasn't a requirement to get any approval prior to the release of a film. Under the Production Code all scripts needed approval. But that approval was not much of a roadblock in practice. Producers had insisted that conflicts over scripts be resolved by a committee of film producers, not censors. While they wanted peace where possible, the ideas the Breen Group put forward were not going to help at the box office. Producers had no intention of letting the Production Code dictate the films they made.

The Production Code didn't stop MGM from dressing Garbo in a costume that left little to the imagination in *Mata Hari* (1931). Photo by Milton Brown.

At the same time the studios were wary of local censorship. The balance point between a racy film that drew audiences and when that same film was censored was rather narrow in practice.

The main unresolved issue was that the film industry thought that it could present sensitive social issues—crime, sex, corruption, and any other form of degeneracy—in the right context and with a good script. As a result, theoretically nothing was off-limits. You just had to have the right presentation. The industry was buying the rights to progressive novels by Hemingway, Lewis, Fitzgerald, and Faulkner. The Catholics involved in the creation of the Production Code didn't want any discussion of social issues at all and condemned these very books. They sought an administrative mechanism to override the public acceptance of progressive art. As Martin Quigley told a bishop, "Our ideas of morality in entertainment differ radically from those held by the vast majority of the public."[818] For example, Daniel Lord's idea was to run only films that covered business, industry, and commerce, plus uplifting biographies.[819]

Catholics, and other forces for censorship, were not only concerned about sex. They wanted to maintain societal order, as they perceived it. For example, the SRC, the department in the Hays organization charged with managing studio compliance with the Production Code prior to the creation of the Production Code Administration, objected to a scene in the film *Drifting Souls* (1932) that had this line: "Do you know that the bank in which your husband had all his money closed?"[820] Over two thousand American banks had closed in 1931, so it was a socially relevant line.

Daniel Lord thought that the film industry's increasing tendency to use plays and novels written for more sophisticated audiences would lower the moral standards of the audience. He didn't think lower-class patrons could handle the material.[821]

The fundamental problem that the Catholic Church was confronting under the SRC was that while the Catholics wanted ever stricter censorship and discretion on the part of the studios, films that crossed over to titillation on virtually any dimension were often resounding successes. James Wingate, who took over the SRC in 1933, demanded cuts to the Mae West film *She Done Him Wrong* (1933), and local censorship boards demanded even more cuts. Yet audiences loved the film, propelling it to one of the top ten box office draws for the year. It was hard to argue for censorship when the public paid for vice. If the advocates for enforced morality seem prudish, they were. Daniel Lord complained about a scene where a married woman took off her dress, revealing underwear, in front of her husband.[822]

In *The Single Standard* Garbo sleeps with her chauffeur.
Photo by James Manatt. Courtesy of the Greta Garbo family archive.

Working to the producers' advantage was the fact that the majority of Americans had no interest in the enforcement of the Code. Outside of a small subset of religious publications, there was no outcry in the media for the Code. The bishops of the Catholic Church, concerned about being perceived as in league with the film industry and with religion-based censorship, delayed in endorsing the Code. When they finally did in late 1930, the moment had passed.

While the newly established Code spoke to how sex was to be portrayed, the realities of early Depression society had made films that depicted sex work or other sexual activity, particularly when the plot then redeemed the woman in question, acceptable to a much broader audience than just a few years prior. Nearly every major actress was cast in these parts and the films did great box office in 1931 and 1932.[823] This was the era of crime films and societal criticism films such as *I Am a Fugitive from a Chain Gang* (1932).

The SRC was always imperfect, and it proved unable to handle changes in the film industry that were the result of the move to sound and the reaction to societal changes flowing from the Depression. Changes would come in 1934.

Chapter 24 – Garbo Talks

"The new Garbo is a greater actress than the old."[824]

— *Photoplay* magazine reviewing Garbo in *Anna Christie*, her first sound film.

MGM created several staged photos of the production of *Anna Christie* that prominently featured a microphone.

In 1929 Greta Garbo was the most popular actor in the world and probably the most proficient as well. However, the industry faced the challenge of converting to sound, and many actors would not successfully make the transition. Foreign actors in particular had the challenge of an accent. As others failed in their attempt to continue their careers in the new sound era, everyone wondered whether Garbo would, or wouldn't, succeed. Garbo was one of the last actors to transition. Instead of a barrier to her career, sound would launch her to new pinnacles of success.

With Garbo's return to Hollywood after nearly four months away, the studio placed her in two final silent films. Notably they both were stronger stories than the silent films she had been in prior to her vacation. The roles were more modern than vampish, while still delivering sex and romance.

As film historian Lucy Fisher notes, "*The Single Standard* projects Garbo's modernity and independence without recourse to exoticism."[825] MGM emphasized the Modern Woman aspect of the plots with title cards like this one:

> For a number of generations, men have done as they pleased—
> and women have done as men pleased.[826]

The Single Standard was based on a five-part serial that ran in *Cosmopolitan* magazine in 1928. It was written by Adela Rogers St. Johns, who knew Garbo through Jack Gilbert's Sunday get-togethers. The Arden Stuart character, which she played, may have been partly based upon her in the first place.

Greta Garbo and Nils Asther looking modern in *The Single Standard*. The photo could be a contemporary Ralph Lauren ad.

The *Single Standard* had its New York premiere July 27. It went on to have a very profitable run in theaters and was one of the top grossing films of the year, even though as a silent with synchronized music and effects, it was competing with sound films.

The *Single Standard* had its New York premiere July 27. It went on to have a very profitable run in theaters and was one of the top grossing films of the year, even though as a silent with synchronized music and effects, it was competing with sound films.

In *The New York Times*, Mordaunt Hall declared, "A third paragraph discussion of Miss Garbo is unnecessary at this date."[827] Garbo no longer needed explaining.

Jacques Feyder had arrived in Hollywood with the script for *The Kiss* already complete. He was already friends with Emil Jannings and his family, as well as with John Loder and his wife, from Europe.

Feyder shared his script with Jannings and, after reading it, Jannings thought that *The Kiss* was an ideal vehicle for Garbo and arranged an informal introduction. While Garbo did not have a contractual veto over scripts, she clearly had some level of script approval. Loder related that Garbo stopped by the Jannings home for tennis, and since Feyder was the only person she had not met, she was persuaded to stay for dinner. The decision to make *The Kiss* flowed directly from this dinner.[828]

Garbo gave the film critic for *The New York Times*, Mordaunt Hall, an interview while on the set of *The Kiss*. Hall, and Ruth Biery, who wrote the multipart story for *Photoplay* in 1928, are the only people with whom Garbo had three or more interview sessions. She was comfortable with them, they treated her fairly, and they wrote intelligently. In the late 1920s and 1930s they were the best at the type of writing each did.

While Hall does not quote Garbo directly when writing about his time on the set of *The Kiss*, he reports on her director preferences (von Stroheim, Lubitsch, and Feyder), her thoughts on sound films, and the scenario of *The Kiss*. Garbo relates that while she likes California, she longed for a change in the weather.[829]

Garbo had a lot of consideration for the other actors on the set. Lew Ayres talked about working with Garbo on *The Kiss*, his first film:

> Throughout the picture she gave me hints that I could have known otherwise only through long experience. Greta is my favorite actress, and I shall always be grateful to her, for she helped me over the hurdles when I was just learning to toddle in this business.[830]

One can get some idea of how Garbo prepared for a role from her preparation for *Anna Christie.* After wrapping *The Kiss* on August 26, 1929, Garbo left for Yosemite. There she booked a room at the Ahwahnee Hotel for two weeks. She brought the script for *Anna Christie* and some other books. Beyond reading, she spent her time hiking around Yosemite. Toward the end of her planned stay, she was found out and left a few days early for Los Angeles to continue preparations.

The small cast (there were only four main parts) rehearsed for two weeks before filming.[831] This step was unusual and was added to help the actors adjust their performance for the sound-film medium. Both theater actors and silent actors had to adjust their technique. While sound-film acting was closer to stage acting than silent-film acting had been, it still required some refinement to come across realistically.

Anna Christie is an intellectual play, not a melodrama as was then typical in American theater. O'Neill won a Pulitzer for it. Adapting popular melodramas for the screen was common in Hollywood. For example, *The Green Hat* (1924) was turned into *A Woman of Affairs*. But *Anna Christie* was a totally different proposition. It was a realistic drama addressing social concerns and the fringes of society. O'Neill was kindred to Ibsen, Strindberg, and Chekhov, not Michael Arlen. With *Anna Christie*, MGM was selling literature to Americans, and they went in droves.

MGM's challenge in bringing this version of *Anna Christie* to fruition was that the O'Neill play directly dealt with alcoholism and sex work, topics that SRC ran from. Frances Marion was brought in to turn the material into a script, as she was the most talented writer at MGM at the time. The script that Marion sent in for approval was only lightly altered from the play. The final act was shortened, and some dialogue was rewritten due to censorship concerns.[832] The sets could be more developed. There was no need for quick scene changes as with a play.

The result was a film that is a play, filmed. There are a limited number of sets. Most of the drama takes place in the conversations. This is an incredibly bold choice. Whereas prior Garbo films featured opulent sets, fashionable clothes, and exciting locations, for *Anna Christie* the dialogue and acting had to carry the film by themselves.

Anna Christie is a simple story. Anna, played by Garbo, has not seen her father Chris, played by George Marion, since she was six years old. After living in the Midwest and spending time as a sex worker, she is coming to visit her father in New York, where he lives on a coal barge. Anna arrives in the harbor-side tavern Chris frequents and runs into Chris's mistress Marthy, played wonderfully by Marie Dressler. Marthy realizes both that Anna is Chris's daughter and that she, like a younger Marthy, has been a sex worker.

Anna presents herself as just down on her luck and moves onto Chris's coal barge. A storm sinks the boat crewed by Matt, played by Charles Bickford, a young sailor who is rescued by Chris. Anna and Matt soon fall in love. This leads to conflict between Matt and Chris, after which Anna discloses the truth of her life. Anna confronts her father regarding how, by not supporting her, he had forced her into sex work. Marthy adds some comic counterpoints along the way. In the end, everyone is reconciled.

The MGM Garbo films up to this point involved fantastical plot points to allow Garbo's character to be a fallen woman, while also pulling off the story. In *Torrent* the simple country girl becomes an opera star, in *The Temptress* she is a well-to-do wife who can seduce men with her eyes, and so on. Even in the later *Susan Lenox* where Garbo plays an orphan country girl, she can go to New York and sleep her way to the top of society. Adrian and Gibbons always get a chance to add their glamour.

Garbo confronts George Marion and Charles Bickford in the climactic scene from *Anna Christie*.

Garbo's role in *Anna Christie* is different. The plot is just a real-life story of everyday, blue-collar people. No one hits the lottery. There is no excuse for her downfall into sex work nor miraculous intervention that drives her moral redemption. She is asking the audience to believe that a woman can be redeemed from sexual transgressions just by moving forward from the point of her conversion, evermore living a good life. It's a stake through the heart of Victorian morality and its immutable virtues.

Anna Christie posed an interesting challenge to censors. Since Garbo's life of sex work occurs before the action of the film, there is no compelling need to have her character pay for her sins so directly. She doesn't have to die. The viewer just has to come to believe she regrets her former life and that she has arrived to the story pure of heart. The real work of the story is for the men to come to love her despite her failings in the past.

This doesn't leave much for the censors to grasp. Some dialogue had to be adjusted, as the play dealt with things more directly. But since allusions to sex work were a stock Hollywood problem solved in numerous films, what were they going to do? Reject the film because two men let a former sex worker into their lives?

The vastness of the audience was one of the problems censors had with film in general. *Anna Christie* as a play premiered at the Vanderbilt Theatre in New York on November 2, 1921, and ran for 177 performances over five months.[833] The Vanderbilt Theatre seated 780 patrons, so only 138,060 people could have seen the play in its original run even if it had sold out every single performance.[834] At five showings per day at just the 5,230-seat Capitol Theatre in New York, that number of patrons was surpassed in just over five days.

New York plays were for the elite of society. So bringing *Anna Christie* to the screen put the question that had made the play controversial a decade earlier before the broadest possible audience: Was women's modern sexual morality functioning under new rules? The film erased all doubt.

We don't know what discussions, both between Garbo and Thalberg and internally at MGM, led to the decision to make *Anna Christie*. The story is a departure from most of the other films made under Garbo's five-year contract. After *Anna Christie* Garbo made four sound films that followed her old silent film template. The final two films of her five-year contract, *Grand Hotel* and *As You Desire Me* (1932) would be somewhat transitional to a higher form of art.

Most of the standard Garbo films had plot holes. The audience came to see Garbo deliver a couple of key scenes. The silliness of *A Woman of Affairs* does not lessen the artistry of Garbo's scene with the flowers. The script was derived from a controversial play, but the controversy was the advertising draw. The play was forgotten.

While at Dramaten, the clear tone of Garbo's voice was considered one of her better attributes for the stage. One instructor wrote, "At least you will not squeak through your professional life like some of the she-rats that infested the theatre."[835]

The quality of Garbo's voice was a great unknown as her first sound film approached. One element expressed in the media was concern over her accent; how pronounced would it be? The other part was the nature of her voice itself. Would it fit with the voice that viewers had been giving her in silent films?

Mordaunt Hall, interviewing Garbo on the set of *The Kiss*, discussed *Anna Christie*. He wrote, "If any voice suits a personality it is that of Miss Garbo. It is deep in tone and her utterances are always distinct."[836]

When talking with Hall about *Anna Christie*, which she already knew would be her first sound film, she told him that it "was a gorgeous story, and we'll see to the accent."[837] Both Hall in *The New York Times* and Harry Evans in *Life* noted that the voice Garbo used for the role of Anna was not her natural speaking voice. She created a unique voice, deeper in tone, to fit the role.[838]

Naturally Garbo was nervous about how her voice would be received. Her friend Wilhelm Sörensen recalled, "Suddenly it occurred to me that she must have stage fright, though she didn't betray herself with a word. . . . Then I heard a voice from underneath the rug beside me in the car [on their way to the studio]. Instead of a rich, deep timbre, I heard the moving plaint of a little girl: 'Oh, Sören, I feel, like an unborn child just now.'"[839]

The advertising department sold against *Anna Christie* being Garbo's first sound film. It succeeded because the product on the screen was a fully modern story with a tight script and the best overall cast she had worked with since *Love*.

MGM wanted to hold off letting the audience hear Garbo speak until they were in the theater. It released the trailer for *Anna Christie* as a silent.[840]

The cast surrounding Garbo for *Anna Christie* was particularly strong. Charles Bickford was an excellent pairing as the love interest. With his stage background and the fact that the film was just the play, he adjusted nicely. George Marion, in the role of Garbo's father, was reprising a role he had played both on Broadway and in the 1923 silent version.

The real unexpected joy of *Anna Christie* is veteran comic actor Marie Dressler as Marthy, the older, alcoholic, former sex worker, who becomes a friend.

Clarence Brown had hesitated to take Frances Marion's suggestion that Dressler was perfect for the role of Marthy because he considered Dressler to be a "Mack Sennett comic."[841]

Dressler herself said that this was a different kind of role for her and that she needed a firm hand to rein in her excesses and ensure that she didn't "play horse with Old Marthy."[842]

Watching a master at work in rehearsals, Dressler altered her acting style for the role. She delivered a more nuanced performance. Film historian Roberta Ann Raider summarized the preparation process:

> She was given a complex character to portray, which included dramatic and comic qualities, instead of a role which was pure farce. Miss Dressler valued the opportunity and worked out a detailed many-faceted characterization which captivated the moviegoers.[843]

Dressler's style in *Anna Christie* was entirely different from her work on earlier sound films. A more nuanced and sensitive acting, working for the camera instead of the audience.[844] That Dressler studied Garbo comes out in her own observations.[845] She focused on the "progressive flowering of the character."[846] At another point in time, she described her approach as trying "to make the most of each little point."[847]

Garbo and Marie Dressler meet for the first time in *Anna Christie*.

Dressler had stripped out her overacted comic style from earlier films to deliver a wonderful, real character. It is no surprise that she took these lessons and earned an Oscar and a second nomination over the next two years.

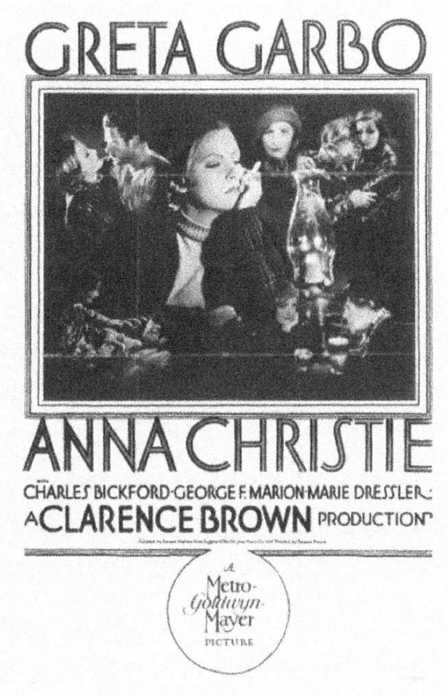

The original movie poster for *Anna Christie* (1930).

Garbo does not appear in the first fifteen minutes of *Anna Christie.* The first scenes set the relationship between Chris and Marthy. Chris speaks about the daughter he abandoned all those years ago. It clarifies that he has a misty-eyed view of what her life must have been like up to that point. For an audience waiting to hear her voice, the buildup to her first words was well orchestrated.

MGM arranged a special screening of *Anna Christie* for film magazine and newspaper writers in a small theater on the studio lot. The writers were most surprised at how little of a Swedish accent Garbo had. MGM told them that it actually had to reshoot some scenes to get Garbo to deliver the lines with more of an accent.[848] Clarence Brown related that after the preview of the unreleased film to a test audience that Thalberg told him, "This is too good to touch."[849]

Reviews of *Anna Christie* are really reviews of the Garbo voice. Mordaunt Hall wrote,

> In her first talking picture, an adaptation of Eugene O'Neill's *Anna Christie*, the immensely popular Greta Garbo is even more interesting through being heard than she was in her mute portrayals. She reveals no nervousness before the microphone and her careful interpretation of Anna can scarcely be disputed. She is of the same nationality as Anna is supposed to be and she brings Anna to life all the more impressively through her foreign accent being natural, because it is something for which she does not have to strive.
>
> Miss Garbo's voice from the screen is deep toned, somewhat deeper than when one hears her in real life. The low enunciation of her

> initial lines, with a packed theatre waiting expectantly to hear her first utterance, came somewhat as a surprise yesterday afternoon in the Capitol, for her delivery is almost masculine. And although the low-toned voice is not what is expected from the alluring actress, one becomes accustomed to it, for it is a voice undeniably suited to the unfortunate Anna.[850]

Variety wrote, "Infinite care in developing each sequence, just the proper emphasis on characterizations and a part that exactly fits Greta Garbo puts *Anna Christie* so safely in the realm of the superlative that nothing less than a rave does justice to everyone concerned, including William Daniels, the cameraman."[851]

It turned out that the silent Garbo had been working with one arm tied behind her back. Sound brought the full range of her skills out. With sound, Garbo's popularity soared even higher.

Robert E. Sherwood, as a playwright, screenwriter, and reviewer, had some insight into what Garbo was accomplishing. Now a syndicated columnist rather than reviewing for *Life*, he stated,

> The Metro-Goldwyn Publicity Department is advertising Greta Garbo as "the greatest living actress," and while it is always a pleasure to any critic to dispute the extravagant claims of press agents, I find myself unable, on this occasion, to utter a word of protest.[852]

Anna Christie marquee in Rochester, New York.

He continued later in his long review:

> Any actor or actress, to deserve that most mis-applied of all epithets, "great," must possess intelligence, grace and power in high degree. Miss Garbo is liberally endowed with the three essential qualities. Her intelligence and grace were revealed in all her silent films, from *The Torrent* to *The Kiss*. Her intense power bursts forth for the first time in *Anna Christie*.
>
> Subject at last to the dangerous exposure of sound, the sinuous Swede displays an abundance of vitality and emotional energy which will be surprising and perhaps shocking to her admirers.[853]

The day after the premiere she brought a bouquet of flowers over to Marie Dressler's house to celebrate her achievement in the role of Marthy.[854]

Garbo's main issue with *Anna Christie* was how it presented Swedish stereotypes. As was her practice she didn't watch the rushes. But she did sneak into the premiere with Feyder and Sören. She told Sören, "Isn't it terrible? Who ever saw Swedes act like that?"[855]

Garbo often watched her films multiple times. A few days later Garbo visited Howard Greer's dress shop and one of Greer's workers said to Garbo, "I'm going downtown in a few minutes to see *Anna Christie*." To which Garbo replied, "How would you like me to go with you?"[856] Off they went to catch the early showing in downtown Los Angeles with another audience clueless to the fact she was sitting among them.[857]

Garbo and MGM had waited and watched how sound worked. They let the technology mature. Then they delivered a film that seemed to demonstrate total command of the medium. Garbo delivered her long scenes and a practiced deeper voice because she had studied sound films for two years.

What followed was an absolute explosion in Garbo's popularity. What does a "popularity explosion" look like? It looks like a graph where you can't keep the line on the chart.

Chapter 25 – Garbo's Popularity Explodes

"Not that she is a poor actress, but that Garbo herself is so much more real and vivid in her audience's mind than the character which she is playing. Her role is like the dress she wears—a sometimes attractive garment which permits her to expose herself decently to the public gaze." [858]

— Clare Boothe Luce, writer

Greta Garbo wearing the headdress from *Mata Hari*.

While Garbo had risen to the top of fan interest and correspondingly to the top position of newspaper and fan magazine reporting before her Swedish vacation, no one could anticipate what was about to happen after *Anna Christie*. It was not just that she was covered by film fan magazines and the general press. The amount of coverage both types of publications gave to movie stars increased dramatically in the late 1920s and early 1930s. From 1927 to 1932 the number of film fan magazines doubled. General newspapers, benefiting from improved technology, printed more photographs and responded to reader demand by writing more about Hollywood. Garbo's image was everywhere.

In its April 1931 issue, *Screenland* magazine captioned a full-page photograph of Garbo with an apology to readers for not having a single article or photograph of her in the January issue. Other stars were fully involved in maximizing their publicity. Paradoxically for Garbo, this happened while she was trying to avoid publicity.

The films of other actors made good money, but that is different from fan engagement. From *Anna Christie* to *Grand Hotel* Garbo made six films (excluding the German version of *Anna Christie*). During roughly the same time Crawford made ten and was the second-most-mentioned female actor in *Photoplay.*

To start, I want to just compare the *Photoplay* mentions of Garbo and Crawford, as they dominated the magazine's attention. In 1932 Garbo was mentioned 780 times in *Photoplay*, a rate of 65 mentions per issue. This is the era where Crawford was appearing in three great films, *Possessed* (1931), *Grand Hotel*, and *Letty Lynton* (1932). From 1933 on Garbo was spending half her time away from Hollywood and making one film per year while avoiding publicity. Yet it is not until 1936 that their names are mentioned at something approaching a similar frequency. During this timeframe, from 1933 to 1940, Crawford was basically making two films per year.

This is in a context where Crawford, at least through the mid-1930s, was one of the other great stars of the era. It is only from 1938 on that Crawford films don't deliver profitability, and this is primarily due to increased production costs. Crawford film revenues stay about the same.

The average domestic revenues of the Garbo films were about a third higher than the Crawford films. Fan interest in Garbo as measured in *Photoplay*

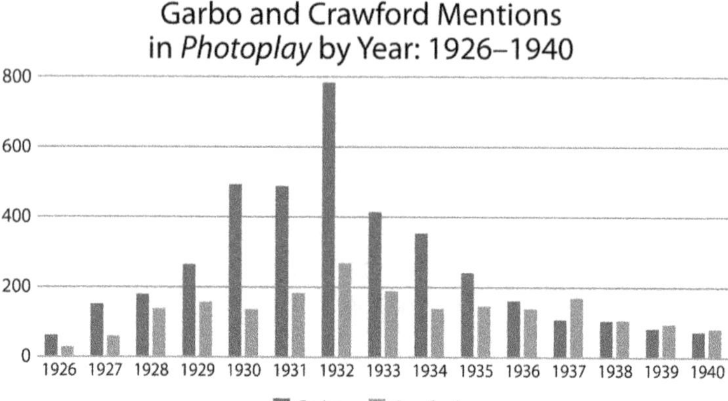

mentions is much more pronounced, with Garbo garnering about three times the mentions as did Crawford. Crawford was Garbo's nearest challenger in magazine interest. Everyone else was laps behind.

When compared to a broader set of popular stars from the 1927 to 1940 era (fourteen years), Garbo still dominated coverage in *Photoplay*. For example, take Joan Crawford, Marlene Dietrich, Janet Gaynor, Norma Shearer, Shirley Temple, Ginger Rogers, Claudette Colbert, Carole Lombard, and Katharine Hepburn. Of the forty-nine times one of these female stars received more than one hundred mentions (as a measure of fan interest) during a year in *Photoplay*, twelve times it was Garbo. Eleven times it was Crawford and eight times it was Shearer. Garbo would have a string of four years, 1930 – 1934, during which she would be mentioned over three hundred times per year. This run was bracketed on each end with a year where Garbo generated over two hundred mentions. Only Dietrich (2), and Hepburn (1) would ever generate over two hundred mentions in a year.

The new wave of stars couldn't generate the interest Garbo could. It would not be until 1938 that other female actors consistently matched Garbo in *Photoplay* mentions. Other actors wouldn't reach the heights of attention Garbo had experienced. Rather, Garbo's mentions would drop to their level. She remained one of the most mentioned actors. This transpired while Garbo was taking long breaks from Hollywood and making only about a film per year.

It seems odd now, but in 1932 as Garbo left for Sweden on her second trip home, journalists were incensed that Garbo would leave without addressing

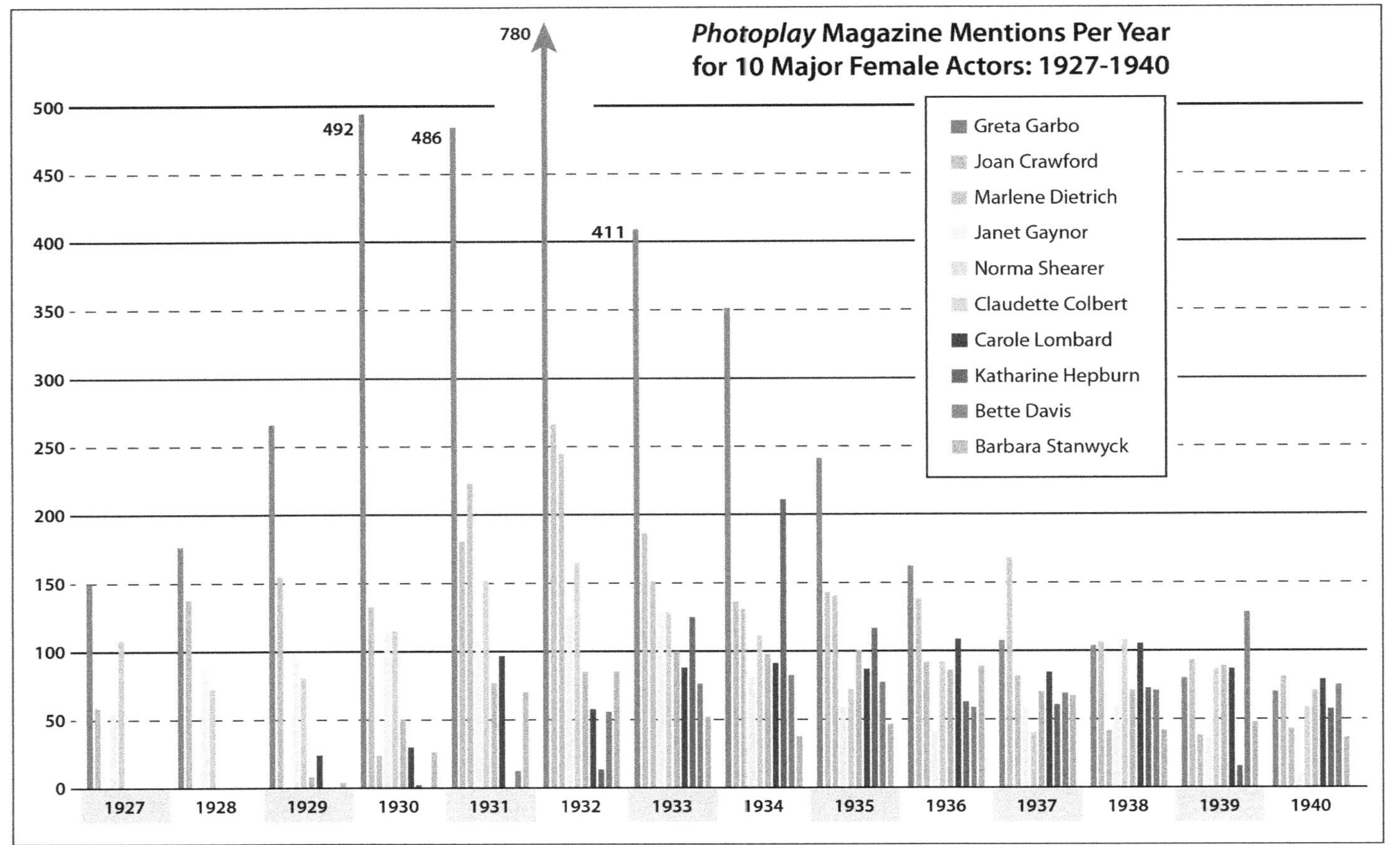
Photoplay Magazine Mentions Per Year
for 10 Major Female Actors: 1927-1940
780
492
486
411
500
450
400
350
300
250
200
150
100
50
0
Greta Garbo
Joan Crawford
Marlene Dietrich
Janet Gaynor
Norma Shearer
Claudette Colbert
Carole Lombard
Katharine Hepburn
Bette Davis
Barbara Stanwyck
1927
1928
1929
1930
1931
1932
1933
1934
1935
1936
1937
1938
1939
1940

them in some public forum. I am sure someone knows where Taylor Swift is going this week, but no one believes she is obligated to announce her travels.

The reaction to Garbo's desire for a private life contrasted with the reaction to a famous male contemporary. Charles Lindbergh was also reluctant to talk to the press when it was not directly related to his flying. Though his attitude changed in the mid-1930s when he decided to publicly champion isolationism. He ignored reporters' questions while traveling. He didn't sign autographs, rarely gave interviews, and was reluctant to be photographed. To avoid the press and fans, he had a pair of glasses (with no prescription) he would put on as a disguise.[859]

Like Garbo, he was used by the media to boost circulation and readership. His reluctance to engage was noted publicly, but it didn't generate anywhere near the backlash that Garbo felt.

The addition of Garbo's voice transformed her career. A strange statement for an actor already at the top of the profession. Now Garbo stood distinctly apart from everyone. Underlying this was her acting skill. Naturalistic acting is best with sound. The character is more complete. As Hollywood acting became more naturalistic overall, Garbo's performance fit into the storytelling of sound films even more than in silent films.

Anna Christie premiered only four years after *Torrent*, but the acting landscape had been transformed. Garbo herself, as described earlier, had driven part of this transition. The conversion to sound led to yet another different acting style. One no longer had to communicate only through action. Just as silent film acting had to differ from stage acting, sound film acting had to differ from both.

Garbo in costume for *Susan Lenox.*

New York stage actors were becoming familiar with naturalistic acting. Konstantin Stanislavski had brought a touring company of the Moscow Art Theatre to the United States from 1923 to 1924. The troupe used an early version of Stanislavski's naturalistic acting method and had been welcomed warmly. For America, the precepts of naturalistic acting flowed from Konstantin Stanislavski and his disciples. Not from Sweden.

By the time sound arrived, Garbo's acting style was no longer remarkable. But she was still the best actor in Hollywood. A parallel would be rock guitar. Jimi Hendrix revolutionized the playing of the instrument. Then many followed in his footsteps. After Hendrix's breakthroughs, other guitarists learned and became his equal. At some point, ranking artists of any kind after the breakthrough becomes an exercise in personal preference. The initial brilliance hasn't been eliminated. The gap has merely been closed.

Garbo continued to mesmerize her audience. She had the technical ability to always be the character she was portraying in a role. Sound freed her to deliver more nuanced portrayals. Still, she was always "Garbo," with all that meant to her audience.

People in the industry could now look at Garbo's work from the position of understanding naturalistic acting. They may not have been able to do what Garbo did on-screen, but they could perceive how she did it.

While evaluations of Garbo's acting in the silent era reflect some befuddlement as to what exactly she is doing to achieve the effect, the sound era brought a new intelligence to other film professionals' insight into her craft.

Garbo built her roles from elements she created. Hyltén-Cavallius would recount, "Stiller had all but anything tried to convince the Metro-Goldwyn directors that Garbo was no 'diva' as they wanted to portray her—but a character actor."[860]

Director George Cukor said,

> It's hard to talk about Garbo, really, for she says everything when she appears on the screen. That is GARBO . . . and all you say is just so much chit-chat. There she is on the screen. How she achieves those effects may or may not be interesting. She is what she is; and that is a very creative actress who thinks about things a great deal and has a very personal way of acting.[861]

Garbo developed a walk for each character, sometimes more than one. MGM executive Samuel Marx watched her develop it for *Grand Hotel*:

> One afternoon I heard footsteps outside my office window, a pacing back and forth, back and forth. It varied each time, in the speed and rhythm of the steps. Finally I got up to look and there was Garbo in the alleyway, deep in concentration. She would do a length, stop, put her hand on her chin and puzzle there for a while, then go at it again. I realized she was working, figuring out how her character would move. She was making *Grand Hotel* at the time, and when you watch that movie today, notice her entrance, the way she sort of floats into the scene. That's what I saw her perfecting that day.[862]

Garbo in costume for *Susan Lenox.*

The walk for *Camille* was completely different. George Cukor described a walk she developed for one of the establishing shots in *Camille*:

> One of the first shots of *Camille* is when she is walking through the glittering halls of the Opera. There are a lot of men standing around smoking, with their hats on, top hats. There was a problem: how should Garbo walk through this group of arrogant men? She was a courtesan, had a certain reputation and couldn't walk through the crowd like a "respectable" woman would. Garbo moved through them marvelously—she carried herself proudly. Almost slipped through as if to avoid their glances. Garbo invented this.[863]

Garbo in costume for *Inspiration.*

Lubitsch talked about her variety of smiles. "She had the most beautiful smile. What am I saying? She had a whole collection of smiles."[864]

The addition of sound just gave Garbo one more tool to work with in building a character. For example, this review by Skinner of the way she uses her voice in *Anna Christie* captures the intentionality of her choices:

> Many of her phrases are whipped out as quickly as if English were her native tongue. In the long speech in which she dominates both men, holds them to unbroken silence, and confesses what her real life has been, she reaches a dramatic power which needs to ask no indulgence. Above all, a speaking part adds noticeably to the rounded perfection of Miss Garbo's art. It breaks through the still mask which was her chief characteristic in the silent films, but this proves an advantage. It enables her to time gestures and facial expressions more accurately, to give them added distinctness and purpose, and to increase the impact of her occasional and rare moments of explosive action. Moreover, the relaxation which inevitably comes with the spoken lines brings a new grace and charm to her lighter passages, adding to the varied pattern of her work without detracting from its essential quality of strong reserve.[865]

Garbo could then pull all these elements together into a cohesive character and build from all of the parts of portrayal: walks, smiles, gestures, speech, everything. The best actors could see this and admire it.

In a rare interview about working with Garbo, Lewis Stone (who appeared in seven Garbo films) said, "She submerges her personality in her work so that you see only the character she plays and never the real individual—this in spite of her sympathetic interest in everyone working with her in the film."[866]

George Marion, co-star in *Anna Christie,* described that concentration on the character as falling in love with it. "She has genius where characterization is concerned; she falls in love with the intellectual aspect of the part and by reason of this sympathy literally slips into her characters. In my opinion this is what is meant by real art."[867]

George Cukor told film historian Gene Phillips,

> Garbo went through a great deal to get a scene right, and I once said to her that she seemed to act a role so easily. She laughed and said that she would kill me for saying that. You have to know how much to rehearse and not overdo it, so that the finished performance in the film will look spontaneous. Garbo knew how to do this. The proper amount of rehears-

> ing does not diminish the spontaneity of a scene, however. When the moment of creation comes on the set, if it has been carefully prepared for, things will happen.[868]

Garbo in a thoughtful pose for *Mata Hari.*

Basil Rathbone told an interviewer the following:

> During the filming of *Anna Karenina*, I watched Garbo and learned from her what I think is the secret of good screen acting; play your part with the least possible physical movement, and the greatest possible mental projection. . . . In films mental projection means everything. And Garbo has this power of mental projection to a superb degree. I learned from her how little to do in order to get the greatest results. My work improved one hundred percent. Now, when I play a part, subconsciously I ask myself, "What would Garbo do with this?"[869]

Rathbone described a specific scene in which he was able to observe her skill: "[Garbo] made a tiny movement . . . the slightest possible drawing away from me, so that she did not touch me as we sat. That little gesture could not have been more effective."[870] However, he could only pick it up watching the rushes. On set he had been puzzled that Garbo had seemingly been doing nothing.

In *Commonweal* the reviewer wrote, "Garbo achieves an extraordinary harmony between facial expressions and bodily movement and speech. Actresses of the older emotional school might find fault with her perpetual understatement. But this, I believe, is her great concealed strength. Outbursts. Such as those which Nazimova once indulged in, are hardly part of her equipment. Her facial expression accomplishes more than a torrent of words. This, of course, reflects one of the benefits of the screen as a medium. The human face is so small in a large theater that many of its finer modulations are lost. But the screen, through enlargement, enables the actor to transcribe the most delicate shades of emotion, of pity, of love, scorn, irony, or rippling humor, with perfect fidelity and the assurance that it will be seen and understood."[871]

Mary Pickford, doyen of all female actors, commented, "Physicality has given way to artistry. Greta Garbo's success in *Anna Christie* has shown conclusively that a great talent can rise above limitations supposed to be insurmountable. But she could not have succeeded without real artistry, and that did not come from any butterfly existence, but from laborious sustained effort, day in and day out."[872]

The completeness of nearly every portrayal in her entire career was the connection point with the audience. Hyltén-Cavallius wrote the following:

> Not until later would I understand that the secret about Garbo's incredible success was that she represented the "romantic woman" as imagined by both the young and the old in the 20s and 30s, perhaps now as well, but you cannot demand too much of a prophet. Also, she turned into that kind of actress after a couple of years, and they are the best—who by intuition, in a sleepwalker's confident way, walks, or rather floats into her roles.[873]

The effect of Garbo did not just happen to the audience in the theater. Melvyn Douglas later said, "I have never played with a woman with such an ability to arouse the erotic impulse. The fact that an actress lets her partner take her in his arms or presses her lips against his does not make a love scene; you have to also see the emotion that drives her to do it, and it is this Garbo conjures forth at the right moment."[874]

Garbo had not been entirely happy with the way the English version of *Anna Christie* had turned out. She got together with Feyder to make changes to the script and to select a new, more European wardrobe.

The surrounding cast had to be changed out for actors who could deliver the lines in German. Garbo's friend Salka Viertel played the role of Marthy. Known in America primarily as a writer, she had an extensive career on stage prior to relocating with her husband to Hollywood in 1928. Marthy was her second, and final, Hollywood role. The initial discussions regarding what would become the film *Queen Christina* happened between Garbo and Viertel at this time.

While Garbo was the focus of her productions, she cared about the ensemble brought together for each project. She helped Gavin Gordon work through a broken collarbone on *Romance*, and when Erich von Stroheim was recovering from back surgery while filming *As You Desire Me*, she would call in sick if

Greta Garbo and Salka Viertel in the German language version of *Anna Christie.*

he was in too much pain to work.[875] Garbo stuck by her co-stars when she could have had them replaced. It makes the later issue with Laurence Olivier's casting in *Queen Christina* unique, the one time Garbo didn't think an actor could overcome an impediment to delivering a role in one of her films.

In addition to filming *Romance* between the two versions of *Anna Christie*, Garbo made *Inspiration*, *Susan Lenox*, and *Mata Hari* in late 1930 and in 1931. The second version of *Anna Christie* (1930) was rather unique in the history of multi-language film production, because the two versions were not shot either simultaneously or sequentially.[876] The reason was that MGM felt it was more important to capitalize on the public reception of *Anna Christie* as a sound film with an immediate follow-up than it was to exploit a small segment of the export market with the release of the German version of *Anna Christie*.[877]

Mata Hari would mark the beginning of a transition in Garbo's career. Though she would make two final films under her five-year contract, MGM would give her roles in different kinds of films. Once free from her long contract, Garbo would approach filmmaking in an entirely new way, and the industry would once more transform due to censorship.

Chapter 26 – Independence

"You can't quit now; we won't let you.
You're at the very peak of your career."[878]

— Unnamed MGM executives to Garbo

Garbo requested Von Sternberg for the role of Carl Salter in *As You Desire Me.*

As the end of Garbo's five-year contract approached, MGM veered from its Garbo film template and cast her in *Grand Hotel* (1932).

Grand Hotel is the first Hollywood ensemble film, with several interlocking plots. Films with multiple storylines were not common before *Grand Hotel*, so for audiences it was a unique experience. In addition to Garbo, John Barrymore, Lionel Barrymore, Joan Crawford, Jean Hersholt, and Wallace Beery were major stars.

Garbo plays Grusinskaya, an aging ballerina who is fretting she has lost the ability to draw fans. She surprises Baron von Geigern, played by John Barrymore, who while royal, is down on his luck. He is in her room to steal her pearl necklace. By odd coincidence they fall in love and Grusinskaya finds the nerve to resurrect her career.

Modern critics focus on the scene where Garbo speaks about being alone, while holding a phone. While this allows them the ability to make commentary about Garbo and solitude, it is not the key scene in the picture. The scene after John Barrymore reveals himself to Garbo is more important and more vivid. We watch as the idea that she is falling in love with the baron slowly crosses her mind. It is classic interior Garbo.

Garbo and John Barrymore falling in love in *Grand Hotel*.

In *McCall's, Grand Hotel* was well received, with kudos to all its stars. But Garbo still stood above them:

> The story is really motivated by Grusinskaya, the dancer, played by Garbo, who in actual footage seems to be on the stage very little of the time, but she proceeds to make it entirely her picture. That scorching quality of her beauty when she walks through the hotel lobby blazing with her happiness; the naked isolation her spirit when she believes her career is over; the tormenting quality of her love—where was I? Oh yes, the rest of *Grand Hotel.*[879]

MGM barely had the time to cast her in *As You Desire Me.* Perhaps with an eye toward showing Garbo it could be a flexible partner once her contract ended, MGM acquiesced to her desire to bring Erich von Stroheim in as the character of Carl Salter. He had had a difficult relationship with Thalberg when working as a director. What von Stroheim could deliver in a role was the sadistic personality of Salter.

Garbo provided a startling new look in *As You Desire Me* by wearing a short blonde wig at the beginning of the film.

As You Desire Me is based on the avant-garde play *Come tu mi vuoi* (How you love me, 1929) by Luigi Pirandello, who won the Nobel Prize in Literature in 1934 for "his almost magical power to turn psychological analysis into good theatre."[880]

As *Variety* noted in its review of *As You Desire Me*, the plot is unlike the standard Hollywood fare.[881] The review says that Garbo carried the film through but that MGM had taken a business risk by selecting such an unusual story.[882]

Most reviews found Garbo's role wonderful. Their issue was with von Stroheim's portrayal of the villain in the story. Probably because he was in pain from a recent back surgery, he takes a line almost everyone found too vehement and brusque.[883] His movement was stilted.

Reviewer Neysa McMein found *As You Desire Me* "lovely and mystifying," and thought the film revealed once again that Garbo defied comparison to any other woman.[884]

It is difficult today to understand the vehemence of some conservatives regarding the presence of European actors in American films. Modern reaction to immigration is more clearly tied to race. In 1927 Perceval Reniers wrote an essay savaging foreigners in film and calling for intervention:

> The influence of the foreign element on the so-called American films—we must face this horrid truth sooner or later—is sufficient just now to make many of them anything but pristine, one hundred percent American films. What with leading men and comedians from England, directors from Germany, Sweden and France, and leading ladies from whatever countries engender such names as Banky and Garbo, it is doubtless high time for some sort of action by the Klan.[885]

Garbo would come to represent all that was wrong with American society to social conservatives. She played women who violated their conception of moral standards and were too free with sex, and she was considered to be so in real life. She represented and encouraged the more modern view of women's role in society. She was foreign. As the Depression slowly led to a socially more conservative America, and as the appeal of Fascism and Communism grew around the world, social conservatives gained power, and their disaffection with Garbo was expressed in the media. Calling on the Klan for intervention was extreme, but not that far removed from how many social conservatives felt.

Garbo was a target. She was quoted in accent when she spoke or was imagined to speak. Even though she now spoke with only a slight Swedish accent. She was lampooned. Taking down Garbo was just part of how one got women to fall in line. Garbo stood quietly against this growing social conservativism. Now that she was on the cusp of being able to choose her own roles, she made a series of assertively feminine and modern choices.

That Garbo was a target was not a secret. After *Susan Lenox*, Garbo was interested in making a film based on the George Bernard Shaw play *Saint Joan* (1923). She asked the German director Ludwig Berger if he would consider directing the film. Berger, clear on what Garbo represented to social conservatives, responded, "Of course [he would direct it]. If you had been born in the fifteenth century you would certainly have been burned."[886]

The woman that Garbo created in *Torrent* was not expected by Thalberg or MGM. She transcends a mediocre script through her portrayal. Beyond that, she created the essence of a Modern Woman, with thought and consideration.

Throughout Garbo's career, before the end of the five-year contract, Thalberg sought to use this ability and the fact that "woman" as portrayed by Garbo was unique and resonated with the audience. He matched her with scripts that called for her to deliver at least a few scenes in which she could work her magic.

Of the films made during Garbo's five-year contract, only a handful of the fifteen films are interesting. *Love* was a great film to start off the contract. Of the silent films that followed, only *The Kiss* really stands out. Since *The Divine Woman* is lost it is hard to evaluate, but it didn't have strong contemporary reviews. The rest—*The Mysterious Lady, A Woman of Affairs, Wild Orchids,* and *The Single Standard*—have great scenes featuring Garbo, but were not great films.

Anna Christie was an inspired choice for Garbo's first talking film. Both versions are wonderful. The sound films that followed—*Romance, Inspiration,* and *Susan Lenox*—are similar to the pedestrian silent films MGM cast Garbo in. *Mata Hari* only rises slightly above the others.

When MGM then decided to make *Grand Hotel* it broke quite a few industry rules. It had multiple interlocking plots, it was an all-star cast, and Garbo played a different role than was usual. While *As You Desire Me* didn't quite work as a film, at least it showed that MGM could use Garbo in different kinds of stories. Going forward after the end of her five-year contract, Garbo's roles became much more interesting.

This shift in the quality of material at the end of the five-year contract was important for three reasons. One issue was that MGM had to position itself as the studio she would be best signing with for her next film. By assigning her to better-quality projects Mayer and Thalberg were demonstrating that they could work outside the formula they had used to maximize her five-year contract.

The second issue was that as great as Garbo was, the public had noticed there was a sameness in her roles. The market was beginning to insist on any kind of different Garbo role.

The third element was that the industry was cribbing from her. While articles pointing out how actors were copying her physical look were amusing, actors were professionals working on their craft. Everyone tried to learn the techniques Garbo used, and many did rather well in this.

Marie Dressler created a totally different kind of screen persona, using a different acting style, after several weeks of rehearsing and filming with Garbo, and it was not a one-off.

After completing *As You Desire Me* Garbo finally had control of her career. She could have done anything. She had money. She could have retired, gone to smaller specialty studios, or returned to theater. She chose to make films at MGM, one of the largest studios. But in control, Garbo made films differently. Instead of three films per year, over the next nine years Garbo made seven films. In five of them she tried to create great art. It didn't always work out. Film is a tricky medium, as so many variables come into play to create the final work.

Garbo later told Cecil Beaton, "I don't hate Hollywood any more than I hate Louis B. Mayer. I don't like Mr. Mayer—although I see his point and I don't blame him for doing to me what he did. . . . He made me sign a long contract—five years—and I was terrified and very unhappy, for it seemed like a life term. When I had finished the contract I said to him: 'This is the end. I don't want to continue. I want to get out of pictures.' He and his minions were so worried! They had these long discussions with me, and we walked up and down outside the soundstage."[887]

In the end Garbo chose Hollywood. Clearly the ability of Hollywood to make the biggest-budget pictures, to deliver the largest audience, and to hire the best technicians mattered to Garbo. Europe made films, but they were just a minor part of the industry. While Hollywood could pay Garbo more than

German, Swedish, or British film companies, Garbo did not need to base her decision just on the money. She had been well compensated to this date, and even in Europe she would still be paid well.

Some writers have hypothesized that Garbo had to sign with MGM because she had lost all her savings in a 1932 bank failure. Rumors ran as high as $1 million ($22.5 million). Garbo did have a significant account at the bank, and she would lose about $100,000 ($2.2 million). Garbo had significant other assets, though clearly this was a painful loss. The financial details that are known are in appendix 4.

For Garbo, the advantage of Hollywood was that it was the best vehicle for reaching her audience. As noted earlier, just a one-week run of *Anna Christie* in the Capitol Theatre in New York delivered a larger audience then the entire Broadway run of the play. Going forward Garbo had choice of material for most if not all her roles. She was looking for the best way to make the films she wanted to make.

In his early biography of Garbo, British author E. E. Laing called his final chapter, which covered her films from *Queen Christina* on, "*The Genius*." He grasped that from this point forward Garbo was the person most in charge of her own career, and he thought it marvelous.[888]

What has been missed in telling Garbo's story from this point in her career is how she chose film projects with intent. They were feminist projects in a time when feminism was in retreat. They directly addressed adultery, marriage, and moral standards. In the two films that don't feature adultery, *Queen Christina* and *Ninotchka*, Garbo plays the boss. A woman in charge. Sex is definitely on the table in these two films, which is problematic enough, but there is no adultery. In this time of tightening censorship controls and with Garbo representing everything social traditionalists now wanted to sweep away, Garbo was the burr under their saddle.

At the same time, Garbo was difficult to attack. She was clearly the greatest actor of the era. The vehicles she chose were literate. Her audience loved her, though this regard did not extend to every corner of America. Her movies made money and Loew's protected her.

Her choices were mostly bold. Even as society became more conservative, she chose projects that addressed female emancipation, equality, and morality. Thalberg worked with her to subvert censorship. The issue of what story could be told, and how, would be central to this part of her career. The epic censorship battle that revolved around *Two-Faced Woman* marked the triumph of the censors, not just over Garbo, but over the industry.

She seems to have tried to work with a new type of director. Rouben Mamoulian, Richard Boleslawski, and George Cukor had achieved their initial success as stage directors. Boleslawski was a major acting theorist, having worked in Moscow with Stanislavski. Ernst Lubitsch had a rather brief early stage acting career before becoming one of the most accomplished directors of his era. Garbo and Lubitsch had known each other socially for years.

Clarence Brown directed two of these films, adding to the five prior Garbo films he had helmed. But we can see from the records that Brown was a substitute. He was now an acceptable backup.

Whatever one thinks of the individual films Garbo made with Mamoulian, Boleslawski, Cukor, and Lubitsch, their career output eclipses that of Garbo's earlier directors, who were workmanlike professionals. Of her other MGM directors, only Sjöström, Goulding and Feyder had great careers. Brown is somewhat in between; he is clearly not of the same rank as Garbo's best directors. But Brown could direct her well and a few films from his career, amid a sea of average films, were excellent.

Stepping back and looking at the nine years Garbo spent working independently, one can see her deliberateness. By independent I don't mean that Garbo produced her films independently. This was still the Studio Era. Rather I mean that she had an independence of action inside MGM. She only made films she wanted to make. It goes beyond the choice of projects. For most of these films she didn't rush into production until the scripts and censorship approvals were in place. The exception was *Conquest*, which became a production nightmare for MGM.

Garbo signed a contract in July 1932 for *Queen Christina* and *The Painted Veil*. She then left for eleven months in Sweden.

Kaj Gynt would report what the pursuit of Garbo in New York in July 1932 was like:

> Garbo and [Ludwig] Berger tried to escape the newspaper men through various stairs—and into a taxi—while at least the photog-

raphers of the scandalous papers hurriedly slipped into other taxis. And then it took off!

Up the avenue and down the street in fanatical zeal not to lose the precious loot at the traffic lights. Out through the Bronx, up the Bronx River Parkway as fast as the cars could go in the rush of traffic, and then "miles and miles and miles" out of the city—and then back again—into the city and out again into Bronxville to the very exclusive and very quiet Hotel Gramatan, located high on top of a cliff. There, Garbo jumped out of her taxi—while the photographer hunters' taxis swerved again at wild speed.

Frightened, Garbo ran back into his car—and it sped off down Bronxville and the Bronx River Parkway and onto Webster Avenue.

Now, had Webster Avenue not been under repair in a couple of places, the cabin would probably have been saved. But as it was, Garbo's taxi had to stop—and the photographers were lucky.

Garbo got out of the car—and was "shot" from three, four different directions. Then she was promised to be left alone.[889]

After being chased by the press, Garbo posed for photos in New York while on her way to Sweden in 1932.

On July 30, 1932, Garbo sailed on the MS *Gripsholm*. *The New York Daily News* sent a reporter to sail to Sweden with her. Though she was onboard with Garbo for the trip, it didn't result in any significant articles.

Garbo arrived in Sweden on August 8, 1932. There ten thousand people turned out for the arrival of the MS *Gripsholm*. On docking Garbo decided to give a press conference in a bid to lessen interest in her visit. She met the reporters in the ship's saloon and spoke extensively. As she surveyed the assembled press she began with, "This looks dreadful."[890]

Asked if she was afraid of the press, Garbo responded thoughtfully, "I am not exactly afraid of the press, but I do not like so much written about me."[891]

When asked what her plans were, she responded, "I haven't any. You get holidays too, don't you?"[892]

There was a set of questions about things that had been speculated as to her next steps. She responded that she had not planned or done any of them. She didn't buy Ivar Kreuger's house, she wasn't going to act in England, and she wasn't starting a film company with Victor Sjöström.

Garbo rented a house in the Stockholm archipelago for the rest of the summer. There she relaxed with her family: her mother, brother, sister-in-law, and their three-month-old daughter. (This daughter is the author's mother. Born Ann-Marguerite, she changed her name to Gray when she was naturalized as an American. When she had first attended school in America, at age seven, her class had been filled with girls named "Ann." As is the way with children's nicknames, Marguerite was transformed by her classmates into "Gray." I will primarily refer to her as Gray.)

Garbo hosting a press conference on the MS *Gripsholm* upon her arrival in Gothenberg August 8 1932.

While Garbo found Sweden a comfortable place to spend time because of her family and friends, she was conscious that she could not return to her former life as an anonymous person walking the streets of the city. Laing nicely summed up her situation: "The crowds, the cars, the flowers, the phone calls and the curious feeling of being Gulliver in a Lilliput filled her world. Sweden as remembered ceased to be."[893]

She wrote to Salka Viertel that "I walk around here like a stranger and can't believe that everything that used to be there is gone. That I am so changed for all of life, for people, for everything. It's so hopeless I'm desperate but that doesn't change anything. I have met four or five people."[894]

Garbo had spent over three years away from Sweden and her family. She was delighted to be home and to be able to stay for nearly a year. Her new contract did not obligate her to start filming until July 1933 at the latest. While she had been gone her brother Sven had gotten married and she now had a three-month-old niece.

Sven had met Ethel Marguerite Baltzer (Peg was what everyone called her) in London in 1930 and they married in May 1931. Ethel Marguerite Svahn had been born in Mishawaka, Indiana, to Swedish parents in 1902. She was orphaned at the age of nine. Two years later she was adopted by August and Tillie (Mathilda) Baltzer, who lived in Kenosha, Wisconsin.

August Baltzer was a successful engineer. In 1918 he was recruited by the Swedish company SKF to be its chief engineer and relocated to Gothenburg, Sweden. Before Tillie and Marguerite could follow, Tillie died of influenza. Peg then left for Sweden and joined her father in Gothenburg. Less than a year later Peg was orphaned again when August suddenly died. By this time she was seventeen and she lived for a time with August's brother and trained as a nurse. When Sven and Peg met, she was the nurse for the Swedish embassy in London.

Peg Baltzer was a nurse when she met and married Sven Gustafson.

Garbo and Peg hit it off right away and became lifelong friends. The importance of Garbo's family has not been delved into by other writers, but it is key to understanding her. The addition of Peg to the family was very comforting to Garbo as she felt that she was a kindred spirit.

Garbo trusted and relied upon her family. She had relatively few close friends in life, and at this point even those were reduced in number with the passing of Mauritz Stiller. In the 1930s both John Gilbert and Mimi Pollak became less central to her life, and she was just meeting Gayelord Hauser and George Schlee. Lilyan Tashman succumbed to cancer in 1934.

Peg, Anna and Gray on a balcony in Stockholm, about 1935.

Garbo originally intended to leave Sweden earlier, but she had been unwell and postponed her departure until March.[895] The MS *Annie Johnson* departed March 26, 1933. The ship only had sixteen cabins, all in the middle third of the ship, with freight carried fore and aft. The ship called on ten different ports before arriving in Los Angeles.[896] The captain reported that Garbo went ashore in Cartagena, Colombia, and Punta Arenas, Chile.[897] The final port of call before San Diego was Colón, Panama, where the MS Annie Johnson spent some days in port.

Deciding to return to the United States on a freighter traveling a roundabout route was an interesting choice for Garbo. World famous, able to buy any ticket she wanted, the expected choice would be a first-class stateroom on a high-end passenger liner. That is how she got to Sweden in July.

Garbo easily fit into "first-class" transportation, accommodations, or vacation locations. She dined at some of the finest restaurants and stayed at some of the most exclusive hotels and resorts. But she also was happy camping or at a rustic vacation home. She had no problem whipping together a meal from what she found in the kitchen. She wandered through the streets and shops of many cities: New York, London, Paris, and Los Angeles, but also those of Klosters; East Brunswick, New Jersey; Oconomowoc, Wisconsin; Santa Fe, New Mexico; and small towns in New England. It is not that Garbo was always accessible. Rather, she had the ability to be accessible when it suited her.

Garbo was an active participant in shipboard games.

Garbo enjoyed the sea, and the idea of spending an extended period on a smaller ship with fewer passengers obviously appealed to her.

Her fellow passengers talked to the press about what Garbo did on the MS *Annie Johnson.* Ture Steen told reporters, "She was very good at deck games. She was a formidable opponent in shuffleboard."[898] He found her approachable and friendly. Other passengers reported that she read voraciously: the Michael Arlen novel *May Fair* (1925) and books on Buddhism and Jenny Lind, among others. When the weather was nice, she liked to sunbathe in a lifeboat on the top deck. Relaxed and casual for most of the trip, she became nervous as they approached San Diego.[899]

Garbo arranged for Salka Viertel to meet her in San Diego when she reached America on April 30. There she met with the press and fans who had figured out her arrival date from news reports. There were two hundred fans at the dock to greet her.[900] Garbo said to them, "I am very happy to be back."[901]

From April 1932, when she finished filming *As You Desire Me,* through August 1939 when she wrapped up *Ninotchka,* she would make six films. She also spent nearly three years in Europe and took many other trips. During this period Garbo lived much of her life away from Hollywood. The star who wasn't there.

Chapter 27 – *Queen Christina*

"Its portrayal of the queen is dangerous because queens have authority, acceptance."[902]

— Martin Quigley, censorship advocate and trade magazine publisher

Ian Keith as Magnus paying obeisance to *Queen Christina*.

Salka Viertel and her husband Berthold had come to Hollywood at the request of director F. W. Murnau in 1928 so Berthold could help him write scripts. Their house in Santa Monica became one of the main centers of expatriate European life in Hollywood. By the time Viertel was filming the role of Marthy for the German version of *Anna Christie*, she and Garbo had been friends for two years. They were both women with an understanding of the dilemmas modern life posed for women of the time, and they sought to address these issues.

Before she left for Sweden, Garbo had been reading Salka Viertel's treatments and draft script for *Queen Christina*. They had conceived of the project on the set of *Anna Christie*. *Queen Christina* was a truly feminist film, and the original script, lost to history, was even more so. Of Garbo's seven independent productions, Viertel wrote at least part of the script for five of them. She also wrote scripts for three unrealized Garbo films.

After signing her new MGM contract, Garbo brought Viertel to meet Irving Thalberg at his beach house in July 1932. Thalberg expressed his interest in the manuscript that Garbo had given him and said he would find Viertel a partner to write revisions.[903]

Queen Christina was the first script that Salka Viertel developed for Garbo. As was the custom at MGM, many hands touched a script and the exact amount of the final product that was Viertel's is impossible to discern. She worked with two or more writers on scripts, most notably Sam Behrman, who added dialogue. While *Queen Christina* and *Conquest* had books to underpin the factual elements of the story, the original film concepts came from Viertel.

Two Garbo films from her independent era were written by famous writing teams, putting Viertel in rather fast company. *Camille* was written primarily by Frances Marion and Zoe Akins. *Ninotchka* by Billy Wilder, Charles Brackett, and Walter Reich. Though she didn't write any of the screenplay, Viertel was responsible for MGM purchasing the rights to the idea that *Ninotchka* is based upon expressly as a Garbo project.[904]

Garbo told Cecil Beaton, "If there was ever any argument about a script I always had this woman to fight for me. She was indefatigable and worked on them to saturation point and always found something good that others wouldn't bother about."[905]

Female writers feature prominently as screenwriters for Garbo films. Marian Ainslee worked on eight different silent Garbo films, writing titles before there was dialogue. Well-known screenwriters Frances Marion, Zoe Akins, Bess Meredyth, and Dorothy Farnum all worked on multiple Garbo films.

While preparing to start *Queen Christina*, Garbo moved into a house at 1201 San Vicente Boulevard in Santa Monica. After filming finally started she wrote to Hörke Wachtmeister:

> I have been suffering the most sleepless anxious period I've had for ages. I hope to God that the worst is over. I have just moved into a house, and I hope I will get a bit of peace behind my closed gates. Marvelous, "wild" garden—it's huge. The only thing worthwhile here. There are chickens as well. God help me if Hollywood finds out that I am a farmer. I have been struggling mightily with *Christina*.[906]

Queen Christina was an important Swedish historical figure, and any Swede would have been aware of her significance. Outside of Sweden few people knew who Christina had been. Her life was three hundred years in the past. It is a story Garbo had an affinity toward since she was Swedish and because it was the historical story of a female ruler.

In Harry Edington's original memo to MGM communicating her return from Sweden, he presented Garbo's proposal that *Queen Christina* start filming on May 15, 1933.[907] This timeline would have brought the production of *The Painted Veil* to a conclusion around October 1933. As events developed, *Queen Christina* did not wrap up filming until October 1933 and filming of *The Painted Veil* was not completed until September 1934.

Garbo had negotiated the option of filming *Queen Christina* in Europe, and she seems to have intended to film it there originally. Garbo visited the Svensk Filmindustri studios out in Råsunda. Garbo also went to London and Paris with Wachtmeister and looked at studios. She saw that they were not as developed as what was available at MGM. She therefore decided to make *Queen Christina* in Hollywood. She wrote to Viertel, "Salka, I know that I am an impossible person but I can't do *Christina* in Europe."[908]

Garbo was deeply involved in production. She had brought the initial story to MGM and had substantial input into the script. She didn't direct, though MGM needed her approval of Rouben Mamoulian as the director. Of all the Garbo films, it is clearly the closest to a story Garbo herself wanted to tell.

Garbo on her way back to Hollywood after deciding she couldn't film *Queen Christina* in Europe.

Garbo had done her own research for *Queen Christina* while in Sweden. She returned to Hollywood with notes on historical architecture and clothing. As well as artifacts from Sweden to contribute to set design. Howard Strickling said that "Garbo was the technical advisor as well as star of *Queen Christina*".[909]

At first Garbo had envisioned a rather true-to-history version of the story, and after Viertel and Bess Meredyth had created a script, Garbo and Thalberg reviewed it. Thalberg, who had produced every Garbo film up to this point and had run the initial development of *Queen Christina*, had a mild heart attack and temporarily withdrew from studio work. Walter Wanger was assigned the job of producing *Queen Christina* in his place. Wanger had come to MGM from Columbia while Garbo was in Sweden, so they had not known each other before the *Queen Christina* project.

Wanger did not think the Viertel/Meredyth draft was "Hollywood" enough. He hired Ernest Vajda and Claudine West to transform it. They did, and then Wanger hired H. M. Harwood, another writer, to craft yet another version. Harwood intended his draft to put forth "the prototype of a modern woman, who shrinks from both marriage and maternity."[910]

Viertel recalled, "The *Christina* script was shaping into the very Hollywood vehicle Garbo had hoped to escape."[911] In a meeting between Garbo, Wanger, and Viertel on May 5 Garbo demanded that the story hew more closely to the original Viertel script. The entire Vajda version was shelved, and the Viertel and Harwood versions were melded together.[912]

It took almost three months to finalize the script after Garbo had arrived in Hollywood from Sweden, leading to production delays. By contrast, resolving the cast issue with Laurence Olivier took two weeks.

After MGM's first two choices for director proved unavailable, a slew of other directors were considered. Finally, MGM asked Garbo if she would accept Rouben Mamoulian. After a trip to the Paramount lot to see a rough cut of *The Song of Songs* (1933), she agreed.[913]

Mamoulian and Wanger had dinner on May 10.[914] Wanger met with Mamoulian again at the studio on Sunday, May 14, and they signed a deal for him to direct *Queen Christina* the next day. The initial May 15 start date for *Queen Christina* was now well out the window.

Mamoulian was not completely satisfied with Viertel and Harwood's script and brought Samuel Behrman in to assist in modifying it. Wanger had originally intended for Viertel and Behrman to work separately, with Viertel giving pieces of the script to Behrman to polish. Behrman destroyed that strategy by marching down the hall to Viertel's office and introducing himself.[915] With their complementary skills, they got on rather well, beginning their productive partnership. With the addition of Behrman for dialogue, a script acceptable to all parties finally emerged. He and Viertel kept ahead of the filming by a day or two as they fine-tuned it.[916]

Years later Mamoulian was interviewed for a television special on Garbo. He had initially insisted that Garbo rehearse scenes, and she demurred. He rehearsed most scenes with just the other cast. He recalled,

> She could really act. She was an intuitive actress. It was something of a miracle, a divine gift. The point is that with her intuition she was able to capture all sorts of emotional states. You did not have to tell Garbo to look like this or that, for this reason or that. No, you just had to tell her which emotion you wanted to have produced for the scene in question. . . . She

Garbo in a thoughtful pose for *Queen Christina*

> produced the emotion on her face, she produced it in her bodily movements—which is more than you can say about many actors. What is absolutely extraordinary about Garbo was that she was both photogenic and intuitive. Garbo was simply unique.[917]

On July 24 Laurence Olivier arrived to complete the cast.[918] Filming started on August 10, but both Wanger and Mamoulian recorded in their datebooks that there was a problem.[919] That problem was Laurence Olivier. Many have speculated that Garbo demanded that MGM get rid of Olivier and bring in Gilbert as a favor to an old friend. Since she had approval power over the main cast, this makes no sense. She had screened his films and approved Olivier as her co-star before production started. The real explanation is that they had no other option. He was supposed to work out, but he just couldn't act against Garbo at that stage in his career. Given how great a career Olivier was to go on to have, it perhaps shows how difficult it was to cast around Garbo. The other lead had to be at the top of their game. Mamoulian recounted the failure of Olivier the following way:

> We rehearsed it at great length and in full costume, and did an elaborate test, but you couldn't "see" him; he was too callow. Sir Laurence and I laugh about it to this day. He told me in London recently: "I resented it for a long time, but you were right, you're absolutely right."[920]

Olivier himself wrote that he realized that he was "too nervous and scared of his leading lady."[921] While he tried to find a way to pull himself together, he couldn't. MGM paid Olivier his full salary and sent him on vacation to Hawaii for two weeks.

A portrait of Garbo for *Queen Christina.*

Given that John Gilbert had totally worn out his welcome at MGM, why did he get brought back for *Queen Christina*? There were no other options. Other male lead actors were working on or committed to other projects. Possible in-house options at

MGM might have been John Barrymore, Clark Gable, Nils Asther, Herbert Marshall, and Robert Montgomery. All of whom had, or would eventually, star with Garbo. None were available. While there were other male actors under contract, they didn't have personalities that fit the character. Lionel Barrymore, for all his talent, was not a fit.

The best fit among non-MGM actors probably would have been Gary Cooper, who was under contract to Paramount and committed to *Design for Living* (1933). Another logical fit, Ronald Colman, was involved in a contract dispute and therefore unavailable. While John Gilbert wasn't anyone's first choice, he was talented enough, fit the role, and was available.

Wanger ended up being the one to call John Gilbert. Gilbert recalled, "He told me to come right over. . . . I laughed. I said I was sorry I couldn't, but I was working. He said over the phone, very low, 'Better come, Jack, they want you for the Garbo picture.'"[922]

Gilbert was able to speak about Garbo's growth as an actor. In an interview after *Queen Christina,* he said, "And I want to tell you that she was magnificent to me while we were working together. She is greater than she ever was, greater to work with, greater in her work."[923]

In the story that was filmed, after all the script revisions, Garbo plays Christina, the queen of Sweden. She has been the queen from a young age. She now faces a royal court that would like to see her get married and produce an heir. While her subjects love her as a queen, the court is interested in succession.

While traveling in the country disguised as a man, she meets a Spanish diplomat, Antonio, played by John Gilbert, who is on a mission to propose Christina's marriage to his king. His carriage has become stuck in the snow. Christina helps explain to his retainers how to extricate the vehicle. Antonio tips her for her counsel, a coin with her image. Circumstances soon throw them together at an inn with only a single room for them to share. As Christina is in men's clothing and not visibly royal, she has no way to dodge the situation. It soon emerges she really does not want to. Antonio and Christina spend three romantic days snowed in together at their inn.

They part, and Antonio continues his journey to give the marriage proposal to the Swedish queen. To his total surprise, he meets her at the palace as queen and realizes what has transpired. Her councilor, Magnus, played by Ian

Garbo and Gilbert snowbound at the inn.

Keith, had hoped to marry her off to a Swedish noble, and sets about trying to replace Garbo on the throne. He works to turn the people against Christina, at which he fails, and then against Antonio, at which he succeeds. In the end, Christina renounces the throne to leave for Spain with Antonio. However, Magnus kills Antonio in a duel. Christina takes the dying Antonio in her arms and decides to leave anyway.

Queen Christina has been seized upon as a rare major Hollywood film from the Studio Era that framed out women from a different vantage point. It told a different kind of story. It was not a purely experimental film made to the wishes of a star, but in the end it had lots of experimental elements. It was as much a vanity project as King Vidor's *The Crowd* (1928), another film that was made by MGM to cater to an important employee's desires. Rather than ending up as a niche specialty film, *Queen Christina* was spectacularly successful.

Garbo wears a very masculine wardrobe for most of *Queen Christina*. The wardrobe reinforces that Christina is, in most respects, like a man. She is the ruler of a country.

Film historian Betsy Erkkila explained what made *Queen Christina* unique:

> Working against the grain of the typical "women's picture" of the Hollywood years, Garbo was able to imagine a female heroine who did not move toward either marriage or tragedy. In tracing the movement of a female figure—a queen—beyond romance and patriarchy toward the open sea, where she is about to embark on a solitary quest for a life that has yet to be written, Garbo created a new kind of female heroine and a new kind of female plot.[924]

In *Queen Christina*, she is the one on a quest. She has her romance with Antonio, but it is a romance that frees her from the straitjacket of royal court expectations. What matters is the resolution of the intersecting desires of Christina's life. After Antonio's death, Christina still wants to sail away into her future.

Queen Christina closes with one of Garbo's best scenes across her entire career. In it, with Antonio dead and her throne renounced, she sails from Sweden. The entire scene is Garbo staring forward as the camera slowly tightens on her face.

The famous final scene of *Queen Christina*.

This is not the ending in the original script. The script, dated July 31, called for Christina to stand beside the body of Antonio and look out to sea. The closing shots that followed were to be of the ship sailing into the sunset. Instead Wanger had Christina walk to the ship's prow.[925]

The final scene is set up by Christina's reaction to the death of Antonio. He is not yet dead when she arrives. She lifts her head from his corpse with a tear in her eye, and a steely resolve then crosses her face.

This famous closing shot presented a technical problem. There was no lens that existed to seamlessly move from such a wide angle to a close-up focus. Mamoulian solved that problem by developing a glass interface that changed the resolution of the lens by being slid across. The idea came from magic lantern slides he remembered from his childhood.

In the scene the camera settles on Garbo's profile at a distance and slowly zooms in. Garbo asked Mamoulian, "What do I express in this last shot?" Mamoulian replied, "Nothing. Absolutely nothing. You must make your mind and your heart a complete blank."[926] Which she does for forty-two seconds.

This is an echo of Stiller's old instruction to allow the audience to paint in the details.

When we get to this final scene, Christina's thoughts are not those of a woman wondering who she is going to date when she gets to Spain. She is an individual on a journey. The viewer gets to imagine going on that journey themselves.

Christina is a new type of female heroine. She is an independent woman acting for her own account. You can't have a modern female superhero film without first having *Queen Christina.*

There are several themes that arise in the screenplay for *Queen Christina* that make it a multidimensional story. There is Christina's conflict between her personal interests and her public duty. This issue is constantly before her. Christina must make a related choice between spiritual fulfillment and material things.

Christina is in conflict with her advisors, all male, regarding the best way to improve the lot of Sweden. They are for war. Christina is for culture and trade.

Queen Christina wades into sexual politics. When Christina and Antonio embark upon their affair at the rural inn, Antonio presumes that as a royal emissary, he is in a superior social position to his as-yet-unidentified lover. This is of course reversed when Antonio appears at court and realizes Christina is the queen. Even in the seduction itself, it is Christina who seduces Antonio.

Christina is an androgynous role. When initially seen, she is dressed as a man and carries herself as one. She is always the ruler of her kingdom and the decision-maker. Even after she encounters Antonio, Christina remains androgynous, never strictly female. As Christina finds love, she never loses her manner to become a classic, dependent female character.

While sex with other men is referred to early in the film, when Christina meets the Spanish Ambassador Antonio, the denouement of their evening at the inn is played for sexual ambiguity.

Christina and the royal party arrive at the inn. Antonio is strangely drawn to her, though he thinks her a man. Then, when Christina removes her jacket, finally revealing her sex, Antonio says, "Life is so gloriously improbable." He is happy to discover his sleeping companion a woman, but it seems he was accepting of a man as the romantic alternative. Love is love.

Once the now heterosexual relationship of Christina and Antonio is embarked upon, there is now the problem that it is an out of wedlock affair. They spend three days in their room. Garbo famously goes around the room touching and memorizing it.

Mamoulian described making the bedroom scene as follows: "The whole bedroom scene in *Queen Christina* I rehearsed with Garbo in metronome and I put music in later. It's like a choreographed visual sonnet."[927] Mamoulian said, "Of course I had Miss Garbo. Not many actresses could do this scene with such grace."[928]

Joseph Breen had taken over the enforcement of the Production Code in December 1933, but he did not have the tool of the yet to be created Production Code Administration. One of his first tasks was to review the proposed script for *Queen Christina*. By late March he had already objected to the scripts of seven films. Working under the original Production Code producer's jury system, of these seven only *Queen Christina* was left relatively intact.[929] This was the beginning of a series of censorship battles between Breen and those producing Garbo's films, and in a sense, because Garbo had chosen the stories, with Garbo.

As a queen Christina was problematic because she seemed to reject marriage and her duty to produce an heir. She clearly had sex out of wedlock, often. She dressed and lived as if she were a man. She was in a lesbian relationship with her maid Ebba. Salka Viertel and Irving Thalberg added the scene where Christina kisses Ebba after watching a similar lesbian kiss in the German film *Mädchen in Uniform* (1931), with the express intent of creating controversy.[930] Garbo was all for it. The very concept of a queen who ruled as Christina did was offensive to the conservative view of the place of women.

Queen Christina was written, filmed, and released under the SRC censorship regime. Based on the correspondence that exists, the film would have been gutted if it had been released under the PCA, which was only six months into the future. Breen wanted extreme cuts to the film and was overruled by the Producer's Committee.

In his letter to Mayer of January 8, 1934 Breen would,

> Respectfully suggest that, beginning with the scene in which the chambermaid seeks to unloosen Garbo's boots, down to the scene in which Garbo is discovered munching grapes in front of the fireplace, you delete all of the intervening scenes, action and dialogue which are played in the bedroom. This means that all of the business of undressing and the dialogue which accompanies it; and the entire sequence of the servant inquiring about the chocolate, should be deleted. The action which has Miss Garbo wandering about the room caressing the furniture, the bed, the wall, etc., *should be curtailed.* We feel we should insist especially that Miss Garbo in this scene *keep away entirely from the bed and fondling the pillow.* We also feel that the following dialogue between Garbo and Gilbert should be deleted;
>
> Christina's lines, "This is how the Lord must have felt when he first beheld the finished world—with all his creatures breathing—living. You are going to Court. What if the Queen keeps you there?"
>
> Antonio's reply "Let her try."

> Christina's line "If one-half her reputation is well founded."
>
> Antonio's answer "After you she will be tiresome."[931]

This would have erased the central pivoting point of the plot. Not to mention about 10 percent of the film.

Since under the SRC regime a film was evaluated for censorship after completion, this letter is basically demanding that the finished film be reshot and recut.

The history of how Breen got to this January 8 letter is illuminating, as Mayer, Thalberg, Wanger, and Mamoulian ignored the SRC from start to finish.

On August 7, 1933, the day filming started, SRC employee James Wingate wrote to Eddie Mannix after reviewing the script for *Queen Christina*.[932] He gets right to his main problem with the script, the scene in the bedroom at the inn. Wingate writes,

> Aside Aside from some details, the script presents one major difficulty from the standpoint of the Code, as well as censorship and policy. This is the sequence in which it is indicated that Christina enters into an intimate sex relationship with Antonio and spends three days in the same room at the Inn with him. It seems to us that the explicit portrayal of any such liaison between these two characters is inadmissible under the Code and likely to endanger the entire story from a censorship standpoint.[933]

There were several other points in the letter regarding lines and scenes that remained in the final version. One was the line "I have no intention to. I shall die a bachelor." Wingate found that suggestive, because it indicates that a woman avoiding marriage was an appropriate lifestyle choice.

A file memo from August 11 shows that Jason Joy, head of the SRC, and Wingate met with Walter Wanger to discuss the objections.[934] Joy suggested that the problematic scenes be shot in several versions as to manage any censorship complaints. Wanger lied and said these complaints would be addressed.

Instead of going back to the SRC, MGM took its final version of *Queen Christina* to the New York State censor on December 21. With some cajoling by MGM, *Queen Christina* was approved by New York with only three minor cuts.[935]

Queen Christina premiered on December 26, to take advantage of the holiday crowds. Then MGM released it broadly with just the New York State revisions. In early January Will Hays wrote not one, but two, letters to Nick Schenck objecting to this. On the same day as the second letter, Breen wrote his letter to Mayer with all of the changes he demanded.[936]

He didn't get them. The Producer's Jury of Ben Kahane, Jesse Lasky, and Carl Laemmle Jr. overrode the SRC and approved *Queen Christina* for broad release. In actuality, MGM had already released the film. Once out for viewing, the public and local censorship boards didn't have the same qualms that the SRC had about the inn scene. No province or state required any significant changes.

Breen had two basic problems in trying to censor films the way he and his censorship group wanted. Martin Quigley, a central figure in the Catholic push for more censorship, wrote, "Our ideas of morality in entertainment differ radically from those held by the vast majority of the public."[937] Breen couldn't appeal to the will of the majority because the majority was not in favor of censorship.

The second issue was his lack of power. After his defeat over *Queen Christina*, Breen wrote to FitzGeorge Dinneen, "I can scold and argue and coax and threaten *but I have no real authority to stop* the dirty pictures."[938]

There was a total lack of public perception that MGM and Garbo went too far with *Queen Christina* regarding sex and appropriate feminine roles. The editorial offices of America were not overwhelmed with complaints about a libertine film. Censorship was the province of a loud minority.

Queen Christina generated $767,000 ($18.9 million) in domestic revenue for MGM. Some historians have pointed out that this was less than several earlier sound films made under Garbo's five-year contract. *Anna Christie, Mata Hari,* and *Grand Hotel* all generated a bit over $1 million ($24.6 million) in domestic revenue. The domestic revenue from Garbo's other early sound films fall in the neighborhood of that for *Queen Christina.*

This analysis misses the fact that despite the arrival of the Depression in 1929, studio revenues held up until 1932. With domestic revenue of $767,000, *Queen Christina* was rather handily outperforming what one would expect a 1933 Depression film to do (one would expect about $100,000 ($2.5 million) less per film after 1932). This also misses that Loew's was still benefiting from

Garbo's particular audience of people who attended its first-run theaters.

Queen Christina did mark a shift for Garbo films. From this point forward foreign film rental revenue for Garbo films was higher than domestic revenue. *Queen Christina* made an astounding $1.8 million ($45.3 million) in export markets. In total *Queen Christina* delivered the largest film rental income of any Garbo film to that date.

Garbo's dominance of the foreign market spanned her career. From *Queen Christina* on, it defined it. Export revenue was $500,000 ($12.3 million) more than either *Grand Hotel* or *Mata Hari*, the only earlier Garbo films to generate more than $1 million in foreign markets. Of all the Garbo films, only *Ninotchka* and *Camille* generated more export revenue for MGM than *Queen Christina*. During the absolute depth of the Depression, *Queen Christina* delivered solid revenue just when Loew's needed it the most.

Garbo had picked a quirky project, developed the concept with Salka Viertel, and while it was made in the MGM system, it was done more or less her way. It intentionally tweaked the nose of the social conservatives. The result was a commercial triumph.

Even at this late date there were reviewers who did not like Garbo's understated method of acting. William Troy in *The Nation* decried the bedroom scene in *Queen Christina*, which he found inappropriate and badly directed. He pointed out Garbo's acting in *Anna Christie* and *Romance* as too understated when compared to the acting of the original stage roles. He hoped that she could find a way to act in a more histrionic fashion. Though he conceded that this would probably go against both her nature and training.[939]

Harry Evans, writing for *Life*, found Garbo's acting in *Queen Christina* the finest she had done to date. He noted that she had more warmth and human appeal than ever.[940]

In Detroit the *Free Press* wrote, "Never has Miss Garbo looked more mysteriously alluring nor acted her role with greater intelligence, delicacy and feeling. She has a warm fervor not always present in her acting."[941]

Modern reviewer Danny Reid at pre-code.com considers *Queen Christina* "a movie that's built to be larger than life. A weird sort of epic not built on battles between armies but that ensconced within a woman's soul."[942]

Martin Quigley wrote about what he wanted to see in films from his view of morality in a book intended to justify the PCA, written three years after *Queen Christina's* release. It was one of his examples of an immoral film:

> *Queen Christina.* A rewriting of history that transcends dramatic license, presenting among other objectionable incidents a bedroom sequence which registers with voluminous and unnecessary detail the fact of a sex affair. The sequence is emphasized and dwelt upon beyond all purposes legitimate to the telling of the story, thereby assuming a pornographic character. Its portrayal of the queen is dangerous because queens have authority, acceptance.—Released February 1934.[943]

The primary reason that Garbo was important to the export market was that the educated working women living in New York and Chicago could find a mirror of themselves in the cities around the world. For example, a review from Australia *(The Sydney Morning Herald)* seems like it could have been written in America:

> Greta Garbo acts magnificently in *Queen Christina.* In its dignity, its sympathy, and its emotional directness, her performance lifts the film to inspired heights. To express the personality of the Queen of Sweden, who blended womanly feeling with such practical authority and force, she had heightened her acting into a harder and brighter key. Yet there is nothing metallic about it. That is the supreme achievement. In the episodes where Christina wears male attire, there is boyishness without angularity.[944]

European reviews were like those in America. *The Karlsruher Tagblatt* is an example, pointing out that several key scenes, the bedroom after Christina and Antonio's romantic night and the closing scene, are powerful for using more or less silent film acting skills:

> The secret of today's success is none other than that the great and beautiful artist Greta Garbo gives a soul painting with metaphorical conquest and with unconditional spiritual grasping, which all carries the partly not unkitschy, even alarmingly that comfortingly, grazing events in real artistic height and ennobles the material poetically. In addition, the specifically cinematic requirement, i.e. the silent mimicry, comes into its own again more often in a pleasing return, whereby Greta Garbo can rise to her greatest ability.

> Greta Garbo's greatness lies in the predominantly silent film performance. This is her most effective and irresistibly moving artistic device.[945]

Garbo herself was not completely happy with the final film. She reiterated this during an interview on the MS *Kungsholm* on her return to Sweden in 1935. When asked about the film she replied, "That picture never was done the way I wanted it—at all."[946] She had also worried that Sweden, where Christina was part of the national origin myth, wouldn't take kindly to the liberties taken with the story to create the film. Keil-Möller wrote about the reaction in Sweden:

> It was a strange experience of the Swedish public to see her characterize a portrait of one of our best known queens and to be able to observe that every feature of this portrait was a perversion of historical fact, every line a distortion, that the story teemed with what for the Swedish audience were thoroughly grotesque, ludicrous and false elements—and in spite of all this to bow before the might of the personal radiance that emanated from Garbo herself. The Swedish public ignored completely the fact that this was supposed to be a recreation of a familiar historical figure. People simply rechristened the film "Garbo" in their minds and were thus able to preserve their mental composure and enjoy her creation.[947]

Garbo on her trip with Rouben Mamoulian to Arizona and New Mexico in January 1934.

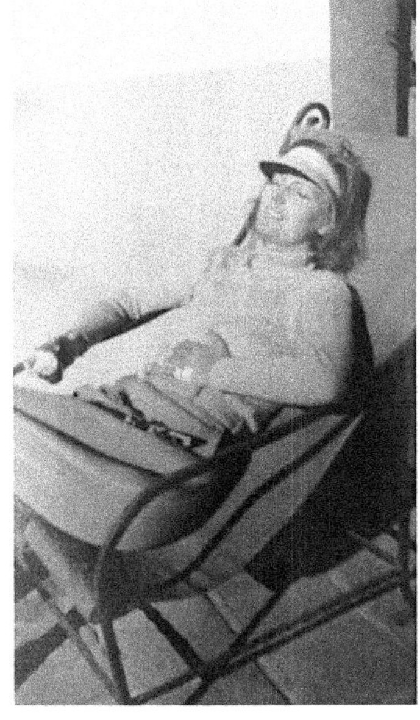

Garbo and Mamoulian had started dating during the filming of *Queen Christina*. They were frequently seen dining around Los Angeles. The couple took a vacation to Arizona and New Mexico. Based on Mamoulian's calendar, the trip began about January 6.[948] On January 12 they were recognized at a hotel in Holbrook, Arizona, despite their cover names of Mary Jones and Robert Bonji. They departed before anyone from the press arrived, but shortly thereafter they were found at Grand Canyon National Park, where they had gone hiking. Reporters then blanketed the state looking for them.

At some point Mamoulian and Garbo had an interaction with the Arizona Highway Patrol. Mamoulian walked away with a card wishing him a pleasant visit and a small five-pointed cardboard badge with a typed note on the back to take care of him as he was a friend of Garbo's, signed by the superintendent of the Arizona Highway Patrol. Mamoulian took some snapshots of Garbo during their trip in which she seems utterly relaxed.

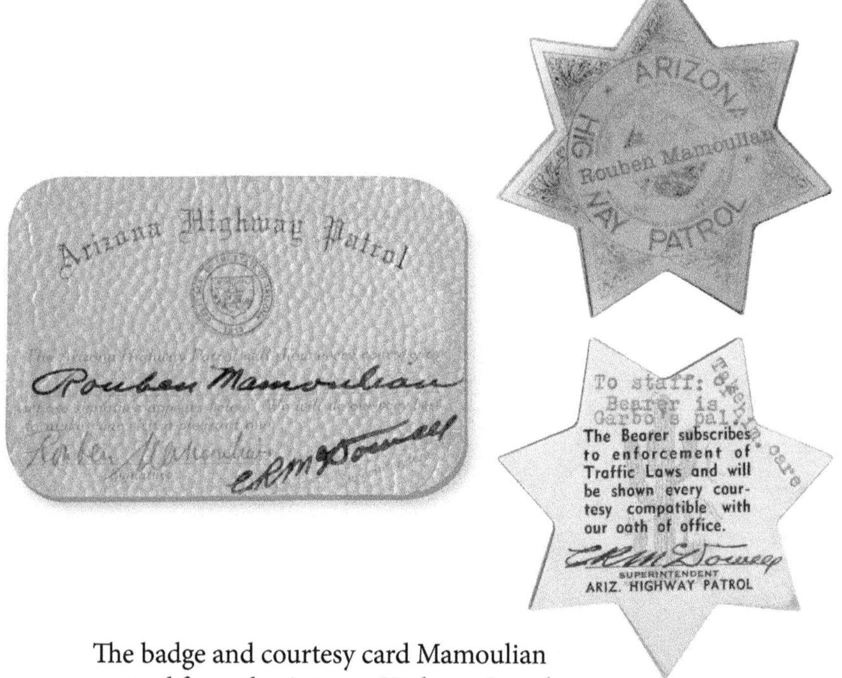

The badge and courtesy card Mamoulian received from the Arizona Highway Patrol.

Chapter 28 – Censorship

"The moving picture industry can be improved. Great pressure can be brought upon the producers at the present time under the National Recovery Act. Further, if betterment can also be made by the bankers, the Bank of America will help us here. The Chase National Bank loans a great deal of money, and young Rockefeller could talk in an effective manner to the producers. A few announcements from Federal Judges would also be helpful."[949]

— Bishop John Cantwell of Los Angeles in a letter to Rev. John Burke, September 1933

In ***The Painted Veil*** Garbo falls in love with the husband she cheated on. Photo by Clarence Sinclair Bull. Courtesy of the Greta Garbo family archive.

The studios were able to manage early censorship rather handily. It was a local market issue. In a technical sense it was easy for silent films to accommodate local variations in censorship. Title cards could be changed and film scenes dropped out or rearranged with less effect on the final story than was possible with sound films. Those desiring censorship were not as organized before 1930, and had differing objectives. For example, some Protestant and women's pressure groups wanted to restrict portrayals of drinking in film, while Catholic pressure groups were unconcerned by it.

Even with the early weak form of censorship, film companies were responsive to the issues in particular films. Studios held previews for interested parties, which sometimes led to changes in films before release. The studios had no interest in public confrontations.

Social conservatives pushed for national standards. With the development of first the "Don'ts and Be Carefuls" in 1927 and their evolution into the Code in 1930, the industry had a set of guidelines for making films that was acceptable to many forces for censorship, at least in theory. The problem for the pro-censorship forces was the weak enforcement mechanism. All the SRC was able to do was show studios where they were likely to be censored based on these standards and communicate with local censorship boards. The decision of whether or not to self-censor based on this input was then an economic one for the studio that weighed the audience interest in the racy scene in question versus the likely cost in revenue from exhibition prohibitions. In most cases the censors were "protecting" the audience from scenes that did not trouble them.

There was a realization by some censorship advocates that if strict censorship was fully implemented, the result would be boring films that audiences did not go to see. Jason Joy, head of the SRC, was content to accept a system of coded meaning in film "from which conclusions might be drawn by the sophisticated mind, but which would mean nothing to the unsophisticated and inexperienced."[950]

Thalberg, who chaired the committee that developed the Code, was focused on protecting the urban first-run market, where the industry made almost half of its revenue.. This market was comprised of the working women whose morals the censors claimed they wanted to protect. They were happy with a lower level of censorship than what any of the social pressure groups hoped to achieve.

Once Garbo was a star MGM tried to persuade censors that Garbo films were special, and this was often successful. Where it ran into local concerns, MGM pointed to other markets that had accepted the original version and pulled out reviews lauding the film and Garbo's acting. Though it edited when necessary. MGM had offered alternate happy and sad endings to *The Temptress* and *Love*. Real problems for Garbo films mainly occurred later, with the arrival of the Production Code Administration (PCA).

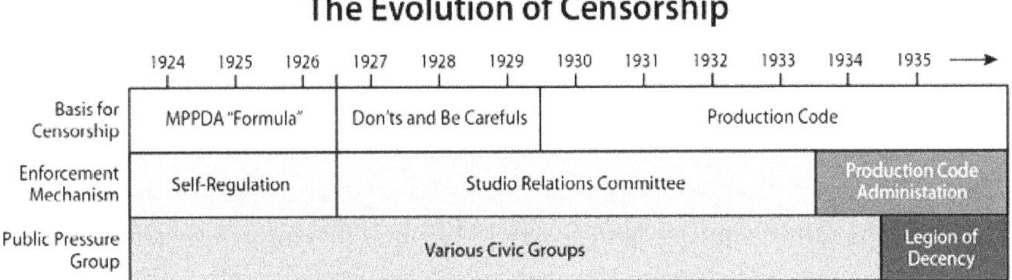

A chart showing the evolution over time, from 1924 through 1936, top row: the document that was the basis for censorship, middle row:the enforcement mechanism, and bottom row: the emergence of the Legion of Decency as a public pressure group.

The driving force for increased censorship was a self-organized group I will refer to as the Breen Group. It was comprised of five people. The three priests were Daniel Lord, FitzGeorge Dinneen, and Wilfrid Parsons. The lay Catholics were Martin Quigley and Joseph Breen. All five had been involved in attempts over the years to set limits on what the film industry made and released. They were all unhappy about how the Code was enforced under the SRC. They were not all of one mind as to how to structure censorship. For example, Martin Quigley would write to Charlie Pettijohn, a PCA employee, in November 1934: "Father Dinneen's outfit, there in Chicago, continues in what I believe to be an unfair manner in slugging the industry continually and embarrassing us in various of the things that we seek to accomplish."[951]

The Breen Group, the formal church hierarchy, and the extended group who had organized the implementation of the Code became progressively unhappier with the way that the SRC enforced it.

After the failure of the SRC to alter either the script or the final edit of *Queen Christina*, the Breen Group realized that the initial implementation of the Production Code had not achieved the objectives they had set out for it. Breen felt that the underlying problem was that Hays "was a compromiser who sold us a first-class bill of goods."[952] The group made a plan to put teeth into the enforcement of the Code by replacing the SRC with the PCA and creating the Legion of Decency They conspired, met in secret, and laid out a series of steps that took months to implement.

In a set of remarks to the annual assembly of the American Catholic hierarchy Bishop Cantwell, in a speech ghostwritten by Breen, laid out the issues. The film companies were making films that contained "sexual irregularity, free love, prostitution, illegitimate children, race suicide, native nudity and the freedom of women."[953] Too much objectionable material was being permitted to get through the process.

One of the main architects of both the Legion of Decency and the Production Code Administration, Martin Quigley, cited *Queen Christina* as a picture that violated moral standards in his 1937 book justifying censorship. He had two points against the film. One was about sex and the other about female role models.

Regarding sex, he found the hotel room scene, which features no visuals of sex, offensive because on the morning after, Garbo wandered about the room seeking to memorize its contents so she could remember the night. He is offended that her character might have had a good time:

> Presenting among other objectionable incidents a bedroom sequence which registers with voluminous and unnecessary detail the fact of a sex affair. The sequence is emphasized and dwelt upon beyond all purposes legitimate to the telling of the story, thereby assuming a pornographic character.[954]

Since the point of the story is that due to this tryst Garbo's character falls in love with the Spanish envoy, in a love so deep she will abdicate her throne, a description of the effect of the evening on her psyche seems warranted. But the complaint is in line with the underlying Catholic belief that enjoying sex is not the point of sex, so any enjoyment of it should not be discussed.

The other point Quigley makes is often overlooked. He found Garbo's portrayal of the queen subversive because she doesn't act the way she should by his view of royal behavior. Her actions as an authority figure who abandons authority, are "dangerous."[955]

Here Quigley is upset with the fact that since Garbo plays a queen, her actions in the film—the rejection of marriage, the rejection of authority, and the famous lesbian kiss—will inspire women both to pursue sinful pleasures in real life and to reject conservative gender roles. He is upset with the permissions granted.

The creation of the PCA was dictated by the bankers who did business with the film industry. The Depression had reduced revenues just as the film companies had increased their financial borrowing to convert to sound. The Breen Group buttonholed the bankers and told them that their investments were at risk if the SRC was not replaced by the PCA. In the depth of the Depression they threatened the bankers with a Catholic boycott of theaters.

The Breen Group worked to coordinate the statements made by Catholic archbishops, and even the pope himself, to give the perception of greater unanimity among Catholics than there actually was regarding censorship. Then they organized the normally fractious archbishops behind the creation of the Legion of Decency. When the Legion was initially created in April 1934, it was only a device to have Catholics pledge to watch wholesome films. Over time it became the unified voice of Catholicism regarding film.[956]

The Breen Group designed a new two-part mechanism to enforce the Code. First, the SRC was replaced by a new office, the Production Code Administration (PCA). The PCA had the authority to pre-approve scripts before they went into production. Another difference was that, instead of going to a producer-driven committee to resolve differences, they were resolved by the board of directors for the MPPDA. Any film not approved by the PCA could not be shown in MPPDA theaters and there were fines to enforce this rule.

The organizing meeting for the legion was discussed in letters by Joseph Breen to John McNicholas. In a letter to McNicholas on May 12, 1934, Breen seeks to alter, to his liking, the composition of the Episcopal committee that created the legion.[957]

Catholic bishops did not want to create a record of their efforts to censor films. For example, the meeting of Catholic archbishops in Cincinnati on June 21, 1934, expressly to discuss the film industry seems to have produced no notes. At a minimum Bishop Cantwell of Los Angeles, Martin Quigley and Joseph Breen all attended this meeting, as their correspondence coordinating their arrival can be found. According to the archivists it is unusual that the discussions that took place during such a meeting are not recorded in the Cincinnati archdiocese archives.[958]

The film industry was aware of the meeting of archbishops, and Will Hays asked to be included. In a June 9 letter to Quigley, Dinneen makes it clear that Hays's request to be present has been rejected. He writes, "We got stung once. No one trusts Hays and I think that it would be quite ridiculous for him or

ARCHBISHOP'S HOUSE
5418 MOELLER AVENUE
NORWOOD, OHIO

March 25--1934

My dear Mr. Quigley:-

If it is convenient for you to come to Cincinnati any time during the week April 15-April 22, I shall be happy to see you and to discuss the motion picture question.

Kindly let us know the time and train of your arrival. There are many stations in Cincinnati, and this is often very confusing for a stranger. It will be best for you to come into the Union Station, the principal one of the city.

It is very gratifying to know that the Church has men like yourself, willing and anxious to help in the cause of souls.

I wish you would feel the greatest liberty in mapping out a program which in your judgment it would be wise for the Episcopal Committee to follow. If you have any suggestions that you wish me to submit to the Committee, I will have occasion to see Bishop Boyle and Bishop Noll in Washington on April 11th, when we have a meeting of the Administrative Committee of the N.C.W.C. One would think it might be well for us to meet you at Washington during our conference; but this never works out well. We literally have hundreds of things to consider and to decide. We have neither the time nor a favorable opportunity to weigh seriously such a question as the evils of the moving pictures.

Wishing you a joyous and blessed Easter, I am

Faithfully yours,

John T. McNicholas
Archbishop of Cincinnati

Mr. Martin Quigley,
Quigley Publishing Company, Inc.
1790 Broadway,
New York City

The details of a Catholic meeting that led to the Production Code Administration and the Legion of Decency were not recorded. This letter from Archbishop McNicholas to Martin Quigley inviting him to it is one of the few pieces of evidence that the secret meeting took place. Photo by the Martin Quigley archives. Courtesy of Georgetown University.

any other representative of the industry to expect to head off this campaign with beautiful promises. Let Hollywood do real penance and show results of genuine reform over an extended period."[959]

As the public development of the Legion took shape, discussed in newspapers and from pulpits across America, Hays responded by appointing one of the Breen Group, Joseph Breen, as the chief of the Production Code Administration (PCA) office in June 1934, replacing the SRC. This change made Breen the censorship officer of the Motion Picture Producers and Distributors of America (MPPDA). Breen would be an effective administrator who was capable of compromising with the studios. Unlike some censorship advocates, Breen understood that films had to draw an audience. Yet his underlying attitude was hostile. In a letter to Martin Quigley from May 1, 1932, he wrote about Hollywood, "But the fact is that these damn Jews are a dirty, filthy lot. Their only standard is the standard of the box-office. To attempt to talk ethical values to them is time worse than wasted."[960]

The studios didn't really have a choice about the replacement of the SRC by the PCA because their bankers insisted upon it. The other new reality was that with the onset of the Depression the country became more socially conservative. New external threats, fascism, and Communism arose. The rights of women became a secondary concern.

The Episcopal Committee on Motion Pictures (ECMP), which Archbishop John McNicholas chaired, planned to operate in the background. The idea was to create a public separation between the ECMP and the Legion, which was ostensibly nondenominational. Though in practice the Legion was entirely controlled by the ECMP.

The Legion started working cooperatively with the PCA to bring public pressure to bear on films that pushed boundaries of the Code through what was eventually a single national rating system. The Catholic Church had de facto control of both the PCA and the Legion of Decency. From 1934 on, the rules of censorship were then slowly tightened, with ever stricter guidelines for acceptance of storylines and scenes.

It took over a year for the organization of the Legion of Decency to crystalize, as the relationship between the local offices and a central authority had not been created. The Chicago office in particular developed an idiosyncratic way of classifying films that took months to resolve. So, during this initial period a film like *Anna Karenina* could receive a PCA approval, be rated as acceptable for adult viewers by the New York Legion of Decency, and be condemned by the Chicago Legion.[961] In November 1935 the Breen Group finally was able to get agreement for the creation of a single national list of film ratings created by a national Legion office in New York.

Hays sent an assistant, Lupton Wilkinson, around America in late 1934 to assess what people thought about the legion and censorship. Wilkinson reported back that censorship served primarily to drive increased ticket sales. Bans were either ignored or circumvented. In the South, members of the Klan considered legion bans to be a papist plot. Of the major cities, only in Philadelphia did the legion control theater attendance to any degree. Everyone wanted to talk about immorality in the movies, and then go to see them that evening.[962]

Breen was concerned with both personal and societal ethical values. Films that showed a character's crimes or sins had to be balanced by "sufficient good." In portraying sex, Breen severely curtailed what action could be shown on-screen. Even kissing couldn't be overly passionate. Films could not be pro-Communist, antiwar, or antibusiness. Law enforcement had to be respected, and characters could not be contemptuous of society, patriotism, or social conventions.

In the period between 1934 and 1941 the PCA reviewed scripts and had changes made. Once blessed by the PCA, the films were almost uniformly then approved for audiences by the Legion. The Legion merely sorted them into categories, A1, A2, and B. During these years the C (condemned) category was basically reserved for objectionable non-Hollywood films.

Turning back to the PCA regime and the portrayal of sex, the first rule was that the sexual behavior in question had to be essential to the plot. The general stricture that the sympathy of the audience should never be thrown to the side of "wrongdoing" led logically to the presumption that illicit or unconventional sexual behavior should only be shown in order to be condemned.[963] The sanctity of the marriage bond was paramount. The dependent status of women was a given. Children outside of marriage were not allowed. Neither was adultery. Divorce, which was legal in some states, was also out because of the Catholic influence on the PCA. Women couldn't leave their husbands, no matter what they did, even if they strayed with a lover.

There is sex in all the Garbo films. The key in terms of skirting censorship in the PCA era was the way it was presented. In the eyes of her fans Garbo was redeemed through love in story after story, even if her character was punished, or almost half the time, killed off. While she sometimes ends up married, Garbo characters don't move toward marriage. They move toward honesty. Thalberg and Garbo seem to have happily added the maximum possible societal condemnation and the commensurate punishment for sins that the PCA demanded to approve the scripts. These just made Garbo's purity of action as a woman clearer. She did it even though everyone condemned her character, even though she knew she was going to suffer. The audience loved the inner truth of Garbo's characters.

Six Garbo films were governed by the PCA. While *The Painted Veil* was released under the PCA, it had been developed under the SRC, and was handled as a transitional film and therefore more or less waved through because of that. Though *The Painted Veil* still had significant censorship issues.

The final five Garbo films were classified by the Legion after that. *Anna Karenina* received a B rating, meaning it was found "morally objectionable in part for all audiences." Though the Chicago Legion condemned the film. *Camille, Conquest,* and *Ninotchka* were all rated A-II, which meant that the legion found them "morally unobjectionable for adults and adolescents." This is interesting as *Camille* and *Conquest* are about a sex worker and an adulterer who had a child out of wedlock respectively.

Two-Faced Woman was famously condemned by the Legion as unfit for any audience, which will be discussed later in the text.

Though not directly related to censorship, the newly ascendant conservative press aggressively attacked people considered to be homosexual, Communist, or too libertine. While sexual orientation was always used as a weapon to disparage people, in the 1920s it was mostly done as a gossip item that was written using allusion and code. The reader could choose to believe it, or not.

As social conservatives gained ascendance during the 1930s, accusations of homosexuality could be career threatening. If an allusion to homosexuality was believed, the assumption was that it reduced the drawing power of an actor. At the time views on homosexuality were not as accepting as they are today.

For many people, being attacked as homosexual was tied to being perceived as rejecting conservative values. In the minds of social conservatives, the Victorian age was composed solely of heterosexual couples living within the bounds of marriage. The emergence of the modern age had led to a boundless increase in the reported frequency of homosexuals and homosexual sex, and this could be remediated by a return to Victorian values.

In this view of the world, women with modern values were suspect. They were the main cause of society's problems and were either libertine or out being lesbians themselves. Therefore, accusations of being a lesbian were a way of putting any woman in her place. The proof of her lesbianism was any behavior that was modern.

If this seems incredibly simplistic, it was. Writing that someone was out on the town with their "gal pal" could be interpreted as an allusion to lesbianism, or just that two women were friends. Beyond that, public association with someone who was homosexual led the press to assume that you might be as well. The "cooties" theory of sexuality.

Virtually every woman with power or social significance in America at this time was labeled as lesbian by someone in the press. Usually by the set of conservative gossip columnists who came to be arbiters of what was acceptable behavior for a star. Some of the accused women were lesbian, or bisexual, but this status was hardly as universal as the accusation was. Garbo—foreign, quirky, famous, and modern—was the biggest target around. This process of othering her was common for these conservative columnists and would accelerate during the McCarthy era after the war.

Garbo had friends who were gay or lesbian, and she stood by them when it became increasingly politically difficult for them in the forties and fifties. She remained their friends publicly at a time when many only visited their gay and lesbian friends through a back door.

The fact that Garbo was friends with known gay people, and didn't hide it, led to a feeling that she was at the very least a fellow traveler, if not gay herself. After all, she had not married.

Garbo was an icon for gay and lesbian people from early in her career. The direct use of same-sex kisses in Queen Christina certainly got people's attention. Though John Gilbert contemplating that he is aroused by what he believes is a man is just as subversive. With her next set of roles, MGM and

Garbo created a set of characters who choose the purity of their love over the damnation of society and the loss of social standing. The appeal of this to the gay and lesbian community before the greater acceptance of their sexuality today is self-evident.

Garbo referred to herself frequently as a man or boy. Using this to assign sexuality is a leap with no basis.

She referred to herself as a boy with virtually everyone with whom she had a significant friendship. It was just her convention. For example, when she writes to her sister-in-law referring to herself as a boy, and wrote to her niece as "My Boy." There is no sexual context. For example here is the English translation of her letter of March 4, 1962 to her sister-in-law.

> Dearest,
>
> Imagine that I never get around to writing. I never know if I will stay or go or anything. Schlee, who is never leaving N.Y. in the winter suddenly decided to go to Europe. So, I had to meet him and went to Switzerland for some days, and to the Riviera for some days. It was too cold, you should only go there for other times. And then I left again for Stockholm. And I continue at Nanna's. In the apartment that was empty before, there are now two servers that destroy my life. I head out before lunch and get home at nine at night because I do not want to see them. I am eating at Nerman's. But it is really boring. The servers will go abroad, but it looks like it will take a while for them to get a permit, they are Italian.
>
> So, I have to leave for Manhattan soon. I am not doing anything here either other than walk the streets just like in N.Y. Strange that I cannot find any interests for anything but streets. Single minded boy. Sad, but I can actually not do anything about it. And I do not think Mamma can either. Nerman is confused as always, since he lost Kajsa. I pity the humans, Strindberg said.
>
> If Peg wants to write, so do that fast because I probably have to leave in a couple of weeks or sooner.
>
> Love [964]

The list of people with whom we can be relatively sure Garbo was in a romantic relationship is not that long: Mauritz Stiller, Jack Gilbert, Rouben Mamoulian, George Brent, Leopold Stokowski, Erich Maria Remarque, Gilbert Roland, and George Schlee. Every other hypothesized romance, straight or gay, has a lack of factual underpinnings. The fact that she had platonic male friends ((Beaton, Hauser, Sörenson, etc.) complicates creating a list of romances. Though some of the possible romances written about likely occurred, and quite probably some that have never been spoken about as well. Garbo kept quiet about her romantic relationships.

Garbo made *The Painted Veil* as the second film in her first independent deal. It was based loosely on the Somerset Maugham novel. The interactions between MGM and the PCA show that the issue of how to deal with the energized censorship regime of the PCA had not been figured out as regards Garbo films, where issues of love and sex were essential elements.

Garbo, as Queen Christina, kisses her attendant.

The first problem that MGM had in getting censorship approval for a script was that the novel was on a list of books and plays banned under a resolution from 1930 that all the producers had agreed to. Fortunately, there was a mechanism to get approval despite the original blacklisting.

On August 2, 1932, while Garbo was still in Sweden, Thalberg sent a memo to Will Hays asking that the committee with the power to permit the filming of *The Painted Veil* approve production. In his letter to the committee Hays pointed out that *The Painted Veil* had not become well known or notorious since its publication in 1925.[965]

By April 1934 the Production Code Administration was reviewing a script. The main issue was that it "contains some pretty strong sex situations."[966] All this time Joseph Breen had been unaware that *The Painted Veil* had been approved for production by his employees. On June 1, 1934, he sent McKenzie, a PCA official, an irate telegram asking after the stars of the project.[967] Later that month he was sent the script.

After Breen had read the script there was a meeting between Geoffrey Shurlock, Breen's assistant at the PCA, and Louis B. Mayer, Eddie Mannix, and Hunt Stromberg for MGM. *The Painted Veil* was already in production, but Shurlock was requesting the deletion of the seduction scene that was apparently in the script at that point. Reinforcing that the buck stopped in New York, not Hollywood, the PCA archive shows that Nick Schenck at Loew's was periodically sent copies of the correspondence between the PCA and MGM.[968]

A preview for *The Painted Veil* was originally scheduled for September 26, but it was then postponed. MGM was unhappy with the way that the film started and rewrote the first five pages of the script. Breen didn't like one sentence of dialogue in the rewrite and demanded it be changed. Preview of *The Painted Veil* took place in Glendale on November 4 and the PCA approved it for release.

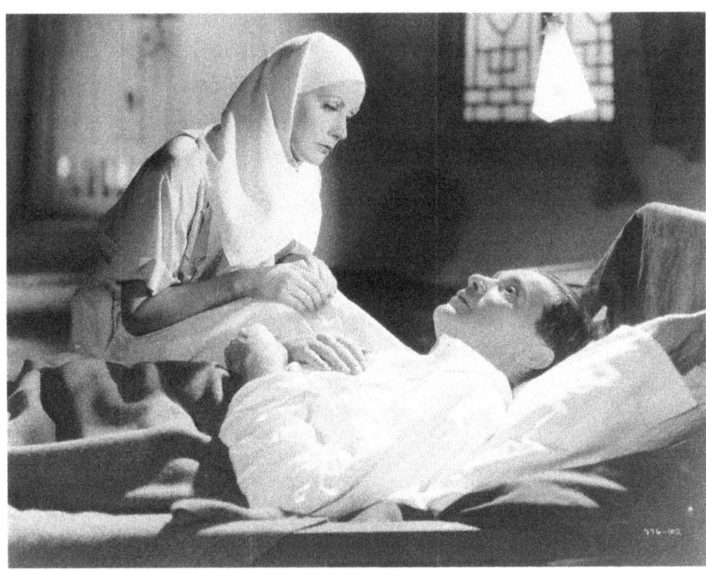

Garbo and Herbert Marshall in *The Painted Veil*.
Photo by Milton Brown. Courtesy of the Greta Garbo family archive.

But on November 7 Joseph Breen wrote to Will Hays: "We reviewed this picture and issued a certificate. However, after previewing the picture twice, the company was not satisfied with the direction of the first half of the picture, and we understand they are making extensive retakes. We will review it again."[969]

The Painted Veil was not a great film. The critic E. E. Laing thought that the fatal flaw in the film was that the story itself did not translate well from page to screen because it was too narrow and turned on the internal thoughts of revenge by the lead characters.[970] It would generate the least revenue of any independent Garbo film. After the film Garbo began a short romance with George Brent, who had co-starred.

The story didn't captivate viewers, even after the substantial retakes. But Thalberg learned from this, and the next three Garbo films were stories that address the issues of adultery and love exceptionally well while still getting PCA approval. Reviewers were starting to elucidate what Garbo did for the audience with greater insight. For instance, William Troy observed astutely,

> It is the background of sorrow, the atmosphere of disenchantment, the mood of frustration. And it may be in the impingement of frustration on beauty, in the breathing of the unhappy contemporary psyche into the classic form, that the alliance which we have been looking for will someday be found. It may be that Miss Garbo has really owed her renown to having given back to her generation a beautifully touched-up version of its own image.[971]

Chapter 29 – The Costume Drama Strategy

"In a story such as this, where transgressions result in suffering, in tragedy, and in death and punishment of the guilty, acceptability under the Code depends pretty generally upon the flavor created by the atmosphere, and the handling of the details." [972]

— Joseph Breen, in a letter to Louis B. Mayer

An Australian poster for *Camille* makes it clear that it is "not suitable for children."

The next three Garbo films seem rather similar in retrospect, and in a sense they were. *Anna Karenina, Camille*, and *Conquest* are all costume dramas set in Europe. Garbo made one costume drama each year from 1935 to 1937. The advantage of these three pictures for MGM and Garbo were twofold. First, MGM made a lot of money in the export market, and both costume dramas and Garbo films were strong export earners. The second advantage was more subtle. All three films gave MGM and Garbo leverage in their negotiations with the PCA. *Anna Karenina* and *Conquest* are directly about adultery. *Camille* is the story of a sex worker. Since *Anna Karenina* and *Camille* were derived from classic novels, MGM could, and did, argue to the censors that the story couldn't be changed to eliminate the "moral failing" of the Garbo character. The story of *Conquest* was not as famous, but MGM could argue that it was true history, so it had to include the adultery.

The costume drama strategy would deliver two of Garbo's great films, *Anna Karenina* and *Camille*. Thalberg's death during the production of *Camille*- would quickly reveal how much his deft touch in story development and navigating censorship mattered. The production of *Conquest* would become a legendary financial disaster.

MGM was able to produce all three films despite censorship concerns because it was willing to have Garbo's character pay a high price for her sins. Because Garbo could sell her characters' inner honesty, the sins didn't matter to the audience, and they took all the social and personal penalties the censors demanded as proof of the depth of Garbo's love. The punitive consequences became, in part, the villain of each story.

It was not just that Garbo could successfully die at the end of a film. While the usual solution to the story in a Code film was to have the heroine realize the evil of her ways and atone, Garbo didn't have to. In fact, the story was stronger because she didn't. Her character had always been true to her heart, so there was nothing to atone for.

No one dreams of throwing themselves in front of a train because their life has run out of viable options. Yet Garbo did so successfully in *Anna Karenina*. While the PCA focused on the objective events, Garbo sins so Garbo is punished, Garbo and Thalberg contrived to tell their stories in such a way that her character's truths overwhelmed the story action. Women watched Anna lose her marriage, her child, her love, and her life, and walked away believing they knew more about true love than when they entered the theater.

On the set of *Anna Karenina*. Photo by William Grimes.

For most of the audience these stories do not create dislike of Garbo's character. She has their sympathy. In an interesting dichotomy, social conservatives may have watched the same films and arrived at different conclusions about the Garbo character. Different audiences could read the same text different ways. For the audience of Modern Women, Garbo's adultery could be pure love. That her character was willing to accept all the consequences of her desire was her triumph, not her fate.

Studios had another way to deal with the new censorship realities. There was a new role model for a female star, the screwball actor. She was a woman who was outwardly self-assured but at the same time hopelessly naïve, who comically stumbles into love. These roles were the specialty of actors like Katharine Hepburn, Carole Lombard, Irene Dunne, and Claudette Colbert. The beauty of these roles for the studios is that they sidestepped censorship issues. The women almost seem unaware of sex as they pursue love.

Anna Karenina was derived from the famous book by Leo Tolstoy. Garbo had already made a silent version of it in the film *Love.* Producer David Selznick hired Salka Viertel and Clemence Dane to write the screenplay. When Selznick found their version too long, he brought in Sam Behrman to tighten up the dialogue. Viertel and Behrman once again fine-tuned the script during production, keeping a few days ahead of the filming.[973]

It would be impossible to carry the entire sweep of the intertwined plots in the book into a two-hour film. Much of the task for the scenarists was to simplify, pare down, and focus. Since the script had to be submitted to the PCA, the issue of how to bring the novel to the screen under the Code was a challenge. It had sex, adultery, illegitimate children, suicide, and other violations of social mores.

Selznick and the screenwriters took a bold approach to managing the PCA: They emphasized the inevitability of Anna's fate, the disapproval of society, and her punishment. Audiences only found Garbo more sympathetic. The filmmakers had pulled a judo move, using the power of the ostracism, condemnation, and punishment Anna faced and making that the story. Breen didn't even realize he had been subverted.

A portrait of Garbo from *Anna Karenina.* Photo by Clarence Sinclair Bull.

Russian military officer Vronsky, played by Fredric March, sees Anna Karenina when she visits Moscow. Smitten, he follows her to St. Petersburg. As Anna is married to an unfeeling husband, played by Basil Rathbone, Vronsky sweeps her off her feet. After a confrontation between Anna and her husband, she and Vronsky run off to Venice. Anna's pregnancy in the novel is one of the many plot points that was eliminated.

The love of Anna and Vronsky does not endure, and they return from Venice. The relationship is doomed from this point as Vronsky wants to return to military service and Anna becomes less important to him.

Interestingly, Anna's death is followed by a scene between Vronsky and a friend. This serves to frame out a view of adultery from a male perspective that is seemingly different from the resonance with Anna's dilemma that every female viewer seems to feel. Thus, male censors can believe that cinematic Anna has paid the proper price for her adultery while female viewers can feel that cinematic Anna lived nobly with her choices.

Censoring *Anna Karenina* was one of the first challenges the early PCA faced. It would prove to be a guide for later films. Since the bare bones of the story were widely known, bowdlerizing it to eliminate adultery, or any of the main elements of the story, would be laughed at. Breen's solution was to insist that the details of the affair between Vronsky and Anna be minimized on-screen. Hand-holding, kissing, and passionate embraces were all kept short and used only fleetingly. The film had to reinforce that their immoral actions were condemned by the entire society. Producer David Selznick would write, "We had to eliminate everything that could even remotely be classified as a passionate love scene; and we have to make it perfectly clear that not merely did Anna suffer but that Vronsky suffered."[974]

Film historian Lea Jacobs observed that "one of the most interesting aspects of censorship in this case is that the condemnation of adultery is not limited to any one character, or isolated didactic speeches. There are several scenes in which this judgement is rendered indirectly, woven into the fabric of the text."[975]

Part of what Selznick took advantage of was the natural sympathy that the lead characters generate within an audience. Breen was aware of this. In a letter to Hays summarizing censorship for the year, he wrote that this was a problem for censors: "Undue sympathy for the sinner is liable by association of ideas and momentum of emotion to lead to sympathy for the sin itself."[976] But MGM also modified the character of Anna. Most people find her less sympathetic in the book. She is more selfish and self-centered.

Breen was proud that MGM had been cowed into submitting an initial script that embodied the Code throughout. It bowed to his direction that it eliminate some kissing and erotic touching. The film does allow for ambiguous interpretation of some scenes. There was sex there if you want to see it in your mind's eye. As Anna and Vronsky are never shown to be happily romantic and Anna is constantly suffering as a result of the affair, Breen believed he had achieved a story that would serve as a parable of the dangers of sex outside marriage. He could not have been more wrong.

Breen changed his mind about *Anna Karenina* in March 1935, and he withdrew his approval while production was underway. Breen wrote a letter to Mayer with a detailed list of additional changes that he now required. When Selznick got the list, he exploded. In a letter sent directly to Breen, Selznick listed all the pre-approvals he had obtained, all of the changes he had already made, and then got around to the basic point that without the underlying adultery, there was no story to speak of. Breen backed down.[977]

A portrait of Garbo from *Anna Karenina*. Photo by Clarence Sinclair Bull.

Anna Karenina was the perfect PCA film about adultery. Yet Garbo subverted it. Her transgressions are for love. Otherwise, no one would have watched it. Jacobs points out that while the relationship between Vronsky and Anna is condemned, they are also pointed out by observers as an ideal couple. Jacobs also points out that Anna's punishment and condemnation exist to further her idealization. This is done through close-ups of Garbo's reactions to each loss and embarrassment.[978]

The treatment of adultery in *Anna Karenina* would define how the PCA handled it for the next fifteen years. Geoffrey Shurlock, Breen's assistant, would comment about the significance of how *Anna Karenina* was handled years later when he stated that "before then (the script for *A Streetcar Named Desire*, 1951) we had considered *Anna Karenina* a big deal. *Streetcar* broke the barrier."[979]

By trying to suppress any possible avenue for Anna to find joy in her life, the censors made it easier for Garbo to play a woman trapped in a horrible life for the crime of being a woman. Women across America certainly noticed. By insisting that the Catholic doctrine that marriage could never be dissolved would be portrayed in film, the PCA enabled Garbo to flip it to a story where a woman's life is tragically suppressed by an unjust and unthinking society.

The audience, at least the women in it, could empathize with why a woman would want to escape from this life. This resonated broadly and the film did well in theaters. The fact that Basil Rathbone played a wonderfully obtuse and unfeeling Karenin certainly helped.

Anna Karenina was a financial and critical success, earning Garbo the New York Film Critics Circle Award for Best Actress (though not even an Oscar nomination). Garbo's next step was to leave Hollywood for nearly a year.

Before Garbo departed, she signed a contract in May 1935 to make both *Camille* and *Conquest* upon her return from a trip to Sweden. The salary was $257,500 per film ($6.1 million). The reason for the odd non-round salary is unknown. MGM was to submit the names of two possible directors, and Garbo got to select the director she preferred. Though she had the option to reject both. She also had the right of approval for the male co-star. MGM developed the scripts during the year she was in Europe.

In *Camille* Garbo plays Marguerite Gautier, a French sex worker from the mid-nineteenth century. She is slowly dying from tuberculosis. She falls in love with a young diplomat, Armand, played by Robert Taylor. Armand con-

Lionel Barrymore convinces Garbo to give up her love of Robert Taylor in *Camille*. Photo by William Grimes.

vinces her to give up Parisian life for the country. But this is short lived. Armand's father, played by Lionel Barrymore, arrives and convinces her that she should end her romance as it is destroying Armand's professional prospects. Armand is crushed by this and thinks it is just Marguerite being fickle, as he does not realize she is soon to die. They are reconciled just before her death.

After viewing a rough outline of the story, the PCA found the film problematic. In May 1936, before production began, Breen wrote a letter to Mayer with some guidelines. He had six points:

1. No courtesans other than Marguerite. The role of Olympe should be married to an old duke, not as his mistress.
2. De Varville should not live in the same house as Marguerite, which he clearly does in this script.
3. Cut to a minimum suggestions that Marguerite profits enormously from a sinful life. Omit all scenes with jewelry, necklaces etc. she receives as gifts.
4. No condoning of Marguerite's life by Armand's father. He should be used as a voicer of morality. Conversation in the country is problematic as written.
5. Armand and Marguerite can't live together in the country. He must visit, not live with her.
6. After Marguerite breaks with de Varville, she must be repentant about her former life. She should have no thought of resuming her former life.[980]

He closed the letter with a final thought: "We recommend that one or two observations be written for Marguerite in her scene with Armand on her death bed, in which she acknowledges the folly of her way—in a sort of 'sin doesn't pay speech.' It would be helpful if you could inject a note of repentance and regeneration. This is important."[981]

On May 20 Breen had a call with Thalberg regarding his letter. Thalberg agreed to all of Breen's points except the first. Since Olympe and the duke were to be played as comic characters, Thalberg thought she should remain a sex worker. In addition, why would a "respectable" Olympe associate with Marguerite?[982] Breen relented. From this point production of *Camille* proceeded with minimal issues from the PCA.

While Breen's objective is to punish sin, Garbo's is to show that her sin is for love. Marguerite's final line is "perhaps it's better if I live in your heart, where the world can't see me if I am dead. There'll be no stain on our love." Breen didn't even realize he had lost, because he didn't understand the mind of the character.

Lenore Ulric as Olympe providing comic relief in *Camille*. Photo by William Grimes.

The death scene at the end of *Camille* is one of the greatest scenes ever filmed. Garbo later recalled the following:

> We had to make two different endings to the film—well, actually there were three. In one version I got to say more on my death-bed. In another version I had to be quieter and just slowly slip away. They plumped for the later version and we were all in agreement on that point. It didn't feel very natural talking that much when you've just about given up the ghost.[983]

After Cukor was hired to direct *Camille* he had to learn how to work with Garbo. His discussion from right after the filming reflects the degree of control Garbo had over the project even though she was not the director:

> After I saw how she wanted to play a scene, I talked it over with her, and made suggestions from my mental picture of the scene. But at the same time, I made it clear that I respected her conception, and that she had given me fresh ideas which I was more than willing to blend with my own. Nor was this merely a kind of artistic compromise. She, as a woman and sensitive artist was, I found, always prolific of ideas, and when she finally admitted me to her confidence and friendship—which she did quickly when the initial barrier of distrust was broken down—we formed an ideal collaboration for our mutual benefit as actress and director.[984]

Garbo suffered from poor health as she made *Camille*. Garbo's health issues will be covered in more depth below. David Lewis and Eddie Wheeler, who worked on the film, ascribed some or all of Garbo's health problems during production to menstrual issues or ovarian cysts.[985] She wrote to Hörke Wachtmeister, "I'm lying in bed—as usual when the moon is walking about."[986]

Rex O'Malley, who played a supporting role in *Camille* as her friend Gaston, delayed production when he had to undergo surgery himself. He recalled that he and Garbo "had lots of fun discussing our aches and pains, and symptoms together."[987]

O'Malley later said that he had never been a fan of Garbo before working with her on *Camille*. It was only when he was forced to modulate his own acting to synchronize with Garbo's restrained delivery that he finally understood her skill:

> She doesn't act; she lives her roles. She was Camille during the entire filming of the picture. . . . Beautiful beyond words of description.[988]

Irving Thalberg, who had never been in good health, died as the main filming of *Camille* was wrapping up in September 1936. David Lewis had been handling the day-to-day producing on the film, but MGM veteran Bernard H. Hyman was assigned to finish the project as the producer.

Fortunately, the initial direction for *Camille* was set by Thalberg before his death and was in the capable hands of Cukor and Lewis. *Camille* succeeded in spite of Hyman's involvement in the film.

Hyman didn't like the edit that Thalberg and Lewis had settled upon, and he recut the film. This version was received poorly in preview. Eddie Mannix, now overseeing *Camille*, decided to let Lewis shoot more scenes and return the edit to something closer to the original Thalberg vision. Garbo wrote to Wachtmeister that she was shooting retake after retake in November and December.[989]

Rescued from Hyman's wayward vision of the story, the final version was magnificent. *Camille* at the time, and now in retrospect, was one of the Studio Era's greatest films. Newsweek wrote in its review, "Yet Garbo, who has never been more vivacious and attractive, brings the hackneyed role to life again."[990]

A Portrait of Garbo in costume for *Camille*.
Photo by Clarence Sinclair Bull.

Theatre World compared Garbo's performance in *Camille* to the multitude of actors who had played the part: "Garbo alone has contrived to impart something fresh to this stereotyped demimondaine who battles mainly with consumption and frustrated love for that nitwitted gentleman, Armand Duval."[991]

Carlo Keil-Möller, in *The American-Scandinavian Review*, wrote,

> This is indeed the triumph of a great artist. It is hard to imagine that further perfection can be possible in the art which she has made her own and which she has raised to a height that none other of its practitioners has hitherto achieved. For ten years she has held her position as the recognized queen of the films amidst ceaseless and severe competition, and she has done so by power of her unique gifts and by no other means. I have never seen Garbo so acid, so transparent in her acting as in this particular role. One can follow an emotion as it passes over her face, one can see the gusts of feeling flurry forth in the play of the muscles over this countenance which is as beautiful as it is ethereal. It is not merely a perfect woman that accords us these moments, it is far rather a great artist. All that film can give at the present time of the measure of a soul, Garbo gives us.[992]

Camille earned Garbo an Oscar nomination for best actress. The film won best picture of 1937 from the New York Film Critics.

Often on repeated viewing, the viewer can see flaws in a performance, even a fine one. Modern film critic and writer Mick LaSalle thought *Camille* was such a fine role for Garbo that he wrote,

> To begin to appreciate what she does in *Camille*, one needs to see the movie more than once. Five, ten times isn't too much. Why not? One would listen to a great operatic performance more than once. Garbo in *Camille* is a great operatic performance. Its scale is huge, and yet its psychological subtleties continue to unveil themselves with each viewing.[993]

The third costume drama was *Conquest*. Viertel had pitched her idea for *Conquest* to Thalberg in 1935. It took two years to bring it to production. The first challenge was to get the factually based story approved by the PCA. In a conference with Thalberg and the PCA staff Viertel, the initial scriptwriter, explained the story.[994] The PCA staff were clear that they thought the two adulteries and the illegitimate child were going to be too much for the PCA to accept. Thalberg got combative. According to Viertel his response was "then I'll go ahead without your okay. This is a great love story and I am determined to produce it."[995]

The PCA staff backed down and gave Thalberg permission to proceed, but only after telling him that this didn't guarantee a final approval.[996]

In response to censorship issues, several major plot points would eventually be changed. For example, in the original story, when Napoleon pursues Marie initially, her husband encourages her to have an affair with him in order to get a guarantee of Polish independence. In the final version her husband is offended that she commits adultery.

Eventually, Thalberg added Sam Behrman to the writing team. They had just finished a final script in September 1936 when Thalberg died.

Countess Marie Walewska, played by Greta Garbo, is a Polish noble married to a much older husband, played by Henry Stephenson. French forces under Napoleon Bonaparte, played by Charles Boyer, drive Russian troops off her estate. Marie meets Napoleon, and then encounters him again at a formal ball in Warsaw. He tries to seduce her, but she resists.

Seeing Napoleon's desire for her, Polish nobles ask Marie to use an affair with Napoleon to pressure him to guarantee the independence of Poland. Marie eventually agrees and embarks on the affair. Her husband disowns her and goes to Rome to get an annulment of their marriage.

Napoleon and Marie are in love. He divorces the Empress Josephine. But instead of marrying Marie Walewska, he decides to marry Archduchess Marie Louise of Austria for political reasons.

Marie leaves Napoleon, not telling him that she is pregnant with his son. Napoleon's mother, who knows Marie is pregnant, sides with Marie. Though Napoleon and Marie meet again in the following years, he never grasps at a chance for happiness with her, instead pursuing glory on the battlefield. She even travels to him in exile, offering him a chance to escape to America with her. Marie, living alone, dies from pneumonia. Napoleon then escapes from Elba and loses at Waterloo.

Garbo had been fortunate with her producers before *Conquest*. Stiller had basically acted as an independent producer/director. The exact relationship of Pabst to the financial backers of *Die freudlose* Gasse is not known, but it seems he produced independently. At MGM Garbo had Irving Thalberg as her producer from the start. Thalberg was the greatest producer of the Studio Era.

A portrait of Garbo for *Conquest*. Photo by Clarence Sinclair Bull.

When Thalberg died in September 1936 during the final days of filming *Camille*, much of the work on it had already been done. Hyman still almost destroyed it.

In a December 1935 letter to Thalberg, almost a year and a half before filming of *Conquest* began, Breen made a few points that he thought addressed his issues with the moral tone of the story:

> It seems to us that the flavor of the story should be one of tragedy. If our audiences get out of it the feeling that living as a mistress even to Napoleon ends in disaster and unhappiness, the picture is likely to be thoroughly acceptable.[997]

The long letter went on to say that the main concern is therefore regarding the adultery. The recommendations were to minimize the scenes where the Polish nobles encourage Marie to sleep with Napoleon. In the initial script they were too extensive. He suggested that they use the character of d'Ornano as a moral voice against her actions and delete the implication that Marie's husband is aware of and encourages her infidelity. Breen asks for a line to be added after Marie and her son return to the Count that he is taking her in out of pity, and he does not condone her actions. Marie should also reject Napoleon's attempt to resurrect their affair. Finally, on her deathbed Marie should repent her actions as foolish.[998]

After Thalberg's death MGM assigned Bernie Hyman to produce *Conquest*, and he disliked the screenplay that Viertel and Behrman had written. Gottfried Reinhardt told Viertel that Hyman was insecure about anything that had not been developed under his supervision.[999] Hyman hired Sam Hoffenstein to rewrite the script. After he read the Viertel version, Hoffenstein went to Viertel and declared her version to be fantastic.[1000] Viertel and Hoffenstein then proceeded to rewrite the script with the minimum number of changes possible.

However, Hyman couldn't resist meddling and several additional writers were brought in. In total seventeen writers worked on the script at some point.[1001] The fundamental issue was that Hyman thought the audience should be led to sympathize with Napoleon, while the writers thought sympathy should be directed toward Walewska, as she was the one who had given up everything to try to save her country. They had Garbo for the role, after all. Hoffenstein finally said to Hyman, "If you want to feel sorry for Napoleon then let Garbo play him."[1002]

Director Clarence Brown and Hyman had trouble getting along. The script constantly evolved during production and the censors at the PCA had changes they demanded for almost every revised page of dialogue. Eventually *Conquest* was three months behind schedule and significantly over budget.

Garbo was still close to the crews she worked with. Gil Perkins, who performed stunts on *Conquest*, recalls a morning they spent waiting for filming to start:

> She sat out there [in an old whaling boat on location] and talked to us about our lives, our wives, our children. I thought to myself

'Boy, if this had been Crawford or Bette Davis, they'd have been screaming; what the hell are you doing keeping me out here?' Because she was there from about 8:30 until noon before we ever got a shot. She just sat there and talked; it didn't bother her.[1003]

Garbo and Charles Boyer listening to Clarence Brown go over a scene in *Conquest*. Photo by William Grimes.

Production of *Conquest* ran for 127 days beginning March 27, 1937. This is longer than any Garbo film at MGM, even *The Temptress*, which was basically made twice. Compared to other Garbo sound films, the next-longest production schedule was that for *Camille*, which ran 75 days. This production problem can be squarely placed on Bernie Hyman for his insistence on rewriting the script constantly during production. Hyman kept changing his view of the story. New scenes were filmed after the initial production and then in turn cut or replaced.

The PCA office received a steady stream of script revisions in March, April, and May.[1004] On August 7, after the main filming had been finished, MGM sent the PCA twelve pages of new script.[1005]

The total cost for *Conquest* was an astronomical $2.7 million ($60.9 million). It cost more than *Anna Karenina* and *Camille* combined. MGM lost $1.4 million ($31.6 million) on *Conquest*, not counting what Loew's made on it in exhibition. Due to the budget overruns *Conquest* was the most expensive film production since *Ben-Hur* in 1925.[1006] (*Ben-Hur* had cost $3.9 million [$73.2 million] and took 214 production days.)[1007] Though in just two years it lost this distinction to the even more expensive *Gone with the Wind* (1939).

Variety reviewed *Conquest* rather positively. The reviewer thought that the spectacle of the sets, costumes, battles, and crowd scenes were opulent and captivating. While they found Garbo's acting good, Boyer delivered a wonderful Bonaparte.[1008]

The Detroit Free Press wrote that "*Conquest*, starring Greta Garbo is reported to have cost $2,800,000, and it looks like it."[1009] Though they thought the story itself was dull.[1010] *Conquest* wasn't a bad film for its time. It just wasn't a great film. Certainly not the equal of *Queen Christina, Anna Karenina*, or *Camille.*

Conquest's earnings from film rentals—$2.1 million ($47.1 million)—were about average for a later Garbo film. It lost MGM money because the production costs came in at about $1.5 million ($33.6 million) over budget (author's estimate). *Conquest* was a financial failure for MGM's executives, and it was their own fault.

Now in charge of the pace of filmmaking, Garbo spent more time with her family in Sweden. She had to manage significant health challenges and she made new friends. Her life was also permanently transformed by public scrutiny.

Chapter 30 – Garbo Turns Thirty

"If you're going to die on screen,
you've got to be strong and in good health."[1011]

— Greta Garbo

A snapshot of herself that Garbo kept.

When Garbo embarked upon the independent phase of her career, still only twenty-eight, several things happened in her personal life. The most important thing was that she slowed the pace of work and made fewer films. From *Queen Christina* through *Two-Faced Woman* Garbo made only seven films in nine years. This was not completely intentional—several projects experienced delays—but Garbo also took yearlong breaks and returned to Sweden.

During the sixty months of Garbo's five-year contract, she spent about half that time on set and made fifteen films. She took one four-month trip home to Sweden. She was sick for one month that we know of. The rest of the time, about twenty-five months, she prepared for roles and relaxed. She took a one-month trip to New York in December 1931 and frequently visited Yosemite, Arrowhead Lake, and Palm Springs.

Once Garbo began functioning as an independent, she slowed her work pace and both Garbo and MGM invested more time in developing projects. Script development began as early as two years before production. The first thing she did after signing to make *Queen Christina* and *The Painted Veil* was to leave for almost a year, while MGM got to work on pre-production. She signed her contract for *Conquest* and *Camille* in 1935 and again left for a year. From June 1932 until she finished *Ninotchka* in August 1940 Garbo spent about fifteen months filming six films. She also spent time functioning more or less as a producing partner: reviewing scripts, selecting directors, reviewing costumes and sets. Things that had previously been done by just MGM. Work dropped from about half her time to something closer to a quarter.

The main adjustment Garbo made in the use of her time was to spend almost three years in Europe, mostly in Sweden. She was also sick at times, probably related to her pernicious anemia. The most notable episode was for several months while in Sweden during 1935 and 1936. More frequently she was indisposed for a few days at a time.

She spent time in New York. Garbo began to visit Gayelord Hauser in Wisconsin. When Garbo was in California, she walked all over western Los Angeles. She started spending time in the low desert east of Los Angeles and at the La Quinta resort, as she could ride there undisturbed.

From 1935 to 1939 there were only about twelve to fifteen months for Garbo to be at leisure and in California. Most of them in 1939. This makes it much more understandable that people in Hollywood say they never saw Garbo during this era. She wasn't there to be seen.

After the 1931 publication of the Palmborg biography, which relied heavily on interviews with her household staff and a few friends, Garbo became wary of people she thought would gossip about her to the press. She still had an active social life and made important new friendships during the thirties. As a researcher I was struck by how many identifiable friends of Garbo never talked about their friendship, mentioned it in an understated way, or only mentioned it toward the end of their lives. Dolores del Rio and her husband Cedric Gibbons were intimate friends from early in her career, and del Rio only briefly spoke of her in the sixties, in Spanish for Mexican magazines. Garbo had breakfast with Jessica Dragonette about sixty times a year for over two decades, and Dragonette tells one Garbo story in her autobiography.

Her publicity problems really began with the effect sound had on her general popularity. Garbo snuck away from Hollywood for the Christmas season in 1931, just before she had to report to the set of *Grand Hotel.* When Garbo was found to be in New York, she drew a crowd. When she came down to the lobby of the St. Moritz hotel, a throng of reporters and fans awaited her. She first tried to deny she was Garbo. Reportedly she said, "I am not Greta Garbo. No, you must be mistaken. Go away, please let me alone." But the crowd didn't leave and she quickly changed tack. "Yes, I am Greta Garbo. Now are you satisfied? I came here from Hollywood for a rest, not to exhibit myself."[1012] What was the dimension of the throng? Apparently, sixty reporters.

In the 1920s, when a star, politician, or other newsworthy person appeared for a public event, there was a formal photography session. For event photos, they arranged a line of people standing in a row. Or they had the movie star standing precisely for the cameras before they went on with their speech or journey.

Up until the mid-1920s there was no camera that allowed photojournalists to regularly capture news as it happened. The development of fast, light, and inexpensive cameras changed this. Photojournalism arrived, capturing crime scenes and courthouse appearances.

Garbo's trip to New York in 1931 marked the expansion of photojournalism to the entertainment world. It was no longer sufficient to just have posed photos of the stars. They were now captured out on the streets and outside clubs.

The final post-war evolution would be paparazzi.

Berthold Viertel would describe the scene years later: "The lobby, all exits, the surrounding streets were occupied every day and night hour by storm troopers—admirers and reporters—who chased the artist everywhere."[1013]

During Garbo's trip to New York in December 1931 news photographers sought her out to photograph, marking the beginning of candid celebrity news photography. The photographer walking with her is holding one of the new lightweight cameras that gave photographers more freedom.

After her 1931 New York City Christmas trip Garbo became increasingly wary of crowds and strangers. Garbo had been stalked, chased, and threatened by the press. Individuals had accosted her, insisting she autograph a photo, insisting they should go to dinner, insisting they were related, insisting they should get married, insisting they were already married.

While Garbo was in New York, the radio gossip columnist Walter Winchell sent Garbo a message inviting her to be on his New Year's Eve broadcast. She politely turned him down, after which Winchell attempted to blackmail her into appearing by threatening to be unkind to her on his show.[1014] Which he proceeded to do. This was the beginning of socially conservative gossip columnists targeting her for her lifestyle and film roles. Winchell would hardly ever have a positive thing to say about her for the rest of his career.

After the Palmborg book, Garbo didn't hire household staff. She did have personal assistants who were MGM employees, and Garbo was one of the few stars who would hire Black assistants. At least two Black women worked for Garbo at MGM. The media described them as "maids," yet the actual tasks performed were far beyond this simple sobriquet. They were the star's secretaries, business affairs managers, and bodyguards.

Most female stars had White female assistants. In 1929 only about two dozen assistants in Hollywood were Black "maids."[1015] They were also the only assistants called maids.

Garbo's first Black assistant was named Alma and she worked for Garbo from at least *The Temptress* through at least *Grand Hotel*. When Alma was hospitalized during the filming of *Grand Hotel*, Garbo flooded her hospital room with flowers.[1016]

Hazel Washington would work for Garbo from April 1933 until she left for Sweden in June 1935. Washington had her own fascinating life. She was married to the first Black police lieutenant in the Los Angeles Police Department. She would go on to be Rosalind Russell's assistant, and then the two of them would partner in a successful set of apparel businesses in Hollywood.

Washington also wrote a Hollywood column for Black newspapers in the 1950s. She would recall that she spent most of her time as Garbo's "sort of protector or bodyguard, keeping the general public away from her and acting as a buffer between her and those who would bother her."[1017]

She also reported that Garbo would do her own makeup and then Washington would help her get into her costume. She didn't use the regular studio makeup or wardrobe staff. They also occasionally snuck out of the studio to shop at the local army/navy store.[1018]

Over the years Washington worked for Garbo she found that "she possessed a deeply enigmatic personality that challenged you to try to solve it with an answer for this human puzzle. She was moody at times, but not unpleasant; thrifty but not stingy, conservative but not tight."[1019]

Washington told a story of a day when Garbo's usual driver was not available. She asked Washington to drive her home in her car. "The car, an old Dodge Roadster, was about 12 years old, with the seat springs poking up through holes in the upholstery which I had covered with an old threadbare blanket. Greta got in and when she sat down the springs underneath her went b-o-i-n-g and she laughed about as hard as she could."[1020]

Garbo could be playful. Colleen Moore remembers that before the preview of *Mata Hari*, the film's director George Fitzmaurice held a dinner party. When the group prepared to leave for the preview at a theater in Glendale, Garbo demurred and said she would remain at the Fitzmaurices' and await their report back with what she assured everyone would be bad news.[1021]

Instead, the audience loved the film. The happy party returned to the house to find Garbo sliding across the fifty-foot living room on a small oriental rug she had commandeered after pushing aside all the furniture. She was having so much fun sliding on the rug that she had no interest in reports regarding the audience.[1022]

Garbo called Max Gumpel out of the blue one day in 1932. While they had socialized after meeting on the set of *Herrskapet Stockholm ute på inköp*, they had not been in touch since Garbo left for America. Gumpel would recall that she telephoned him at work and asked if he knew who was calling. After Garbo eventually identified herself, Gumpel assumed it was a prank organized by a friend. He invited her to dinner, and still thinking the joke was on, asked her to look as much like Garbo as she could. He was pleasantly surprised when Garbo herself showed up for dinner.[1023]

Garbo spent a fair amount of time with Edmund Goulding and his wife Marjorie. He observed that when Garbo had not been as famous that "she lived as others do, surrounded by a few friends and having a life of her own." Goulding found her unchanged when they were together: "Many an evening she will sit with Mrs. Goulding and myself and discuss the problems of her profession, and all her varied interest in the world of art." However, "She becomes restless if the bell rings and, with the advent of visitors, she will immediately leave."[1024]

Garbo on a train on her way back to Stockholm in June 1936.

Garbo arrived in Sweden after completing *Anna Karenina.* She sailed from New York on June 4, 1935. She was twenty-nine years old. She mostly dodged the press before her departure, posing for a single photograph. She granted a press gaggle an interview on the MS *Kungsholm* before it docked in Gothenburg. When asked if she was happy to be home, she replied, "Yes, indeed.[1025]

While she answered questions, those answers were guarded. A Stiller manuscript had recently been discovered and the assumption was that it was intended for her. When asked about it she gave an answer that may have revealed more than the reporters knew. "How can I make any statement about that off-hand? It is entirely too important—maybe—and very near to my heart."[1026]

When asked if she saw Swedish pictures while in Hollywood, she responded that she saw a few, but then asked the reporters, "They all seem to move in the same circle. Why?" Amused when the reporters had difficulty answering that question, she said, laughing, "Now, you see how difficult it is to answer some questions."[1027]

One journalist decided to interview the other passengers about Garbo on the trip. She had spent the voyage playing deck games, and she swam twice a day in the pool. On several days she kept to her stateroom for the entire day. She ate primarily a vegetable-heavy diet at meals. One passenger who swam with her in the morning said, "She is the most fascinating person I have ever met—and ever expect to meet. There is no one like her."[1028]

Garbo rented a small cottage north of Stockholm. Local farmers reported that she was up early, walking in the woods picking berries for breakfast.[1029] Sweden has a law, *allemansrätten* (every man's right), which gives anyone the right to pick berries and roam on private property, so she could wander the fields and woods. When the local store opened at eight in the morning, Garbo stopped in and bought simple things like fish, bread, and bananas.[1030]

A photo Garbo kept of her mother and sister-in-law. Photo by Sven Gustafson.

She spent time in Stockholm and at a cottage on the archipelago outside the city with her brother and his family. She visited Hörke Wachtmeister in Tistad, which is close to Hårby, a rural estate she and Sven bought the following year.

Mimi Pollak threw a dinner for Garbo with all her old Dramaten classmates. While there she was asked to tell of the further adventures of her two imaginary rabbits. Over a decade before, Garbo had regularly entertained her classmates with the ongoing adventures of these rabbits.[1031]

Garbo reconnected with Nöel Coward when he visited Stockholm, and they became close friends. Coward would drag Garbo to parties she didn't want to attend, at which she invariably ended up having a great time. Carlo Keil-Möller, who may have introduced them to each other, recalled them sitting in his living room during January 1936 discussing the sacrifices that they had each made to work in Hollywood, and what they thought of the place.[1032]

In September 1935, right after her thirtieth birthday, Garbo became gravely ill. She spent months in bed and was in the hospital from time to time. Even right before she returned to Hollywood in April 1936 she was writing to Mimi Pollak that she was still out of sorts.

The exact nature of what ailed Garbo has never been disclosed, or if it was related to her pernicious anemia. At one point her doctor suggested surgery, but it is not known if she underwent it.

In October 1935 Garbo wrote to Mimi Pollak that she had been sick since her birthday (September 18). She had been running a temperature and primarily lying in bed. She was waiting to see a doctor to get a diagnosis.[1033]

A second letter to Pollak in December made it clear that her illness was serious. She wrote,

> I've been sick since September. I've only been up a few days sometimes and then in bed again. Now I have been in bed for a five week stretch but I'm still not well. I'm not allowed to walk. I'm desperate but that doesn't help. My doctor says I should be operated on but I am resisting as long as possible. It is my lower abdomen that is causing trouble.[1034]

In a third letter written April 20, 1936, Garbo briefly writes about having been sick and that she is still tired. She has "been out of sorts the whole time—only gone to doctors or the hospital."[1035]

Garbo wrote several letters to Salka Viertel during this trip to Sweden. They are undated and the correct sequence is not clear, though some letters can be placed before others based on topics such as the socialite Mercedes de Acosta.

In one letter Garbo is unhappy that she has read that Frances Marion is working on the screenplay to Camille instead of Viertel, and she is going to ask her lawyer to address this and get Viertel assigned to the project. She mentions that she has met Nöel Coward (in the summer of 1935). Garbo has also received a telegram from Mercedes de Acosta offering to travel with her back to the US. Garbo intends to duck her by not responding.

Garbo did eventually extend de Acosta an invitation to visit, not thinking she would come. She did travel from America to Sweden just to visit and Garbo was then unsure of how to handle her. She took de Acosta to the Wachtmeisters' at Tistad because "I didn't know what else to do." Garbo was clearly trying to cut her off. She found de Acosta "more queer [probably in a behavioral rather than sexual sense] than before. But otherwise the same."

De Acosta wrote about her trip to Sweden in her normal fabulist fashion. For example, according to her Garbo took her to see the house in which she was born. Garbo was born in the Södra Maternity Hospital.

Garbo gave a press conference in the lounge of the MS *Gripsholm* while arriving in New York when she returned from her vacation. She arranged to answer questions for ten minutes.

When asked her reason for evading the press for so many years she replied,

> I don't think it's necessary to see the press so much when one is in motion picture work. People ought to feel that which you want to express.[1036]

When questioned as to whether she would go on the stage, she replied,

> I'm so terribly nervous. I'll never go on the stage because of that. To be seen in the movies is enough; I will not speak on the radio.[1037]

She said that she had the flu in Sweden and did not enjoy her long holiday there. "I haven't been well," she said. "I was sick most of the time."[1038]

Garbo didn't mention that she had been either bedridden or hospitalized over a four-to-six-month period of time.

When asked if she had spent her time at her home in Sweden, Garbo responded, "I have no home. I am just a wanderer."[1039]

When asked if she was glad to be back, Garbo responded, "Very much. When one has been so long in a country one grows to like it."[1040]

Reporters observed that Garbo was "still showing the effects of her illness."[1041]

In December 1936 Garbo and her brother together purchased an old Swedish estate called Hårby, located near the small town of Gnesta. Sven had led the search for a suitable property, as Garbo had already departed for Hollywood. It was purchased by Sven with the help of a loan from Hörke, which Garbo repaid.[1042]

After the purchase Sven and Peg lived there with their daughter Gray, and they ran the forestry and farm operations. Garbo's mother, Anna, lived there as well once she decided to leave Stockholm.

Hårby is beautifully situated just across the line into Södermanland County. It lies about forty-five miles (seventy kilometers) southwest of Stockholm County. It is on the west shore of Lake Sillen, a picturesque, long, narrow lake.

Hårby in winter

Garbo's niece Gray on a plow horse during fall at Hårby.
Lake Sillen is visible in the background.

Hårby was a working farm of two hundred acres, with additional forests. The house itself was beautiful and took full advantage of its location on the lakeshore. Sven went to forestry school so he could manage the business. He asked the Wachtmeisters for ideas based on their management of the Tistad estate. Sven bought additional acreage on the other side of the lake.

Garbo intended to make Hårby a major part of her life. When she next returned to Sweden she spent basically nine months of her eleven-month break there. Instead, it was sold as World War II began. Years after Hårby was sold, Garbo wrote to Peg about wanting to return to Sweden and live with the family on a farm while she produced films.[1043]

While Garbo's career was in Hollywood, when one looks at the pattern of visits, it is evident she was committed to living at least part of the time in Sweden until relatively late in her life. The ongoing importance of her family is also clear.

Garbo came to realize that the pressure of celebrity was hurting her mental health. She saw a series of psychologists in the late thirties. Not much is known about this other than a somewhat humorous mention in a letter to Hörke Wachtmeister in which Garbo relates that her doctor caught himself up short after agreeing with her that life was depressing:

> My latest physician is a little hunchbacked man who I am dragging down into the abyss of pessimism. He sees me as an "interesting case of depression." He says he is a psychologist and wants to help me in that way. He keeps me for an hour and a half every time. We sit there fencing with words and keeping a watchful eye on one another. One day when I was very tired I said, "Everything is futile."
>
> "Yes, that's true," he said.
>
> But then he realized that was not the right way to treat a "depression," so he gave me a piercing look and said one had to look at life with a sense of humor.[1044]

Dr. Eric Drimmer, a Swedish-born psychologist who had Garbo as a patient in Los Angeles, confirmed that Garbo's intent in the 1930s was to live most of her life in Sweden with her family. She would return to Hollywood for film projects. This plan changed with the beginning of World War II, when instead her family relocated to America.[1045] He wrote about her in a 1959 Swedish article. He related,

I say this with absolute conviction: Greta Garbo herself never had anything to do with creating the myth of her solitude. It was created by other people.[1046] Drimmer went on to relate details of her therapy, information that would be considered HIPAA protected today:

> The more I came to know about her past and story, the more convinced I became that Garbo was a normal, ambitious and cheerful girl when she left Sweden. Hollywood was solely responsible for her inhibitions. No matter how paradoxical it may sound, her life took a wrong direction just at the point at which her fame and wealth were created.[1047]

Drimmer counseled her to acknowledge and confront her shyness and fears. One can see in shipboard interviews from the time how Garbo tried to do so. He summed up that Garbo's difficulties with English upon her arrival made things hard, as she felt misunderstood and ridiculed in published interviews.[1048]

Despite the publication of this article, Drimmer and Garbo remained friends into the sixties. They had breakfast at his house one morning in 1962 when Garbo was visiting Stockholm.[1049]

Garbo was more gregarious after her return from Europe in November 1938. She did not have numerous intimate friends, nor did she go to the more public film industry events. She did meet almost everyone who spent any significant amount of time at the social events hosted by Salka Viertel, Anita Loos, and Vicki Baum. Garbo was spotted at theaters, restaurants, and nightclubs.

Film director Robert Parrish[1050] recalled visiting the Viertel house:

> I walked in the back door one day and there was a guy with short hair cooking at the stove. In the living room, Arthur Rubinstein was tinkling on the piano. Greta Garbo was lying on the sofa, and Christopher Isherwood was lounging in a chair. "Who is the guy in the kitchen," I asked no-one in particular. "Bertolt Brecht," came the reply.[1051]

The modern equivalent might be to walk into Jon Batiste on the piano with Kate Winslet and Matt Damon in the living room and Lin-Manuel Miranda at the stove.

One adjustment Garbo made that many other Europeans did not was she increasingly socialized with Americans. One of the more important Garbo circles of that time was one based around Anita Loos.[1052]

Loos recounts one famous story where she, Garbo, Charlie Chaplin, Paulette Goddard, Aldous Huxley, Bertrand Russell, Christopher Isherwood, the Indian guru Krishnamurti (philosopher, speaker, and author of several books), and others were picnicking on the dry riverbed of the Los Angeles River.[1053] A sheriff's deputy demanded that they cease trespassing and move on. Huxley tried to impress the deputy with the presence of some casually dressed film stars. The deputy told Huxley not to take him for a fool, as these were clearly not the film stars he was referencing, and they had to pack up and leave. The picnic was reassembled in the Huxley backyard.[1054]

When Orson Welles moved to Hollywood in 1939, he rented a house on Rockingham Drive and soon discovered that Garbo was his neighbor. She sent word that she wished to use his pool, with the proviso that she wanted to use it privately. Welles agreed, but temptation overcame him and one day he showed up poolside while Garbo was swimming laps. Welles had worried that she would be upset. Instead she was delighted to meet him and they often sat poolside after her laps to talk.[1055]

Garbo didn't enjoy fame. She resented the intrusions into her personal life and tried to find a way to live as normal a life as possible given her circumstances. She limited her interviews, instead holding press conferences when the ship she was traveling on docked in New York or Gothenburg. She also held one in Italy. She worked with psychologists to find balance in her life.

Garbo met Gayelord Hauser through friends in 1934 and by 1939 magazines were writing about them as a couple, though they never were. They traveled together. For example, in February 1940 Hauser, his business and romantic partner Frey Brown, and Garbo were in Palm Beach, Florida.[1056] After being discovered, they departed for the Florida Keys.

Gayelord Hauser was an early dietician. He was a strong believer in natural food and the importance of eating vegetables, fruit, and specific supplements. Not everything that Hauser advocated has turned out to be accurate, but he was ahead of his time in focusing on the benefits of good nutrition. His admonitions to minimize sugar consumption, avoid processed foods when possible, and limit meat consumption seem perfectly reasonable today.

Hauser was a positive influence on Garbo, getting her to go out to see and do things, including attend dinner parties he hosted. She had been working with Dr. Drimmer on managing her fear of crowds and strangers, so Hauser's efforts were an extension of her facing her fears. Garbo even had him visit her on set while she was making *Ninotchka*, breaking her mostly enforced but occasionally waived "no visitors" rule. Because Hauser contended that not going out was part of a negative feedback loop that kept her from going out, Garbo worked to go out more frequently, and while she had always socialized within smaller groups of people she was comfortable with, from the late 1930s on Garbo was out in public more frequently and was more gregarious than she had been since her early days in Hollywood.

Given her health issues, Hauser provided ideas about how to eat a healthier diet. Garbo ate a primarily vegetarian diet when they met. Hauser added more protein to her diet, which helped her immensely. He was a proponent of exercise, so they had that in common as well.

Garbo spent time with Hauser in Wisconsin. Garbo and Hauser had visited Hauser's brother in Milwaukee in December 1941.[1057] They also invested in Wisconsin real estate together.

For several summers Garbo rented a house on Islandale, a small island in Lac La Belle.[1058]

One great advantage for Garbo in Wisconsin was that few ever realized who she was while she was visiting Hauser. She wrote to Peg in the mid-1940s that,

> I have ended up in Wisconsin for some days. But it is too late in the year, here is no summer any more. Rain and fall. But it is a bit of a change of air. . . . I have been incredibly tired, so it was best to go here. Nobody recognizes me here, I can just waddle around for a little while and breathe now and then.[1059]

Gayelord Hauser spent significant time at his homes in Coldwater Canyon and Palm Springs, in addition to Wisconsin. Garbo would visit him at these locations until his death in 1984.

Garbo and Gayelord Hauser in Wisconsin.

Through Gayelord Hauser Garbo met singer Jessica Dragonette, with whom she became close friends. Dragonette recounted a story from right before the 1940 election where Garbo jumped up on a bench in Dragonette's living room and asked those assembled, "Will you vote for me for President of the United States? I'm a good man. Besides I'll have to do something important after having been in films."[1060]

As before, Garbo also struck up unexpected friendships. Dancer and actor Fred Astaire was stunned to learn his mother Anne had become good friends with Garbo after being introduced to her by Hauser. When Astaire asked his mother if Garbo knew of him, she reported that Garbo had said: "Oh yes, he's the boy who dances, isn't he?"[1061]

Leopold Stokowski and Garbo met at a Sunday lunch hosted by Anita Loos sometime in the fall of 1937. Loos recalled, "I was the one person he knew at MGM and I introduced him—not that I remember it at all. There was a certain group of us out there: Aldous Huxley, Christopher Isherwood—let me think who else—a group of high-powered intellectuals, and, of course, Stokowski belonged to it, and they met at my house at lunch on Sundays and she just happened to meet Stoki. So, he joined the group and she belonged to the group. It didn't strike me as a romance because everybody was busy working and he was making film tests concerning sound."[1062]

Stokowski is the person who opened classical music to new ideas in the early twentieth century. He created the pops concert while he was the conductor of the Cincinnati Symphony Orchestra. He brought many contemporary composers attention by premiering their works. In 1912 he was hired as conductor of the Philadelphia Orchestra, where he remained as principal conductor until 1936. He came to Hollywood in 1937 and appeared in two films. Then in 1939 he collaborated with Walt Disney on the animated classic *Fantasia* (1940).

Their relationship was gossip column news and reporters chased after them whenever they went out. One reporter did catch up with her at the front door of George Cukor's house after following her car for miles. When he presented himself Garbo asked, "How did you find me? Did you follow me from my house?" When the reporter admitted that he had done so, she responded, "How sad. How sad." This was half the resulting interview. The other half was Garbo's answer to the question regarding the possibility of marriage to Stokowski. Garbo responded, "No, no, I will not marry. I won't deny that Mr. Stokowski and I are very good friends, but as for marriage to him—no. That is out of the question."[1063]

Whereas Garbo was shy and disliked publicity and public events, Stokowski was just the opposite. He was a public figure and relished the attention of music fans, the press, and the public. Adding film acting gave him exposure he could never receive from just conducting.

Even with this difference, they had a lot in common. Garbo loved music and had many musicians among her friends. They both sought to eat a healthy diet, liked to be out in the sun, and liked to walk.

Garbo left for Europe in December 1937. She was away from Hollywood for an entire year. During her trip (between *Conquest* and *Ninotchka*, December 1937 to October 1938), Hattie Grimstead, a Swedish journalist, spent extensive time talking to people in Sweden who knew Garbo and wrote about it. She began her story with Garbo's press conference on the MS *Gripsholm*. She quoted her regarding the upcoming Ninotchka project, and Garbo demonstrated a light touch:

> I am tired of period pictures and I want to do something modern now. My next film is to be a comedy, as I expect you know. Will I be allowed to keep my lover in it? Certainly I am hoping so! Don't you think it is high time they let me end a picture happily with a kiss? I do. I seem to have lost so many attractive men in the final scenes![1064]

The reporter got people who frequented Hårby to talk about its inner workings. Garbo goes about the farm with Sven attending to things. It is revealed that Garbo is able to embroider "exquisitely."[1065] Hårby was furnished in a traditional Swedish fashion. Her bedroom is simple, with lots of books.

Garbo went to Stockholm and stayed with friends there. Together they went about watching skate sailing, ice hockey, and skiing. She went ice skating. When she talked about Söder, it was as "my part of the city."[1066]

The writer pointed out that despite living in America, Garbo remained essentially Swedish in her nature. The only thing that kept Garbo away was her work:

> Only the fact that she loves her work to the exclusion of everything else keeps Garbo in Hollywood—she makes no secret of it to her friends. She counts the screen as the most important thing in the world and she abnegates herself and her own desires to the demands of her art just as did Duse and Bernhardt and the famous actresses before them.[1067]

Garbo is living at Hårby at this point. She looks forward to seeing Stokowski. She wrote to Viertel:

> But somewhere in this world are a few beenes [beings] who do not have it as we have of that I am certain. And if I would stop making film I could go and see if I could find out a little about it.[1068]

On February 24, 1938, Stokowski and Garbo rendezvoused in Rome, departing for a villa they had rented in Ravello the following day. The press tracked them relentlessly whenever they left the Villa Cimbrone. Film fans descended on the town to catch a glimpse of her. The local police ended up guarding the villa to deter unwanted visitors. The Italian government ordered its press to stop covering Garbo and Stokowski, but that still left an army of international reporters.[1069]

Finally, on March 17 Garbo agreed to a press conference under the condition that afterward, the press would leave her alone. The press was ushered in and Garbo answered a few questions. The first few questions focused on whether she and Stokowski were going to marry. Garbo responded that she intended to remain single.

The most interesting topic reporters asked about was her friends. Garbo said she had about a dozen friends, split between Europe and America. She said that "I haven't many friends. I haven't seen much of the world either. My friend, Mr. Stokowski, who has been very much to me, offered to take me around to see some beautiful things. I optimistically accepted."[1070]

The press didn't leave them alone as agreed. They left for Rome shortly after that point and then Garbo and Stokowski departed for Tunisia on March 30. They rented a villa in Hammamet, a coastal resort south of Tunis. Here they finally were able to disappear. They were sighted again in Casablanca at the end of April, just as they were departing for Sweden, where they joined Garbo's family at Hårby.

While in Stockholm, Stokowski did attend to some music publishing business. Lennart Reuterskiöld, who owned Reuter and Reuter, ended up asking publisher Åke Bonnier to lunch. After a wonderful lunch with Garbo and Stokowski, Bonnier asked them to dinner at his father's (famous publisher Karl Otto Bonnier, who first published August Strindberg and Selma Lagerlöf, among many notable authors) house that Friday. Bonnier had assumed that this would present no problem. However, he had not reckoned with his father's reluctance to meet her. The eighty-two-year-old elder Bonnier was not a filmgoer at all. Only after rather persistent entreaties was the dinner agreed to.

Friday arrived and Åke Bonnier related how dinner went:

> Garbo arrived wearing white trousers, which were considered rather startling in those days. My father was obliged to have Garbo sit next to him. Garbo turned out to be in a very lively and pleasant and talkative mood. After dinner she said to my father, "Now you must show me the garden." And she took him under the arm and they took a tour round the garden and had a look at the greenhouse. They were gone a good while and then we sat in the library and chatted, before Eva and I drove our guests home.
>
> It got quite late and it was gone one in the morning when we got home. The telephone suddenly started to ring and I thought: who could it possibly be ringing at this time of night?
>
> It was my father, who said in that aged, trembling voice of his: "Thank you, dear Åke, for forcing me to have Greta Garbo to dinner, you see, I have fallen so dreadfully in love with her."[1071]

The family enjoyed having Stokowski as a guest. He taught Garbo's niece Gray to swim in the lake. Later that summer Stokowski flipped the car he was driving in with Garbo near the town of Södertälje, between Hårby and Stockholm. Fortunately, neither was hurt.[1072] Then at the end of July Stokowski left Sweden while Garbo remained at Hårby until September.

Garbo arrived in New York on the MS *Kungsholm* on October 7, 1938. Leopold Stokowski arranged for his friends Dick Hammond and Reggie Allen to meet her on arrival. After being escorted to Garbo's stateroom, Hammond convinced her to talk to the press before disembarking, so as to give them less reason to chase her around the city. Garbo was by now accustomed to a shipboard interview when she either arrived or departed. She spent a few minutes answering questions posed by reporters. Refusing to answer questions about her private life, she responded to a question about whether she hated reporters by saying she might "like all of you, removed from your jobs and your newspapers."[1073] She wished that she had two faces, one for the movies and one for her private life.

Two other questions stand out. One reporter asked Garbo if she ever planned to marry. Her response was "if I could find the right person to share my life with perhaps I would marry."[1074]

The second question of note was rather pointed, and Garbo's response was clever. The reporter asked, "Do you think single blessedness the proper state for a professional woman?" The patriarchal assumptions underlying the question were a direct challenge to the single life Garbo was leading. Her response was simply "if you are blessed, you are blessed, whether you are married or single."[1075]

Hammond and Allen had not accounted for the throng of fans and additional reporters waiting on the dock. Many were waiting in taxis with their meters running to follow Garbo into the city. Hammond and Allen contrived to sneak Garbo into, of all things, a newsreel car while they separately marched down the gangway with a tightly packed entourage of Swedish people, with some entering the car of the Swedish consul.

The ruse almost worked. But as the crowd descended on their car, someone recognized Garbo in the newsreel car, and the chase was on. It ended abruptly in a few blocks when one of the pursuing vehicles took the bumper off the Swedish consul's car, blocking all traffic.[1076]

Garbo spent a couple of weeks in New York without being found out. She traveled up to Gloucester, Massachusetts, with Hammond for a relaxing week, and then boarded a train to California.[1077]

Fans had been copying Garbo's evolving hairstyles ever since she had become a star. When Garbo returned to America that October with straight hair, that proved problematic to the hairdressers of America. Were women to wear their hair so simply, the financial implications for the hairdressers would be significant. A national hairdressers association passed a resolution criticizing her decision to not perm her hair because if this became the popular style, it "would have the effect of working vast injury to the hair stylists and hairdressers of the United States."[1078]

When Garbo chose to not perm her hair, it rocked the hairstyling industry.

Chapter 31 - *Ninotchka*

"Thanks Peggy for offering to come over. But if it is just because you would like to help, it is not necessary. If it is because you would like to be here, you are very welcome. You are the only people I can stay calm with."[1079]

— Garbo letter to her sister-in-law, June 20, 1945

In *Ninotchka* political opposites Garbo and Melvyn Douglas fall in love.

After nearly a year in Europe, spent primarily at Hårby, Garbo returned to America in October 1938. In December she signed a one-picture deal for *Ninotchka*, which had been in development for her.

Filmed in 1939, *Ninotchka* breaks every norm in the Hollywood of the era. It's astounding that it got made. It was not just that Garbo was cast in a comedy, totally against type. It's everything about the film. It's a subtle satire. It is also political. Garbo is cast as a Communist. Not one who is a caricature or overdrawn, but rather a true believer who falls in love with a capitalist.

While *Ninotchka* mocks elements of Stalin's rule, it treats Communists as people. One reviewer wrote, "It is the first movie with any airiness at all to discover that Communists are people and may be treated as such in a story."[1080]

Garbo doesn't play any old Communist. She has a very feminist role. She is a woman with professional responsibilities. She is the boss, serious and hard. The jokes are witty and sophisticated. How hard is it to deliver a line that makes purges funny? Garbo delivered "The last mass trials were a great success. There will be fewer but better Russians," as comedy.

It was a personal risk for Garbo as well. She socialized in the European émigré community in Hollywood, which included plenty of Communists and Socialists. Hollywood intellectuals were still pro-Communist because they were anti-Nazi. In 1939, those who had fled Germany considered the Soviets anti-Nazi first and foremost. The full extent of Stalin's atrocities of the mid-1930s were just coming to light. The Russian-German non-aggression agreement was signed after filming, but before the premiere in New York on October 9, 1939.

Melchior Lengyel developed a three-sentence story at the request of Bernie Hyman. Hyman and Salka Viertel had come up to him at lunch and asked if he had a comedy idea suitable for Garbo. He said no, but the next day called Viertel and said an idea had come to him overnight. She asked him to come right over and pitch it to Garbo.

Garbo was swimming in Viertel's pool naked. Nonplussed, he nevertheless delivered his three-sentence plot: "Russian girl saturated with Bolshevist ideas goes to fearful, capitalistic, monopolistic Paris. She meets romance and has an uproarious good time. Capitalism not so bad after all." This earned Lengyel $15,000 ($336,000).[1081]

However, several writing teams failed to turn this basic idea into a script. MGM brought in Ernst Lubitsch, whom Garbo had known from the German social circle when she was new in Hollywood. Lubitsch refocused with a new writing team of Charles Brackett, Billy Wilder, and Walter Reich, who then wrote their classic script.

Lubitsch wanted to show Garbo how the new script for *Ninotchka* had evolved, so they met for lunch at a restaurant. Lubitsch had ordered a huge spread for them to eat while they discussed the film. Garbo demurred, saying she was dieting. So, Lubitsch began explaining to Garbo the plot of *Ninotchka* and how he viewed what she could bring to the film. Garbo got so carried away with Lubitsch's descriptions that she ate the entire spread over the hour that Lubitsch was talking.[1082]

Garbo signed a contract for in December 1938. From the initial concept developed by Lengyel back in the fall of 1937, development had proceeded for the entire year she was in Europe. Production began in June 1939.

Garbo meets the three Russian emissaries who provide comic relief in *Ninotchka*.

Garbo and Melvyn Dougls consult a Paris map together.

Garbo is Ninotchka, a Soviet representative sent to Paris to reclaim jewels smuggled out of the Soviet Union by Grand Duchess Swana, played by Ina Claire. The grand duchess is in a relationship with Léon, played by Melvyn Douglas. The three prior Russian emissaries have been seduced by the charms of Paris and corrupted by Léon, who intends to romance Ninotchka in order to deflect her from her mission. Ninotchka arrives in Paris to set the emissaries straight and meets Léon. A romance blossoms between them.

Ninotchka is torn between her new love and her Communistic ideals. The duchess steals the jewels while Ninotchka and Léon are together. Then the duchess gives the jewels back to Ninotchka on the condition that she leave Paris and Léon. She does and returns to Moscow.

However, Moscow is dreary. There is censorship, fear, and hunger. Ninotchka reunites with the three emissaries she had met in Paris, and in a classic scene they bring eggs to make an omelet in her apartment. Léon contrives to reunite with Ninotchka, with the assistance of the three Russian envoys.

Lubitsch thought he had to find ways to keep Garbo loose and relaxed. At one point he contrived to have a book made that would open with a small explosion. Garbo noticed the book, titled *Parisian Nights*, one day and with curiosity as to what Lubitsch was reading during production, moved to pick it up. She sensed that Lubitsch was standing nearby with a studied obliviousness and stopped. There the book lay for several days, Garbo glancing at it and Lubitsch pretending not to notice.

After several days Garbo walked over to the book saying, “I know it’s a trick, but I’ve got to see what’s in this thing.” She opened the book, which went off with a bang. Everyone dissolved into laughter.[1083]

Garbo and Ernst Lubitsch share a laugh on the set of *Ninotchka.*

Theatre Arts Magazine thought that *Ninotchka* (along with *Mr. Smith Goes to Washington*, which was released the prior month) marked a coming age of new maturity in Hollywood. It celebrated it as a "grown-up film for grown-ups."[1084] *Ninotchka* holds up well to this day.

Ninotchka was a contemporary film. The events, though fictional, would have been the recent past. It was political, skewering communism and the Soviet Union. Political leftists were not amused. *New Masses* magazine wrote, "I cannot remember a picture so industriously twisted back and forth to cover every single slander of socialism."[1085]

Comedy requires different skills than dramatic acting to be successful. So, the natural question was whether Garbo could translate her talents to comedy. Most reviews thought so. Allen Bishop wrote,

> Any good actress could play Ninotchka—it is not a particularly exacting part—and make the film amusing. Miss Garbo not only makes it amusing, confounding critics who thought she could never adapt her peculiar magic to the exigencies of comedy by showing herself to be as deft a comedienne as she is a tragic actress. . . . Miss Garbo effects the transition between two basically different

> characters with great subtly and technical skill—not only by a change of expression, of gesture and tone of voice, but in the whole line of her body. Although Miss Garbo—thank God—is always Miss Garbo, you have only to see her in such contrasting roles as Camille and Ninotchka to realize that she is an actress of radiant quality and ability.[1086]

A portrait of Garbo from *Ninotchka*.

Upon completing *Ninotchka*, Garbo remained in the United States. Germany had occupied Czechoslovakia in March and war seemed inevitable to many people. World War II formally started with the invasion of Poland on September 1. At this point, and for the first few years of the war, an invasion of Sweden did not seem out of the question.

So Garbo's family moved to the United States in October 1939. Her mother, brother, sister-in-law, and niece initially came to California before relocating, through several intermediate locations (including Tucson, Arizona; Manchester, Vermont; Gloucester, Massachusetts; and Bronxville, New York), in Santa Fe, New Mexico. Originally the family did not intend to stay in America permanently.

Garbo had spent considerable time with her family in Sweden, and Sven had visited her in America in 1935, spending three months there. His visit overlapped in part with the production of *Anna Karenina*. Laing's early biography, which relies more on his contacts in Europe, sums up what he learned from these contacts: Sven and Garbo, in addition to being siblings, were best of friends.[1087] As events in Europe became more tense, she had made arrangements for her entire family to escape to America before war began. They had to convince Garbo's mother that she should leave, but eventually she agreed.

Sven and Garbo made plans to sell Hårby before the war started. Then Germany invaded Poland. A buyer thought that made Hårby an attractive investment as its timber had suddenly become more valuable, and a deal was quickly finalized.

An undated letter sent after 1942 clarifies that the decision to sell Hårby was made by Sven and Peg.[1088] While they liked Hårby, many people thought Sweden might be invaded by Germany. Keeping Hårby while living outside the country was a financial risk.

Even after the war had fully engulfed Europe, Garbo wished there were a way to be in Sweden. "Sweden really isn't safe. I do so long to go home, but the oceans so unsafe now."[1089]

In October 1939, with the Hårby deal done but not closed, Sven, Anna, and Gray left Sweden for America. Peg stayed behind to supervise the sale closing and then she departed in December. The family was finally together in America. However, Anna didn't like Los Angeles. In January 1940 Anna, Sven, Peg, and Gray moved to Tucson, Arizona. They did not like it there either and by May they had relocated to Santa Barbara, California. Garbo wrote to Wacht meister:

> The family is living here only a day's journey away. Peg is having a lot of trouble with her joints and my brother and Mum want to go home. . . . If peace comes, what I want most is to go home and not to make another film. I don't want to even think about it.[1090]

In a separate letter she wrote to Wachtmeister that she saw her family weekly after they returned from Tucson.[1091]

Garbo also met George Schlee in 1939, and it developed into the final romance of her life. George and his wife Valentina were Russians who fled the revolution in 1920. The Schlees arrived in New York in 1922 with a Schlee-managed theater troupe that had been hired to perform their successful Paris-based show in New York. Right after the opening in October, the Shubert Theater group experienced a financial reversal, and announced to Schlee that they couldn't guarantee payment. Schlee arranged for an engagement in Chicago, which was successful, but after that the troupe disbanded. He arranged for most of the other actors to work with various other productions in America, and he and Valentina returned to New York.

After a few years the Schlees began a couture business under Valentina's name featuring her designs. For the next thirty years Valentina was one of the premiere dressmakers in America, with a side business designing costumes for stage, opera, and film. George ran the business side of the company in the background until the venture closed in 1957. He invested in numerous other ventures, including plays, and worked with Gloria Swanson, a Hollywood contemporary a few years older than Garbo, on her non-Hollywood Multi-prises business, which operated from 1939 to the mid-1940s.

Gayelord Hauser had brought Garbo to Valentina's showroom in 1939, and she found both Schlees to be interesting. A complicated relationship developed between the three of them. Valentina was at the time involved romantically with Jack Barrett, the president of the Bollingen Foundation.[1092] Their relationship was a long-term one. Now Garbo and George Schlee became romantically involved, while the Schlee marriage continued. It took several years after their initial meeting for their relationship to fully mature. In 1940s letters to Peg, Garbo still clearly views Schlee as a bit of an outsider.

Perhaps the most interesting letter regarding Schlee that Garbo sent to Peg Gustafson is an undated one that was sent sometime during the war. Garbo clearly has expectations regarding how much a man should be contributing around the house, and so far, Schlee hasn't measured up:

> And you little boys, how are you going to believe that Schlee will probably come in a short while. Then he will have to help me with the house. If he doesn't, I will ask him to leave again. I will write later if he comes and will tell you how he behaves with the dishes.[1093]

Apparently, Schlee adjusted. Garbo would mention him in her letters to Peg frequently.

In June 1945 Garbo wrote to her sister-in-law regarding her caution around her relationship with Schlee:

> Kata is now very scared. Schlee is thinking about coming over so I will probably have to host him as a guest. If that works and the old lady does not mind. Too much work "you know." It is terrible to have them around.[1094]

Just before Christmas later that same year Garbo again wrote about Schlee to Peg, indicating she was not yet totally comfortable with him:

> I am invited to Schlee for Christmas, but I do not feel like going. I think I will stay in my room. It is not fun to go to strangers for Christmas. And they don't celebrate Christmas the way we do, and don't eat the same things as us, so perhaps I will go to Nyborg and Nelson and get something there. Who knows. Thanks little Peg for the bread, it was fantastic! [1095]

By June 1946 Garbo wrote a letter to Peg indicating that she had become much more comfortable with him.[1096] She planned to travel with him to Sweden on her first post-war trip.[1097] He was one of the few people she ever brought to her brother's home.

In the late 1930s and early 1940s, the world was changing. Europe was at war and America was unsettled. The consequences of these changes would upend Garbo's career.

Chapter 32 – End of an Era

"Immoral and un-Christian attitude toward marriage and its obligations; impudently suggestive scenes, dialogue and situations; suggestive costumes.[1098]

— John McClafferty, executive secretary of the Legion of Decency,in a letter to Archbishop John McNicholas, describing his view of *Two-Faced Woman*

Garbo dancing was a more contemporary presentation of the star.

Back when the Production Code was created in 1930 Irving Thalberg had written,

> People influence pictures far more than pictures influence people. The motion picture does not present the audience with tastes and manners and views and morals; it *reflects* those they already have.[1099]

In 1941 the American audience, buffeted by the Depression and war, had become more conservative. The ideas of equality and emancipation for women had been set aside. The consequences of this societal shift would alter the trajectory of Garbo's career.

Change would come when the Legion decided to alter the status quo. There were a variety of reasons for the Legion of Decency to push for stricter and more intrusive censorship in 1941. The film industry had pushed the boundaries with some recent film content, challenging the PCA. There was a change in PCA leadership. The Legion and the PCA had disagreed on the censorship of some films, with the Legion rejecting PCA approvals as too lenient. Garbo's final completed film, *Two-Faced Woman*, got caught in the crossfire.

After a seven-year run, Joseph Breen had resigned from the PCA in March 1941. His replacement was Geoff Shurlock, his former assistant. Shurlock didn't have the political nous or respect that Breen had earned from all sides.

Conservatives at the Legion of Decency were looking for a way to assert their control. They weren't just concerned about the portrayal of sex and male/female relationships. They wanted more control over every aspect of how society was portrayed on the screen. The Catholic Church was not alone in the push for returning women to a place of subservience and sexual modesty. Christian premillennial fundamentalists were a rising social force in America. Their fundamentalist solution to the Depression was to commit to a "Christian" home where the wife remained at home while the husband worked, and his authority governed the household.[1100] Their concern for this husband-led order was a foundational issue for them.

Casting Garbo in *Two-Faced Woman* came about because of the changing nature of the business. At one point Garbo was intended to get the role of Marie Curie in the film Madame Curie, which eventually was filmed by MGM in 1943 with Greer Garson in the main role.

Salka Viertel suggested the story to Bernie Hyman in 1938. He didn't think Garbo even knew who Curie was, but when Salka cabled Garbo to assess her interest her reply was "Love to play Marie Curie. Could not think of anything better."[1101] The MGM story department was against buying the rights to the story because they didn't think a female actor would want to play a scientist.[1102]

MGM shelved the Curie film as a Garbo project with the start of the war. Producer Bernie Hyman thought a comedy was a better option for a Garbo vehicle given the times.[1103] That decision led to *Two-Faced Woman*. With the Continental European market closed off by war, MGM executive Benny Thau was tasked with asking Garbo to make two pictures for the price of one. Garbo's response was to offer to make one picture at half price.[1104]

After *Madame Curie* was shelved, Salka Viertel briefly left MGM in a contract dispute, signing with Warner Brothers. Eddie Mannix convinced her to return, and she was assigned the task of coming up with another comedy for Garbo to star in. They settled on *The Twin Sister* (1901), an old European play by Ludwig Fulda. Salka adapted the story into a screenplay with Sam Behrman and George Oppenheimer, a comedy specialist.

In *Two-Faced Woman* Garbo plays a double role of a woman and her fabricated sister. The real one is Karin, who is a ski instructor in Idaho. Melvyn

Garbo and Melvyn Douglas find love in Idaho.

Douglas is Larry Blake, a publishing executive on vacation. Sparks fly between them, and they end up snowbound in a remote cabin. They marry, but then work calls Larry back to New York. Karin is concerned that Larry misses his old urban life, and that she might lose him. She is particularly concerned about Griselda, played by Constance Bennett, an old love interest of Larry's.

Karin travels to New York, obtains a fancy wardrobe, and goes looking for Larry at the rehearsal of Griselda's new play. There she ends up presenting herself as Karin's imaginary twin sister Katherine.

The rest of the film resolves the relationships between Karin, Larry, Griselda, and several minor characters.

Garbo and Constance Bennet face off over Melvyn Douglas.

Originally the plot did not have Karin marrying Larry before he returns to New York. The PCA rejected the storyline because it presumed premarital sex between Larry and Karin. Producer Gottfried Reinhardt's solution was to have Larry and Karin marry while in Idaho and then to have Larry leave her and return to New York. Being married, Larry is now a cad, but the premarital sex issue was addressed. The PCA approved.[1105]

The film we see today is not the film originally released. The most likely idea is that Garbo was intending to play the twins as a commentary on how men perceived a woman based on how she behaved. A scene with Larry eavesdropping on his wife's telephone call, which gives the game away, was added after initial release to placate the Legion of Decency. This makes the story pointless. In the original version, with Larry unaware that Karin and Katherine are one and the same, the material naturally revolves around both his differing perceptions of the same woman in different guises and her perception of how he relates to her in each guise.

The film suffered from disagreements between producer Gottfried Reinhardt and director George Cukor. They bickered about details and fought passive aggressively over co-stars, wardrobe, and film locations.[1106]

In one of the most surprising and consequential censorship developments of the era, the Legion of Decency condemned *Two-Faced Woman* after its release. How this came about was only partly related to the film itself. The events marked the ascendancy of social conservatives for the next three decades.

As discussed earlier, the Legion of Decency was not officially part of the industry censorship bureaucracy. It was an ostensibly independent, but in practice Catholic, monitor of films with no formal powers.

After the Legion of Decency rated a film, the only other action taken was publicizing the rating in each archdiocese through newsletters. The Legion had three ratings for films of varying levels of acceptance: A-I, A-II, and B. Films rated C were condemned, another matter entirely. During the conversion to the censorship regime in which the PCA and Legion worked in tandem, there was a brief turbulent period, but from 1935 to 1939 no Hollywood studio films earned a C rating.[1107] Non-Hollywood studio films, typically but not exclusively imports, sometimes received a C rating and subsequently achieved little distribution. Typically these condemned films were seen only in the biggest cities, at smaller independent theaters. In a market sense they were irrelevant.

The Legion issued three C ratings to Hollywood studio films from 1939 to 1941, and the underlying issue that it was attacking in censoring two of these films was regarding a couple presenting their sexual relationship one way when in fact the obverse was true. The Legion objected to the false presentation of affairs.[1108]

In the third film, *Strange Cargo* (1940), the character who was the fulcrum for each other character's redemption, Cambreau, turned out to be the issue for the Legion. Its reviewers thought that the Cambreau character was a filmic stand-in for Jesus, and therefore sacrilegious.[1109]

Two-Faced Woman was approved by the PCA under its new head Shurlock. To the PCA reviewers the story device of Garbo playing both Melvyn Douglas's wife and her twin sister who seduces him was considered "obviously farcical."[1110]

The Legion claimed an entirely different point of view. Because of the plot dynamic, the Legion objected to the casual treatment of marriage. It also objected to one costume, several love scenes, and many instances of dialogue it found too risqué.

The Legion had a couple of other objectives that attacking *Two-Faced Woman* conveniently solved.

With the departure of Breen, the Legion wanted to make sure that the PCA under Shurlock would not steamroll it into approving what it considered to be questionable films. *Two-Faced Woman* gave it an opportunity to reiterate the power of the Catholic Church to wreck economic havoc if it was challenged. There was also an issue with Garbo playing yet another free-spirited woman, or in this case two.

During the three prior C classifications of Hollywood films after 1939, there had been a broad objection voiced to the Catholic Church being in the position to set public policy. The Catholic Church responded strongly, accusing its detractors of religious discrimination (invoking the Klan), as it was merely upholding American values.[1111] Therefore it was in no mood to compromise.

When the Legion looked around for a target to bring the film industry further to heel, MGM was probably the best one. It was one of the majors, so both the industry and the public would clearly notice. MGM did push the envelope more than the other majors. After all, MGM strategy was to give Loew's films that would fill its first-run theaters with urban women. The Motion Picture Department of the IFCA reported that of the 1,271 films reviewed by the Legion of Decency between February 1936 and November 1937, MGM had the highest percentage of films receiving a B classification of any of the majors.[1112]

Garbo as her imaginary twin.

Further, Time magazine hypothesized, not unreasonably, that the condemnation of *Two-Faced Woman* was due to the fact that the annual signing of the Legion of Decency pledge was scheduled for mid-December.[1113]

The question one must ask is whether the condemnation of *Two-Faced Woman* made any sense on the merits of the film. Melvyn Douglas, who starred in both films, pointed out that *The Chocolate Soldier* (1941), released just weeks before, had a similar plot to *Two-Faced Woman*, with one person in the couple testing the loyalty of the other by pretending to be a third individual, and that it had no censorship problems at all.[1114]

Newsweek wrote that the Catholic Church had telegraphed a desire for more restrictive censorship at its fall conference in Philadelphia, where Archbishop McNicholas had stated that films were "too suggestive and sexy."[1115] The Legion had in 1941 undertaken an internal review of its work over the past five years, and found itself deficient.[1116]

No other condemned movie had received such official Catholic attention to the fact of its condemnation. Archbishop Francis Spellman of New York issued his only pastoral letter regarding films to call viewing *Two-Faced Woman* "an occasion of sin and dangerous to public morals."[1117]

On Wednesday, November 26, the day before Thanksgiving, the Legion released its official C rating for the film. In coordination with the Legion, Archbishop Spellman sent out a release that it was to be announced at all services that Sunday that *Two-Faced Woman* was dangerous to public morality. It was immediately banned in Providence, and then Boston.

On December 1 the Catholic Church decided to go after MGM VP of Publicity Howard Dietz. He had commented a few days earlier that "there is no exact science in the production of motion pictures. People do at various times differ as to the effect of a given line or scene, particularly in a picture such as this, which is a comedy and designed primarily to amuse."[1118]

Apparently, this bromide was an offense to the perfection of the Legion of Decency's process, in which its interpretation of the film could not be questioned.

McClafferty's meeting with J. Robert Rubin occurred on December 2. Rubin caved to every demand McClafferty put forward. Rubin agreed to release a statement, pre-approved by the Legion, reaffirming MGM's commitment to the Code and the Legion's interpretation of it.[1119] For the first time the Legion was pre-eminent.

MGM immediately submitted a list of changes to McClafferty. The main change was to alter the underlying story of the film. To address the Legion's concerns, MGM suggested adding a scene in which Larry calls home to check on Karin, only to learn that she has followed him to New York. Thus, Larry is able to figure out that Karin and Katherine are one and the same, waving away the whole issue of adultery (other than the unaddressed fact that Garbo, as Katherine, still pretends she is engaged in adultery). There were also eleven proposed cuts to scenes in the film.

Though *Two-Faced Woman* has historically been dismissed as a poor film, that seems to reflect the negative effect of the censorship on public perception. In spite of the bad publicity, the film received a featured recommendation from the National Board of Review on November 15, and Garbo was nominated for the New York Film Critics Circle Award for Best Actress in 1941 for the role.

Catholics were careful to not reveal how direct their control of censorship was, though their letters are clear enough. After the confrontation over *Two-Faced Woman*, Joseph Breen would write to Martin Quigley, "It looks, though, that a new day and a new deal is on its way." [1120]

Two-Faced Woman didn't quite deliver the same revenue for MGM as the other Garbo independent productions. Only *The Painted Veil* had lower total revenue. The Legion boycott was not the main issue. Most of the domestic revenue was generated before the original version of the film was withdrawn, three weeks after the release. The Japanese attack on Pearl Harbor suppressed theater attendance nationally that December. *Two-Faced Woman* suffered along with every other film released at that time. The war had also totally eliminated access to many foreign markets, which affected Garbo more than most stars.

Garbo and the industry were unaware that *Two-Faced Woman* would be her last film. She shrugged off the entire episode and signed a contract with MGM to make *The Girl from Leningrad* (1941).

Chapter 33 – The War Years

"I remember the four of us sitting around this table.
Greta sat there; I sat here; George Cukor sat next to me;
and L.B. sat at that end. We were trying to sell him on the idea of
letting Greta and me star in Mourning Becomes Electra,
which George would direct. Well, we didn't get very far.
We could tell right away that we were not heating up the room.
So George nodded to me and Greta, and we got up and left.
That was the end of that idea.[1121]

— Katharine Hepburn, actor

Garbo by her swimming pool

The trope is that Garbo's last film failed, and she walked away from Hollywood. Those who say that ignore the very public record of projects Garbo was involved in up to 1949. There is another fascinating project that she agreed to in 1955, *The Miracle*, that has been hidden for decades. But it too fizzled out by 1957. Garbo spent fifteen fruitless years trying to make another high-quality film about an interesting woman.

Yet the fact remains that *Two-Faced Woman* was Garbo's last film and when it was released, she was only thirty-six.

Several factors led to Garbo not making that next film. American censorship was in its most restrictive phase. The Studio Era was over, and after World War II production budgets shrank as theater attendance dropped. MGM itself was transformed, run by a new generation of managers.

The country became even more conservative. Women's rights slumbered until the 1970s and social conservatives constrained American life. There were few roles for middle-aged female actors. A quick survey of twenty of Garbo's contemporaries who kept working after the war shows that three-quarters of them appeared mostly in television after the mid-1950s.

While Joan Crawford, Katharine Hepburn, Bette Davis, and Marlene Dietrich made films as stars later in life, few of the roles allowed for explorations of sex and relationships, Garbo's stock-in-trade. She was aware of the kind of roles that fit her best. When RKO offered her the role of the mother in *I Remember Mama* (1948), her telegram back was simply "no mamas, no murderers."[1122] She also turned down *The Paradine Case* (1947).

Occasionally the roles for mature female actors were great lead roles. Bette Davis and Joan Crawford in *What Ever Happened to Baby Jane?* (1962) were wonderful, but unusual.

Garbo didn't walk away from Hollywood until sometime after 1957. The Garbo projects that never got made are themselves fascinating. They primarily would have been bold projects challenging female stereotypes.

Garbo wrote many letters to Peg during this period. Peg's return from Sweden marks the beginning of the bulk of these letters. They were close friends and the letters reveal much about Garbo's inner thoughts during the 1940s and 1950s.

There were many letters that were mundane and addressed topics like the transferring of ration coupons between them. Garbo wrote to thank Peg for the frequent food packages, primarily ginger cookies, that were sent to her. Garbo also asked what kinds of gifts the family would like for Christmas and birthdays, later asking if they had been well received.

In an undated letter written in 1941 Garbo wrote that she was sad to learn of her mother Anna's health problems. She thought Anna might have worked too hard in her years of taking care of the family. Garbo responds to having learned that Peg is going to return to Sweden:

> I don't know what to say about going. I should think it is a bad time now. Perhaps there will be a terrific bang in Europe and everybody would be drawn into it. Perhaps even Sweden.[1123]

In this earliest of the surviving letters from Garbo to her sister-in-law she talks about perhaps renting a house in Nantucket for the summer and she could join them there.[1124]

In a separate undated letter, also before Peg's departure, Garbo relates that she might be going to Europe for a prospective British production (probably *Saint Joan*). Though she once again counsels Peg not to go to Sweden. Garbo writes that she is still filming *Two-Faced Woman*.[1125]

Garbo had seen the original Russian film *Frontovye podrugi* (The Girl from Leningrad, 1941) upon its US release and wanted to remake it in Hollywood.[1126] The story was about a wounded soldier and a nurse set during the 1939 Russo-Finnish War. Bernie Hyman asked Viertel to develop a script. The trade press announced that MGM was developing this project.[1127]

The dust had hardly settled from the condemnation of *Two-Faced Woman*, and Garbo signed a one-picture deal with MGM to make *The Girl from Leningrad*. The sudden death of Bernie Hyman on September 7, 1942, led MGM to drop the project. Garbo had already been paid the 50 percent advance. Clarence Brown told several interviewers that Mayer offered to pay Garbo the balance due under the contract, but that Garbo turned him down because she didn't think she deserved to be paid any more money if they were not going to make the film. According to George Cukor, Mayer was "lost in admiration over the splendid way she behaved about it."[1128] Then in 1943 MGM terminated Viertel's contract. Garbo's historic production relationship with MGM would no longer be her preferred option.

In the midst of war Garbo intended to make a film version of *Saint Joan* from the play by George Bernard Shaw. Shaw vetoed the idea of an established Hollywood actor playing the role. Though Garbo had written to her sister-in-law Peg that "the man from England will come in the beginning of next week, and then we will find out what is happening."[1129] However, producer Gabriel Pascal never made the trip.

Her brother Sven and mother Anna moved to Manchester, Vermont, as Peg and Gray returned to Sweden in October 1941 to celebrate Christmas with friends. America's entry into the war delayed their return for a year.

Garbo's mother and niece in Manchester Vermont.

While living in Manchester, they spent summers in the vacation communities of East Gloucester and Brewster, Massachusetts. In the fall of 1943, the family moved to Bronxville, New York. Once the family decided to move to the New York area, Garbo was excited that they would be closer:

> September 10 [1943, Anna Gustafson's birthday]
>
> Angels. I hope momma had a good day today. I have been thinking about you all morning and been wondering how you have been doing. It would be fantastic if you would find a house close by so that I could visit you every day. I really hope so! Since you are staying here now, I will come a bit later. Between the 1st–5th is when I will travel.
>
> I hope you will live in Greenwich Village or something similar. I sold my little house yesterday. "God bless the king." It is in escrow already, so I hope there won't be any backfire. With a little bit of profit too, but not so much. Perhaps 14 hundred, I have not had the

> time to count it yet. But I am so happy that the house is out of my hands. I always have to go there to water the plants now and then, so it will not dry out completely.
>
> My dear sweet little children, smack yourself over to New York soon so that we can stay together for a while. I am writing this today to let Anna know that I am thinking about you too, and I am sending her an extra hug right now.
>
> Love, and will write again soon.
>
> Love love[1130]

After they had settled in, Garbo visited them, coming out from the city by train:

> Dearest,
>
> I boarded the train in time. So now I am here, coughing at the hotel. Call me as soon as you can, and thanks for everything this weekend.
>
> Kata[1131]

Another undated letter from during the war covers all the usual topics in a single short note. Rationing and items sent back and forth; Garbo's sewing, which she spent a lot of time on during the later part of the war; George Schlee, to whom she was gradually growing closer. As is usual at this time, her letter to Peg is chatty:

> Dearest,
>
> First of all, thanks to my little sister in law for being such a sweety. I have received the gloves and a coupon and map of New York. Peggy never forgets nothing. Do not send me coupons because I can manage fine. I am still so occupied with the house and garden. Soon I have to rest. Sewing curtains by myself too. Large stitches—completely fabulous. But you can't see them. And you little boys, how are you going to believe that Schlee will probably come in a short while. Then he will have to help me with the house. If he doesn't, I will ask him to leave again. I will write later if he comes and will tell you how he behaves with the dishes. I have not read the letters I have sent along. It is easier to send then without the envelopes.

> Live well my dearest and rest and paint and have a good time. Das leben ist so kurtz.
>
> Will write soon again
>
> When I opened the letters I read (?) anyway
>
> Love[1132]

Garbo and Peg shopped in the city from time to time. In one letter Garbo invites Peg in to look for coats:

> Thanks for having me over. If Peg will come to the city tomorrow, Tuesday and would come at 11 we could look for coats until 2 PM. If you have to go to the doctor, do not forget to eat a good breakfast and no lunch.
>
> Love to you all.
>
> Let me know in time or I will do something else.[1133]

While on a train back to Los Angeles, Garbo writes that "if it is not going well out here now, I will close the house up and come again."[1134] So while she was spending more time in New York, she returned to Hollywood to see what career opportunities were present.

When Garbo was planning to work on *Women of the Sea*, she wrote back to Peg about her concerns regarding not having been before the camera for several years:

> I don't have much time work on it, most of it will not be taken care of until work is over. If it will happen, but I think it will. In that case I am going to Canada for two months, but perhaps not for that long. I am shivering at the thought. I have been away from it for such a long time that I can't imagine standing in front of a camera again. My face has probably changed over time, and it will not be easy. I believe it is called La Vie.[1135]

She wrote a second letter about *Women of the Sea* while she awaited a completed script, proposing that the family come out to Los Angeles again.

After the plans for *Women of the Sea* fell apart, Garbo wrote to Peg that her desire was to return to Sweden, as Peg also hoped to do. For the first time she mentions that she might try her hand at directing.

Her mother Anna was a dedicated angler and the whole family sometimes went fishing. Gray (Lillan) spent part of the summer of 1944 at a music camp:

> Dearest little fishermen,
>
> Thanks for Peg's letter. It was fun to hear from you and that Anna gets to go fishing again, praise the Lord. I think Peg will write and tell me what the doctor has to say. I also want to go back to the old country. You would build a nice home. We could rent an apartment with two extra rooms with a separate entrance for me. Hope in h-ll, that would not be bad.
>
> Everyone believes there will be peace in Europe in a few months at the end of the year. Then there's the Japanese left and then there will be peace, we hope. I want to be a director back home, or just sit and stare at the surroundings. Would you like me to send you some crispbread, since you can't buy it there?
>
> I can't imagine that Lillan is at camp. And writes home with such wonderfully bad spelling. And is big as a giant. I don't have any Victory garden. I just have a little piece of grass as a garden, and drive around in my clonky Victory car. Vive la Victory.
>
> Thanks Peg for getting the information. I don't think it will take long before we can go home. And that will be the best. Home to Mrs. Janson and the potato dumplings [kroppkakorna]. Anyway, it is so boring here that I have to come your way for a while. I want some cucumbers and brännvin [Scandinavian vodka] but it will be sudden. Stand up for yourself Anna girl, soon freedom and Janson will come. Hugs to my fishers and Love [1136]

Salka Viertel recalled that Lester Cowan first approached her with the idea of making a film about a Norwegian female ship's captain in early March 1944. Cowan had talked the Norwegian government into lending him a ship. From that beginning the project to make a film called *Women of the Sea* began.

After Viertel related her meeting to Garbo, she agreed to meet with Cowan to discuss it. Viertel recalled that Garbo was adamant that she would not sign a contract until there was a shooting script.[1137] Cowan hired Viertel to write that script, and Vladimir Pozner was added to the screenwriting staff. The target date for completion was July 15.

Garbo was very positive about the project, assuming the script would be acceptable. But early on, she clearly had some concerns about all of the elements coming together. She wrote to Peg that "I am supposed to do a Norwegian sea story. To be shot in Canada, as soon as it is ready. If it will come off."[1138]

Lester Cowan now had a project, with a ship from the Norwegian government and the part of the captain filled by Garbo. Viertel and Pozner were writing the screenplay and Joris Ivens, a respected documentary filmmaker, was to direct.[1139]

Cowan was under pressure to get everything turned into a signed contract so that he could get the commitment to their use of the ship and other resources from the Norwegian government. As the screenplay was not complete, he asked Viertel and Pozner to write a treatment of the end of the story from where they currently were in the screenplay, hoping that this would be enough to get Garbo to sign a contract. This was presented to her on June 20, and she did not like it. Garbo then withdrew from the project. She said that the focus was too much on the love story element.

George Cukor tried to interest MGM in making *Mourning Becomes Electra* in 1944 with Garbo and Katharine Hepburn in the lead roles. Mayer listened to their pitch and turned them down. Cukor probably thought he could sell the idea of Garbo and Hepburn together. One can only imagine how great this could have been. But it certainly did not fit with the new conservative social tide.

Garbo on the MGM lot during World War Two

After the collapse of these projects, Garbo was unsure of what to do next. The war was still in progress, but it seemed clear that Allied victory was inevitable. She summarized her options and her indecision in a letter to Peg:

> Dear,
>
> Thanks for letter. Yes, we are now there in chaos. I have the same thoughts as you. If I would sell the house and go to Sweden. Or get started on a new movie, or go to New York. So there you see that I am in the same predicament. How would I be able to give you an answer on anything when I don't know myself. It is also a . . . that you don't know what to do. If I didn't have the house it would be easier. But it is so langweilig [boring] here that it is pointless to stay. If you've settled for Santa Fe, just go for it. I don't know it well enough. And then you'll see what happens. Perhaps I will go to New York and take a flat there. But as I said I don't know a thing. Probably a shame that you sold the car because it would probably come handy now. I am at least anchored here for a month or two so we should stay in touch. Other than that, no news. Apart from Hörke who says that I am welcome to stay there. It is probably difficult to get housing in Sweden.
>
> Love love [1140]

Later Garbo wrote Peg with her decision to move to New York. While she had been getting offers for roles, she found she no longer felt like making films. She had been spending her time working on her new house in California, which she realized she would probably sell. She enclosed a Swedish-language article on postage to Sweden and travel.

Garbo clearly took months to ruminate over her options and how she felt about the best way to continue her career, if at all. While she planned to move to New York, the possibility of moving back to Sweden was still on her mind. It was only after her first post-war return to Sweden that Garbo would definitively choose New York. Until then, she was undecided:

> Dearest little Peg,
>
> Finally, a little sign of life from a lonely single girl. God, I have worked so hard. My hands are completely wrecked. I have not had the time to do anything but work on this house. I am terribly good when I have to. I don't know what to do with this place. No curtains, nothing but chaos. But it will probably work out in the end. But the sad thing is that I do not want to stay here. Away but

where? I will probably move to New York again. I have not seen a single person here regarding jobs. I have offers to the right and left, but I have not been able to think of anything but to get things in order here, and sadly I do not feel like making movies any more. All of this is really very silly, actually. So, I think I will return to New York, you'll see. It is such a pity not to stay and get some rest at some point. I am incredibly tired mentally. I would like to have a little change of air. But at some point, I will get everything in order. I hope so anyway. I got a letter from Fente, and I will write to him soon. I hope you will have a nice time there. Live well my little friend.

Send my greetings to Fente when you write—and Lillan.

Love—

(In ink: Not so well, it seems)[1141]

Chapter 34 – A Parasocial Life

"I am jealous of regular, decent people who are left in peace and quiet. How stupid it is to have fallen into this life that gives me no right to have another life than to lock myself in.[1142]

— Garbo, in a letter to her sister-in-law

Garbo returning to New York in 1952.

Was Garbo a recluse? The short answer is no. The use of the term has a historical context. In early Hollywood reporting, a "recluse" was someone who didn't attend the almost-public social parties that thrived in Hollywood. Garbo was one of a set of stars who rarely attended, and they were all called reclusive.

Later Garbo was called a recluse in a way that was truer to its use in psychology. This was just a media construct. Garbo wasn't isolative like Howard Hughes, the business mogul who spent four years in a hotel room in Las Vegas without ever leaving. She wasn't even living in an isolated rural location, avoiding the world, like J. D. Salinger. Garbo lived most of her post-war life in Manhattan, attended parties, traveled widely, and had a circle of friends. People saw her out and about all the time.

She would fall among the legion of artists who valued their privacy when not performing. Dave Chappelle retreats to his home in Ohio when he is not performing. Harrison Ford lives a private life when he is not promoting his latest film. Perhaps the closest modern parallel is Jodie Foster, who doesn't give interviews when not promoting a film and who reveals nothing about her private life.

While Garbo never made a film after 1941, she tried to for at least another fifteen years. In a way Garbo accidentally slid into retirement because she refused to compromise on roles. Society had become socially conservative. No one was financing films about women challenging the social order of the day.

Garbo signed on to make *The Girl from Leningrad, Women of the Sea, The Duchess de Langeais,* and *The Miracle.* They just didn't get made. Garbo committed to *Saint Joan* and *Mourning Becomes Electra*. Garbo was clearly discussing other projects. For example, Tennessee Williams would relate that he pitched *The Pink Bedroom* to her. After hearing him out she said to him, "Yes, it's wonderful, but not for me. Give it to Joan Crawford."[1143]

The role would have been a better fit for Crawford. *The Pink Bedroom* is about lust, not love. Garbo had a clear sense of the role she wanted. There is no way to know how many roles she seriously considered, but based on other people's memoirs she listened to pitches into the 1960s.

For a world-famous celebrity, she was able to make her life rather normal. She was wealthy, had a luxurious apartment with door attendants, was friends with the rich and famous, and traveled frequently. She also never hired security, walked the streets on her own, cooked for herself, often ran her own errands, and talked with shopkeepers and neighbors.

She just didn't talk to the press. Yet she did talk at length to Swedish reporter Sven Broman, so even that is not true. For a while she would ruin photographs by raising her hand, and when she stopped that, photographers waited for her to accidentally block their shot, perhaps using a tissue or brushing away her hair. It paid better.

For Garbo, an interesting media phenomenon developed after World War II. Garbo was private and avoided media. She gave no interviews. But she was publicly out and about, at home in New York and on her travels in Europe and elsewhere. She socialized with her friends. Yet the media developed a penchant for presenting her as a recluse.

She had always used portrait photography to present herself to the world. This did not end with her MGM career. Her seven portrait sessions with Cecil Beaton all took place after her final MGM film, and she knew Beaton would publish them. She also sat for notable photographers George Hoyningen-Huene, Horst Horst, and Antony Beauchamp in the fifties, all of whom published the images. She created a curated public image of Garbo even as she was avoiding paparazzi and press interviews.

When Garbo arrived in Hollywood the studios were already creating staged photographs that were represented as portraying the actual life of the subject. Stars would stand in make-believe kitchens for photographs. They posed at the beach. The unifying theme of this work was that it was created, edited, and released by the studio. It was marketing.

After Garbo's Christmas visit to New York in 1931, photojournalism expanded to include celebrities. The final step would be the paparazzi, photographers who created the story instead of just reporting it. Staged photos, intentional provocations to get a reaction to shoot, and imagined narratives to sell the photo were the final evolution.

> The paparazzo Tazio Secchiaroli recalled this about shooting celebrities in the 1950s: We discovered that by creating little incidents we could produce great features that earned us a lot of money. That way we could break the humiliating barrier of earning only three thousand lira from the newspapers for a photograph, and instead earn as much as two hundred thousand lira.[1144]

Regarding Garbo, the paparazzi portrayed her as hiding. Lots of people tried to ruin the paparazzi's work by obscuring their face.[1145] Garbo's raised hand was captioned "reclusive." It was their Garbo story.

This photo would be captioned that Garbo was hiding, not that Schlee was raising his hand to block the shot.

As an example of the primacy of the recluse narrative, there is one paparazzi photo with Garbo just standing and Hauser lifting his hand to block the shot. The caption states that Garbo is hiding from the press.

Garbo was out and about with her friends through this period, but she was not seeking press exposure. Though she was jokingly referred to as "the hermit about town" in New York, the public perception of Garbo was derived from articles like one in The Indianapolis Star in 1960. The headline for the rather public activity of Garbo walking into the El Morocco nightclub with hair stylist Sydney Guilaroff leads with the word "recluse." [1146]

There is no question that writers ignored facts, or her friend's statements, about Garbo to fit their narrative. John Bainbridge intentionally ignored a fact he knew about Garbo's employment at PUB so he could include Petschler's fanciful story about discovering Garbo. He also purposefully misquoted Carey Wilson. When Bainbridge's biography was serialized in Life magazine, Wilson complained:

> Sirs:
>
> By elision LIFE has perverted a quote from me about the days when Garbo, John Gilbert and I were friends.[1147]

Garbo's biggest problems after *Two-Faced Woman* were to find a good script that could get past the censors and a competent producer. The roles that had made her career were now considered risqué in this more conservative era.

The America Garbo helped to create, where the Modern Woman was a fixture, disappeared. It had been gravely wounded by the Depression and vanished completely with the start of World War II.

After the Victorian era, it was assumed that emancipated women would be working side by side with men. When the Depression threw a quarter of all men out of work, it seemed a hollow promise.[1148] The idea that women would "wife it" as one role out of many was replaced by a generation more committed to a family-based life with more traditional boundaries.

But relations did not return to the Victorian era. Men and women were now marital partners. They had dated and selected each other. The separate spheres never returned. While the man was the breadwinner and the woman the homemaker, it was a partnership of often slightly dissatisfied people. For women, while they often worked, perhaps even just part-time, their jobs were secondary to their main role as the housewife if they were well-off.[1149]

After World War II women coming of age thought that being a housewife was more emotionally satisfying than having a career.[1150] Self-supporting women came to be viewed as almost un-American, as they could find freedom within American domestic marriage, with all of the modern conveniences. In part this generation viewed marriage as a bulwark against economic deprivation (for these were the children of the Depression) and nuclear annihilation.[1151] Communism, as represented by the Soviet Union, was conflated with sexual risk of all kinds. Further, moral weakness led to Communism.

This view of women's roles was not uniform. Working-class women had to work even as they raised families. They were clear on the unfairness of their wages for identical or similar jobs men held. Female union membership tripled in the two decades before the mid-fifties.[1152] But working-class and minority women didn't get portrayed in movies or written about in magazines. There was an unresolved contradiction in magazine non-fiction stories about women as they portrayed both professional women and housewives as successful. There was never a return to a simplistic division of male and female spheres and roles.[1153]

There also was a set of anti-feminist authors who wrote that women shouldn't compete with men because of the fundamental differences between the sexes. Their basic message was that domesticity was the road to fulfillment, and they tended to append derogatory tags (narcissistic, unfeminine, domineering, etc.) to professional women.[1154]

Women in the 1930s had admired screen stars as independent women. After the war women wanted role models they could admire as wives. The idea of equality of the sexes while courting had ruled the screen in the thirties, but it had not proposed any model of marriage that contained that equality.[1155]

Despite decades of pursuit by the media and the attention of her fans, Garbo kept going out in public, often by herself. She clearly didn't want the attention, but she refused to isolate herself. The paparazzi and other media othered her, painted her as antisocial, while she was living a rather active social life. She just wasn't working.

The question that arises from this is why they persisted in this storyline when it was demonstrably untrue, and why the public enjoyed it and perpetuated it.

One thread is the trope that someone as artistic as Garbo must be damaged. Conservative columnist Walter Winchell would write of Garbo, "Where there is artistic temperament there is extreme sensitivity. Where there is extreme sensitivity, there is emotional stress."[1156] In an extended newspaper serial on Garbo Roby Heard would write, "There she remains today the enigma fleeing

Garbo laughing with friends.

about the earth, the shadowy 'Harriet Brown' compelled to obey the commands of a strange, deep-rooted complex that makes her cringe."[1157]

Conservative columnists would write about Garbo's absence from the screen as somehow her fault. The rewriting of the Garbo story didn't end there. Garbo's impact on women was devalued, part of the conservative, anti-feminist times. She was in the headlines for being famous, rather than her accomplishments.

From the end of the war through about 1960 Garbo was one of the celebrities who spent part of the summer on the Riviera. She was both photographed with friends and portrayed as "hiding" from the press. Since the market paid more for the hiding/recluse caption, that became the focus of the media over time. Garbo didn't really change.

The Hollywood celebrity industrial complex built a Garbo story on memes about reclusiveness and isolation that did not reflect her lived life. It was lazy and easy. Supposedly liberal editors did not value women's contributions to culture and society. They mostly didn't believe in feminism or emancipation anyway.

Garbo on the Rivera

Garbo refused to react to it publicly. Realistically, what would she achieve with a public response? She would have been fighting the tide.

Charles Ponce de Leon would write that public figures discovered the celebrity press was not particularly concerned with accuracy, and attempts to correct these misrepresentations took an inordinate amount of effort, and opened the subject up to additional questions. [Katharine] Hepburn would say it was futile to give a reasonable explanation for anything she did; the mills grinding out the Hollywood chatter were operating on a different principle.[1158]

The press came to care so little about Garbo, the person, and to lose all sense of her accomplishments, that after her death Simon & Schuster would publish a book about Garbo by an author whose prior two books were (1) a biography of Polish politician/musician Ignacy Paderewski disparaged as untrue by all who knew Paderewski and (2) a book about Pope John Paul II that the publisher withdrew from distribution because it was "fraudulent."[1159]

Antoni Gronowicz's Garbo book was actually written before the book on the pope. The original publisher returned it to the author after it failed fact checks. Somehow Gronowicz then sold it to Simon & Schuster in 1977. The problem was if it published the book while Garbo was alive, it would be sued for libel and lose. Garbo had sworn an affidavit that she didn't know Gronowicz. Since a dead person can't be libeled, legally speaking, Simon & Schuster simply waited until after her death to publish it.

The question that arises is would a reputable publisher ever publish a similar fraud about a famous man? Are women just fair game? Could you imagine a reputable publisher releasing a fraudulent book about Henry Fonda (who died in 1982)?

Shamelessly *The New York Times*, whose integrity failures would soon be revealed by several fraudulent reporting scandals, happily vouched for the book. I like to think the price was a year of college tuition for the reviewer, but it was probably just a lunch. The key question remains, why would *The New York Times* positively review a book that was an obvious fraud? Were its supposed "journalistic standards" waived for eighty-five-year-old women? And since that seems to have been the case, why?

Barry Paris would dedicate a nine-page appendix to debunking the Gronowicz book.

It is fair to ask what Garbo did for the last forty years of her life. It developed a rhythm. She stayed active for as long as she could.

After her family moved to the United States, Garbo spent about four to six weeks with them every year. When they were in Bronxville, she came out from New York for dinner and to see Peg, or met her in the city to shop. She visited them in Santa Fe and Palm Desert as well. When her niece Gray settled in New Jersey, she went out there, or Gray came into the city, either alone or with a child or two. From 1970 on, Garbo took a two-week vacation with Gray every winter.

The annual four to six weeks Garbo spent with her family over more than forty years were a way of grounding herself. Her family didn't care that she was famous and had no interest in celebrity. She usually visited by herself. The only person known to have traveled with her to Santa Fe was Schlee.[1160]

Some of her friendships from her Hollywood days endured. These friends didn't announce their friendship. They wrote about her obliquely, sparingly. Or the information came out in a roundabout way. Other people, Charlie Chaplin for example, just didn't write about her in their autobiographies.

She remained connected to her old Hollywood friends, though she saw them less frequently. When Colleen Moore was seeking to rent out her longtime home, Garbo came to look at it. When they went into the bathroom that Harold Grieve had designed for her in the 1920s, she said, "Ah Colleen, those were the good old days."[1161]

In the 1950s Irene Mayer Selznick and her adult sons Jeff and Danny were invited to a Christmas Day get-together with Garbo at Sam Spiegel's apartment in New York. She greeted the sons with the line "Did you know I knew your mother before you did?" (A line the author heard from Garbo on more than one occasion.) She then went on to regale Jeff and Danny with tales of meeting their grandfather in Berlin and additional stories from her Hollywood days with both their father and grandfather.[1162]

Garbo would visit California regularly. She tended to avoid hotels and stayed with friends. Usually Brian and Eleanor Aherne, Harry Crocker, Minna Wallace, or Gayelord Hauser. She also would rent houses in the Palm Springs area or stay at the La Quinta resort.

Garbo moved to New York, first living at Hampshire House, and then buying an apartment at 450 East 52nd Street in 1954. From this New York base she traveled, either with friends or to visit friends. After the war she could be found in California, Santa Fe, Wisconsin, Europe, and vacation spots New Yorkers frequented. In Europe she spent time on the Riviera and on yachts in the Mediterranean, with frequent stops in Paris and London. After reconnecting with Viertel in 1960, she would spend every fall in Klosters. After Schlee died in 1964 Garbo spent less time on the Riviera, and in the 1970s she began an annual winter holiday to the Caribbean with her niece Gray. While she still visited California, she spent most of her time in Palm Springs and the smaller surrounding towns.

One of Garbo's great friendships was with the singer Jessica Dragonette. Dragonette retired from starring on radio as a singer when she married Nicholas Turner at age forty-seven. For the thirty-three years until Dragonette's death in 1980, if she and Garbo were both in New York, they got together three times a week for breakfast.[1163]

Through the Gouldings Garbo met Cecil Beaton in 1932. The British photographer was just one year older than Garbo. He and Garbo would become close friends, and he would take a number of photographic portraits of her at different times.

She was part of social circles revolving around actors Montgomery Clift, Jean and Dusty Negulesco, David and Hjördis Niven, and producer Sam Spiegel and his wife Betty. These friends would mostly remain silent about Garbo, though one story that was told relates a 1955 dinner Clift hosted with Garbo and Schlee as guests, along with Libby Holman, Kevin McCarthy and his wife Augusta, Arthur Miller, and Thornton Wilder. At that dinner Garbo talked to them extensively about her love of Hammacher Schlemmer, whose eclectic store in New York closed in 2023.[1164]

The silence of her friends sometimes leads to interesting tidbits that seem totally out of context. In the biography of Sam Spiegel there is a story told by director George Stevens about going to Spiegel's apartment to discuss a possible project. His account, which has Stevens and his son arriving to have drinks with Spiegel and Garbo, completely misses the fact that her presence at such a meeting in 1970 was remarkable.[1165]

Not all of Garbo's friends in New York were in the film industry. She was close to cartoonist Charles Addams after meeting him in 1960 and was friends with the author John Gunther, antique dealer Joseph Lombardo, lawyer Eustace Seligman, and their spouses. The point being, these friendships alone would hardly be the mark of a recluse, and the list is much longer.

In 1960 she first visited Klosters, a small ski town in Switzerland. Salka Viertel had made this her home. Visits here replaced the Riviera. Garbo arrived at the start of the fall off-season and stayed until the end of November or beginning of December most subsequent years. Garbo joined the circle of friends Viertel had there. Peter, Salka Viertel's son, and his wife Deborah Kerr were good friends. Irwin Shaw, Robert Parrish, and Gore Vidal were part of this group.

While some of the Klosters circle mentioned that they socialized with Garbo there, for the most part none of them provided any details beyond the most basic. She took nearly daily hikes in the mountains around the town and occasionally visited friends who had their own homes in nearby Swiss towns.

Garbo with friends in Klosters

The even longer list is of people who may have met her, but embellish the depth of their relationship. Often these writers presume the accuracy of prior media commentary about her. Therefore, a writer recalling meeting her in the mid-fifties might state that "she said she would never act again" because they were oblivious to The Miracle project. They were leveraging the Garbo mystique for themselves.

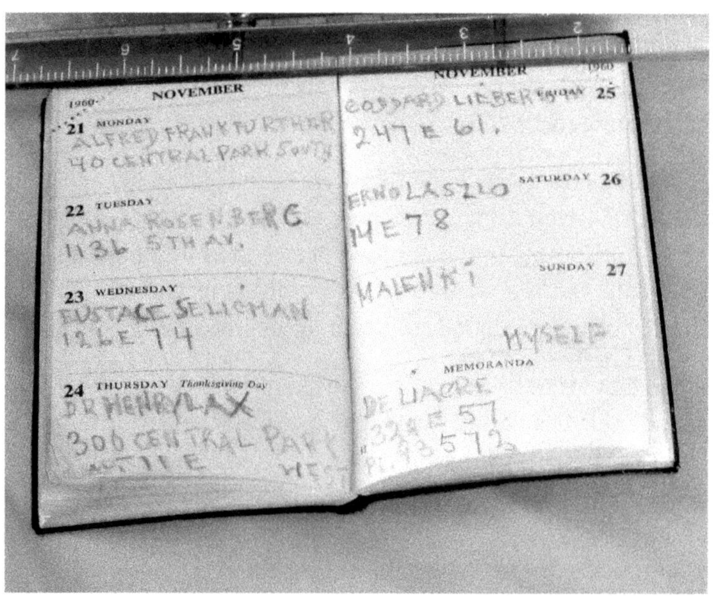

1960 NOVEMBER

21 MONDAY
ALFRED FRANKFURTHER
40 CENTRAL PARK SOUTH

22 TUESDAY
ANNA ROSENBERG
1136 5TH AV.

23 WEDNESDAY
EUSTACE SELIGMAN
126 E 74

24 THURSDAY Thanksgiving Day
DR HENRY LAX
300 CENTRAL PARK

NOVEMBER 1960

FRIDAY 25
GODDARD LIEBERSON
247 E 61.

SATURDAY 26
ERNO LASZLO
14 E 78

SUNDAY 27
MALENKI
MYSELF

MEMORANDA

Pages from Garbo's 1960 datebook.

Rather than go through all the events in Garbo's private life for the years from the end of her career to her death, it is more useful to just look at a sample year, 1960.

In her datebook for 1960, Garbo's entries are written in a mix of English and Swedish. Her datebooks are an imperfect guide for several reasons. It is often hard to understand what an entry really means. For example, she writes "Hotel Urban Zurich" on December 31. Has she unexpectedly gone to Switzerland, even though she had appointments in New York the previous day? Is it to call someone there on that day? Is it a reminder to book a reservation? The interpretation of some entries becomes subjective. While Garbo enters some of her travel, she doesn't enter every trip. She returns from Vermont, but there is no entry for her departure. The first half of the year has significantly fewer entries, seemingly capturing less of her life.

Garbo's datebook begins with an entry before the 1st of January, with her niece's new address in New Jersey. She has a number of medical appointments in January and a lunch with Gray Reisfield (she had married by this point). In February a few more medical appointments, and a note that she has to pay one hundred dollars to pick up a ceiling light. She notes she hurt her hand on February 29.

The datebook is rather empty until a note that she was admitted to Flower Hospital, then located in New York City, on May 23 and released on May 26. She noted in June when it was thirty days after the operation, so the assumption is that she was admitted for surgery of some type. She noted that on June 1 George Schlee (nicknamed "Malinki") departed for Europe.

Through the rest of the first half of the year are some appointments that can be hard to place specifically. Scattered through are notes like "Greenburg 4," "Call Japan 11," and "121 E 60 TE. 85917." They might be social or medical. There are notes like "Put Up Blinds."

There is a note on July 18: "Leave Vermont." We don't know how long she was there or with whom, though she was probably visiting the Gunthers' summer home.

In August Garbo flew to Nice and in the following months there are sketchy notes as to her whereabouts. She leaves Cap-d'Ail for Paris on September 20 and on September 30 Garbo arrives in Klosters, where she stays for all of October. This was her first visit to Klosters. On November 1 she flew to London for nine days. In London she had visited Sydney Guilaroff and then took the train out to Reddish in Wiltshire, England, to visit Cecil Beaton. They went to Salisbury Cathedral, a favorite building of hers, and Beaton took some photographs of Garbo there and at his home.

She flew to Paris on the 10th. After two days in Paris, she returned home to New York. Upon returning to New York she had an active calendar with quite a number of social events through the end of the year.

While there are large blank spots in the 1960 datebook, there are a couple of things that are likely but are not recorded.

Garbo at her brother's vacation home in Palm Desert.

Garbo visited her brother and sister-in-law regularly. Their longtime residence was in Santa Fe, New Mexico. In 1960 they purchased a small winter home in Palm Desert, California. This home was in the Cahuilla Hills above the desert floor, at the time a remote location. In all likelihood she would have visited with them in one of these locations.

Garbo with Gayelord Hauser

At some point in the year Garbo usually visited Gayelord Hauser, either at his home in Los Angeles or at his lake house in Wisconsin. A local gossip columnist had Garbo checking into a Los Angeles hotel in January.[1166]

Based on this report and her hospital stay in New York in May, her likely travels were to fly out to Los Angeles in January and after some time, go out to visit Sven and Peg. This letter from either 1960 or 1961 is typical:

> My Dear Boys,
>
> I hope the weather is weather for you, but it probably too early for that. I have pulled a muscle in my back. Or whatever it is that has happened. But I have been in terrible pain. I am getting better now. Just as I got the card from Reud promising nice things. But that card might have been sent too early, and now all the good things might happen now. So here I am waiting. I still have a bit of a cold, so I wonder if it is too cold in the desert for me. Didn't Peg tell me something about sulpha baths somewhere in Palm Springs? Have you tried it?
>
> Now Peggy must not bombard me with questions, because then I will just get nervous. But I will try to come when my back has healed. I can stay over at Ahernes I hope, and from there get someone to drive me to Palm Springs and we can meet up there. As always I say, I hope. Could Peggy please tell me what the weather is like and how cold it is. Do you have warm sleepwear and everything else needed?
>
> My dear boys, here is hoping we will see each other soon.
>
> Good morning[1167]

Her West Coast trip probably was four to eight weeks, perhaps longer if her back injury took more time to heal.

Given her May surgery that year, she may not have visited all of her usual places. But for many years this was Garbo's pattern. She spent Christmas in either California or New York. In the winter or spring she traveled to California, visiting Hollywood and Palm Desert or La Quinta. Sven and Peg spent winters in Palm Desert, so they were close by. Occasionally she visited San Francisco.

Depending on whom she had already seen on this trip, Garbo visited Hauser in Wisconsin or Sven and Peg in Santa Fe in the early summer. She took a car out to visit Gray in New Jersey as she was just an hour away. The kids were at school through June, so they could talk among themselves uninterrupted before a family dinner.

In early summer she might take small trips in the Northeast. In 1960 she went to Vermont. She went to Cape Cod, Martha's Vineyard, Long Island, and Bermuda at different times.

Then in late summer she went to Europe. In the 1940s and 1950s she went primarily to Italy. After Schlee bought Cap-d'Ail, just west of Monaco on the French Riviera, she shifted her travels to France rather than Italy. During this time she might sail on a yacht through the Mediterranean for some of her trip. Schlee might rent one or friends might invite her aboard. She sailed with both Sam Spiegel and Ari Onassis. While the Riviera was the main point of the trip, Garbo stopped in Paris or London frequently. After her two post-war trips to Sweden, she did not return there very often.

Chapter 35 – *The Duchess de Langeais*

"I have to go to N. York in a hurry. My new boss is there, and they have cooked something up that I have to help them with.[1168]

— Garbo, in a letter to her sister-in-law

Screen capture from Garbo's 1949 screen test for *The Duchess de Langeais*

Finally, Garbo found a project she wanted to make. Its failure would have two main causes. The PCA would not approve a script, which threw the project into disarray. The other issue was that the producer, Walter Wanger, was working on a shoestring. He didn't have the resources or credibility of a Studio Era producer working for a major studio.

In late 1947 or early 1948 George Cukor approached Salka Viertel about making a film of the life of George Sand. Viertel and Cukor then met with Garbo, and she liked the idea. After this meeting Viertel spent six months developing a script. They shopped the project in Hollywood and to independent British producers.[1169]

In the context of the times and the social conservatives' drive for conformity, choosing George Sand was provocative. The House Un-American Activities Committee had just begun investigating Communists and homosexuals in Hollywood in 1947. It was also the beginning of the Lavender Scare, which resulted in thousands of federal employees being fired for their sexual orientation. Garbo's response was to sign on to a project about a cross-dressing bisexual who wrote subversive and wildly successful novels.

In 1948 Walter Wanger, who had produced *Queen Christina*, bumped into Salka Viertel in Los Angeles. Wanger told Viertel that he was eager to produce a Garbo vehicle. In early 1948 they discussed and discarded several options. Wanger brought in Eugene Frenke, a minor producer married to Anna Sten, to help with financing.[1170] By late July they were focused on the Viertel script about the life of George Sand that had been discussed with Cukor. Garbo wrote to Peg:

> We are trying to find a fitting "thing" for me (work) but no luck so far. I probably should have let everything go and held some kind of peaceful existence for all future. This whole industry is so dirty, it is difficult to comprehend for those who are not in it. I have nightmares at times when thinking about having to join the circus again. I am probably not made the right way to get mixed up with all this any more. But the gauntlet is thrown, is that the saying?[1171]

Viertel recalled, "Everything began to move rapidly. Wanger called again, Frenke called five times a day and I spent hours on the phone. Then we dined in his house, Greta, Wanger and I and during a most fantastic dinner everything was set. [Cukor was] signed, the story bought, Greta happy, etc. etc."[1172]

Garbo signed the letter of intent for *George Sand* on August 4, 1948. Her deal was for $150,000 ($2 million) and 15 percent of the producer's share of profits.[1173] The project was announced to the press with filming to begin in May 1949. On August 5 she wrote to Peg, "I'm about to get a job again."[1174]

In September 1948 Eugene Frenke and George Schlee, representing Garbo, traveled together to Europe with a laundry list of tasks. They were looking for investors and locations. As Wanger thought that it might be possible to find a better vehicle than George Sand, they were also looking for alternate stories and writers. Cukor proposed switching to Sapho, and this was briefly considered.[1175] Meanwhile, Schlee and Frenke successfully got everything lined up for *George Sand.*

At this point Wanger had a script, a star, a director, and financing for *George Sand.* If he had just proceeded, he would have produced Garbo's return to the screen. But he thought the story was too small, and in the fall of 1948, he finally found a replacement.

Wanger screened the French film *La Duchesse de Langeais* (1942), based on the nineteenth-century novel by Honoré de Balzac. He proposed that the project be switched from *George Sand* to *The Duchess de Langeais*, and Garbo, who had already seen the French film, agreed.

Garbo asked Cukor if he would direct *The Duchess de Langeais*, but he found the story old-fashioned, and Cukor withdrew from the project.[1176] This changed the start of production from May 1949 to September 1949. Wanger needed a script, and in May 1949 he hired Sally Benson to write it. Then he departed for Europe to pin down everything else: director, funding, and production locations. Garbo did her screen tests.

After deciding on production in Italy, Wanger returned to the first disaster. Sally Benson had been fronted the money for the script, and Wanger discovered she had been on a two-month drinking bender. There was only the vaguest sketch of a script for the $15,000 ($204,000) advance.[1177]

With George Cukor withdrawn from the project, Schlee asked Josh Logan, who he knew socially, to meet together with Garbo to discuss directing. They met in the French town of Vézelay on July 26, 1949.[1178] Logan relates that they discussed the project for hours. Garbo liked the work he had done directing the play *South Pacific* (1949).[1179]

Humorously, given the problems with the Benson script, Wanger telegrammed Logan that the first version of the script was better than he had expected.[1180] Since Logan was already involved in a Helen Hayes project,[1181] while he was interested, he needed time to finish up his existing commitments.[1182] Production was still scheduled for September. The day after his meeting with Garbo, Logan sent Wanger a telegram turning down the project.[1183] Casting around for another option, Wanger turned to Max Ophüls.

Looking now at the documentation that survives, it is amazing how little regarding *The Duchess de Langeais* was settled. The revised production start date slid to October 10, but with two months to go Wanger had just settled on a director. Ophüls's first task was to write the script, so that wasn't settled either.

Financing for the project was in disarray. While the framework seemed clear, the details eluded the participants. New players were being brought to the table as late as August 19, when suddenly Pathé was mooted as a financing partner.[1184] Just three days later the Italian partners wanted to veto James Mason as the co-star.[1185] Proposals to change the financing appeared as late as September 7, a month before the scheduled start of production.

All this time Wanger had been accruing costs. He had paid Viertel $6,475 ($88,000) for the George Sand script and Sally Benson $15,000 ($204,000) for her basically useless script. Then an additional $4,000 ($54,000) to other writers for script work.[1186] Garbo and Ophüls were in Italy, ready to work, which required money. The endless meetings and telegrams were all costs.

Wanger announced that Italian publisher Angelo Rizzoli would finance the film on August 30, 1949. Garbo and Schlee agreed to meet with Rizzoli and Wanger to help cinch a deal.

One does not know what script Wanger submitted to the PCA, or when. There is only a single letter in the Wanger files, and uncompleted projects are not in the PCA files at the Herrick Library. The PCA sent Wanger a devastating letter referencing a September 9 telegram Joseph Breen had already sent to Wanger denying PCA approval for the script for *The Duchess de Langeais*.

Breen's letter to Wanger made production impossible. He saw absolutely no way that the PCA could approve the script. He wrote, "In our considered judgement this story is completely, and thoroughly, unacceptable under the provisions of the Production Code."[1187] That left little room for misinterpretation. Breen went on to explain that not only is the story one of "acceptable adultery," but there are no compensating moral values and no voice for morality. Breen pointed out that in the original novel, the duchess does not commit adultery, giving him no reason to accept it in the script.[1188] Breen went on to attach a full eight pages of specific script objections.

Wanger once again didn't have a script. It seems that Wanger did not disclose this information to Garbo or Rizzoli. Within days of receiving Breen's telegram Wanger, Garbo, Frenke, and Schlee met with Angelo Rizzoli, ostensibly to finalize the deal. The most likely event is that Wanger just played hardball on financing during the meeting to allow the deal to die while ducking the blame.

If Wanger was honest with Rizzoli, the press reports would have been about the script issues derailing the deal. Contemporaneous reporting focuses on the supposed intransigence of Garbo and Schlee. News reports went into detail regarding failed financing negotiations, supposedly because of Garbo's attitude.[1189] Significant effort was made by Wanger to blame Schlee in the press for the failure to obtain a deal. This despite the fact that he had been instrumental in moving the project forward, encouraging Garbo to proceed and trying to line up Josh Logan.[1190]

Garbo in Rome to discuss financing *The Duchess de Langeais.*

On September 22 Garbo agreed to shift the project into 1950 in exchange for two-and-a-half weeks' salary.[1191] The key provision in the extension was that Wanger had to demonstrate financial commitments were in place for the project by January 1, 1950. If she knew that the issue was Wanger's mismanagement of the script development, rather than the financing, would she have signed the extension?

Another revealing document is a letter from Eugene Frenke to Walter Wanger dated October 5, 1949. At this point they have identified two options to finance the project, one based on RKO and one based on Columbia. He wants Wanger to tell him which one to pursue first:

> I am stressing the O'Connell deal because he is willing to lay out any money necessary for the development and completion of the script which, after all, has been the real source of all our troubles. This deal allows us to prove our ability to finance before completion of the script, whereas any other source of financing, I am afraid, will be contingent upon an acceptable screenplay. As you know, the time between now and January 1st, (our date of proving financial stability) is growing short.[1192]

Wanger and Frenke's relationship seems to have deteriorated at this point. Wanger sent a telegram to Garbo's agent at MCA, Roy Meyers, claiming that Schlee was causing problems, Garbo was not accommodating enough on approving other cast, and that Schlee was manipulating Frenke.[1193] In November Frenke sent a letter to Wanger asking why he was not responding to his calls, and Wanger responded with a letter blaming Frenke for all the problems.[1194]

Wanger finally thought he had a deal in December with financing from Romulus Films and Telinvest Inc. But it was to be finalized after the January 1 date specified in the contract. Garbo withdrew at that point. She cited instances where Wanger had not complied with the terms of the contract.[1195]

Garbo walking with Cecil Beaton in London in 1951.

It is clear that the deal was in no way secure even later in January. On January 23 Y. F. Freeman wrote to Wanger on behalf of Paramount that "at the time I talked to New York I had no intimation of the type of security which would be offered." And whatever element of the deal Paramount was going to be a part of was off.[1196]

On January 25, 1950, Eugene Frenke sent Wanger a letter with the transcript of a radio broadcast by entertainment reporter Sheilah Graham. This was clearly a placed item to put the fault for the failure of *The Duchess de Langeais* project on someone else. It contained a report of Wanger and Frenke's conditions for proceeding with the film that Garbo had already abandoned:

> And one of the conditions of the movie with Garbo this year in Paris is that she leaves her dress maker boy friend, George Schlee behind in America. The last time George saw Paris he interfered so much, the backers of the picture backed out. But Mr. Wanger is trying so hard to make Greta happy. He's trying to land Sir Laurence Olivier to play her lover.[1197]

How Frenke and Wanger thought this public relations placement helped their case with Garbo is unfathomable. Not only was Schlee her romantic partner, he was a trusted business advisor who had been involved in theater production and financing since the 1920s.

Garbo relaxing at Cecil Beaton's home. Photo by Cecil Beaton.

Chapter 36 – *The Miracle*

"It will be a miracle if she accepts!"[1198]

— Harry Saltzman, in a letter to Norman Bel Geddes

Garbo leaving an airplane in 1957.

In July 1954 Norman Bel Geddes met with Harry (Herschel) Saltzman and proposed making a film version of The Miracle, based on the Karl Vollmoeller play written in 1911.

Norman Bel Geddes had worked primarily as a theater set designer. One of his early successes was developing *The Miracle's* set design in 1924 for Max Reinhardt at the Century Playhouse in New York. There had been silent film versions of *The Miracle*, but it had not been remade as a sound film. Now, closer to the end of his career, Bel Geddes believed that he could acquire the rights.

Harry Saltzman had the far more colorful background. A Canadian, he found himself in Europe working as a talent agent for music halls and circus performers in 1938. His agency had two million marks ($13.3 million) in German banks that it couldn't get out of the country. Harry volunteered to travel to Berlin to see if he could find a solution to this problem. Instead of repatriating his agency's money back to Paris, Harry set about using the company's money to obtain exit visas, tickets, and identity cards for the Jewish artists trapped in Germany. Saltzman left only when the funds were almost depleted and the authorities were closing in on him.[1199]

Garbo standing on the dock in Nice in 1953.

When war broke out, Saltzman eventually ended up with the US Office of Strategic Services (OSS), the precursor to the CIA. He was naturalized as an American in March 1939, the standard waiting period being waived. In 1945 he traveled to Paris for an OSS front company to "hasten the resumption of normal trade relations between France and the United States."[1200]

In 1954 Saltzman began working with screenwriter Ben Hecht on film projects. Saltzman and Hecht were represented by agent Ray Stark, who worked for Charles Feldman at Famous Artists, who was also now Garbo's agent.

Norman Bel Geddes first proposed *The Miracle* to Garbo in November 1955. Garbo agreed to a letter of engagement on December 21, 1955. Her compensation was to be $250,000 ($3.4 million) and 20 percent of the producer's profits. The script was to be written by Christopher Fry, and Laurence Olivier was proposed as the director and co-star.[1201]

Fry had made his mark as the leading British dramatist for the decade after the war, known for his wit and poetic verse. In the mid-fifties he turned to writing scripts for films, most notably *Ben-Hur* (1959). Fry was an interesting choice. The alternative they considered was Samuel Beckett. Clearly the goal was to deliver intelligent dialogue.

Feldman seems to have attempted to cut Saltzman, who as the executive producer was responsible for raising the funding, out of the deal so he could take over responsibility for the financing himself. Bel Geddes and Saltzman realized this and were prepared to contain Feldman by formalizing their relationship as executive producer and producer.[1202]

Over the New Year weekend in 1956 Charles Feldman, as Garbo's agent, met with George Schlee and Norman Bel Geddes about *The Miracle*. Feldman recommended Garbo undertake the role.

On January 17, 1956, Charles Feldman wrote George Schlee that he had confidentially spoken with Bill Paley, the president of CBS, about making *The Miracle* as a television special for the network. The idea was to create a holiday event that could be rebroadcast every Easter. Feldman and Paley had discussed a budget of about $1.5 million ($18.1 million). After his discussions with Paley, Feldman learned from Saltzman that his conception of the project had a budget of $4.5 million ($54.4 million) and would be for theatrical release. Feldman was able to confirm to Schlee that the production company Cinerama was interested in a theatrical project. However, he cautioned that Cinerama would take longer to finalize a deal than Paley.[1203]

Eventually CBS bowed out, but then NBC developed an interest. At this point in time no television production had ever cost more than $500,000 ($6.0 million). NBC was willing to invest up to $2.5 million ($30.0 million) to create a unique event.[1204]

On January 26 Bel Geddes sent a telegram to Saltzman directing him to engage Olivier as an actor only, not as director.[1205] Until this point no one had actually spoken to Olivier about the project, and they discovered that he was unsure about working with Garbo because of his *Queen Christina* experience.

On February 8, 1956, Saltzman sent a letter to Ray Stark that was a summary of developments to date. Bel Geddes, Saltzman, and the writer Christopher Fry had worked out a revised second act that they thought resolved censorship issues. Saltzman wrote that he and Schlee thought it was now time to finalize Garbo's contract, and she had agreed to a basic deal. However, they wanted the contract to be written by Feldman, as he was her agent.[1206]

There was much jostling between Bel Geddes and Saltzman on one side and Feldman and Stark on the other about which interpretations of meetings were discussed, but by the end of February Feldman had told Bel Geddes that he would have Garbo sign a commitment that they could take to NBC.[1207]

Then suddenly the Bel Geddes/Saltzman partnership blew up. On March 9, 1956, they signed an agreement dissolving the partnership and Saltzman agreed to leave the deal in exchange for $4,000 ($48,000).[1208] The parting was amicable, as they spoke in mid-March to manage the fallout when Feldman learned of it. One assumes that the issue was whether to pursue either a television or a theatrical release.[1209]

In mid-March Bel Geddes interested John Huston in directing the project for Warner Brothers, which wanted to finance it.[1210] This took place while he was still developing the NBC deal. NBC wrote Bel Geddes on May 25, 1956, that it had decided to withdraw from the project.[1211]

Garbo at Orly airport in Paris in 1955.

At this point the project was now solely conceived of as a blockbuster for theatrical release. Bel Geddes was working with Cinerama, theatrical producer Blevins Davis, and other studios to piece together financing. *The Miracle* was intended to be the first film using Cinerama's new CinemaScope 55 high-definition technology. But Bel Geddes didn't have Saltzman's touch for finalizing a deal, and negotiations dragged on with multiple potential partners.

The script was rewritten to reflect this new direction. Fry had written a spare internal script, but Bel Geddes hired Michael Dyne to rewrite it so as to take advantage of the high-definition CinemaScope 55 technology. Bel Geddes submitted a working script draft to Garbo, and she and Schlee did not like it. Schlee told Bel Geddes,

> I think instead of a simple and touching, subdued story of inner feelings of humanity and the battle against the worst, it's a terrific production with cavalry, battles, checker games. . . . I'm talking from your point of view and My God . . . it's a hot potato. . . . This is a terrific involved story with a lot of action and people, extras, battle scenes—it's Cecil DeMille all over, but how the hell one can do it so that it wouldn't be schmaltzy.[1212]

Bel Geddes had taken the project in a more standard Hollywood direction without understanding why it appealed to Garbo as a more thoughtful film project.

It is interesting to wonder whether if Harry Saltzman had remained involved, he could've salvaged the project. In 1958 Saltzman co-founded Woodfall Film Productions, the most important British film producer of the 1960s, with Tony Richardson and John Osborne. After obtaining the rights to *Look Back in Anger* (1956), Saltzman was able to persuade Richard Burton to take the main role at $100,000 ($1.1 million), half his usual rate. Saltzman then successfully took the project to Warners.[1213] This was the beginning of a string of critical and financial successes for Woodfall.

Saltzman had a financial creativity and interpersonal smoothness that Bel Geddes was not blessed with. Karel Reisz described him as a "charming, exuberant rascal."[1214] Saltzman would go on to partner with Albert Broccoli on the James Bond franchise.[1215]

The content of *The Miracle* was always going to concern the censors. While the 1924 Reinhardt play had been accepted, in fact praised, by Catholic clergy, the times had changed, and both the Catholic Church and industry censors were more rigid in their approach to how Catholic belief was portrayed.

The story basics were that Sister Beatrice, a nun, leaves her thirteenth-century convent for the love of a knight. As she leaves, the statue of the Virgin Mary takes her place as a live being. There is a storyline about the Virgin Mary and the convent and a storyline about Sister Beatrice and her difficult life for the twenty-five years she is gone from the convent. She sins frequently. Eventually Beatrice returns to the convent and the Virgin Mary reassumes her statue form. The miracle is divine forgiveness for her sins. Obviously, avoiding religious controversy required a deft touch.

Bel Geddes asked Monsignor Devlin to review the script in March 1957 and to render an opinion as to its appropriateness. Devlin had three major demands. He wanted Beatrice to be a novice, not a nun. In Catholicism a novice is free to return to normal life, while once she becomes a nun, she is pledged to God. Devlin's second demand was that Beatrice should not leave the convent willingly. She should be abducted. Finally, Devlin required that Beatrice not sin while absent from the convent. Her return, repentance, and forgiveness of sin are the whole point of the story. But Devlin wanted to gut this to preserve the idea of Catholic clergy perfection.[1216]

This was where the censorship regime had gone, to a point where the Catholic Church could dictate that no Catholic nun could sin and repent, because Catholic clergy were too perfect for that.

There was no one involved in the project with the stature of Thalberg, whom Breen had trusted to follow a guideline once they had agreed to it. Bel Geddes was unable to convince Devlin or other Catholics that he could be trusted to be nuanced and sensitive. There was also no one at the PCA who understood how to read a nuanced story.

Garbo and Schlee walking together in 1958.

Somewhere at the end of 1957 or beginning of 1958 the Bel Geddes version of *The Miracle* died. Instead, Warner Brothers made a version of its own that was released in late 1959. It was a minor film relocated in time to the Napoleonic era. Other than the miracle of the statue replacing Beatrice (now Teresa in this version) the plot is radically transformed from either original story.

The Miracle is the last project for which a Garbo agreement has been found.

The problem for Garbo was always regarding the role. She wanted to play women who were interesting, who behaved in a noble way, at least from her more feminist point of view. The Legion of Decency had not seen the nobility in a film like *Camille* that Garbo saw. Or she might have played women who had a modern sensibility regarding their role in life, as in *Ninotchka*. Hollywood in the 1950s just wasn't making many films with interesting female roles. Garbo was no longer a fit for roles that required a female lead two decades younger than she was. It is hard to identify many roles from the end of World War II through at least the mid-1960s that featured a mature woman confronting her sexuality and romantic choices as the core of the plot.

Chapter 37 – Fade to Black

"Lillan is of course willing to go. I took for granted she couldn't, but no sir she is raring to go. So we will see what happens with everything plus me. You have probably called Lillan today so she perhaps has some news from you. This is only to let you know I am thinking of you. Love"[1217]

— Garbo, in a letter to her sister-in-law

Garbo walking in New York in 1981.

Garbo's niece went east for college in the fall of 1950. Garbo's whole family had become American citizens, while Garbo herself became an American citizen in 1951. Gray graduated from Bryn Mawr in 1954 and then began at Yale Law School that fall, where she met her future husband Donald Reisfield. He was at Grace-New Haven Hospital for a medical internship.

While Gray was at Yale, Garbo invited her to visit in New York. She made a point of shifting their relationship to a more adult footing, writing for a visit in March 1955:

> You can come on Saturday the 5th at six or Sunday the 6th at five for cocktails. What would you like to drink? I hope that I will be all right. One never knows in advance what the heavens is planning for us, but I can always send a telegram if something unexpected is happening.
>
> Let me know whenever you're coming, and remember to let me know what you would like to drink so that I have that prepared. It was really well done that you passed the exams. Good boy! Welcome![1218]

Gray transferred to Columbia Law School for the final two years because Don undertook his residency at Columbia Medical Center in New York. She graduated in 1957.

After a year in Europe for a fellowship, the Reisfields settled in New Jersey. This proximity allowed Garbo and my mother to remain involved in each other's lives. Garbo told Sven Broman that "my niece is the person in my immediate circle I rely upon the most."[1219]

Somewhere between the collapse of *The Miracle* and the death of George Schlee in 1964, Garbo lost her interest in making films. At the time she was somewhere between fifty and sixty years old.

After Garbo died I was touched that she had several photographs of me in a drawer. They spanned from when I was a baby until one from college. I didn't know that she kept them. I was born in 1958, and Garbo was already fifty-two. She had suggestions for my name, which thankfully were not taken up. If I had been Patrick, I am not sure I would have enjoyed the Ricepaddy nickname in middle school. My mother told me she favored Patrick:

> Names for Lillan's baby:

Philip, Peter, Patrick, Paul[1220]

I remember her visits, the earliest ones not as distinctly. I do remember walks around the neighborhood. First with my mother and Garbo, and then just with her. I took her to nearby Farrington Lake and showed her the shoreline path that wound around the entire lake. We walked to my school, and I showed her how I could climb the monkey bars. We were not peers, and having Kata in my life was akin to an extra grandparent.

I remember a time that my grandparents visited. Sven and Garbo were constantly making us laugh. My parents were putting aluminum siding on the house, and my grandfather built a bonfire with the shingles that you could see from a block away. It cracked the brick fireplace my father had built in the backyard, and I don't think he was happy about it. But it was an awesome fire.

I am not the only one who remembers Garbo's visits to my parents' house. My next-door neighbor from that time recounted this to me:

> One spring day, I remember your mother had a guest at the pool, and your mom invited me to meet her guest and go swimming. When I arrived at the pool, I was greeted by an older woman in a black and white floral dress with a big floppy hat and sunglasses. Your mom introduced her guest as Aunt Kata. I said hello and received a smile. I think that your mom had explained that I was the older boy next door who had taken an interest in her children.
>
> I thought nothing of this. Aunt Kata was another of your relatives. I went home after the swim and told my mom that I had met Mrs. Reisfield's aunt. My mother said nothing about who Aunt Kata might be as your mom had confided in her about who Aunt Kata was and asked that my mom keep the confidence. I did not know that I had met Greta Garbo until almost 30 years later.[1221]

At her apartment she had a collection of small trolls. Several people who visited her apartment found them and wondered why they were under the furniture. As young children my siblings and I played with them. I think that they kept us out of trouble while the adults talked. I have kept one.

When I started my career I had a difficult situation with my first employer. I spent most of a morning listening to Garbo tell me the story of her contract walkout from 1926–27. Her point was to know your value and get it. I changed employers.

The last big party she attended with all the family was a Thanksgiving in the mid-eighties. My aunt and uncle hosted and my cousins, siblings, and I traveled to their Fort Lee, New Jersey, condo from the various places life had scattered us. My wife and I came from California. Garbo was the life of the party.

She was ill and in failing health when my son was born, but Garbo wanted to meet him. We brought him to her apartment. She had trouble holding him, and he was but two months old. She clearly enjoyed meeting the next generation.

Beginning in 1970 Garbo began to take an annual winter trip to the Caribbean with Gray Reisfield. Typically, this was for two weeks. Garbo spent less time in California from this point on. Initially they went to Barbados, but eventually they started going to the adjacent islands of Antigua and Barbuda on a regular basis. In later years Garbo sometimes spent Thanksgiving with the Reisfields.

This routine, with some variation depending on the year, was Garbo's life from the end of World War II until 1986, when she became too frail to travel as often after her heart attack.

Garbo with her niece in Barbuda in 1976.
— Billy Cunnigham image.

Garbo walked. When she was home in New York she was always seen in her West Side neighborhood. She loved Central Park and ventured all over Manhattan. She could turn an errand to Macy's into a half-day exploration of Murray Hill. She walked with companions and by herself. New Yorkers in the thousands let her be. They might recognize her, often in a startled way. The vast majority then moved on. They had seen Garbo and it would be a topic at dinner.

She preferred this, though sometimes she playfully interacted. The thing that bothered her was when people made a big deal of her presence. She could never take her safety for granted.

Despite her preference for solitude, hundreds of New Yorkers had Garbo stories. She was physically striking, remaining beautiful for her age well into her seventies.

When photographer Billy Cunningham snapped a photo in December 1978 of a stylish seventy-three-year-old woman wearing a nutria coat he recalled, "I thought: 'Look at the cut of that shoulder. It's so beautiful.'" He later wrote, "All I had noticed was the coat, and the shoulder."[1222] That woman turned out to be Garbo, and this unintentional Garbo photo op turned out to be his big break in street-fashion photography.

The media dichotomy that had developed in the fifties was still there. On one hand Garbo was just an elegant woman out walking who caught the eye of the greatest street-fashion photographer, but in the next article she would be a recluse once more.

Garbo had the ability to make a conversation about anything interesting. Part of it was that she had a wide range of knowledge and could converse on topics from gardening to how the Brooklyn Bridge was built. Regardless of the topic, the conversation was fascinating.

The photo of Garbo in a nutria coat that boosted Billy Cunningham's career.

Garson Kanin was witness to a conversation Laurence Olivier had with Garbo at George Cukor's house in 1938 (five years after Olivier was removed from the cast of *Queen Christina*). He had arrived with his fiancé Vivien Leigh, and she was jealous of the time Garbo and Olivier had spent walking around the garden. In his book Kanin recounts Olivier's retelling to Leigh of this conversation, with Olivier taking both parts in the appropriate voice. The jealous Leigh didn't believe that they spent ten minutes talking about which fruits and vegetables they had in their home countries.[1223] But anyone who had a conversation with Garbo about anything would not have been surprised at all.

An example of Garbo's humor when she was engaged with a group of people is her visit to the White House at the invitation of President Kennedy. Garbo went to the White House as part of a prank, attending a dinner on November 13, 1963. Lem (Kirk LeMoyne) Billings was an intimate friend of John Kennedy and the other Kennedy brothers. He was Kennedy's roommate at Choate.

Billings had met Garbo in France in the spring and summer of 1963 and spent quite a bit of time with her. Though he worked in New York, he was at the White House most weekends. He had spent the fall talking about the wonderful times he had with Garbo in Europe.

Garbo had already met Jackie Kennedy a few times in New York. In addition to the president, Jackie, and Lem, the balance of the guest list included Lee Radziwill (Jackie's sister) and Florence Mahoney (a health policy advocate). Mahoney knew Garbo socially and had convinced her to be part of this elaborate prank. She would relate,

> The small dinner was set in the new President's Dining Room upstairs. Lem was invited without being told the identity of the other guests. Miss Garbo was tipped off about his admiration and asked to pretend that she had never met him. Lem was rocked on his heels when she came through the door. He started forward eagerly, but a cool voice cut him short, "Have I ever met you before?"[1224]

Billings was in shock. He didn't understand how Garbo didn't recognize him. He tried jostling her memory with places they had gone together. President Kennedy came up with helpful suggestions as to how Billings could be so mistaken. Perhaps he had met someone with an uncanny resemblance? Eventually, laughter ended the ruse as no one could keep a straight face any longer.[1225] The rest of the dinner was apparently great fun.

After dinner the president had given Garbo a personal tour of the White House. At some point they had gotten into a conversation about scrimshaw. Another topic Garbo could talk about in depth. There was a surprising array of such topics. It all depended on what she had read or with whom she was speaking. For example, I know that Garbo was well versed in the New York City water system, its history, where the water came from, and when the pipes had been built. After their deep dive into scrimshaw, Kennedy spontaneously gave her a piece from his collection that they had been admiring.

This is the unguarded Garbo feeling at ease. She was in a small group of people, and the two she did not already know were the president and his sister-in-law. She was part of an elaborate joke, which would have appealed to her. Kennedy told the group he had stayed up with them later than he was accustomed to. Another sign the party was a success. Reading about Garbo at ease is completely different from reading about situations where she is on her guard.

450 East 52nd Street
New York 22, New York

November 18, 1963

Dear Mrs. Kennedy,

It was a most unusual evening for me that I spent with you in the White House. It was really fascinating and enchanting. I might believe it was a dream if I did not have in my possession the President's "tooth" facing me.

I shall forever cherish the memory of you, the President and the evening.

With all my affection,

Greta Garbo

To: Mrs. John F. Kennedy

Garbo letter to Jacqueline Kennedy after her November 1963 dinner. Courtesy of the John F. Kennedy Library.

Upon returning to New York, Garbo wrote a letter to Jackie thanking her for a wonderful time at the White House.

George Schlee's health was failing in 1964. He had been hospitalized twice early in the year, for depression and then for pneumonia.[1226] In October he and Garbo were in Paris, and he died after suffering a heart attack.

Garbo was clear that the press would report the death focusing on her presence with Schlee, to whom she was not married. She panicked and left the hotel for the house of her friend Cécile de Rothschild to get assistance in taking care of the situation. De Rothschild took charge of managing the details. Valentina Schlee flew to Paris and claimed George's body, then returned to New York. According to friends she held it against Garbo that she had not been able to reach her nor had Garbo been available when she was in Paris.

Garbo was not invited to the memorial service, and for years Valentina did not talk about her or say her name, referring to her only as "the fifth floor." For several years door attendants at the Campanile made a point of never putting them on the elevator together. But in time they reconciled. Before passing away in 1989, Valentina placed her customer files, with every clients' measurements, with Garbo.

Garbo wrote a note for herself about Schlee that she kept. Her sadness comes through:

> Where is my friend—who's hand I could have held
> Walking life's road together.
> He is gone.
> Life is sad and empty.
> He has gone so far away my beloved friend
> He has gone to heaven
> Life is unbearably sad and empty
> I keep seeing his hand
> The hand I could have held
> Walking through life together
> The hand of my beloved friend
> I am not allowed to touch it again
> Oh Lord—Why?[1227]

Her brother Sven died in 1967. Garbo would outlive most of her friends. Those who did not pass before her were mostly in poor health by the time of her death.

Garbo broke her wrist in a fall while walking in Klosters in October 1971. She was in a large hard cast for five weeks, graduating at that point to a small cast for a few more weeks. She wrote about her fall and cast in letters to Peg.

Just after that *Life* magazine ran a photo spread taken before her fall of her doing calisthenics on her balcony in Klosters, including handstands.[1228] She was sixty-six. Garbo tried to manage her health issues by exercising, walking, and eating well. Her pernicious anemia had to be managed her entire life.

Sam Green recalled that Garbo had a problem with one of her front teeth in 1978. Garbo didn't have a dentist, so Green arranged for his dentist to look at her tooth. Which he did, on a park bench on the edge of Central Park. She didn't want to go to his office.

PEGS. DEAR. I
HAVE BROKEN MY
WRIST. RIGHT ONE
I AM IN A CAST.
CANNOT LEAVE OF
COURCE UNTIL IT
IS BETTER. I AM
WONDERING WHY
THAT HAS TO HAPPEN
I DIDN'T THINK I NEEDED
ANY MORE LESSONS
BUT I MUST HAVE BEEN
WRONG. WILL WRITE

WHEN I SHALL LEAVE.
LOVE TO YOU ALL
K.

NOV. 2. 1971

Garbo wrote to Peg after she broke her wrist in 1971.
Written with her off hand. Courtesy of the Greta Garbo family archive.

Garbo decided to use a different dentist. Gray's husband Don arranged for his cousin, Joe Fertig, to attend to her problem. Reisfield had not identified Garbo by name, and as Joe's sister recounts,

> So, someone had escorted her over to his office [Reisfield's and Fertig's offices were in adjacent buildings]. In walked your great aunt, and it was unbeknownst to my brother, what her name was. My brother told me he worked on a certain lady that day. He said her eyes were mesmerizing. He knew there was something about the woman that was captivating . . . still not knowing her name. When she left, my brother's office staff had already gone crazy . . . they knew! They said to Joey, "Do you know who that was?" He had no idea he had done some dental work on Greta Garbo. He said she was lovely.[1229]

In 1984 Garbo had a mastectomy and successfully beat breast cancer.

Not long after her mastectomy, Garbo was staying at the guest house of Gayelord Hauser at his Los Angeles home when he died of pneumonia on December 26, 1984. After a memorial service for Hauser, Garbo served as the host for a reception for his friends at the house. Anthony (Tony) Palermo, who had been Hauser's business associate and heir, but was part of the younger generation, was the executor of his estate.[1230] Palermo was financially savvy and continued Hauser's Modern Products business.

Garbo had invested with Gayelord Hauser in Rodeo Drive retail property and with Hauser, Palermo, and other investors in the Glen Bay Plaza shopping mall in Glendale, Wisconsin. She worked with Palermo to unwind what remained of these investments after Hauser's death.

In 1985 Garbo met Sven Broman and his wife in Klosters. She found them companionable and enjoyed being able to speak Swedish with them. Garbo was aware that Broman was a journalist, but she opened up to him anyway. He turned their discussions into a book.

In 1986 she had a mild heart attack while in Switzerland. Gray went over to Klosters and arranged for her care there and her return to New York.

In her final years Garbo's lifelong health problems caught up with her. She became frail and was no longer able to take the long walks that she loved. Travel became difficult. In 1988 Garbo became ill while in Klosters and Gray had to fly to Switzerland to arrange her transport back to New York. She didn't travel again.

To justify casting the barely known Greta Garbo in *Gösta Berling's* Saga, Mauritz Stiller told Charles Magnusson, "You get a face like that in front of a camera only once in a century."[1231] It wasn't just her face. He meant her whole person. He perceived right at the outset that Garbo had a talent that was unlike anything experienced before. He was right.

Salka Viertel once showed Jack Larson (actor and playwright) a letter Garbo had written to her where she closed the letter with a drawing of herself as a tightrope walker and the words "I guess I can't complain because after all, I'm only a circus lady."[1232]

The master of understatement, Garbo was so much more than just a performer. She had transformed the world around her. The changes to the world that Garbo had either initiated, such as in photography, or merely moved along, such as the modern conception of female life, were important and Garbo's role was intentional. She knew what she was doing. When social conservatives tightened censorship in America, she challenged it by taking roles that subtly fought back.

In the decade after the war Garbo couldn't find a project worth making. Censorship destroyed interesting stories and financing a film without an MPPDA certificate was difficult. The female characters were uninteresting. They didn't have sex out of wedlock. Their romantic lives weren't messy. Finally in the 1970s the feminist movement arrived and the stories Garbo told, and tried to tell, could be filmed again. But Garbo was now in her seventies. The at least twenty, or possibly thirty, years of her career that never happened would not be reclaimed. When she applied to Dramaten, she had wanted to be an actor. She ended up being so much more.

After Garbo died, New Yorkers started to tell their Garbo stories. As she walked around the city, she was not uninvolved. She interacted with people. Dozens of people wrote their Garbo stories, and hundreds told them. They came out in letters to the editor and around dinner tables.

Harlan Conti told the story of shopping an Abercrombie & Fitch sale and trying to decide if a coat would fit the mother of the friend shopping with him. They asked a woman about the same size as his mother to try the coat on so they could decide. The woman gladly modeled the coat, striking poses so they could evaluate it. Only when they went to pay did they learn from the cashier that their model had been Garbo.[1233]

Author and journalist William Safire wrote about the day he missed two major scoops. The jewelry store below his office at the *Herald Tribune* was robbed in the middle of the day while he was trying to meet a deadline. When a secretary tried to motivate him to go downstairs to cover the story, he waved her off, citing the deadline without grasping her point.

He finished his work and then went downstairs to realize he had missed an opportunity for breaking a major story, all because he would not listen. He recounted,

> A woman in a wide-brimmed black hat came out of the jewelry store. Saw me looking desolate, and stopped. "Are you all right?" she asked. I made a despairing grunt. She took off her dark glasses and tried again; "Can I help you?"
>
> I looked up at this woman, who had a striking face but must have been over 40, and said thanks, lady, but all I wanted was to be let alone.
>
> She put her glasses back on, trotted down the steps and disappeared into Madison Avenue. A moment later, one of the jewelry managers came out and said he would put up with robberies as long as he had customers like Greta Garbo.
>
> The other shoe dropped on my head: not only had I missed a breaking news story, but when Fate offered a consolation interview with the most sought-after interviewee in the world, my response was to tell Garbo—famed for her movie line "I want to be alone"—that I wanted to be alone.[1234]

That was Garbo. She cared about people. The fact that she went up to a distraught stranger and asked if he was all right would not surprise her friends.

She cared about her craft. She worked diligently for years to become the best actor in the world. Then she used her art to intentionally address the position of women in modern society. She worked with the best people in the business, and they liked working with her. She was the key cog in a system that delivered films that had an impact on their audience around the world.

She dealt with a level of celebrity she had not anticipated and that no one before her had experienced. She was the face of a century. Yet outside of work she aspired to a quiet private life.

For her friends and family, she was an intelligent and funny companion. Having beat pernicious anemia, cancer, and a heart attack, Garbo died of kidney failure on April 15, 1990. She is buried in Skogskyrkogården cemetery in Stockholm, two kilometers from Dalen in the Enskede district where she and Alva used to farm their allotment.

The Garbo photo closest to how the author pictures her in his mind.

Appendix 1: General Notes on Garbo Biographies

The point of these notes is to show the vast extent of misinformation that crept into prior Garbo biographies. It is not meant to be comprehensive.

Several people, notably Erik Petschler and Arnold Genthe, told their stories of Garbo in ways that portrayed them as having "launched her career." These two tales in particular have become canonical. Removing these fanciful stories from the history of Garbo is addition by subtraction. The Petschler story has been addressed earlier. Genthe didn't understand that Garbo remained in New York because her contract was not finalized. He created the idea that MGM was not sure if it wanted her as his explanation of that fact. The idea that the decision to hire Garbo was made at the Loew's offices in New York is not correct. It was an MGM decision. Genthe wrote a scenario in which his photos arrived as MGM was having a board meeting. Executives don't open mail during board meetings. ***Vanity Fair's p***ublication of Genthe's photo in the November issue flows from the normal timing of print production from when Garbo signed her contract. Genthe didn't convince the magazine to run the photo.

The story of her childhood circumstances has been misconstrued either because the social conditions in Stockholm are misunderstood or because of fake articles that portray the family as impoverished. The Gustafsons were a rather typical working-class Swedish family. Laing, relying on European sources, relates the story correctly. Garbo finished primary school in 1919 at thirteen, as was the Swedish standard. There was no opportunity for working-class Swedish women to go to high school. The deprivations the Gustafson family felt during World War I were issues all Swedes dealt with, as the country was embargoed. Everyone in Stockholm experienced food insecurity. There were hunger marches in the city.

Many people were asked about Garbo years after they were a part of her life. Their memories are often roughly right, but details are incorrect. In 1933 one of her childhood friends recalled getting together with Garbo over Christmas in 1924. It is a warm and joyful story. The memory was actually from 1928, the first Christmas she returned to Stockholm. Garbo spent Christmas 1924 in Istanbul.

Several people have attributed the stage name Garbo to Mauritz Stiller, or others. It is clear from the newly discovered Molander notebook that she started using Garbo at Dramaten in September 1922, over a year before she officially changed her name.

Without understanding the contract issue, the eight-week sojourn in New York becomes a mystery in need of explanation. The usual explanation written by many is that MGM simply had no idea what to do with Garbo.

Biographers have turned to an article written by Adela Rogers St. Johns in Liberty magazine, spread across two August 1934 issues. In it, "Kaj Gynt" explains that MGM didn't know if Garbo actually fit into its plans. Kaj Gynt and Greta Garbo were, in fact, familiar with each other from Stockholm. Gynt emigrated to America when Garbo was two, but returned to visit. She had trained at Dramaten and in New York she worked on Broadway. The Rogers St. Johns article has a ten-year-old Garbo in Stockholm ostensibly having schoolyard conversations with what was in reality a thirty-year-old living in New York. Gynt did serve as her translator in 1925 and they remained friends for years after.

The ten-week gap between Garbo's arrival in Hollywood and the start of production for Torrent is about standard when compared to other European actors. Stiller was always assigned to *The Temptress* as his first MGM film. He was waiting for the arrival of Einar Hanson, who originally was to be the co-star, so *Torrent* was filmed first.

Lillian Gish wrote in her memoir that, after Alva died, she consoled Garbo, who had earlier spent time on the set of *The Scarlet Letter* when Gish was filming the story with Lars Hanson. Most writers have used this vignette. The problem with this tale is that Gish departed Los Angeles for New York on April 19. Alva died on April 21.

The scene stills show that Stiller had filmed about three-fourths of *The Temptress* when he was fired. The Stiller sequence that was retained was not the beginning party scene. Rather, it was the whip fight scene in Argentina, and possibly some of the scenes around it. I was able to use MGM payroll records to give an accurate accounting of the dates Stiller worked on The Temptress.

Some writers have taken seriously the notion that Garbo would marry Gilbert after knowing him for twenty-four days.

It has been written that Garbo intentionally rejected Olivier after he had been cast in *Queen Christina*. Garbo had the right to approve her co-star and selected him in the first place. Both Wanger and Mamoulian confirm Olivier couldn't act against Garbo.

Garbo's independent films frame out the evolution of the censorship regime of the Production Code Administration. While the approval of the final cut of *Queen Christina* over the objections of the SRC is understood, how *Queen Christina* in part triggers the implementation of the PCA has been missed. While the costume dramas didn't have big censorship confrontations, they pushed the formal boundaries of censorship. MGM didn't fight to reduce the demand that Garbo's characters suffer for their sins. Garbo made those characters sympathetic, cleverly subverting the censor's intent.

Prior biographies don't explore the forces that led to the condemnation of *Two-Faced Woman* by the Legion of Decency and exaggerate the impact on both Garbo and revenues.

While most biographies understand that Garbo did not retire after *Two-Faced Woman*, none understands the full extent of her attempts to make more films.

The fact that Walter Wanger's script for *The Duchess de Langeais* was rejected by the Production Code Administration has been overlooked.

No biographer has ever written about *The Miracle*, a film Garbo signed to make in 1955.

The following are specific observations regarding the significant Garbo biographies:

- **Palmborg, Rilla Page—*The Private Life of Greta Garbo* (Doubleday, Doran & Company, 1931)**

Palmborg interviewed Garbo twice for fan magazines, and these interviews, along with information from Garbo's household staff and some of her friends at the time, are the basis for this book. Her history of Garbo in Sweden leans heavily on *Lektyr* articles. In Hollywood, she has trouble getting things right chronologically. For example, Palmborg has Garbo going out on Gilbert's yacht when they first meet in 1926. Gilbert didn't buy the yacht until the fall of 1927, a year later. There is a section where Palmborg quotes others as saying Garbo didn't have friends in Stockholm, when clearly she did.

Palmborg describes Garbo's house at 1027 Chevy Chase Drive, Beverly Hills (which she moved into in April 1929) in great detail as she had information from the staff. So it is probably rather accurate. She adds the Norins' (housekeepers) reminiscence of their time working for Garbo. Probably also accurate. She was able to get Wilhelm Sörensen and John Loder to talk to her about Garbo, and this information is probably mostly accurate. They probably did not realize they were going to be quoted.

Where the book relies on her interviews, it is strong. The other parts rely on bad magazine articles.

■ **Laing, E. E.—*Greta Garbo: The Story of a Specialist* (John Gifford Limited, 1946)**

A Garbo biography writer who was a British theater and film critic. His comments on her acting career and the industry are valuable. Written from a distinctly European perspective.

Laing writes a mini-review of each film. Somewhat chatty in tone.

Laing is lazy about the chronology of films and this is a pretty major error. He seems to be writing about them from memory. He does talk to some Swedes about Garbo's first visit home, and he has the Swedish media reports. He has clearly spoken with people who knew her from both Sweden and Germany, but who is unclear. This information is the strongest part of the book.

■ **Bainbridge, John—Garbo (Doubleday, 1955)**

The first full biography written after the end of her career. It suffers from a lack of footnotes and contains some intentional errors. It is based primarily on mag azine and newspaper articles. He did unearth some new information and he interviewed people who knew her. If it were not used as a source by subsequent authors, it would not matter at all as a book.

■ **Billquist, Fritiof—*Garbo: A Biography* (G. P. Putnam's Sons, 1960) (English Translation)**

Fritiof Billquist was a Swedish actor who had a long career in theater and film. He would work with many of the people who figured into Garbo's brief stage and theater career in Sweden.

The early part of his book is based on unreliable Lektyr series, and magazine articles. Information from her life in Hollywood is pulled from other biographies and film magazines. He does have access to the Mimi Pollak and Lars Saxon letters. He quotes them without attribution and sometimes combines letters.

His detailed summary of her first return to Sweden has more depth than other coverage. The best part of the book, and probably the most accurate, is where he describes the play she considered with Gösta Ekman, whom she knew.

Billquist is the only author to detail Garbo's summer in Sweden in 1935, when she rented a small place north of Stockholm. He adds a few stories told by friends from that summer.

■ **Zierold, Norman—*Garbo* (Stein and Day, 1969)**

Zierold is somewhat similar to Laing in that he was a professional observer of the entertainment industry. He was the editor of two industry magazines: *Theatre Arts Magazine* and *Show*. He states clearly that his focus is not on Garbo's early life and career, and he uses earlier biographies to fill in this part of her life.

Zierold's book delivers an appraisal of Garbo as an actress and person. He interviews many of the people who worked with her and those who knew her socially. These interviews are wonderful. This was the first book that added significant first-person accounts of Garbo since Palmborg's biography.

■ **Sands, Frederick and Broman, Sven—*The Divine Garbo* (Grosset & Dunlap, 1979)**

The strong part of this book is a set of interviews by Broman with Swedes who knew Garbo back when she was young and starting out. Unfortunately, the majority of the rest of the book is a poorly constructed assembly of the same magazine articles everyone has used, plus extensive use of Lektyr.

■ **Walker, Alexander—*Garbo* (Macmillan, 1980)**

Walker was given access to the MGM files regarding its relationship with Greta Garbo. However, the files seem to have been rather scant. (These files were reputedly raided by collectors.) For example, Walker remarks on the six-month hiatus between the end of *The Divine Woman* and the start of *The Mysterious Lady*, and he theorizes about it. But he couldn't provide a single memo.

Walker does reference some fascinating MGM internal correspondence. For example, the memos around the start of *Queen Christina* show how the plan for filming the movie was delayed. One only wishes there were even more. Walker's brief section about her early life before Hollywood is pulled from the standard material used before.

■ **Daum, Raymond and Muse, Vance—*Walking with Garbo: Conversations and Recollections* (HarperCollins, 1991)**

This book takes some quotes from the time that Raymond Daum and Garbo were friends and walking companions (from 1963 to 1983, when he moved from New York to Austin). Attached to this is Vance Muse's retelling of the conventional Garbo biography.

■ Broman, Sven—Garbo on Garbo (Bloomsbury, 1991)

Sven Broman has assembled his remembrances of conversations he had with Garbo over the years from 1963 until her death. While these conversations are not extensive, they are great material. He has added letters, interviews, and remembrances of several of her friends to try to paint a more complete picture of her. For the most part it succeeds. Since much of this was written down after the fact, some of the details are probably inaccurate. A few stories are at odds with known facts. But for the most part, he has assembled a range of useful memories from people who knew her.

■ Paris, Barry—*Garbo: A Biography* (Knopf, 1995)

The first biography of Garbo to include footnotes. Paris adds some important new research. For example, he is the first biographer to realize that *Die freudlose Gasse* was considered an important film, and Garbo an important actor, at the time it was released. However, Paris didn't challenge any of the errors in prior biographies and never checked timelines to make sure the story he was telling was plausible. Paris often tosses two recountings that are mutually exclusive onto the page and asks the reader to figure it out. This presents anything ever written about Garbo as equally plausible. But he did find some new material that is valuable. He conducted some interesting interviews with contemporaries who were still alive.

Paris understood the power of the Genthe portraits, and he wrote about how Garbo's arrival transformed female acting in that everyone had to compete with her success. Though he doesn't understand why she was successful. He settles on her being a unique "type."

He simplifies and gets wrong Garbo's walkout and the events that led up to Gilbert starring in *Love*.

Paris also postulates on Garbo's frame of mind with no basis for his speculation. He constantly attributes motives to her as if his speculative conception must be self-evident to a reader. He makes some misstatements that seem sloppy. For example, he writes that *Two-Faced Woman* was produced on a cheap budget. While Garbo did make the film for half of her previous fee, the total cost of the film is in line with most other Garbo films.

■ Swenson, Karen—*Greta Garbo: A Life Apart* (Scribner, 1997)

Swenson also wrote a solid biography with footnotes. As with the Paris biography, which was written around the same time, the biggest issue is with the sources she chooses to use. She did the research, but she didn't know what to believe. For example, she uses Genthe's autobiography.

Lots of Swenson's information comes from the same suspect magazine sources. Swenson discredits Mercedes de Acosta, as have most serious writers, then quotes her liberally. While de Acosta can provide a provocative quote, that doesn't make it accurate.

■ Gottlieb, Robert—*Garbo* (Farrar, Straus and Giroux, 2021)

Gottlieb's recounting of Garbo's life during her career is taken from prior biographies with little additional research. Gottlieb adds conjecture where he doesn't have the relevant facts. For instance, he has a theory that Garbo did not get along with her family. His premise is based on comments from Mercedes de Acosta and Cecil Beaton. Both de Acosta and Beaton were famously jealous of others who Garbo spent time with. Gottlieb positions Salka Viertel as the mother Garbo never had, without any basis for his conclusion. Gottlieb misses the actual collaborative relationship between the two.

When discussing Garbo's later films, he focuses on his reviews and presents them as the final, definitive take. He also ignores the many months Garbo was not in Hollywood.

■ Dance, Robert—*The Savvy Sphinx* (The University Press of Mississippi, 2021)

Robert Dance cowrote my earlier book, so any review by me of his later book is somewhat biased. As with other biographers, he gives too much credit to the inaccurate but repeated stories of Garbo's early life. He does a better job sifting through the material from America. The strength of his biography is that he is the first author to focus any significant time on Garbo's work with photographers. He has the best history of when photographic sessions took place. He understands how technology was evolving and that photographers had styles they brought to their work. He overstates the amount of control Garbo had over her roles and co-stars before she began negotiating per-film deals with *Queen Christina*.

Appendix 2: Garbo's Transformational Approach to Photography

Garbo and Arnold Genthe

July 21, 1925

The portrait created on July 21 was a standard celebrity portrait from that era.

(Below) July 27, 1925

Garbo and Genthe would transform portrait photography when Garbo would act for the camera on July 27. Going through a range of emotional poses she would set the stage for the evolution of the relationship between the camera and the subject.

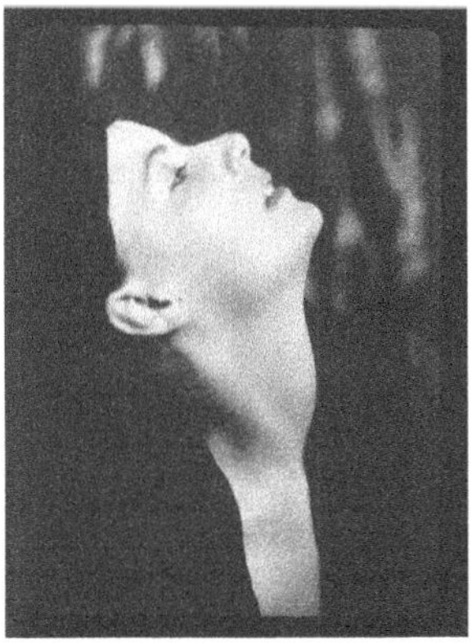

July 27, 1925 Continued

July 31, 1925

In a final portrait session on July 31, Garbo and Genthe found a balance, delivering a session where Garbo seems to relate directly to the viewer.

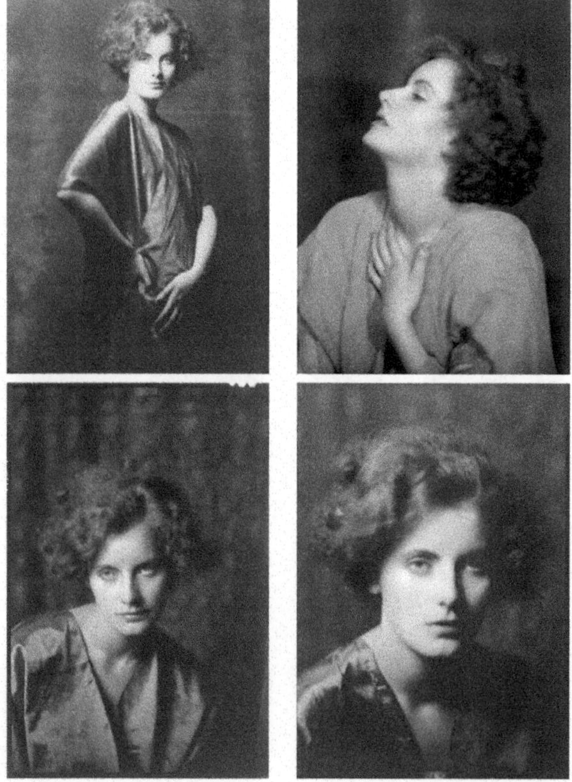

The brilliance of what Garbo and Genthe achieved can be seen by looking at these photos in comparison to the other photos of female actors that appeared in *Vanity Fair* during 1925. *Vanity Fair* used the leading photographers of that era.

Elsie Ferguson - January
Raquel Meller - January
Pauline Lord - February
Laurette Taylor - April
Lillian Gish - April
Mary Ellis - April
Pola Negri - June
Jane Cowl - September
Carol Dempster - October

Clare Eames – October

Gertrude Lawrence – October

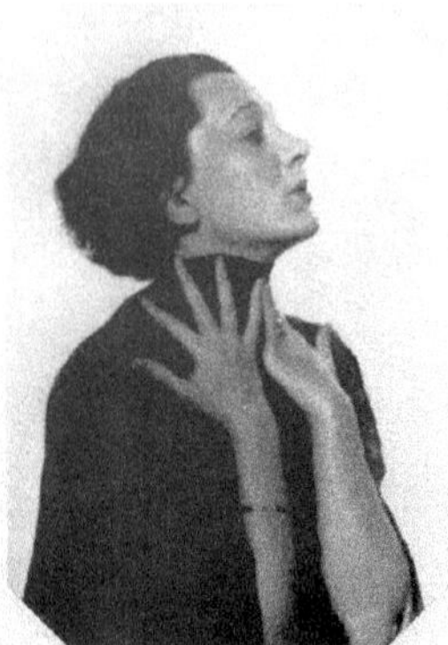

Alice Brady – November

Helen Wills – November

Iris Tree – November

Ethyl Barrymore – December

Gloria Swanson – December

Appendix 3: Run-Zone-Clearance and the Profitability of First-Run Theaters

Information presented in the 1946 case of *Bigelow v. RKO Pictures*, a fight over market conditions in 1939, is illustrative of how the run-zone-clearance system concentrated profits in first-run theaters, regardless of theater size. Conveniently, the three sample theaters representing first-run, second-run, and third-run theaters had comparable seating capacities.

As one can see from the chart below, the Chicago Theatre made substantially more money than the other two theaters while being only marginally larger. Even though the Chicago paid more for films because it was a first-run house, it paid a lower percentage of its revenue for the films than the other two theaters. The calculation of film rental expense as a percentage of box office shows that while distributors made more money from first-run houses, their take from rentals did not grow at the rate of the added box office revenue.

Extending the analysis to look at revenue per seat, the Chicago Theatre was making three times the revenue of the second-run Avalon Theater. It was making more than six times what the third-run Tower brought in.

Even when adjusted for ticket prices, it is clear that what drives the profitability of first-run theaters is that they fill a higher percentage of seats, or run more shows per week, or both. At equalized seat prices (using the contracted minimums from the exhibition agreement), the Chicago Theatre still generates twice as much revenue per seat as does the Avalon Theater and over three times as much as the Tower Theatre.

Representative Chicago Theaters for Top Three Run Tiers

	First run	Second run	Third run
Theater	Chicago	Avalon	Tower
Owner	Paramount	Warner	Paramount
Seats	3,852	2,385	3,013
Contracted minimum admission	$0.75	$0.50	$0.40
1939 box office	$1,709,562	$352,576	$209,850
1939 film rental expense	$307,336	$105,152	$69,580
Rental expense as % of box office	18.0%	29.8%	33.2%
Box office per seat	$443.81	$147.83	$69.65
Box office per seat adjusted to flat admission of $0.40	$236.70	$118.26	$69.65

Source: Michael Conant, *Antitrust in the Motion Picture Industry* (University of California Press, 1960), 160.

This chart demonstrates the cumulative effect of each of the key differentiators. Intuitively, higher ticket prices led to higher revenue. This was compounded by higher occupancy, as demonstrated by the box office revenue per seat remaining significantly higher when adjusted for ticket price.

Because this example came from a large city, it was possible to use a large third-run theater in the comparison. Most third-run theaters were smaller. While larger theaters had higher operating expenses, the expenses for management, building, advertising, and amenities increased at a slower rate than revenues. So, larger theaters such as these had expense advantages over the thousands of smaller theaters, regardless of their place in the run-zone-clearance hierarchy.

While in general little detail regarding daily profits from individual theaters has survived, one data set from Philadelphia in the mid-1930s confirms both that first-run theaters took in the lion's share of revenue and that films that ran in these first-run theaters made outsized profits.

As with Chicago, first-run theaters in Philadelphia generated more revenue per seat because of higher ticket prices. First-run theaters generated $4.42 in average weekly per-seat revenue while second-run theaters only averaged $2.51. In the case of Philadelphia, as with Chicago, first- and second-run theaters were about the same size. The difference in pricing power was due to a combination of first-run films, theater amenities, and better live shows.

■ How Film Rental Revenue Hides the Value of First-Run Customers

Film rental information summaries have been found for most studios. This is often confused with modern ticket sale information, and they are not the same. Historical ticket revenue information is patchy and, even when printed in historical trade magazines, unreliable.

Fortunately, we can use the data from the Bigelow v. RKO Pictures case to get a general picture of how much more valuable a film that did proportionately better in first-run theaters was compared to a film that did better outside the big cities. For example, a Garbo film would skew to first-run theaters compared to a Western.

The intent here is to show in a general sense how much extra value first-run theaters delivered to their owners that is not captured in film rental data from the Studio Era, not to develop an exact formula. Films that are seemingly equal when viewed only through the prism of film rental income have significantly different revenue potential at theaters, even when the rental expense is the same. Shifting one day's worth of tickets to a first-run theater from a comparably sized second-run theater was worth around $3,000 ($70,000).

The Box Office of Theaters Based on Run Priority

	First run	Second run	Third run
Theater	Chicago	Avalon	Tower
1939 box office	$1,709,562	$352,576	$209,850
1939 film rental expense	$307,336	$105,152	$69,580
Film rental expense adjustment	0.23	0.66	1.00
Equalized rental effect on box office	$387,040	$233,303	$209,850
Box office revenue gain due to run tier	$1,322,522	$119,273	$0
Per day	$3,623.35	$326.78	n/a

Source: Bigelow v. RKO Pictures, Inc., 327 U.S. 251 (1946).
Note: n/a is short for "not applicable."

For example, look at the thirty-eight more days that *Love* ran in first-run theaters compared to the Norma Shearer vehicle *The Student Prince in Old Heidelberg* in just Brooklyn and Queens (discussed in chapter 18). If *The Student Prince* ran those same days in a comparable second-run theater, it would have potentially earned $100,000 ($2.3 million) less ticket revenue from Brooklyn and Queens.

We don't know for a fact that *Love* ran in more first-run theaters than *The Student Prince* nationwide. We just know it for Brooklyn and Queens. We do know based on industry reports that Garbo films delivered the first-run audience. When looking just at the available film rental data, the importance of the box office data, now lost, is missing.

Appendix 4: The Failure of the First National Bank of Beverly Hills and its Effect on Garbo

On June 4, 1932, the First National Bank of Beverly Hills failed. Rumors quickly developed in newspapers that Garbo had over $1 million on deposit there. Since the five-year contract she had just completed paid her $975,000 cumulatively, this was impossible. But the rumor is oft repeated to this day. There was even a rumor that a large withdrawal by Garbo led to the bank's failure.

A few days after the bank failed, Garbo's manager Harry Edington would address these rumors: "Miss Garbo had only an insignificant amount in the bank, a few thousand dollars at most—and this was in a checking account. Her money is invested principally in United States bonds." [1241] This statement is patently false, as Garbo had a significant amount in her First National Bank account.

According to correspondence between Laurence W. Beilenson, her lawyer, and the bank's receiver, Garbo had $364,597.94 on deposit when the bank failed.[1242] Garbo had not spent the $610,000 balance of salary she had received from MGM to that point. She had diversified her investments.

As Edington stated, she had invested in U.S. government bonds. She sent money back to her family in Sweden. She paid for medical care for her sister Alva. She helped her mother move to a nicer apartment. Garbo had a Swedish bank account and a Swedish insurance policy. She probably had at least one other American bank account or investment account.

Wilhelm Sörensen would tell Garbo friend and biographer Sven Broman that Garbo had taken most of her money out of her original bank and opened another account sometime before his departure for Sweden in late 1931. [1243]

Another point of reference is a note to Garbo from Charles Greene, who was an accountant, that summarized her accounts at First National Bank the prior year. In April 1931 she had $74,500 there, almost all in a savings account.[1244] She had only a little over $1,000 in a checking account. So in 1931 she had assets somewhere other than in First National Bank.

The most likely scenario is that prior to 1931 Garbo diversified her investments, though new salary payments continued to go to the First National Bank.

Garbo did not lose all of the money she had on deposit in the bank. The receiver recovered 40 to 50 percent of it. Garbo was allowed to claim half the loss, just over $182,000, against her 1933 income.

All income over $88,000 was taxed at 50 percent or more. Accounting for all various income brackets, Garbo saved another $80,000 in tax offsets by writing off this bad debt. Still, her net loss of about $100,000 was significant.

Acknowledgments

So many people helped me research and craft this Garbo project that I want to apologize up front to anyone I may leave out. Creating a complete list is complicated by the fact that I started to informally (at first) research Garbo in 2000 and I didn't decide to write the book until Covid.

Anders Kallner, my Swedish cousin, did some of my translations and found Swedish material I was looking for on my behalf. Johanna Eriksson was more than just my main Swedish translator. She read an early draft and helped me address some Swedish colloquialisms and cultural issues. Cliff Campeau, Frank Drees, Dan Sved, Dennis Smithenry, Jane Hartsock, Lynn Wohlwend, and Melody Chu all read early versions of the book and helped me focus and correct it. Frank also translated German and provided lots of great questions and information. Lillemor Ring was kind enough to answer my questions about her grandfather Ragnar Ring. Cornelia Löwenhielm also helped with some Swedish translations.

Meg Toth and Jacob Whiten edited my book. Mike Hamers provided the layout and cover design. Lana McAra and Devi Barnard at Vendela Publishing helped make the book a reality.

I want to thank Patrick Vonderau (Martin Luther University) and Bo Florin (Stockholm University), the authors of *A Tale from Constantinople: The History of a Film that Never Was*. They both gave me some of their time and helped me flesh out the *Odalisque* project and Garbo's relationship with Trianon-Film.

Regarding Garbo's life in Sweden, a number of people at the Swedish Film Institute were a great resource. The late Margareta Nordstrom was my introduction to SFI. Later I was assisted by Ola Törjas, Magnus Rosborn, and many others.

Musikverket provided new and previously unused information thanks to the work of Rikard Larsson and Virve Polsa.

Agnes Sjöbrandt at the University of Stockholm Theatre Archive and Dag Kronlund of the Swedish Royal Dramatic Theatre provided me with information about Garbo's years at the Royal Dramatic Theatre. Rikard Hoogland at the Stockholm University Theatre Studies Department, Hélène Ohlsson at Stockholm University, theater historian Willmar Sauter, and Linnea Stara of the Finnish Theatre Information Centre provided me with a historical understanding of Swedish language theater in Sweden and Finland.

Maria Stanfors at Lund University helped me understand the social context of Garbo's childhood. Kristine Falk at the Swedish Salvation Army and Hans Nordlund and Angelica Tillaeus in the Filipstad municipality helped me research Garbo's aunt Sigrid.

Åsa Mähring at the City Museum of Stockholm provided an array of information about the Gustafson family. Both archives within Riksarkivet helped me. For censorship documents, Kristina Eriksson and other staff at the Täby archive were invaluable. In Stockholm, archivist Bo Lundström was my key contact. There were quite a few librarians at the National Library of Sweden who helped me in my research.

While I never found a missing Tullbergs industrial film with Garbo, Petteri Kalliomäki at the Finnish National Audiovisual Institute and Vennlig Hilsen and Laila Johns at Nasjonalbiblioteket Norway were kind enough to look through their film archives.

In Germany I was assisted by Debora Classen, Jens Kaufmann, Christof Schöbel, and Simon Lames at Deutsches Filminstitut & Filmmuseum. At Deutsche Kinemathek I was assisted by Cordula Döhrer, Gerrit Theis, Lisa Roth, Birgit Umathum, and Julia Riedel.

Christoph Albers at the Newspaper Archive of the Berlin State Library helped me find key German newspapers. Nico Spilt answered my questions about historical train schedules. Andrea Haller filled in some rudimentary German history for me.

Though American, Sara F. Hall at the University of Illinois Chicago gave me additional information on Hugo Bettauer and The Joyless Street.

In the United States no film history archive rivals the Margaret Herrick Library, and I can't remember all the staff who helped me over the years. I do want to call out the late Robert Cushman, Howard Prouty, and Louise Hilton. At the Louis B. Mayer Library, Emily Wittenberg was exceedingly helpful. At USC Cinematic Arts Library, the late Ned Comstock was a great resource. While not in a building, the Media History Digital Library was invaluable.

Other film history archives where I spent a fair amount of time include the University of Kentucky Clarence Brown archive and the Wisconsin Center for Film and Theater Research at the University of Wisconsin, where several people, including Amanda Smith, helped me in my research. At the Harry Ransom Center at the University of Texas at Austin, Steve Wilson, Amy Wagner, and Michael Gilmore were wonderful. Ben Harry at Brigham Young University made my visit easy.

Dana Nemeth and John King at the Browne Popular Culture Library at Bowling Green State University helped me with their collections of film fan and gossip magazines. I also did lots of research at the libraries of the University of Michigan, Eastern Michigan University, and Michigan State University. Among public libraries, I researched elements of the book in New York, Denver, and Ann Arbor. I was able to unravel the story of John Gilbert's 1927 car crash thanks to the assistance of Matthew Nye at the San Diego Public Library.

Richard Abel, professor emeritus at the University of Michigan, Patrick Keating at Trinity University in San Antonio, Ross Melnick at University of California, Santa Barbara, Spencer Howard at the Herbert Hoover Presidential Library, and Gregg Tripoli at the Syracuse Historical Society each provided information in their field of study.

My guide to the censorship information at the Catholic University of America was Brandi Marulli. I would also like to thank the staff at the Booth Special Collections at Georgetown University, where the Martin Quigley papers are kept.

About the Author

Scott Reisfield is the grandnephew of Greta Garbo.

He has used his access to family documents and overlooked archive collections to write this book. While he had casually researched Garbo after she passed away, with the free time created by COVID he decided to write the definitive biography.

Reisfield focuses on Garbo's real achievement, being a beacon of how to live a more modern life for millions of women. Garbo used her talent and training as an actor to create more believable characters. People believed they understood what Garbo was thinking on the screen. Garbo informed their idea of modern romance and love.

Scott has a BA from the University of Pennsylvania and an MBA from the University of Michigan. He spent forty years in business, thirty of them in senior management, working in companies ranging from large corporations to startups. He also managed marketing for a national association. He lives in Ann Arbor, Michigan.

He cowrote the 2005 book *Garbo's Garbos: Portraits from Her Private Collection.* That book was a coffee-table companion to the museum exhibit of the same name.

A photo of the author as Garbo remembered him. Courtesy the Greta Garbo family archive.

Scott Reisfield. Credit Heather Nash.

Endnotes

1. Robert Morley, *Tales from the Hollywood Raj* (Viking, 1983), 152.
2. Coco Point Lodge was destroyed by Hurricane Irma in 2017.
3. Lionel Barrymore, *We Barrymores* (Appleton-Century-Crofts, 1951), 246.
4. Cal York, "One More Garbo Fan," *Photoplay*, May 1932, 95.
5. Whitney Stone, *I'd Love to Kiss You . . . Conversations with Bette Davis* (Pocket Books, 1990), 146.
6. Sarah L. Navins, archivist, Franklin D. Roosevelt Presidential Library, email to author, April 17, 2025. This was taken from an unpublished article by Eleanor Roosevelt titled "Mail of a President's Wife." In addition to 300,000 pieces in 1933 she received 90,000 in 1937 and 150,000 in 1940.
7. Robert Gottleib, *Garbo* (Farrar, Straus and Giroux, 2021), 4
8. "Rockville Girl Speaks," HiLo Brow, updated September 23, 2011, https://www.hilobrow.com/2011/09/23/rockville-girl-speaks/.
9. Sven Broman, *Garbo on Garbo* (Bloomsbury, 1991), 25.
10. Börje Lundberg, *Expressen*, June 17, 1999.
11. Lundberg, June 17, 1999.
12. Pernilla Jonsson and Fredrik Sandgren, "Statistics on the Occupational Structure of Sweden 1800–1920: Censuses a Way to Capture Shifts in Regional Employment?," *International Network for the Comparative History of Occupational Structure* (July 2009): 7.
13. John Gilmour, *Sweden, the Swastika and Stalin* (Edinburgh University Press, 2010), 16.
14. John Lewis Austin, "Intima Teatern and the Formations of Theatrical Modernity in Sweden" (thesis, University of Illinois Urbana-Champaign, 1997), 70.
15. Austin, "Intima Teatern," 74.
16. Michael Jonas, "'Time of Turmoil': Sweden, Undeclared Emergencies, and the Experience of Crisis and Transformation in and around the First World War," *First World War Studies* 14, nos. 2–3 (2023): 325–26.
17. Gilmour, *The Swastika and Stalin*, 16.
18. Gilmour, *The Swastika and Stalin*, 20.
19. Maria Stanfors, "Women in a Changing Economy: The Misleading Tale of Participation Rates in a Historical Perspective," *The History of the Family* 19, no. 4 (2014): 517–18.
20. Goeran Lindberg, secretary, Hyltinge hembygdsforening, email to author, June 15, 2021.
21. Åsa Mähring, curator, City Museum of Stockholm, email to author
22. Mähring, email to author.
23. Mähring, email to author.
24. Mähring, email to author.
25. "Välkomna till koloniföreningen Dalen som ligger i Enskededalen/Kärrtorp i södra Stockholm," Koloniföreningen Dalen, accessed August 22, 2025, http://koloniforeningendalen.se/om%20oss.html.
26. Lesley Acton, *Growing Spaces: A History of the Allotment Movement* (Five Leaves, 2015), 22.
27. Acton, *Growing Spaces*, 32.
28. Broman, *Garbo on Garbo*, 36.

29. "Greta Garbo Inherits $772," *Baltimore Evening Sun*, March 20, 1956, p. 1.
30. Greta Garbo to Peg Gustafson, letter, undated, but from either 1956 or 1957, author's personal collection: "If you could give the amount to Sigrid. But from what I understand it is not as simple as Peg thinks it is to just tell them to deposit the money to my bank. They probably need some kind of release signed by me. Could Peg make that happen in some way."
31. Anna Maria Katarina "Kata" Dalström (née Carlberg), 1858–1923.
32. Broman, *Garbo on Garbo*, 35.
33. Jonas, "'Time of Turmoil,'" 325.
34. Broman, *Garbo on Garbo*, 36.
35. Jan-Olof Drangert et al., "Why Did They Become Pipe-Bound Cities? Early Water and Sewerage Alternatives in Swedish Cities," *Public Works Management & Policy* 6, no. 3 (January 2002): 178.
36. John Bainbridge, *Garbo* (Galahad Books, 1971), 19.
37. Broman, *Garbo on Garbo*, 35.
38. Broman, *Garbo on Garbo*, 37.
39. Ruth Biery, "The Story of Greta Garbo," *Photoplay*, April 1928.
40. Biery, "The Story of Greta Garbo," April 1928.
41. Robin Hood [Bengt Idestam-Almquist], "'Keta' en riktig vildbasare Älskeade leka Tarzan på tak," *Stockholms-Tidningen*, January 27, 1954, p. 1.
42. Biery, "The Story of Greta Garbo," April 1928.
43. Biery, "The Story of Greta Garbo," April 1928.
44. Biery, "The Story of Greta Garbo," April 1928.
45. Biery, "The Story of Greta Garbo," April 1928.
46. Broman, *Garbo on Garbo*, 39.
47. "High School Graduates, by Sex and Control of School: Selected Years, 1869–70 through 2019–20," National Center for Education Statistics, accessed August 22, 2025, https://nces.ed.gov/programs/digest/d10/tables/dt10_110.asp.
48. Börje Lundberg, *Expressen*, June 18, 1999.
49. Broman, *Garbo on Garbo*, 37.
50. Biery, "The Story of Greta Garbo," April 1928.
51. Broman, *Garbo on Garbo*, 39.
52. Broman, *Garbo on Garbo*, 37.
53. Broman, *Garbo on Garbo*, 37.
54. Broman, *Garbo on Garbo*, 37–39.
55. I have presented all financial data in the original amounts, and I have converted them to 2025 US dollar amounts. I used the website https://www.measuringworth.com to convert currencies to dollars, if necessary. Then I adjusted that value using a price inflator (https://www.usinflationcalculator.com) to get to 2025 dollars. Going forward I will present the historic original amount and then the current value in US dollars in parentheses.
56. John Bainbridge, *Garbo* (Knopf Doubleday, 1995), 23.
57. John Bainbridge, *Garbo* (Knopf Doubleday, 1995), 24.
58. Karen Swenson, *Greta Garbo: A Life Apart* (Scribner, 1997), 33.
59. "Vaxholm Grenadier Regiment," Wikimedia Foundation, last modified August 17, 2025, https://en.wikipedia.org/wiki/Vaxholm_Grenadier_Regiment.
60. Biery, "The Story of Greta Garbo," April 1928.
61. Rilla Page Palmborg, *The Private Life of Greta Garbo* (Doubleday, Doran, 1931).

62. John Bainbridge, *Garbo* (Doubleday, 1955), 40.
63. Ruth Biery, "The Story of Greta Garbo," *Photoplay*, April 1928.
64. Sven Broman, *Garbo on Garbo* (Bloomsbury, 1991), 39.
65. Maria Stanfors, conversation with author, March 3, 2022.
66. Susan Porter Benson, *Counter Cultures* (University of Illinois Press, 1986), 131.
67. Benson, *Counter Cultures*, 132.
68. Benson, *Counter Cultures*, 165.
69. Greta Garbo to Eva Blomqvist, letter, July 7, 1920, Swedish Film Institute Archives, Stockholm.
70. Greta Garbo to Eva Blomqvist, letter, August 16, 1920, Swedish Film Institute Archives, Stockholm
71. Garbo to Blomqvist, August 16, 1920.
72. Greta Garbo to Eva Blomqvist, letter, August 7, 1920, Swedish Film Institute Archives, Stockholm.
73. Garbo to Blomqvist, August 16, 1920.
74. Robin Hood [Bengt Idestam-Almquist], "Garbo var 'rapp tvålflicka' Lönen hos söderfrisör 7 kr," *Stockholms-Tidningen*, March 3, 1954, p. 1.
75. Frederick Sands and Sven Broman, *The Divine Garbo* (Grosset & Dunlap, 1979), 24.
76. Sands and Broman, *The Divine Garbo*, 25.
77. Broman, *Garbo on Garbo*, 39.
78. Greta Garbo to Eva Blomqvist, letter, August 27, 1921, Swedish Film Institute Archives, Stockholm.
79. Stig Berg, *Dä årner säj* [Stories from my childhood] (NWTs, 1987), 38–39.
80. Lillemor Ring, *Kapten Ring* (temporis acti Stories, 2016), 163.
81. Ring, *Kapten Ring*, 238.
82. "Svenska Dagbladet-Tullbergs Industrial Division Creates Foreign Editions," *Svenska Dagbladet*, January 2, 1920.
83. "Garbo jubileum," *Aftonbladet*, September 8, 1940, p. 11.
84. Ring, *Kapten Ring*, 243.
85. "Filmning Hos Paul U. Bergström," *Aftonbladet*, December 2, 1920, p. 7.
86. Ring, *Kapten Ring*, 250.
87. Karen Swenson, *Greta Garbo: A Life Apart* (Scribner, 1997), 38.
88. Swenson, *Greta Garbo*, 38 (brackets in the original).
89. "Filmning Hos Paul U. Bergström," p. 7.
90. Ring, *Kapten Ring*, 250.
91. Ring, *Kapten Ring*, 241.
92. The Library of Congress estimates that 75 percent of silent films are lost and no copies remain. "American Silent Feature Film Database," Library of Congress, accessed August 29, 2025, https://www.loc.gov/programs/national-film-preservation-board/preservation-research/silent-film-database/. This analysis focuses on theatrical films. The percentage of silent industrial films that are lost might easily be higher, as fewer positive copies were made of each film
93. Mats Björkin, "Industrial Greta: Some Thoughts on an Industrial Film," in *Nordic Explorations: Film Before 1930*, ed. John Fullerton and Jan Olsson (John Libbey, 1999), 263–68.
94. Björkin, "Industrial Greta," 263–68.

95. *Biografbladet*, 1922, p. 527.
96. Swedish Film Database, accessed August 29, 2025, https://www.svenskfilmdatabas.se. They are not all filed under Tullbergs Film (or a variant). Some are only filed under director Ragnar Ring. The PUB film is filed under three titles, and there is another title that is a 1930s compilation of scenes from the PUB film and the co-op films that I have not counted.
97. Statens biografbyrås arkiv, Riksarkivet, https://sok.riksarkivet.se/.
98. Statens biografbyrås arkiv, Riksarkivet, https://sok.riksarkivet.se/.
99. "Industrifilm Apropå den Tullbergska *'Tokio-filmen,'*" *Biografbladet*, Feb. 1, 1922, p. 105.
100. "17-årig Garbo fick 1000 kr. för vekors filmning," *Svenska Dagbladet*, April 9, 1942, p. 12.
101. "Industrifilm Apropå den Tullbergska *'Tokio-filmen,'*" p. 105.
102. "Garbo jubileum," p. 11.
103. Ring, *Kapten Ring*, 251.
104. Sands and Broman, *The Divine Garbo*, 29.
105. Sands and Broman, *The Divine Garbo*, 29.
106. Biery, "The Story of Greta Garbo," April 1928.
107. Stanfors, conversation with author, March 3, 2022.
108. Paul Bergström to Ragnar Ring, letter, 1922. An excerpt from this letter was in a Garbo biography formerly available at PUB. The store has now been closed.
109. Stanfors, conversation with author, March 3, 2022.
110. "17-årig Garbo fick 1000 kr. för vekors filmning," p. 12.
111. Jeremiah Laurent, "Great Expectations: Women's Help Wanted Ads in Kansas City, 1920–1936" (thesis, University of Missouri–Kansas City, 2014), 54.
112. "Garbo jubileum," p. 11.
113. Carla Waal, *Harriet Bosse: Strindberg's Muse and Interpreter* (Southern Illinois University Press, 1990), 54.
114. John Bainbridge, *Garbo* (Doubleday, 1955), 40.
115. John Bainbridge, *Garbo* (Doubleday, 1955), 39.
116. Ingrid Luterkort, *Om igen, herr Molander! Kungl. Dramatiska teaterns elevskola*, 1787–1964 (Stockholmia förlag, 1998), 143.
117. *Svenska Dagbladet*, August 19, 1922, p. 8.
118. *Svenska Dagbladet*, August 19, 1922, p. 8.
119. Announcement, *Svenska Dagbladet*, August 30, 1922, p. 12.
120. Biery, "The Story of Greta Garbo," April 1928.
121. Erik Petschler, archives, A123, Music and Theatre Library of Sweden, Stockholm.
122. Petschler, archives.
123. Petschler, archives.
124. Greta Garbo to Mimi Pollak, letter, September 1, 1926, author's personal collection.
125. Throughout this book, "class year" refers to the year of arrival, not graduation.
126. Alf Sjöberg, "Hon fick avgiva ett heligt löfte att aldrig vidare ägna sig åt film" [She had to make a sacred promise never to devote herself to film again], *Hänt i Veckan*, January 9, 1970, 16.
127. Sjöberg, "Hon fick avgiva," 18.
128. Fritiof Billquist, *Garbo: A Biography* (G. P. Putnam's Sons, 1960), 48.
129. Ingrid Luterkort, *Om igen, herr Molander! Kungl. Dramatiska teaterns elevskola, 1787–1964* (Stockholmia förlag, 1998), 143.

130. Sven Broman, *Garbo on Garbo* (Bloomsbury, 1991), 7.
131. Ruth Biery, "The Story of Greta Garbo," *Photoplay*, April 1928.
132. Gustaf Molander, archives, 1922–23, A553, Music and Theatre Library of Sweden, Stocholm (brackets in the original).
133. Molander, archives.
134. Greta Garbo to Mimi Pollak, letter, undated, but possibly 1923, author's personal collection.
135. Luterkort, *Om igen, herr Molander!*
136. "Dramaten's Archive Role Book," Dramaten, accessed August 29, 2025, https://www.dramaten.se/rollboken?detail=&type=&search=. I did an analysis of the Dramaten online role book, which lists all performers in named roles.
137. "Greta Garbo-Successful Student at the Dramaten Student School," Dramaten, accessed May 2021, https://www.dramaten.se/kronlunds-kronika/greta-garbo-framgangsrik-elev-pa-dramatens-elevskola.
138. A play by Pär Lagerkvist still in development at that time.
139. Alf Sjöberg, "Hon fick avgiva ett heligt löfte att aldrig vidare ägna sig åt film" [She had to make a sacred promise never to devote herself to film again], *Hänt i Veckan*, January 9, 1970, 17.
140. Lena Cederström, "Innan Hon Blev Stjärna," *Scenen*, no. 19 (1930): 521.
141. Cederström, "Innan Hon Blev Stjärna," 521 (brackets in the original).
142. "Greta Garbo-Successful Student."
143. Billquist, *Garbo: A Biography*, 48.
144. Billquist, *Garbo: A Biography*, 50.
145. Billquist, *Garbo: A Biography*, 220.
146. Susan Flakes, "Theatre in Swedish Society," *The Drama Review* 26, no. 2 (Fall 1982): 84.
147. Edward F. Sundberg, "The Swedish Theatre-1900–1950" (thesis, University of Wyoming, 1954), 84.
148. John Lewis Austin, "Intima Teatern and the Formations of Theatrical Modernity in Sweden" (thesis, University of Illinois Urbana-Champaign, 1997), 87.
149. Austin, "Intima Teatern," 87.
150. Austin, "Intima Teatern," 79.
151. Austin, "Intima Teatern," 79-80.
152. Lennart Forslund and Sverker R. Ek, *Teater I Stockholm 1910–1970* (Almqvist & Wiksell, 1982).
153. Frederick J. Marker and Lise-Lone Marker, *A History of Scandinavian Theater* (Cambridge University Press, 1996), 299.
154. Alrik Gustafson, "The Scandinavian Countries," in *A History of Modern Drama*, ed. Barrett Clark and George Freedley (D. Appleton-Century, 1947), 2.
155. Robert Knopf, "Intimate Theater/Chamber Drama," in *Theater of the Avant-Garde, 1890–1950: A Critical Anthology*, ed. Robert Knopf (Yale University Press, 2001), 105; Gustafson, "The Scandinavian Countries," 1–2.
156. Marker and Marker, *Scandinavian Theater*, 231; Austin, "Intima Teatern," 108.
157. Marker and Marker, *Scandinavian Theater*, 228.
158. Sundberg, "The Swedish Theatre," 102–4.
159. Bengt Forslund, *Victor Sjöström* (New York Zoetrope, 1988), 179.
160. This film is also known as The Saga of Gösta Berling, The Story of Gösta Berling, and The Atonement of Gösta Berling.

161. Willmar Sauter, email to author, March 28, 2021.
162. John Lewis Austin, "Intima Teatern and the Formations of Theatrical Modernity in Sweden" (thesis, University of Illinois Urbana-Champaign, 1997), 56.
163. Forslund, *Victor Sjöström*, 96.
164. Gustaf Molander, archives, 1922–23, A553, Music and Theatre Library of Sweden, Stockholm.
165. Victor Sjöström, *As I Remember* (Varen, 1951), 2.
166. Bo Florin, *Transition and Transformation: Victor Sjöström in Hollywood 1923–1930* (Amsterdam University Press, 2013), 19.
167. Anders Marklund, "The Golden Age and Late Silent Cinema," in *Swedish Film*, ed. Mariah Larsson and Anders Marklund (Nordic Academic Press, 2010), 72.
168. Bo Florin, "Victor Sjöström and the Golden Age," in *Swedish Film*, ed. Mariah Larsson and Anders Marklund (Nordic Academic Press, 2010), 82.
169. Forslund, *Victor Sjöström*, 97.
170. Forslund, *Victor Sjöström*, 118.
171. Hans Pensel, Seastrom and Stiller in Hollywood (Vantage Press, 1969), 51.
172. Forslund, *Victor Sjöström*, 98.
173. Forslund, *Victor Sjöström*, 109.
174. Victor Sjöström is an important element of this story. When he signed with MGM and moved to America his name was anglicized to Victor "Seastrom," but they are one and the same person. I have used Victor Sjöström except where I am quoting other writers.
175. Forslund, *Victor Sjöström*, 107
176. Forslund, *Victor Sjöström*, 112.
177. Victor Sjöström to Hjalmar Bergman, letter, November 9, 1922, author's personal collection.
178. Forslund, *Victor Sjöström*, 120-121.
179. Forslund, *Victor Sjöström*, 120-121.
180. Forslund, *Victor Sjöström*, 122.
181. Mauritz Stiller to Charles Magnusson, letter, August 2, 1925, Stiller file, Swedish Film Institute, Stockholm.
182. Alexander Walker, *Garbo* (Macmillan, 1980), 22.
183. Lennart Forslund and Sverker R. Ek, *Teater I Stockholm 1910–1970* (Almqvist & Wiksell, 1982), 95.
184. Lillemor Ring, email to author, November 18, 2021.
185. Rilla Page Palmborg, "The Mysterious Stranger," *Motion Picture*, May 1926, 15.
186. Faith Service [Gladys Hall], "Greta Garbo: Find," *Movie Magazine*, September 1925, 15.
187. Ruth Biery, "The Story of Greta Garbo," *Photoplay*, April 1928.
188. Biery, "The Story of Greta Garbo," April 1928.
189. Service, "Greta Garbo: Find," 90.
190. Ragnar Hyltén-Cavallius, "Hur Stiller 'upptäckte' Greta Garbo," *Stockholm Dagblad*, October 26, 1933.
191. Ragnar Hyltén-Cavallius, *Följa sin Genius* (Lars Hökerberg, 1960), 221.
192. Biery, "The Story of Greta Garbo," April 1928.
193. John Bainbridge, *Garbo* (Doubleday, 1955), 53.
194. Ruth Biery, "The Story of Greta Garbo," *Photoplay*, May 1928.

195. Elizabeth A. de Noma, "Multiple Melodrama: The Making and Remaking of Three Selma Lagerl of Narratives in the Silent Era and the 1940s" (thesis, University of Washington, 2000), 52.
196. Sandra Walker, "A Formal and Stylistic Analysis of the Early Films of F. W. Murnau Within the Context of Swedish and German Cinema" (thesis, University of Zurich, 2006), 49.
197. Stephan Brecht, ed., *Bertolt Brecht Letters 1913–1956* (Methuen, 1990), 78.
198. A separate shorter version was created for those markets where the longer version was deemed too long for the audience.
199. Biery, "The Story of Greta Garbo," May 1928.
200. Biery, "The Story of Greta Garbo," May 1928.
201. Karin Swanström interview, *New York Herald Tribune*, December 20, 1936.
202. Ragnar Hyltén-Cavallius, datebook, Stiller file, Swedish Film Institute, Stockholm.
203. Hyltén-Cavallius, *Följa sin Genius*, 221.
204. Swanström interview, December 20, 1936.
205. "Bakom Gösta Berlingsfilmens Kulisser," *Filmnyheter*, April 7, 1924.
206. Robin Hood [Bengt Idestam-Almquist], "Halvårs ateljétortyr för Garbo när 'Gösta Berling' spelades," *Stockholms-Tidningen*, March 7, 1954, p. 1.
207. Inga Gaate, "De unga grevinnorna Dohna," *Filmjournalen*, March 16, 1924, p. 85.
208. Gaate, "De unga grevinnorna Dohna," p. 85.
209. Gaate, "De unga grevinnorna Dohna," p. 85.
210. Hyltén-Cavallius, "Hur Stiller 'upptäckte' Greta Garbo."
211. Biery, "The Story of Greta Garbo," May 1928.
212. Dag Kronlund, conversation with author, September 14, 2021.
213. Gladys Hird, "Daniel Hjort: Classic or Outdated Nationalist Drama?," *Scandinavian Studies* 54, no. 2 (1984): 124.
214. *Stockholms Dagblad*, February 18, 1924.
215. "Greta Garbo-Successful Student at the Dramaten Student School," Dramaten, accessed May 2021, https://www.dramaten.se/kronlunds-kronika/greta-garbo-framgangsrik-elev-pa-dramatens-elevskola.
216. "Dramaliska teaterns elevmatiné," *Dagens Nyheter*, February 18, 1924, p. 9
217. *Stockholms-Tidningen*, February 18, 1924.
218. "Vem Är Greta Garbo," *Filmnyheter*, January 14, 1924, 10.
219. *Filmnyheter*, March 17, 1924, cover
220. *Filmjournalen*, March 30, 1924, p. 229.
221. Karen Vedel, "The Performance of Pictorialist Dance Photography," *Nordic Theatre Studies* 29, no. 1 (2017): 144–45.
222. Leif Wigh, "Henry B. Goodwin's Women," in *The Frozen Image: Scandinavian Photography*, ed. Martin Friedman (Abbeville, 1982), 98, 100.
223. Eva-Lena Karlsson and Magnus Olausson, "Henry B. Goodwin—A Visual Artist with the Camera as His Tool," in *Art Bulletin of Nationalmuseum Stockholm*, ed. Ludvig Florén, Magnus Olausson, and Martin Olin, vols. 24–25 (Susanna Pettersson, 2017–18), 89–90.<?>.
224. Rolf Söderberg, Henry B. Goodwin (Alfabeta, 1987), 11.
225. Karlsson and Olausson, "Henry B. Goodwin," 24–25:90.
226. Vedel, "Pictorialist Dance Photography," 153 (brackets in the original).<?>.
227. *Filmbladet*, April 19, 1924, 14.

228. "Den Första Delen av Gösta Berling Premiär Går," *Svenska Dagbladet*, Mar. 11, 1924, p. 7.
229. Biery, "The Story of Greta Garbo," May 1928.
230. Carla Waal, *Harriet Bosse: Strindberg's Muse and Interpreter* (Southern Illinois University Press, 1990), 198.
231. I will use Constantinople where the city is referred to by that name in historical documents. Otherwise I will use the modern name Istanbul.
232. "Greta Garbo Filmar Även I År," *Filmnyheter*, August 18, 1924, 1.
233. Ruth Biery, "The Story of Greta Garbo," *Photoplay*, May 1928.
234. Ragnar Hyltén-Cavallius, "Hur Stiller 'upptäckte' Greta Garbo," *Stockholm Dagblad*, October 26, 1933.
235. Ragnar Hyltén-Cavallius, *Följa sin Genius* (Lars Hökerberg, 1960), 221.
236. Greta Garbo to Mimi Pollak, letter, July 1924, author's personal collection.
237. Mauritz Stiller to Greta Garbo, letter, September 13, 1924, author's personal collection.
238. Greta Garbo to Mimi Pollak, letter, September 1924, author's personal collection.
239. Garbo to Pollak, September 1924.
240. Garbo to Pollak, September 1924.
241. David Schratter to Mauritz Stiller, letter, March 20, 1924, no. 24, Victor Sjöström arkiv/Mauritz Stiller papper, Swedish Film Institute, Stockholm.
242. Robin Hood [Bengt Idestam-Almquist], "Rysk flyktings inkliv genom fönster påBragevägen ledde till Greta Garbos USA-färd mot berömmelse," *Stockholms-Tidningen*, March 10, 1954, p. 1.
243. Robin Hood [Bengt Idestam Almquist], "Rysk flyktings," p. 1.
244. Robin Hood [Bengt Idestam-Almquist], "Rysk flyktings," p. 1.
245. *The New York Herald*, October 15, 1921, p. 22.
246. Bo Florin and Patrick Vonderau, *A Tale from Constantinople: The History of a Film That Never Was* (Brutus Östlings Bokförlag Symposion, 2019), 33.
247. Florin and Vonderau, *A Tale from Constantinople*, 44.
248. Mauritz Stiller, financial information, 1924, no. 24, Victor Sjöström arkiv/Mauritz Stiller papper, Swedish Film Institute, Stockholm.
249. Stiller, financial information.
250. Mauritz Stiller to David Schratter, handwritten note, May 22, 1924, no. 24, Victor Sjöström arkiv/Mauritz Stiller papper, Swedish Film Institute, Stockholm.
251. Stiller, financial information.
252. Florin and Vonderau, *A Tale from Constantinople*, 61.
253. Florin and Vonderau, *A Tale from Constantinople*, 61-62.
254. Florin and Vonderau, *A Tale from Constantinoplee*, 63.
255. "Regissör Stillers nya film," *Aftonbladet*, August 15, 1924, p. 10.
256. Biery, "The Story of Greta Garbo," May 1928.
257. Stiller to Garbo, September 13, 1924.
258. Biery, "The Story of Greta Garbo," May 1928, 127.
259. Biery, "The Story of Greta Garbo," May 1928, 127.
260. Biery, "The Story of Greta Garbo," May 1928, 127.
261. Florin and Vonderau, *A Tale from Constantinople*, 66.
262. "Gösta Berling," *Der Film*, August 24, 1924, 49.
263. "Gösta Berling," 49.

264. Fred Hildenbrandt, "Gösta Berling," review of Gösta Berling, *Berliner Tageblatt*, August 20, 1924.
265. "Gösta Berling," *Vorwärts*, August 21, 1924.
266. Kurt Pinthus, "Gösta Berling als Film," review of *Gösta Berling, 8 Uhr-Abendblatt*, August 19, 1924.
267. Biery, "The Story of Greta Garbo," May 1928.
268. "Greta Garbo-Successful Student at the Dramaten Student School," Dramaten, accessed May 2021, https://www.dramaten.se/kronlunds-kronika/greta-garbo-framgangsr-ik-elev-pa-dramatens-elevskola.
269. Greta Garbo to Mimi Pollak, letter, September 15, 1924, author's personal collection.
270. Mauritz Stiller to Greta Garbo, letter, October 19, 1924, author's personal collection.
271. Greta Garbo to Mimi Pollak, letter, November 1924, author's personal collection.
272. Greta Garbo to Mimi Pollak, letter, October 1924, author's personal collection.
273. Florin and Vonderau, *A Tale from Constantinople*, 248.
274. Garbo to Pollak, September 15, 1924.
275. Garbo to Pollak, October 1924.
276. Garbo to Pollak, October 1924.
277. MGM to Mauritz Stiller, telegram, November 8, 1924, author's personal collection.
278. Alma Söderhjelm, *Mina sju magra år* [My seven lean years] (Albert Bonniers Förlag, 1932), 199.
279. Gustaf Molander, archives, 1922–23, A553, Music and Theatre Library of Sweden, Stockholm.
280. Irene Selznick, *A Private View* (Knopf, 1983), 60.
281. Biery, "The Story of Greta Garbo," May 1928.
282. Florin and Vonderau, *A Tale from Constantinople*, 83.
283. Hyltén-Cavallius, *Följa sin Genius*, 228.
284. Hyltén-Cavallius, "Hur Stiller 'upptäckte' Greta Garbo."
285. Stiller, financial information.
286. Hyltén-Cavallius, *Följa sin Genius*, 233.
287. Ragnar Hyltén-Cavallius, overwrap to Odalisque manuscript, Swedish Film Institute, Stockholm.
288. "Sex nationer berätta julseder," *Svenska Dagbladet*, December 20, 1938, p. 7.
289. Greta Garbo to Vera Schmiterlöw, letter, January 1, 1925, author's personal collection.
290. Biery, "The Story of Greta Garbo," May 1928.
291. Garbo to Schmiterlöw, January 1, 1925.
292. "Heft 3," *Das Tagebuch*, January 27, 1925, p. 103.
293. "Heft 3," *Das Tagebuch*, January 27, 1925, p. 103.
294. Biery, "The Story of Greta Garbo," May 1928.
295. Loew's had owned the Metro Pictures studio as a wholly owned subsidiary. It acquired and merged Goldwyn Pictures and Louis B. Mayer Pictures with Metro Pictures. Originally named Metro-Goldwyn, it eventually changed its name to Metro-Goldwyn-Mayer, or MGM.
296. Mauritz Stiller to Greta Garbo, telegram, January 20, 1925, author's personal collection.
297. At the time the official name of the company was Metro-Goldwyn. It was not changed to Metro-Goldwyn-Mayer until January 1926. To simplify the narrative I will use Metro-Goldwyn-Mayer, or MGM, throughout, unless the use is part of a quote.

298. Victor Sjöström to Mauritz Stiller, telegram, February 7, 1925, author's personal collection.
299. Michael Wolffsohn, "Die Lichtbildbühne und Karl Wolffsohn," November 9, 2015, https://www.wolffsohn.de/cms/images/Snippets_pdf/rede-gedenktafel-lichtbildbuehne.pdf.
300. "Here Is 'Miss Sweden,'" *Oakland Tribune*, August 27, 1924, p. 12.
301. H.D. [Hilda Doolittle], "The Cinema and the Classics I: Beauty," *Close Up*, July 1927, 28.
302. Alexandra Seibel, *Visions of Vienna: Narrating the City in 1920s and 1930s Cinema* (Amsterdam University Press, 2017), 111–13.
303. Seibel, *Visions of Vienna*, 111–13.
304. Sara F. Hall, "Inflation and Devaluation—Gender, Space and Economics in GW Pabst's Joyless Street," in *Weimar Cinema: An Essential Guide to Classic Films of the Era*, ed. Noah Isenberg (Columbia University Press, 2009), 136. It was published as a novel in 1924 and sold three hundred thousand copies in that year. It was then printed in several languages for other countries.
305. "Memories of Assistant Director Mark Sorkin," *Die freudlose Gasse = The Joyless Street* (Film und kunst GmbH, 2015), DVD disc 2, quoted in Vasiliki Sakellariou, "The Representation of a Society in Distress: Hugo Bettauer's Novel *The Joyless Street* Through its Filmic Adaptation" (thesis, University of Caen, 2020), 10. Mark Sorkin (1902–1986) was G. W. Pabst's film editor and a close associate.
306. Hall, "Inflation and Devaluation," 137.
307. Lee Atwell, *G. W. Pabst* (Twayne, 1977), 35.
308. Natalia Poljakowa, "The Distribution, Censorship and Reception of German Films in Soviet Russia of the 1920s" (thesis, University of London, 2015), 80–81.
309. Sakellariou, "Representation of a Society," 11–12.
310. Murray G. Hall, "Hugo Bettauer," in *Elektrische Schatten: Beiträge zur österreichischen Stummfilmgeschichte*, ed. F. Bono et al. (Filmarchiv Austria, 1999), 159, quoted in Seibel, *Visions of Vienna*, 113–14.
311. Bernd Widdig, *Culture and Inflation in Weimar Germany* (University of California Press, 2001), 215–16.
312. Widdig, *Culture and Inflation*, 213–15.
313. Hall, "Inflation and Devaluation," 142.
314. Widdig, *Culture and Inflation*, 215–20.
315. Seibel, *Visions of Vienna*, 118–19.
316. Jenelle Troxell, "'Light Filtering Through Those Shutters': Joyless Streets, Mnemic Symbols, and the Beginnings of Feminist Film Criticism," *Camera Obscura* 34, no. 3 (2019): 88.
317. Troxell, "'Light Filtering,'" 75.
318. Hall, "Inflation and Devaluation," 151.
319. Hall, "Inflation and Devaluation," 152.
320. Paul Rotha, *The Film till Now: The Film Since Then* (Spring Books, 1970), 37.
321. Jan-Christopher Horak, "Film History and Film Preservation: Reconstructing the Text of *The Joyless Street* (1925)," in *Screening the Past: Film and the Representation of History*, ed. Tony Barta (Praeger, 1998).
322. Matthew D. Harrington, "G. W. Pabst and the New Objectivity: Social Criticism and the Loss of Idealism in the Weimar Republic" (thesis, Virginia Polytechnic Institute and State University, 2002), 44.
323. "The Joyless Alley in Staaken," *Der Film*, March 1, 1925.
324. Greta Garbo to Mimi Pollak, letter, March 9, 1925, author's personal collection.
325. Garbo to Pollak, March 9, 1925.

326. Sandra Walker, "A Formal and Stylistic Analysis of the Early Films of F. W. Murnau Within the Context of Swedish and German Cinema" (thesis, University of Zurich, 2006), 80.
327. "Latest Movies—*Die freudlose Gasse*," *Der Film*, May 24, 1925, 20.
328. "*Die freudlose Gasse*," *Reichsfilmblatt*, May 23, 1925.
329. "*Die freudlose Gasse*," *Reichsfilmblatt*, May 23, 1925.
330. "*Die freudlose Gasse*," *Deutsche Filmwoche*, May 29, 1925, 14.
331. "*Die freudlose Gasse*," *Film-Kurier*, May 19, 1925.
332. Patrice Petro, *Joyless Streets* (Princeton University Press, 1989), 206–9.
333. Petro, *Joyless Streets*, 159.
334. Hall, "Inflation and Devaluation," 137.
335. Bryher [Annie Winifred Ellerman], "G. W. Pabst, a Survey," *Close Up*, December 1927, 58.
336. H.D. [Hilda Doolittle], "An Appreciation," *Close Up*, March 1929, 61.
337. H.D. [Hilda Doolittle], "The Cinema," 26–27.
338. Guido Seeber, "Die taumelnde Kamera," *Die Filmtechnik*, no. 5 (1925): 92–93.
339. Barry Paris, *Louise Brooks* (Alfred A. Knopf, 1989), 290.
340. Richard Abel, *French Cinema* (Princeton University Press, 1984), 260.
341. Poljakowa, "German Films," 107–8.
342. Greta Garbo to Mimi Pollak, letter, June 21, 1925, author's personal collection.
343. Greta Garbo to Mimi Pollak, letter, March 9, 1925, author's personal collection.
344. Garbo to Pollak, March 9, 1925.
345. Mauritz Stiller to Greta Garbo, letter, March 20, 1925, author's personal collection.
346. "Den svenska filmen i dödvatten," *Aftonbladet*, April 26, 1925.
347. "Goldwyn vill engagera svenskar!," *Svenska Dagbladet*, February 20, 1925, p. 9.
348. Robin Hood [Bengt Idestam-Almquist], "Skickligt, stilla och omärkligt dirigerade Garbo Hollywoodresan" [Skillfully, quietly and imperceptibly, Garbo directed the Hollywood journey], *Stockholms-Tidningen*, March 14, 1954, p. 16.
349. Bengt Forslund, *Victor Sjöström* (New York Zoetrope, 1988), 205.
350. Mauritz Stiller to Charles Magnusson, letter, August 2, 1925, Stiller file, Swedish Film Institute, Stockholm.
351. Greta Garbo archive, Swedish Film Institute, Stockholm.
352. Jürgen Spiker, *Film und Kapital* (Berlin, 1975), 125–26.
353. "German Film Wages Reduced," *The Film Mercury*, April 16, 1926, 7.
354. Garbo, archive.
355. Greta Garbo to Mimi Pollak, letter, April 11, 1925, author's personal collection.
356. Greta Garbo to Julius Pollak, letter, June 5, 1925, author's personal collection.
357. Garbo to Pollak, June 5, 1925.
358. Garbo to Pollak, June 5, 1925.
359. Kristen Thompson, *Exporting Entertainment* (British Film Institute, 1985), 113.
360. Dieter Baretzko, *Illusionen in Stein* (Reinbeck, 1985), quoted in Klaus Kreimeier, *The Ufa Story* (University of California Press, 1996), 123.
361. Joseph Garncarz, "Art and Industry: German Cinema of the 1920s," in *The Silent Cinema Reader*, ed. Lee Grieveson and Peter Krämer (Routledge, 2004), 394.
362. Alma Söderhjelm, *Mina sju magra år* [My seven lean years] (Albert Bonniers Förlag, 1932), 199.

363. Söderhjelm, Mina sju magra år, 199.
364. MGM to Mauritz Stiller, telegram, February 25, 1925, author's personal collection.
365. Stiller to Magnusson, August 2, 1925. This letter is a unique document. The topics go back over several years. It reads as somewhat of a stream of consciousness and references communications, decisions, and events that are unknown other than being mentioned in the letter.
366. Stiller to Magnusson, August 2, 1925.
367. Stiller to Magnusson, August 2, 1925.
368. Garbo to Pollak, June 21, 1925.
369. Greta Garbo to Lars Saxon, letter, June 24, 1925, author's personal collection.
370. Bernard Rosenberg and Harry Silverstein, *The Real Tinsel* (Macmillan, 1970), 122.
371. *Variety*, April 8, 1925.
372. *Aftonbladet*, August 9, 1925, p. 6.
373. Ruth Biery, "The Story of Greta Garbo," *Photoplay*, May 1928.
374. Darla Miller, "Publicist Recalls Glamorous Days of Crawford and Garbo," *Boca Raton News*, March 20, 1979, p. 6B.
375. Ruth Biery, "The Story of Greta Garbo," *Photoplay*, June 1928.
376. Biery, "The Story of Greta Garbo," June 1928.
377. Arnold Genthe, "Rebellion in Photography," *Overland Monthly*, August 1901.
378. Genthe, "Rebellion in Photography."
379. Genthe, "Rebellion in Photography."
380. "Genthe Collection," Library of Congress, accessed September 19, 2025, https://www.loc.gov/collections/genthe/about-this-collection/. Upon his death in 1942, Arnold Genthe donated all of the negatives and prints in his possession to the Library of Congress.
381. Isadora Duncan, *My Life* (Boni & Liveright, 1927), 327.
382. Elspeth H. Brown, *The Corporate Eye: Photography and the Rationalization of American Commercial Culture 1884–1929* (Johns Hopkins University Press, 2005), 206.
383. "Greta Garbo's Favorite Photographer," *Popular Photography*, March 1938, 96.
384. Karen Vedel, "The Performance of Pictorialist Dance Photography," *Nordic Theatre Studies* 29, no. 1 (2017): 143.
385. Matthew Reason, "Still Moving: The Revelation or Representation of Dance in Still Photography," *Dance Research Journal* 35, no. 2 (Winter 2003) and 36, no. 1 (Summer 2004): 43.
386. Arnold Genthe, *As I Remember* (Reynal & Hitchcock, 1937), 166.
387. Robert Dance and Bruce Robertson, *Ruth Harriet Louise and Hollywood Glamour Photography* (University of California Press, 2002), 161–62.
388. Gerben Bakker, "The Decline and Fall of the European Film Industry: Sunk Costs, Market Size and Market Structure, 1890–1927" (working paper no. 70/03, Department of Economic History, London School of Economics, February 2003), 22.
389. Hans Pensel, *Seastrom and Stiller in Hollywood* (Vantage Press, 1969), 56.
390. Rilla Page Palmborg, "The Mysterious Stranger," *Motion Picture*, May 1926, 51.
391. Nick Schenck, written response, Bosley Crowther papers, Special Collections, Brigham Young University.
392. Greta Garbo to Mimi Pollak, letter, October 4, 1925, author's personal collection.
393. Louise Brooks, "Gish and Garbo: The Executive War on Stars," Sight and Sound, Winter 1958, 15.

394. Bosley Crowther, *The Lion's Share* (E. P. Dutton, 1957), 124.
395. Ruth Biery, "The Story of Greta Garbo," *Photoplay*, June 1928.
396. Dan Van Neste, *The Magnificent Heel: The Life and Films of Ricardo Cortez* (BearManor Media, 2017), 66.
397. William Daniels, oral interviews, Margaret Herrick Library, Academy of Motion Picture Arts and Sciences, Beverly Hills, CA.
398. *Exhibitors Herald*, January 9, 1926, p. 40.
399. C. E. N., review of *Torrent*, *Hollywood Daily Citizen*, February 6, 1926, p. 3.
400. *Variety*, January 27, 1926, 29.
401. "Irving Thalberg May Make More Stars," *Variety*, January 27, 1926.
402. *Exhibitors Herald*, December 25, 1925, p. 85.
403. Andrea Comiskey, "The Sticks, Nabes, and the Broadways: U.S. Film Distribution, 1935–1940" (thesis, University of Wisconsin, 2015), 86.
404. Stuart Galbraith, *Motor City Marquees* (McFarland, 1994), 56.
405. Henry Aldridge, "Live Musical and Theatrical Presentations in Detroit Moving Picture Theaters: 1896–1930" (thesis, University of Michigan, 1972), 232.
406. "*Torrent*—(Original Trailer)," Turner Classic Movies, accessed September 23, 2025, https://www.tcm.com/video/95031/torrent-original-trailer/.
407. Unsigned review of *Torrent*, *Photoplay*, May 1926, 118.
408. While film rental grosses can be found for most studios, there were no national box office reports. Variety compiled ticket sales from a sample of first-run theaters, but film historians believe that these reports were not always correct. Days booked per theater is a squishier statistic, but it is the best proxy.
409. Fred, review of Torrent, *Variety*, February 24, 1926, 4.
410. *Exhibitors Herald*, March 20, 1926, p. 60.
411. Laurence Reid, *Motion Picture*, May 1926, 65
412. Lea Jacobs, *The Decline of Sentiment: American Film in the 1920s* (University of California Press, 2008), 258.
413. Jacobs, *Decline of Sentiment*, 259.
414. Fred, review of *Torrent*, 42.
415. Alexander Walker, *Stardom* (Stein and Day, 1970), 140.
416. NIE, review of *Torrent*, *St. Louis Post-Dispatch*, March 1, 1926, p. 17.
417. L. E. Sanborn, "$10.00 Letter," *Photoplay*, June 1926, 10.
418. *Variety*, March 10, 1926, 33.
419. *Variety*, March 24, 1926, 28.
420. *Variety*, March 3, 1926, 30. Rube Wolf was a band leader and comedian.
421. Betsy Erkkila, "Greta Garbo: Sailing Beyond the Frame," *Critical Inquiry* 11, no. 4 (June 1985): 598.
422. *Santa Monica Outlook*, January 10, 1927.
423. Greta Garbo to Lars Saxon, letter, February 14, 1926, author's personal collection
424. Greta Garbo to Mimi Pollak, letter, March 4, 1926, author's personal collection.
425. .Garbo to Pollak, March 4, 1926.
426. Garbo to Pollak, March 4, 1926.
427. Garbo to Pollak, March 4, 1926.

428. Garbo to Pollak, March 4, 1926.
429. Garbo to Pollak, March 4, 1926.
430. Helen Louise Walker, "A Woman Alone," *Picture Play*, October 1937, 16.
431. Irene Selznick, *A Private View* (Knopf, 1983), 60.
432. Unsigned review of Torrent, *Long Beach Press-Telegram*, February 28, 1926, p. 43.
433. Laurence Reid, *"Ibanez' Torrent," Motion Picture*, May 1926, 65.
434. Robert E. Sherwood, *"The Temptress," Life*, November 4, 1926, 26.
435. Mordaunt Hall, "Greta Garbo's Intelligent Acting," *The New York Times*, December 4, 1927, sec. X, p. 7.
436. Frederick Smith, "The Celluloid Critic," *Motion Picture Classic*, May 1926, 50.
437. Elise Dufour, "Imagination in the Motion Pictures," *Hollywood Topics*, Jan. 15, 1927, 30.
438. Greta Garbo to Mimi Pollak, letter, September 1, 1926, author's personal collection.
439. Mordaunt Hall, "Hollywood Surprises New Swedish Actress," *The New York Times*, February 28, 1926, p. X4.
440. Roberta Pearson, *Eloquent Gestures: The Transformation of Performance Style in the Griffith Biograph Films* (University of California Press, 1992), 21.
441. Pearson, *Eloquent Gestures*, 1–17.
442. Marguerite Tazelaar, "The Garbo as Seen by Her Cameraman," *Queenslander*, July 25, 1935, 3.
443. Barry Paris, *Garbo: A Biography* (Knopf, 1995), 549.
444. Robert Gottlieb, *Garbo* (Farrar, Straus and Giroux, 2021), 3.
445. Sven Broman, *Conversations with Greta Garbo* (Viking, 1991), 64–65.
446. Ragnar Hyltén-Cavallius, *Följa sin Genius* (Lars Hökerberg, 1960), 226.
447. Alexander Walker, *Stardom* (Stein and Day, 1970), 145.
448. 448 Betsy Erkkila, "Greta Garbo: Sailing Beyond the Frame," Critical Inquiry 11, no. 4 (June 1985): 599–601.
449. Rilla Page Palmborg, The Private Life of Greta Garbo (Doubleday, Doran, 1931), 173–74.
450. Mordaunt Hall, *The New York Times*, July 28, 1929, p. 101.
451. "Garbo a New Type of Actress For Film World," *Santa Monica Outlook*, April 25, 1928.
452. Sergei Eisenstein, *Immortal Memories* (Houghton Mifflin, 1983), 156.
453. Greta Garbo to Peg Gustafson, letter, after May 25, 1945, based on dated enclosure, author's personal collection.
454. Ruth Waterbury, "The Revolt of the Angel," *Photoplay*, March 1927.
455. Norman Zierold, *Garbo* (Stein and Day, 1969), 86.
456. Paul Hawkins, "A New Slant on Garbo," *Screenland*, June 1931, 20.
457. Harold Benton, "Bless You My Children," *Photoplay*, March 1933, 71.
458. Whitney Stone, *I'd Love to Kiss You . . . Conversations with Bette Davis* (Pocket Books, 1990), 146.
459. Erkkila, "Sailing Beyond the Frame," 596.
460. Adela Rogers St. Johns, *Liberty*, July 27, 1929.
461. Scene stills, 1926, Photography Archive, Margaret Herrick Library, Academy of Motion Picture Arts and Sciences, Beverly Hills, CA; Scene stills, 1926, author's personal collection.
462. Sven Broman, *Conversations with Greta Garbo* (Viking, 1991), 62.
463. Greta Garbo to Lars Saxon, letter, March or April 1926, author's personal collection.

464. John Bainbridge, *Garbo* (Doubleday, 1955), 101–2.
465. Ursula Hardt, *From Caligari to California* (Berghahn Books, 1996), 96.
466. Hans Pensel, *Seastrom and Stiller in Hollywood* (Vantage Press, 1969), 62.
467. Ruth Biery, "The Story of Greta Garbo," *Photoplay*, June 1928.
468. Greta Garbo to Mimi Pollak, letter, December 16, 1925, author's personal collection.
469. Pensel, *Seastrom and Stiller*, 72.
470. "MGM Releases Set," *The Film Daily*, July 30, 1926, p. 1.
471. "Editing Rushed on '*The Temptress*,'" *The Film Mercury*, September 10, 1926, 20.
472. "August 22 MGM," *The Film Daily*, July 30, 1926, p. 3.
473. Lea Jacobs, *The Decline of Sentiment: American Film in the 1920s* (University of California Press, 2008), 239–40.
474. "'*Temptress*' with Sad Ending for Ohio Exhibitors," *Motion Picture News*, December 11, 1926.
475. Garbo to Saxon, March or April 1926.
476. "Joel McCrea Once Doubled for Garbo, of All Things!," *Brooklyn Daily Eagle*, March 1, 1942.
477. Greta Garbo to Mimi Pollak, letter, November 23, 1926, author's personal collection.
478. Unsigned review of *The Temptress, Photoplay,* December 1926, 52.
479. Unsigned review of *The Temptress, Los Angeles Times,* October 3, 1926, p. 147.
480. Mordaunt Hall, "Another Ibáñez Story," *The New York Times*, October 11, 1926, p. 18.
481. Greta Garbo to Vera Schmiterlöw, letter, June 29, 1926, Riksarkivet, Stockholm.
482. Frederick Lewis Allen, "Since Yesterday," *Harper's Magazine*, November 1939, 610.
483. Nancy Cott, *The Grounding of Modern Feminism* (Yale University Press, 1987), 3–10.
484. John D'Emilio and Estelle Freedman, *Intimate Matters* (Univ. of Chicago Press, 2012), 189.
485. Liz Conor, *The Spectacular Modern Woman: Feminine Visibility in the 1920s* (Indiana University Press, 2004), 46.
486. Frederick Collins, "What She Wanted, She Got," in *The New American Woman Revisited*, ed. Martha H. Patterson (Rutgers University Press, 2008), 122.
487. Bridgette Søland, *Becoming Modern: Young Women and the Reconstruction of Womanhood in the 1920s* (Princeton University Press, 2000), 9.
488. Ben Singer, *Melodrama and Modernity* (Columbia University Press, 2001). This is a simplification of the argument Singer makes regarding what modernity meant.
489. Peter Filene, *Him/Her/Self: Sex Roles in Modern America* (Johns Hopkins University Press, 1986), 125.
490. Beth L. Bailey, *From Front Porch to Back Seat* (Johns Hopkins University Press, 1988), 19.
491. Paula Fass, *The Damned and the Beautiful* (Oxford University Press, 1977), 262–65.
492. Fass, *The Damned*, 22–23.
493. Bailey, *Front Porch*, 13.
494. D'Emilio and Freedman, *Intimate Matters*, 197.
495. Martha H. Patterson, ed., *The New American Woman Revisited* (Rutgers University Press, 2008), 17.
496. Kate Murphy, *Fears and Fantasies: Modernity, Gender, and the Rural-Urban Divide* (Peter Lang, 2010), 51.
497. Søland, *Becoming Modern*, 89.
498. Gregory Black, *Hollywood Censored* (Cambridge University Press, 1994), 39–40.

499. Martin Quigley, *Decency in Motion Pictures* (Macmillan, 1937), 5.
500. Alexander Walker, *Stardom* (Stein and Day, 1970), 145.
501. Lucy Fisher, "Greta Garbo: Fashioning a Star Image," in *Idols of Modernity: Movie Stars of the 1920s*, ed. Patrice Petro (Rutgers University Press, 2010), 137–38.
502. Fletcher Wilson, "Ricardo Cortez in Spectacles Revealed in '*Torrent*' at Garrick," review of *Torrent, Minneapolis Star Tribune*, February 21, 1926, p. 6.
503. Jim Tully, "Greta Garbo," *Vanity Fair*, June 1928.
504. Mollie Gray, review of *Flesh and the Devil, Variety*, January 26, 1927, 37.
505. Alf Sjöberg, "Hon fick avgiva ett heligt löfte att aldrig vidare ägna sig åt film" [She had to make a sacred promise never to devote herself to film again], *Hänt i Veckan*, January 9, 1970
506. Maureen Honey, "Gotham's Daughters: Feminism in the 1920s," *American Studies* 31, no. 1 (Spring 1990): 25.
507. Mick LaSalle, Complicated Women (St. Martin's Press, 2000), 36.
508. Honey, "Gotham's Daughters," 38–39.
509. Greg Smith, "Silencing the New Woman," *Journal of Film and Video* 48, no. 3 (Fall 1996): 4.
510. Ben Singer, *Melodrama and Modernity* (Columbia University Press, 2001), 221–24.
511. Maureen Honey, *Breaking the Ties That Bind* (University of Oklahoma Press, 1992), 3–6.
512. Jackie Stacey, *Star Gazing: Hollywood Cinema and Female Spectatorship* (Routledge, 1994), 174.
513. Norman Webb, "Story of the Box-Office," *Film Spectator*, August 20, 1927, 12.
514. In the silent era it was common for stars to make four films per year. If the start of Garbo's American career had followed standard form, she would have made six films in her first eighteen months.
515. Patrice Petro, *Joyless Streets* (Princeton University Press, 1989), 218–19.
516. Shelley Stamp, "'Exit Flapper, Enter Woman,' or Lois Weber in Jazz Age Hollywood," Framework: *The Journal of Cinema and Media* 51, no. 2 (Fall 2010): 365.
517. Greta Garbo to Mimi Pollak, letter, September 1, 1926, author's personal collection.
518. Thomas O. Service, review of *The Temptress, Exhibitor's Herald*, December 11, 1926, p. 51.
519. Andrew Sarris, *Confessions of a Cultist: On Cinema 1955–69* (Simon & Schuster, 1970), 141.
520. Lary May, *Screening Out the Past* (Oxford University Press, 1980), 220.
521. Sumiko Higashi, *Virgins, Vamps and Flappers* (Eden Press, 1978), 77.
522. "Title cards from 1:22:00 to 1:23:30," *The Temptress*, directed by Fred Niblo, from *The Garbo Silents Collection* (1926; TCM Archives, 2005), DVD.
523. Betsy Erkkila, "Greta Garbo: Sailing Beyond the Frame," *Critical Inquiry* 11, no. 4 (June 1985): 595–96.
524. Erkkila, "Sailing Beyond the Frame," 596–97.
525. "Women Enjoy Greta Garbo," *Los Angeles Evening Post-Record*, October 19, 1926, p. 2.
526. "Old Styles in Heroines Passé," *Los Angeles Times*, July 15, 1928, p. C29.
527. Tamar Lane, *The Film Mercury*, September 3, 1926, 3.
528. Richard Lippe, "Greta Garbo: The Star Image," *Cineaction!*, Winter 1992, 12–21.
529. Sid, review of Love, *Variety*, December 7, 1927, 18.
530. Waly, review of *The Single Standard, Variety*, July 31, 1929, 17.
531. Molly Haskell, *From Reverence to Rape* (Holt, Rinehart and Winston, 1973), 20.

532. Fisher, "Fashioning a Star Image," 141.
533. Molly Haskell, "Garbo Revisited," *Viva*, January 1974, 36–38.
534. Haskell, "Garbo Revisited," 36–38.
535. Haskell, "Garbo Revisited," 36–38.
536. Erkkila, "Sailing Beyond the Frame," 598.
537. *Photoplay*, August 1932, quoted in Adrienne L. McLean, *Glamour in a Golden Age: Movie Stars of the 1930s* (Rutgers University Press, 2010), 115–16.
538. Helen Appleton Read, "Changing Styles in Women's Beauty," *Brooklyn Eagle Magazine*, September 27, 1931, 81.
539. Adela Rogers St. John, Love Laughter and Tears (Doubleday, 1978), 247.
540. Greta Garbo to Lars Saxon, letter, August 1926, author's personal collection.
541. Garbo to Saxon, August 1926.
542. Garbo is altering the timeline as she did not hire Harry Edington as her agent until December 1926. She may be referring to her lawyer.
543. Ruth Biery, "The Story of Greta Garbo," *Photoplay*, June 1928, 144–45.
544. Doris Markham, "An Idyll or a Tragedy—Which?," *Motion Picture*, December 1926, 100.
545. MGM payroll ledgers, Margaret Herrick Library, Academy of Motion Picture Arts and Sciences, Beverly Hills, CA. They are only extant through August 31, 1926.
546. Gwenda Young, *Clarence Brown: Hollywood's Forgotten Master* (University Press of Kentucky, 2018), 73–74.
547. Eve Golden, *John Gilbert: Last of the Silent Film Stars* (University Press of Kentucky, 2013), 119.
548. Young, *Hollywood's Forgotten Master*, 75.
549. Charles Highman, *Hollywood Cameramen: Sources of Light* (Indiana University Press, 1970), 57.
550. Young, *Hollywood's Forgotten Master*, 77.
551. Markham, "Idyll or a Tragedy," 23.
552. Markham, "Idyll or a Tragedy," 23.
553. Young, *Hollywood's Forgotten Master*, 77.
554. "Forum Opening," *Hollywood Topics*, February 12, 1927, 12.
555. Fred, review of *Flesh and the Devil*, *Variety*, January 12, 1927, 14.
556. Fred, review of *Flesh and the Devil*.
557. *Photoplay*, February 1927, 52.
558. Mordaunt Hall, "The Undying Past," *The New York Times*, January 10, 1927, p. 20.
559. Lea Jacobs, *The Decline of Sentiment: American Film in the 1920s* (University of California Press, 2008), 245–46.
560. E. E. Laing [pseud.], *Greta Garbo: The Story of a Specialist* (John Gifford, 1946), 81.
561. *Variety*, February 23, 1927, 7. Washington, DC had segregated movie theaters.
562. Markham, "Idyll or a Tragedy," 23.
563. Sven Broman, *Conversations with Greta Garbo* (Viking, 1991), 62.
564. . Adela Rogers St. Johns, "Garbo, the Mystery of Hollywood," *Liberty*, July 27, 1929, 35.
565. King Vidor, *A Tree Is a Tree* (Harcourt, Brace, 1952), 135.
566. Basil Rathbone, *In and Out of Character* (Doubleday, 1962), 141.
567. Carey Wilson, "Stars Are Human After All," *Photoplay*, September 1936, 96.
568. *Detroit Free Press*, May 4, 1930, p. 3.

569. Colleen Moore, *Silent Star* (Doubleday, 1968), 204.
570. John Bainbridge, *Garbo* (Doubleday, 1955), 125.
571. Roland Flamini, *Thalberg: The Last Tycoon and the World of M-G-M* (Crown, 1994), 149.
572. Golden, *John Gilbert*, 88–89.
573. Richard Merryman, *Mank* (William Morrow, 1978), 210.
574. Rilla Page Palmborg, "Greta Garbo Has Her Say About These American Men," *Motion Picture*, February 1928, 59.
575. Greta Garbo to Mimi Pollak, letter, December 24, 1926, author's personal collection.
576. Agnes Smith, "Up Speaks a Gallant Loser," *Photoplay*, February 1927, 32.
577. Smith, "Gallant Loser," 32.
578. Adela Rogers St. Johns, *Love Laughter and Tears* (Doubleday, 1978), 247.
579. Moore, *Silent Star*, 201–2.
580. Golden, *John Gilbert*, 122–23.
581. *Coronet*, April 1942, 113.
582. David Naylor, *Great American Movie Theaters* (Preservation Press, 1987), 18.
583. If you do a Google search for "1930 film box office," the results will fall under a headline about box office, but the information will be data on film rentals. This is not the same as the box office information available today.
584. *The Motion Picture Almanac* (Quigley, 1929), 111.
585. Sidney Kent, "Distributing the Product," in *The Story of Films*, ed. Joseph Kennedy (A. W. Shaw, 1927), 216–18.
586. Handwritten spreadsheet of Loew's summary financials, 1921–1953, Bosley Crowther papers, Special Collections, Brigham Young University.
587. Eddie Mannix Ledger, Margaret Herrick Library, Academy of Motion Picture Arts and Sciences, Beverly Hills, CA.
588. Loew's summary financials, 1921–1953.
589. Miriam Hansen, "Pleasure, Ambivalence, Identification: Valentino and Female Spectatorship," *Cinema Journal* 25, no. 4 (Summer 1986): 6.
590. Mark Glancy, *Hollywood and the Americanization of Britain* (I. B, Tauris, 2014), 43–44.
591. Gail Studlar, "The Perils of Pleasure? Fan Magazine Discourse as Women's Commodified Culture in the 1920s," in *Silent Film*, ed. Richard Abel (Rutgers University Press, 1966), 263.
592. Martin Quigley written answers to submitted questions, 1934, GTM-GAMMS142, Martin J. Quigley Papers, Georgetown University Manuscripts.
593. See appendix 3.
594. Exhibitor's Herald, run by Martin Quigley, acquired Moving Picture World in 1927 and the combined publication was titled Exhibitor's Herald and Moving Picture World in 1928. It was retitled Exhibitor's Herald-World in 1929. At the end of 1930 Quigley bought Motion Picture News and the combined publication was titled Motion Picture Herald in 1931.
595. Ad placement, Hollywood Reporter, May 4, 1938.
596. Ad placement, Hollywood Reporter, May 4, 1938.
597. "Theater Man Says Film Concerns Kept Films from Him," *New York Tribune*, September 20, 1922, p. 7.
598. Joel Frykolm, *George Kleine & American Cinema* (Palgrave, 2015), 52.
599. Michael Conant, *Antitrust in the Motion Picture Industry* (University of California Press, 1960), 160.

600. Conant, *Antitrust*), 160.
601. Not all large theaters were first-run theaters. Size is a close enough proxy for being first run for this rough analysis.
602. Conant, Antitrust, 48.
603. Howard T. Lewis, The Motion Picture Industry (D. Van Nostrand, 1933), 150.
604. Kent, "Distributing the Product," 219.
605. *Film Daily Yearbook* (1927), 13. There are statistical briefs on this page.
606. "1930 Census: Volume 4. Occupations, by States. Reports by States, Giving Statistics for Cities of 25,000 or More," United States Census Bureau, accessed October 27, 2025, https://www.census.gov/library/publications/1933/dec/1930a-vol-04-occupations.html.
607. Estelle Freedman, "The New Woman: Changing Views of Women in the 1920s," in Decades of Discontent: *The Women's Movement, 1920–1940*, ed. Lois Scharf and Joan Jensen (Greenwood Press, 1983), 120–21.
608. Carolyn Strange, *Toronto's Girl Problem: The Perils and Pleasures of the City 1880–1930* (University of Toronto Press, 1995), 221.
609. Freedman, "The New Woman," 121.
610. Edward L. Glaeser, "Urban Colossus: Why is New York America's Largest City?," Working Paper No. 11398 (National Bureau of Economic Research, June 2005), 4.
611. Glaeser, "Urban Colossus," 22.
612. "1930 List of New York City's Steamship Companies. White-Orr's Business Directory," Brooklyn Genealogy Information Page, accessed October 27, 2025, https://bklyn-genealogy-info.stevemorse.org/Directory/1930.Steamship.html.
613. *Film Daily Yearbook* (1929), C.
614. John Sedgwick and Michael Pokorny, "The Film Business in the United States and Britain during the 1930s," *Economic History Review* 58, no. 1 (2005): 82.
615. *Pittsburgh Courier*, June 2, 1934, p. 8.
616. Mordaunt Hall, "The Hollywood Hermit," *The New York Times*, Mar. 24, 1929, sec. 10, p. 7.
617. Ruth Biery, "The Story of Greta Garbo," *Photoplay*, June 1928, 145.
618. "Gilbert-Garbo in Studio Tilt with MGM," *The Film Mercury*, November 12, 1927, 3.
619. Biery, "The Story of Greta Garbo," June 1928.
620. Mae Tinée, "This One is All to Merry Save for a Silly Story," review of *Women Love Diamonds*, *Chicago Tribune*, May 2, 1927, p. 29.
621. John Bainbridge, *Garbo* (Doubleday, 1955), 110.
622. *Picture Play*, May 1927, 68.
623. John Bainbridge, *Garbo* (Doubleday, 1955), 129.
624. Karen Swenson, *Greta Garbo: A Life Apart* (Scribner, 1997), 139.
625. Greta Garbo to Mimi Pollak, letter, November 22, 1926, author's personal collection.
626. Mauritz Stiller to Louis B. Mayer, letter, December 18, 1926, author's personal collection.
627. Stiller to Mayer, December 18, 1926.
628. Stiller to Mayer, December 18, 1926.
629. "Greta Garbo Educated on Contract, Resumes," *Variety*, January 26, 1927, 7.
630. "Greta Garbo Educated," January 26, 1927.
631. "Garbo Refuses to Sign 5 Year Pact with Metro-Goldwyn," *Exhibitor's Herald*, February 26, 1927, p. 10; "Garbo Prefers $400 for 1 Year to $2,500 for 5," *Variety*, February 16, 1927, 5.
632. "Varconi Loaned to MGM," *The Film Daily*, January 30, 1927, p. 8.
633. Douglas Gomery, *Movie History: A Survey* (Wadsworth, 1991), 39.

634. "Aileen Pringle's Business Like Claim as Lead," *Variety*, March 16, 1927, 5.
635. Greta Garbo to Robert Rubin, telegram, March 6, 1927, author's personal collection.
636. "J.R. Rubin on Coast," *The Film Daily*, March 23, 1927, p. 2.
637. "Garbo Signs Five Year M-G-M Contract," *Motion Picture News*, April 8, 1927, p. 1257.
638. Biery, "The Story of Greta Garbo," June 1928.
639. "Gilbert Dodges Death," *Hollywood Topics*, February 5, 1927, 1.
640. "Two Women Hurt in Auto Accident," *La Jolla Light*, February 1, 1927.
641. "Film Actors Caught in Overturned Car," *Oakland Tribune*, February 1, 1927.
642. "Film Star in Motor Accident," *Los Angeles Evening Post-Record*, February 1, 1927.
643. Greta Garbo to Mimi Pollak, letter, between April 18 and September 17, 1927, author's personal collection.
644. Greta Garbo to Mimi Pollak, letter, September 17, 1927, author's personal collection.
645. "John Gilbert in Canada," *Variety*, March 16, 1927, 9.
646. Colleen Moore, *Silent Star* (Doubleday, 1968), 203–4.
647. Donald Ogden Stewart, *By a Stroke of Luck! An Autobiography* (Paddington Press, 1975), 157–58.
648. Stewart, *Stroke of Luck!*, 157–58.
649. "Gilbert in Dual Role on Blotter," *Los Angeles Times*, April 16, 1927, p. 19.
650. *Los Angeles Daily News*, April 16, 1927, p. 4.
651. "Cortez Signed by MGM," *The Film Daily*, March 23, 1927, p. 2.
652. "Greta Garbo's Illness May Kill New Film," *New York Daily News*, May 9, 1927, p. 90; Dan Van Neste, *The Magnificent Heel: The Life and Films of Ricardo Cortez* (BearManor Media, 2017), 65.
653. Dorothy Calhoun, "They Learned About Women From Her," *Motion Picture Classic*, August 1927.
654. Ricardo Cortez, interview by Kevin Brownlow, Oct. 28, 1965, quoted in Paris, *Garbo*, 130.
655. Greta Garbo to Mimi Pollak, letter, April 18, 1927, author's personal collection.
656. *Exhibitors Herald*, June 4, 1927, p. 30.
657. Family Search, accessed October 27, 2025, https://familysearch.org.
658. "'Karenina' Suspended for Revision," *Variety*, May 18, 1927.
659. Raymond Daum and Vance Muse, *Walking with Garbo: Conversations and Recollections* (HarperCollins, 1991), 142–43. Garbo to Ray Daum about her pernicious anemia. In people with pernicious anemia the parietal cells in the gut do not manufacture enough hydrochloric acid to accomplish efficient digestion.
660. Unsigned review of *Love*, *The Film Daily*, December 18, 1927, p. 6. Marion is credited with the scenario.
661. "Tolstoi's Objections Explained by Studio," *Variety*, October 5, 1927, 11.
662. Unsigned review of *Love*, *Film Spectator*, March 3, 1928, 9.
663. Matthew Kennedy, *Edmund Goulding's Dark Victory* (Univ. of Wisconsin Press, 2004), 64.
664. *Photoplay*, October 1927, 45.
665. Eve Golden, *John Gilbert: Last of the Silent Film Stars* (University Press of Kentucky, 2013), 48–49.
666. Scene stills, 1926, Photography Archive, Margaret Herrick Library, Academy of Motion Picture Arts and Sciences, Beverly Hills, CA.
667. *New York Daily News*, September 13, 1927, p. 32.
668. Ana Salzberg, *Produced by Irving Thalberg* (Edinburgh University Press, 2020), 150–51.

669. Welford Beaton, "Exhibitors Misled on Cost of Production," *Film Spectator*, October 29, 1927, 5.
670. *Motion Picture News*, December 30, 1927, p. 2015.
671. *Motion Picture News*, January 28, 1929, p. 276.
672. Åsa Jernudd and John Sedgwick, "Popular Films in Stockholm During the 1930s: A Presentation and Discussion of the Pioneering Work of Leif Furhammar," in Towards a Comparative *Economic History of Cinema, 1930–1970*, ed. John Sedgwick (Springer, 2022), 87–142. Ticket sale data for the Capitol, Embassy, and Astor Theatres came from Variety. Exhibition dates for Loew's first-run theaters in Brooklyn and Queens came from The *Brooklyn Eagle* and the *Brooklyn Times-Union*. Theater seating capacity came from www.cinematreasures.org.
673. Also known as *The Student Prince in Old Heidelberg*.
674. The Astor Theatre had 1,141 seats compared to the Embassy with 556 seats. So, the two films delivered similar box office revenue as a special feature, but *Love* did so in a much smaller theater at higher ticket prices. *Love* didn't have the additioanl cost of opening acts as exhibited.
675. Ad placements, *Brooklyn Daily Eagle*, February–May 1928.
676. Eddie Mannix Ledger, Margaret Herrick Library, Academy of Motion Picture Arts and Sciences, Beverly Hills, CA.
677. Sid, review of *Love*, *Variety*, December 7, 1927, 18.
678. "Entire Showing of '*Love*' to Go on Air from Embassy Dec. 20," *Exhibitors Herald*, December 17, 1927, p. 28.
679. Irene Thirer, "Tolstoi's '*Anna Karenina*' Splendidly Filmed by Edmund Golding," review of *Love*, *New York Daily News*, November 30, 1927, p. 170.
680. Unsigned review of *Love*, *The Film Daily*, December 18, 1927, p. 6.
681. Unsigned review of *Love*, *Motion Picture*, March 1928, 60.
682. Mordaunt Hall, "The Screen," review of *Love*, *The New York Times*, Nov. 30, 1927, p. 22.
683. Jack Gilbert interview, *Los Angeles Evening Express*, January 7, 1928, p. 12.
684. Gil Perkins, interview by Ronald Davis, 1986, quoted in Karen Swenson, *Greta Garbo: A Life Apart* (Scribner, 1997), 366.
685. Doris Markham, "An Idyll or a Tragedy—Which?," *Motion Picture*, December 1926, 23.
686. Rilla Page Palmborg, "Greta Garbo Has Her Say About These American Men," *Motion Picture*, February 1928, 59.
687. Palmborg, "Greta Garbo Has Her Say," 59.
688. Jay Brien Chapman, "The Only Man Who Knows Garbo," *Screen Book*, January 1934.
689. Norman Zierold, *Garbo* (Stein and Day, 1969), 79.
690. Clarence Bull, oral interviews, Margaret Herrick Library, Academy of Motion Picture Arts and Sciences, Beverly Hills, CA.
691. Matthew Kennedy, *Edmund Goulding's Dark Victory* (Univ. of Wisconsin Press, 2004), 116.
692. Floyd Porter, oral interviews, Margaret Herrick Library, Academy of Motion Picture Arts and Sciences, Beverly Hills, CA.
693. Swenson, *Greta Garbo*, 210.
694. Adela Rogers St. Johns, *Liberty*, July 27, 1929.
695. Clarence Bull and Raymond Lee, *The Faces of Hollywood* (A. S. Barnes, 1968), 23.
696. Gil Perkins, *Screen Actor*, Winter 1981–1982.
697. Zierold, *Garbo*, 79.
698. Floyd Porter, oral interviews.
699. Marguerite Tazelaar, "The Garbo as Seen by Her Cameraman," *Queenslander*, July 25, 1935.

700. Jean Negulesco, *Things I Did and Things I Think I Did* (Simon & Schuster, 1984), 211–12.
701. Zierold, *Garbo*, 69.
702. Zierold, *Garbo*, 70.
703. Frank Westmore and Muriel Davidson, *The Westmores of Hollywood* (Lippincott, 1976), 75.
704. Marguerite Gustafson, conversation with author, 1990s.
705. Zierold, *Garbo*, 97–98.
706. Howard Gutner, *Gowns by Adrian: The MGM Years 1928–1941* (Harry N. Abrams, 2001), 74.
707. Leonard Stanley, Adrian: *A Lifetime of Movie Glamour, Art and High Fashion* (Rizzoli, 2019), 127–28.
708. Elizabeth Hawes, "New Women Make New Styles," *Scribner's Magazine*, Sept. 1932, 300.
709. Mayme Ober Peak, "Study the Stars & Dress Your Line," *Ladies' Home Journal*, June 1932, 8.
710. Gilbert Adrian, "Setting Styles Through the Stars," *Ladies' Home Journal*, Feb. 1933, 10.
711. Gilbert Adrian, oral interviews, Margaret Herrick Library, Academy of Motion Picture Arts and Sciences, Beverly Hills, CA.
712. James Laver, *Taste and Fashion* (Harrar, 1932), 136.
713. Ruth Goldstein, "The Better Photograph," *The Banner* 3, no. 6 (November 1922): 6–7.
714. Alice Tildesley, "Secrets About the Famous," *Miami Herald*, July 25, 1926, p. 56.
715. Ruth Harriet Louise, portrait of Greta Garbo, photograph, https://www.ebay.ca/itm/373780367031.
716. Bull and Lee, *The Faces of Hollywood*, 23.
717. Zierold, *Garbo*, 80–81.
718. Terrance Pepper and John Kobal, *The Man Who Shot Garbo* (Simon & Schuster, 1989), 24.
719. Bull and Lee, *The Faces of Hollywood*, 23–31.
720. Bull and Lee, *The Faces of Hollywood*, 23.
721. Pepper and Kobal, *The Man Who Shot Garbo*, 24.
722. Pepper and Kobal, *The Man Who Shot Garbo*, 25.
723. Greta Garbo to Mimi Pollak, letter, January 28, 1928, author's personal collection.
724. Garbo to Pollak, January 28, 1928.
725. Eddie Mannix Ledger, Margaret Herrick Library, Academy of Motion Picture Arts and Sciences, Beverly Hills, CA.
726. Bosley Crowther papers, Special Collections, Brigham Young University.
727. Edith & Victor Sjöström to Greta Garbo, telegram, Nov. 7, 1928, author's personal collection.
728. *Paramount Around the World* (February 1, 1928), 2.
729. Hans Pensel, *Seastrom and Stiller in Hollywood* (Vantage Press, 1969), 60.
730. Pensel, *Seastrom and Stiller*, 63.
731. Pensel, *Seastrom and Stiller*, 64.
732. Greta Garbo to Mimi Pollak, letter, December 24, 1926, author's personal collection.
733. Mauritz Stiller to Greta Garbo, letter, Nov./Dec. 1927, author's personal collection.
734. Greta Garbo to Mimi Pollak, letter, January 28, 1928, author's personal collection.
735. Carlo Keil-Möller, "Garbo," *The American-Scandinavian Review* 26, no. 1 (Mar 1938): 42–43.
736. Mauritz Stiller to Greta Garbo, letter, March 6, 1928, author's personal collection.
737. Colleen Moore, *Silent Star* (Doubleday, 1968), 209.

738. Howard Greer, *Designing Male* (G. P. Putnam's Sons, 1951), 271.
739. Mauritz Stiller obituary, *Scenen*, November 15, 1928.
740. Mauritz Stiller obituary, *Goteborg's Post*, November 9, 1928.
741. Biografbladet, November 15, 1928, p. 597.
742. "Red Cross Hospital," Wikimedia Foundation, last modified January 3, 2024, https://sv.wikipedia.org/wiki/R%C3%B6da_Korsets_sjukhus.
743. Victor Sjöström, *As I Remember* (Varen, 1951), 4–5.
744. Sidney Franklin, "We Laughed, We Cried," 1964, Oral History, American Film Institute, Los Angeles.
745. Rilla Page Palmborg, "The Private Life of Greta Garbo," *Photoplay*, September 1930, 92.
746. Fritiof Billquist, *Garbo: A Biography* (G. P. Putnam's Sons, 1960), 156.
747. Greta Garbo to Mimi Pollak, letter, September 29, 1928, author's personal collection.
748. Garbo to Pollak, September 29, 1928.
749. Alexander Walker, *Garbo* (Macmillan, 1980), 89.
750. "Stockholm i Garbo-feber," *Svenska Dagbladet*, December 19, 1928, p. 22.
751. Lillemor Ring, *Kapten Ring* (temporis acti Stories, 2016), 293.
752. Ring, *Kapten Ring*, 293.
753. Billquist, *Garbo: A Biography*, 153.
754. Billquist, *Garbo: A Biography*, 153–54.
755. "Greta Garbo vill spela Jeanne d'Arc och Salome," *Svenska Dagbladet*, Dec. 18, 1928, p. 1.
756. *London Sunday Express*, October 7, 1934.
757. Sven Broman, *Conversations with Greta Garbo* (Viking, 1991), 80–81.
758. Cole Lesley, *Remembered Laughter: The Life of Nöel Coward* (Alfred A. Knopf, 1976), 176.
759. John Bainbridge, *Garbo* (Doubleday, 1955), 150–51.
760. John Bainbridge, *Garbo* (Doubleday, 1955), 131.
761. Broman, *Conversations with Greta Garbo*, 64.
762. *Hufvudstabladet*, March 10, 1971.
763. *Hufvudstabladet*, March 10, 1971.
764. Ragnar Hyltén-Cavallius, *Följa sin Genius* (Lars Hökerberg, 1960), 238.
765. Rilla Page Palmborg, "The Private Life of Greta Garbo," *Photoplay*, September 1930, 90.
766. Mordaunt Hall, "The Hollywood Hermit," *The New York Times*, Mar. 24, 1929, sec. 10, p. 7.
767. Hall, "The Hollywood Hermit," p. 7.
768. Hall, "The Hollywood Hermit," p. 7.
769. Fritiof Billquist, *Garbo: A Biography* (G. P. Putnam's Sons, 1960), 192.
770. *Photoplay*, November 1928, 48.
771. *The Pittsburgh Press*, January 8, 1932, p. 5.
772. Katherine Albert, "Exploding the Garbo Myth," *Photoplay*, April 1931, 98.
773. Leonard Hall, "Garbo-Maniacs," *Photoplay*, January 1930, 60.
774. Barry Paris, *Garbo: A Biography* (Knopf, 1995), 179.
775. Sven Broman, *Conversations with Greta Garbo* (Viking, 1991), 220.
776. *Pittsburgh Courier*, June 15, 1935, p. 5.
777. Rilla Page Palmborg, *The Private Life of Greta Garbo* (Doubleday, Doran, 1931), 210–11.
778. Palmborg, Private Life, 213.
779. Karen Swenson, *Greta Garbo: A Life Apart* (Scribner, 1997), 246.

780. Billquist, *Garbo: A Biography*, 200.
781. "Garbo Admirer Freed," *The New York Times*, October 13, 1933, p. 24.
782. "Greta Garbo Suitor Seized," *Los Angeles Times*, July 10, 1941, p. 1A.
783. "Greta Garbo's Screams Drive Burglars Away," *The Boston Globe*, July 8, 1944, p. 10.
784. "Recluse Wills Estate to Garbo," *Detroit Free Press*, February 18, 1947, p. 1.
785. Irmis Johnson, "Glamourous Garbo's Strange Legacy," *San Francisco Examiner*, April 27, 1947, p. 83.
786. Irmis Johnson, "Glamourous Greta's Strange Legacy," *The Atlanta Constitution*, April 27, 1947, p. 77. This article was in multiple papers.
787. Lilli Palmer, *Change Lobsters and Dance* (Macmillan, 1975), 216–17.
788. William Frye, "The Garbo Next Door," *Vanity Fair*, April 2000, 320.
789. "Gustaf Norin Biography," IMDb, accessed November 11, 2025, https://www.imdb.com/name/nm0635362/bio/?ref_=nm_ov_bio_sm.
790. Palmborg, *Private Life*, 121.
791. Salka Viertel, *The Kindness of Strangers* (Holt, Rinehart and Winston, 1969), 142–43.
792. Palmborg, *Private Life*, 193–200.
793. Norman Zierold, *The Moguls* (Coward-McCann, 1969), 138.
794. Palmborg, *Private Life*, 202–3.
795. *Photoplay*, March 1931.
796. Palmborg, *Private Life*, 220–21.
797. Palmborg, *Private Life*, 228–36.
798. Palmborg, *Private Life*, 171.
799. Tallulah Bankhead, *My Autobiography* (Harper, 1952), 199.
800. Palmborg, *Private Life*, 159–60.
801. Palmborg, *Private Life*, 169–70.
802. Palmborg, *Private Life*, 173.
803. Walter E. Taylor, "I Had Tea with Garbo!," *Christian Science Monitor*, March 25, 1936, p. 16.
804. Taylor, "Tea with Garbo!," 16.
805. Taylor, "Tea with Garbo!," 16.
806. Taylor, "Tea with Garbo!," 16.
807. Paris, Garbo, 319.
808. Frank Walsh, *Sin and Censorship* (Yale University Press, 1996), 63.
809. Leonard Leff and Jerold Simmons, *The Dame in the Kimono* (Grove Weidenfeld, 1990), 8.
810. Walsh, *Sin and Censorship*, 49.
811. Gregory Black, *The Catholic Crusade Against the Movies* (Cambridge University Press, 1997), 11.
812. Black, *The Catholic Crusade*, 11.
813. Walsh, *Sin and Censorship*, 61.
814. Black, *The Catholic Crusade*, 13–14.
815. Black, *The Catholic Crusade*, 15.
816. Black, *The Catholic Crusade*, 20.
817. Black, *The Catholic Crusade*, 20.
818. Walsh, *Sin and Censorship*, 63.
819. Black, *The Catholic Crusade*, 18.

820. Walsh, *Sin and Censorship*, 67.
821. Walsh, *Sin and Censorship*, 69.
822. Walsh, *Sin and Censorship*, 74–76.
823. Colin Shindler, *Hollywood in Crisis* (Routledge, 1996), 19–22.
824. Unsigned review of Anna Christie, *Photoplay*, March 1930, 54.
825. Lucy Fisher, "Greta Garbo: Fashioning a Star Image," in *Idols of Modernity: Movie Stars of the 1920s*, ed. Patrice Petro (Rutgers University Press, 2010), 144.
826. "Title card," *The Single Standard*, directed by John S. Robertson (1929; Turner Entertainment Co., 2009), DVD.
827. Mordaunt Hall, review of *The Single Standard*, *The New York Times*, July 29, 1929, p. 26.
828. Rilla Page Palmborg, *The Private Life of Greta Garbo* (Doubleday, Doran, 1931), 153.
829. Mordaunt Hall, "On the West Coast," *The New York Times*, July 28, 1929, sec. 8, p. 3.
830. Paul Hawkins, "A New Slant on Garbo," *Screenland*, June 1931, 112.
831. "Greta Garbo Talks," *The New York Times*, January 26, 1930, sec. 8, p. 6.
832. "Greta Garbo Talks," p. 6.
833. "*Anna Christie*," Internet Broadway Database, accessed November 5, 2025, https://www.ibdb.com/broadway-production/anna-christie-12677.
834. "Vanderbilt Theatre," Internet Broadway Database, accessed November 5, 2025, https://www.ibdb.com/theatre/vanderbilt-theatre-1371.
835. E. E. Laing [pseud.], *Greta Garbo, The Story of a Specialist* (John Gifford, 1946), 136.
836. Mordaunt Hall, "Greta Garbo Explains Her Next Picture," *The New York Times*, July 28, 1929, p. 101.
837. Hall, "Greta Garbo Explains," p. 101.
838. Mordaunt Hall, "Clever Film Actresses," *The New York Times*, March 23, 1930, sec. 9, p. 5; Harry Evans, "Greta Garbo Speaks," *Life*, March 21, 1930.
839. Gwenda Young, *Clarence Brown: Hollywood's Forgotten Master* (University Press of Kentucky, 2018), 109.
840. "Delay German 'Anna,'" *Variety*, January 22, 1930.
841. Roberta Ann Raider, "A Descriptive Study of the Acting of Marie Dressler" (thesis, University of Michigan, 1970), 198.
842. Young, *Hollywood's Forgotten Master*, 110.
843. Raider, "Marie Dressler," 223.
844. Raider, "Marie Dressler," 220.
845. Marie Dressler, *My Own Story* (Little, Brown, 1934), 252.
846. Raider, "Marie Dressler," 223.
847. Raider, "Marie Dressler," 223.
848. Palmborg, *Private Life*, 217.
849. Hedda Hopper, Hedda Hopper's Hollywood, column, *San Francisco Chronicle*, April 21, 1940, p. 19.
850. Mordaunt Hall, review of Anna Christie, *The New York Times*, March 15, 1930, p. 22.
851. Land, review of Anna Christie, *Variety*, March 19, 1930.
852. Robert E. Sherwood, "The Moving Picture Album," *The Bay City Times*, Mar. 2, 1930, p. 21.
853. Sherwood, "The Moving Picture Album," p. 21.
854. Palmborg, *Private Life*, 218.
855. Palmborg, *Private Life*, 218.

856. News clipping, archive, Museum of Modern Art, New York.
857. Barry Paris, *Garbo: A Biography* (Knopf, 1995), 192.
858. Fritiof Billquist, *Garbo: A Biography* (G. P. Putnam's Sons, 1960), 185.
859. Henry Hemming, *Agents of Influence: A British Campaign, a Canadian Spy, and the Secret Plot to Bring America into World War II* (Public Affairs, 2019), 32.
860. Ragnar Hyltén-Cavallius, *Följa sin Genius* (Lars Hökerberg, 1960), 235.
861. Robert Emmet Long, *George Cukor Interviews* (University Press of Mississippi, 2001), 47.
862. Raymond Daum and Vance Muse, *Walking with Garbo: Conversations and Recollections* (HarperCollins, 1991), 70.
863. Long, George *Cukor Interviews*, 40
864. Garson Kanin, *Hollywood* (Viking Press, 1967), 105.
865. Richard Dana Skinner, "The Play and Screen," review of *Anna Christie*, *Commonweal*, March 26, 1930, 590.
866. "Lewis Stone Gives His Impressions of Garbo," *St. Louis Globe-Democrat*, Feb. 9, 1934, p. 21.
867. Billquist, *Garbo: A Biography*, 171.
868. Gene Phillips, *The Movie Makers* (Nelson-Hall, 1973), 73.
869. Leonard Soule, "Hissed to the Heights—That's Rathbone," *Motion Picture*, July 1936, 37.
870 Basil Rathbone, *In and Out of Character* (Doubleday, 1962), 224.
871. Richard Dana Skinner, "The Screen," review of *Anna Christie*, *Commonweal*, September 3, 1930, 446.
872. Mary Pickford, "Stay Away from Hollywood," *Good Housekeeping*, October 1930, 36.
873. Hyltén-Cavallius, *Följa sin Genius*, 226.
874. Billquist, *Garbo: A Biography*, 187.
875. Arthur Lenning, *Stroheim* (University Press of Kentucky, 2000), 212.
876. Ginette Vincendeau, "Hollywood Babel," in *The Classical Hollywood Reader*, ed. Steve Neale (Routledge, 2012), 137–38.
877. "Delay German 'Anna,'" *Variety*, January 22, 1930.
878. Cecil Beaton, *Cecil Beaton: Memoirs of the 40's* (McGraw-Hill, 1972), 209.
879. Neysa McMein, "Toast to a Lady," *McCall's*, August 1932, 13.
880. Per Hallström, Nobel Prize award speech, December 10, 1934, Swedish Academy, Stockholm, https://www.nobelprize.org/prizes/literature/1934/ceremony-speech/.
881. Rush, review of *As You Desire Me*, *Variety*, June 7, 1932, 21.
882. Rush, review of *As You Desire Me*, 21.
883. Arthur Lenning, *Stroheim* (University Press of Kentucky, 2000), 212.
884. Neysa McMein, "Too Good to be True," review of *As You Desire Me*, *McCall's*, Jan. 1934, 20.
885. Perceval Reiners, "The Foreign Element," *The Independent* 119, no. 4040 (1927): 458.
886. Fritiof Billquist, *Garbo: A Biography* (G. P. Putnam's Sons, 1960), 180.
887. Beaton, *Memoirs of the 40's*, 209.
888. E. E. Laing [pseud.], *Greta Garbo: The Story of a Specialist* (John Gifford, 1946).
889. Kaj Gynt, "Garbo jakt," *Filmjournalen*, August 25, 1932, p. 14.
890. Billquist, *Garbo: A Biography*, 192.
891. United Press International, "Thousands See Garbo Return," August 8, 1932, quoted in Karen Swenson, *Greta Garbo: A Life Apart* (Scribner, 1997), 288.
892. Billquist, *Garbo: A Biography*, 192.
893. Laing, *Story of a Specialist*, 125.

894. Greta Garbo to Salka Viertel, letter, 1933, author's personal collection.
895. Garbo to Viertel, 1933.
896. Oscar Fernbach, "Greta Stars in Big Sea Mystery," *San Francisco Examiner*, April 7, 1933.
897. Druce Stone, "Garbo Comes Back—And Talks!," *Movie Classic*, July 1933, 56.
898. Stone, "Garbo Comes Back," 56.
899. Stone, "Garbo Comes Back," 56–57.
900. Stone, "Garbo Comes Back," 34.
901. Jim Mitchell, "Of All Things! Garbo Returns in New Mood," *San Francisco Examiner*, May 1, 1933, p. 5.
902. Martin Quigley, *Decency in Motion Pictures* (Macmillan, 1937), 37.
903. Salka Viertel, *The Kindness of Strangers* (Holt, Rinehart and Winston, 1969), 169.
904. Donna Rifkind, *The Sun and Her Stars* (Other Press, 2020), 221.
905. Rifkind, *The Sun and Her Stars*, 146.
906. Greta Garbo to Hörke Wachtmeister, letter, Summer 1933, author's personal collection.
907. Alexander Walker, *Garbo* (Macmillan, 1980), 133.
908. Greta Garbo to Salka Viertel, letter, 1932 or 1933, author's personal collection.
909. Rifkind, *The Sun and Her Stars*, 142.
910. Rifkind, *The Sun and Her Stars*, 126–27.
911. Viertel, *The Kindness of Strangers*, 183.
912. Rifkind, *The Sun and Her Stars*, 127.
913. David Luhrssen, *Mamoulian: Life on Stage and Screen* (Univ. Press of Kentucky, 2013), 69.
914. Mamoulian calendar of social engagements, box 14, folder 5, Rouben Mamoulian archive, Library of Congress, Washington, DC.
915. Viertel, *The Kindness of Strangers*, 188.
916. Samuel N. Behrman, *People in a Diary* (Little, Brown, 1972), 149.
917. Sven Broman, *Conversations with Greta Garbo* (Viking, 1991), 123.
918. Walter Wanger datebook for 1933, Walter Wanger archives, University of Wisconsin Libraries, Madison, WI.
919. Wanger datebook for 1933; Rouben Mamoulian datebook for 1933, Rouben Mamoulian archive, Library of Congress, Washington, DC.
920. C. Higham and J. Greenburg, *The Celluloid Muse* (Henry Regnery, 1969), 137.
921. Laurence Olivier, *Confessions of an Actor* (Simon & Schuster, 1992), 71.
922. Eve Golden, *John Gilbert: Last of the Silent Film Stars* (University Press of Kentucky, 2013), 255.
923. John Gilbert, "Don't Send Gilbert into Exile," interview by Gladys Hall, *Modern Screen*, March 1934, 60.
924. Betsy Erkkila, "Greta Garbo: Sailing Beyond the Frame," *Critical Inquiry* 11, no. 4 (June 1985): 615.
925. Script files, Rouben Mamoulian archive, Library of Congress, Washington, DC.
926. Andrew Sarris, ed., *Interviews with Film Directors* (Bobbs-Merrill, 1967), 291–92.
927. Rouben Mamoulian, "An Interview with Rouben Mamoulian," interview by John A. Gallagher and Marino A. Amoruco, *The Velvet Light Trap*, no. 19 (1982): 16.
928. Luhrssen, *Mamoulian*, 71.
929. Martin Quigley to Archbishop John McNicholas, letter, March 20, 1934, box 30, folder 27, National Catholic Welfare Conference, The American Catholic History Research Center and University Archives, The Catholic University of America, Washington, DC.

930. Viertel, *The Kindness of Strangers*, 174.
931. Joseph Breen to Louis B. Mayer, letter, January 8, 1934, *Queen Christina* file, PCA files, Margaret Herrick Library, Academy of Motion Picture Arts and Sciences, Beverly Hills, CA.
932. James Wingate to Eddie Mannix, letter, August 7, 1933, *Queen Christina* file, PCA files, Margaret Herrick Library, Academy of Motion Picture Arts and Sciences, Beverly Hills, CA.
933. Wingate to Mannix, August 7, 1933.
934. Memo to file by James Wingate, August 11, 1933, *Queen Christina* file, PCA files, Margaret Herrick Library, Academy of Motion Picture Arts and Sciences, Beverly Hills, CA.
935. W. D. Kelly to Eddie Mannix, letter, December 21, 1933, *Queen Christina* file, PCA files, Margaret Herrick Library, Academy of Motion Picture Arts and Sciences, Beverly Hills, CA.
936. Will Hays to Nicholas Schenck, letter, January 3, 1934, *Queen Christina* file, PCA files, Margaret Herrick Library, Academy of Motion Picture Arts and Sciences, Beverly Hills, CA; Will Hays to Nicholas Schenck, letter, January 5, 1934, *Queen Christina* file, PCA files, Margaret Herrick Library, Academy of Motion Picture Arts and Sciences, Beverly Hills, CA; Breen to Mayer, January 8, 1934.
937. Frank Walsh, *Sin and Censorship* (Yale University Press, 1996), 63.
938. Luhrssen, *Mamoulian*, 74.
939. William Troy, "Garbo and Screen Acting," review of *Queen Christina*, *The Nation*, January 24, 1934, 112.
940. Harry Evans, review of *Queen Christina*, *Life*, February 1934, 38.
941. Ella McCormick, "Greta Garbo Brings a Glamorous Queen Christina to Life in Moving Romance," review of *Queen Christina*, *Detroit Free Press*, March 2, 1934, p. 19.
942. Danny Reid, "*Queen Christina* (1933) Review, with Greta Garbo and John Gilbert," review of *Queen Christina*, pre-code.com, June 1, 2015, http://pre-code.com/queen-christina-1933-review-greta-garbo-john-gilbert/.
943. Quigley, *Decency in Motion Pictures*, 37.
944. Cinema, "Garbo's Greatness," review of *Queen Christina*, *The Sydney Morning Herald*, April 12, 1934, p. 27.
945. Unsigned review of *Queen Christina*, "Greta Garbo als Königin Christine," *Karlsruher Tagblatt*, November 4, 1934.
946. Greta Garbo, "Garbo Talks—For Publication," interview by Gunilla Bjelke, *Movie Classic*, October 1935, 77.
947. Carlo Keil-Möller, "Garbo," *The American-Scandinavian Review* 26, no. 1 (March 1938): 41–48.
948. Walter Wanger datebook for 1934, Walter Wanger archives, University of Wisconsin Libraries, Madison, WI.
949. Bishop John Cantwell of Los Angeles to Rev. John Burke of the National Catholic Welfare Conference, letter, September 20, 1933, box 30, folder 26, National Catholic Welfare Conference, The American Catholic History Research Center and University Archives, The Catholic University of America, Washington, DC.
950. Richard Maltby, "The Production Code and the Hays Office," in *Grand Design: Hollywood as a Modern Business Enterprise, 1930–1939*, ed. Tino Balio (University of California Press, 1993), 40.
951. Martin Quigley to Charlie Pettijohn, letter, November 1934, GTM-GAMMS142, Martin J. Quigley Papers, Georgetown University Manuscripts.
952. Frank Walsh, *Sin and Censorship* (Yale University Press, 1996), 83.
953. Walsh, *Sin and Censorship*, 87.

954. Martin Quigley, *Decency in Motion Pictures* (Macmillan, 1937), 37.
955. Quigley, *Decency in Motion Pictures*, 37.
956. Gerald Kelly and John Ford, "The Legion of Decency," *Theological Studies* 18, no. 3 (September 1957): 391–93.
957. Joseph Breen to Archbishop John McNicholas, letter, May 12, 1934, box 198, folder 5, United States Conference of Catholic Bishops, The American Catholic History Research Center and University Archives, The Catholic University of America, Washington, DC. The Bishops' Committee on Motion Pictures would be comprised of four conservative and influential members; Archbishop John McNicholas of Cincinnati, Bishop John F. Noll of Fort Wayne, Bishop Hugh Boyle of Pittsburgh and Bishop John Cantwell of Los Angeles.
958. Cincinnati archdiocese archives, email to author, June 2022.
959. FitzGeorge Dinneen to Martin Quigley, letter, June 9, 1934, GTM-GAMMS142, Martin J. Quigley Papers, Georgetown University Manuscripts.
960. Joseph Breen to Martin Quigley, letter, May 1, 1932, GTM-GAMMS142, Martin J. Quigley Papers, Georgetown University Manuscripts.
961. Walsh, *Sin and Censorship*, 131.
962. Gregory Black, *Hollywood Censored* (Cambridge University Press, 1994), 187–91.
963. Ruth Vasey, *The World According to Hollywood, 1918–1939* (University of Wisconsin Press, 1997), 133.
964. Greta Garbo to Peg Gustafson, letter, March 4, 1962, author's personal collection.
965. Production Code Administration file for *The Painted Veil*, Motion Picture Association of America, PCA files, Margaret Herrick Library, Academy of Motion Picture Arts and Sciences, Beverly Hills, CA.
966. Production Code Administration file for *The Painted Veil.*
967. Production Code Administration file for *The Painted Veil.*
968. Production Code Administration file for *The Painted Veil.*
969. Production Code Administration file for *The Painted Veil.*
970. E. E. Laing [pseud.], *Greta Garbo: The Story of a Specialist* (John Gifford, 1946), 213.
971. William Troy, "A New Garbo?," review of *The Painted Veil*, *The Nation*, Dec. 19, 1934, 721.
972. Joseph Breen to Louis B. Mayer, letter, September 25, 1934, Production Code Administration file for Anna Karenina, Motion Picture Association of America, PCA files, Margaret Herrick Library, Academy of Motion Picture Arts and Sciences, Beverly Hills, CA.
973. Salka Viertel, *The Kindness of Strangers* (Holt, Rinehart and Winston, 1969), 198.
974. Gregory Black, *Hollywood Censored* (Cambridge University Press, 1994), 209.
975. Lea Jacobs, *The Wages of Sin* (University of Wisconsin Press, 1991), 119.
976. Jacobs, *The Wages of Sin*, 118.
977. Black, *Hollywood Censored*, 209–10
978. Jacobs, *The Wages of Sin*, 126–30.
979. Leonard Leff and Jerold Simmons, *The Dame in the Kimono* (Grove Weidenfeld, 1990), 177.
980. Joseph Breen to Louis B. Mayer, letter, May 18, 1936, Production Code Administration file for Camille, Motion Picture Association of America, PCA files, Margaret Herrick Library, Academy of Motion Picture Arts and Sciences, Beverly Hills, CA.
981. Breen to Mayer, May 18, 1936.
982. Notes from Joseph Breen's phone call with Irving Thalberg, May 20, 1936, PCA files, Margaret Herrick Library, Academy of Motion Picture Arts and Sciences, Beverly Hills, CA.

983. Sven Broman, *Conversations with Greta Garbo* (Viking, 1991), 148.
984. E. E. Laing [pseud.], *Greta Garbo: The Story of a Specialist* (John Gifford, 1946), 221.
985. Karen Swenson, *Greta Garbo: A Life Apart* (Scribner, 1997), 356.
986. Greta Garbo to Hörke Wachtmeister, letter, 1936, translation in author's personal collection.
987. Swenson, *Greta Garbo*, 263.
988. Swenson, *Greta Garbo*, 263.
989. Garbo to Wachtmeister, 1936.
990. Unsigned review of *Camille*, *Newsweek*, January 9, 1937, 32.
991. David Fairweather, "The Film World," review of *Camille*, *Theatre World*, April 1937.
992. Carlo Keil-Möller, "Garbo," *The American-Scandinavian Review* 26, no. 1 (March 1938): 41–48.
993. Mick LaSalle, *Complicated Women* (St. Martin's Press, 2000), 218.
994. Viertel, *The Kindness of Strangers*, 199–200.
995. Viertel, *The Kindness of Strangers*, 200.
996. Viertel, *The Kindness of Strangers*, 200.
997. Joseph Breen to Irving Thalberg, letter, December 10, 1935, PCA files, Margaret Herrick Library, Academy of Motion Picture Arts and Sciences, Beverly Hills, CA.
998. Breen to Thalberg, December 10, 1935.
999. Viertel, *The Kindness of Strangers*, 213.
1000. Viertel, *The Kindness of Strangers*, 213.
1001. Gwenda Young, *Clarence Brown: Hollywood's Forgotten Master* (University Press of Kentucky, 2018), 202–6.
1002. Donna Rifkind, *The Sun and Her Stars* (Other Press, 2020), 217.
1003. Gil Perkins, interview by Ronald Davis, 1986, quoted in Karen Swenson, *Greta Garbo: A Life Apart* (Scribner, 1997), 366.
1004. Breen to Thalberg, December 10, 1935.
1005. Al Block to Joseph Breen, letter, August 7, 1937, PCA files, Margaret Herrick Library, Academy of Motion Picture Arts and Sciences, Beverly Hills, CA.
1006. *Variety*, October 13, 1937, 1.
1007. Eddie Mannix Ledger, Margaret Herrick Library, Academy of Motion Picture Arts and Sciences, Beverly Hills, CA.
1008. Flin, review of *Conquest*, *Variety*, October 27, 1937, 18.
1009. Unsigned review of Conquest, Detroit Free Press, November 7, 1937, p. 99.
1010. Unsigned review of Conquest, Detroit Free Press, November 7, 1937, p. 99.
1011. Sven Broman, *Conversations with Greta Garbo* (Viking, 1991), 139.
1012. "Street Crowd Chased Garbo," *New York Daily News*, December 27, 1931, p. 3.
1013. Bertolt Brecht, *Schriften zum Theater* (Suhrkamp, 1957), 343–44, quoted in Karen Swenson, *Greta Garbo: A Life Apart* (Scribner, 1997), 264.
1014. Swenson, *Greta Garbo*, 264.
1015. "Colored Maids in Unique Position in Hollywood," *New York Amsterdam News*, May 1, 1929, p. 13.
1016. Harry Levette, "Coast Codgings," *The Chicago Defender*, February 6, 1932, p. 5.
1017. Hazel Washington, "Greta Garbo's Ex-Maid Talks of Famed Film Star's Moods, Fears," *The Chicago Defender*, November 7, 1956, p. 18
1018. Washington, "Greta Garbo's Ex-Maid," p. 18.

1019. Washington, "Greta Garbo's Ex-Maid," p. 18.
1020. Washington, "Greta Garbo's Ex-Maid," p. 18.
1021. Colleen Moore, *Silent Star* (Doubleday, 1968), 202.
1022. Moore, *Silent Star*, 202.
1023. John Bainbridge, *Garbo* (Doubleday, 1955), 200.
1024. Mollie Merrick, "Garbo's Dread of Crowds Actual Mental Suffering," *Los Angeles Times*, May 8, 1932, p. B13.
1025. Greta Garbo, "Garbo Talks—For Publication," interview by Gunilla Bjelke, *Movie Classic*, October 1935, 77.
1026. Garbo, "Garbo Talks—For Publication," 77.
1027. Garbo, "Garbo Talks—For Publication," 77.
1028. Garbo, "Garbo Talks—For Publication," 79.
1029. Fritiof Billquist, *Garbo: A Biography* (G. P. Putnam's Sons, 1960), 209.
1030. Billquist, *Garbo: A Biography*, 209.
1031. Billquist, *Garbo: A Biography*, 220-21.
1032. Carlo Keil-Möller, "Garbo," *The American-Scandinavian Review* 26, no. 1 (March 1938): 41–48.
1033. Greta Garbo to Mimi Pollak, letter, October 7, 1935, author's personal collection.
1034. Greta Garbo to Mimi Pollak, letter, December 1935, author's personal collection.
1035. Greta Garbo to Mimi Pollak, letter, April 20, 1936, author's personal collection.
1036. *The New York Times*, May 4, 1936, p. 9.
1037. *The New York Times*, May 4, 1936, p. 9.
1038. *The New York Times*, May 4, 1936, p. 9.
1039. *The New York Times*, May 4, 1936, p. 9.
1040. *The New York Times*, May 4, 1936, p. 9.
1041. *The New York Times*, May 4, 1936, p. 9.
1042. Broman, *Conversations with Garbo*, 156–57.
1043. Greta Garbo to Peg Gustafson, letter, Summer 1944, author's personal collection.
1044. Broman, *Conversations with Garbo*, 157.
1045. Broman, *Conversations with Garbo*, 177.
1046. Broman, *Conversations with Garbo*, 173.
1047. Broman, *Conversations with Garbo*, 172-77.
1048. Broman, *Conversations with Garbo*, 172-77.
1049. Broman, *Conversations with Garbo*, 173.
1050. Parrish had been a child actor, appearing in a large number of films, including a small role in *Anna Christie*.
1051. Donna Rifkind, "History for Sale in Santa Monica," *Los Angeles Times*, June 18, 2015, p. A21.
1052. Sybille Bedford, *Aldous Huxley* (Knopf, 1974), 359; Lionel Rolfe, *Literary L.A.* (Chronicle Books, 1981), 51; Julian Huxley, *Aldous Huxley: A Memorial Volume* (Harper & Row, 1965), 154.
1053. This picnic can be dated to November 26, 1939, based on a letter Bertrand Russell wrote to his mother.
1054. Huxley, Aldous Huxley, 91–93.
1055. Barbara Leaving, *Orson Welles* (Penguin, 1985), 206.

1056. *The Palm Beach Post*, February 9, 1940, p. 1.
1057. *Milwaukee Journal*, January 4, 1941, p. 1.
1058. Jean Lindsay Johnson, *Illustrious Oconomowoc* (Franklin, 1979), 140.
1059. Greta Garbo to Peg Gustafson, letter, mid-1940s, author's personal collection.
1060. Jessica Dragonette, *Faith Is a Song* (St. Anthony Guild Press, 1967), 254.
1061. *Atlanta Daily World*, February 11, 1940, p. 7.
1062. Oliver Daniel, *Stokowski: A Counterpoint of View* (Dodd, Mead, 1982), 357.
1063. *Los Angeles Examiner*, October 22, 1937.
1064. Hattie Grimstead, "With Garbo at Home," *Screenland*, April 1938, 28.
1065. Grimstead, "With Garbo at Home," 29.
1066. Grimstead, "With Garbo at Home," 80.
1067. Grimstead, "With Garbo at Home," 81.
1068. Greta Garbo to Salka Viertel, letter, February 1938, author's personal collection.
1069. Daniel, *Stokowski*, 363.
1070. "Garbo Won't Wed, Says So Herself," *Daily News*, March 18, 1938, p. 3.
1071. Broman, *Conversations with Garbo*, 168–70.
1072. "Garbo, Stokowski Periled in Crash," *San Francisco Examiner*, June 27, 1938, p. 5.
1073. "Garbo Back; Refuses to Discuss Own Life," *The New York Times*, October 8, 1938, p. 34.
1074. "Garbo Back," p. 34.
1075. Norman Zierold, *Garbo* (Stein and Day, 1969), 109.
1076. Daniel, *Stokowski*, 370.
1077. Daniel, *Stokowski*, 370–71.
1078. "Miss Garbo Chided for Plain Coiffure," *The New York Times*, October 19, 1938, p. 18.
1079. Greta Garbo to Peg Gustafson, letter, June 20, 1945, author's personal collection.
1080. William Paul, *Ernst Lubitsch's American Comedy* (Columbia University Press, 1983), 207.
1081. Maurice Zalotów, *Billy Wilder in Hollywood* (Putnam, 1977), 79.
1082. Norman Zierold, *Garbo* (Stein and Day, 1969), 92–93.
1083. John Bainbridge, *Garbo* (Doubleday, 1955), 242.
1084. Allen Bishop, "Hollywood Comes of Age," review of *Ninotchka*, *Theatre Arts Magazine*, February 1940, 119.
1085. James Dugan, "MGM Lays an Egg," *New Masses*, September 12, 1939, 27–29.
1086. Bishop, "Hollywood Comes of Age," 119.
1087. E. E. Laing [pseud.], *Greta Garbo: The Story of a Specialist* (John Gifford, 1946), 224.
1088. Greta Garbo to Peg Gustafson, letter, after 1942, author's personal collection.
1089. Greta Garbo to Hörke Wachtmeister, letter, March 15, 1940, quoted in Sven Broman, *Conversations with Greta Garbo* (Viking, 1991), 189.
1090. Garbo to Wachtmeister, March 15, 1940, quoted in Broman, *Conversations with Garbo*, 189.
1091. Greta Garbo to Hörke Wachtmeister, letter, August 29, 1940, author's personal collection.
1092. Founded in 1945 by Paul Mellon, the Bollingen Foundation published books, gave fellowships to poets, and created the Bollingen Prize for Poetry. The foundation was subsumed back into the Andrew W. Mellon Foundation in 1968.
1093. Greta Garbo to Peg Gustafson, letter, between 1941 and 1945, author's personal collection.
1094. Garbo to Gustafson, June 20, 1945.

1095. Greta Garbo to Peg Gustafson, letter, December 21, 1945, author's personal collection.
1096. Greta Garbo to Peg Gustafson, letter, June 6, 1946, author's personal collection.
1097. Garbo to Gustafson, June 6, 1946.
1098. John McClafferty to Archbishop John McNicholas, letter, November 21, 1941, box 198, folder 28, USCCB OGS, The American Catholic History Research Center and University Archives, The Catholic University of America, Washington, DC.
1099. Irving Thalberg, *Discussion of the Production Code in Its Draft Form* (Association of Motion Picture Producers, circa 1930), 2.
1100. Betty DeBerg, *Ungodly Women: Gender and the First Wave of American Fundamentalism* (Mercer University Press, 2000), 126–27.
1101. Salka Viertel, *The Kindness of Strangers* (Holt, Rinehart and Winston, 1969), 218.
1102. Viertel, *The Kindness of Strangers*, 218.
1103. Viertel, *The Kindness of Strangers*, 239.
1104. Bosley Crowther, *The Lion's Share* (E. P. Dutton, 1957), 273.
1105. Gottfried Reinhardt, *The Genius* (Knopf, 1979), 104.
1106. Patrick McGilligan, *George Cukor: A Double Life* (St. Martin's Press, 1991), 165.
1107. International Federation of Catholic Alumnae, Quarterly Bulletin (June 1938), 23.
1108. James M. Skinner, *The Cross and the Cinema: The Legion of Decency and the National Catholic Office for Motion Pictures, 1933–1970* (Praeger, 1993), 68.
1109. Frank Walsh, *Sin and Censorship* (Yale University Press, 1996), 167.
1110. Production Code Administration Board report on *Two-Faced Woman*, *Two-Faced Woman* file, p. 4, PCA files, Margaret Herrick Library, Academy of Motion Picture Arts and Sciences, Beverly Hills, CA.
1111. Walsh, *Sin and Censorship*, 172.
1112. International Federation of Catholic Alumnae, Convention Report (1938), 20, The American Catholic History Research Center and University Archives, The Catholic University of America, Washington, DC.
1113. "To See Is to Sin," *Time*, December 8, 1941, 60.
1114. James Bawden and Ronald Miller, *Conversations with Classic Film Stars* (University Press of Kentucky, 2016), 86.
1115. *Newsweek*, December 8, 1941, 70.
1116. *Newsweek*, December 8, 1941, 70.
1117. *Time*, December 8, 1941, 60.
1118. John McClafferty to Archbishop Spellman, memorandum, December 1, 1941, box 198, folder 28, USCCB, The American Catholic History Research Center and University Archives, The Catholic University of America, Washington, DC.
1119. John McClafferty to Archbishop Spellman, memorandum, December 2, 1941, box 198, folder 28, USCCB, The American Catholic History Research Center and University Archives, The Catholic University of America, Washington, DC.
1120. Joseph Breen to Martin Quigley, note, December 1941, GTM-GAMMS142, Martin J. Quigley Papers, Georgetown University Manuscripts.
1121. Joan Kramer and David Henley, *In the Company of Legends* (Beaufort Books, 2015), 109–10
1122. Greta Garbo to Leland Hayward, telegram, 1947.
1123. Greta Garbo to Peg Gustafson, letter, between July 1 and September 30, 1941, author's personal collection.

1124. Garbo to Gustafson, between July 1 and September 30, 1941.
1125. Garbo to Gustafson, between July 1 and September 30, 1941.
1126. *Hollywood Citizen-News*, August 10, 1942, p. 5.
1127. *Variety*, October 28, 1942, 15.
1128. C. Higham and J. Greenburg, *The Celluloid Muse* (Henry Regnery, 1969), 60.
1129. Greta Garbo to Peg Gustafson, letter, 1943 or 1944, author's personal collection.
1130. Greta Garbo to Peg Gustafson, letter, September 10, 1943, author's personal collection.
1131. Greta Garbo to Peg Gustafson, letter, 1943 or 1944, author's personal collection.
1132. Greta Garbo to Peg Gustafson, letter, between 1941 and 1945, author's personal collection.
1133. Greta Garbo to Peg Gustafson, letter, 1943 or 1944, author's personal collection.
1134. Greta Garbo to Peg Gustafson, letter, 1943 or 1944, author's personal collection.
1135. Greta Garbo to Peg Gustafson, letter, Spring 1944, author's personal collection.
1136. Greta Garbo to Peg Gustafson, letter, Summer 1944, author's personal collection.
1137. Salka Viertel, *The Kindness of Strangers* (Holt, Rinehart and Winston, 1969), 276.
1138. Greta Garbo to Peg Gustafson, letter, Spring 1944, author's personal collection.
1139. Harry Waldman, Scenes Unseen (McFarland, 1991), 129.
1140. Greta Garbo to Peg Gustafson, letter, Fall 1944 or Winter 1945, author's personal collection.
1141. Greta Garbo to Peg Gustafson, letter, Winter or Spring 1945, author's personal collection.
1142. Greta Garbo to Peg Gustafson, letter, undated, author's personal collection.
1143. Tennessee Williams, *Memoirs* (Doubleday, 1972), 139.
1144. Diego Mormorio, *Tazio Secchiaroli: Greatest of the Paparazzi* (Harry N. Abrams, 1998), 26.
1145. Ron Galella, *No Pictures* (PowerHouse Books, 2008).
1146. *The Indianapolis Star*, March 20, 1960, p. 112.
1147. Carey Wilson, letter to the editor, *Life*, January 31, 1955.
1148. Peter Filene, *Him/Her/Self: Sex Roles in Modern America* (Johns Hopkins University Press, 1986), 160.
1149. Filene, *Him/Her/Self*, 175.
1150. Filene, *Him/Her/Self*, 168.
1151. Elaine Tyler May, *Homeward Bound: American Families in the Cold War Era* (Basic Books, 1988), 20.
1152. Dorothy Sue Cobble, *The Other Women's Movement* (Princeton Univ. Press, 2004), 11.
1153. Joanne Meyerowitz, ed., *Not June Cleaver* (Temple University Press, 1994), 231–33.
1154. Meyerowitz, *Not June Cleaver*, 247.
1155. May, *Homeward Bound*, 42–44.
1156. Walter Winchell, *The Cincinnati Enquirer*, May 10, 1955, p. 21.
1157. Roby Heard, "A Broken Heart Drove Star into Seclusion," *Pittsburgh Post-Gazette*, August 12, 1954.
1158. Charles Ponce de Leon, *Self Exposure: Human Interest Journalism and the Emergence of Celebrity in America, 1890–1940* (University of North Carolina Press, 2002), 133.
1159. "Publisher Recalls Book About Pope," *Chicago Tribune*, July 31, 1984, p. 9.
1160. Greta Garbo to Peg Gustafson, letter, May 25, 1948, author's personal collection; Greta Garbo to Peg Gustafson, letter, undated, author's personal collection.
1161. Colleen Moore, *Silent Star* (Doubleday, 1968), 211.
1162. Irene Selznick, *A Private View* (Knopf, 1983), 197.

1163. Barry Paris, *Garbo: A Biography* (Knopf, 1995), 163.
1164. Patricia Bosworth, *Montgomery Clift* (Harcourt Brace Jovanovich, 1978), 252.
1165. Natasha Fraser-Cavassoni, *Sam Spiegel* (Simon & Schuster, 2003), 295.
1166. *Los Angeles Evening Citizen News*, January 4, 1960, p. 17.
1167. Greta Garbo to Peg Gustafson, letter, 1960 or 1961, author's personal collection.
1168. Greta Garbo to Peg Gustafson, letter, October 18, 1948, author's personal collection.
1169. Salka Viertel, *The Kindness of Strangers* (Holt, Rinehart and Winston, 1969), 300.
1170. Frenke also had controlled the rights to *The Girl from Leningrad*, so Garbo may have already known him.
1171. Greta Garbo to Peg Gustafson, letter, July 1948, author's personal collection.
1172. Matthew Bernstein, *Walter Wanger, Hollywood Independent* (University of California Press, 1994), 258–59 (brackets in the original).
1173. Letter of understanding between Walter Wanger and Greta Garbo, August 4, 1948, Walter Wanger Collection, University of Wisconsin, Madison, WI.
1174. Greta Garbo to Peg Gustafson, letter, August 5, 1948, author's personal collection.
1175. George Cukor to Walter Wanger, letter, September 13, 1948, Walter Wanger Collection, University of Wisconsin, Madison, WI.
1176. Viertel, *The Kindness of Strangers*, 300.
1177. Bernstein, *Walter Wanger, Hollywood Independent*, 261.
1178. Copy of Greta Garbo's datebook, 1949, author's personal collection.
1179. Joshua Logan, *My Up and Down, In and Out Life* (Delacorte, 1976), 314.
1180. Walter Wanger to Josh Logan, telegram, July 5, 1949, Walter Wanger Collection, University of Wisconsin, Madison, WI.
1181. This was the Broadway play *The Wisteria Trees* (1950).
1182. Logan, My Up and Down, 315.
1183. Josh Logan to Walter Wanger, telegram, July 27, 1949, Walter Wanger Collection, University of Wisconsin, Madison, WI.
1184. Eugene Frenke to Walter Wanger, telegram, August 19, 1949, Walter Wanger Collection, University of Wisconsin, Madison, WI.
1185. Walter Wanger to Eugene Frenke, telegram, August 22, 1949, Walter Wanger Collection, University of Wisconsin, Madison, WI.
1186. *The Duchess de Langeais* accumulated cost worksheet, August 31, 1949, Walter Wanger Collection, University of Wisconsin, Madison, WI.
1187. Joseph Breen to Walter Wanger, letter, September 12, 1949, Walter Wanger Collection, University of Wisconsin, Madison, WI.
1188. Breen to Wanger, September 12, 1949.
1189. "Antagonism Seething Between Garbo, Italians," *Los Angeles Times*, Sept. 12, 1949, p. B6.
1190. Logan, *My Up and Down*, 314.
1191. Agreement to extend contract between Walter Wanger and Greta Garbo, September 22, 1949, Walter Wanger Collection, University of Wisconsin, Madison, WI.
1192. Eugene Frenke to Walter Wanger, letter, October 5, 1949, Walter Wanger Collection, University of Wisconsin, Madison, WI.
1193. Walter Wanger to Roy Meyers of MCA, telegram, October 1949, Walter Wanger Collection, University of Wisconsin, Madison, WI.

1194. Eugene Frenke to Walter Wanger, letter, November 21, 1949, Walter Wanger Collection, University of Wisconsin; Walter Wanger to Eugene Frenke, letter, November 28, 1949, Walter Wanger Collection, University of Wisconsin, Madison, WI.

1195. MCA to Walter Wanger, letter, January 3, 1950, Walter Wanger Collection, University of Wisconsin, Madison, WI.

1196. Y. F. Freeman, VP of Paramount, to Walter Wanger, letter, January 23, 1950, Walter Wanger Collection, University of Wisconsin, Madison, WI.

1197. Eugene Frenke to Walter Wanger, letter, January 25, 1950, Walter Wanger Collection, University of Wisconsin, Madison, WI.

1198. Harry Saltzman to Norman Bel Geddes, letter, December 19, 1955, Norman Bel Geddes Collection, Harry Ransom Center, Austin, TX.

1199. Robert Sellers, *When Harry Met Cubby* (The History Press, 2019), 47–48.

1200. David Kamp, "Harry the Spy," *Vanity Fair*, September 18, 2012.

1201. Copy of internal office memo sent to Charles Feldman, December 22, 1955, Norman Bel Geddes Collection, Harry Ransom Center, Austin, TX; Charles Feldman to Ray Stark, Feldman Famous Artists Corporation inter-office memo, January 9, 1956, Charles Feldman Collection, Louis B. Mayer Library, Los Angeles, CA.

1202. Transcript of telephone call between Norman Bel Geddes and Harry Saltzman, January 3, 1956, Norman Bel Geddes Collection, Harry Ransom Center, Austin, TX.

1203. Charles Feldman to George Schlee, letter, January 17, 1956, Norman Bel Geddes Collection, Harry Ransom Center, Austin, TX.

1204. Harry Saltzman to Norman Bel Geddes, letter, December 19, 1955, Norman Bel Geddes Collection, Harry Ransom Center, Austin, TX.

1205. Conversation between Norman Bel Geddes and Alan Livingston of NBC, May 13, 1956, Norman Bel Geddes Collection, Harry Ransom Center, Austin, TX

.1206. Harry Saltzman to Ray Stark, letter, February 8, 1956, Norman Bel Geddes Collection, Harry Ransom Center, Austin, TX.

1207. Harry Saltzman to Norman Bel Geddes, letter, February 24, 1956, Norman Bel Geddes Collection, Harry Ransom Center, Austin, TX.

1208. Termination agreement between Norman Bel Geddes and Harry Saltzman, March 9, 1956, Norman Bel Geddes Collection, Harry Ransom Center, Austin, TX.

1209. Charles Feldman to Harry Saltzman, letter, February 23, 1956, Charles Feldman Collection, Louis B. Mayer Library, Los Angeles, CA.

1210 Transcript of telephone call between Norman Bel Geddes and John Huston, March 13, 1956, Norman Bel Geddes Collection, Harry Ransom Center, Austin, TX.

1211. Emanuel Sacks of NBC to Norman Bel Geddes, letter, May 25, 1956, Norman Bel Geddes Collection, Harry Ransom Center, Austin, TX.

1212. Norman Bel Geddes memo summarizing Schlee's criticism of script, December 4, 1956, Norman Bel Geddes Collection, Harry Ransom Center, Austin, TX.

1213. James Welsh and John Tibbets, eds., *The Cinema of Tony Richardson* (State University of New York Press, 1999), 26.

1214. Welsh and Tibbets, *Cinema of Tony Richardson*, 26.

1215. Welsh and Tibbets, *Cinema of Tony Richardson*, 26.

1216. Comments by Gerstle Mack on Monsignor Devlin's critique of script, March 29, 1957, Norman Bel Geddes Collection, Harry Ransom Center, Austin, TX.

1217. Greta Garbo to Peg Gustafson, letter, February 2, 1970, author's personal collection.

1218. Greta Garbo to Gray Reisfield, letter, February 26, 1955, author's personal collection.
1219. .Sven Broman, *Conversations with Greta Garbo* (Viking, 1991), 102
1220. Greta Garbo to Peg Gustafson, letter, February 4, 1958, author's personal collection.
1221. Lewis Hoch, email to author, October 9, 2023. Hoch is five years older than the author.
1222. Megan McDonough, "Bill Cunningham, Photographer of New York Street Fashion Dies at 87," *The Washington Post*, June 25, 2016.
1223. Garson Kanin, Hollywood (Viking Press, 1967), 97.
1224. Mary Van Rensselaer Thayer, *Jacqueline Kennedy, the White House Years* (Little Brown, 1971), 122.
1225. David Michaelis, *The Best of Friends: Profiles in Extraordinary Friendships* (Morrow, 1983), 177.
1226. Kohle Yohannan, Valentina: *American Couture and the Cult of Celebrity* (Rissoli, 2009), 261.
1227. Note by Greta Garbo, undated, Garbo's personal papers, author's personal collection.
1228. *Life*, November 12, 1971, 86–87.
1229. Arlene Fertig Granetz, email to author, March 12, 2022.
1230. *Palm Beach Daily News*, January 31, 1985, p. 2.
1231. Alexander Walker, Garbo (Macmillan, 1980), 22.
1232. Jack Larson, "Garbo: Outtakes of a Life," *The Washington Post*, April 22, 1990, p. B2
1233. "Greta Garbo was a Model Too," *San Francisco Chronicle*, April 19, 1990.
1234. William Safire, "My Garbo Sighting," *The New York Times*, April 20, 1990, p. A33.

Index

A

Abbott, George, 278
AB Hasse W. Tullbergs (publisher), Ring employment, 25
AB Svensk Filminspelning (production subsidiary), 60
Adam and Evil (1927 film), 239
Addams, Charles (Garbo friendship), 455
Adrian (costume designer), 261, 267
  Camille costume development, 268–269
adultery
  Anna Karenina/Conquest examination, 382
  censorship/condemnation, 385
  pure love, equivalence, 383
  script inclusion, importance (Anna Karenina), 386
Aftonbladet (magazine), 94
  Garbo coverage, 138–139
Äfventyret (The Beautiful Adventure) (1922 film) (Garbo minor role), 44, 76–77
Ahern,Brian/Eleanor (Gabor visits), 453
Air Dome Theatre (Ellsworth, KS) (photo), 231
Akins, Zoe (screenwriter), 350, 351
Aktiebolaget Svenska Biografteatern (Svenska Bio), 56
  ensember, Molander (joining), 54
  Stiller (director), 54
  Stiller, films (creation), 25
Albert, Kathering (fan displeasure, display), 295
Albert Ranft organization, Garbo employment, 44
Alexander den store (Alexander the Great) (1917 film), 57
Allan, Maud (dancer), 143
Allen, Frederick Lewis, 183
Allen, Reggie, 415–416
Amatörfilmen. (1922 Molander film), 37
American Catholics, impact, 190–191
American films, foreign element (influence), 338
American-Scandinavian Review, The (Camille review), 391
Ames, Marjorie (Gilbert relationship, uncertainty), 245–246
Andersson, Olof (Svensk Filmindustri financial manager), 60
Anna Christie (1930 film), 44, 49, 302, 339
  cast, excellence, 319–320
  censor challenge, 318
  Dressler photo, 320
  English version, Garbo unhappiness, 333
  Garbo concentration, 331
  Garbo photo, 313, 320
Garbo preparation, 316, 320
Garbo role, 313
Garbo success, 333
Garbo/Viertel photo (German language version), 334

Garbo voice, reviews, 321–322
    Marion interview, 173
    O'Neill, adaptation, 321
    original movie poster, 321
    premiere, 328
    production photo, 313, 317
    public reception, capitalization, 334
    revenue, 362
    Rochester marquee, 322
    special screening, MGM arrangement, 321
    Swedish stereotypes, Garbo issue, 323
    versions, 334
Anna Christie (play), Vanderbilt Theatre premiere, 318
Anna Karenina (1878 film), 238–239
Anna Karenina (1935 film), 305
    adultery, examination, 382, 386
    censorship, PCA challenge, 385
    Chicago Legion of Decency condemnation, 374
    Cortez, assignation, 248–249
    Cortez photo, 251
    costume drama, 382
    direction, Thalberg/Buchowetzki opinion (difference), 249
    female audience, empathy, 387
    financial/critical success, 387
    Garbo photos, 252, 384, 386
    Legion of Decency rating, 375
    New York Legion of Decency approval, 374
    PCA approval, 374
    plans, resumption, 248
    production photo, 383
    script, PCA submission, 384
    Tolstoy screen interpretation, 258
    women, viewing/perspective, 382–383
Anschluss, occurrence, 116
anti-feminist authors, impact, 450–451
antisemitism, 308
    Die freudlose Gasse attack, 117
    virulence, 309–310
Antonsson, Ebba
    childhood, recall, 11
    school experience, 15
Apex Club, Garbo visits, 302
Arlen, Michael, 316
Art Deco style, Garbo (relationship), 203
Asögatan barbershop, Gullan employment, 2
Astaire, Fred (actor), 412
Asther, Nils (actor), 301, 302
    Queen Christina consideration, 355
    Single Standard, The (photo), 314

Astor Theatre, *Love* ticket revenue, 255–256
As You Desire Me (1932 film), 318, 333, 348
  Garbo photo, 335, 337
  McMein review, 338
  play basis, 337
  plot, unusualness, 337–338
  Von Sternberg (photo), 335
Atonement of Gösta Berling, The (Mayer screening), 102
audience, Garbo communication, 201
Austin, John Lewis (theatre historian), 47
Austrian National Socialists (Nazis), Bettauer death (relationship), 122
Avalon Theater, revenue per seat, 229–230
Avedon, Richard (photographer), 146
Ayres, Lew (actor), 262
  Garbo, interaction, 315–316

B
Bainbridge, John (Garbo facts, ignoring), 448–449
Balaban & Katz Paradise Theater (Chicago) (photo), 231
Balettprimadonnan (Wolo Czawienko) (Stiller 1916 film), 57
Ball, Russell (photographer), 141
  Garbo photos, 139, 187, 253
  Garbo sessions, 270–272
Baltzer, August (engineer), 345
Baltzer, Ethel Marguerite (Peg)
  departure, 438
  Duchess de Langeais discussion, 461–462
  Garbo correspondence, 426–427, 439–445, 458
  Garbo, friendship, 345–346
  Garbo wrist, break, 481
  Hårby sale, 424
  photo, 345, 346
  Sven, meeting/marriage, 345
Baltzer, Tillie (Mathilda) (death), 345
Balzac, Honoré de, 462
Bankhead, Tallulah (actress)
  dinner, hosting, 303
  public appearance, fan attention, 300
  Read analysis, 207
Bara, Theda (actress)
  caricature, 216
  vamp version, 199
Barrymore, Ethel (actress), 303
Barrymore, John (actor), 262
  Camille photo, 387
  Grand Hotel photo, 336
  Queen Christina consideration, 355
  stardom, 336

Barrymore, Lionel
Camille role, 388
stardom, impact, 336
Barthelmess, Richard, 220
Beaton, Cecil (photographer), 141, 340, 378
Garbo visit, 457
photo, 464
portrait sessions, 447–448
Beaton, Welford, 253
Beauchamp, Antony (photographer), 141
photo sessions, 448
Beaumont, Lucy (*Torrent* photo), 166
Beautiful Adventure, The (1922 production), 45
Beckett, Samuel (playwright), 469
Beery, Wallace (stardom), 336
Behrman, Max (scriptwriter), 17, 351
Viertel, interaction, 353
Bel Geddes, Norman (Miracle, The involvement), 468–470
Bella Donna (1923 film), 179
Bell, Monta (director), 152, 215
Chaplin training, 155
Garbo, interaction, 168
Benavente, Jacinto, 84
Ben-Hur (1925 movie)
production, cost, 396
success, 84
Bennett, Constance (Two-Faced Woman photo), 429
Benson, Sally (scriptwriter) Duchess de Langeais involvement, 462–464
Benson, Susan Parter, 21
Berger, Ludwig (director), 339, 342–343
Bergman, Hjalmar (Sjöström correspondence), 60–61
Bergman, Ingmar, 41, 54
Bergman, Ingrid, 54
Berg, Stig, 24
Bergström, Paul. see Paul U. Bergström
son, Garbo attraction, 22
Berliner Tageblatt (Garbo Gösta Berling review), 98
Berlin, Garbo impressions/tour, 96, 103
Bernadotte, Folke (Manville marriage), 287
Bern, Paul, 220
Bernstein, David (Loew's CFO), 229
Besnard, Lucien, 84
Bettauer, Hugo, 113, 116–117
Riehl assassination, 122
Beverly of graustark (film), 180
Bickford, Charles (actor), 317, 319–320
photo, 317

Biery, Ruth (reporter), 11–12
Garbo interview, 42, 69, 76, 94, 139, 178, 245
Garbo/Mayer contract issue, recollection, 209–210
multipart story, 295, 315
Women Love Diamonds, Garbo recollection, 236
Big Parade, The (Gilbert involvement), 212
Billings, Lem, 479, 480
birth control, impact, 188
Birth of a Nation (Griffith 1915 film), 56
Bishop, Allen (Ninotchka analysis), 423
Blasco Ibáñez, Vicente, 156, 159, 176
Blekingegatan. see Gustafson family
Blomqvist, Eva (childhood friend), 22
Boardman, Eleanor (actress), 220
comparison, 207
Vidor marriage, 218
Boleslawski, Richard (director), 174, 342
Bonnier, Åke, 415
Bonnier, Karl Otto, 415
books, blacklisting (impact), 379
Bosse, Harriet, 84
Bow, Clara (actress), 194
childhood, 10
Bowes, Edwin, 150
Boyer, Charles (actor), 301
Conquest photo, 395
Conquest role, 392
Brackett, Charles, 350
Brecht, Bertolt (writer), 69, 409
Breen Group
Catholic archbishops/pope, coordination, 371
impact, 309, 310, 369
Breen, Joseph
antisemitism, 310
Camille concerns, 381
censorship battles, 360
censorship problems, 362
Cincinnati meeting, 371
draft code document, creation, 309
MPPDA censorship officer, 373
overruling, Producer's Committee (impact), 360
PCA office chief, Hays appointment, 373
PCA resignation, 429, 432
Production Code enforcement responsibility, 359–360
Selznick correspondence, 386
Brent, George (Garbo romantic relationship), 378
Bretschneider, Erich (CEO), 92, 103
Brisson, Carl, 291
Mosebacke Theatre headliner, 16

Broadway musical (Stiller presentation), 278, 289
Broccoli, Albert (producer), 472
Brodnitz, Hanns, 97
Bröllopet i Bränna (Petschler 1927 film), 37
Broman, Sven, 9–11
    Garbo interview, 447, 475, 483
Bronnen, Arnold, 69
Brookhart, Smith (antisemitism), 308
Brooks, Louise (actress), 152
Brosi, Oscar (arrest), 297
Brown, Clarence (director), 209, 213, 320, 342, 438
    Anna Christie screening, enthusiasm, 321
    Conquest photo, 395
    Hyman, interaction (issues), 394
    joke, 262
Brown, Harrier (Garbo alias), 451
Brownlow, Kevin (historian), 248
Brunius, John W. (film director), 30
    Garbo, film extra, 37
Bryher. see Ellerman
Buchowetzki, Dimitri, 238, 249, 253–254
Buhler, Joseph (lawyer), 286
Bull, Clarence Sinclair (photographer), 141, 144, 254
    Garbo portraits, making (responsibility), 271
    Garbo, professional relationship, 270
Bürgel, Heinrich Karl Hugo. see Goodwin
Burton, Richard (actor), 471–472
Busch, Otto (Stiller meeting), 103

C
Calhoun, Dorothy (writer), 248
Cameron, Julia Margaret (pictorialist photographer), 79
Camille (1936 Cukor film)
    American-Scandinavian Review, The (review), 391
    Australian poster, 381
    Barrymore photo, 387
    Breen objections/guidelines, 388
    closed set, Garbo insistence, 265
    costume drama, 382
    costumes, Adrian development, 268–269
    endings, variation, 3889
    Garbo photos, 387, 391
    Garbo role, LaSalle appreciation, 391–392
    Garbo walk, development, 330
    Keil-Möller, review, 391
    Legion of Decency rating, 375
    Marion/Akins (writers), 350
    PCA, impact (limitation), 388–389

photo, 389
production, duration, 396
Taylor interview, 173
Cantwell, John
American Catholic assembly speech, 370
Cincinnati meeting, 371
Capitol Theatre (New York)
Anna Christie showings, 318, 341
Love (running), 256
Student Prince, The (running), 256
Capitol Theatre (New York), Torrent ticket sales, 161
Catholic censorship, 308
Catholic Church
censorship, 308
power, reiteration, 432
Cederström, Lena (actress), 45
celebrities
parallel world, existence, 297
press, accuracy (unconcern), 452
stalkers, characteristics, 297
censorship, 367
attempts, 190
Catholic bishops, record creation (avoidance), 371
Catholic censorship, 308
Catholic Church campaign, 189
Catholic control, hiding, 435
coded meaning, acceptability, 368
evolution (chart), 189, 369
Garbo, relationship, 192
increase, factor, 369
issues, sound arrival (impact), 308
justification, 370
PCA challenge (*Anna Karenina*), 385
regime, presence, 308
self-censorship, studio decision, 368
studio responsiveness, 368
Chaney, Lon (actor), 212, 248
Chaplin, Charlie (actor), 155, 267, 410, 453
acting, Garbo acting (comparison), 172
childhood, contrast, 10
character
creation, Garbo intent, 201
essence (Garbo delivery), 201
Chekhov, Anton (playwright), 316
Cherry Orchard, The (Chekhov), 49
Chevalier, Maurice (actor), 264
Chicago Theatre, revenue per seat delivery, 229–230
Chicago theatres (box office per seat), 230

Chmara, Gregori, 116
Chocolate Soldier, The (1941 film), 433
Christensen, Halfdan, 45
Churchill, Winston, 195
church-run primary school *(folkskolan)*, Garbo attendance, 14
Cinema Shop ad, 269
Clark, Robert (organist), 158
clerical workers, census category, 232–233
Clift, Montgomery (Garbo social circle), 455
closed sets (Garbo insistence), 265
Close Up (magazine), 125–126
Cody, Lew, 245
Colbert, Claudette
  Photoplay mentions, frequency, 326
  screwball role, 383
Colman, Ronald (actor), 220
  Queen Christina consideration, 355
Come tu mi vuoi (How you love me) (Pirandello), 337
Comiskey, Andrea (film historian), 158
Communism, appeal, 338
Concubine from Smolny, The. see Odalisken från Smolna
Connelly, Edward (Torrent photo), 166
Conquest (1937 Brown film), 301
  adultery, examination, 382, 394
  Boyer photo, 395
  Brown photo, 395
  change, PCA demands, 394
  costume drama, 382, 392
  Garbo photos, 393, 395
  Hoffenstein rewrite, 394
  Hyman, producer role, 394
  Legion of Decency rating, 375
  losses, 396
  moral tone, Breen concerns, 393–394
  plot points, changes, 392
  production, cost, 396
  production, duration, 396
  review, 396
  Thalberg approval, 392
  Viertel pitch, 392
conservative gender roles, rejection (Quigley objections), 371
conservative values, rejection (perception), 376
"Constantinople Project, The," 90
Conti, Harlan, 484
Cooper, Gary (actor)
  Garbo appreciation, 302
  Queen Christina consideration, 355

Cortez, Ricardo (actor), 154
Anna Karenina photo, 251
disappointment, 155
Garbo interaction, 248
Torrent photos, 152, 169
Cowan, Lester (film idea), 442
Coward, Nöel (Garbo meeting/friendship), 289, 404, 405
Crawford, Joan (actress), 206, 207, 260, 395
box office appeal, Independent Theatre Owners Association contention, 227
childhood, 10, 436
film roles, continuation, 436
Hurrell portraits, 270
Photoplay mentions, frequency, 326
public appearance, fan attention, 300
Read analysis, 207
stardom, 239, 336
What Ever Happened to Baby Jane? role, 437
Crocker, Harry (Garbo visits), 453
Crosby, Juliette, 220
Crowd, The (Vidor 1933 film), 356
Cukor, George (director), 202, 329, 342, 390, 412, 438
Garbo, interaction/respect, 389
Garbo/Olivier conversation, 478
Mourning Becomes Electra pitch, Mayer rejection, 443
culture (changes), Garbo (impact), 195
"Culture Is Ordinary" (Williams), 195
Cunningham, Billy (photographer), 478
Curie, Marie (MGM film production), 429–430

D
Dagens Nyheter *(newspaper), Garbo acting review, 78*
Dakota Theater (Seneca, SD) (photo), 231
Dalem Allotments (Enskede), Gustafson cottage
farming plot, 10
photo, 8
rent, 7–8
Dalstrom, Kata, 9
Dando, Jill (fan murder), 297
Dane, Karl (actor), 164
Daniel Hjort (Wecksell), Garbo/Sjostrand scene, 77
Daniels, William (cinematographer), 155, 170, 213, 261–262
Garbo gift, 264
Das Tagebuch article (*Odalisque* financing), 107–108
dating, permissions, 187
Daughters of the American Revolution, censorship efforts, 308
Davies, Marion (Polly of the Circus preview attendance), 265
Davis, Bette (actress), 260, 395
film roles, continuation, 436
observation, 173–174

public appearance, fan attention, 300
What Ever Happened to Baby Jane? role, 437
de Acosta, Mercedes, 405
del Rio, Dolores (actress), 220
Garbo, closeness, 268, 399
DeMille, Cecil B. (director), 239
demure heroine, banishment, 201
Den beundrandsvarde Crichton (The Admirable Crichton) (1902 film) (Garbo minor role), 76
Den osynligexi (The Invisible) (Molander stage production), 45
depression, treatment, 408
deranged fans, impact, 297–298
Der Dybuk (Pabst film), 114
Der Film (magazine), 97, 122
de Rothschild, Cecile, 481
Der Tag (newspaper) (*Die freudlose Gasse* serialization), 113
Design for Living (1933 film), 355
desire, infinity (Garbo projection), 204–205
Detroit Free Press
Conquest review, 396
Queen Christina critique, 363
Deval, Jacques (writer), 301
Devil's Circus, The (1926 film)
costs/profits, 163
Shearer appearance, 162
Diamond Handcuffs, 236
Die freudlose Gasse (Joyless Street, The) (Street of Sorrow, The) (1925 film)
audiences, social orientations (differences), 125
Bettauer (author), 113
cast announcement (Film Kurrier special issue), 119
censorship cuts, 116, 120
characters, addition/subtraction, 117
contract, Garbo signing/payment, 108–109
contract, Hanson signing, 109
criticisms, 121–122
Ellerman review, 126
ethical conflict, fantasies, 198
film writer access, 122
financial backers, Pabst relationship (uncertainty), 393
Garbo photo, 112, 116
Haas, Willy (script), 116–117, 124
heroine, virtuousness/complexity, 199–200
interplay, 122
intertitle, insertion, 127
movie still, 115
Pabst/Sorkin editing, 123
parallel story, 115
premiere, Garbo absence, 123
Reichsfilmblatt review, 124
resonance, 125

restored version, Munich Filmmuseum creation, 121–122
script (Haas), 116–117
sexual advantages, men (taking), 120–121
Stiller film project, 108
storylines, hyperinflation (impact), 117
subplots, 114–115
success, 123
U.S. release (truncation), 121
women, powerlessness, 118
Die Stadt ohne Juden (The City Without Jews) (Bettauer), 113
Dietrich, Marlene
extortion letters, receipt, 297
film roles, continuation, 436
Paramount hiring, 205–206
Photoplay mentions, frequency, 326
Read analysis, 207
Dietz, Howard
Catholic Church, attack, 433–434
Gilbert conversation, 222
Dinneen, FitzGeorge, 309, 362
censorship effort, 369
Quigley complaints, 369
Divine Woman, The (Sjöström 1928 film), 52, 172, 273, 339
Divorcee, The (Shearer role), 205
divorce, film presentation (Legion of Decency opinion), 374
Donne, Edgar (estate bequeath/stalker behavior), 298
Donne, Sissy, 298
"Don'ts and Be Carefuls" (pre-production guidance), 190, 308, 368
replacement, 309
Doolittle, Hilda (poet), 112, 125
Dostoevsky, Fyodor, 209
Douglas, Melvyn (actor)
Chocolate Soldier role, 433
Ninotchka photos, 417, 420
Two-Faced Woman photos, 428, 429
Two-Faced Woman role, 430
Dragonette, Jessica
Garbo friendship, 399, 412, 454–455
Turner marriage, 455
Dream Play, A (Strindberg), 49
Dressler, Marie (actress), 317
Anna Christie photo, 320
Garbo celebration, 323
joy, 320
Drifting Souls (1932) scene, objection, 311
Drimmer, Eric (Garbo psychologist), 408–410
Duchess de Langeais, The, 461
Benson, Sally (script, writing), 463

Cukor withdrawal, 462–463
deal, finalization/failure, 465–466
financing, problems, 463–464
French version, Wanger screening, 462
Logan, directing consideration, 463
PCA disapproval, 464
project, dropping, 446, 463
Rizzoli financing, 464
screen capture (photo), 459
Viertel, involvement, 461–462
Duncan, Anna (dance photo), 143
Duncan, Isadora (dancer), 143
Dunne, Irene (screwball role), 383
Dunning, Philip, 278

E

early film industry revenue, source (pie chart), 225
Edén, Nils (prime minister appointment), 5
Edington, Harry (Garbo agent), 237, 238, 245, 301
Garbo new deal, 241
Philharmonic Auditorium, Garbo attendance, 305
Queen Christina (proposal), 351
Einstein, Albert, 195
Eisenstein, Sergei, 172
Ekengren, Arthur F./Sally (barbershop) (Garbo employment), 16
Ekman, Gösta (film actress), 30–31
MGM contracts, offering, 130–131
Ekstrand, Sture (Garbo portrait photos), 79
Ekström, Märta, 41
Ellerman, Annie Winifred (Bryher), 125–126
Die freudlose Gasse review, 126
En Herrgårdssägen (film), name change, 69
En lyckoriddare (A knight of fortune) (Brunius 1921 film), 30–31
En piga bland pigor (A maid of maids) (1924 film), Keil-Möller/Lundell (involvement), 133
Enskede. see Dalem Allotments
En vikingafilm (A viking film) (1922 Ring film), 32–34
Enwall, Frans
health, deterioration, 33
Royal Dramatic Theatre, actor/teacher/head, 32
Enwall, Signe (actress), 84
Garbo acting coach, 19, 33–35
Episcopal Committee on Motion Pictures (ECMP), background operation, 373
Erkkila, Betsy (film historian), 162, 357
Erotikon (1920 Stiller film), 93, 132
Esterházy, Ágnes (actress), 114, 115, 122
Ett Resande Teatersällskap (Hanson/Garbo appearance), 77
Evans, Harry (Garbo acting appreciation), 363
Evens, Harry, 319
Exhibitors Herald

Garbo review, 159
Gilbert crash, mention, 246
Temptress review, 199
Existentialism, Sartre analysis, 195
"Exit Flapper, Enter Woman" article, 198
Expressionist film, 117

F
Fairbanks, Douglas (Swedish film industry dinner), 88, 95
"fallen woman" position, 121
family names, usage, 71–72
Famous Players, Pickford signing, 239
Farnum, Dorothy (screenwriter), 351
Fascism, appeal, 338
Faulkner, William (writer), 311
Feldman, Charles, 469–470
female actors
MGM revenue percentage, 206
screwball roles, 383
female authority, Garbo films (impact), 197
female clerks, number (increase), 233
female heroine *(Queen Christina)*, creation, 357
female purity, Victorian notion, 188
feminine life, Garbo truth, 200
femininity, conception (change), 184
feminism, retreat, 341
Fertig, Joe (dentist), 482–483
Feyder, Jacques (director)
career, success, 342
Garbo preference, 315
The Kiss scriptwriter, 315
Feyder, Jacques/Françoise, 301
Filene, Peter, 186
film
acting, style/melodrama, 169
censors, impact, 189
distribution market, differences, 227
early film industry revenue, source (pie chart), 225
fan magazines, doubling, 325
foreigners, intervention (Perceval insistence), 338
studios, self-censorship decision, 368
theaters, seating capacity, 230
universal popularity, 189
vamp, unreality (Garbo eroticization), 162
Filmbladet (trade magazine), 38
Film Daily
Gilbert crash, mention (absence), 246
industry developments, 227
total box office, 233–234

"Film Europe" creation, 97, 131
Film Europe project, Stiller (involvement), 133
Filmindustri AB Skandia (Svensk Filmindustri), 56
Filmjournalen (Swedish film fan magazine), 18
Film-Kurier (magazine), *Garbo Die freudlose Gasse* review, 124–125
Film Mercury, The (Temptress, The coverage), 179, 201–202
Filmnhyeter (magazine), 74
  Garbo acting review, 78
  Hanson/Garbo scene still, 79
Filmsignale (consumer magazine), 91
Film Spectator
  Love (film), complaints, 252
  Love (film), production, 253
  report, 197
Fimsy (Garbo pet dog), 300–301
  photo, 301
first-run audience, urban/female characteristic, 225
first-run theaters
  clerical workers, display, 232
  exhibitions, film industry revenue, 224
Fisher, Lucy (film historian), 193, 314
Fitzgerald, F. Scott (writer), 311
Fitzmaurice, George (dinner party), 401
Flamini, Roland (biographer), 220
flappers, Modern Woman (relationship), 196
Fleming, Victor, 220
Flesh and the Devil (MGM 1926 film), 153
  boundary, pushing, 191
  communion scene, filming (Garbo description), 214–215
  Garbo acting, Brown recollection, 215
  Garbo character, death, 205
  Garbo/Gilbert characters, romantic rendezvous, 192
  Garbo/Gilbert love scene, 213
  Garbo performance, 171
  Garbo photos, 183, 211
  Garbo, unusual/creative choice, 198
  Lobby Card ad, 215
  love scene, 214, 217–218
  love triangle, basis, 211–212
  National Board of Review criticism, 191
  New York Times review, 216
  Palace Theater, box office results, 217
  Photoplay review, 216
  premiere, Garbo/Gilbert attendance, 246
  production, continuation, 243
  theater display (photo), 240
  visual schema, Brown/Daniels development, 214
Flodin, Ferdinand (Garbo portrait photos), 79
Florin, Bo, 56

foreign film market, Garbo dominance, 363
Fougstedt, Arvid (artist), 284
Fox Studios
    film major, integration, 228
    Gilbert (multi-film contract), 212
Francis, Alex (actor), 173
Free Church movement, 4
freedom, concept, 187
Frenke, Eugene (investor/location search), 462
Frontovye podrugi (The Girl from Leningrad) (1941 film), 438
"Fru fran Hagalund" ("I am the Lady from Hagalund") (cabaret song), 45
Fry, Christopher, 469
Frye, Bill, 299
Fulda, Ludwig, 430
Fuller, Loie (dancer), 143
Funkquist, Georg, 41, 44
Funny Girl (play), Garbo/Frye (audience/fan attention), 299–300
Fürth, Jaro (actor), 114, 124
    Die freudlose Gasse reviews, 124

G
Gaate, Inga (*Gösta Berling* cast interviews), 7676
Gable, Clark (actor)
    Queen Christina consideration, 355
    Susan Lenox photo, 260
Garbo, Alva
    birth, 6, 7
    death, 177, 210
    Greta attachment, 177
    office clerk (job), 15
Garbo, Greta
    8 Uhr-Abendblatt review
    450 East 52nd Street (New York residence), 454
    1717 San Vicente Boulevard house, 303–304
    access, public access, 294
    accomplishments, Sherwood observation, 322–323
    active life, 453
    actress career, long-term plan, 37
    advertising film role, 24
    Aftonbladet coverage, 138–139
    age 9 (photo), 1
    age 109 (photo), 5
    airplane exit (photo), 466
    America, impressions (questions), 288
    American citizenship, 475
    Americans, socialization (increase), 409
    anemia, lifetime management, 482
    Anna Christie photo, 313, 320
    Anna Christie success, 333

Anna Karenina photos, 251, 384, 386
anonymity, preference, 305–306
antisocial behavior, paparazzi opinion, 451
Arizona/New Mexico photos, 365
Art Deco style, relationship, 203
art, perfection, 331
athletic interests, 219
audience connection (Torrent), 160
audience, mesmerization, 329
audience sympathy (Anna Karenina), 384
Ball photos, 139, 187, 253
barbershop assistant, 2, 16–17
Barbuda photo, 476
Beaton photo, 464
beauty (Stiller observation), 66
Berliner Tageblatt review, 98
Biery interview, 42, 69, 76, 94, 139, 178, 245, 295
birthplace (Stockholm), 7
Black assistant, hiring, 401
box office appeal, Independent Theatre Owners Association contention, 227
Broman interview, 447
Brown, Harriet (alias), 451
bumper harvest (Dalem Allotments), 8
California visits, 453
Camille photos, 387, 391
car driving photo, 184
censorship, relationship, 192
character, essence (delivery), 201
characterization ability (Smith observation), 167
character, sins (price), 382
childhood, 2–3
childhood, description, 11–12
cipher, critic viewpoint, 200
clothing, impact, 269–270
Conquest photo, 393
costume, first film role (photo), 26
costume, *Luffar-Petter* film role (photo), 37
Coward meeting/friendship, 289, 404, 405
crew, interaction, 262
crowds, dislike, 11
crowds, following, 290
dancing (photo), 426
datebook (1960) photo, 454
datebooks, entries, 456–457
death, 475, 486
deportation, threat, 237–238
deranged fans, interaction, 297–298
Die freudlose Gasse performance, Doolittle review, 126
Die freudlose Gasse performance, reviews, 123–125

Dragonette friendship, 399, 412, 454–455
Dramaten publicity photo, 50
Duchess de Langeais, The (photo), 459
employment duties, conscientiousness, 23
English, practice, 155
Europe, visits, 398–399, 413
exhibition profits, 254–255
Exhibitors Herald review, 159
facial expressions/bodily movement/speech, harmony, 332
facts, writers (ignoring), 44–449
fame, enjoyment (absence), 410
family, emigration, 423
family, New York move, 439
fashion photo, 140
father, loss, 20
film characters, honesty (importance), 375
film projects, quality (improvement), 340
film projects, selection, 341
Fimsy (pet dog), 300–301
Fingal/Agaton (imaginary rabbits), 46, 404
Flesh and the Devil performance, 171
Flesh and the Devil photos, 183, 211
flim audition preparation, 34–35
foreignness, audience disaffection, 338
fresh image, MGM creation (absence), 254
friends photo, 449
Garbo/Stiller photo, 89
gay/lesbian icon, 376–378
Genthe photos, 144–146
Genthe sessions, 80, 82, 142–147
Gilbert love affair, 212–222
Gilbert meeting, 182, 208
Goodwin photo, 82, 86
Goodwin sessions, 64, 80, 82–83, 142, 145
Gösta Berling Berlin premiere, attendance, 96–97
Gösta Berling performance, reviews, 84–85
Gösta Berling photos, 63, 70, 71, 75
Gösta Berlingg scene stills, usage, 78, 79
Gothenburg harbor arrival (press conference), 287
Gouldings, friendship, 402
Grand Hotel photo, 336
gregariousness, 409
Gullan description, 2
Gumpel dinner, 402
Gumpel friendship, 28
Gurra (nickname), 76
Gustafson (name transition), 43
Gustafson (original acting name), 27, 72
hairstyle, change (photo), 416

Hall (Gladys) interview, 139, 172, 235
Hall (Mordaunt) interview, 168, 292, 295, 314–315
hat, modeling (Bergström hiring), 23
hat, modeling (photo), 24
Hauser photo, 456
health issues, 390, 404, 483
heart attack, 483
height, teenage years (self-consciousness), 13–14
Hollywood arrival, 151, 194, 265
home, burglars (entry), 298
hospital stay, 458
humor, example, 479–480
Hyltén-Cavallius, reconnection, 290–291
illness, 248
imperfect human being, presentation, 171
improvisation ability, Eisenstein observation, 172
Inspiration photo, 330
internment, 2
interviews, cessation, 295
Istanbul photo, 104
Joyless Street photo, 112
Kåge acting advice, 31–32
Kata (nickname), 9, 476
Katrina South School class (photo), 14
Klosters photo, 454
last name, official change (document photo), 72
last party, 477
Life review, 167
Lipke interview, 294
Loos, friendship, 409–410, 412
Los Angeles home (photo), 242
Los Angeles Times interview, 294
Louise photos, 193, 250, 280
Love photo, 259
Lubitsch, interaction, 422
Luffar-Petter premiere, attendance, 38
malady, recovery, 24
Mamoulian, dating, 366, 378
manager, desire, 209
marriage, desire (absence), 221
marriage, plan, 178
Mayer meeting, 102
McCall's review, 337
medical appointments (datebook entries), 457
mental health problems, celebrity status (impact), 408
MGM letter of intent/payment scale, 109–110, 129, 135
MGM lot (photos), 171, 441
MGM salary, weekly terms, 149
"Miss Sweden" crowning, 111

modeling jobs (advertisements), 85
Molander, meeting, 289
mother, accompaniment (photo), 287
mother/brother, time (spending), 291–292
mother/niece (photo), 437
mother/sister-in-law photo, 403
moviegoing, attendance, 13
movie industry, joining (decision), 33
MS Annie Johnson, 346
MS *Gripsholm* (passage/photo), 343, 344
MS *Gripsholm* (press conference), 413
MS *Kungsholm* (interview), 365, 402, 405, 416
MS *Kungsholm* (photo), 286
MS *Kungsholm* passage, 415–416
Mysterious Lady, The (photo), 193
naturalistic acting style, 48, 126
naturalistic performances, 169–170
negotiation refusal, obstinance, 237–238
new contract, original contract (differences), 242
new deal (Rubin/Edington, assistance), 241
news photographer, following (photo), 400
New York arrival (photo), 137
New York photo, pose, 343
New York return (photo), 444
New York, walking (photo), 474
Ninotchka photos, 417, 419–422
Northern Cemetery visit, 290
nutria coat (photo), 477
Oakland Tribune photo, 111
onscreen physical movement, reduction (Rathbone observation), 332
Oscar nomination, 392
Painted Veil, The (photos), 367, 379
Palmborg interview, 295
Palm Desert photo, 456
paparazzi, impact, 400
parasocial life, 446
partial nudity (photo project), 147
peace, reporters (avoidance), 289
pencil carbon light photo, 213
pernicious anemia, attack, 248
personality, public property (fan belief), 295
personal safety, worry, 296
photo essay (Vanity Fair magazine), 204
Photoplay interview, 295
Photoplay review, 159
photo, retention/control, 235
photos, 249, 276, 291, 299, 302, 306
physical activity, 305
physical look copying, 340

playfulness, 401
Polly of the Circus preview attendance, 265
popularity, ranking, 197
Portofino fans, impact/fight, 298–299
portrait photography, usage, 447–448
portraits, businesslike approach, 271
portraits, initiation, 78–79
press availability, limitation, 214–215
press avoidance, reason, 405–406
private life, quest, 293
professional acting lessons, 20
projects, collapse, 443–444
projects, literate aspect, 341
public events, visits, 305–306
publicity, avoidance, 325
public perception, articles (impact), 448
public relations interviews, 158–159
Queen Christina performance, 171
Queen Christina photos, 353, 354, 356, 357, 378
recluse, misnomer, 446
rehearsals, importance, 331–332
reputation, establishment, 182
resonance (Film Spectator report), 197
Riviera photo, 450
Roberts interview, 139
Rodeo Drive investment, 483
role transcendence, Davis observation, 173–174
"romantic woman" representation, 171
runner (job), 10–11
Salvation Army papers, selling, 10–11
sample *Torrent* review, 159–160
San Francisco photo, 150
savings, loss (rumor), 341
Saxon friendship/romance, 164, 165
Schenck meeting, 151
Schlee photo, 471
school graduation, 16
school, initiation, 9
scripts, selection, 197, 449
sense of justice, 11
set closure, insistence, 265
shyness (Bankhead recollection), 303
siblings, birth, 6
sickliness, 15
significance, 261
silent films, studio revenue, 274–275
singing, 9
Single Standard, The (photo), 205, 312, 314
sister-in-law correspondence, 377

smile, Lubitsch appearance, 331
snapshot, 397
social circle, 455
solitude, desire (*New Yorker* stories), 478
solitude, desire (respect), 222
speeding tickets, 164
SS *Drottningholm* passage, 292
SS *Drottningholm* passage (photo), 285
stalkers, 397, 400
star billing, guarantee, 243
Stiller (collaborator/friend/romantic partner), 55
Stiller death, impact, 283–284
Stiller letter, 280–281
Stiller (Abraham), meeting, 290
Stiller (collaborator/friend/romantic partner) meeting, 65
St. Johns interview, 295
Stokowski, meeting/romantic relationship, 378, 412–414
Strand Hotel Christmas dinner, 289
Süleymaniye Mosque photo, 107
Susan Lenox photo, 260, 328, 330
Sven visit, 424
Sweden return (1928), 275, 285–289, 344–345
Swedish accent, reactions, 338–339
swimming pool photo, 434
talent, Molander appreciation, 41
talent, Stiller appreciation, 73–74
talking movies, 313
Temptress, The (photos), 179–181
Temptress, The (reviews), 167–168, 180–181
tennis photo, 175
three-film output, 243
tomboy, 12
Torrent photos, 152, 161, 166, 169, 174
Torrent reviews, 159–167
Tower Road photo, 219
train photo, 402
transcendence, Keil-Moller observation, 279
transcendence, Sjöberg explanation, 194–195
transformation/impact, 484
Trianon contract, termination, 132–133
Tullberg film girl, 30
Two-Faced Woman (photos), 428, 429, 431
type creation, Read analysis, 207
UFA discussions, 132
uniqueness, 160
unusual/creative, choice, 198–199
urban market first-run theaters, performance, 217
urban women, first-run tickets, 254–255
U.S. arrival, 130, 136

U.S. existence, depression, 165
U.S. plan, audacity, 134–135
U.S. silver certificate, 128
Viertel/Santa Monica photo, 296
voice, clarity/quality, 319, 321–322
voice, impact, 328
Wachtmeisters, meeting, 289
walk, style (development), 329–330
West Coast trip, 459
West interview, 294
White House tour, 480
Winchell attack, 400
Winchell perception, 451
Wisconsin photo, 411
Woman of Affairs, A (performance), 171
Woman of Affairs, A (photo), 221
work pace, deceleration, 398
work, Stiller instruction, 170
wrist, break, 481–482
Yosemite trip, 316
Garbo, Greta (acting skill)
acknowledgement, absence, 170
Chaplin acting, comparison, 172
Evans appreciation, 363
Gilbert analysis/appreciation, 259, 355
intuitive feeling, 27
love, 12
Mamoulian appreciation, 353–354
skill, female audience resonance, 50
Stiller encouragement, 3
Tullberg appreciation, 27
Garbo, Greta (career)
control, 340
MGM control, 197
transformation, voice (impact), 328
Garbo, Greta (contract)
comparison, 241
extension, reasons, 273
negotiations, 245–246
signing (1935), 387
Garbo, Sven
baker (job), 15
birth, 6
childbirth (out of wedlock), 17
death, 482
Hårby sale, 424
job flexibility, importance, 17
military service, 17
photo, Garbo house display, 303

Garson, Greer (actress), 430
Gaynor, Janet (*Photoplay* mentions, frequency), 326
General Federation of Women's Clubs, censorship efforts, 308
Genthe, Arnold (photographer), 140–141
Garbo photos, 144–146
Garbo sessions, 80, 82, 142–147
George Sand
  letter of intent, 462
  project, dropping, 462
German film firms, export market difficulties, 134
Germany
  film companies, capital access difficulties, 91
  hyperinflation, cessation, 91
  women, role, 120
Gert, Valeska (actress), 114, 115
  Die freudlose Gasse reviews, 124
Gibbons, Cedric (set designer), 220, 243, 261, 267
Garbo friendship, 268, 399
tennis, Garbo win, 305
Gibson Girls, Modern Woman (relationship), 196
Gilbert, John (Jack) (actor), 204, 213
  Ames, relationship (uncertainty), 245–246
  arrest, 247
  car accident, 245
  description, 212
  drinking, impact, 219–220
  Flesh and the Devil, 209
  Flesh and the Devil photo, 211
  Garbo, intimate scene *(Flesh and the Devil)*, 214
  Garbo love affair, 212–222
  Garbo meeting, 182, 208
  Garbo romance, 216–218, 378
  hiring *(Queen Christina)*, 354–355
  jail, release (Los Angeles Times conversation), 247–248
  jail, sentencing, 248
  Love photo, 259
  marriage, Garbo avoidance, 220
  pencil carbon light photo, 213
  Polly of the Circus preview attendance, 265
  social group, Garbo presence/distance, 218
  Tower Road photo, 219
  Woman of Affairs, A (photo), 221
Girl from Leningrad, The (1941 film)
  contract, Garbo agreement, 435
  Garbo rejection, 436
  project, dropping, 438, 446
Gish, Lillian
  salary, 110
  Scarlet Letter, The, 164

Glazer, Barney/Alice, 220
Goddard, Paulette (actress), 410
Godsol, Joe (Sjöström negotiations), 61
Golden, Eve (biographers), 220
Goldwyn, Frances Howard, 220
Goldwyn, Frances Howard (Garbo visit), 302
Goldwyn Pictures, Sjöström distribution rights deal, 61, 130–131
Goldwyn, Sam (Goldwyn Pictures chair), 61, 267
Garbo visit, 302
Gone with the Wind (production expense), 396
Goodwin, Henry (Heinrich Karl Hugo Bürgel) (photographer), 146
  creative process, description, 81
  Garbo photo, 82, 86
  Garbo sessions, 64, 80, 82–83, 142, 145
  negative, artistic manipulation, 81
  pictorial presentation, concern, 79
  portraits, storytelling effort, 81
Gösta Berling (Stiller 1924 film), 52
  advertising campaign, Schratter creation, 94
  Berlin premiere (Stiller/Garbo/Lundequist attendance), 95–96
  cast, announcement, 71
  dramatic tension, 69
  filming, initiation (difficulty), 73
  Garbo (Dohna role), 55, 63–76
  Garbo (Dohna role) (photos), 63, 70, 71, 75
  Garbo, Mayer screening, 153
  heroine, virtuousness/complexity, 199–200
  magazine article (photos), 67
  profits, international distribution deals (importance), 92–93
  reception, unevenness, 132
  reviews/reception, 83
  scene, production effort (Filmnyheter description), 74
  scene stills, usage, 78
  shooting windows, 75–76
  subplots, impact, 70–71
  success, 83–84
  vamp role, antithesis, 238
Gösta Berling's Saga (The Saga of Gösta Berling), 64
Gotgatan barbershop, Garbo (employment), 2, 16
Goulding, Edmund (director/producer), 252, 262
  career, success, 342
  Garbo friendship, continuation, 301
  tennis court, Garbo usage, 305
Goulding, Edmund (producer), 220, 253
Goulding, Edmund/Marjorie (Garbo friendship), 402
Graham, Sheilah, 467
Grand Hotel (1932 film), 318, 325, 336, 399
  Astor Theatre marquee photo, 223
  filming, 262
  Garbo/Barrymore photo, 336

Garbo, taciturn behavior, 262
Garbo walk, development, 329–330
McCall's review, 337
revenue, 362
storylines, 336
Great Depression
film revenues, reduction, 371
impact, 33, 362–363, 428, 449
Green Hat, The (1924 film), 316
Green, Same, 482
Greer, Howard (clothes shopping), 282
"Greta Garbo Educated on Contract, Resumes" (Variety headline), 238–239
Grieve, Harold, 453
Grimmie, Christina (fan murder), 297
Grimstead, Hattie (journalist), 413
Gronowicz, Antoni (author) (fact-check problems), 452
Guilaroff, Sydney (Garbo visit), 457
Gumpel & Bengtsson (construction company), 25
Gumpel, Max
Garbo friendship, 28, 402
Olsson marriage, 28
Gunnar Hedes Saga (The Blizzard) (Stiller 1923 film), 60, 69
Söderhjelm (script involvement), 134
Gunther, John (Garbo friendship), 455
Gurra (Garbo nickname), 76
Gustafson, David (Karl's half brother)
interview, 10
Stockholm relocation, 9
Gustafson family
apartment (Blekingegatan 32), 7–8, 10
cottage. see Dalem Allotments.
Greta protectiveness, 17
Gustafson, Greta. see Garbo
Gustafson, Johan/Joanna (paternal grandparents), 7
Gustafson, Karl Alfred (father), 3, 6
death, 20
employment status, 7
Frinnaryd (birthplace), 6
household, discipline/love/support (presence), 11
illness, 15–16
kidney disease, progression, 17
poverty, 10
Gustafson, Maria (Karl's half sister) Stockholm relocation, 9
Gustafson, Peg, 172, 265
Garbo correspondence, 303
Gustaf V. see King Gustaf V
Gustav III. see King Gustav III
Gynt, Kaj, 342–343

H

Haas, Willy (*Die freudlose Gasse* script), 116–117, 124
Hagerman, Elsa
  Garbo correspondence, 17
  Sven partner, 17
Hall, Gladys (Faith Service)
  Garbo interview, 139, 172, 235
  Stiller interview, 64–65
Hall, Mordaunt, 167
  Flesh and the Devil, The, 216
  Garbo acting, discussion, 180–181
  Garbo interview, 168, 292, 295, 314–315, 319
  set visits, Garbo allowance, 265
Hall, Sara F., 118, 120–121
Hammond, Dick, 415–416
Hansi (cabaret star), Garbo imitation, 46
Hanson, Einar (actor), 94, 105, 114–115, 176
  death, 277, 278
  MGM deal, 130–131
  Süleymaniye Mosque photo, 107
Hanson, Lars (actor), 49–50, 57, 73, 278
  Gösta Berling performance, 84, 209
  MGM deal, 130–131
  photo, 276
  Scarlet Letter, The, 164
  scene stills, usage, 78, 79
  stage return, 290
  Stiller meeting, 277
Happiness in Marriage (Sanger), 188
Hårby estate, 415, 419
  Garbo/brother purchase, 407
  inner workings, 413–414
  photos, 406, 407
  sale, 408, 424
Harrison, George (fan stalking/injury), 297
Harrison, Rex, 298
Harwood, H.M. (screenwriter), 352
Haskell, Molly (film historian), 203–204
Hasselquist, Jenny (actress), 57
  Goodwin photography, 83
Hauser, Gayelord, 378
  Garbo visits, 297, 346, 411–412, 425, 453, 458, 460
  influence, 410–411
  memorial service, 483
  photos, 411, 456
Hays, Wiliam Harrison (Will), 190
  archbishop Cincinnati meeting appearance request, rejection, 372
  compromises, Breen dissatisfaction, 369–370

Parsons, perception, 309–310
Production Code acceptance, efforts, 309–310
Heard, Roby, 451
Hearst, William Randolph (*Polly of the Circus* preview attendance), 265
Hecht, Ben (Saltzman collaboration), 469
Hedqvist, Ivan (MGM contracts, offering), 130–131
Hellberg, Fredric (store manager), 22–23
Hellberg, Magdalena, 23, 31, 84
Hemingway, Ernest (writer), 311
Hendrix, Jimi, 329
Hepburn, Katharine (actress), 206
box office appeal, Independent Theatre Owners Association contention, 227
film roles, continuation, 436
Mourning Becomes Electra discussion, 436
Photoplay mentions, frequency, 326
screwball role, 383
heroine, emergence (Photoplay critique), 206
Herr Arnes Pengar (Sir Arne's Treasure) (Stiller 1919 film), 68–69
Herrskapet Stockholm ute på inköp (Mr. and Mrs. Stockholm go shopping) (1920 film), 27, 29, 402
Hersholt, Jean (stardom), 336
He Who Gets Slapped (Sjöström 1924 film), 212
Hildenbrandt, Fred, 98
Hiller, Lejaren à (photographer), 143
Hjort, Daniel, 48
Hoffenstein, Sam (scriptwriter), 394
Hollywood Daily Citizen, Torrent review, 156
Hollywood, Garbo selection, 340–341
Holman, Libby (dinner), 455
homosexuality, accusations (impact), 375–376
Honey, Maureen, 195
Hornblow, Jr., Arthur, 220
Horst, Horst (photographer), 141
photo sessions, 448
Hotel Imperial (1927 film), 177–178, 277
cinematographic effects, 177–178
House Un-American Activities Committee investigations, initiation, 461
Hoyningen-Huene, George (photographer), 141
photo sessions, 447–448
Hurrell, George (photographer), 141
Garbo, problems, 270
portraits, 270
Husing, Ted (*Love* action description), 258
Huxley, Aldous, 409–410, 412
Hyltén-Cavallius, Ragnar, 329
description (Garbo), 73–74
Garbo reconnection, 290–291

Garbo secret, 171
Garbo success, secret, 333
observations (Stiller), 65–66, 76, 87–88
Stiller/Garbo involvement, 88
Süleymaniye Mosque photo, 107
Hyman, Bernard H. (producer), 390, 420, 431
Brown, interaction (issues), 394
Conquest involvement/interference, 394
death, 438
I
I Am a Fugitive from a Chain Gang (1932 film), 312
Ibsen, Henrik, 48–49, 57, 316
Idestam-Almquist, Bengt, 90, 131
Idiot, The (Dostoevsky), 209
Idun (magazine), Garbo appearance, 75
IFCA. see International Federation of Catholic Alumnae
I livets virvlar (Swirls of life) (Semitjov), Stiller film rights purchase, 90
immigration (reaction), race (relationship), 338
immutable virtues, concept, 185
imperfect human being, Garbo presentation, 171
Ince, Thomas, 212
Independent Theatre Owners Association (1938 ad), 226, 227
industrial economy, clerks employment (photo), 232
inflation, sex (parallel), 117–118
innate male advantages, absence, 186
Inspiration (1931 film), 262–263, 334
Garbo photo, 330
Intermezzo (Molander 1936 film), 54
International Federation of Catholic Alumnae (IFCA)
censorship efforts, 308
Motion Picture Department report, 433
interpersonal relationships, change, 188
Intimate Theater (Strindberg), 48–49
Stiller management/director, 49, 53
I Remember Mama (1948), Garbo refusal, 437
Isherwood, Christopher (writer), 409, 412
Istanbul
Garbo enjoyment, 106–107
Garbo photo, 104

J
Jacobs, Lea (film historian), 385
Jaenzon, Julius (cinematographer), 25, 105
Garbo meeting, 68
MGM, offering, 131
Jannings, Emil (actor), 277, 300, 315
Jannings, Ruth, 300–301
photo, 301

Johansson, Axel (uncle) death, 9
Johansson, Gullan, 2
Johansson, Selma Sigrid (Sigrid) (maternal aunt), 9, 24
Johnson, Mary (film actress), 30–31, 89
Jordahl, Anders, 61
Joy, Jason (SRC head), 361
  coded meaning, acceptability, 368
joyless street, physical navigation, 118
Joyless Street, The. see *Die freudlose Gasse*

K
Kåge, Ivar (stage/film actor), 31, 84
  Garbo friendship, 37
Kahane, Ben (Producer's Jury member), 362
Kanin, Garson, 478
Kaper, Bronislaw (composer), 267
Karenina, Anna (role, Garbo refusal (lie)), 240
Karin, Ellyn (film director), 69
Karlsdotter, Anna Lovisa (mother), 3, 6
  bread, baking, 16
  death, 9
Karlsdotter, Greta (patronymic descriptor), 71
Karlsdotter, Sigrid (sister), 7. see also Johansson
Karlsruher Tagblatt (*Queen Christina* critique), 364–365
Karlsson, Sven (patronymic descriptor), 72
Katrina South School
  Garbo attendance, 15
  photo, 14
Keil-Möller, Carlo (scriptwriter), 133, 279
  Camille review, 391
  Garbo conversation, 404
Kennedy, Jackie (Garbo meeting/letter), 479–480
Kennedy, John F., 479
Kent, Barbara (actress), 214
Kent, Sidney (Paramount executive), 224
Kerr, Deborah (actress), 264
  Garbo friendship, 455
Kerry, Norman (actor), 251
Kinematograph, 96
King Gustaf V, Conservative Party prime minister appointment (failure), 4
King Gustav III
Kungliga Dramatiska Teatern founding, 46
  story, screenplay (Stiller involvement), 133
Kiss, The (1929 film), 262, 323, 339
  Bull portrait gallery, Garbo entry (emotional state), 271
  Feyder (scriptwriter), 315
  Hall interview, 319
  set, Hall allowance, 295
Klosters (Garbo friendship), 455–457, 482

Knock or the Triumph of Medicine (Garbo appearance), 100
Kodak Brownie cameras, usage, 141
Konsums nya bageri (Konsum's new bakery) (1921 Tullberg film), 29
Konsumtionsföreningen (co-op/productions), 29–30
Konsumtionsforeningen Stockholm med omnejd (Consumer's association, Stockholm and surroundings) (1921 Tullberg film), 29
Krauss, Werner (actor), 114, 121
    Die freudlose Gasse reviews, 124
Kreuger, Ivar (film investor), 59, 131, 344
Krishnamurti, 409
Kuhle Wampe (1932 film), pro-communism aspect, 120
Ku Klux Klan
    intervention (call), 338
    legion bans perception, 374
Kunsky-Publix stage presentation, 158

L
Ladies' Home Journal, Modern Woman definition, 196
Laemmle, Jr., Carl (Producer's Jury member), 362
Lagerlöf, Selma, 64, 68, 415
    Gösta Berling film rights, Brecht ownership, 69
    novels, adaptations, 68–69
    novels, changes (issues), 68–69
Laing, E.E. (author), 216, 341
    Painted Veil, The (critique), 380
La Malquerida (The Unloved Woman) (Benavente), 84
Lane, Tamar, 201–202
Lang, Fritz (film director), 90, 134
large cities, industrial economy (emergence), 232–233
Larson, Jack, 484
LaSalle, Mick (Camille appreciation), 391–392
Lasky, Jesse (Producer's Jury member), 362
Lasse Ring. see Ring
Lavender Scare, initiation, 461
Laver, James (Garbo clothing impact analysis), 269
lead characters, audience sympathy (Selznick understanding), 285
Legion of Decency, 370–371, 473
    Catholic Church control, 373
    rating categories, impact, 374, 431–433
    strictness/intrusiveness, increase, 429
    Two-Faced Woman (1941 film) condemnation, 431–433
Leigh, Vivien, 478
Lektyr (Swedish magazine), 17–18
Lengyel, Melchior (Ninotchka encapsulation), 420–421
Lennon, John (fan murder), 297
lesbianism, proof, 376
Letty Lynton (1932 film), 325
Lewin, Albert (director), 137, 177
Lewis, Sinclair (writer), 311

Lichtbild-Buhne (film magazine), 110
Lind, Agnes, 10
Lindbergh, Charles, 328
Lindberg, Hugo (Stiller executor), 290
Lindwall, Tore, 41
Lipke, Katherine (Garbo interview), 294
Littlefield, Lucien (actor), 154
Loder, John (actor), 284, 292, 301, 315
Loder, Sophie, 301
Loew, Marcus (Loew's president), 157, 223
  first-run theaters, acquisition/building, 231
  illness, 151
  Zukor meeting, 228–229
Loew's
  exhibition profits, 243–244
  gross/net income, 225
  Love revenue generation, 256–257
  Paramount, theater sales, 229
  Swedish distribution rights, obtaining (Magnusson attempt), 135
Loew's-MGM company, integration (formation), 244
Loew's State Theatre, Torrent premiere (ticket sales), 161–162
Logan, Josh (Duchess de Langeais direction consideration), 463
Lombard, Carole (actress), 206
  Photoplay mentions, frequency, 326
Lombardo, Joseph (Garbo friendship), 455
Lönn, Oscar (playmate), 12
Look Back in Anger (Saltzman rights, obtaining), 471
Loos, Anita, 220
  Garbo friendship, 409–410, 412
Lord, Daniel
  censorship effort, 369
  complaints, 311
  draft code document, creation, 309
  film ideas, 311
  moral standards, reduction concern, 311
Lorensberg Theatre, 49
Los Angeles Times, The
  Garbo interview, 294
  Queen Christina (ad), 202
  The Temptress review, 180
Louis B. Mayer Productions, Gilbert (long-term deal), 212
Louise, Ruth Harriet (portraits), 141
  Garbo photos, 193, 250, 280
  Garbo, professional relationship, 270–271
  MGM exit, 271
love
  adultery, pure love (equivalence), 383
  marriage (comparisons), 186

realities (display), 204
redemption, 375
Love (1927 film), 203, 232
audience characteristic, 258
audience, Variety analysis, 258
distribution treatment, 255
endings, variation, 369
exhibition dates, comparison, 256
Film Spectator complaints, 252
Garbo character, death, 205
Garbo/Gilbert photo, 259
Garbo photo, 250
Gilbert direction, Photoplay report, 252
Louise portrait, 280
Motion Picture review, 259
new name, 251
picnicking (photo), 272
production, Film Spectator article, 253
stage shows, cost effectiveness, 254
Tolstoy (Ilya) complaints, 252
Lowe, Edmund, 220
Lowenthal, Alma (Schratter marriage), 91
Lubitsch, Ernst, 315, 331
dinner, 301
Garbo, interaction, 422
Ninotchka photo, 421
stage acting, 342
U.S. arrival, 90
Luce, Clare Boothe, 324
Luffar-Petter (Peter the Tramp) (Petschler 1922 film), 34, 36, 38, 43
scene stills, usage, 78
Lundborg, Einer/Margareta (photo), 291
Lundell, Nils, 133, 288
Lundequist, Gerda (actress), 73
Gösta Berling Berlin premiere, attendance, 96–97
Gösta Berling performance, 84

M

Macpherson, Kenneth, 125–126
Madame Curie (film), postponement, 430
Madchen in Uniform (1931 film), 360
Magnusson, Charles
American films, distribution rights (negotiation), 135
epic films, management, 59–60
film company owner, 54
funding, Stiller request, 108
revenue stream, directors (perceptions), 62
Stiller correspondence, 61
Svenska Bio production manager, 56–57

Mahoney, Florence, 480
male/female relationships, Legion of Decency (control, desire), 429
Mamoulian, Rouben (director), 342, 358
  Arizona Highway Patrol badge/courtesy card, 366
  director, MGM approval (need), 351–352
  Garbo, dating, 366, 378
Mankiewicz, Herman/Sarah, 220
Mannix, Eddie (senior manager), 155, 361
  Camille oversight, 390
  Painted Veil, The (meeting), 379
Manville, Estelle (Bernadotte marriage), 287
Manville, Hiram (industrialist), 287
March, Fredric (actor), 384
Mare Nostrum (film), 180
Marion, Frances (screenwriter), 251, 316, 351
  role reprisal, 320
Marion, George (actor) (Anna Christie role), 173, 317, 331
  photo, 317
Markham, Doris (fan magazine writer), 214, 261
marriage
  Garbo plan, 178
  journey, restructuring, 186–187
  love, comparisons, 186
Marshall, Herbert (actor)
  Painted Veil, The (photo), 379
  Queen Christina role, consideration, 355
Mårtenson, Mona (film actress), 37, 41, 44, 75
MGM contracts, offering, 130–131
Marx, Samuel, 329
Mata Hari (1931 film), 334
  Fitzmaurice dinner party, 401
  Garbo headdress (photo), 324
  revenue, 362
Maugham, Somerset, 378
Mayer, Irene, 102
Mayer, Louis B., 101, 150, 157
  Atonement of Gösta Berling, The screening, 102
  betrayal, Garbo feeling, 209
  Garbo little "chat," 237–238
  Garbo on-screen performance, observation, 167
  Mayer/Thalberg/Rubin trio, basis, 244
  The Painted Veil meeting, 379
  Polly of the Circus preview attendance, 265
  Stiller/Garbo meeting, 102
  Stiller/Garbo meeting, follow-up, 108
  Stiller letter, 238
May Fair (Arlen), 348
McCarthy, Kevin/Augusta (dinner), 455

McClafferty, John
Rubin meeting, 434
Two-Faced Women, opinion, 428
McCormick, John, 220
McCrea, Joel (actor), 180
McLain, John (writer), 267
McMein, Neysa (review), 338
McNicholas, John
Breen correspondence, 371
ECMP chair, 373
movie objections, 433
secret meeting invitation, 372
Meredyth, Bess (screenwriter), 351, 352
Merry Widow, The (von Stroheim film), 216
Gilbert involvement, 212
Metro-Goldwyn-Mayer (MGM)
creation, 212
gross/net income, 225
letters of intent (Garbo/Stiller signing), 109, 129, 148
long-term contract, Garbo signing pressure, 236
revenue, female actor percentage, 206
salary offer, Garbo refusal, 237
Stiller, contract negotiations, 139, 148
Swedish distribution rights, obtaining (Magnusson attempt), 135
target, Legion of Decency attack, 433
Metro-Goldwyn-Mayer (MGM), Garbo contract negotiations, 139
contract fight, 236
extension, MGM request, 148–149
signing, 150
unenforceability, 148
Metropolis (Lang 1927 film), 134
Miller, Arthur (dinner), 455
Minneapolis Star Tribune (Torrent review), 194
Miracle, The (film project), 436, 468
censor concerns, 472
Fry script, 469–470
Monsignor Devlin script review, 472
NBC interest, 470
Olivier, involvement, 469–470
project, death, 473
proposal, 469
Mirande, Yves (writer), 301
Mockery (1927 film), 248
Modern Women
Garbo representation, 194
Gibson Girls/flappers, relationship, 196
ideas, audience projection, 200
Ladies' Home Journal definition, 196
MGM emphasis, 314

pre-marital sex, awareness, 188
presentation, movie screen stories (impact), 188–189
redefining, 184
Moje (Stiller nickname), 88, 89, 136, 170, 276
Molander, Gustaf, 35, 53–54, 289
contract, Garbo release (Stiller request), 101–102
notebooks, 43
photo, 53
Råsunda studio (photo), 51
Molander, Harald, 52
Molander, Karin, 278
photo, 306
Molander, Olof (Garbo meeting), 289
Molander, Edith (photo), 276
Mon ami Teddy (Min vän Teddy/My friend Teddy), Garbo/Kåge/Enwall performances, 84
Montgomery, Robert (Queen Christina consideration), 355
Moore, Colleen, 220, 281, 453
Fitzmaurice dinner party, 401
home, Gilbert visit, 247
moral crusaders, impact, 189
morality, prewar codes, 120
moral standards, *Queen Christina* violation (Quigley opinion), 370
Moreau, Jean (cabaret star), Garbo imitation, 46
Moreno, Anthony (actor), 179–180
The Temptress photos, 181
Mors Rival (Mother's Rival), Garbo/Bosse performance, 84
Moscow Art Theatre (Stanislavski), 40, 49, 329
Mosebacke Theatre (cabaret theatre), 13, 27, 47
Brisson, headliner, 16
motherhood, Victorian conception, 186
Motion Picture (magazine)
Love review, 258
Torrent review, 167
Motion Picture Classic (Smith), 167
Motion Picture Herald (Quigley ownership), 308
Motion Picture News, Gilbert crash, mention (absence), 246
Motion Picture Producers and Distributors of America (MPPDA)
Breen (censorship officer), 373
certificate, need, 484
film company creation, 190
PCA film rejection, impact, 371
self-censorship programs, design, 190
Mourning Becomes Electra
Cukor pitch, Mayer rejection, 443
Garbo/Cukor/Hepburn discussion, 436
project, dropping, 446
Movie Magazine (Garbo interview), 139
movie ticket sales, Depression (impact), 234

Moving Picture World, Gilbert crash, mention (absence), 246
Mozartsaal theatre, Brodnitz directorship, 97
Mr. Smith Goes to Washington (film), 423
MS Annie Johnson, Garbo passage, 346
  photo, 347
MS *Drottingholm* (Garbo/Stiller passage), 138
MS *Gripsholm* (Garbo passage), 343
  press conference, 413
  press conference photo, 344
MS *Gripsholm* (Stiller/Hanson/Molander passage), 278
MS *Kungsholm*
  Garbo passage, 415–416
  Garbo passage (photo), 286
  interview, 365, 402, 405, 416
Mundelein, George, 309
Munich Filmmuseum, Die freudlose Gasse (restored version), 121–122
Murnau, F.W. (film director), 90, 93, 350
Murray, Nickolas (photographer), 141, 142, 146
Mussolini, Benito (war entry announcement), 267
My Life (Duncan), 143
Mysterious Lady, The (1928 film), 273–274, 339
Garbo photo, 193

N

Nagel, Conrad (actor), 156, 265
När larmklockan ljuder (When the alarm bell sounds) (Stiller 1913 film), 25
narrative
  closure, 204–205
  non-Victorian gender roles basis, 195
  stories, emergence, 196
National Catholic Welfare Conference (NCWC), censorship efforts, 308
naturalistic acting, 49–50, 126, 169, 329–330
naturalistic performances, 169
naturalistic style, 170
Negri, Pola (actress), 177, 179, 277
Negulesco, Jean (director), 264
Negulesco Jean/Dusty (Garbo social circle), 455
"New Man" evolution, implication, 120
New Objectivity (Neue Sachlichkeit) style, 113, 117
"New Woman" concept, 120
New York City
  clerks, employment, 233
  first-run market, importance, 233
New York Daily News
  Garbo/Stiller New York departure, coverage, 138
  Torrent premiere (ad), 157
New York market, Loew's domination, 232

New York Times, The
Flesh and the Devil, The (review), 216
Garbo, Hall interview, 292, 314–315
integrity failures, 452
Temptress, The (MGM 1926 film), 180–181
Niblo, Fred, 180, 215
demure heroine, banishment, 201
Garbo interaction, 168
primary photography, 177
Temptress, The (reshoot), 178
Nielsen, Asta (actress), 114, 115, 122
Die freudlose Gasse reviews, 124
Nilsson, Axel (lawyer)
negotiation, program, 148
U.S. arrival, 138, 147
Ninotchka (1939 Lubitsch film), 341
Bishop analysis, 423
completion, 348
contract, Garbo agreement, 421–422
Douglas photo, 417, 420
Garbo photos, 417, 419–422
Garbo project, 350
Legion of Decency rating, 375
Lubitsch photo, 421
New Masses critique, 423
rights (MGM purchase), Viertel (impact), 350
Theatre Arts Magazine appreciation, 423
Niven, David/Hjördis (Garbo social circle), 455
Norin, Gustaf, 172, 305
Norin, Gustaf/Sigrid (Garbo household staff), 300, 303
Normal Theater (Chicago) (photo), 228
Northern Cemetery, Garbo visit, 290
Novarro, Ramon (actor), 255
Hurrell portraits, 270
Nygren, Karl (speech instructor), 46
Nykroppa (Varmland County), Garbo visit, 24

O
Oakland Tribune (Garbo photo), 111
Odalisken från Smolna (The odalisque from Smolny) (The concubine from Smolny), 90
Odalisque project, 87, 90
budget/revenue projections, 103
failure, 104–106, 132
final agreement, 101
financing, Das Tagebuch article, 107–108
financing, issues, 102–103
Garbo role, explanation, 100–101
locations, scouting, 101
production, initiation, 94

script, donation, 105
script, Hyltén-Cavallius/Stiller refinement, 103
Stiller delay/sickness, 99–100
Stiller mistakes, 105
Office of Strategic Services (OSS), Saltzman involvement, 468
Olas Grande Inn (Garbo visit), 304–305
Olivier, Laurence, 352
Garbo conversation, 478
Miracle, The (involvement), 469–470
problems, 354
Olmstead, Gertrude (actress), 154
comparison, 207
Olsson, Ingeborg Oskara (Gumpel marriage), 28
O'Malley, Rex (actor), 265
Camille role, 390
Onassis, Ari (Garbo sailing), 460
O'Neill, Eugene (playwright), 49, 290, 316, 321
O'Neil, Sally (actress), 156, 207
Ophüls, Max (director) Wanger contact, 463
Orient (1924) production, problems, 94
Osborne, John, 471
Oscar Theater, Broadway musical (Stiller presentation), 278

P

Pabst, Georg Wilhelm (director), 170
appraisal, 116
Die freudlose Gasse reviews, 123–124
films, completion, 114
Stiller meeting, 108
Pacific Palisades (photo), 305
Paderewski, Ignacy (politician/musician), 452
Painted Veil, The (Boleslawski 1934 film), 174
censorship issues, 375
contract, Garbo signing, 342–343
Garbo coat, Cinema Shop ad, 269
Garbo photos, 367, 379
Hays production approval, Thalberg request, 379
Laing critique, 380
Marshall photo, 379
PCA approval, Breen awareness (absence), 379, 380
pre-production, Garbo absence, 398
preview, 380
production, conclusion, 351
rewrites, 380
Troy critique, 380
Palace Theater, Flesh and the Devil box office results, 217
Palermo, Anthony (Tony), 483
Paley, Bill, 469–470

Palmborg, Rilla Page, 17, 64, 284
Garbo biography, 300, 400
Garbo interview, 295
Palmer, Lilli, 298
paparazzi, impact, 400, 448
Paradine Case, The (1947), Garbo refusal, 437
Paramount, theaters (sale), 229
Paramount Theatre (Seattle) (photo), 228
Paris, Barry, 15, 170
Gronowicz book debunking, 452
Parrish, Robert (director), 409
Garbo friendship, 455
Parsons, Louella, 199
Production Code opinion, 301
Parsons, Wilfrid
censorship effort, 369
draft code document, creation, 309
patriarchal bourgeois moral order, women (exclusion), 121
patriarchal power structure, existence, 198
Paul U. Bergström (PUB)
amateur theatre club, employee usage, 31
film, 26–27
film, Garbo (first film role), 26–27
Garbo employment (continuation), Ring advice, 32–33
Garbo resignation, 34–36
Ring client, 25
Paul U. Bergström AB Stockholm (Tullberg 1920 film), 29
Paul U. Bergström (PUB), Garbo employment, 20–23
hat modeling, 23
regulations, violation, 21
PCA. see Production Code Administration
Pearl Harbor, Japanese attack, 435
Pelican, The (Strindberg), 49
Perkins, Gil, 260, 263
Garbo conversation, recollection, 394–395
personality, depth, 198
personal satisfaction, impact, 187
personal/societal ethical values, Breen concern, 374
Petro, Patrice (film historian), 198
Petschler, Erik (stage/film actor), 34, 36, 38, 64
patronage/efforts, 37
Pettijohn, Charlie (Quigley correspondence), 369
petting, socially acceptability, 187
Phillips, Gene (film historian), 331–332
photographers, subject (portrait photography), 144
photographs, use (change), 80
photography (evolution), Garbo (impact), 80–081
photojournalism, changes/expansion, 399–400, 448

Photoplay (magazine)
  actresses, mentions (chronological comparison), 327
  coverage, Garbo domination, 326
  Garbo/Crawford mentions, comparison, 325
  Garbo driving article, 294
  Garbo interview, 295
  Garbo review, 59
  heroine, emergence, 206
  Love (Gilbert direction), 252
  Temptress review, 180
Pickford, Mary (actress), 194, 333
  stage appearance, 239
  Swedish film industry dinner, 88, 95
pictorialism, technical advances, 80
pictorialist era, static images (output), 141
pictorial presentation, photographers (concern), 79
Pines, Romain (film distributor/financier), 114
Pink Bedroom, The (Williams pitch), 447
Pirandello, Luigi, 337
plays, blacklisting (impact), 378
plot elements, 195
Pollak, Mimi (film actress), 41, 45, 133
  actors (observation), 46
  Amatörfilmen lead, 37
  Dramaten dinner, 403–404
  Dramaten publicity photo, 50
  Europe movie making, Garbo desire, 273
  Garbo correspondence, 37, 44–45, 88–89, 95, 99, 164
  Garbo/director interaction, correspondence opinion, 168
  Garbo illness, seriousness, 404
  Garbo marriage, correspondence discussion, 178
  Garbo, reunion, 288
  Garbo self-blame (letter), 129
  Garbo unhappiness, recollection, 249
  Luffar-Petter premiere, attendance, 38
  Mårtenson/Garbo correspondence, 64
  Royal Dramatic Theatre, student life changes (Garbo observations), 100
  Stiller/Garbo relationship, 278
Polly of the Circus (Davies film preview), 265
Pommer, Erich (producer), 177, 277
Ponce de Leon, Charles, 452
poor women, jobs (need), 185
Pope John Paul II, 452
Porten, Henny (actor), 132
Porter, Floyd (gaffer), 262
portrait photography, movement/emotion (capture attempt), 142–143
Possessed (1931 film), 325
Pozner, Vladimir, 442
Princes Gustavus/Sigvard, Garbo meeting, 287

Pringle, Aileen, 239, 245
Producers' Jury, impact, 362
Production Code, 190
American Catholics, impact, 190–191
Breen enforcement, 359–360
creation, Thalberg insight, 428
development, 309
enforcement, American interest (absence), 311–312
evolution, 368
impact, 307
implementation, Breen Group organization, 369
studio compliance, Hays management, 311
Production Code Administration (PCA) (1934), 360
Anna Karenina script submission, 384
arrival, 369
Catholic Church control, 373
creation, 310, 371
film rejection, impact, 371
script pre-approval authority, 3712
Selznick management, 384
Protestant denominations, censorship concerns, 308
PUB. see Paul U. Bergström

Q
Queen Christina (1933 film), 349, 398
androgynous role, 359
attendant kiss (photo), 378
censorship issue, 192
changes, Breen request, 360–361
contract, Garbo signing, 342
Detroit Free Press critique, 363
female heroine, creation, 357
filming, group morale, 263
final scene, shooting, 358
foreign film rental revenue, domestic revenue (contrast), 363
Garbo involvement, depth, 351–352
Garbo performance, 17
Garbo photos, 353, 354, 356, 357
Garbo queen portrayal, subversiveness (Quigley opinion), 370
Gilbert, hiring, 354–355
Gilbert photo, 356
heterosexual relationship/bedroom scene, 359
immoral film, Quigley opinion, 364
Karlsruher Tagblatt critique, 364–365
Los Angeles Times ad, 202
moral standards violation, Quigley opinion, 370
premiere/release, 362
pre-production, Garbo absence, 398
production, geographic considerations, 273

Reid critique, 363
same-sex kisses, direct use (attention), 378
screening, audience thrill, 234
scripts, changes/completion, 352–353
sexual politics, approach, 359
Strickling (technical advisor), 352
Swedish reaction, 365
Sydney Morning Herald, The (critique), 364
Troy criticism, 363
Viertel treatments, Garbo (reading), 350
Wanger (producer), 352–353, 461
Quick, Lawrence, 170
Quigley, Martin (censorship advocate), 189, 307–309, 349, 367
Cincinnati meeting, 371
complaints, 369
draft code document, creation, 309
entertainment morality, ideas (differences), 311
immoral film, example/opinion, 364
secret meeting invitation, 372
Quintanilla-Perez, Selena (fan murder), 297

R

Radziwill, Lee, 479–480
Raider, Roberta Ann (film historian), 320
Ranft, Albert, 44, 48
theatre, Molander management, 53
Råsunda (Svensk Filmindustri sets), 49, 59
Stiller/Garbo discussions/arguments, 76
Rathbone, Basil (actor), 218–219, 332, 384
Read, Helen Appleton (actresses, analysis), 207
Reason, Matthew, 145
Reichsfilmblatt (trade magazine), 123–124
Die freudlose Gasse reviews, 124
Reichsmark, introduction/impact, 91
Reich, Walter, 267, 350
Reid, Danny (Queen Christina critique), 363
Reid, Laurence (*Torrent* review), 167
Reinhardt, Gottfried (playwright), 267, 394, 430–431, 472
Reinhardt, Max (touring productions), 49
Reisfeld, Donald, 475
Reisfeld, Gray, 475
Garbo lunch, 457
Garbo trip, 477
Garbo visit, 460
Reisz, Karel, 472
Remarque, Erich Maria (Garbo romantic relationship), 378
Reniers, Perceval (foreigner intervention essay), 338
Reuterskiöld, Lennart, 415
Richardson, Dorothy, 126

Richardson, Tony, 471
Riehl, Walter, 122
Ring, John Magnus Ragnar (Ragnar Ring) (Lasse Ring)
  AB Hasse W. Tullbergs employment, 25
  advertising film casting, 24
  book foreign sales supervision, 25
  films, categorization, 28
  Garbo employment, 37
  Garbo interaction, recollection, 30
  Royal Västernorrland Regiment officer, 24–25
  Stiller meeting, 25, 64
Ring, Lillemor (Ragnar granddaughter), 26
Ring, Ruth (Lasse wife) Garbo attentiveness/appearance, 26
Rizzoli, Angelo (*Duchess de Langeais* financing), 464
RKO (film major, integration), 228
Roberts, W. Adolphe (Garbo interview), 139
Rockefeller, John D., 142
Rogers, Ginger (*Photoplay* mentions, frequency), 326
Roland, Gilbert (Garbo romantic relationship), 378
Romance (1930 film), 262–263, 333–334, 339
  Hurrell portraits, 270
"romantic woman" (Garbo representation), 171
Rosenberg, Oscar (Sjöström/Jordahl deal negotiation), 61
Rosenthal, Artur, 96
Rothstock, Otto, 122
Royal Dramatic Theatre (Dramaten) School
  1922 class (Molander notebook) (photo), 43
  acting, unique approach, 40
  building (photo), 40
  building, opening, 47
  compressed timeframe, 35
  contract, Garbo (signing), 99
  Enwall (Signe), graduation, 33
  Enwall (Frans), health (deterioration), 33
  Garbo admission/attendance, 20, 29, 32
  Garbo application, 23, 32
  Garbo audition, 35
  Garbo/classmates (photo), 39
  Garbo enjoyment, 41–42
  Garbo tardiness, 42–43
  Keil-Möller (director), 133
  Kungliga Dramatiska Teatern (king founding), 46
  Molander, joining, 54
  student life, change (Garbo observations), 100
Royal Västernorrland Regiment, Stiller film involvement, 25
Rubens, Alma, 155
Rubin, J. Robert (general counsel), 139, 140, 147–149
  Garbo cable, 239–240
  Garbo deal, signing, 150

Garbo new deal, 241
McClafferty meeting, 434
Rubinstein, Artur (pianist), 409
Russell, Bertrand (philosopher), 409
Russell, Rosalind (actress)
public appearance, fan attention, 300
Washington, assistant role, 401
Russian Eagle, Garbo visits, 302

S
Safire, William, 485
Saint Joan (Shaw), 339, 438
Saldana, Theresa (fan stalking/injury), 297
salesclerks, training, 21
salespersons, powers of persuasion (importance), 21
saleswomen, skilled selling (importance), 21
Salinger, J.D., 446
Salkin, Michael (film distributor/financing), 114
Sally, Irene and Mary (Crawford/O'Neil role), 207
Saltzman, Harry (Herschel), 468
financial creativity, 472
Hecht collaboration, 469
same-sex kisses, direct use (attention), 378
Sanborn, L.E., 161
Sand, George, 461
Sandrich, Mark, 270
Sången om den eldröda blomman (Song of the scarlet flower)(Molander/Stiller cowriters), 54
Sanger, Margaret, 188
San Simeon, MGM crowd (photo), 266
Santa Monica Outlook, Sjöström interview, 172
Sartre, Jean-Paul, 195
Saxon, Lars (publisher), 18, 136
Garbo correspondence, 136, 209
Garbo friendship/romance, 164–165
Scarlet Letter, The (1926 Sjöström film), 164
Schaeffer, Rebecca (fan murder), 297
Schenck, Nick, 292
Garbo/Stiller meeting, 151
Hays correspondence/objections, 362
PCA/MGM correspondence, receipt, 379
Schlee, George, 298, 346, 457, 460
death, 454, 481
Garbo meeting, 425
Garbo romantic relationship, 378, 440
health, failure, 481
investor/location search, 462
Miracle, The (film project) involvement, 469
photo, 471

Schlee, George/Valentina (couture business), 425
Schlee, Valentina, 425
  George body, claim, 481
  showroom, Hauser/Garbo visit, 425
Schmiterlöw, Vera (film actress), 37, 41, 44
  Garbo correspondence, 106
Schratter, David, 89–91
  distribution efforts, 110
  film deal (Stiller), 93
  Lowenthal marriage, 91
Schratter family, US arrival, 110
Schratter, Herman (birth), 110
Schratter, Mary (birth), 110
Schytt, Eric (playmate), 12
Screenland (magazine), Garbo photo (inclusion), 325
Secchiaroli, Tazio (paparazzo), 448
sekelskifte (turn of the century changes), 3–4, 47
Seles, Monica (fan stalking/injury), 297
self-censorship, studio decision, 368
self-expression/self-determination, right, 187
self-supporting women, US perception, 450
Seligman, Eustace (Garbo friendship), 455
Selznick, David, 220, 385
  tennis game, Garbo win, 305
Selznick, Irene, 167
Selznick, Irene Mayer, 453
Semitjov, Vladimir, 90
Sennett, Mack, 38
Service, Faith. see Hall
service jobs, condition, 21
sex
  censorship concerns, 311
  Garbo films presence, 375
  Legion of Decency, control (desire), 429
  offensiveness (Queen Christina), Quigley opinion, 370
  portrayal, Legion of Decency (impact), 374
  portrayal, Production Code (impact), 312
sexuality
  cooties theory, 376
  Garbo, impact, 197
sexual mores, change, 188
sexual orientation, weaponization, 375
sexual passion/courtly love, fusion, 204
sexual politics, *Queen Christina* approach, 359
sexual power dynamics (Garbo truth), 200
sexual purity, importance, 186
Shaw, George Bernard, 339, 438
Shaw, Irwin (Garbo friendship), 455

Shearer, Norma (actress), 147, 162, 164, 196, 220, 255
comparison, 207
Divorcee, The, 205
Hurrell portraits, 270
Photoplay mentions, frequency, 326
salary, 110
stardom, approach, 239
Student Prince in Old Heidelberg, The, 205
Thalberg, marriage, 256
She Done Him Wrong (1933 film), 311
Sheik, The (1921 film), 225
Sherwood, Robert (Garbo review), 167
Sherwood, Robert E. (playwright/screenwriter/reviewer), 322–323
Shurlock, Geoffrey
Anna Karenina, impact (perception), 386
Painted Veil, The (meeting), 379
PCA leadership, 429, 432
silent films, editing ease, 308
Singer, Joseph, 229
Single Standard, The (1929 film), 339
filming (photo), 263
Garbo/Asther photo, 314
Garbo photo, 205
modernity/independence, projection, 314
movie still (photo), 312
New York premiere, 315
premiere/profitability, 314
Variety review, 203
Sir Arne's Treasure (Molander/Stiller cowriters), 54
Sjöberg, Alf (director/Garbo classmate), 38, 41, 45, 194
Sjöstrand, Arnold (actor), 41, 44, 77
Sjöström, Edith, 55, 61, 301
Sjöström, Victor (film director/actor), 4, 49, 51–54
career, success, 342
debts, 61
directing (photo), 58
Magnusson, filmmaking relationship, 57–58
Magnusson telegram, 131
photo, 52
Råsunda studio photo, 51
Santa Monica Outlook interview, 172
Stockholm arrival/Stiller hospital visits, 282–283
storytelling conventions, development, 54–55
U.S. arrival, 57, 59–60, 90
Sjukhus, Maria, 17
Skandiaateljén (film studio), 31
Skogskyrkogarden (Forest Cemetery), Garbo internment, 2
small-town theaters, weekend operation, 230–231

Smith, Frederick, 167
social changes, 185
social conservatism, growth, 33–339
social group, Garbo (presence/distance), 218
social issues (film industry presentation issue), resolution (absence), 310–311
social problems, play creation (relationship), 48
social space, industrialization (impact), 225
Soderhjelm, Alma, 101, 134
Södermalm (Garbo family location), 7
Söderman, Ingalill (Dramaten publicity photo), 50
Södra Theatre, 13, 47
Song of Songs, The (1933 film), 353
Sörensen, Wilhelm, 284, 289, 301, 319, 378
    Philharmonic Auditorium, Garbo attendance, 305
spectator/star relationships, 196–197
Spiegel, Sam, 267
    Garbo sailing, 460
    Garbo social circle, 455
    get-together, 453
SRC. see Studio Relations Committee
Stacey, Jackie (film historian), 196–197
Stadsmuseet Stockholm, Garbo headshot (possession), 82
Stalin, Josef (rule), *Ninotchka* (mockery), 420
Stanislavski, Konstantin, 40, 49, 329–330, 342
    naturalistic acting process, 49–50
Stark, Ray (agent), 469
    Saltzman correspondence, 470
Steen, Ture, 348
Steichen, Edward (photographer), 141, 142, 146, 147
Stein, Gertrude, 125–126
Sten, Anna (actress), resonance (absence), 206
Stephenson, Henry (actor), 392
Sternberg, Josef (director), 205–206
Stevens, George, 455
Stewart, Beatrice, 247
    Gilbert car accident, 245
Stewart, Donald Ogden (screenwriter), 247
    Gilbert car accident, 245
Stiller, Abraham (Garbo meeting), 290
    photographs (Garbo house display), 303
Stiller, Mauritz (film director), 4, 30, 37, 49, 53–54, 170
    acting encouragement, 3
    Broadway musical (presentation), 278, 289
    Busch meeting, 103
    contract advice, 237
    death, 275, 276, 282
    death, Garbo (devastation), 283–284
    Europe, return, 178

film development, 24–25
financial terms, proposal (delivery), 238
Finland, escape, 53
firing, 277
firing, Thalberg (impact), 176
Garbo (break), 129–130
Garbo (collaborator/friend/romantic partner), 55
Garbo (film discussions/arguments), 76
Garbo audition/meeting, 65
Garbo, romantic dynamic, 279, 378
Garbo/Stiller photo, 89
German reviews/comments, 97
Gösta Berling Berlin premiere, attendance, 96–97
Gösta Berling scene, filming (photo), 75
Hollywood arrival, 151
Hollywood exit, 278
home (photo), 130
hospital stay, Sjöström visits, 282–283
Hyltén-Cavallius impression, 65–66
Intimate Theater management, 49
letter (to Garbo), 280–281
Magnusson, filmmaking relationship, 57–58
Mayer meeting, 102
Mayer meeting, follow-up, 108
MGM deals, 130–131
MGM, falling out, 135
MGM letter of intent/payment scale, 129
Moje (nickname), 88, 89, 136, 170, 276
murder, Gilbert consideration, 247
New York arrival (photo), 137
Nilsson meeting, 131–132
Pabst meeting, 108
photos, 53, 276
Ragnar Ring meeting, 25
Råsunda studio (photo), 51
San Francisco photo, 150
Schenck meeting, 151
Schratter film deal, 93
sickness, 99
Sjöström directing (photo), 58
Sjöström telegram (MGM treatment), 110
Stiller/cat photo, 95
storytelling conventions, development, 54–55
Svensk Filmindustri financial claims, 62
Sweden return, 277
Thalberg, meeting, 177
U.S. arrival, 57, 136

Stinnes, Hugo, 131
St. John, Adela Rogers, 175, 218
  Garbo/Gilbert relationship consideration, 221–222
  Garbo interview, 295
  Single Standard, The (scriptwriter), 314
Stockholm
  Bonnier lunch/dinner, 415
  cottage, Garbo rental, 403
  house, Garbo rental, 344
  population, increase, 3
  theatres, variety, 48
  working-class people, deprivation, 10
Stockholms Dagblad (newspaper), 65
  Garbo acting review, 77–78
Stockholms-Tidningen (Idestam-Almquist), 90
Stocklassa, Ingrid, 176–177
  Garbo meeting, recollection, 218
Stokowski, Leopold
  car accident, 415
  Garbo meeting, 412
  Garbo romantic relationship, 378, 412–414
Stone, Lewis (actor), 274, 331
Strand Hotel
  Garbo Christmas dinner, 289
  Royal Dramatic Theatre party, 45
Strange Cargo (1940 film), Legion of Decency objections, 432
Strange Interlude (O'Neill), 290
Street of Sin, The (1928 Stiller film), 277
Strickling, Howard (technical advisor), 352
Stridsropet, selling, 1
Strindberg, August, 48–49, 77, 84, 316, 415
Stromberg, Hunt (*The Painted Veil* meeting), 379
Stuart, Henry (actor), 114, 115
Student Prince in Old Heidelberg, The
  audience characteristic, 258
  distribution treatment, 255
  exhibition dates, comparison, 256
  Novarro/Shearer vehicle, 255
  Shearer role, 205
Studio Era, 342, 356, 390
  cessation, 4326
  Thalberg, impact, 393
Studio Relations Committee (SRC), 190
  creation (1930), 310
  overriding, SRC (impact), 362
  Queen Christina (ignoring), 361
  replacement, 373
  Wingate leadership, 311
studios, censorship wariness, 310

Sudermann, Hermann, 211
Susan Lenox (1931 film), 317, 334, 339
  forced sex, movie still, 307
  Garbo/Gable photo, 260
  Garbo photo, 328, 330
Svahn, Ethel Marguerite, 345
Svenska Bio. see Aktiebolaget Svenska Biografteatern
  Kreuger investment, 59
  Magnusson (production manager), 56
Svenska Dagbladet (newspaper), 71
Svenska Teatern
  company, Stiller (joining), 53
  Molander (Haralld) management, 52
Svensk Filmindustri. see Filmindustri AB Skandia
American market, value, 59
  Andersson (financial manager), 60
  financial claims, 62
  financial problems, 87
  profits, international distribution deals (importance), 92–93
  Sjöström debts, 61
  Stiller director role, 49
  studios, Garbo visit, 351
  Swedish style, development, 55–56
Sverige och Svenska Industrier (Sweden and Swedish Industries) (1921 Tullberg film), 29
Swain, Mack (actor), 154
Swanson, Gloria (actress), 194
Swanström, Karin (actress), 73
Sweden
  demographic/social upheaval (1850–1911), 3
  films, actor/actress pay scale, 36
  food shortages/worker unrest, protest marches, 9
  Garbo return (1928), 275, 285–289, 344–345
  Garbo trip, *New York Daily News* reporter (accompaniment), 343
  GDP, doubling, 3
  imports, British blockade, 4–5
  King Gustaf V, Conservative Party prime minister appointment (failure), 4
  Liberal Democratic Party, election win, 5
  modernity, claim (advertisement), 47
  movements, appearance/impact, 4
  nationalism, resurgence, 4
  political crisis, World War I (impact), 5
  post-war economic situation, problems, 6
  Social Democratic Party, election win, 5
  society, theatre orientation, 47
  Stiller return, 277
  theatre/film, cross-fertilization, 50
  trade, dependence, 4
  women, economic opportunities (increase), 3
  workforce, women (entry), 6

Swedish Film Institute, *Odalisque* film script (donation), 105
Swedish films
  access/arrangements, difficulties, 62
  industry (golden age), 56–57, 59, 93
Swedish National Romantic movement, 4, 68
Swedish Romantic movement
  progression, 47
  stories, usage, 55–56
Swedish-Russian War (1808–1809), 52
Swedish sphinx, 263
"Swedish Style," 55–56, 62
Swedish Transportation Association, Tullberg films, 28–29
Swenson, Karen (biographer), 218
Sydney Morning Herald, The (Queen Christina critique), 364

T
Tale from Constantinople, A (script), 90
Talmadge, Norma, 102, 166
  popularity, ranking, 197
Tashman, Lilyan, 220, 281–282
  death, 346
tasks, freedom, 185
Taylor, Robert (actor) (*Camille* film), 73, 387–388
Taylor, Walter (writer) (Garbo meeting), 304
Teje, Tora, 44
Temple, Shirley (*Photoplay* mentions, frequency), 326
Temptress, The (MGM 1926 film), 153, 165, 277, 317
  boundary, pushing, 191
  endings, variation, 369
  Exhibitors Herald review, 199
  Film Mercury coverage, 179, 201–202
  Garbo acting, Dufour review, 167–168
  Garbo acting, *New York Times* review, 180–181
  Garbo acting, *Photoplay/Los Angeles Times* review, 180
  Garbo photos, 179–181
  importance, 176
  men, destruction, 199
  Moreno photos, 181
  opening postponement, *Film Mercury* mention, 179
  sidesaddle horse riding (Garbo), 179–180
  Stiller, firing, 176
Terje Vigen (A Man There Was) (Ibsen)
  rights, Magnusson acquisition, i
  script (Molander/Sjöström cowriters), 54
Thalberg, Irving (MGM head of production), 55, 130–131, 151, 199, 220
  death, 390, 393
  Garbo casting, 153
  Polly of the Circus preview attendance, 265
  Shearer, marriage, 256

Stiller, meeting, 177
Variety magazine interview, 156
Thau, Benny (MGM executive), 430
Theatre, Libre, 48
Thomas Graals bästa (1917 film), 54, 57
Thomas Graals myndling (1922 Molander film), 54
Schmiterlöw participation, 37
Three Sisters (Chekhov), 49
Thulstrup, Karl-Magnus, 41
ticket revenue, analysis, 234
Tildesley, Alice (interview), 270
Tokiofilmen (The Tokyo) (1922 Ring film), 29
government project, 30
Torrent (1926 film), 151–154, 317, 323, 328
advertising, 157–158
attention, 159
booking, risk, 158
Capitol Theatre (New York), ticket sales, 161
character creation, Garbo intent (demonstration), 201, 339
costs/profits, 163
domestic strength, 163–164
first-run theater run, 159
Garbo abilities, Erkkila observation, 162
Garbo/Cortez photo, 152
Garbo photos, 161, 166, 169, 174
Garbo recollection, 155
Hollywood Daily Citizen review, 156
Loew's State Theatre, premiere (ticket sales), 161–162
Minneapolis Star Tribune review, 194
New York premiere, New York Daily News ad, 157
one-minute trailer, 159
Photoplay review, 159
pre-publicity, absence, 157
response, 174
sample review, 159–160
St. Louis Post-Dispatch review, 160
success, Garbo surprise, 165
Variety/Film Daily reviews, 160
Tösen från Stormyrtorpet (The Girl from the Marsh Croft) (1917 film), 57, 59
Tourneur, Maurice, 212
Tower Theatre, ticket sales, 230
Tree Is a Tree, A (Vidor), 218
Trianon (German film company), 87
arrears, 132–133
bankruptcy/absorption/debacle, 110, 148
contract, Garbo termination, 132–133
financial issue, Stiller resolution (Garbo expectation), 107
funds, source, 92
Gösta Berling exhibit license agreement, 92

loan obligations, payment inability, 94
success, 91, 93
Trianon-Film AG (German film company)
Johnson (actress), hiring, 89
Trianon-Film-Ateliers GmbH, Schratter founding, 91
Trianon-Film Verleih GmbH, Schratter founding, 91
Trilby (novel), 279
Troxell, Jenelle, 120
Troy, Wiliam
Painted Veil, The (critique), 380
Queen Christina criticism, 363
Tullberg, Hasse, 27
Tullbergs Film
Business unit, Ring creation, 25–26
initiation, 64
Turner, Nicholas (Dragonette marriage), 455
Twin Sister, The (Fulda), 430
Two-Faced Woman (1941 film), 299, 342, 398, 438, 449
adultery, issue, 435
censorship, negative impact, 435
Douglas photo, 428
Garbo photos, 428, 429, 431
Legion of Decency condemnation, 431–433, 438
Legion of Decency rating, 375
McClafferty opinion, 428
National Board of Review recommendation, 435
New York Film Critics Circle Award for Best Actress, 435
PCA approval, 432
storyline, 430

U
UFA (German film company)
competing offer, 149
contract, Garbo negotiation, 129
financial challenges/bailout, 133–134
telegram, 131
UFA (German film company), financial problems, 108
Ullstein (publishing company), 110
Ulric, Lenore (*Camille* photo), 389
Uncle Vanya (Chekhov), 49
Undying Past, The (Sudermann), 211
United States, clerical workers (percentage), 234
urban market first-run theaters, Garbo performance, 217

V
Vajda, Ernest (screenwriter), 352
Valentino, Rudolph, 212, 225

Vanity Fair
actors, Genthe portraits, 143
female actor portraits, 147
photo essay, 204
Varconi, Victor (actor), 239
Variety (magazine)
Gilbert crash, mention, 246
"Greta Garbo Educated on Contract, Resumes," 238–239
industry developments, 227
Love audience, analysis, 258
Single Standard review, 203
Stiller, moviemaking comments, 277
Thalberg interview, 156
Torrent review, 160
Värmlänningarna (Värmlanders) (Petschler 1921 film), 36
Vaxholm Grenadier Regiment, Sven Garbo training, 17
Vedel, Karen, 145
Veidt, Conrad (actor), 104–105, 108
Versace, Gianni (fan murder), 297
Victorian age
moral clarity, 188
new order, impact, 187
overthrowing, 185
Vidal, Gore (Garbo friendship), 455
Vidor, King (director), 220, 356
Boardman marriage, 218
Viertel, Berthold (Garbo meeting), 301–302
Viertel, Salka (scriptwriter), 267, 303, 442
Behrman, interaction, 353
Garbo correspondence, 344–345, 351, 404–405
Garbo meeting, 301–302, 348
Garbo reconnection, 454
photo, 302
set admittance, prevention, 265
social events, 409
Viking Shoe Polish, film/advertisement (1922), 32
Violins of Autumn, The (Garbo performance), 89
visual representation, concept, 141
Voight, Hubert (MGM publicist), 139
Von Sternberg, Josef (actor)
movie involvement, Garbo insistence, 337
As You Desire Me photo, 335
von Stroheim, Erich, 216, 315, 333
vote, right, 184

W

Wachtmeister, Horke (Garbo correspondence), 408, 424–425
Wachtmeister, Nils/Horke (Garbo meeting), 289, 402
wages, increase, 185

Walker, Alexander (film historian), 160, 171
Wallace, Minna (Garbo visits), 453
Wanger, Walter (producer), 461
    Frenke correspondence, 467
    Joy/Wingate meeting, objections discussions, 361
    Queen Christina, 352–353
Warner (film major, integration), 228
Washington, Hazel (Garbo assistant), 401
Weber, Lois (director/story editor), 198
Wecksell, Josef Julius, 77
Wecksell, Julius, 48
Weimar constitution, German women (vote right), 120
Weimar cultural context, 117–118
Welles, Orson, 267
    Hollywood residence, 410
Wengel, Max (detention), 298
Wengeroff, Vladimir, 131
Werner, Eduard, 158
West, Claudine (screenwriter), 352
Westi Film, 131
    operations, cessation (1925), 133
West, Mae
    box office appeal, Independent Theatre Owners Association contention, 227
    She Done Him Wrong (1933 film), 311
Westmore, Perc (Polly of the Circus preview attendance), 265
West, Myrtle (Garbo interview), 294
What Ever Happened to Baby Jane? (1962 film), 437
Widdig, Bernd, 117–118
Widestedt, Ragnar, 27
Wilder, Billy, 350
Wilder, Thornton (dinner), 455
Wild Flowers in Southern California (Richfield Oil guide), Garbo/Taylor usage, 304
Wild Orchids (1929 film), 273–274, 296, 339
Wild Strawberries (Bergman 1957 film), 54
Wilkinson, Lupton (legion/censorship assessment), 374
Williams, Hope (Read analysis), 207
Williams, Raymond, 195
Williams, Tennessee (playwright) (Pink Bedroom pitch), 446
Wilson, Carey (screenwriter), 219, 220, 237, 247
    Bainbridge misquote, 449
    party invitation (Garbo refusal), 222
Wilson, Carmelita, 220
Wilson, Lois, 172
Winchell, Walter, 451
    attack, 400
Wingate, James (SRC leader), 311, 361
Wochenschrift Probleme des Lebens (Weekly problems of everyday life), Bettauer articles, 113

Wohnstätten GmbH
Bretschneider (CEO role), 92
Trianon absorption, 110
Wohnstätten, loan
cessation, 106
exposure (reduction), 103
Wolffsohn, Karl, 110
Woman of Affairs, A (1928 film), 273–274, 316, 339
Garbo/Gilbert photo, 221
Garbo performance, 171
Hays Office, impact, 192
intertitle, 196
silliness, 318–319
Woman on Trial, The (1927 film), 277, 278
women
clearer, Garbo purity (relationship), 375
contributions, appreciation (absence), 451–452
derogatory tags, 451
economic opportunities, increase, 4
employment, increase, 6
equality/emancipation, delay, 428
legal marriage equality (1921), 5
modern values, perception, 376
powerlessness (Die freudlose Gasse), 118
role, perception (nonuniformity), 450–451
self-supporting women, US perception, 450
sexual purity, importance, 186
social groups, organization (freedom), 4
subservience/sexual modesty, Catholic Church insistence, 429
Women Love Diamonds (1927 film), 236
set, Garbo arrival (refusal), 236
Women of the Sea
Cowan idea, 442
Garbo consideration, 440–441
project, dropping, 446
Woodfall Film Productions, co-founding, 471
Wray, Fay, 277
Wyler, William, 301

Z
Zukor, Adolph (Loew meeting), 228–229